LIFE AND LSE

LIFE AND LSE

Roger Alford

Book Guild Publishing
Sussex, England

First published in Great Britain in 2009 by
The Book Guild Ltd
Pavilion View
19 New Road
Brighton BN1 1UF

Typesetting in Garamond by
Keyboard Services, Luton, Bedfordshire

Printed in Great Britain by
CPI Antony Rowe

A catalogue record for this book is available from
The British Library

ISBN 978 1 84624 345 5

Contents

v

CONTENTS

CONTENTS

1

Arrival and Early Years

Arrival

Early October was reasonably warm in 1926, but the weather was turning colder. On the 17th the *Sunday Times* performed its usual duty of reporting the stresses and strains of the world: Mussolini was claiming a mandate, M. Poincaré was having difficulties and there were anxious days in Tangier. These were all far away, but nearer home, in Chester, a lorry carrying fifteen couple of foxhounds had collided with a cyclist. However the hounds were unhurt so there were no domestic worries to disturb what was to be a quiet Sunday for most people, but a most eventful one for me. Although I was present for part of the time, I have to call upon others to describe what happened. First, my older brother Michael:

> Then on a day full of whispers and winks, I was packed off to spend a few days with my cousin, Elizabeth. When I returned, I was invited to peer into a flouncy cot containing a bundle of swaddling clothes out of one end of which protruded a small, wizened head. It purported to be my new brother. I must say, left to me, I'd have chosen something a bit bigger. Anyway, its name was Roger. (Michael Alford, *The Paradise Rocks*, p. 28)

Then the more down-to-earth account from the diary of Alice Florence Davey, my maternal grandmother, always Nana to us as children, who was then living with my parents:

1

Oct 17 [*1926*]

Baby born, fine boy. 9½ lbs, 21 in. long, 14¼ round chest; pains began about 8 a.m. Frank [*my father*] took Michael up to Bertha [*mother of Elizabeth*] & fetched nurse; child born at ¼ to 4 [*p.m.*]. Doris [*my mother*] looks well.

Following these first-hand accounts of the earliest me, I must have been fed, weighed, cleaned up and loved by my proud parents and admired, with diminishing sincerity, by successively more distant members of our circle of family and friends. The only source which records my earliest remarks and emerging character is again my grandmother's diary in which they follow her account of the first steps towards the building of a holiday bungalow at Aldwick, on the western edge of Bognor in Sussex, which my parents had decided upon and which was to play a large role in my childhood. Here I simply report what is in her diary. However factual such an account of any child's early remarks and character may be, they do leave the reader (and the subject himself) feeling really just a touch queasy. Perhaps our coarser cynicism is embarrassed when faced with such loving pleasure in childish innocence.

April 13 [*1929*]

Frank went to Bognor, took plans [*of the bungalow*], engaged workmen, put everything in train; they expect to start digging in a week's time.

Roger: [*then aged 2½*] 'Me not go to bungalow, all cold and windy. Make my hair all blow about. Mama and Dada go, me stay at home with Nana and Michael and Mrs Clark and Phyllis' [*the latter two, home help and maid respectively*].

[*Doris*] told Michael to be quiet at dinner and not to talk so much. Every time that Michael spoke after that, Roger: 'Michael be quiet, I want to eat my din-din.' [*See 'Baby Talk' at the end of Chapter 23.*]

Roger is a generous and forgiving child; Michael hit him on the nose (he said Roger hit him, but he had no mark and they were playing trains quite happily). [*Doris*] slapped him [*Michael*]. Roger tried his best to comfort him 'Have a sweet, Michael' and wiped M's spectacles and tried to put them on him, hovering round him

2

so lovingly and so upset to see him cry. If I give him a sweet he always asks for one for Michael and takes it to him.

April 18 [*1929*]
Doris said 'I am going to see Phyllis Hine [*a friend*] now.' Roger from his cot: 'What about me? I want to go see Phyllis Hine ... I like Phyllis, she's a nice girl.'

What little else there is to be said about my earliest years has to depend upon what my mother told me many years later. One of her memories was that when I was only a year or two old she used to sit me on the edge of the table, kneel down in front of me with her arms outstretched and sing to me:

> I don't like little you-dle-oo
> Your eyes they are too blue-dle-oo
> Whatever shall I do-dle-oo
> With naughty little you-dle-oo

At which point with a gurgle of delight I would fall into her arms. Many variants followed – Your hairs/teeth they are too few-dle-oo, I'll put you in a stew-dle-oo, turn you into glue-dle-oo etc, but to me they were all equally delightful reasons for falling into her arms. Soon I was too heavy for this game and then I can remember enjoying these rhymes on their own, combining as they did teasing and love in a very satisfying way.

Then there are my own hazy early memories. Washing day, with a galvanised bath in the garden, Sunlight soap and a strong laundry smell. Sammy, our cat, was there but he had the good sense to avoid small children. Also in the garden was a line of low iron hoops along the edge of the lawn, ineffectually aimed at protecting it; too late, of course, because Michael had already begun reducing it to the sad state I remember later. However, I found these iron hoops highly entertaining and I remember clanking up and down the path with one, banging it on the ground.

The location of these memories is the house in which I was born: 20 Avenue Road, Isleworth, Middlesex (although mother always thought Osterley sounded better than Isleworth), telephone number: HOUnslow 1566. It was on the corner of Avenue Road and Grove Road but, despite its Avenue Road address, its front door was in Grove Road; and to further confuse posterity its number was much later changed to 30 Avenue Road. The house was found for us by Auntie Bertha, who on 7 November 1922 was walking from her house at 16 Thornbury Avenue (which really *was* in Osterley) to London Road, Isleworth, to catch a tram to Shepherd's Bush to visit her cousin Doris, my mother. Her route took her down Avenue Road and, noticing this suitable house for sale, she mentioned it to my mother who mentioned it to my father; then things moved quickly and they bought it on 14 November 1922 for, I believe, £1,000. It was well placed, just the length of Avenue Road – something under two hundred yards – from London Road with its trams (later trolleybuses) taking you to Hounslow in one direction and to Chiswick and Hammersmith in the other, together with the number 37 bus to Richmond and the Green Line bus (used only on rare occasions) up to Kensington and the West End. On the other side of London Road was a parade of shops – Watkins (the pharmacy, but 'chemist' to us), Zeeta (cakes), Lillyman (butcher), Fenn (jeweller), MacFisheries (fish shop) together with a greengrocer, a bank and some others covering most of our day-to-day requirements. Next to them was Isleworth Station leading to Waterloo. Altogether, our house had a very convenient location and, with the many fine horse chestnut trees along our roads, a very pleasant one.

The house itself was semi-detached but generously proportioned, and built around 1904; it had a double front door which was painted green, letting into a hall with Lincrusta on the walls and a typical floor of encaustic tiles in a coloured pattern. Facing you was the staircase with a passage past it to the right, leading round behind to the kitchen and the breakfast room which was warmed by a large coke stove; by the 1930s this provided our central heating – something of a novelty at that time. Off this passage to the right was my father's study which contained our telephone. On the left of the hall was what would have been the dining-room, but since we had all our meals in the breakfast room, it had become the family room. It had French windows letting out into the back garden containing a pear tree which produced inedible fruit and an apple tree named 'The Forge' which produced very large and delicious cooking apples, two old trees left over from the orchards and market gardens which had once helped to feed London. To the right of the hall was the sitting-room, for use only when there were visitors, with pale green walls, gilded outline panelling and heavy green brocade curtains; there was a bold bolection moulding round the fawn tiled fireplace and over it, set as a panel on the wall, an English landscape by an artist named Gallon, clearly influenced by Constable. The stairs, with a thick fawn carpet, led up to a half-landing with a very large unframed mirror above it, then a 180 degree turn and half a dozen steps up to a generous first-floor landing, four bedrooms and a bathroom. In the far right bedroom there was later a narrow wooden staircase up into a large loft. There, as the building conventions of the day dictated, the water tank was located in the north-east corner where it and its attendant pipes were most likely to freeze up in the winter. To me as a child, 20 Avenue Road was spacious, warm and comfortable, and above all it was home.

Body and mind were both growing and memories become clearer. In the afternoons Phyllis, our maid, used to take me out in a pushchair. This had a leather strap to keep me in, the end of which had a delicious leathery taste. I can remember being wheeled by her down St John's Road to the little park opposite Isleworth Brewery, the latter notable for its deep rich malty smell. It was on one such outing that Phyllis, our maid, asked me how many fingers I had on one hand; I replied five; no, she responded, you have four fingers and a thumb. I enjoyed this exchange so much that I insisted on it being repeated again and again throughout the rest of our walk. On another occasion I was wheeled on past the brewery to a church hall with a garden in front of it; there was a fête of some sort, but I can only remember running and sliding on the grass, to what I fondly imagined was the admiration of all those around. Still later, I remember going with Michael past Isleworth Station, under its iron railway bridge and into Linkfield Road. This was a rather downmarket road, containing a very small and decrepit sweet shop aiming at the smaller consumer; there we could buy gobstoppers and Sherbet Fountains and flimsy comics, one printed on pale green paper and another on pale pink. Mother rather frowned on these.

Aldwick

In 1928 my father and mother bought a site at Aldwick to have a bungalow built. It was started in April 1929 and by midsummer of 1929 it was just about habitable; almost immediately we had the excitement of moving into our very own seaside holiday bungalow. It cannot have been much of a holiday for my mother and father, as there was much still to be done to make it comfortable, but for Michael and me it was the first of the many holidays we were to spend there. And not only holidays, for Nana (her name pronounced as if it was spelled 'Nannah', with an equal stress on both syllables) soon adopted it as her permanent residence and, to reduce the pressure on mother (who was still working hard at home as a very successful freelance fashion artist), it was decided that I would stay there with her for what turned out to be something over a year. Living at Aldwick cosseted by a much-loved grandmother, and with mother and Michael being driven down by my father for frequent weekends and all the school holidays, it must have seemed to me the very best of both worlds.

When my father was down with us there were many things for him to do at the new bungalow, including building the stone-capped brick fountain at the bottom of the garden. This had a pond some six inches deep in front of it, and my father frequently warned us not to fall into it. Once when he was mowing the lawn, he got to the far end, turned the mower round and stepped back – into the pond! Mother said that she had never seen a child laugh as much as I did – wheezing and slapping my thigh to try and get the laughs out before I burst. It must have been around this time that we invented a new game called 'Mother and Child', to be played after I had cleaned my teeth before going to bed. I would make a horrible face in the bathroom mirror and mother would make the face of the mother who would have produced such an ugly child.

In the early days at the bungalow I slept in one of the front bedrooms, and when newly arrived for a holiday, mother would put into it a Valor oil stove to give a little warmth. Around it would be placed our mattresses and blankets ready for bedtime (no sheets for the first night or two – damp sheets were dangerous). At night this oil stove threw a characteristic pattern on the ceiling which I found comforting as I snuggled into the prickly blankets; later, headlights would throw a pattern of light which moved around the room as the occasional car went past, competing with the Valor's fixed pattern. I used to wonder who could be driving past at that time of night, and where to and why.

Even Aldwick was not without germs, and my occasional infant sore throats were treated with the usual sock pinned round my throat at night. One night, sleeping uneasily and whimpering, in came mother to see what was wrong; a brief investigation revealed that the brooch (in the shape of a duck followed by three ducklings) used to pin the sock had come unfixed and was stuck in my toe. Similarly, an uncomfortable walk with me complaining that my wellington boot hurt revealed that I had been walking on Dismal Desmond, a rubber toy Dalmatian dog.

On a more cheerful note, I can recall one Christmas when there were two plastic pencil cases, one each for Michael and me; one was an acid red, the other a violent blue, but the thought of owning either of them gave me a glow of excited expectation. At Christmas the presents from our parents were placed under the Christmas tree; we were allowed into the sitting-room just to have a glimpse of them before we went to bed on Christmas Eve and I remember them as being tightly wrapped in crisp pale mauve paper. There would also be presents from aunts and other members of the family, and this meant the penance of writing thank-you letters. Auntie Marjorie lived along the coast at Ferring-on-Sea, and I can remember having to write such a letter which I addressed to her at 'Ferring-No-Sea'. Such were the simple events which impressed themselves on my early memory.

Our bungalow was officially 3 South Avenue, Aldwick Gardens, Bognor Regis, Sussex, but surely it should have a name (I am not really sure why, since 20 Avenue Road had never needed one). Having recently disturbed a rabbit on the adjoining land I suggested 'The Running Rabbit', but this was rejected as suitable for a pub rather than a home. Instead mother chose 'Idlewylde'; I have been unable to trace the source of this name or why she chose it. By now some further houses were being built around us. I used to visit one, where the builders clearly appreciated my company. Mother was doubtful and suggested that I might get in their way and that they might not really like me visiting them. I was outraged: 'Mother! Some builders are *very* affectionate.'

For me life with Nana at Idlewylde was comfortable and secure. We went shopping in Bognor by the Red Rover bus which, on the return journey, would obligingly diverge from its scheduled route to drop us nearer our bungalow. In Bognor a band would sometimes play in the old cast-iron West Bandstand opposite the Royal Norfolk Hotel; Nana would sit and listen, but when it played 'Here Comes the Galloping Major' I galloped enthusiastically around the bandstand to the admiration of elderly ladies in deckchairs. Nana and I would walk together across Aldwick Road to

Yeoman's Acre to buy tomatoes from a man with a military moustache and a greenhouse filled with the scent of his crop. And on summer evenings we would play bezique, sitting by the window of her bedroom, looking out on to a silent South Avenue.

There was another member of the Idlewylde household: Joan Boxall. Each day she came in from Rose Green where her family lived in a thatched house whose eaves came down almost to the ground. I liked her, and can remember her giving me for breakfast a fried egg on fried bread, all cut up neatly into squares – absolutely delicious; my mouth still waters at the memory.

Starting School

But the stern realities of life began to intrude, and while I was there with Nana, at the age of four I started school. In fact I attended two schools, the first being one run by Miss Spiridion at her house a few doors along on the other side of South Avenue. There I can only remember lustily singing 'Rule Britannia' with about five other pupils, all girls. One of these was Jean Hazelrigg who lived nearly next door to the school and was – apart from Michael – the earliest playmate I can remember. Jean's ambition was to be a naval officer, and in her garden a small enclosure of young conifers surrounding a compost bin became a ship to be boarded and captured or to be defended and saved from the enemy. All this exciting and victorious naval action was carried out by a crew of just two – Jean and me.

Then I moved to Miss Clear's tiny school in Aldwick village, one of about eight pupils. I quote from Michael's book:

> For a description of its single, low-ceilinged classroom, I have to thank Roger. Stone-floored, he says, and smelling of cheese, mid-morning cocoa, rising damp and, in winter, of camphorated oil. The only other feature in the room he could recall was a black-tongued cockatoo, which gave out ear-splitting screeches.
>
> Miss Clear's curriculum included teaching her pupils to read with the help of gaily coloured ABC books and to write (particularly pothooks) on slates with squeaky slate pencils. In pursuit of numeracy, they recited their multiplication tables in sing-song

unison and furrowed their little brows trying to grasp the mysteries of short division, explained with the aid of an abacus (for in those days, teachers taught the hard way). When winter drew her icy patterns on the window panes, he tells me, Miss Clear used to move her pupils to the cosy warmth of her kitchen, where a large iron kettle murmured on a black-leaded range. It was while my seven-year old brother was attending at the village school, it was found, to the family's shame, that he had been dabbling in an unacceptable enterprise.

Each day on his way to 7th Cottage [*Miss Clear's home*], Roger used to call upon Mr Roberts, proprietor of the village sweetshop, to buy a 1d chocolate wafer biscuit for break. One day he noticed a clematis looped over the fence of *Almora*, Mrs Firminger's house, next to the footpath. Being a sweet-natured child (he assures me) he picked one of the flowers and presented it to Mr Roberts. Much affected by this cherubic gesture, the kindly Mr Roberts responded open-handedly with a Sharp's toffee. Obviously this was a profitable practice to be made full use of, and so it was until it came to the ears of Miss Clear who saw it as verging on blackmail rather than charming spontaneity and brought the career of a promising young con-man to an abrupt end. (Michael Alford, *The Paradise Rocks*, p. 112)

I must add in my defence that all of this occurred when I was five, rather than seven as he suggests.

My daily journey across the big field, following the footpath to Aldwick village, brought me into contact with the cows who regarded it as their domain and had no hesitation in lying across the footpath while they chewed the cud. But Michael and I had already 'helped' with the cows at Aldwick Farm and at about six years of age I now felt (fairly) confident in dealing with them. Some fifty years later, and more than twenty years ago, an elderly Miss Tarrant reminded me of how she and her mother hesitated at the stile, wondering whether to risk crossing the big field with its threatening cows, when I appeared and boldly announced that they need not be afraid – I would escort them across. And this I did, marching in front and boldly shooing the dim and gentle cows off the path to make way for them.

Tales from Mother

Memory has strange and random processes and although so much from this time at Aldwick has faded from my mind, two memories still stand out clearly. The first is seeing in Nana's *Daily Mail* a photo of a gipsy wedding, with the groom pushing his bride along in a wheelbarrow; for decades afterwards the words 'wedding' or 'marriage' instantly brought into my mind a gipsy pushing his bride in a wheelbarrow. The second was coming home by bus from shopping in Chichester with mother, where I had been attracted by a small green and yellow china frog ('Made in Japan'). Mother bought it for me and on the way home she began to tell me tales about my new acquisition. I was told that her name was Matilda Topobus (we were on the top deck of the bus at the time), clearly a Latin name, appropriate for a china frog bought in the once Roman city of Chichester. Matilda, she told me, always went to bed with a hot-water bottle, but one containing cold water and with a leak in it – to keep her feet cool and moist. I was charmed by such stories. Matilda, up on a bookshelf in my study at home, still looks down at me as I write. One incident that mother recalled was waiting in our parked car when the car in front began to back towards us. Mother and Auntie Bertha cried out that it was going to collide with us but, aged about five, I leant across, sounded our horn and saved the day.

Mother also told us tales about her own childhood with the Doré cousins who, after the early death of her father, were warm and supportive. There were seven of these cousins but it was the three youngest, Dorothy, Gilbert and Sibyl, who played a large part in mother's childhood – and later. She was introduced to Bognor when, aged eleven, she went there with them in 1904 on the first of three holidays. Looking after them was their nursery nurse Wonnie, with definite views on good behaviour but much loved by all of them. (For many of our mother's childhood memories and an account of these holidays see *The Paradise Rocks*, Chapter 1.) However, there were a few of mother's tales that Michael missed, and Gilbert figured largely in them. When very young he took to biting his sisters; Wonnie had her own cure for this – next time he did it, she bit *him*. Hardly politically correct, but the effect was immediate and he never did it again. For holidays at Bognor they travelled by train from Victoria Station; to keep their train compartment to themselves, Gilbert would put his face against the window and blow out his cheeks, making what they called 'boony' faces. This was evidently very successful, although one would suppose that few passengers would really wish to travel cooped up with four lively children. (Many years later I mentioned this tale in conversation with some of my colleagues and this led to a discussion on the most effective ways of discouraging others from entering your compartment; the best suggestion was to stare hard at them out of the window and beckon them in.) When they reached the house where they were staying, Gilbert complained that his bed had been used by the preceding tenants and demanded that Doris, our mother, should sleep in that bed for the first night 'to purify it'.

Wonnie used to read to her charges from a book about the adventures of Little Ug; they loved these tales and were warm supporters of Little Ug. Many years later mother found the book; it was called *The Adventures of Little Hugh*. She suddenly felt her childhood had been robbed of the charm of these tales of Little Ug, and wished that she had not found it. Some of mother's memories did not include her cousins, and one of these was of attending a birthday party; there she was given a Coconut Pyramid, a rather uninteresting cake but redeemed by having a glacé cherry on the top. She carefully removed this cherry and placed it on the side of her plate to be eaten as the final special treat. The horrid boy next to her then leaned over, took her special treat and ate it. Mother could still vividly recall her outrage at this dastardly act. I can only remember going to one birthday party; there the table was dominated by two large and impressive jellies, one pink and the other green, with scrolls of cream on top. I could hardly believe that anyone was going to disturb their colourful symmetry by taking great spoonfuls out of them.

2

Growing Up

Wyndham School

It was now time for me to move back to be with the rest of the family at Isleworth and, in January 1931, to join my older brother Michael at a much larger educational establishment – Wyndham School, with its cap and scarf in the school colours of black and red. Michael had been there for some time and was due to leave so we only overlapped for one term. Our records show that for most of my time there the fees were £5 5s 0d per term. The school, some ten minutes' walk from home, along very quiet suburban streets lined with great horse chestnut trees, was in a tall dark-brick late Victorian house with a semi-basement and a generous flight of stone steps leading up to the front door. The headmistress was the dumpy, bustling, grey-haired Miss Béroud (to my ears 'Misberoo' – all one word). Each morning, dominating the assembly, she seated herself at a table in the largest schoolroom and called the roll for all sixty or so boys and girls; she used a heavy crayon, red at one end, blue at the other, and a squared attendance book. If you were present you received a firm upward red stroke; the next day your record was marked in the next square along, by an equally firm downward stroke, red again if you were present, blue if you were absent. In this way a horizontal zig-zag line of mainly red strokes, but occasionally blue ones, marked the passage of each one of us through the term, and our susceptibility to infections. Every day during the first lesson Miss Béroud used to visit each class with a galvanised hand-sprayer and 'woosh woosh' – two strokes of some alleged germ-killer aimed to keep us all healthy; the resulting mist gave me a fizzy sensation in my nose. At break time (marked like the lesson times by a clanging brass handbell) we went up to the generous hallway by the front door where there was a table with a glass of hot milk and a biscuit for each of us; behind the table was one of the intimidating big girl prefects (aged about fifteen), to keep order. Then out into the walled back garden which was our playground; it backed onto a similar playground of a similar school whose boys had caps of pale blue, but we viewed these other children beyond the wall with mild distrust and did not fraternise with them. In the corner of the garden was a large tree close to the wall but with just enough room for one to squeeze all the way round it – most satisfying.

The teacher at Wyndham I remember most clearly was Miss Kay, a gentle, hesitant, pale lady who wore a long light-brown silky dress with coffee-coloured lace inserts at the neck and cuffs; with her greying hair piled up on top she looked as if she were about to attend a Edwardian tea party. Discipline was not her strong point; when one of the class was disobedient she would take his hand and exclaim weakly, 'You are a naughty boy, a very naughty boy', and make smacking motions which stopped about two inches above the offender's hand. Miss Garry, who later made efforts to teach me Latin, was very different; she was pale, bony-faced, red-headed and Irish; ill-humour was never far below the surface. Thank goodness she was soon replaced by a short, plump, kindly teacher, but any real grasp of Latin had to wait until later in my education. Of other teachers at Wyndham I have only fragmentary memories: Miss Hilliard, short, dumpy, good-humoured, who was second in command to Miss Béroud; Miss Pike, who used to walk up Avenue Road on her way to school and whom I sometimes accompanied, feeling she deserved some entertaining conversation on the way; the elegant Miss Cummings whose classroom was right at the top of the house and indeed seemed to me dangerously high up. And there was the head girl, grown-up, tall, masterful Beryl Stribling, who had her mahogany-coloured hair in a heavy, glossy, perfectly plaited pigtail and who sometimes rang the school bell. (There was no head boy since the the school only took boys up to the age of ten or so.)

In the lowest forms lessons were interspersed with periods of free time when we could play with plasticine or draw. The plasticine, which had started life in various colours but was by then in its greeny-grey terminal state, was in worn wooden boxes; we were each given a box (which usually contained the crumpled artworks left by the previous user) to turn into our own range of misshapen objects. For drawing, we each had a pale brown covered 'rough book'. I can still remember my drawing of a canoe containing some explorers going up the Amazon; so far, so good. But they would need supplies, and in a stroke of genius I drew a second canoe towed behind the first one and in it I drew boxes of supplies, each with its contents written on the side: Bread, Tea, Sugar, Milk, Biscuits. But they might need more supplies, so I added another canoe to carry these: Matches, Meat, Apples, Tizer (a popular fizzy drink). Suddenly I had found a most rewarding formula for creating an unlimited wealth of supplies for my explorers. (Decades later I rashly revealed this discovery of canoe-based wealth creation to my wife. When I could not resist buying extra items from Sainsbury's, she gently suggested that I was still trying to fill up the canoes of my childhood.)

As part of the family archive, my mother carefully preserved some of my exercise books, and a brief look at these shows that education was taken seriously at Wyndham. Early in 1935 (aged eight) in mental arithmetic I could work out that 7 half-crowns = 17s 6d, that 30 farthings = $7^{1}/_{2}$d and (since we had learned the 13 times table) that $(13 \times 6) + 10 = 88$. Probably later in 1935 I was able to do long multiplication and work out $4939 \times 978 = 4,830,342$. On 23 October 1934 for Dictation I had to write down the following passage:

Like most reptiles, the lizard changes its skin, but it is not <u>dun</u> so cleanly as a snake; the lizard<u>'s</u> skin comes off bit by bit.

(One spelling mistake and one omitted genitive ending, both underlined by the teacher; graded B) while for Writing on 15 November 1934:

The mother earwig watches her young with attentive care, and provides for all their wants.

(This looks unusually well written to me, far better than my later writing, but it was only graded B and the letters t, c, p and f – although perfectly well-formed to my eye – were underlined by the teacher and each had been written out five times.) Altogether, tough correcting and grading. I also made literary efforts on my own; mother noted as 'entirely original' a poem I composed at the age of $6^{1}/_{2}$:

15

> You can always be quite happy
> In a little country house
> With the birds all singing gladly
> And the name of them is grouse

Each day I walked home for lunch; in the summer the table was laid by the open French windows into the back garden and just myself and mother lunched on salmon pie – tinned salmon (very cheap at that time) with mashed potatoes on top – perfectly delicious. This was followed by loganberries from our garden with sugar and top-of-the-milk (cream would have been regarded as extravagant). Life was good.

Then back to school in the afternoon: out of the front door, left along Grove Road, then turn right up the long curve of The Grove, on past the large grass triangle pointing up Osterley Road to the Great West Road, then another hundred yards and on the right was Wyndham (which was the name of the house as well the name of the school, although I do not know which came first). I can remember clearly this walk back to school in the summer afternoons; there was not another soul to be seen, no cars, no aeroplanes, no birds, nothing but me and a summer silence so profound that I could feel it pressing warmly upon me.

At Wyndham the only other boy I can remember with any clarity was Raymond Castle, who varied between friend and enemy and whose route to school led past our house. He lived in Wood Lane in a house backing on to St Mary's Sports Ground which his bedroom overlooked. He told me that at night his bedroom would be lit momentarily by the headlights of cars as they topped the hill at Hindhead some thirty five miles away. It was on St Mary's Sports Ground that Wyndham held its games each Wednesday afternoon in the summer, the pupils walking there in a 'crocodile'. Our journey took us past my own front door, and it seemed strange to go past it in this way, as if for a moment our house disowned me. For this activity we were divided into 'Houses'; there was Milton (my House, with a pink badge), Longfellow (red) and some others. The badges were small coloured rectangles with a narrow 'gold' margin and a pin across the back. Their only significance was that you had to have your badge pinned on to play games and this led to frequent tearful emergencies as the badge was mislaid. The last resort was to buy a new badge (ninepence at the time) – a small but useful source of income to the school.

16

Life at Isleworth

St Mary's Sports Ground ('the field' to us) was much more than the venue for Wyndham's games. Both Michael and I were members, which cost five shillings a year (or a reduced fee of nine shillings for the two of us), and we played there regularly while we lived at Isleworth. It was some five acres in size, only a few hundred yards from home, with an somewhat neglected entrance between two large pillars with a short drive flanked by dejected privet bushes. There on Saturday afternoons in winter we would watch the Old Isleworthians playing their football matches in some local league; in the summer older boys played bicycle polo, and a group of us would sometimes play cricket. I can remember one occasion when, unusually, our father came with us to the field and joined in a game. His turn came to bat, and after one or two strokes he hit a really powerful drive; the ball went high into the air and came down straight through the glass canopy of the small brick cricket pavilion. There was an appalled silence, but his response was immediate: 'A pound to anyone else who can do that!' and instead of ending in guilty flight the game went on more keenly than before.

Along the back of the field was a long brick wall with a large dead tree up against it in the middle. We spent quite a lot of time climbing that tree and from it we could see over the wall and into an orchard. Just occasionally we would jump down, collect a few rather sour apples, and then escape back on to our own side of the wall before we were caught by the fierce and active keepers whom we were certain lay in wait for trespassers. In fact this orchard was totally uncared for, a relic of the time when Isleworth was a fruit-growing area, and I doubt if the owner or anyone else entered it from one year's end to the next. Beyond the orchard and over the railway line we were certain that there was a motor racing track because we could often hear the cars racing round it. Unaware of their role in our imaginings, the mechanics at the Frazer Nash garage on London Road continued to tune up their sports cars. In one corner of the field there was St Mary's Tennis Club with three red clay courts and two grass courts (on which I later learned to play tennis). It had a wooden clubhouse where, surrounded by a Saturday afternoon scent of warm wood and fragrant tea, the older lady members prepared refreshments for the players. These ladies were also in charge of the key to a glass-fronted case which was a miniature sweet

17

shop, from which even the junior members of the field could buy a sustaining penny bar of chocolate.

Isleworth was not without its dangers, chief of which was Norman Jones. He was a tall and (in my view) dangerous boy, who with his two or three henchmen only occasionally came into my distant view, but to me there was always the possibility that I might meet them at close quarters. When they wore school caps, these were like those of Wyndham, black with red radial stripes, but whereas Wyndham's stripes were broad and generous, those of Norman Jones's school were appropriately narrow and mean. I was once on the flat roof of our garage (an excellent vantage point overlooking the road which ran next to our house) when this gang happened to pass; they saw me and Norman Jones suggested that I should descend to the road where they could talk to me. Certainly not! But look, said Norman Jones, they were only weak and harmless, and to prove this he picked up a stone and pretended to try to throw it, but allowed it to simply fall out of his hand as proof of his weakness and harmlessness. Dangerous <u>and</u> cunning. No sweet words from him would tempt me off the security of our garage roof.

Our part of Isleworth – Spring Grove – had originally been designed around Sir Joseph Banks' noble house and grounds (long since converted to house an educational institution) with The Grove forming a semicircle round the north side of it. It was he who planted the noble horse chestnut trees which gave our area a green and leafy character and gave us a large autumn supply of conkers. They also provided a generous fall of leaves, and I can remember walking with Michael from Auntie Bertha's house in Thornbury Avenue, Osterley (telephone number: HOUnslow 3082), each of us with one foot on the pavement and the other most satisfyingly in the gutter, pushing through great mounds of these leaves on our way home.

In our living-room at 20 Avenue Road there was an open coke grate which, in addition to the central heating, made it very warm and cosy on winter days. A bookcase contained my grandfather's bound copies of *Punch* from the 1880s and 1890s, and I can remember lying on the hearthrug as a child, propped up on my elbows, looking through them and enjoying their visual variety of text and cartoons – some humorous, some political – but not really comprehending the significance of either. Also in the bookcase was a set of the works of Rudyard Kipling bound in red and with a gilt motif of an elephant's head and a small swastika on the front cover.

In Kipling's time this was an ancient and innocent symbol of good luck, popularised by Schliemann's discovery of it in the ruins of Troy. It was only later that Hitler adopted it as the deadly and ill-starred symbol of the Nazis.

Of the bedrooms in our house my own was the smallest, on the left as you arrived at the top of the stairs. My bed was along the wall opposite the door, and when I stood on it I had a fine view out of the window over our end of Avenue Road and its junction with Grove Road. I can remember standing there one evening and watching a thunderstorm which produced lightning in faint shades of pink and green. I liked my bedroom, but sometimes as I lay in bed I would think of the world extending westwards over Hounslow and far beyond; this all seemed uncomfortably boundless, and I would turn over to face into the house, which gave me a feeling of cosy security. Mother told me that at the age of six or so I was sent up to my bedroom for some misdemeanour; 'Best place, this weather', was my parting shot as I went up the stairs.

In their bedroom next door my parents had a large double bed with a dark wooden headboard. My mother sometimes went to bed early and then I would be allowed to snuggle in next to her and we would read from a large and colourful book – most cosy and delightful. After Judy, our springer spaniel, arrived she would sometimes be allowed to lie on the bottom of mother's bed and then, when I tried to get in, her instinct to guard mother would take over and she would stand up red-eyed and growling furiously until I had got in. Since I was then clearly a friend, she would collapse into grovelling apology and wagging welcome. After I grew out of the highly coloured book our cosy evenings would sometimes be spent in word games, one of which was making up advertisements for unlikely products; the only one I can remember was my own contribution: 'Try Slymo – the new green, gritty margarine!' Next to the double bed was a gas fire against the wall, and a radio on a small table. The gas fire had its name, 'Veriot', cast into its enamelled top, and mother felt it was a rather upmarket name, like 'Cheviot'; then one day it dawned on her that it was really claiming to be 'Very Hot' and she never again felt the same way about it. To me the main use of the radio was for *Children's Hour*, to listen to this I used to lie across the bed with my face a few inches from it so as not to miss a word spoken by Uncle Mac or Larry the Lamb in *Toy Town*.

Before we had a dog of our own we were intrigued by a chow dog – mother used to say it was tastefully lined in blue – which lived a few doors away down Avenue Road. It usually sat at the open window of a first-floor bedroom, taking an interest in passers-by. One day its interest was so stimulated that it fell out of the window. Apparently none the worse for its misadventure it was soon back at its post, but the incident was eagerly noted by us children. I was once emerging from our front door when I was surprised to see a cat dash round our corner pursued by three miscellaneous dogs, which seemed instinctively to have formed a primitive hunting pack. The cat made straight for the horse chestnut opposite, and from bounding along the road it bounded vertically up the tree trunk. The dogs were quite unprepared for this evasive manoeuvre and raced on past the tree and up the road, apparently enjoying the momentum of the chase and oblivious of the fact that their quarry had disappeared. The cat meanwhile got some dozen feet up the tree, was no longer able to hold on, performed a graceful arc and landed flat on its back in the road sending up a small cloud of dust. So much for cats always landing on their feet.

In due course we acquired our very own dog, Judy, a liver-and-white springer spaniel, as well as other pets: a tortoise (which showed a marked preference for expensive cos lettuce) and two rabbits belonging to Michael, one black, the other grey. These latter required rabbit supplies which came from a tiny general store in the middle of a row of shops along London Road towards Hounslow, just past the granite horse trough which used to stand at the generous junction with Spring Grove Road. Whenever mother went there she would find herself paying bills for various rabbit items bought by Michael and charged to the family's account. This store had a row of biscuit tins with glazed lids, from one of which it sold broken biscuits which were not only cheap but also promised fragmentary but exciting discoveries; it also sold unusual items such as liquorice twigs and pods of locust, or carob, beans. We once bought some of the latter and fed them to an appreciative giraffe at a zoo and it was there that a friendly giant anteater licked chocolate off my fingers with its long prehensile tongue. In this row of shops the very first one had special attractions: it was triangular in plan, had a most appealing display of cheap toys, and sold paregoric sweets with a lovely tangy flavour. Only decades later did I discover that paregoric is camphorated tincture of opium and has long been withdrawn from the market, as have the tiny spherical aconite pills (containing the deadly poison aconitine, hopefully in a very tiny therapeutic amount) which my grandmother sometimes dosed us with in preference to the newfangled aspirin. On the other side of the road from the tiny general store was a wooden shack occupied by Mr Legge, our cobbler, who always wore a cap to cover what was evidently a perfectly bald head. He had a very good memory for his customers and later was to greet us warmly after a mainly wartime absence of some eight years.

Mother used to take Judy out for walks, often going through an alleyway next to Isleworth School for Boys. On one occasion Judy found a bag of sausages dropped by someone and ate the lot before mother could intervene. From then on we always referred to it as Sausage Alley and Judy was always eager to go along it – just in case... Mother managed to train Judy to 'Wait!' when preparing to cross a road; when all was clear she gave the order 'Over!' and Judy would bound across. We boys would sometimes tease Judy by saying 'Over!' when there was no road to cross, and she would duly bound away and then stop and look confused – very naughty of us. Mother's training did not always work. Again near Sausage Alley, faced with a newly tarred road which mother was not going to cross, Judy forgot her training and started to cross the road; a car was approaching – slowly and still some way away – but mother tried to bring her back, crying 'Judy!' in a cross voice. Judy's apologetic side now took over, and she promptly rolled over guiltily on the freshly tarred road, leaving mother struggling to pick up an inert and apologetic dog covered with tar to save it from the not very likely danger of being very slowly run over. I was once walking past one end of Sausage Alley when I came across a man and his dog waiting there. The man looked ill-humoured but the dog seemed pleased to see me, so I patted it on the head and looked at the name-tag on its collar; this said 'Slade', and gave a phone number. To my childish eye it was clear that the dog's name was Slade, so as I patted it I said 'Good Slade, nice old Slade', while Mr Slade looked increasingly ill-humoured.

On my walk to Wyndham School I went along Grove Road and then turned right into The Grove. On this corner was a tall dark Victorian house with a beech tree in its back garden which in season used to shed beech mast all over the pavement, and in the basement of the house lived Mrs Green, an elderly retired musician. Mother inflicted on the unfortunate Mrs Green the penance of teaching Michael to play the piano, and perhaps it was the hopeless and depressing nature of this task that led mother to feel some responsibilty for Mrs Green in her final years; when the old lady died she left mother her violin – perhaps as a gesture of forgiveness. Along

The Grove lived a schoolfellow named Kenneth Inwards (nicknamed 'Guts' for obvious reasons). His house was large and square with a long garden. He had a younger sister, Cynthia, and two older brothers who caused us much delighted terror by limping down the garden after us waving two ancient sabres and roaring out piratical threats. At the further end of Avenue Road lived the Willment family and I played with them occasionally. What really remains in my mind is their storeroom over the coach-house which was filled with the wonderfully intense scent of apples.

Mother took us on occasional outings, and one of these was to London Zoo where we saw the chimpanzees' tea party. She said later that the chimps were much better behaved than her own children. In the display cabinet in our sitting-room at home she had a scroll (on an ordinary piece of paper tied up with a ribbon) which she claimed had been presented to her by the Prince of Wales congratulating her, in very bad verse, on managing to bring up three such naughty boys ('How very good must this mother be/To cope with such naughty boys three'). The Prince had even placed her portrait on it – drawn, curiously enough, in her own very characteristic fashion-artist style. The fraud was clear but the mock seriousness with which she parried all our doubts reduced us to helpless and disbelieving giggles.

There were occasional excitements at Avenue Road, such as the Crystal Palace fire in 1936. We were taken up into the loft and, held by Dad, were allowed to lean out through the skylight to see the glow in the sky. There was also the case of the ventilation pipe rising out of the pavement in Avenue Road just outside our house. One day the Council removed it but left a sharp piece of metal sticking up; I duly fell over this, Dad complained, and a team of Council workmen came with what seemed to me to be a large and noisy steam hammer, and hammered it down. Less dramatic but still exciting were the occasions when we were allowed to take out a carrot or a small potato and feed it to the milkman's horse, which had a soft 'moosey' nose – a phrase mother adopted from her early time in the fashion studio with the lively Miss André. The latter, after a shopping trip to Barker's in Kensington, enthralled her studio of girl fashion artists with the tale of seeing a shop detective watching her, and how she picked up some item and seemingly put it in her bag – the detective stiffened – but she then replaced the item and walked out of the store still being watched suspiciously. This risk-filled adventure was greeted by cries of 'Ooh, you didn't really, did you?' from her excited audience.

22

Father had a taste for the occasional practical joke. Our neighbours facing our front door from the other side of the road were the Longmates. Mr Longmate was short and very pleasant (I believe he had been commissioned in the field in the First World War) and someone in the family was concerned with the manufacture of hypodermic needles (or in the inspired Spoonerism of one newsreader, 'hypodeemic nerdles'). Dad took a long piece of cotton thread, led it through our letterbox and surreptitiously attached it to the knocker on the Longmates' front door. All of us watched with bated breath; two quick pulls, 'Knock, knock'. The front door opened – no one there, must have misheard – the door closed. Again 'Knock, knock', again the door opened and Mr Longmate looked out, now puzzled. 'Knock, knock', and the door was opened instantly by a now very suspicious Mr Longmate, but still nothing. At this point father went over and confessed to a now rather relieved neighbour.

Colet Court

But I was now of an age when I had to move on from Wyndham, and at the beginning of the summer term of 1937 I started at Colet Court, the preparatory school for St Paul's; I now wore a dark blue cap bearing the silver outline of a Maltese cross. Each schoolday (which included Saturday mornings) I walked down Avenue Road to London Road to catch the number 657 trolleybus (which by now had replaced the trams) to Turnham Green. Perched on a front seat on the top deck I could enjoy a bird's-eye view of our progress. There was the great wall round Syon House and the little green gazebo which stood level with the top of a wall on the opposite side of the road, built to view the excitements of the plodding horse-drawn traffic of an earlier era. The railway bridge and the Grand Union Canal marked the start of Brentford High Street – very run-down and with many junk shops – followed by the great Gas Light & Coke Company's works and the end of Kew Bridge marked by the Kew Theatre. Then past Brentford market, along Chiswick High Road to Turnham Green with a First World War tank in its nearest corner. There I left my perch in the 657 trolleybus and at the same stop caught the number 27a bus (and with luck my same pole position on the upper deck) which took me along the rest of Chiswick High Road, much more prosperous than Brentford High Street, and past the large Commodore Cinema on the right marking the beginning of King Street, Hammersmith. Then over Hammersmith Broadway and finally to the bus stop just outside Colet Court. This was a journey I never ceased to enjoy. At the time I had no idea that it took me past the place where St Peter's School had once been at 219–221 King Street, and where my paternal great-grandfather had been Headmaster between 1871 and 1891; or that it passed within a few hundred yards of where my father had worked as assistant to Frank Brangwyn in his studio at Temple Lodge in Queen Caroline Street.

Of school work at Colet I have only a few memories; in a spelling lesson we had to correct Mr Renton for spelling cement 'ciment'. I received a very good mark for an English essay on 'A Rubbish Dump' – very anthropomorphic, with each new item arriving on the dump being expected to entertain the older inhabitants with the story of how they came to be there (a formula which allowed unlimited sub-stories). But this was one of my better performances, for the harsh light of the form lists shows me hovering a bit below the middle. Looking at the names on these lists, many faces still come clearly to my mind. At one time our form master was Mr Mather, and for one late afternoon lesson he came in his Territorial Army uniform and polished his Sam Brown belt ready for a parade after school; and there were a few boys with German names whose families had recently moved to Britain. But these tiny clues to the future passed unnoticed by me.

Colet Court was built of deep red brick (as was St Paul's School on the other side of the road). There was a front building with the art school on the first floor and a dining-room in the basement, and behind that the main school building with a large central hall and some three tiers of galleries off which were the classrooms. Behind this main building were a gymnasium, a large hard-surfaced playground and then a playing field suitable only for cricket in the summer (for which there was a wooden pavilion) and our annual sports day. On the playground, apart from the chatting and games played in small groups, there were larger games. One of these was Chain He. This started as a normal game of He, but when caught you joined hands with the catcher so that as the game progressed the chain of catchers became longer and more difficult to control, while the efforts to escape became more desperate and more hopeless, till at last all were caught; then someone else was elected as the new He and it began again. Another game was King, played with a tennis ball. The first person with the ball aimed to throw it and hit a victim; the two then cooperated, passing and throwing, with successive victims joining the throwing team, and the efforts of the others to avoid the ball led to wild scrambles out of the way. All very good exercise, and fortunately all the ground-floor windows looking over the playground were covered with stout wire mesh. Another game was very different; one boy stood near a wall hunched as if for leapfrog, then another would stand similarly with his hands on the first boy and then another and another; then the rest of the boys in the game each in turn took a long run and leapfrogged as far up this chain as they could in an effort to make it collapse under their combined weight.

On weekdays we had lunch at school in the dining-room in the basement of the front building. There if you wanted a second helping you put your knife and fork on your glass and raised it up for one of the dinner ladies to see. On one memorable occasion the catering arrangements overdid things. There were hot doughnuts with hot jam sauce for pudding and it suddenly became evident that there were a very large number being left over and we were invited to have as many as we liked. I ate six. On a few occasions I went to lunch at Lyons, which was not far up Hammersmith Road towards Olympia. There you could have chips with everything; like several other items they were served in small white rectangular dishes and the price label under them said '2d per por'; so obviously this small white china dish was a 'por' and for pudding one could have a por of stewed plums or a por of tinned peaches. It was only many years later that I realised that the chips had been 2d per portion and these neat white dishes had no name of their own. These lunches at Lyons were usually on a Wednesday, and after lunch there were games; for some of these we had to go by the tube from Hammersmith out past Turnham Green. As it approached Turnham Green station the train passed over a narrow viaduct without any side railings so that as you looked out of the window there was nothing between you and the ground some way below; this always gave me a rather worrying feeling of insecurity. Otherwise, when school was over it was out on to Hammersmith Road for the journey back home over the same route that I had followed in the morning. Sometimes the number 27a bus was rather full, and then two of us might crowd into the luggage hole under the stair – regarded as a rather adventurous thing to do.

Hobbies and Interests

Beyond school and prep, there was much going on at home. My trips in the pushchair had been overtaken by trips with mother by number 37 bus to the River Thames where we fed the ducks and walked upriver to Richmond Lock; or we might get off the bus earlier and walk through Old Isleworth to the London Apprentice, a riverside pub, where there were different ducks to feed and a ferryman with a green-painted boat who for a few pence would row us across the river to Richmond Old Deer Park. From there we could walk downriver to Kew Gardens; but this was more of an expedition and was only done when I was older. On Sundays Michael and I were sometimes taken by mother to the chapel at the beginning of Hounslow High Street, where we were allowed out before the sermon to browse in the windows of a large toy shop opposite. Sometimes we were sent off on our own to this chapel with a penny each for the collection. But we did not much like going to chapel and on some occasions, I regret to say, we would spend these pennies on two ounces of Packer's Crispits and idle away our morning instead.

Throughout my childhood in Isleworth I spent quite a lot of time playing with friends at the field – St Mary's Sports Ground. In due course I became a junior member of the Tennis Club there and, wielding my 5-shilling tennis racket, was given lessons on the grass courts by some kindly older members. I can remember the springy feeling of well-being as I walked with newly whitened tennis shoes up College Road to the Tennis Club. But we could be more adventurous; Michael had a friend, Haigh, who lived in Norwood and I remember the two of us going by bus into Hounslow and then up Lampton Road to play football with him on Norwood Green. On one of these journeys, probably looking rather deprived, I was given a penny by a kindly old gentleman.

At the age of eight or so I joined the Cubs which met in the Parish Hall about half a mile away. Walking there on winter evenings along London Road seemed to me to require a torch, and one of the larger silver ones with two new batteries produced a most satisfying beam of light through the mist. I also had a torch like a pistol – you pulled the trigger and it lit up; that gave me some small cachet amongst my fellow Cubs, but it did not have the distance-conquering beam of my more conventional torch. At Cubs we learned to tie knots, we played games, won badges for various minor skills and prepared to help old ladies across roads. I enjoyed it all very much.

Like so many children, I began to collect stamps. In her wardrobe Nana had some old German stamps which were a start; but the real pleasure was to take one's Saturday pocket money (6d) and walk past our line of shops and down St John's Road. There, past Woodlands Road (down which lived Mrs Bearman who gave up trying to teach me to play the piano), were some shops on the right. The last shop seemed to me uncomfortably narrow and tall, but it sold packets of stamps of several sizes and commensurate prices. Generally I felt I could only afford a 2d packet, but even this gave a delicious sense of expectation as I carried it home and opened it to reveal the full extent of its philatelic treasures. Then, particularly if it was winter and wet, sitting at the table by the fire with my 'XLCR' junior stamp album (from the same shop), identifying, sorting, hingeing and admiring these colourful new additions to my collection – this was bliss indeed. As I grew older my ambition grew; opposite Colet Court there was a tiny shop which seemed somehow to have inserted itself into a corner of the grounds of St Paul's School. There on Saturday mornings after school I was tempted by a much more sophisticated range of stamps which took a correspondingly larger share of my pocket money. I could not resist some of the flamboyant stamps of Edward VII or the classic simplicity of Victoria's penny reds; my collection grew.

But then I became interested also in coins, and my expenditure began to shift towards them and away from stamps. I found that the downtrodden junk shops along Brentford High Street each seemed to have a box of coins, and after a little persuasion Dad would drive me along to one of these shops and wait while I picked out a few of the less worn ones for a penny each. These shops yielded chiefly George III copper coins, including one or two of the large 'cartwheel' twopenny pieces, but also some earlier pennies and farthings. In our local parade of shops was Fenn's, which sold jewellery and watches. Mr Fenn also sold soft suede leather watch pouches very cheaply and I bought some of these to hold my coins. These pouches and their precious contents were kept in a green metal box which was divided into compartments of just the right size

Again the pleasures of possession drove me on, and I bought *Seaby's Standard Catalogue of British Coins* (1/6d); then I saw an advertisement: twenty Roman denarii from some recently discovered hoard for £2. With help from mother (and probably from an imminent birthday) I wrote off, enclosing a postal order. A few days, and then a small packet came through the door; the excitement of opening it – and there were the promised twenty coins, all in good condition and requiring much careful inspection, classification and listing. They were all rather late (after AD 200), clean silver in colour though in fact somewhat debased, but they were really and truly Roman. The only Roman coin I can clearly recall finding in a junk shop around this time came from the one opposite the Commodore Cinema in King Street, Hammersmith; I got off the bus on my way home one Saturday lunchtime and crossed the road to see if it had any coins. A bearded old man pulled out a box and left me to look through it; I found one Roman coin and paid him the usual penny for it. Then he said: 'Tell your mum I let you look through that box on your own; I wouldn't let many boys do that.' I left his shop with my Roman coin and a distinct feeling of rectitude.

By this time our father had become developer to the Duke of Newcastle's estate at Dorking in Surrey and was preparing to build the small Castle Gardens development. One of the first tasks was to demolish a factory building on the site next to the River Mole just east of Dorking. This had a tall brick chimney and we were taken there one day to see it taken down. As a preliminary treat we were invited to throw stones at the condemned building's glass windows, which we did with enthusiasm. (Was this setting us a bad example, or allowing us to work off our destructive instincts?) Then we all stood well back; the temporary wood chocks now holding up the tall chimney were pulled out by a long cable, and down it came with a tremendous thump and a cloud of dust. A most satisfying day.

Meanwhile back at home Dad was busy at weekends building a large model electric railway; it went round the whole loft on a wooden shelf nearly 2 feet wide, enough to take four or more sets of tracks, and these with all their points were hand-made by him: wooden sleeper, steel rails and metal rail-shoes and even flint chippings to emulate the ballast. It was a large undertaking and I can remember watching and grunting in sympathy at Dad's efforts as he worked away; he once remarked: 'Now old chap, we'll change over – you do the work and I'll do the grunting.' At last enough of the model railway was finished to allow a beautiful green scale-model Basset-Lowke locomotive and its equally beautiful carriages in Great Western Railway livery to run round the whole layout. It was most exciting, although noisier than we expected – the whole house rumbled slightly. Alas, the extensive layout was nearing completion when the war started and after several years of work it was used on only a few occasions before 20 Avenue Road was partly let, partly closed down, as we left it for what my parents believed would just be the duration of the war; in the event they were never to live there again.

There were two parts of our house which had attractions all of their own: the garage and the loft. I can never remember anyone coming to either of these to see what I was doing, which gave them a pleasant sense of privacy. The garage was at the bottom of the garden and ran its whole width; on the left were the garage doors letting directly on to the pavement; in the middle was a pit about 3 feet deep to allow my father to do maintenance under the car – it was covered by removable planks and gave off a dank and musty smell. On the right was a sturdy workbench across the whole width of the garage with a vice, all sorts of old tools, and on shelves a number of red painted ex-sweet boxes full of nuts, bolts, nails and oddments; just the place for hammering and sawing at pieces of wood in my attempts to make things. Here also, but under my father's supervision, we melted old lead pipes into wonderfully heavy ingots by pouring the molten metal into the frog – the indentation – of a brick, so that they emerged bearing an enigmatic inscription which in fact was the reverse image of 'LBC' (London Brick Company). We also melted shards of glass until they formed a drip which fell and then, as the glass cooled, stopped at the end of a thin and hopelessly fragile stem. The garage provided me with many happy hours of activity.

Mother thought it would be instructive for her children if our springer spaniel – St Judith of Osterley to the Kennel Club, but just Judy to us – had a litter of puppies. Judy was in due course taken off to be introduced to Broomwood Baritone and the result was a litter of six, produced in her dog basket in one corner of the breakfast room. As they grew and became more adventurous they and Judy took over the garage, with a tea chest on its side as a kennel. Judy was now often given a few hours of freedom from family life. Then I could go into the garage where all six plump and eager puppies would straggle up to me, obviously very pleased to have a visitor. Best of all was to step over them, run to their tea chest, back into it on my hands and knees, hide my head in my hands and wait to be inundated by this crowd of soft, warm, licking, nibbling puppies. They also bought popularity, as two of the really senior girls at the tennis club (aged about eighteen) asked if they could come and see them.

The loft was quite different; it too had a characteristic smell – dry and dusty. It was a large room panelled with softboard, painted cream and reached by a rather ad hoc wooden staircase. On the wall at one end were bookshelves on which were a miscellany of elderly books passed down from my maternal grandfather, including nearly 150 of the small (6 in x 4 in) volumes of Cassell's National Library published in the 1880s. They cover literature (including all Shakespeare's plays), history, travel and the classics, and must have been a true treasure-house of culture in their time. Picking out some of the volumes recently I found *Thoughts on the Present Discontents* by Edmund Burke, *Table Talk* by Martin Luther, *The Voyages and Travels of Sir John Maunderville*, the *Poetics* of Aristotle, *Sketches of Persia* by Sir John Malcolm and the *Autobiography* of Benjamin Franklin. The advertisements they contain give some idea of what was worrying people in the 1880s: Dredge's Heal-All (Cure for Rheumatism, Lumbago, Chilblains); The Mexican Hair Renewer (prevents the hair falling out); Himrod's Asthma Remedy (gives instant relief also for Bronchitis and Colds); Harness's Electropathic Belt (an agreeable, natural and certain remedy for … well, nearly everything, including Rheumatism, Nervous Affections [*sic*], Paralysis and Constipation).

And in the middle of the loft room surrounded by our slowly growing model railway was a child's desk, painted white. It was there that I invented 'secret' codes, used them to produce 'secret' documents, drew a map of ancient Greece and took my first steps in learning about Ancient Egypt. For this I copied out lists of pharaohs in their dynasties as well as lists of hieroglyphs and their transliterations, and later pondered over Renouf's *Ancient Egyptian Grammar* (a much-prized birthday present). All of this gave me an agreeable feeling that in some way I had a personal stake in Ancient Egypt.

One of mother's relaxations was the occasional matinée at the Kew Theatre and her usual companion was Auntie Bertha. After the performance it was over the road to a small café, tea for two, then home by trolleybus. On one journey home Auntie Bertha said that she must now pay her share of the tea, but mother thought Auntie Bertha had paid. On their next visit to the café they confessed to their lapse and paid up; but the staff of the café remembered the event vividly and gathered round to look at the two respectable ladies whose apparent dishonesty had made such an impression upon them at the time. Apart from the Kew Theatre there were other nearer entertainments; in London Road not far from our house was an impressive new Odeon Cinema. For a time mother and Dad went there every Monday evening, and Michael and I were allowed to go to the Saturday morning children's programme as well as to see selected grown-up films. One of these was *Sanders of the River*, and inspired by it we invented a new game. It required two long garden canes as spears and our two family dustbin lids as shields. Michael would go into the garage; I remained in the middle of the garden. Michael then emerged from the garage, emitted the war cry 'AY-EE-O-KO' (taken from the film), flung his spear at me, I parried it with my shield, flung my spear at him, he threw up his arms and fell down dead. We then changed places and the same scene was enacted again and again. Not without risk, but short, simple, dramatic and greatly enjoyed by both of us.

3

Holidays

Aldwick

Nearly every year we spent most of the Easter and summer holidays down at Aldwick, arriving there by car after a journey in which oily smells and the motion of the car always made me feel sick. This required a stop at the top of Bury Hill either for brief recovery in the open air or for a more compelling reason. But once we arrived at Idlewylde recovery was rapid, and Michael and I would soon be ready to see what had changed around Aldwick in our absence. Michael, five years older than me, had much clearer memories of these holidays at Aldwick, particularly the earlier ones. While he was writing his book *The Paradise Rocks*, an evocation of our childhood at Aldwick, we would have several late-night telephone conversations each week, normally beginning with Mike asking: 'Do you remember...' and we would stir up each other's memories, extending and correcting recollections of persons, places and incidents. With so much in common our recollections flowed effortlessly and were a source of great pleasure to both of us. In this way many of my childhood memories were absorbed into Michael's book, where I am happy to see them preserved.

For a long time after we arrived, South Avenue was an undulating waste of pale grey chalky mud, in winter full of puddles which froze over, producing sheets of hollow ice from which the water had receded; I spent many enjoyable hours crashing through these in my wellingtons. In summer it was a dusty waste and I pedalled over its hummocks on a very old tricycle, too small for me really, which looked like a leftover from some Victorian nursery, which it probably was; it lacked any paint but was well furnished with rust. At the age of six or so, I was pedalling along West Avenue when

33

I first ran into Billy Gill, leader of a gang of eight-year-old desperadoes, some three of them. (He was Aldwick's equivalent of the threatening Norman Jones and his gang at Isleworth.) One of the newly built houses in West Avenue had an outside storeroom; cunningly they persuaded me to leave my tricycle and look inside; trustingly I did so; treacherously they closed the door and imprisoned me; bravely I fought my way out (by simply pushing the door open again) and ran home. One should never trust Billy Gill. It was more than a week before I ventured back to West Avenue to recover my tricycle, which I found on the pavement exactly where I had left it. Billy Gill was now a recognised threat, as shown by a letter I wrote from Isleworth to our friend Jean Hazelrigg, who lived a few doors away in South Avenue. It shows no sign of parental intervention and its literary weakness suggests that I was about seven at the time:

> Dear Jean I hope you are all right becos I am. has billy Gill bean around, if so, I hope you have been on the look out for him and not let him catch you and take you home, but I dont want to [*hear*] all a bout that all the same. I am having a lovy time up hear.
>
> good by
> Roger sant searley,
> good by
> and good hopes
>
> a picture of a house

To make it more entertaining the bottom half of the sheet is taken up with a picture of a house, helpfully labelled as shown above. It is not clear whether this letter was ever sent (although the way it has been folded suggests that it could well have been), but it is contemporary evidence of my view of Billy Gill.

Over time (and when we weren't otherwise occupied) tension grew between us and Billy Gill. We were not a large force, our strength consisting of Michael, myself, Jean from up the road, Julian (our younger brother, who only counted as a half) and one or two others loosely attached; we had no idea of the number of Billy Gill's followers. By some diplomatic process now forgotten we came to believe that on the next Saturday afternoon Billy Gill's force would appear for battle on the wasteland (a rather small undeveloped building plot) next door to our bungalow. We began our preparations for the conflict. First we excavated a dugout at the back of the land which we stocked with balls of damp clay as ammunition; we then worked on our secret weapon, a smallish hole which we filled with stinging nettles from the ditch and then camouflaged. We were confident that many of Billy Gill's gang would fall into this hole, and would then have to retire from the battlefield for dock-leaf treatment, leaving us victorious. But it was possible that we might capture some of his by then weakened gang; in preparation for this we practised tying prisoners to a rather feeble buddleia bush near our dugout. We mainly experimented on Julian, but found that if we tied him too tightly he threatened to go home and tell mother, and if we tied him up gently enough to avoid his objections he simply escaped. Clearly our technology needed improvement, but there was no time. The day of battle came, our gang (or at least several of us) assembled after lunch, a final set of clay balls was prepared and the stinging nettles in our secret weapon were renewed. But Billy Gill and his followers never turned up. As the afternoon wore on we got bored and drifted off to do other things, feeling that this was an anticlimax rather than the positive victory we had anticipated. As I had learned earlier, never trust Billy Gill; however from that time on his shadow was lifted from South Avenue and he ceased to play any part in our concerns. For the anticipated battle I had kept in reserve one of my prized possessions – a rubber dagger. Much of the paint was missing from its once black handle and rather bent silvery 'blade' with its alleged bloodstain of an improbable pink. On one occasion I proudly showed this fearsome weapon to Mrs Prior next door but her reaction of simulated horror was so disconcertingly realistic that I had to hastily run home.

It was at Aldwick that I first began to notice cars; at that time my father had a Wolseley and what most impressed me about it were the decorative pink flowers painted on the wooden frames inside each door. Nearby lived a young man who owned an SS Jaguar sports car. He used to do minor things to this car, and aged five or six I would go over and take a friendly interest in what he was doing. He obviously appreciated my interest and on one memorable occasion he drove me into Bognor and bought me an ice cream at Sait's Dairy in London Road. In due course my father moved over to Citroen cars and then in the late 1930s to a Packard Straight Eight which was to live on blocks in our garage for most of the war. These cars were chosen chiefly because they had the garages of main agents conveniently nearby on the Great West Road.

In due course I had transport of my own, a Fairy Cycle on which I would sometimes cycle into Bognor by myself, which indicates the lack of traffic on the roads. But the weather was not always suitable for such trips and when it was cold or raining I could always resort to our bookcase with its well-thumbed copy of *Sarah Crewe* by Frances Hodgson Burnett. The gist of this story is firmly, if inaccurately, fixed in my mind: Army officer in India sends daughter Sarah Crewe back to fashionable girls' school in England; in some way father is disgraced, loses all money, dies; no fees paid, Sarah relegated to role of ill-used pupil-teacher; lives in cold unhappy garret at top of school; friend of father's hears of this, knows father was innocent, resolves to save Sarah; Indian servant climbs over roof, converts garret into charming room with warm fire; cold, damp Sarah returns glumly to usual misery but *tableau*! all is warmth and comfort, and all ends well for her. I found it a most satisfying tale. Another book was *Bevis, the Story of a Boy* by Richard Jefferies. It was filled with adventures – Bevis and his friends made a gun, had a catamaran, were really rather rough and did all sorts of exciting things, most of which I did not fully understand, in a rural setting I could not really envisage. I found it all enthralling.

In September 1935 dear Nana died. I have no memory of the event, shielded from the sadness by my mother and father. Over the years mother told us some tales about her, and the one I remember was about their puppy and the little puddles each evening in the kitchen where it slept. The traditional method of rubbing the animal's nose in it had no effect and Nana was about to send it away when their maid revealed that filling her hot-water bottle each evening was the cause of the puddles, leaving my grandmother feeling very guilty about the poor puppy. Perhaps that puppy grew up to be Music, so named by my grandfather after one of his enthusiasms; he was once going over Richmond bridge on the top of a horse-bus when looking over the side there was Music, also crossing Richmond bridge, many miles from home. In those days with only horse-drawn traffic, it was quite safe for a dog to be let out to 'go walkies' on its own. (It is often said that there was a current of anti-Semitism in Britain at that time, but my grandmother expressed the opinion that a touch of Jewish blood did wonders for a family.)

Apart from our own Judy, there were several other dogs of note around Idlewylde. There were Karl and Dimmy (Dmitri) the two borzois belonging to the visiting cousin of Miss Pullen, our other next-door neighbour, and with him we would take them across the field and down Dark Lane to the beach for a run. He once took me over to West Wittering in his car to let them race along the sands there. Afterwards he treated me to an ice cream, and while left in the car Dimmy managed to eat most of the green blind covering its rear window. Then there were two red setters with wonderfully glossy coats which belonged to a family who came down to a house on the other side of the road for summer holidays; their two boys and the dogs sometimes came down to the beach with us. But in particular there was Black-Elastic Dog, so named by mother because in his pleasure at the prospect of coming to the beach he would bounce up and down from his back legs to his front ones. When we got to the beach he would espy some doggy friend up at the pier nearly a mile away and would race up there to say hallo, and then come racing back ready for more fun with us. He was a charming bundle of energy and *joie de vivre*. And just round the corner in East Avenue there was Mrs Ackford (whose husband was the editor of the *Bognor Observer*) and her golden spaniel; I liked both of them and when on occasion I paid a social call she seemed pleased to see me and would offer me lemonade and biscuits. To show solidarity with her spaniel I claimed to like dog biscuits; I did try eating one or two, but solidarity has its limits and I soon reverted to the more conventional ones that she offered.

Across the large field behind Idlewylde, across Fish Lane and down Dark Lane, was the beach. With almost no traffic Michael and I were left to go there on our own. Later the footpath across the large field was edged with trees and I can remember entertaining the men doing the planting by turning head-over-heels and ending up in one of the holes. It was then enclosed with palings and became a shady and tidy alleyway rather than a country path. At the beach there was always something to do. There was the pleasure of digging sand castles or paddling (only at high tide did we swim, and then generally with an adult to watch over us) or leaping sure-footedly over the large cluster of rounded rocks and searching the pools beneath them for the sea life they contained or the sea-borne detritus that had washed into them. We did sometimes wonder at the apparently fossilised bulgy jute sacks that were scattered thinly around (only much later did we learn that these came from the *Carnot*, a small ship carrying cement in sacks which was wrecked on Aldwick beach in 1912). Emerging from the shingle was 'the Pipe', a large and long iron land water drain with a down-turned end. We could teeter along it at high tide, surrounded by sea and feeling very adventurous, or throw stones at it when the tide was low, creating most satisfactory sonorous clangs. And there was always the ice cream man and the possibility of a Wall's Snofrute of triangular cross-section in its blue and white chequered cardboard sleeve. We never tired of these pleasures. Then wandering back from the beach as the afternoon drew to a close, salty from the sea, rather sandy, filled with sun and fresh air, looking forward to teatime when we got home; we were filled with well-being and all was right with our world.

Away from the beach there was Aldwick Farm and the fields stretching from Mrs Duffin's tiny shop towards the Downs. With Michael in the lead we often visited the farm, watching the cows being milked and sometimes 'helping' to herd the cows back to their meadows – how tolerant and kindly were the farm workers. And opposite the barn was the hollow oak – not an oak but certainly with a hollow top, which felt like a natural wooden castle. Sometimes we would meet our milkman in his horse-drawn two-wheeled cart which he drove standing up. Occasionally he would let one of us join him and then the real pleasure was moving on to a more distant customer which required the horse to trot along, making all the milk bottles clink in unison. Or we would range over the ditches and hedgerows of our local fields, always finding something new and interesting to us. But as Mike began to develop other interests I did more exploring on my own. I found that the fencing posts round these fields were a favourite basking place for small brown lizards, and carefully approaching from the other side of the post I could occasionally catch one. I vaguely hoped that it might discard its tail, but they were clearly keeping this trick for more serious adversaries. Once I spotted a larger pale green lizard; I stalked it and – surprise! – caught it. Even bigger surprise – it turned its head, bit my finger and I hastily dropped it. Several fields away was a pond – really a wider section of ditch – where we had hunted newts in the past; on one of these later visits I saw a leech making its black sine-wave progress through a clear patch of water.

Far beyond our local fields was Tangmere, which we regarded as our very own RAF airfield. Michael and I must have visited it on several occasions and to get there we used to go into Bognor to catch the rural Silver Queen bus which went past the airfield boundary. The visit I can remember most clearly was an unsuccessful one where rain and cloud meant that there was no flying. Michael and I came back to Bognor cold, damp and with no money; desperate times required desperate measures, and we summoned up the courage to borrow a penny each for the bus fare home from our neighbour Mr Gentle, whose estate agency was nearby. Home at last, we were soon warm and dry and enjoying tomato soup in front of the fire; the contrast made our earlier discomfort almost worthwhile.

Julian now was getting bigger and began to acquire his own circle of friends. It was some time later when they were all playing football on the wasteland next door to Idlewylde that Dad heard cries of sporting encouragement drifting over the fence – 'Come on Ju', 'Pass the ball Ju', 'Shoot, Ju, shoot'. To him this all had a vaguely anti-Semitic sound and he decreed that in future Julian's name, having been shortened by his playmates to Ju, would now be finally shortened to just J, and to the family he has been J ever since.

As our holiday at Aldwick drew to a close it was time for mother to prepare us for going back to school. This meant a visit to Mell's Gents & Boys Outfitters, up by Bognor railway station. The shop smelt of new clothes and in it were some model figures, one of which was a man with sandy hair, a fixed smile, a rather unnatural forward-leaning posture and hands slightly raised as if preparing to save himself when he finally toppled over. Mr Mell himself would serve us and I would be cajoled into trying on short grey flannel trousers (of a size that I would 'grow into') and various other items. Finally there was a dark blue school macintosh; mother pushed and adjusted me into it and then stepped back to observe the effect. It was at this moment that Mr Mell revealed that the mac had a yellow waterproof silk layer in the shoulders to ensure that its owner was kept dry. Suddenly the mac took on an entirely new character; I could see myself out in pouring rain but kept warm and dry by my mac with its waterproof layer. Then I imagined myself in a rowing boat in pouring rain with not only my wonderful new mac but also a scarf with the same waterproof layer – the rain could not harm me! We left Mr Mell with me wearing my super-macintosh and dreaming of new and dramatic situations of pouring rain which I could now face with warm and dry bravado.

For new school shoes I was usually taken to Daniel Neal somewhere near Kensington High Street, but on one occasion I was taken to Babers, a very upmarket shoe shop in Regent Street (no doubt because my father's team of workers had recently finished redecorating it). There the shoes were, as always, rather heavy and unforgiving in their harsh newness (and size that I would 'grow into'); but when I tried them on I was allowed to slide my feet into a machine which presented me with an x-ray picture of my feet inside the new shoes. I could see that there was indeed space for me to grow into, and if I waggled my toes I could see my bones move; this added an entirely new interest to the rather dull business of equipping me for the return to school.

We spent a considerable part of our childhood at Aldwick; we loved our holidays there and looking back on them, they were for us a golden age.

Neath

Not all my holidays were spent at Aldwick. At Easter in 1937 my parents arranged for me to go down to Neath in South Wales to spend two weeks with my paternal grandparents. My grandfather, James Alford, had an interior decorating business which included a shop selling paint and wallpaper, managed by Auntie Kate – short, dark, fiery, feared by everybody in the firm (including, I suspect, by my grandfather) but kind to me. I spent quite a lot of my time with her in the shop; there I enjoyed rearranging the tins of Eau-de-Nil paint (I don't recall any other colour) and working the machine which cut the edges off wallpaper rolls. The back room looked over the Great Western Railway line leading into Neath station, and as Michael was a keen trainspotter, I supported his interest by recording for him the names of Castle Class locomotives as they passed. I am not sure how ethical this vicarious trainspotting was to a true aficionado like Michael, but I gained some small pleasure from noting down names like *Manorbier Castle* and passing them on to him, hoping he would enter them in his neatly written notebook.

There were other attractions of being with Auntie Kate; nearby was a cake shop where I went to buy cakes for elevenses and for tea, and the covered market where one stall in particular held my interest because it had the complete works of Shakespeare in a set of tiny volumes about an inch square. And further away were the cinemas, which I was allowed to go to on my own. One film that I saw was *King Kong*, and I fortified myself for the experience by buying four ounces of Rowntree's blackcurrant gums which were handed over the counter to me in a crisp pale mauve paper bag. By the end of the film, with half these sweets gone, I felt I could never again face a blackcurrant gum. But it was another film which made such an impression on me that later at Wyndham in my Composition exercise book (21 September 1936, aged nearly eleven) I wrote an essay on it. Here it is, as booksellers say, with all faults:

> My favourite film was 'Escape from Devil's Island'. It was a British film made in the Gaumont British film ~~studiose~~ studios. I saw it at the Windsor cinema, ~~ne~~ Neath, in South Wales. I liked it because of the thrills of getting through the jungle being trailed by bloodhounds. In the centre of the jungle one was crushed by a ~~baa~~ boa constrictor and another shot down and torn to pieces by a panther. Eventually reached England where on was caugh again.

There were several red marks from my teacher and a final damning comment in large red letters: 'Rewrite'.

I think that my presence provided my grandfather with a welcome excuse for some trips which he enjoyed. We went to a big boxing match in Swansea – a local lad against an Egyptian; with my interest in Ancient Egypt it was clear whom I should support. He also took me to an evening of local boxing matches held in a field with a raised baulk of earth marking out the ring. We went to the agricultural show at Brecon where I saw some louche fellow smoking two cigarettes simultaneously, and grandfather left me outside a tent while he went inside for a glass of beer; it was tacitly understood between us that nothing should be said about this at home – Grandma had strong feelings about drink.

Back at Fernleigh, my grandparents' house, I would watch as Grandma prepared Grandpa's supper for his return from work – it was a large plate impressively heaped with the food required by a large and active man. After supper he would settle down at the dining table and cut himself some pipe tobacco from a large curved bar with a wonderful strong tangy smell. Then it was up to bed for me, where I was allowed to read for a while. One book I found in the bookcase there was *Biffel, the Story of an Ox*, set in Southern Rhodesia. I was captivated by the story of Biffel's life from calf to fully

41

grown ox, ending up yoked to a creaking wagon, trekking over the dusty trails of Mashonaland with the cries of the drivers and the crack of their long whips. I can remember almost nothing of it in detail, but the atmosphere it created has remained with me ever since.

When I was not out with Auntie Kate or Grandpa I used to play in the garden. This sloped up quite sharply from the house and had a small lawn with a laundry line stretched across it; on the middle of this line I hung a garden cane on a string and then with another cane I attacked it, parrying, cutting and thrusting my way to victory after victory, engrossed in a world of my own. I am afraid that my letters home reveal the usual shortage of money and emphasise the arrangements for meeting me at Paddington on my return. Although everyone was very kind to me, I was evidently feeling rather homesick and was relieved to be on the train back to Paddington. On the journey a very kind man took pity on an obviously abandoned child and took me to the restaurant car for an ice cream, and at Paddington handed me over to my father.

Tavistock

It must have been in 1938 that mother felt we deserved a change from Aldwick, and for the summer she rented a house in Tavistock which was run as a small school by a Miss Potts. It was a grey stucco building with a bay window on each floor and a bedroom for each of us. On the other side of the road were Tavistock's municipal tennis courts and bowling greens (both about 2d per hour), behind them a narrow canal, a grass park and finally the river Tavey. When Dad came down he took us out in the car to visit all the local sights – Dartmoor and the tors, and other local beauty spots including Lydford Gorge, a dramatic combination of rock and rushing water. At other times we spent hours playing tennis and bowls, and exploring the river. On the river was a weir, and masses of elvers – baby eels – were struggling up its weedy face. I felt these needed some help, and often spent time lifting them over the weir and getting wet and chilled; my reward for this humanitarian action was an acute attack of earache, after which the eels were left to fend for themselves. For a while we were joined by Auntie Bertha and cousin Elizabeth, and with them we took bus rides to various beauty spots. I can remember a tall railway viaduct, a very shallow rocky river where we made life difficult for baby salmon (although we never caught one) and a cold, dark and forbidding reservoir where Elizabeth wanted us to swim; I was relieved when swimming was vetoed by our elders.

With the house came a maid, a kindly soul who made a saffron cake specially for us. I am afraid none of us liked its strange taste, but to show that we appreciated her gesture we cut a slice or two each evening after she had gone home and stoked them into the boiler. As we should have foreseen, its diminishing size led her to make us another one and the rest of the holiday was spent in a carefully calculated process of stoking enough of it into the boiler to show that we were eating it, while leaving enough to persuade her not to make us another one. The back garden of Miss Potts's house ended up against what I remember as almost a cliff; one day there was a heavy rain shower and the water poured over this cliff and down the garden path, threatening to flood the house. Michael and I managed to divert the flow, getting thoroughly and enjoyably soaked in the process and gaining much praise from mother. Shortly after this a small spring appeared in the garden path; mother was charmed and urged us to avoid stepping on this example of nature's bounty. But a few days later some Water Board men arrived and nature's bounty was repaired out of existence.

We sometimes walked the few hundred yards into the centre of Tavistock where we bought very large pale pork sausages from a pork butcher. We visited a chemist's shop which gave free samples of Pain Reliever tablets; we did not need these, but we felt we might need them at some future date, so we collected quite a useful supply. And there was the local cinema, very small and a real fleapit, which early on a Saturday evening was filled with teenage footballers, still in their sporting gear, relaxing after their matches. Its most popular features were the films that came in weekly episodes, and even at my age I was conscious of the strange discontinuities from week to week. These did not even have the credibility of those ending one episode with the hero bound hand and foot to a railway line, and 'With one bound he was free . . .' as the beginning of the next. But somehow it didn't seem to matter in that fuggy, crowded space where everyone was determined to enjoy themselves.

Monville

Joan Webster, Elizabeth's elder sister, had friends in France and in 1939 mother felt that a short holiday abroad would broaden my horizons. On 9 August I went with Joan from Newhaven to Dieppe and then by rail to Monville and then to the chateau of La Boucaille, which was the home of Joan's friends, the de la Moissonière family. It was a substantial country house surrounded by an estate, some of it farmed and other parts left as woodland. The family consisted of elderly Madame, Myrée (her daughter and Joan's friend), another daughter Raymonde (married but staying there with her own small daughter) and Mano (her son, who had a tandem bicycle on which he and I occasionally toured the local roads). There were also some servants who spoke a strangely guttural Norman patois. Several things made an impression upon me; the frogs in a small pond behind the chateau would chirrup and grunt noisily, quite unlike British frogs; and the food was different and delicious, eaten at a large dining-table in a handsome dining-room. At our first dinner I was served with cider; it seemed harmless enough, but later that night I was very sick and after that I politely declined it. Breakfast also was a family meal, but in the warm weather we had this in our dressing-gowns out on the large gravel drive in front of the chateau. I only remembered much later that it must have been Myrée who had come over to Osterley to stay with Joan some years earlier; when introduced to her I sought to display my French by greeting her with 'Bonjour, cochon', but fortunately she appeared to have forgotten my ill-judged effort to improve Anglo-French understanding.

To keep me entertained I was provided with a small-bore shotgun and a handful of cartridges and was invited to go out into the estate, quite unsupervised, to shoot something. I enjoyed this grown-up freedom, and am I glad to say that I had only one victim, but sorry to say that it was an innocent blue tit. Joan and I went out on trips – I particularly remember going to Rouen where I wanted to buy mother a small plastic tortoise which took my fancy, but on Joan's gentle suggestion I bought her instead a silver thimble. It must have been coming back from this trip that we were greeted excitedly by Myrée and Mano who were holding some pieces of cloth; did Joan recognise them? Yes she did, and then the full story emerged. Not far from the pond with its noisy frogs was a clothes line and before we went out Joan had left sundry garments on it to dry; a small herd of heifers had come to investigate them and had then eaten the whole lot except for the parts under the pegs. It was these fragments which Myrée and Mano had invited Joan to identify. I was enjoying this holiday, but unknown to me the storm clouds were gathering.

Only through Michael's account (*The Paradise Rocks*, p. 358–9) did I learn much later of my father's efforts to get in touch with me by telephone as the international crisis worsened. Over several days from 22 August 1939 his increasingly urgent attempts had all failed, but then:

> ... at last, to everyone's relief, we were advised through a roundabout route that young Roger had been put on a boat in the care of a kind and reliable stranger. On the Monday afternoon [*26 August*], happily oblivious of all the fuss he had caused, my brother arrived back in his Motherland for a dockside reunion of hugs and kisses from his thankful parents.

My own memory of my return is of my father standing behind the glass window at the ferry arrival point at Newhaven, his head bobbing about as he anxiously scanned the passengers coming off the channel ferry to see if I was there. At last we saw each other; I had a great sense of relief that he was there to meet me, but then the memory fades. It was very nice to be home, but still the crisis did not really impinge on me and it was back to our summer holiday as usual. However, under pressure from mother, the first thing was to write a thank-you letter to my hostess at La Boucaille enclosing what seemed to me at that age to be very suitable gifts – three picture postcards of Bognor beach and some chocolate. On the next Thursday Mike and I went fishing on the pier, something we had done many times with little success; however this time I caught a red mullet, my best catch ever, and mother cooked it for my supper. But then came Sunday the 3rd of September (again I draw on *The Paradise Rocks*, p. 262):

> Like millions of other families that Sunday morning, we gathered round the wireless; Downing Street and eleven strokes of Big Ben. Then the Prime Minister's crumpled voice; the melancholy reasons for the failure of the British Government's negotiations, the ultimatum sent to Hitler. At last came the kernel of his announcement, '... I have to tell you now that no such undertaking

has been received and that, consequently, this country is at war with Germany.'

Some two weeks later I received a picture postcard (showing the front of Rouen Cathedral) from Madame, written in her thin sloping hand and sent to me via Dad's office at 19 Hanover Square:

La Boucaille
Monville
Seine Inf
France   16 Sept. 39

Dear little Roger

I have been very happy of your cards of sea shore and kindest letter and very nice chocolate – thank you very much for all these things. You are a very good and gentle boy. I hope you are well and your family too. Kindest regards for all. I kiss you with love.

Jenny de Prévost de la Moissonière

4

1939 – War and Evacuation

Radley College

The summer holiday drew to a close and school began to loom; it was then that we all began to experience the upheaval of war. I had no idea that preparations had been made for Colet Court to be evacuated from London; my parents had been informed of the plans (indeed they had attended a preliminary meeting as early as September 1938) and had agreed that I should be evacuated with the school. Now it was not just a few items of clothing for the new term, it was more like kitting out an expedition: a new camp bed with blankets and sheets, washing kit and a long list of specified clothing, everything marked with my name in red on Cash's name tapes. Then, instead of the familiar 657 trolleybus and 27a bus, I was driven by my father to Radley College near Oxford and, a few weeks before my thirteenth birthday, given over to the care of a very different Colet Court.

Looking back, the unsung heroes of this evacuation were the teachers; from comfortable family homes or bachelor flats around Hammersmith they suddenly found themselves not just teaching forms of rather homesick boys in entirely new and unfamiliar surroundings, but also having to take on some of the less appealing role of parents. In the following term, when the school had moved to Danesfield, I can still see Mr Ingoldby, a rather aesthetic bachelor, coming into our crowded dormitory to see that the lights were out. Half of us were already suffering from chickenpox (caught from a local barber brought in to cut our hair, who told us to shut our eyes as he blew into our faces to remove the cuttings) and Mr Ingoldby was greeted by, 'Please Sir, I have got the squits', 'It's true, Sir, he's been to the bog three times already', 'Sir, Sir, Suddaby says he is feeling ill' ... On Mr

Ingoldby's face was a mixture of distaste and resigned determination to do his best in circumstances he could never have foreseen even in his wildest nightmares. Somehow they, Mr Ingoldby and all the other teachers, not to mention their wives, managed to deal with these domestic emergencies, console the homesick, keep their teaching going, supervise games, organise the writing of letters home, check that weekly laundry was properly bundled up, and arrange activities to occupy us in the evenings and over weekends – all in new and often very trying circumstances. Looking back, for sterling work in adversity they all deserved A+.

Arriving at Radley I found many of my friends and many other faces I had known at Hammersmith, but everything else was utterly different. We were scattered amongst various makeshift dormitories around the college, and had to find our way to the important places: our own scattered classrooms, football pitches, the tuck shop and the dining hall, where our meals had to alternate with those of the Radley boys (who used to flick butter pats up onto the high wooden ceiling, and periodically these plopped down on us as the room heated up). I think all of us at the start felt a sense of rootlessness because suddenly there was no natural centre to our lives; but we came to terms with our new situation, life assumed a pattern and we settled down. Eagerly we awaited letters from home, which soothed the dull ache of homesickness which most of us felt but all of us tried to conceal. My own letters home show this, with the recurring theme: 'Please write to me whenever you can'.

At Radley I was placed initially in the cricket pavilion which had become a dormitory for about thirty boys. I found this rather stark and overcrowded and somehow managed to get myself a transfer which took me to the house of Mr Brodie, the Radley College chaplain, where there were already two other boys. I still have a picture postcard of this period house which I sent to mother on 5 October 1939; it has the traditional X marking the window of the bedroom shared by the three of us. Mr Brodie's housekeeper was Mrs Hughson, tall and nicely spoken, and down in the warm kitchen was Joyce the maid, sometimes helped by her mother (who could not tell the time – she would turn away from the clock and just casually ask Joyce what the time was); all were very kind to us. One evening towards the end of term Mr Brodie invited the three of us into his private sitting room – wonderfully woody and cosy, with an uneven polished wooden floor nearly black with age and a log fire lighting up an ancient cast-iron fireback. But it was to the warm kitchen that we gravitated when we were at a loose end. This had a large table in the middle and we would sit there and talk while Joyce got on with her work, which she felt included keeping us supplied with extra items of food. In one of my letters home:

I am in the kitchen now, we have just been toasting bread and putting dripping and salt on it.

and I added

P.S. It is Joyce's birthday etc so please send Postal Order (BIG ONE)

I am afraid that such requests for money were a recurring theme in my letters. As an excuse I can only say that many things that would be readily available at home – from marmalade, biscuits and sweets (although these latter were generally rationed by mother) to toothpaste or a bottle of ink – I now had to buy for myself, and this required money. I can remember the pleasure I got from buying my very own pot of Golden Shred marmalade from the Radley tuck shop. A less pleasurable occasion was when I was hauled off by ambulance to hospital in Oxford with suspected appendicitis, only to be sent back the next day as a false alarm.

It would be impossible to reconstruct our daily round from memory, but fortunately I set this out in one of my letters home:

Colet Court
Radley College
Radley
Berks

Dear Dad
I promised to write to you to give an account of a days work, so here it is. We get up at 6.30, wash, dress, make our beds etc, then breakfast at 7.30. First lessons start at 8.20 till 9.40 then chapel and assembly in the gymnasium. Then there is football till 12, we change for dinner which is at 12.40 till 1.00, rest period at 1.00 till 1.30 then lessons again till 3.30. Tea is next at 3.55 (it is only milk and biscuits), lessons again till 5.30, supper 6.30, bed 7.00,

so you see we have a full day. The weather is warm, except in early morning. There is a big tuckshop at the college, and it sells all kinds of things from jam to chewing gum and from drinks to ham sandwiches. The meals are very nice, well cooked and nice ingredients. But now and then there are not quite enough second helpings. We work on all days except on Wednesday afternoon and on Sundays. My bed is very comfortable and I sleep very well indeed. We make our own beds, and I am getting good at making mine. The Rev Brodie, our host, is very nice indeed, and so is Mrs Hughson and Joyce the maid. Is there a war on? Somehow it does not seem like it down here, as we dont see the papers very often. Now I must sign off, so good bye, good health and good luck etc. Yours with tons of love

Roger

X X X X X X X X

P.S. Thanks for the 10/-

The grounds of Radley were extensive and soon we were exploring them in our free time. Beyond the playing fields there was a rough area and there we found that poachers had set snares for rabbits, which we carefully removed. Coming back carrying them we met one of the senior Radley boys; we showed him the snares only to be told that these were set legitimately by the senior boys, and we hastily handed them over to him to be returned to their owners. Catching rabbits was one of the country pursuits which were approved by the college. Behind one of the college buildings were cages where the seniors were allowed to keep ferrets and where we sometimes went to watch them being fed; later we watched these boys netting burrows and using the ferrets to flush rabbits out into the nets. Another wildlife feature was the early-morning sight of dozens of large hermaphrodite worms pairing on the dewy grass of the lawn between the main buildings and the cricket pavilion. We looked at them with interest, but we were careful not to disturb them.

As term went on we ventured outside the Radley grounds and on one of these expeditions we came across an isolated summerhouse, deserted and run-down, with broken stained glass scattered around it. We could not resist picking up the best small pieces of rich reds and blues. Not far away was RAF Abingdon and we often saw their black Whitley bombers moving slowly across the sky. I was a member of the Colet Court choir and as it came up to Christmas 1939 we went to this aerodrome to give a carol concert in the Officers' Mess; I now wonder how many of the aircrew who listened to us were destined to die in the war. Our choir also sang before an audience from both schools as part of the end-of-term entertainment. This was held in the large gymnasium where the stage lights and curtains were managed by Radley seniors. I was impressed by their muscular management of the curtains and by the way they led the appropriate audience response by clapping and cheering behind the scenes as they lowered the curtains after each item on the programme. Being in the choir also led to me and a few others being invited by the Radley music master – was his name Mr Borgni? – to his panelled rooms where for an hour he talked to us and played on a grand piano; we very much enjoyed this and were greatly impressed by his performance.

At last term came to an end and there was all the relief of going home to one's family, with the added bonus of Christmas – not quite the ample Christmases we had known in the past but not yet the sparse ones of the later wartime years. By this time my parents had moved to our bungalow at Aldwick 'for the duration of the emergency', the official euphemism at that time for the war, so that it was in our familiar holiday home that we spent Christmas. One of my Christmas presents was a small diary; this I managed to keep for the first three days of the new year, noting that I went into Bognor on each of these days, went fishing (caught nothing), saw *The Lion has Wings* (very good), had a friend to tea and returned a stray dog to its home. At that point my diary discipline failed, but this is enough to show that this holiday was much like so many other holidays we had spent there. The war still seemed a background, rather than a foreground, to our lives.

Danesfield

At last the holiday had to end and I was faced with another change. Colet Court had moved from Radley to Danesfield, a large country house belonging to the wealthy Garton family of Garton's HP Sauce. It was a fine house made of white chalk blocks, in large grounds on a low bluff overlooking the Thames; its postal address was Medmenham, which was some two miles west of Marlow on the road to Henley. We were now all accomodated in rather crowded dormitories (previously the servants' quarters) at the top of the house. Near our dormitory was a butler's pantry containing a large sink with a draining board on each side. I and a boy named Cook sometimes used to fill up the two large bowls in the sink, one with hot water and one with cold. Then each sitting on one of the draining boards, one put his feet in the hot bowl, the other in the cold one. At a signal we then each put our feet into the other bowl, which gave us a strange but agreeable sensation, and in this way we would switch our feet between the bowls until the novelty wore off; at least it was a game leading to clean feet. Our classrooms were on the ground floor, some of them in sections of the long gallery overlooking the gardens. I think the school must have contracted considerably because in my form there were now only eight boys. Our dining hall in the warm weather was a set of open-sided converted stables round a yard; as we sat eating, there was nothing between us and the swallows swooping down to collect mud from around the puddles in the yard and taking it up to build their nests under the eaves opposite. But there was one thing we really missed – Radley's tuck shop. Now all we had was a table set up each Saturday in one corner of the very large sitting room which served as our assembly room, with a rather limited selection of sweets which we could buy with our pocket money. A distinct comedown. Lessons went on as usual and we quickly settled in to our new surroundings.

At school, singing was one of our regular activities. At Danesfield we had a new music master and I can remember the pleasure of singing Handel's 'Where'er you walk'; however, writing it down raised difficulties. The most popular spelling is that used above, the apostrophe showing the dropped 'v' from the single word 'Wherever'; a runner-up is 'Where e'er', a contraction of 'Where ever'– two words rather than one (and the version I prefer, since in singing it emerges as two words); but, courtesy of Google, I found also: 'Where'ere', 'Where ere', 'Where er', 'Where E'er', and finally 'Where-er-you-walk'. Clearly apostrophes can be a problem. This reminds me of a different conundrum of one's schooldays which arises with Macaulay's poem *Horatius*. The hero, after holding back the Tuscan army, just manages to swim across the foaming Tiber to reach the further bank,

'And even the ranks of Tuscany could scarce forbear to cheer'. Let Richard Morrison, Cultural Editor of *The Times*, clarify matters:

Cheers to all our readers

If I have learnt nothing else in my 23 years on this newspaper, I have come to realise that there is no query so esoteric or erudite that several dozen *Times* readers don't leap forward with the answer. Not always the same answer, mind, but that's a mere detail. In this space last week I wondered whether Macaulay's great line in *Horatius* – 'And even the ranks of Tuscany could scarce forbear to cheer' – meant that the Tuscan hordes did cheer or didn't cheer. Well, exactly 50 per cent of your replies argue with incisive logic that, if you take Macaulay's syntax literally, the Tuscans *didn't* cheer. Unfortunately, the other 50 per cent or you marshal no less brilliant arguments to deduce that they *did*.

Back to square one, then? Not quite. I've just had a postcard from Sue Handoll, of Berwick-upon-Tweed – who is, she tells me, none other than Macaulay's great, great, great grandniece. 'They cheered,' she writes authoritatively.

That's good enough for me. Or as her great, great, great grand-uncle might have put it: I can scarce forbear to agree. (*The Times*, 27 February 2007)

That first winter of the war was cold, with many days of snow. It was on one of these days that my father came down to Marlow by train (petrol rationing was now very tight) and I met him at the station; it is hard to describe my pleasure at seeing him. He took me to a restaurant for lunch, of which I remember only the suggestion by the waiter that I might care for a jam omelette for dessert – it was an inspired suggestion. After much talk it was time for Dad to return to town, so back to the station, and as I regretfully saw him onto the train he gave me a half-crown. I walked back to the bus stop but, horror of horrors, I found that my half-crown was missing and I had no other money. There was nothing for it but to walk the two miles back to Danesfield – a small figure in a dark blue mac trudging along a snowy and deserted road through a bleak white landscape. But salvation was at hand; a car pulled up, driven by the estate manager of

Danesfield who had recognised the Colet Court uniform, and in this vehicle of mercy I was delivered to the front door of the school.

On the winter evenings, after prep, we used to devise our own entertainments and one of these was a small cardboard theatre. Four of us, myself, Cook, Suddaby and an Indian boy named Homi (in those days it was all surnames) cooperated on this. It consisted of a shallow stage with an upright rear wall about six inches square, all behind a proscenium arch some twelve inches square. In the rear wall were two slots and through these were threaded a long strip of paper four inches wide and marked off in sections of about five inches. Then in these sections we drew successive scenes of a story we made up. When we had finished and had done a bit of rehearsal we would invite a few other boys (and because of its size it had to be only a few) to a performance. Then one of us told the story in words, two of us were in charge of moving the picture tape along section by section, and the fourth was there to keep an eye on the other three and to correct any errors by the storyteller. We devoted quite a lot of our free time to this theatrical venture and got a great deal of pleasure out of it; how our audiences felt, I cannot recall.

We ventured around the estate in the cold weather and threw snowballs at each other on the snowy days, ending up with chilled hands inside sodden woollen gloves. My diary suddenly comes to life again on 19 February 1940 and records that 'Lyon and Kissin fell in the river'; this must have been an uncomfortable experience because it is only on the following day that it records 'Thaw. Played football', and this is the last thing I could find to enter about the momentous year of 1940. It wasn't until the weather warmed up that we began to realise just how pleasant our surroundings were. Then, although lessons went on as usual, we spent most of our time in shirts, shorts and sandals, with a lot of freedom to roam around the estate. We saw almost no newspapers, I cannot remember any radios, and the war seemed far away.

Danesfield had large gardens ending in a steep overgrown slope down to the river with a zig-zag path leading to a boathouse; in it was a skiff in which, accompanied by a master, we were allowed to paddle up and down the river, sometimes landing by a weir to lie on the grass and just watch the river flowing by. On one occasion two of us were going down this path when we found a fire in the undergrowth; we managed to put it out at the expense of a few burns from hot ashes, and were commended for our action. Not far from the house was a sloping field on which the whole school, divided into two teams each led by a master (Mr Berry and, I believe, Mr Legh), once enacted a battle of movement. Having the masters joining in added greatly to the afternoon's enjoyment. On warm summer evenings Mr Evans our headmaster would read chapters of Arthur Ransome's *Swallows and Amazons* to a large circle of boys seated on the grass, all listening with rapt attention. Further away from the house was a large shallow pit, almost a small quarry, which was used as a dump for some of the family's rubbish; also in the pit was a large and very climbable tree, blown over and lying on its side. A group of us went regularly to this tree, clambering all over it in games of three-dimensional He; when we needed a rest we would descend to the ground and read the family's letters which had been dumped there.

But time was coming for another change; all of us in the top forms were due to take the Common Entrance exam and to move on from Colet Court, most going on to St Paul's. One of my particular friends was going to another school and I wrote home urging that I should be sent there as well. Somehow or other I was reasoned out of this, passed Common Entrance (which I feel was rather a formality at that time) and became destined for St Paul's the following September. At last term ended, there were farewells to friends going on to other schools, none of whom did I ever see again, and then it was joyfully home for the summer holiday of 1940. But it was home to find a world of threatening events which we had hardly been aware of in our quiet backwater of Danesfield.

At Aldwick were mother, Mike and J, with Dad having to spend many weekdays at 20 Avenue Road, having closed his office at 19 Hanover Square, and slowly closing down his business as architect and property developer which could not function under the restrictions of wartime. Mike was attending Chichester School of Art and, five years my senior, was much more conscious of the tumult of events and now kept a regular diary. This enabled him in Chapter 21 of *The Paradise Rocks* to give his own first-hand account of these dangerous but exciting summer months of 1940 as seen from Aldwick. The increasing level of air activity culminated in the Battle of Britain, which we watched together from the garden of Idlewylde, often standing on the fountain to get a better view of history being made in the summer skies above us. With many of my own memories incorporated in Mike's book, here I need to do no more than repeat a few of them and add some further details.

Summer Holiday 1940 – The Battle of Britain

I must have arrived home in the middle of July; with the fear of invasion, the beach had already been closed off, the pier had a section cut out of the middle so that it could not be used for enemy landings, and stout poles were erected in the fields beyond Yeoman's Acre to deter glider landings. However, by now I was nearly fourteen and the earlier pleasures of field, farm, beach and pier no longer exercised the same attractions. But there was still Bognor with its shops, cinemas and library; after the seclusion of Danesfield such urban facilities were an agreeable change. Above all there were aircraft and air battles to be watched and eagerly discussed. Like so many boys at that time, Mike and I had our aircraft recognition handbooks and had become adept at immediately identifying all the main aircraft on both sides. We had our air raid shelter, and at mother's insistence we opened it whenever there was a warning but I can only recall going into it for a short time one night – there was too much to see and we were unwilling to miss any of the action. We had our record of air raid warnings in the form of a piece of wooden board into which we hammered a nail for every warning; already it was quite a forest of nails. We had our record of Eric Coates' *Four Ways Suite* with *Northwards*, a rousing march, as our preferred musical background for watching air battles, and we had the BBC Nine O'clock News in the evenings to chronicle the successes of the RAF by day. Fortunately we were not aware of the perilously narrow margin by which the Battle of Britain was to be won.

It is difficult to remember all the warnings, sounds of air battles over Portsmouth, sightings of enemy aircraft, squadrons of Hurricanes going off to intercept enemy bombers, high-level air battles revealed only by patterns of contrails and miscellaneous explosions near and far. Michael gives the most coherent account of this, but one particular event stands out above all others. Some five miles north of Bognor was Tangmere, an RAF fighter station where in earlier years Mike and I had admired Hawker Furies and Gloster Gladiators, but which was now home to squadrons of Hawker Hurricanes, the backbone of Britain's air defence at that time. It was the attack on Tangmere on 16 August 1940 which for us marked the climax of the Battle of Britain. As so often at that time there was a warning on, and our ears picked up the sound of aircraft high overhead, clearly not our own. Straight away Mike and I were out in the garden and

I can recall staring up into the hazy sky trying to identify the planes as they flew northwards. Then the engine note changed and we saw the dark and sinister shapes of Stukas – Junkers 87b's – diving down on Tangmere with their sirens howling. It was a dive-bombing attack of the kind which had shattered armies during the German attacks on Poland and France. Thunderous explosions and a great pall of brown smoke, then sudden silence.

Out of sight the Stukas were hedgehopping their way back from the target. We now ran into the front garden to get a better view of what was to happen next, and suddenly over the houses opposite surged the Stukas at near rooftop height. Simultaneously from our left came a force of Hurricanes and Spitfires. I can do no better than to quote Mike:

> Before our astonished eyes, across the skies over Aldwick, Rose Green and Nyetimber, a roof-top air-battle developed, savage and patternless; a melée of aircraft flying in all directions to the chattering accompaniment of machine-guns and the sound of tortured engines.
>
> The combined fire-power of a Hurricane and a Spitfire, took it in turns to knock bits off one of the Stukas; another raider was being chased back towards Tangmere before suddenly turning south again, dropping earthwards. Attempting to avoid its assailant's guns yet another, its swastikas clearly visible, jinked and twisted desperately over our heads before it was lost to view beyond the Dark Lane elms. At Runcton spent bullets broke green-house panes and links of ammo-belt tinkled down in Rose Green Road.
>
> Within minutes it was all over. As the sound of aircraft died away, a deep silence descended upon Aldwick Gardens. Soon, the loudest sounds were the voices of neighbours as they emerged from their houses, many of them suggesting hopefully that all the German planes had been shot down. (Michael Alford, *The Paradise Rocks*, pp. 276–77)

My own most striking memory is of a Spitfire close behind a Stuka, its crosses and swastika markings clearly visible, with the Spitfire banking left and right as it fired burst after burst, tearing pieces off the Stuka with its withering fire.

The attack on Tangmere started at about one o'clock and later that afternoon Mike and I, having heard about a crashed Stuka, cycled the two miles over to Sefter School and there on the other side of the Pagham Rife was the Junkers 87b, badly damaged but still dark and menacing even in defeat. The dying pilot and dead gunner had already been removed, but the bullet holes and blood-spattered canopy told their story clearly enough. We walked round it absorbing all the details of our first close-up view of an enemy aircraft. Later Mike collected a dive brake from this Stuka and I collected (and still have) an aluminium panel, gold in colour, with a bullet hole through it and marked with the plane's production number: 5618. For years it carried the acrid smell of the aircraft's synthetic oil.

In the following days there were other attacks in the direction of Portsmouth and then one on the airfield at Ford. We would see Hurricanes and Spitfires going off to intercept these raids but the air-fighting was too far away for us to see any detail; for most we heard only the distant explosions of the bombs, louder in the case of Ford. Two hours after the latter attack two Junkers 88s came over us, evidently on reconnaissance to assess the damage. As soon as we heard the now familiar note of German engines I ran out into the garden to see what was happening. Mother called to me, saying it might be dangerous; my hasty reply was: 'Don't worry, he's got no more droms to bop, I mean no more bops to drom.' The firemen at our local Slated Barn Post next to Mrs Duffin's little shop had gone to help after the attack on Ford and that evening they showed Michael and me the hose nozzle from Ford's own fire engine, battered out of shape by a bomb.

Slinfold

By now mother in particular was becoming seriously worried that we might find Aldwick in the front line of a German invasion, compounded by receiving official instructions on what to do if such an invasion did happen. It was decided that we would move some thirty miles back to Slinfold in the north of Sussex where Dad had earlier bought a plot of land (in fact a field of about five acres on a south slope and surrounded by coppiced woodland) in Hayes Lane with the intention of building a country cottage there. We had visited the field several times before the war and had eaten our picnic lunches there (I particularly remember the liver sausage sandwiches). It was now arranged that we would rent a large room from Mr Pocock at The Chalet, Hayes Lane, which adjoined the bottom of our field (Mr Pocock had been a craftsman at the London workshop of Fabergé). In addition there were the components for a substantial wooden hut ready to be erected on our land; Dad had bought this as a site office for the time when he would start building his country retreat.

For our move to Slinfold I return to Mike's account in *The Paradise Rocks* pp. 285–86:

...having made sure we'd left nothing in the air-raid shelter – whose main purpose so far had been to keep the milk cool – the bungalow was locked up. The chickens had been sent on in advance. On the strength of our last few petrol coupons, my parents, little Julian, a sack of oatmeal from Isted's and Judy, drooling in anticipation of meeting a better class of rabbit, set off in the car to the safety of the north Sussex countryside. Detailed to carry a couple of cardboard attaché cases, a meat mincer and the dinner plates, Roger and I followed by train.

...on Barnham station, my plates slipped their packaging, fell to the platform and proceeded to cut noisy figures-of-eight around the empty Nestlés Chocolate machine, under the station trolley and behind a crate of disbelieving Khaki Campbells before describing a gracious *pas-de-deux* at the feet of an astonished ticket-collector. Phew! – and not one broken!

But that only presaged a disagreeable journey of stops and starts due to the exigencies of war. At Christ's Hospital we arrived just in time to see the 'Slinfold Flyer' disappearing out of the station leaving us two hours to wait until the next. Then it started to rain. Nor had we brought our macs. And we'd finished the Spam sandwiches.

To burden the reader with yet another vicissitude that befell these two bedraggled refugees upon arrival at their rural asylum, would be an uncalled-for imposition. So let it suffice if I say that it hinged on the discovery of a circular twelve-inch hole in the ground a few yards from The Chalet's wall.

The village bobby stood up, brushed the grass from his trousers, replaced his tin hat and turned to my father. 'An unexploded bomb, sir!'

It is difficult to reconstruct the details of this move. In my memory, it is clear that at some stage Mike and I spent a few days on our own at Slinfold, living in the hut, with a hole a foot deep and some two feet across in front of it in which we cooked over a wood fire. Needing food, Mike and I walked down to the butcher in Slinfold village; all he could offer us was a rather grisly sheep's head. Outside the hut we built a good-sized fire in our cooking hole, put the sheep's head in a large and heavy iron cooking pot inherited from Nana's kitchen, covered it with water, put the lid on it and waited for lunch. And waited and waited. The water had become warm but it seemed clear that our cooking effort was not going to succeed; disillusioned, we left it, walked down to the village again, caught the bus into Horsham and consoled ourselves with a visit to the cinema. Back to Slinfold again, and we were trudging up Hayes Lane when we noticed a distinct and appealing smell of cooking. Reaching our hut, there in our large iron pot and smelling delicious was a perfectly cooked sheep's head. What a welcome home! Some of our other efforts at cookery were less successful; a squirrel, shot by Mr Pocock, emerged from the pot with its limbs outstretched and looking disconcertingly like a human baby. We tried eating it, but it was rubbery and tasteless; perhaps we should have gone to the cinema.

We were now installed in the heart of the countryside, lodged in one large room of The Chalet together with a wooden hut, lacking most of our accustomed amenities and in particular without a car because of the stringent petrol rationing. We might be less exposed to the dangers of invasion but we were certainly exposed to many other straining discomforts. Amongst these, Mr Pocock was excavating an air raid shelter under his kitchen and as his excavation grew my father could see a real danger of half the bungalow collapsing into it and leaving us homeless. There were minor compensations; Mr Pocock gave us a black-and-tan guinea pig named Wommet, a perfect watch-dog who whistled loudly whenever he (?) heard the front gate being opened. When I had some minor indisposition I was allowed to have him in bed with me. Soon after we arrived a blue tit flew into a closed window, knocked itself out and lay flat on its back on the floor with its beak open. Mother, ever kindly, gave it a single drop of brandy

– such a surprise that it recovered and flew away. However, because I was away at school I shared our rural hardships only during the holidays. Indeed, shortly after we arrived at Slinfold I had to go back to school with my camp bed, bedding roll, suitcase and bicycle. All these things had to be carried along the rough track over a few fields to Slinfold's tiny station, itself a very Adelstrop. From there it was to Guildford, change to the Reading line and then on to Crowthorne, for now I had moved on to St Paul's School. On Crowthorne station I was grateful to see Psycopoulos, a boy whom I knew only by sight at Colet Court, who had come down to the station and formed himself into a one-man welcoming committee for any arriving Paulines.

St Paul's at Crowthorne

Crowthorne was a very small town in Berkshire with two main claims to fame: the widely known, or notorious, Broadmoor Criminal Lunatic Asylum and Wellington College. I think that the majority of St Paul's boys were billeted around the town, but while our science teaching was done in the old science block thoughtfully preserved when Wellington had a new one built, our other teaching was done at Easthampstead Park, some three miles away; bicycles were our essential means of transport. My first billet in Crowthorne was with Colonel Page (ex-Indian Police) and his family at a house named Geneina (Arabic, we were told, for garden) in Ellis Road, a substantial 1920s house which had a large garden with a stream running through it. In this billet there were five of us – two Weston brothers, two Winterbotham brothers and me. We shared a small sitting room on the ground floor while the elder Winterbotham, working for Higher School Certificate (A Level), had a study-bedroom of his own, leaving the other four of us to share a large front bedroom. Our routine was simple; on most days, through every kind of weather, we cycled some three miles up to Easthampstead Park, an imposing country mansion originally belonging to the Marquis of Downshire, and approached by an impressive drive which passed through meadows and was lined with trees (although we used a more convenient tradesman's entrance at the back). There, in a very large reception room, we attended morning assembly for prayers, a hymn and announcements by W.F. Oakeshott, the High Master, and then it was lessons as usual in large and airy rooms. (The High Master used to initial documents with WFO, popularly interpreted as 'What a Funny One'.) Science lessons were concentrated on certain mornings or afternoons in the old laboratories in the grounds of Wellington, where there was also a gymnasium given over to our use. As always, the teaching – the main reason for being there at all – has left the least impression on my memory; our teachers were good, the work suitably demanding and, I would guess, our progress mainly satisfactory. But the memorable incidents in the classroom were few if any, and it was incidents outside this routine which remain in my memory. One of these was the announcement that sweets were going to be rationed; I went to one of the sweet shops in Crowthorne to buy some before they disappeared behind a barrier of coupons, but others had been there before me and all they had left were some elderly and stale bars of Clarnico marzipan so, without enthusiasm, I bought two of these. All of us had to manage our very small finances, and it was at the nearby Post Office that I opened my first Savings Bank account, identified as Crowthorne 4562. I still have my later deposit book which reveals that I have been lending the government 7 shillings and 11 pence since March 1951. The Post Office also sold cards, one having the inscription: 'Here's good luck to/My boy in Air Force blue'; not all wartime verse reached sublime heights. Very different was the stationer's shop near an entrance to Wellington which was not far from Crowthorne railway station. It had everything to make schoolwork appealing: exquisite fountain pens of every marbled colour, crisp and virginal pads of paper, sets of geometry instruments on dark blue velvet and bottles of perfumed Quink in a rich shade of blue (washable). Shamelessly this shop sold pride of possession, and just going into it made one feel academically eager. Very different, but vital, was the bicycle shop, which smelt of oil. We were entirely dependent on bicycles and I had a Raleigh with Sturmey Archer gears where the gear change went through a small chain fitment into the rear hub. My fitment broke, and there was mild panic because in wartime there was no certainty that I would be able to get a replacement; I had a wonderful sense of relief when the bicycle shop came to my rescue. For those whose cycles were out of action the school had a green lorry, open and with low sides, which left each morning from the middle of Crowthorne and took them to Easthampstead Park; it was no soft option because you sat on the hard wooden floor up against hard wooden sides and were bumped along for three miles.

Some of our free time was spent playing in the garden of Geneina. It was large and bushy enough for good games of Hide and Seek; over the stream was a wooden bridge and under it I found a hiding place which in all our games was never discovered. The stream had banks a few feet high and once we dammed it with clods of earth; after a day or two we had created quite a large pond. Then one evening as we were doing our prep there was a rumble and a rush of water and our dam had collapsed, sending a miniature Severn Bore downstream. But the war was still around us. Cycling to school one afternoon we watched a large formation of enemy bombers going towards Reading. And each evening when the four of us went upstairs to bed in the large bedroom, we undressed, put on our pyjamas, turned off the lights and took down the blackout screens. Then we would look out at a great red glow on the horizon; this was the London Blitz (which lasted from 7 September 1940 to early May 1941) with the docklands burning some thirty five miles away. We heard occasional enemy bombers flying over us, saw flak in the distance and had some fairly random bombing. On one journey to school I noticed something in a field, went to investigate and found an unexploded bomb. I could see its fins about five feet down and the sides of the entrance were smeared with paint; I duly reported it. But not all these random bombs fell harmlessly. One night (it was 8 October 1940) we were looking out at the great red glow of the blitz when across the low birch trees in front of us raced a ripple of white accompanied by a loud explosion; this was the leaves being turned up in the moonlight by the blast of the bomb which killed the headmaster of Wellington as he returned from ensuring that all was well with his boys.

Decades later these memories of watching the distant Blitz were reawakened by finding a copy of *Citizens in War – and After*, an upbeat history of Britain's Civil Defence by Stephen Spender, an author usually associated with the literature of social protest, who was active in the Fire Service during the Blitz. In my copy I have placed a quotation from page 300 of Edmund Wilson's *The Fifties*: 'Spender ... was rather vain of his experience in the fire brigade...' Evelyn Waugh's mocking vision of Spender and those like him appears on page 1 of *Officers and Gentlemen*: 'On the pavement opposite Turtle's [*Club*] a group of progressive novelists in firemen's uniform were squirting a little jet of water into the morning room.'

By now I was a member of the Junior Training Corps, which conducted military training that was amateurish but serious. On one exercise we spent a night in the open guarding the mansion at Easthampstead Park against an imaginary enemy; next day, as a training in self-sufficiency, we were divided into small groups, given some ingredients and told to cook ourselves a meal. My group made a stew, but the failure to stir it right down to the bottom while cooking led to it having a distinctly burnt flavour. At this time much of the area south of Easthampstead Park had become a large ammunition dump, with neat and regularly spaced piles of ammunition boxes covered with tarpaulins. Less warlike, but a practical contribution to the war effort, was the school's farm. We had to cycle there once a week to work for an afternoon; on one such occasion I dug up potatoes which were infested with wireworm but were quite suitable for feeding to our pigs. Some boys had the more exotic task of giving the piglets a bath which they – the boys at least – rather enjoyed. Fortunately there were some real farmworkers to keep the whole operation running properly. As we cycled to school we saw a large and ancient steam plough with long vertical rotating blades churning up a long-established hay meadow, another sign of the wartime drive for food production.

We also had to cycle for some of our pleasures; one trip was to California in England, a lake near Wokingham where we were going to swim. Unfortunately one of our group fell off his cycle and had an epileptic fit – really rather worrying – and we never got there. But we did get to Eversley to visit the church where Charles Kingsley had been vicar; he was author of *The Water Babies* which I had read with mother when I was younger. In another book at home I remember seeing a print of him writing, accompanied by his cat which used to sit on his desk watching him. I remember the church as being entirely white inside except for a wonderfully contrasting frieze of coats of arms in their heraldic colours. In the floor at the back of the church was a sheet of glass revealing a pre-Christian altar stone over which the church had been built, a sign of the long-standing veneration of the site and of the victory of Christianity over paganism.

Looking back, my sympathy is with Colonel and Mrs Page; after long service in India, they returned to a deservedly quiet retirement at Crowthorne, only to have it disrupted by active and hungry evacuees. But they rose to the challenge. I had taken to imitating the whining tone of a comedian called Cyril Fletcher; Colonel Page did not approve of this and I was made to sit on the stairs each evening and read to him for a few minutes in a proper voice. I am very grateful to him for his remedial concern. And Mrs Page introduced us to a pudding called Plum Brown Betty, sponge with plums in it, smothered in rich chocolate-flavoured blancmange.

Hard Times in Sussex

Back home in Slinfold for the half-term holiday, Mike and I were standing around outside our wooden hut when out of the low cloud came a Heinkel 111 – blue-grey in colour, swastika and crosses standing out clearly, yellow leading edges to its wings; five seconds later it disappeared into the next cloud. It was dangerously low and I imagine the pilot was as surprised as we were. On an earlier occasion there were vapour trails in the blue sky high above us; we couldn't see what was going on, but a scattering of ammo-belt clips fell around us. A few hundred yards down Hayes Lane towards the village was a row of small cottages, the first of which was a tiny general store run by Mrs Birchmore, a woman of unfailing kindness and good humour on whom we depended for most of our everyday needs. Just past these cottages was the railway bridge carrying the single branch line from Horsham to Slinfold station and then on to Guildford. Neither this bridge nor Mrs Birchmore's stores could have been priority targets for the Luftwaffe, nevertheless some weeks before I came home for half-term they dropped two bombs close to them, one of which made the largest crater I ever saw. Mike hardly heard what must have been a very large explosion, but he did hear the thumping of clods of earth falling on the cottages. This was something very different from the bomb which wrecked Mr Esdaile's garage just up Hayes Lane; that was, as Michael said, very feeble. The raiders did not have it all their own way and one bomber that was shot down hit the ground not far away at Slaughter Bridge in a great burst of flames.

One of our hopes had been that we could grow enough vegetables on our field to keep ourselves supplied. Mike and I tried digging a vegetable patch but the heavy clay was appallingly difficult to cultivate; in addition the field sloped south and millennia of run-off seemed to have robbed the soil of any fertility it might once have had. In the end it was our meagre rations, the eggs from mother's hens and her large sack of oatmeal (bought as a last-minute thought from the herb-scented shop of the seedsman E.H.

Isted in London Road, Bognor) that kept us going, together with a morale-raising pudding consisting of a layer of blancmange with a layer of jelly over it. A final blow was when our local carrier – the vital channel for the ordering and delivery of goods around the countryside – disappeared into the forces.

As soon as we got to Slinfold, Dad and Mike, really with nothing else to do, started working hard to build a house; not quite the ample weekend country retreat originally envisaged by my father, but what would be a comfortable country cottage – when it was finished. They were helped on and off by various workers from the village, but Dad still had occasional trouble with a recurrent rupture and Mike, who loved anything to do with building, carried a large part of the burden. They had to use almost entirely second-hand materials, with the result that people looking at this cottage later took it to be a genuinely ancient building. Amongst these recovered materials were old doors. Before the war Dad had visited a demolition yard and had seen half a dozen old doors; he thought these might be useful and bought them for four pounds or so, with delivery to Slinfold. What duly arrived was a large lorry containing more than a hundred doors – the six he saw had just been specimens. In the event these were invaluable and fifty years later there were still a few lurking in various dark corners behind the cottage.

Mike and Dad started by providing our cottage-to-be with that fashionable wartime amenity, a deep air raid shelter. Mother was sceptical and felt it was unnecessarily deep; her scepticism was well founded and a wet spell led it to collapse into a muddy pool, which at least allowed efforts to be concentrated on the cottage itself. By the summer of 1941, after many vicissitudes and shortages, it had windows and was tiled so that we could at least live under our own roof. But even so it was mainly a shell with no timber floors (timber was in very short supply); on the ground floor we did indeed live at ground level, in fact on the concrete oversite slab which was the base of the cottage. Most of our time we spent in what would be the sitting room, where, without the timber floor, the fireplace on which mother did our cooking was some two and a half feet up, placing it at a very convenient level. Mother and Dad now moved out of The Chalet and had their bedroom on the ground floor of the cottage; but for me, when home on holiday, there was just enough flooring on the first floor to allow me to reach my bed, and after dark we could hold three-dimensional conversations perfectly easily. (J continued to use the room in the Pocock's bungalow as his bedroom.)

It was to the various stages of this slowly progressing building work that I came home for holidays, including what must have been our most comfortless Christmas of the war. Back at school and Geneina, life was more comfortable and went on much as before. At Easter German bombers were still throbbing over Slinfold at night on their way to London, although some seemed to drop their bombs at random; Mike and I were near the top of Hayes Lane listening to the nightingales when a stick of bombs came whistling down onto the open Sussex countryside. German bombing left quite a number of unexploded bombs – UXBs – three of which had fallen in the field next to ours. These had to be dealt with by Bomb Disposal Units which drove around in well-labelled trucks with red mudguards. One of these units was based on a vacant plot in a row of houses near Horsham Station, bringing the bombs back there and then using pressurised steam to remove the charge. There was a cherry tree on this site and the steaming had covered it with a crisp coating of German explosive, like a very heavy frost. On this site I picked up a fist-sized lump of discarded explosive which I took home to experiment with; without a confining bomb casing it simply burned rather slowly with a reddish flame and thick black smoke; not really a wise experiment.

School Again

Back at school, I was moved to a billet in a house in the grounds of Broadmoor Criminal Lunatic Asylum occupied by one of the warders and his family. This led mother to exclaim: 'All these school fees, and when anyone asks where Roger is, I have to say he's in Broadmoor'. The warder's wife was not very congenial, but the warder himself was very kind. He took me into the asylum to buy things from the shop run by the inmates (which always seemed well stocked, even with things that were becoming hard to buy outside). As a shop assistant served us he would murmur biographical details quietly to me: 'Murdered his wife in Brighton, cut her up'. He also took me to a concert party there with songs and sketches; again he was a mine of information; during a duet – '*He* killed his chauffeur and *she* poisoned her husband and children'. He was a keen gardener and grew wonderful runner beans. In the loo at their house there was (for whatever purpose) a book called, I believe, *A Welsh Singer*. This I read in my necessary moments which became more and more protracted as I was gripped by the story. It was simple: Welsh boy loves Welsh girl, promises marriage; goes to London to make fortune, succeeds; she proves to have wonderful voice, goes to London, succeeds; in London she meets same Welsh boy – *he does not recognise her!!!* – he falls in love – again, will she marry him? – ah, but he has told her of his Welsh intended back in the Valleys; Welsh singer says do honourable thing and ask Welsh intended to release him; he goes back to Valleys to do this; Welsh singer gets there first; reverts to being Welsh intended, with head down, so unrecognised; successful Welsh boy confesses all, proves himself honourable, Welsh girl raises head, recognition, true love, marriage, happy ever after. Not great literature, hardly realistic, but to me at that age a tale sufficiently compelling for me to remember it after all these years.

Then it was back to Slinfold for the summer holiday. By now Mike, awaiting call-up, was in the Home Guard doing night patrols on the lookout for German parachutists; he often did these patrols with Valentine Dyall, an actor living further up Hayes Lane, who was the BBC's Man in Black and well known for his scary stories at night on the radio. It was while I was still away at school that we sadly lost Judy; we believed that she died from eating poisoned bait which a nearby farmer had been putting down to kill foxes.

Meadhurst

At school I was now moved to Meadhurst, a large house in Crowthorne with some twenty five boys presided over by Chris Heath, a maths teacher, ordained minister and keen scoutmaster. It was a very well-organised house with rotas for all sorts of household chores. One of these was shoe-cleaning, with all outdoor shoes kept in a small conservatory to be cleaned by the boys on the rota; some minor disagreement led to one boy taking a handful of black shoe polish and squashing it into the golden hair of his fellow cleaner, but otherwise this like other duties was done with good grace. The house kept chickens, and those on the rota mixed up their mash each day to feed them, but collecting the eggs was another matter. The chickens did not want their eggs taken away from under them and defended their next generation with determined pecks to the fumbling hands. A number of boys on the rota declined this painful duty, and here my experience with mother's hens allowed me to go boldly egg-collecting where other boys had, one might say, chickened-out. Indeed I became a mainstay of this part of the chicken rota. Food in the house was reasonable, given the exigencies of wartime. Sugar in particular was short, and we each had our own jar containing part of our ration, the rest being contributed to the general catering. It was evident that not much of this went into the notorious Prune Bounce, a dessert of prunes and gelatine and gelatine and gelatine, named from its tenacity in retaining its shape even when dropped from a considerable height. Amongst the many other incidents, I can remember Carruthers, a senior boy aiming to do medicine, causing some fuss by dissecting a dead cat in the kitchen, and the affair of the sock, bearing my name tape, which was found in the bed of Chris Heath's four year old daughter. Despite having assistance from the rotas, one can only wonder at the resilience of Mrs Heath and her minions who had to keep the house in order and some thirty boys fed and laundered.

Chris Heath took his duties towards us very seriously. He gently pressured all of us to join the Scouts, indeed a new wartime variety called Air Scouts (parallel to Sea Scouts), with patrols named after birds – I was in the Gannet patrol, commonly referred to as the 'messy birds'. In our spare time we did all sorts of scouting activities which we enjoyed; we were happy to be vaguely connected with the air, but of course we had not heard the then current piece of gallows humour: 'Join the army and see the world, join the Air Force and see the other world'. Chris Heath was of a religious nature; on Sundays our day ended with the service of Compline, and I think he was the mover in many of us becoming confirmed. Later on I even went once to Early Service at St Richard's Church in Aldwick; but without any breakfast I felt rather wobbly afterwards and I never tried this risky experiment again. My own religious roots were rather shallow then and became non-existent later. Chris Heath even tried giving some of us, perhaps those who seemed particularly unworldly and pure, and therefore needing it, a bit of sex education. I can only say that his rather religious approach seemed a bit short on both sex and education.

With the ending of the Blitz on London in May 1941, there was a significant decline in the amount of air activity that we saw at Crowthorne and at Slinfold, but the war still delivered some nasty surprises. Facing the bottom of the main staircase in Meadhurst was a noticeboard on which main items of war news were posted. I can remember the shock of seeing that our battleships *Prince of Wales* and *Repulse* had been sunk off Malaya on 10 December 1941. I can also remember us all crowded round a radio in one of the dormitories listening eagerly but derisively for the broadcast interventions of the German propagandist Lord Haw-Haw, who for a time broke into some of the BBC news bulletins, demanding 'Where is the *Ark Royal*?' (an aircraft carrier that the Germans claimed to have sunk).

Back to Aldwick

Having done sterling work on the cottage Mike was called up in late 1941, going to the 60th Training Regiment, Royal Armoured Corps, at Tidworth on the edge of Salisbury Plain in Wiltshire. There he became 7947947 Trooper Alford M.G. and in due course at Dhond in India he joined the 7th Queen's Own Hussars, who had just been driven out of Burma by the Japanese. With them he went to Iraq (where in Baghdad he bumped into Dr Gray, our family doctor from Bognor) and then to Italy until the end of the war. He then contrived a transfer to the Royal Engineers as a means of getting back to his real love – architecture and building. This took him to Athens, where in his spare time he was able to sketch the Parthenon entirely alone on the Acropolis; he was demobbed in 1946.

Fears of invasion had ended with the German attack on Soviet Russia on 22 June 1941 (indeed, had we but known it, Hitler had called off any plans for invasion not long after we went to Slinfold). This and the prospect of another winter in a partly finished house in the heart of the countryside was too much for mother, already overstrained by our refugee lifestyle, and late in 1941 mother and Dad decided to return to Aldwick. Only a short time before this a landmine had gone off near Hammond's Barn, some 500 yards from Idlewylde, damaging its roof and breaking many windows. It was this landmine which first showed me one of the typical signs of blast damage – a door with a mixture of irregular indentations and precise parallel-edged cuts, depending on how the glass had been blown into it. But the damage was not enough to put off our return. I was told that when she arrived back at Idlewylde mother was so relieved that she kissed the front door as she would have kissed an old friend. All this happened while I was away at school, and it was to Aldwick that I came back for Christmas 1941; there my parents were to remain for the rest of their lives.

It was nice to be home again, if only briefly. This wartime Christmas provided no luxuries; we had one of mother's chickens and a 'Christmas pudding' made with only a few of the traditional ingredients; but it did contain one particular non-traditional item. When I started helping mother to do the mixing by hand I had a small adhesive plaster on a cut finger; after we had finished and the pudding was boiling, I noticed that my plaster was missing. I felt it better not to mention this. Christmas presents were minimal but I was at home, and that was pleasure enough.

After the war my father sold the Slinfold cottage and field, and my next visit, more than fifty years later, was out of idle curiosity when we happened to be passing. It was then that I had to explain that the seemingly 'ancient' cottage at the top of the field dated only from 1940–41.

5

Aldwick and the City

Leaving School

In 1942 I came home to Aldwick for the summer holiday and only then did I become aware that my father's income had declined to the point where he could no longer afford to keep me at St Paul's. In retrospect it seems strange that I was not simply transferred to one of the local schools (for example, Chichester High School for Boys). But at the time I certainly saw nothing odd in my parents' decision that at the end of the summer holiday I should not go back to school but should get a job in the City. My father sounded out some possibilities and in due course he took me up to see Vanderfelt & Co, Stockbrokers; he talked to the elderly Mr Vanderfelt and it transpired that a relative on my mother's side had been one of Mr Vanderfelt's first partners. I was accepted and in August 1942 (two months before my sixteenth birthday) I started travelling up each day from Bognor to Vanderfelt's offices in Austin Friars in the City. Initially I was simply an office boy; I came under Miss 'Binnie' Barnes, a trusted clerk, who was very kind to me and later offered to put me up temporarily if bombing made travel too difficult. I did miscellaneous duties around the office, including rounds delivering stock and collecting cheques from other Stock Exchange firms, many of them in the rabbit warren of old and fusty offices called Draper's Gardens where the buildings were linked together by high-level walkways. From this I soon learned my way around the City, which at that time was still grimy from the great conflagration of the Blitz and had many gaps where buildings had been demolished by bombs. Indeed, in front of our own office building in Austin Friars there was a great heap of rubble which had once been the Dutch Church.

One task I remember was being given some twenty old white £500 Bank of England notes, each of which I had to cut in half across the middle. The reason for this was that the two sets of halves would then be taken to two different bank branches for safekeeping as a precaution against one branch being destroyed by a bomb. Normally the Bank of England would pay out on damaged notes provided the Chief Cashier's signature was present, but I would guess that if those halves were destroyed by wartime bombing the Bank would pay out on the other halves. A few weeks later I had to join the halves together with sticky paper and then take them down to the Bank of England and pay them in. Amongst many other things I learnt that the *Stock Exchange Official List* was always referred to as Wettenhall, this being the name of the original publisher. Each day I had lunch at a Mecca restaurant, to me a rather adult treat which I enjoyed, although 'Vienna Steak' and other dishes of unidentified minced-up meat were prominent in the restricted menus. Several times I was sent off to the West End by Miss Barnes to collect theatre tickets, which formed pleasant outings. While I was with Vanderfelt's some fraud occurred at the office and we were visited by a detective named Prothero. Dad sat up when I mentioned this, telling me that Prothero was a well-known detective who often had his name in the papers in relation to high-profile cases. A few weeks later Mr Vanderfelt came into the office angrily waving a letter and announced that the perpetrator of the fraud had written to him saying he was short of money and could the firm help him!

The Floor of the Stock Exchange

I enjoyed working at Vanderfelt's, but I was now becoming attuned to the business of the Stock Exchange and wished to move up. In March 1943 I applied successfully for a job as a 'Blue Button' – an unauthorised clerk – with Ogle & Mudie, a very small firm of brokers. A Blue Button was identified by a circular blue badge with a white rim worn in his lapel which was always concealed when leaving the City. Thus identified I had entry to the dealing floor of the Stock Exchange and could do all sorts of tasks there except actually buying and selling shares; it was the conventional first step to becoming an authorised clerk who could deal, usually referred to as a dealer, and possibly in due course a full member of the Stock Exchange.

Mixing with members and dealers was much more interesting and enjoyable than just working in an office. I now spent most of each working day on the floor of the Stock Exchange, a very large and well-lit space with a wooden floor and many large pillars supporting the roof and each surrounded by seats. It was round these pillars and along some of the walls that jobbers had their pitches, and displayed their current share price lists against the wooden panelling. This panelling, the seats, the waiters' stands, the doors and our desks were all of a medium brown oak (or so I see it in my memory). In addition to this wood panelling there was in places marble of a kind which led to the dealing room being nicknamed 'Gorgonzola Hall'. There were always a great many people on the floor, nearly all dressed in dark grey, with constant movement, and the murmur of voices often overlaid by the waiters calling the names of people for whom they had messages and occasionally by a bustle of excitement in some part of the market.

My day started in the office, which consisted of only some three clerks, collecting the limit books (which contained a record of the orders to be executed for clients when the price of a share reached a particular level) and a few other items and taking them down to the 'House' (as the floor of the Stock Exchange was always referred to by its habitués). There one of my first duties consisted of going round jobbers' pitches checking the prices of a list of securities and collecting price lists, particularly the daily lists for gilt-edged (British government stocks). Some of these opening prices I then telegraphed to certain country brokers using the telegraph counter which opened onto the floor; at the end of the day there would be a similar collection of closing prices. During the day, as buying and selling orders came in, I would do an initial price check for each security with two or three jobbers and pass this information over to our only dealer, who was Mr Mudie himself. One problem was knowing which jobbers dealt in which securities; there was small privately produced booklet which gave some of this information, but quite a lot I somehow picked up for myself.

I began to feel a need for a rather wider horizon and in September 1943 I secured the job of Blue Button in a larger firm, Gerald Hodgson & Co, whose office was on the second floor of 2 Copthall Buildings in Copthall Avenue. Like all firms at that time their office was staffed mainly by male clerks too old to serve in the forces, some six of them. Most were veterans of the First World War and one told me that he still had tiny pieces of shell splinter emerging from his rather battered face – he would become aware of the latest one when he felt his razor snag on it as he was shaving. There was one older woman, three young girl clerks/typists and then two office boys and myself, each waiting to go into the forces. The people with whom I had most contact were our two dealers, Hand and Mackintosh, with whom I spent most of each day on the floor of the House, and Mr Levick (a fighter pilot in the First World War) who was one of the partners. I found all of them pleasant,and Mr Levick in particular took a kindly but demanding interest in me. From the office it was a walk of something over one hundred yards down Angel Court to Throgmorton Street and the Stock Exchange.

While most pillars, or stands, were surrounded by jobbers, some were mainly used by brokers like Gerald Hodgson. In David Kynaston's four-volume history of the City of London, volume 4, *A Club No More, 1945–2000*, there in Plate 6 (between pages 278 and 279) is a photograph of our stand – number 8 – taken in 1947, quite unchanged from when I knew it in 1944 and with the very same waiter whom I remember so clearly, in his uniform of dark blue with a red collar. Above him on the pillar, as on many others, is the large glazed screen with numbers; one of my jobs was to watch, from anywhere on the floor, for our number to light up, which meant that a phone call had come through for us; then it was quickly to the phone room behind our stand, where two girls in blue overalls (who soon came to know that I was with Gerald Hodgson) would direct me to one of a series of numbered wooden kiosks to take the call. When a member or dealer was wanted in person our waiter would sonorously intone the name of the firm and the person's name (I particularly remember 'Strauss Turnbull – Cox'). Near stand 8 was a set of stand-up desks with drawers, one section of which on the side nearest the stand was ours. It was at this desk that I spent my time when not going round the market getting prices or chatting with others on the floor, always with an eye on our telephone light and ready for any messages or instructions. This set of stand-up desks appears in Plate 8 of the same volume of Kynaston, on the left at the edge of the dome with one man leaning his back against it and another leaning over it. And beyond it you can see jobbers' price lists on the wall where in my day there was a jobber in shipping shares; I remember him because I took down an order wrongly, leading us to sell him £15,000 of some stock instead of £15 (the thousands were often understood rather than stated and hence my mistake). I was sent to apologise to him and he agreed to amend the deal. He did this by taking his dealing book, some seven inches tall by three inches across with a smooth black leather cover, opening it, rubbing out the wrong deal, writing in the correct one and amending his net position in that stock. All the jobbers seemed to have these same dealing books which were nearly always in their hands. Beyond him was a jobber in rubber companies who had very thin business in those days of the Japanese occupation of Malaya, but I remember the firm because one of the partners was a tall older man named Herring who had won the Victoria Cross in the First World War. Somewhere behind our stand was the firm of Stocken & Concanon; Concanon was a very jovial man with a rather large nose, who was referred to by his fellow members as 'the man who put the conk in Concanon'. Lunchtimes now could not be too long, so I patronised Lyon's Long Room, underground and well described by its name, which was only on the other side of Throgmorton Street from the Stock Exchange; there I soon had my favourite table and the same kindly waitress.

There was a pleasantly social overtone to life on the floor, and this was enhanced by several factors. Business at this time was at a low ebb, although what there was had to be done quickly and efficiently. There were occasional bursts of activity but these were rare, so that there was quite a lot of time for chatting and good-humoured banter. Nearly all the people on the floor were either elderly members brought back from retirement to carry on the business in place of all those of military age who were in the forces or else were, like myself, too young to serve but were awaiting call-up; this all made for a fairly relaxed atmosphere outside business. I remember seeing two elderly members – both dark suits and silver hair – one sitting against a stand reading a newspaper; the other, standing close by, unobtrusively set fire to the newspaper and then looked innocently in the other direction; the reader waited till it was well alight and then unhurriedly folded up the paper, putting out the fire, put the paper down next to him and looked equally innocently away from the arsonist. And I think it was on May Day that one particular member (was his name Caro?) always appeared on the floor in a straw boater which was ceremonially snatched from his head, kicked around the floor to loud cheers and then kicked out into Throgmorton Street. Strangers were at particular risk, because one feature of the floor was that the exits were not at all obvious, so that a stranger wandering in could not easily get out again even if he realised his mistake. If he was seen on the floor a cry went up, either 'Strangers!' or 'Fourteen Hundred' (dating from a time when there were supposedly 1,399 members of the Stock Exchange so that 'Fourteen Hundred' meant that there was a stranger on the floor). The intruder traditionally had his trousers removed and was pushed out into Throgmorton Street with his trousers thrown after him; this nearly happened once when I was there, but the stranger was rescued and bustled out, still trousered, by one of the waiters. I once ran this risk of debagging before I became a Blue Button. Mr Marks was a pleasant member of the Stock Exchange who got on to our train at Horley and whom I often talked to; he kindly offered to let me see the floor of the House. I met him at one entrance, was warned to walk quickly across the floor keeping close to him and not to look around; then it was in, across and out. Quick, but to me a very interesting foretaste of what was to come.

On the floor, one regular matter to be discussed first thing in the mornings was *The Times* crossword and its more difficult clues (one clue that I can remember was just 'gsge' – answer: 'scrambled eggs'); then there were the latest bomb experiences, the prospects for that day's 3.30 at Newmarket, problems with roses, and many other important topics. But looming behind all this was always the war news which we saw minute by minute on the Reuters and Exchange Telegraph tapes which were pinned up on green baize noticeboards not far from our stand. It was in a news item on one of these tapes that I first saw the term 'Fiduciary Issue'; this stuck in my mind but it was only many years later when I became concerned with monetary economics that I came to understand what it meant.

During my time on the floor all of the many dealers and members with whom I came in regular contact were pleasant and helpful. One person whom I particularly remember was Mr Pierce of Seymour, Pierce – with a crisp iron-grey moustache, very well dressed in black jacket, pinstriped trousers and often with a top hat. He always spoke very kindly to me as I passed him in the gilt-edged market and to me he personified many of the best aspects of the Stock Exchange community. However there were some people from whom I tended to keep my distance; these were a small number of other Blue Buttons whom I found too coarse for my taste and too keen on smoking and drinking. Their unappealing example was one influence that helped to push me in the opposite direction and I became a lifelong non-smoker and non-drinker. They sometimes came out with unpleasantly squalid conversation and although I understood it well enough it was not to my taste and I soon developed an uncomprehending look which made me an unrewarding audience who would not become involved.

Life on the Train

Coming up to the City each day from Bognor meant that a significant part of my day was spent on the train. For most of my time in the City I left home at 7.30 a.m., caught the bus to Bognor station and the 7.55 to London; changed at East Croydon for the train to London Bridge and then by bus to the office where I generally arrived some time before 9.45, making it two and a quarter hours door to door. On occasions there were delays and disruptions due to air raid damage, but on the whole the trains ran with remarkable regularity throughout the war. On our Southern Railway line we had comfortable Pullman carriages which were usually warm, although there were occasions when fuel-saving left them rather chilly. Business hours in the House were short at that time and I generally had only to take the limit books back to the office and I was then free to go home. Occasionally I caught the 4.07 p.m. train from London Bridge, but more often I varied my return journey by catching the number 11 bus from Bank to Victoria Station and catching the 4.18 or 5.30 to Bognor, so that I was generally home by 6 o'clock or 7.15. This meant four and a half hours travelling each day of which three hours was spent on the train, some one and a half hours each way. I was very fortunate in having a number of travelling companions whose company made many of these hours a pleasure.

For my first few months in the City I used to catch the later 8.28 train to London Bridge and on that I usually travelled with two elderly gentlemen, one a plump, pipe-smoking solicitor, the other a rather slight and bearded manager of some charity organisation; both of them retired, but brought back to work in order to take over from younger men who had gone into the forces. They were very kind to me and we talked and exchanged newspapers. My journeys home from London Bridge were more solitary. All of these journeys took me through some beautiful Sussex countryside, but also past Gatwick, at that time a military airfield with aircraft which were of interest to me. It also took me past Faygate where next to the railway line was an enormous dump of crashed aircraft, British and German, probably a hundred yards long or more and some thirty feet high – as high as a house.

After I became a Blue Button I had to catch the earlier train, the 7.55, and there I soon found another group of travelling companions. In 1943 Audrey Whitehead and Barbara Bech were travelling up to town each day to their secretarial courses at St James' Secretarial College. Who picked up whom on the train may be a matter of dispute but what is certain is that soon we were regularly travelling together and filling our journeys with congenial talk. There were others who sometimes travelled with us: Michael Rowe, and less frequently his brother Dickie, both working for the jobbers Donnison; Geoffrey Oxley, also on the Stock Exchange; Daphne Burke, a very pleasant and attractive physiotherapist, and others who joined us less often. But it was Audrey and Barbara who were now my main travelling companions and with whom I also shared various other social activities around Bognor. All of this began over sixty years ago and we have maintained contact with each other ever since. It was from Audrey that I learned many years later that Daphne had married an army officer and just after the war they went out to Kenya where tragically she died in childbirth.

Occasionally I would stay on in town to go to the cinema with a friend and this meant coming down to Bognor on a late train. On one of these journeys I was in the first carriage and the train gave a distinct lurch and quickly came to a halt. We learned later that it had hit a woman crossing the line in the blackout and killed her. On another occasion we arrived at Barnham, the last stop before Bognor, where a number of young people got on to the train, obviously going home after a dance. One girl sat down opposite me and and I saw her slip an engagement ring back on to her proper finger.

Life at Bognor

I now settled into a routine, with my life shared between the City, the train and Bognor. I became a member of the Nyewood Lane Tennis Club and played there frequently at weekends and often in the summer evenings after I came back from London. Both Audrey and Barbara made their appearance on these courts. Apart from games with friends and other members, there were also American tournaments. In one of these I partnered Audrey and came fourth; in another I drew as my partner a local garage owner, solid of torso but slim of leg, who was a very good player and we (or rather he) won. Tennis balls were a difficulty because they were in short supply. We thought at one time that this problem was over when Ken Keeling, who was in the Merchant Navy and brother of one of our members, appeared with brand new tennis balls which he had 'acquired' as Rangoon fell to the Japanese. Unfortunately these were designed for the hot climate of Burma and proved rather soft and sluggish in Bognor's summer. I suspect that our standard of tennis was rather moderate, but it gave us all a lot of pleasure and another social circle.

Saturday always started with coffee at Leslies', a pleasant restaurant in Bognor's High Street; I could be pretty sure of meeting friends there, sometimes Audrey, Barbara or Michael Rowe, but often others also. Then there was the library, at that time located behind a shop (Hansford's menswear) in London Road, where apart from books there was a charming fair-haired librarian named Barbara Bostock; sadly, after a while she left the library and went into the WAAF. The books I took out ranged widely, but two I remember particularly were *I, Claudius* and *Claudius the God* by Robert Graves, which (unwisely perhaps) I found completely convincing as Roman history and which strengthened my interest in Roman coins. *Place Names of Sussex* was another book I borrowed (and by mistake left in the phone kiosk outside the station, where I found it untouched and still waiting for me a month later). Here I would also mention another book, this time one which I bought for myself: *From the Greek* edited by Headlam. This slim book contained translations of some of the best short poems of Ancient Greece. In those years of wartime uncertainties these latter two books offered consoling certainties, one introducing me to the deep roots of the place names in my part of what I then regarded as my own county of Sussex, the other in revealing the finest spirit of the Greeks – I can still remember the thrill of buying it and reading it for the first time. In other fields also the war saw a sudden and widespread upsurge in the desire to hold onto the certainties of our own historical and cultural roots.

War produced many things, some of them potentially lethal and all of them of great interest to boys like myself. Pieces of German aircraft were treasured and machine-gun rounds from German aircraft that had been shot down were eagerly collected, as were shell fragments and 'Z' Battery rocket fins from our own flak. More exciting were incendiary bomb tails, arming wires from exploding booby trap incendiary bombs and fragments from German bombs; I have one of the latter that was given to me by one of our office boys named Swallow. It is almost an inch thick, 8 inches long by 4 inches wide, savagely jagged and weighing 4½ pounds. None of these was dangerous any longer, but this cannot be said of German 13 mm cannon shells of which I acquired two; these had bright brass cartridge cases, yellow shells and a copper tip with a flat head of copper foil covering the fuse – beautifully made, very appealing, but potentially deadly.

In wartime the cinemas were a wonderful source of escapism, and for every film they seemed nearly full of people and equally full of cigarette smoke. On Saturday afternoon, if I wasn't playing tennis, I would often go to the Pier Cinema, the Picturedrome or the Odeon (and not only on Saturday afternoon). The names of the films I saw are mostly, and probably deservedly, forgotten. Of the few I recorded, *Coney Island* gained my accolade of 'Not bad' while *Stage Door Canteen* I rated as 'Lousy with sentiment'. But I always felt a thrill of anticipation as the curtain slowly rose to reveal the screen. And there were the newsreels which gave us some visual sense of the impact of the war.

But it was not only at Bognor that I went to the cinema; at Victoria Station there was a News Theatre which showed newsreels and cartoons. Sometimes I went to it because I had missed my train and had an hour to wait, and sometimes I just went to it. On one occasion I met a friend from school, Terry Downey, in town; my diary records:

Monday 16 August 1943
... We had lunch at Lyons and then saw *Bataan* at The Empire Leicester Sq. It was absolutely first rate, and by far the best film I have seen. It made Terry jump at one place where a gun suddenly went off. It thrilled and frightened me much more than the blitz last night. Also saw a comedy about a cat and three kittens. We then went to an exhibition at Dorland Hall of bomb damage pictures of Germany, also saw bombs including 4000 lbs and 8000 lbs. They looked horribly big and when I thought of the row the small bombs made last night and then imagine one of those going off it made me feel quite queasy.

Civil Defence

Finally would come Saturday evening, but not quite the Saturday evening of a young man about town because I was always on duty with the Civil Defence, initially as a member of a First Aid Party and then as First Aid member of a Rescue Party. I had begun taking an evening course in first aid with the Bognor Red Cross when I started going up to the City, and after I passed certain tests this qualified me to join the Civil Defence as a member of a First Aid Party. I continued with the course but was now required to take an ARP (Air Raid Precautions) course which covered more advanced first aid and a range of other relevant subjects such as dealing with incendiary bombs; these courses often took up two evenings a week. Most First Aid or Rescue Parties went on duty in rotation: Monday night one week, Tuesday night the next week and so on. Because I was going up to town each weekday I was allowed to do every Saturday night instead, which brought me in touch with most Parties as they rotated through my duty night. Officially I had to belong to some Party and in early August 1943 I recorded the first entry in the red notebook which I used for my Diary:

Rescue Party .6.B.

Leader	C Stephenson
Deputy	F. Cole
Driver	Light

| Richards | Buckland | R. Alford |
| N. Cheney | G.A. Gutsell | |

There was always some shuffling around of people between Parties and the names crossed out probably arose from this. As a member of the Civil Defence I had my dark blue battledress with yellow flashes and yellow lanyard; I felt pride in wearing this, and often wore it for much of Saturday on the excuse that I was going on duty in the evening. I also had my tin hat, black with R for Rescue in white, back and front; this I still have, hanging up in the loft.

Apart from training courses we also had periodic exercises. A mock incident would be staged and, under the eye of Dr Ayres (Medical Officer of Health for Bognor Regis), we would be called in to deal with it. The 'victims' were allowed to tell us only a few key symptoms and the rest was up to us. I quote from my diary:

Wednesday 17 November 1943
... Had practice in evening. Went to Rank's kennels at about 7.45 [*p.m.*], Called at 8.15. Arrived at Pavilion where incident was staged at Ambulance post. Charlie, myself and another made reconnaissance, there were:

> 1 Fractured base [*of skull*]
> 1 broken collar bone
> 1 Coal gas poisoning
> 1 Fractured pelvis
> 1 Crushed abdomen
> 1 Compound Fractured Femur
> 2 Minor cases
> 1 Fractured jaw

I had to deal with the fractured jaw which was Mary Inskipp. After the practice at which Dr Ayres, Mr Searle and Sgt Dowling were present, we went over everything again while drinking tea and eating cake. Dr Ayres said it was an excellent show, got home at 10.30.

In another similar practice one of the 'victims', down in a narrow entrance to an air raid shelter, was supposed to be dead and we had to carry him out to get to the others. However, he claimed that rigor mortis had set in, and with his arms and legs stiff at all angles he managed to give us great difficulty in removing him.

Around Bognor there were a number of Civil Defence posts and over time I spent my Saturday nights in several of these. The first was the Ambulance Post, referred to above, at the north-east corner of the Pavilion, which was brick-built and supposedly blast-proof. This had a door into the main hall of the Pavilion and I used to go in and watch the crowded Saturday night dance with its small band, including a blind pianist. Nearly all the people there were in the forces, with pretty WAAFS spending much of the evening behind the rows of seats round the dance floor fending off licentious soldiery; the only exception were a civilian couple, an older woman and a much younger man, who were by far the best dancers on the floor and were there every week. Another advantage of this post was that one of our ambulance drivers there was the delightful Barbara Bostock from the library. Other posts had fewer amenities, although the Aldwick Farm Post (also known as Rank's Kennels) did have its own emergency mortuary ('Shrouds to be used in order from the top of the pile'); other ones were at the Old Fire Station in the High Street and at Limmer Lane. The senior one, however, was the post in the more professional surroundings of the Ockley Road Depot (Bognor's main Council Yard); there it was next to the town mortuary and was surrounded by much of the equipment needed for any larger air-raid incidents. There too we had practices:

Sunday 14 November 1943
Had practice in morning, washed Rescue Lorry, dusted inside, cleaned tools, inspected First Aid kits, washed water bottles etc. First Aid kits contain:

> 4 Large Mines dressings
> 4 Small ditto
> 8 Triangular Bandages
> 2 Pkts pins
> 1 Pkt labels
> 1 Pr Scissors

Reserve box contains about enough for 5 other complete kits.

I probably spent most time at the Aldwick Farm Post, which was in a building only yards from the cowshed where Mike and I had 'helped' the cowmen when we were children, some eight years before, but now seeming a world away. There I now spent the night in a large room which was surrounded by two levels of bunks and had a table in the middle. I can still see myself, on one particular occasion, in an upper bunk looking down on on the other Rescue Party members while they played cards and filled the room with the smoke from their Woodbines and Weights. All of this particular group were Council employees – road workers, dustmen and depot staff, sturdy, dependable and all veterans of the First World War. One of them let me feel the only partly healed break in his shin which was his legacy from that war. The only direct reference to them in my diary is: '... borrowed blankets from Sid. Argued with Taffy about politics'. I had total faith in them as members of our Rescue Party; they were unfailingly kind to me and I enjoyed being on duty with them.

One windy Saturday night our Rescue Party was called out from the Ockley Road Post, not for any bomb damage but because a tree had been blown down across the access to the Ice House in the grounds of Hotham House. Into our Rescue lorry and off to the scene; then a quick recce with torches (there was the usual blackout) and out with the axes ready to chop up the tree. At this moment some, shall we say, very cheerful Canadians soldiers appeared, claiming that they were lumberjacks and would show us how to do it. And, using our axes, they did just that while we lounged against our lorry and watched. Then with many thanks and farewells we went back to Ockley Road, our duty done. One evening just after D-Day I was standing outside our post at the Old Fire Station in the High Street watching one of the great bomber streams going out on a raid in support of the invasion armies in Normandy; I was chatting to some British Commandos, and it became clear to me they had in mind the grim implications of this massive and thunderous display of potential destruction, while to me it was just a heartening display of Allied air power.

Warnings and Raids

Towards the end of 1943 both Audrey and Barbara finished their secretarial courses in London; Audrey, now in the Foreign Office, continued to travel up for a while before moving back with her mother to Wimbledon, coming down to Bognor only occasionally. Barbara took a job with a firm of publishers at West Dean, north of Chichester; as she continued to live in the Farm House near Aldwick Farm, we still often met for coffee at Leslies' on Saturdays. I now travelled more frequently with Michael Rowe, who also sometimes joined us at Leslies', as well as with a number of other people, and I sometimes came down with Susannah Solomon, a very charming girl who was also doing a secretarial course in London and whose father was on the Stock Exchange. They lived at the small village of Sutton (in, I seem to remember, The Old Poor House!) with Pulborough as Susannah's nearest station.

Also towards the end of 1943 I met Roy Chiverton – always Chiv to me – who was in the sixth form at Chichester High School for Boys; we soon became friendly and in him I found an academic rapport which I had missed after I left school. We cycled around together, played chess, discussed books and also, I see from my diary, discussed discussions. Many years later he reminded me that on one of his visits to our house my mother gave us some of the newly available whale meat to try; what Chiv felt about it I do not know, but I didn't like its strange fishy–meaty taste. To me it seemed just another of the minor disadvantages of wartime. Through Chiv I met some of his school friends, in particular Dennis Wood. This gave me another enjoyable social circle at Bognor.

Meanwhile the war rumbled on. In 1942 and into 1943 there had been tip-and-run raids on Bognor, by Me 109s (with yellow noses), Fw 190s and also by bombers, on one occasion a single He 111. In each case they dropped a few bombs, and machine-gunned the streets, causing casualties. All of these raids occurred on weekdays when I was up in the City. In response there were low-level standing patrols by Hawker Typhoons; their engines had powerful torque so that they flew slightly crabwise up and down the coast at low level. I also saw that machine guns had been mounted on top of the Gas Company building at the top of Argyle Road. Another, more friendly, low flying visitor at around this time was a Vickers Wellington carrying a large circular frame and known as a Flying Christ; it was intended to set off German magnetic mines, but there were evidently none in the sea off Bognor. There was a burst of air activity at the time of the Dieppe Raid in August 1942 and the Germans dropped propaganda leaflets, many of which we found around Aldwick and collected as further souvenirs of the war; they were filled with pictures of Canadian prisoners, and the shingle beach of Dieppe littered with Canadian dead and disabled Churchill tanks.

Bognor's large gasholder was was an obvious and tempting target for the Luftwaffe and it was attacked a number of times, most dramatically on Thursday 17 December 1942 when a German bomber collided with it, falling inside, killing all its crew, setting it on fire and leaving a large gash for me to see when I went past it coming home from the City that evening. This prominent 'war wound' remained there for several years. It must have been around the same time that a Dornier bomber, probably a Do 17, crashed at Lagness. It came down in a very shallow dive, just missing cottages on the Lower Bognor Road and ending up in a field on the other side of the road. One of the cottages had a wall only about three feet high along the road and one engine of the Dornier knocked a crescent-shaped piece out of this wall; the repair was still visible decades later. When I visited this crash site shortly afterwards the only recognisable parts of the aircraft were the two engines; the rest was just a mass of fragments, and the ditches round the field all contained the yellow-green dye intended to mark the plane's position if it came down in the sea. In 1943 German air activity lessened and the later 'Baby Blitz' of early 1944 seemed to us little more than a series of nuisance night raids aimed mainly at London; the only result we saw was the scattering of 'Window' strips dropped to confuse our radar. These fell all around us at Aldwick and came in two sizes, dark metallised strips about two centimetres wide and thin silver strips; many of both kinds we collected as war souvenirs. These, together with the Dieppe leaflets, and my collection of shell and bomb fragments, cannon shells, bullets and pieces of the Stuka shot down at Sefter School after the raid on Tangmere, gave a physical presence to the war.

Events and Interests

Up in the City business on the Stock Exchange remained at a low level, but we had a number of visitors around this time. The most important of these was Mrs Churchill, who appeared on the gallery at the Capel Court end of the floor, to great acclaim. Her first words were 'I have never seen so many bald heads together in one place', and this was greeted with much laughter and applause. But perhaps more telling was a day just before the invasion of Normandy when men who had been dealers and Blue Buttons but who were now in the forces were invited to revisit the floor. One I particularly remember was a Lieutenant with the bold flashes 'Beach Signals'.

My journey home now nearly always started by catching the number 11 bus from the City to Victoria, but frequently breaking this journey to visit Baldwins, the coin dealers, who were in John Adam Street just off The Strand. There I enjoyed the kindly company of Albert Baldwin and spent quite a lot of my pocket money on Roman coins (all of which I still have), but also branching out into Anglo-Saxon coins (which student penury later forced me to sell back to Baldwins). There I also met some American aircrew who were relaxing from operations over Germany by building up coin collections. They were about as far from brash Yanks as you could imagine and they impressed me enormously. I enjoyed talking to them and one – tall, calm and softly spoken – showed me a flak splinter which was removed from his thigh only a few days earlier after a raid over Germany. Occasionally I broke my journey to go up the Charing Cross Road to look in the bookshops and a few times to go to Seaby's, another (somehow less congenial) coin dealer located rather inconveniently north of Oxford Street. It was at Baldwin's that I was introduced to Harold Mattingley, then Keeper of Coins at the British Museum. He was very kind to such a junior collector and invited me for a private visit to see some of the museum's collection; he suggested that I should join the Royal Numismatic Society, which I did. I received a letter confirming my election as a Fellow dated 16 November 1944, the day on which I joined the Army. It was only when pressure of work began to outweigh my interest in coins that in 1951 I felt I had finally to withdraw from the Society.

At home we now had a new pet. At that time farmers would 'shoot-out' rooks' nests, believing that these birds were a pest (now, of course, it is recognised that in fact they destroy pests). My younger brother J was there when they were shooting-out the rookery in the Rank's grounds and he rescued a baby rook which had fallen out of its nest. He brought it home and we fed it and watched it grow. Clearly it had to learn to fly, so we placed him (?her) on the back of a kitchen chair, and offered him food at the back of another chair a little way away. Raucus (named by mother) hopped across to the back of the second chair for the food, and by offering food in this way and gradually moving the chairs apart, he was soon hopping and using his wings. Then one day he simply took off and flew round the bungalow. But he did not then fly away; he flew back to his accustomed perch – and we had acquired a delightful pet. He was very intelligent and inquisitive; it was almost impossible to take a photograph of him because he would come and stand on the camera to investigate all its nooks and crannies with his long black beak. He loved joining in when I whitened my tennis shoes; every lace-hole had to be checked and he would end up with white all over his beak. When sitting in the garden reading the paper, this black beak would sometimes come suddenly through the sheet as he tried to investigate the letters on the other side. Mother's gardening was on a small scale and sometimes she would bring out a bowl of water and, kneeling down, would give favoured plants a rather small drink. Once when she was doing this Raucous came up and dropped a pebble into the bowl; clearly an accident, and mother picked it out and threw it away. Off hopped Raucus, collected the pebble, brought it back and dropped it into the bowl again – he had discovered a new game to play with mother! Coming home one evening, I can remember him perched on the roof of our bungalow as I alighted from the bus at the end of the road; immediately there was a loud 'CAW!' and he flew off the roof, glided low down over the road and then up to land on my shoulder. There was only one downside to dear Raucus – he liked butter; this was rationed and he often had to be shooed away from the butter dish. As time passed he became more independent, going away for several hours but always coming back, until one final day when he went off as usual but never came back. We speculated sadly on what might have happened to him; we had become very fond of Raucus and we greatly missed him.

6 June 1944 – The Invasion

Meanwhile evidence grew of the impending invasion of Europe. Out at sea off Bognor a concrete city appeared to be growing on the horizon, with blocks of various sizes; what it was, we had no idea. From the train I saw a new road being constructed to allow heavy vehicles to avoid the town centre of Leatherhead; military traffic signs appeared along the roads while the bridges began to sprout notices with their weight limits. Cycle trips up onto the Downs along Fairmile Bottom revealed growing numbers of encampments filled with troops, field hospitals, parked military vehicles and, at Fontwell, a surprisingly small field containing a flight of artillery-spotter Auster light aircraft. Around us at Bognor were stationed Canadians – the Regiment de Maisonneuve – and later the 8th Hussars, who arrived in the west car park, chewing up Aldwick Road at Hammonds Corner with the steel tracks of their Cromwell tanks. The officers of the 8th Hussars wore very distinctive dark green side-hats with gold edging – most colourful – and there was often a group of them in Leslies' on Saturday morning. The south coast including Bognor remained a prohibited area for anyone not actually living there. The events which followed seemed to me at the time sufficiently important to deserve a longer entry in my diary.

Tuesday 6 June 1944

INVASION! Allied forces landed on the continent in great strength this morning. At 01.30 this morning the planes carrying paratroops came over going South, all carrying green lights; at 03.00 planes were returning.

05.30 Awakened by forces of planes flying in all directions, Mitchells, Spitfires etc. Weather is rather overcast with slight rainy tendency. Clouds low. Noticed some of the concrete things in sea are being towed out also jetty built out from Selsey is very clear. There are about twenty tugs etc in the sea off Bognor now. [*These concrete things were Mulberry, which was now in the process of being towed over to Normandy to form a harbour to supply our invading armies.*]

Caught 7.55 up. Noticed that planes on way up had curious white markings on sides and wings. On Gatwick all Spitfires and Mustangs had black and white stripes on sides of fuselage, and top and bottom of wings. Also saw stripey Mitchells. Saw two chars [*office cleaners*] on 43 bus, one mentioned that Germans said invasion had started. This was not mentioned on the 7 o/c news but it was on the 8 o/c. I saw the official news from Eisenhower on Exchange Telegraph board at 9.50 in the Stock Exchange. Everybody was discussing it. Things fairly normal all day, but there were always groups round the Ex Tel and Reuter boards. The 12 o/c news was broadcast in the House. Went home by 5.30 with Charles and one of his friends – Jessica Wright. I saw Susannah as the train pulled out. Went to Red Cross [*lecture*] at 8 o/c and met Chiverton. We saw 68 Albermarles each towing a Horsa [*troop-carrying glider*], Stirlings each towing a Horsa and Halifax IIIs each towing a Hamilcar [*a larger glider*]. One Horsa broke loose from an Albermarle; we had seen it [*the glider*] was in difficulties, and it only just managed to get to land near Felpham after dropping half a dozen parachutes of all colours. All were proceeding SE by E at varying heights, but all fairly low and going pretty fast. At about 10.15 we saw roughly a dozen Fortresses heading NW; one, behind the others, carried a red light mid-way along the port wing denoting wounded on board.

6

Diary: Flying Bombs and a Few V2s

Flying bombs played a considerable part in this next phase of my time in the City. Here I use a selection of entries from my diary to give some idea of their impact on daily life but also show how ordinary activities went on despite the flying bombs. I leave it to the reader to skip over their repetitions and banalities.

Friday 16 June 1944
3 warnings last night. Up to town by usual train. Went to Baldwins. Heard first news of new type of pilotless planes. Went to Plaza, saw *Lady in the Dark*. Went to Spinks. Bought Utchat & Scarab [*Ancient Egyptian faience beads*] for 5/- & 2/-

Saturday 17 June 1944
Had coffee at Leslies, there saw Michael Rowe who told me Audrey Whitehead was down from London. Saw her, and she told me they had a bad time in London last night. Then went riding. We rode to Middleton from Felpham. Played tennis in afternoon. On duty all night. Up 4 times at 11.50, 01.15, 03.00 & 05.15. One flying bomb (FB) passed over very low, and landed at Bosham.

These entries record my first awareness of Hitler's attack on London using the V1, usually referred to as the flying bomb or doodlebug, the first of which came over on Tuesday 13 June. On the Monday I had just started a fortnight's holiday but, having a season ticket, I went up to town on several of these days. I first heard about this new weapon on the Friday (above) when visiting Baldwins, the very congenial coin dealers. Soon we all became familiar with the characteristic harsh, organ-like, reverberant note of the flying bomb – once heard, never forgotten.

When I went back to work on Monday 26 June, on the floor of the Stock Exchange I heard many flying bomb stories from those who had experienced this new German weapon at first hand. As the seriousness of this threat to London became evident, my parents told me that they were quite willing for me to remain at home rather than going up daily into what was, after all, the target area. However, I felt that this was a new and exciting phase in the war and I had every intention of seeing it at first hand. In addition I was buoyed-up by the simple-minded belief, shared by so many, that while some people might get hurt, these would not include me. For a major city the size of London this belief had some justification, and this feeling was a major factor in making it possible for so many people to carry on in the face of this new threat.

Monday 26 June 1944

Dad said there were 12 flying bombs over last night. Up as usual with Michael and Audrey. Rather busy with one thing and another. Alert 12.50. Had lunch. Flying bomb exploded in Holborn direction. All clear 1.15. Alert 1.30. Went up to office. [*At this time everybody had to leave the House – the Stock Exchange – when there was an alert.*] Got closings [*closing prices*] in Throg Street [*Throgmorton Street, next to the Stock Exchange, where the jobbers and many brokers congregated when they were kept out of the House*]. Got books from House, names from Checking Room. 7 doodlebugs exploded up to 3.30, no all clear yet. In Throg St when one came over low we could not see it, but we all moved to cover. Rather low cloud & rain occasionally. 3.50 2 further doodlebugs have gone off. 7.53 [*home at Aldwick*] another doodlebug gone off.

Tuesday 27 June 1944

Up as usual. Warning on E. Croydon platform. Train very late, got to house at 10.20. Warning 10.50. One came down quite near. I was talking to Levick [*in the office*] and we could hear it distinctly [*whistling overhead*]. I tried to get to a window to see it but could not. Wellington [*bomber*] flying about over City. All clear 11.30. Alert 12.00. We were just getting into Throg St when one came over very low going Holborn way. It exploded some way away, then there was another explosion at about the same distance. All clear 12.30. Alert 12.40 flying bomb over close. Stopped but no explosion. Warning 2 o/c. Just before it went Mr Lightfoot told Howe that S. London had had a warning, and 3 flying bombs were coming this way. Nothing happened. All clear 2.30. Another warning after hours. Down by 5.30 with Susannah Solomon. Went to Red Cross, but as they were getting ready for Fête at the Hawthorns; I left. Had argument on religion with Nicholls. Saw Chiv. He showed me his Higher School Certificate papers. Came home from station with Michael [*Rowe*] in Taxi. Went to bed at 9.30 and got on with Tacitus *Annals*.

Wednesday 28 June 1944

Up as usual with Audrey. Warning 10.50. One flying bomb came over and exploded some way away. Some time later another came over very close but went away into the distance and we did not hear it explode. All clear 11.58. Alert 12.25. Had lunch. One flying bomb over 1.17, another flying bomb over, it exploded fairly near. 11.25 another flying bomb, it came right over us, and I saw it just as it went into a cloud, but I could not distinguish its shape. The noise was very loud. Another flying bomb at 1.40 but some way away. 2.18 flying bomb came near but went off at some distance. 2.22 another flying bomb, but not near. All clear 3.10. I was running all round Throg St gathering prices from 2.30–3.00. 5.30 Warning as we were leaving Victoria. Came down with Susannah. Levick starts his holiday tomorrow.

Friday 30 June 1944

At Horsham we went on to the Dorking line. Train stopped at Balham, and we were told All Change so Michael and I got tube to Bank, got to office at 10.20. Alert on. Checked bargains at Northgate House. Got lists in Throg St. Had lunch with Joyce Cray at Lyons at 12.10. Flying bomb landed at 12.45. All clear 1.15. Went down to House and got prices. 1.35 Alert. Flying bomb landed at 2.10. Exploded 2.11 fairly near. All clear 2.28. Alert 2.50. 3.25 imminent danger whistles. 4.38 two have exploded. 5.15 I was on the East side of Victoria Station. One went off about 200 yds away in Warwick Way. Lots of smoke billowed up, and the blast gas gave me a funny feeling in my forehead.

I had gone to Victoria station as usual to catch the 5.30 train home but found that no trains were leaving due, I believe, to some ordinary signalling problem. With flying bombs coming over, waiting with hundreds of others on the crowded concourse seemed to me to be asking for trouble so I had gone for a walk outside the station until the trains started again.

At first when there was a warning we all had to leave the floor of the House and go out into Throgmorton Street or back to our offices, returning to the floor after the all-clear. The reason, I understood, was that the Stock Exchange was an old building and it was feared that if it were hit the whole thing would collapse. Going back to our offices on the second floor of Copthall Buildings I often met a pleasant American who was with the US brokers Fahnestock; his office was near ours and he seemed quite composed about working in the City despite the flying bombs. But this traipsing to and fro wasted a lot of time and soon watchers were placed on the roof of the Stock Exchange to allow us to stay on the Floor during the frequent warnings; if the watchers saw flying bombs heading left or right of the building they did nothing, but if they were coming straight for it they blew whistles – the Imminent Danger signal – and everybody had to get out – and quickly. Even the oldest members showed a surprising turn of speed on such occasions. The Bank of England, which was on the other side of Bartholomew Lane and just opposite the Capel Court entrance to the House, also had an Imminent Danger signal, at one time a bell and later a klaxon.

Monday 3 July 1944

Two alerts last night. One doodlebug went over, and we had a good view of it. One heavy explosion woke me up. Up by 7.05, got to Victoria at 8.45. Waiting for No. 11 bus when doodlebug went off. Had coffee in Throg St ABC restaurant with Garwood and then Dick. All clear 9.50. Alert 10.20. All clear 11.25. Alert 11.50. It is terrible weather, low cloud and pouring rain. Various doodlebugs have gone off in the distance all day. 3.22 doodlebug over. 3.30 Doodlebug came very near, then stopped dead. Loud explosion. It broke glass quite near.

One fortunate aspect of the flying bomb was that its engine usually stopped a few seconds before it went off, giving people some chance of getting down on the ground or under cover. My understanding is that this was a design fault. At the end of its pre-set time of flight, explosive tabs blew down the elevators, putting it into a steep dive onto its target; this dive threw its fuel to the back of the fuel tank, starving the engine which then cut out. However later flying bombs were modified and had their engines still running as they went off.

Tuesday 4 July 1944

Got to London Bridge at 9.30. Warning was sounding. Saw that doodlebug had gone off at top of building next-door but one to Adelaide House [*on the north side of the Thames next to London Bridge*]. All clear 9.50. Got lists. Alert 10.15. All clear 11.30. Alert 11.50. Down with Mike by 5.30. No all clear when we left.

Wednesday 5 July 1944

Up with Mike and Audrey. Got to office 10 o/c. Alert 12.35–1.50. Mac is away. One doodlebug came over at 12.55, we did not hear it go off. Alert 2.15. One came over low at 2.20. Hand and I were in Angel Court, so we stopped by a doorway and it went over, the engine stopped with a grinding sound, and a few seconds later it went off.

Friday 7 July 1944

Up to town. Saw doodlebug last night v. close. Many explosions some way away. Dull & cloudy today, and its raining. Alert 12.15. Lunch 12.35–1.10. All clear 2.10. Alert 2.27. All clear 3.00. Alert 3.17. Went to Baldwins, bought Claudius Æ 1 [*Æ indicates a coin was of brass or bronze and the number 1 here shows it was of the largest size*] 3/- rev SC. ROMA. Vespasian Æ 1 2/6. Tiberius Æ 2 2/6 rev PONTIF MAX. All clear 5.43. [*On the journey home*] We passed a crater made by a doodlebug, about 20 ft across, 2–4 ft deep on railway lines. It had blown the roofs off about a dozen houses. Bits of the doodlebug were still in the crater. Got to Bognor 7.55. Alert 7.43. 9.00 Lancasters, Marauders and Bostons going out. 10.30 Lancs coming back. 10.45 V. heavy explosions. I am staying up till about 3 o/c because Dad is going up to town tomorrow.

Around this time we saw the large bomber streams going out to bomb in support of our armies in Normandy. On one occasion I counted 700 Lancasters and Halifaxes as they passed over; the noise, and sense of sheer power and weight, were most impressive. One of these streams went out to bomb Caen, and after it had passed over us there was a pause and then in Idlewylde our French windows began to rattle as the bombs went off on the other side of the Channel. And one morning a number of Canadian wounded were ushered onto our train at Horsham, another reminder of the battles in Normandy.

Tuesday 11 July 1944

3 alerts last night, 9 doodlebugs over at various times. All went over Selsey, but too far north for Portsmouth or Southampton. There was a very large concentration of Bofors gun fire. Searchlights were on and we could see the doodlebugs as bright spots, accentuated by their own tail light [*from the engine*]. Ordinary AA was firing too, also some bursts which were shaped so: [*horizontally spread star*], in brilliant orange, larger than the ordinary 3.7 or 4.5 [*calibre*] bursts. Up by 7.55 with Michael and Audrey. Caught steamer from Tunbridge Wells at E. Croydon. Got to London Bridge at 9.30. Caught 17 bus to Bank. Alert on. All clear 9.50. Had coffee in ABC, got lists. Alert 11.23. Doodlebug came over at 11.25, came very near, exploded loudly fairly near (it landed in City Road). When we first heard it Throg St was crowded with Brokers and Jobbers, but as it came nearer the street cleared like magic. We heard the Bank of England bell go off which means imminent danger. There is rather low cloud which hides the doodlebugs. Took lock of coin cabinet to locksmith in Copthall Avenue to have key made for it. 1.05 alert. Hand, Mackintosh and I were in Throg St and we could hear one coming. It got nearer and nearer till it sounded right on top of us, when suddenly I saw it disappear across Throgmorton St at terrific speed. Then suddenly it stopped and there was a hell of a bang, it raised the dust in Throg St, and we saw a huge pall of smoke come up from the direction of London

Wall. I hurried up Copthall Court, then up Copthall Avenue. The glass in the Copthall Pharmacy was gone, and in several other shops, also in some buildings near ours. Lots had been broken in London Wall, and Moorgate and Finsbury Pavement were smothered in broken glass. As I crossed London Wall to see the damage Fire Engines were coming from Finsbury Circus ringing their bells. The smoke from the flying bomb was everywhere. The blast tore a lot of boarding out of the Cable and Wireless place on the corner of Moorgate and London Wall. The doodlebug landed on a blitzed site behind Moorgate tube. It broke glass next door but one, but not in our offices. I got my key and lock back from the locksmith at 12.30, it cost 2/3d and works beautifully. All clear 1.37. Flying bombs 2.40, 2.42, 2.48. The last one went off went off quite loudly. Caught 4.07 from London Bridge. Alert just before we left. Home by 6.20. Went to Red Cross. Acted as casualty for fake incident. Had fake wound on my leg, v. well done by Mr Hoad. He gave me a small thunderflash.

Hand and Mac, our two dealers, were shorter than me, and the dust thrown up in Throgmorton Street by the explosion of the doodlebug that landed behind Moorgate Tube came up to their heads and left them coughing and choking, but my head was just above it. The explosion was followed immediately by the crash of glass from the tobacco kiosk in Throgmorton Street, followed only a few seconds later by the sound of the glass being swept up by the bearded old man who ran it.

Wednesday 12 July 1944

Six doodlebugs over last night. I saw one being attacked by a Mosquito over Bersted way. The Mosquito only used its machine guns and no tracers, then it gave up and turned away. The flying bomb was heading towards Guildford. Another came low almost over the house. It made a terrific row. I woke up and ran out to see it disappear between the two houses opposite. There were two alerts. Up by 7.55 with Michael and Audrey. Got to London Bridge at 9.30. No alerts during business hours. Alert 3.16. One came fairly close then stopped. We did not hear it explode. 3.22. One coming over. It stopped and exploded some way away. Another also went off some way away. Another, engine running until it actually went off, but not too close. 3.30 Another doodlebug. No bang. 3.34 flying bomb gone off in distance. It is quite sunny now with a few large white patches of cloud. 3.46 All clear. Caught 5.15 down from London Bridge. Another Alert was on, and at about 5.10 I was in a v. small [*end*] compartment with only four seats [*and I was up against the window*]. Two people were standing when a doodlebug began to come near. It got very near, then the tone of its engine changed and it began to dive. One could not move, the train was so full, but fortunately it landed some way away. It blocked the line though, and we went round by Peckham etc. As we went past Croydon (?) one went off in the distance and another exploded on the Downs as we went through Amberley. I think it landed on Bury Hill. We got to Bognor at 7.45. Went round to see Chiv; we went and watched the [*members of the Church*] Fellowship playing tennis. We saw Mary Gray there. Then we went to my house and looked at my books.

Wednesday 19 July 1944
Caught steamer at E. Croydon. Got to London Bridge at 9.30. All clear at 9.40. Found that a doodlebug had landed in Budge Row, Cannon St, at 8.30. Another had landed in Old Jewry at 9.20. Cannon St and Gresham St were cordoned off, and lots of glass out in Princes St, Moorgate and Gresham St. It blew several panes of glass out in our building. Alert 10.08. One doodlebug went off. 10.15 doodlebug exploded, 10.46 another about the same place. All clear 1.05. Alert 1.25. All clear 1.50. Alert 2.32. One bang a long way off. All clear 2.55. Angel Court lost quite a bit of glass from this mornings bombs. Alert 3.30, 3.34 doodlebug gone off. Went up on roof and found two small pieces of doodlebug; I suppose it was the Old Jewry one. 3.40 All clear. Went to Baldwins. Down by 5.30. Went and watched Church Fellowship playing tennis. Barracked Sykes.

Friday 21 July 1944
Up as usual. It was raining at Bognor. We got to East Croydon at about twenty minutes past nine. The 69 [*train*] came in and we

got into it. Then we heard a doodlebug diving (45°), and we looked out and Michael and I saw it distinctly. Someone said it looked as if it landed near Waddon. Its engine was still going and it was banking slightly to the <u>RIGHT</u>. It made quite a big bang and a cloud of smoke. We got to Moorgate at 9.50. All clear 10.00; Alert 10.10; All clear 10.45; Alert 11.10; All clear 12.13; Alert 12.20.

Tuesday 1 August 1944

Up as usual by 7.55. Alert 9.48. One [*flying bomb*] came over and landed in Aldgate. From Throg we could see the smoke coming up behind Old Broad Street, also between Copthall Buildings. I was just getting the books, and when it went off it closed the door, which I had left open. 2.20 Alert, 2.30 All clear. Heard nothing. 3.25 Alert. 3.24 Quite a loud bang, but we heard nothing coming. 3.31 one came over. I heard the engine stop and could hear it coming down. It fell quite close with a very 'pointed' explosion, I dont know where it dropped. 3.55 one coming, 3.55½ it has stopped. I went into Mr Levick to see if he wanted anything and he was down behind a desk. He said 'Get down, its coming'. Then sure enough I heard it gliding over giving a shrill weak whistle so I got down. It seemed to come over, then it exploded but curiously enough it was not particularly loud. All clear 4.03. It has been rather a tiring day running up and down from the Stock Exchange. Went to *Financial Times* for Dad. There seemed some smoke up towards Finsbury Pavement. Perhaps one dropped there. Down by 5.30. Went to Red Cross. Hoad gave us some 'Incidents'. I did quite well as leader.

Tuesday 8 August 1944

Up as usual. Had coffee. Mac was back from his holiday. Fairly quiet day. Nice weather, down by 5.30. I went to Red Cross but they were getting ready for the Fête so I did not stay. Went to Chiv's. On the way there I saw a lot of our Heavy Bombers going out high up. One had a thin stream of smoke coming from its starboard outer engine. I called for Chiv but he was at tennis. His mother came out to look at the planes, and she called out Chiv's brother to see them. We watched the plane that was trailing white smoke, and as it got fairly well out over the sea the smoke seemed to get thicker, then the plane wobbled a bit. I mentioned that the wing where the smoke came from seemed to glitter. Suddenly the the smoke streamed out in a thick white track, the plane swerved to the right, began to dive and the whole thing burst into flames. The tail came off and also other pieces, the fuel tanks fell away blazing – they burnt with a brilliant orange flame, leaving a plume of fire behind them – and the fuselage came falling down going over and over; nearly half way down two parachutes appeared, but one seemed to be falling much too fast, and I think it had failed to open properly. A little while later we saw a colossal pall of black smoke coming up from where the plane went into the sea. I did not hear any bombs go off. I think the men in the plane must have known that there was something wrong, and I hope that all the others baled out further inland, leaving the Pilot and Co-Pilot to get it over the sea before ditching it. I cycled to the tennis courts to see Chiv. Played Battle of Jutland with Faith. She won. 9.45 Bombers coming back. Michael Rowe counted 179.

Friday 11 August 1944
Up as usual. Hand is away today. Things quiet in the House. Alert 2.30. Doodlebug approaching 2.35. As it came nearer I poked my head out of the window by my desk. It came nearer and nearer and I was just about to duck when I saw it travelling very fast at about 1000 feet from East to West parallel to London Wall. It was a little way to my right and it must have just about gone over the Stock Exchange and the Bank. I had a very good view of it for a good four seconds, but it seemed much longer. The doodlebug had short wings with leading and trailing edges parallel. The body looked very long and I could see the jet motor at the rear easily. It appeared to be black, but as the sky was bright it may have been any colour. There was no trail or flame of any kind behind it, and it just touched the base of a patch of cloud as it went over. I could see the fluffy wisps of vapour against it. Down by 5.30.

This next entry is rather long, but it does give some idea of the things that had to be done after a bomb had gone off.

Sunday 27 August 1944

[*On duty at the Rescue Party Post at Rank's Kennels, next to Aldwick Farm*] I was woken up by a distant explosion. I lay in bed for a few moments, then the warning went. I jumped out of bed, and everybody followed suit. Then we heard a doodlebug coming. With one accord we all rushed out; Ted, the Party leader saw it but I did not; it came nearer and nearer, straight towards us, then it stopped. We heard it come whistling down amazingly clearly, then there was a terrific explosion from the direction of Bognor (7.30 approx). We saw the smoke coming up. [*This doodlebug went off in the gardens between Shelley Road and Tennyson Road in West Bognor, just under a mile from where we were standing.*] Soon the All clear went. Ted told me I could go after we had waited for about ten minutes and no call had come through, so I went straight home, but Mr Field said it was in Nyewood Lane, so I got on my bike and cycled towards it. I turned up Richmond Avenue West, and there was a cordon across Elm Grove. They let me through [*I was in Civil Defence uniform*] and as I turned into Shelley Road I saw No 1 Rescue Party lorry so I left my bike by it. Then the driver asked me to help take a stretcher and blankets and an extra blanket to a nearby house. I did so and as they were busy and wanted more men they let me stay with them. Ayres asked me who I was with and without waiting for a reply told me to report to my leader; so as by this time No 2 Party had arrived I went to them. Then Searle divided us into pairs to search the badly damaged houses for casualties, and also the gardens. I was with Jock. We went to two houses, all the windows were out, there was glass and plaster all over the place, things were thrown, china on the floors, Silver and books strewn about. The stairs were unsafe and the landing was all askew and the room by it had had the outer wall blown away. In one of the bedrooms the bed was stained with blood and altogether it was properly messed up. Then we went to the other house. The inside was wrecked. After that we searched the gardens and I found a blackbird, with its wings badly hurt, its tail blown to bits and half its beak gone. I had to kill it, it was so badly hurt. After that we had to search one house for jewellery, rings etc. I found a £1 note, a 10/- note, four 2¹/₂p stamps and two pairs of glasses, one pair bust, in an upstairs sitting-room, one wall of which was smashed. The others found a small case by a bed full of rings, watches etc. Les of No 1 Party found two handbags, one containing ration books. Everything was handed to the Police. When we had finished that we went into Shelley Road again. Just as we got there Sgt Davis of the Ambulance came running out of Elm Grove and said that he wanted a sitting case car, so I was told to go down to Nyewood Lane and get one. I ran down and found Searle there. I asked for a car but he said that none were available and told me to get an Ambulance. I got on to the running board of the front one and directed them to Davis. Then I got off, but Sgt Bailey said that Davis needed an assistant so I ran after it and jumped on again. We went into Tennyson Rd and stopped there. I went in with Davis and helped an old lame woman out into the Ambulance. Then Osborne came up and began to help so I went back to Shelley Rd and put my bike in Wood's garden [*Dennis Wood was a friend; his house was damaged by the flying bomb*]. Then I went back to the Nyewood Lane end of Shelley Road and Searle told me to go with him. We went up Nyewood Lane and Searle asked me if I had any dressings. I told him I had several in my battledress, so he told me to enquire at every house in Nelson Road for minor casualties. At the third house, called Woodlea, I was told that a man had cut his foot. I was shown upstairs and on the landing there was quite a bit of blood and glass, and the man came walking out of a bedroom with a limp. He had a bandage round one foot, and the woman who led me upstairs took us both into his bedroom. He sat on the bed and I unwound the bandage which was a piece of cloth just wound loosely round his foot. He had quite a nasty horizontal cut on the inside of his right foot behind the big toe joint. Some fool had put two pieces of sticking plaster over it, but I thought perhaps there was some glass in it, so I wrapped the cloth loosely round it again, made him get back into his bed which was spotted with blood and told him to keep warm. Then I ran down into the road and saw Osborne and another First Aid man coming from Nyewood Lane, so I told them where the casualty was and they said they would attend to him, so I took them to the house and left them to get on with it. Then I searched the rest of the road helped by Chiverton and Wale [*two friends*] who had just come. I searched all one side and half the North side when the sergeant of No 3 or 4 Party told me he had done the rest, so I went back and found Searle again and told what I had done. He said that was all right and told me to do the same to Glencathara Rd. There were no casualties, but at No 10 their water tanks had been shifted and they were leaking, so I finished the road, finding nothing else to report. I then went to the Incident Officer in Ellasdale Road and told him that they needed the Water Co. man. He told me to look in Shelley Road, which I did, but could not find him, so I told the I.O. [*Incident Officer*] who said he would attend to it. Searle then told me I was wanted to help search Wood St, so I went there and searched it with some of No 1 Party. After that I went and had tea at the mobile canteen. There were as many sandwiches and biscuits as you liked, all free. Then Harry Nicholls turned up and we all went and helped Dennis Wood clear up his house [*which was on the other side of the road from the two badly damaged houses*]. Left incident at a quarter to twelve. The crater was about 20 ft across by 4 ft – 5 ft deep. Chiv came home with me.

Played tennis in afternoon.

[*In my diary there is a map of the incident*]

Mother's comment in her diary was just the jocular note: 'Flying bomb on Bognor. Roger to the Rescue!' This incident in Bognor was really the end of my experience of flying bombs; only two more are mentioned in my diary, both distant ones. It is worth noting that nearly all of my experience of flying bombs in the City was on weekdays and in working hours. Things could be much more tense for those living in central London as can be seen from *Prophesying Peace, Diaries 1944–1945* by James Lees-Milne, pages 78–158.

This left the V2s which started on 8 September and had continued sporadically since. These rockets arrived unseen and there was no defence against them, so people simply carried on as usual, just as they did with the flying bombs. However the V2 did produce a sonic bang which could be heard over a wide area, but this was no help, unlike the normal few seconds of silence before a flying bomb went off, because at the target this sonic bang and the explosion of the warhead occurred at virtually the same time. This warhead contained about one ton of explosive, very like that of the flying bomb. Of the 7,000 flying bombs launched against London some 2,500 got through and many of these fell in Kent and some on other targets, while around 500 V2s hit London. Altogether, from the German point of view, the flying bomb was much more cost-effective; indeed Albert Speer himself regarded the V2 as a very serious waste of Germany's wartime resources. For most Londoners the V2 was a minor nuisance but one which did cause a significant number of casualties.

Thursday 26 October 1944
Up by myself. We got to East Croydon and we were told that London Bridge station was not working. It was quite foggy. I got into the next Victoria Train, then I got a tube from Balham to the Bank. Went straight to the House and got lists. Time was 10.30. Levick is away today, so it does not matter. Down by 5.30.

Friday 27 October 1944
Up as usual. Saw V2 damage near Shuttleworth's factory which caused hold up yesterday. Busy day. V2s at 11.15 (?), 11.50 and 12.15. Down by 5.30.

Monday 6 November 1944
Up by 8.28. V2 had landed by viaduct at London Bridge, almost exactly where the one landed by Shuttleworth's on 27.10.44. It knocked out quite a large piece of the viaduct and the rails festooned down to the ground. Men were working with oxy-acet. welding gear as we passed. Got to office at 10.45.

As the train inched carefully into London Bridge station I could look straight down into the great hole where the rest of the brick viaduct had been, with the rails now looping down into it. Continuing to run trains over a brick viaduct when nearly half of it had been demolished by a V2 says something for the willingness at that time to accept some risk to keep things going. But my acquaintance with V2s was not quite finished.

On 9 February 1945, by then a trooper in the army up at Barnard Castle in County Durham, I was given seven days' leave. Arriving at King's Cross in the evening I was struck by the number of RAF bomber crews going back to their bases. For taxis there was a queue managed by a porter; when an empty taxi pulled up he would ask the first person in the queue where he was going to, in my case Victoria Station, and he would then shout down the queue: 'Anyone else for Victoria?' In this way every taxi was used to capacity. I spent most of my leave with my family at Aldwick, but for the last two days I went back up to town to stay at the Royal Armoured Corps Club which was in a Georgian house in Grosvenor Square where the US Embassy now stands. I was on a 38a bus going from Victoria station along Grosvenor Place on the way to this club and looking idly up into the sky over the Buckingham Palace gardens. Suddenly, in front of my eyes, a V2 went off prematurely, high up in the sky. But others did not, and my two days in London were punctuated by their sonic bangs and explosions.

7

The Army

Shorncliffe

Note in my Diary

My last day at the office was Friday 10 November 1944. Then I had a holiday till Wednesday 15 November, when I went to London by the 16.15 [*train*] and was met by Michael Rowe at Victoria. We went to Collins [*Music Hall in Islington on that evening, and I spent the night at Michael's family flat. Next day, 16 November, carrying a rail warrant and with a number of other recruits*] I caught the 9.15 train from Charing Cross to Shorncliffe [*near Folkestone in Kent*], where we arrived at 11.25. We were then marched to Moore Barracks [*and there began my military service, which was to last for just over three years*].

Moore Barracks was rather down-at-heel (the rumour was that it had been condemned after the Crimean War). Most of it was of grim Victorian red brickwork and in need of some interior decoration. There were the usual guardroom, cookhouse, parade ground etc and a battery of barrack-rooms which each held about twenty soldiers in a line of beds down each side. Included was a washroom with lots of hand-basins but not a single plug; lesson one for survival in the army – always carry your own plug. The only other furniture was one's own kitbag which held everything that was not in use or set out on the bed for daily inspection.

Our acquaintance with real army life began with a long queue filing past a sergeant who allocated each of us to some branch of the army – most went into the infantry, but my request to join the Royal Armoured Corps because I had a brother in the 7th Hussars was granted without any question. We were then each given our Pay Book (Soldier's Service Book, Army Book 64); mine, brown and now rather tattered, shows that I was enlisted at Shorncliffe on 16 Nov 1944, 'For the National Service Act, Duration of Emergency'. It shows my army number: 14867566, and I signed it on 17 November. It gives my trade on enlistment as 'Student'; I suspect I put this down on Dad's advice – certainly 'Unauthorised Clerk' (the proper title of a Blue Button) would not have looked very impressive. It also shows that I weighed 128 pounds and had a birthmark on the outside of my right buttock; I soon realised that this was not a very convenient identification mark to show in public and later managed to change it to a birthmark on the inside of my right elbow. Next we were kitted out – battledress, denims, boots, underwear (traditionally available in two sizes, too big and too small), mess tins, eating irons (knife, fork, spoon) etc. I don't recall any attestation or swearing to fight for my country; certainly the spirit of the time made it seem superfluous. We were then allocated to platoons, this being done by alphabetical order (which accounts for all my friends in A platoon having names beginning with A). Finally to our barrack-room where I began trying to turn my bedspace into a rather cramped temporary home.

On this first evening most of us wandered down to the NAAFI, warm and smoky, where we crowded round tables drinking tea and eating meat pies (despite having had quite a reasonable supper in the cookhouse) and started getting to know some of our fellow recruits. One at my table was the proud owner of a khaki-coloured cigarette case which held twenty cigarettes; this was handed round the table and much admired. Such were our simple pleasures of ownership in wartime, when there was not much money for luxuries and indeed very few luxuries to buy. In another group someone had brought a ukelele and was imitating George Formby. Then back to our barrack-room for our first night sleeping on 'biscuits', the three squares which made up a mattress. We were all pretty well worn-out by the events of the day and sleep was no problem, but all too soon it was 'Wakey, Wakey', and our new life truly began.

Our platoon was in principle commanded by Lt Nunn, but for all day-to-day purposes it was commanded by Corporal Buss of the East Surreys – solidly built, fair bristling moustache and a healthy complexion. That is, unless he perceived some idleness or stupidity by one of the soldiers in his platoon; then quite frightening red-faced anger took over. Our very first experience of this made it clear to all of us that doing your very best and doing it instantly was the only safe strategy. He was supported rather feebly by Sergeant Geraghty, small, elderly, kept in service only because of the war and blind in his right eye, so that he fired his rifle left-handedly, aiming with his good left eye. These two NCOs were supported even more feebly by a rather pale and thin-faced soldier who lived in our barrack-room with unclear duties which he systematically neglected, being a true specialist in skiving. He had been court-martialled in Italy for desertion but had been found not guilty because he had been kept in the front line for an unduly long period. The feebleness of these two was of no account, for Corporal Buss needed no support in his total and unquestioned command of our platoon.

One of my main impressions, looking back, was of constant rushing to and from our barrack-room, changing from battledress for drill, into denims for training, then into physical training (PT) kit, back into denims and so on through the day. Drill on the square, PT (taken by instructors in red and black striped jerseys – the army was very keen on physical fitness) together with arms training filled most of our working day. We were each issued with a rifle (I chose one with rather pale woodwork which would be easily recognisable) and with these we trained in marksmanship and fired on ranges, but which we mostly cleaned and kept lightly oiled. We also used Bren guns, which we dismantled and reassembled until we could do it in our sleep; and my paybook shows that I passed the Tests of Elementary Training Nos 1, 2 and 3 on the rifle and 1 and 2 on the Bren. We learned about the 2 inch mortar, hand grenades and gas; we learned map-reading and judging distance, and we were indoctrinated with the battlefield infantry mantra: *Down – Crawl – Observe – Sights – Fire* as well as being inoculated and vaccinated. And we blancoed and cleaned and polished, and we read the Company Detail which gave us our training programme for the following day. These six weeks at Shorncliffe were ones of unremitting activity and getting used to army life and discipline.

Wednesday 29 November 1944
Company Sergeant Major in a good temper all the morning. Had an argument with him during a period of judging distance about the distance of a chimney. Ayler, Ardagh and I won. Had a very

interesting demonstration for all 'A' Coy. down by the ranges. It was done by people in German uniforms, and was very well done. They dug trenches, and attacked through a smoke screen, and all sorts of other things, and we had to guess what was going on. A brass hat arrived and watched too. Went to get our things from drying room. Found we had not got key, so I had to double back and get it. Read in quiet room all the evening with Ayler and Ardagh. Got letter from Mother. Fairly nice weather. There was a convoy quite close in at about 4.30 PM. [*The camp was on high ground overlooking the sea.*]

Thursday 30 November
Fairly normal day, CSM in a good temper. Played football in the afternoon and he joined in. Good fun. Company detail makes us blanco from now on, and we have inoculation tomorrow.

Friday 1 December 1944
In morning Gas, Foot Drill Competition, Rifle lesson and Foot drill. In afternoon PT, Gas Chamber, then No 75 Innoculation. Hurt a bit after needle was withdrawn. We have now had three inoculations and the Vaccination. My turn with Aldridge and Anderson to scrub forms and table. I did two forms. Arm beginning to get sore towards evening. Lt Nunn talked to us in evening. We are to be allowed out tomorrow from after lunch till 23.00 hrs. We get 48 hours light duties because of inoculation.

Saturday 2 December 1944
Had rather a bad night, bedclothes came unstuck. Arm not too bad. Had pay parade in morning, got £1. Went into Folkestone in afternoon, long bus queue, but we caught an empty Relief bus in Shorncliffe. There were three of us, Ardagh, Ayler and myself. I bought *What Happened in History* by V. Gordon Childe. Had tea at Odeon café, and saw *Tampico* [*film*] at the Central [*Cinema*]. Lts Nunn & Fox were in the row ahead of us. Got back at 9.14 and reported to CQMS office. Had a letter from Dad, enclosing a nice letter from Gerald Hodgson & Co.

Misfortunes of War

Our training routine was punctuated by three particular events which remain in my mind. The first of these was to me a surprising observation. We were firing our rifles on a 30-yard range in slanting afternoon sunlight and I could see the bullets – like rods of silver – as they were fired down the range.

The second particular event occurred one Sunday:

Sunday 3 December 1944
Got up at 7.30. Spent the morning cleaning a Bren gun with some other blokes. Ayler and I assembled and stripped it several times. At about 12.15 two planes [*both Typhoons*] crashed on the west side of the playing fields. The lights went out but came on a few seconds later, and I ran out and saw a shed burning near the gym. I ran across to it, and there by the road was a mass of pieces of one plane, and the wings and petrol tanks were burning. Several cooks were putting water on the burning parts, when an officer found the pilot close to the burning wing, and with two other men he dragged him clear. Somebody washed all the dirt off his face with a bucket of water, crude but effective. However the poor bloke was dead. I helped carry him away from the flames. The lower part of his nose was torn, and he had several deep gashes in his forehead and cheek, but they were not bleeding, and his legs were burnt. His flying boots were torn off and his clothing was also torn about. It was a curious thing, but somehow the poor chap did not seem human, but more like a doll.

Parts of the plane were still burning and there was ammunition scattered all around but there was nothing more we could do, so for a while we just stood around the wreckage and the dead pilot with the sadly dramatic scene impressing itself upon our memories. (We found the pilot's name on his identity disc – I seem to remember that it was Callaghan.) We then drifted back to the barrack-room and our Sunday morning tasks. It was a salutary reminder of the realities of war. My diary continues:

I did feel a little squeamish but not much, and I managed to eat a good lunch. Went to Hythe with Ardagh and Ayler. Saw *Vessel of Wrath* [*film*], quite good.

Later it was confirmed that another Typhoon had crashed at the same time outside the camp. It seemed likely that coming back in mist from a strike, they were flying low under the impression that they were coming in over the low ground of Romney Marsh. Unfortunately they were too far east and hit the high ground at Shorncliffe.

In the army much time is spent in training on weapons which may be dangerous to the enemy, but which can certainly be dangerous to you and your own side, and long experience had led to very strict range discipline. We received training on dummy hand grenades, but the time came when we were to practice throwing live ones. For this several platoons were taken out to a gently sloping field to the west of Shorncliffe. There a roughly U-shaped enclosure of sandbags had been erected; the thrower of a bomb stood inside this enclosure, threw his bomb and ducked down below the sandbags as it went off. Outside the enclosure with their own sandbag protection were on one side a corporal looking after the boxes of grenades and responsible for arming them and handing them to the thrower, and on the other another corporal with a blanket; if anybody should accidentally drop a grenade it was his task to smother it with the blanket (and get away quickly) to reduce the danger from the flying fragments. Everything was ready for the third particular event which punctuated our training at Shorncliffe.

We all lined up well back from the sandbags, and one by one were called forward to throw a grenade. When you reached the enclosure the corporal handed you an armed grenade. For all of us this was the first time we had held an truly lethal object and a certain tension was understandable. The corporal with the blanket stood ready and yet another corporal stood behind the thrower quietly making comforting remarks: 'Now you know about grenades – no need to be nervous – just do exactly as you have been taught – when I say "throw" pull out the pin with your left thumb and throw the grenade.' The corporal would then step back a pace and say 'throw'. The bomber did as he had been taught, throwing the grenade round-armed with his right hand; everyone around the throwing bay ducked, the grenade went off, the base plate whined off into the distance, and it was the next man's turn to throw.

All went well until one soldier was given the command 'throw'. What nobody realised was that he was fatally left-handed. On the command he did indeed pull out the pin with his left thumb, but then his left-handedness took over: he dropped the grenade from his right hand and instinctively tried to throw the pin with his left. After a frozen second one corporal dragged him behind one arm of the sandbags and the corporal with the blanket threw it over the grenade, but it went off before he could get fully behind his wall of sandbags and he received a leg full of splinters. There was a pause while he was carried off, and we never saw him again. The rest of the afternoon's grenade throwing went on; when we arrived back in our barrack-room there was much discussion of the day's events.

After six weeks our primary training was complete and it was time for us all to move on to our arms training regiments. Corporal Buss came to our barrack-room on our last evening, sat on a bed and said goodbye to us; by now we knew exactly where we stood with him and it was a congenial occasion. He had certainly given us a very effective introduction to military discipline.

Barnard Castle

Each of us now received a movement order and a rail warrant to our next unit. I left Shorncliffe on Friday 22 December and at 17.30 the same day arrived at the 61st Training Regiment, Royal Armoured Corps, at Stainton Camp just outside Barnard Castle in County Durham. As we arrived we passed concrete standings with lines of Sherman tanks, and my spirits rose at the prospect of training on these impressive looking machines. The camp itself seemed nearly new, and a great contrast with Shorncliff; neat huts were set out along wandering tarmac paths, and everything was crisply clean and tidy. This extended to the inside of what now became our troop hut, which had the usual line of beds down each side, clean white walls and a really beautiful gleaming pale fawn linoleum floor. We were extremely proud of our floor (which we felt made a very good impression during hut inspections) and willingly devoted part of each Sunday to cleaning the whole of it with white spirit and repolishing it; its state was helped by the fact that being in a tank regiment our army boots had no studs in them, as these could slide dangerously on a tank. But it was further helped because pride in our floor led us to protect it with sacking, cardboard and anything else we could find, all of which had to be hidden away before inspections.

Having arrived at our new hut we left our kit and, hungry after our journeys from different Primary Training Centres, we went for our first meal in the clean and modern cookhouse. There our troop of twenty four began to get to know each other. Transformed from privates into troopers and feeling now like seasoned soldiers, we soon settled into our new camp. Next day we met our squadron leader and, much more important, the two sergeants who had day-to-day responsibility for our troop. One seemed to us rather old and fatherly, the other, rather younger, had a distinct sense of humour; both we found to be helpful and kindly but very firm. Almost the first thing the older one told us was 'If you must shag, shag clean; don't come to me with a prick like the end of a pepper pot and expect any sympathy'.

At some point we received further inoculations. For this we were paraded at one end of a long instructional room, all feeling a little nervous. In the middle of the room was a large table for the medical officer and his helpers with all their alarming equipment together with a corporal clerk. The first man was called forward, received his jab in the upper left arm, had this recorded in his paybook and was told to wait at the other end of the room. Then the next man was called forward and so on. As, perhaps, the tenth man was receiving his jab, one of the earlier ones waiting at the further end of the room collapsed, then another and another; this was not lost on those waiting for their jabs who began to feel more nervous. What exactly happened next I cannot remember, but clearly we all survived. One rumour circulating at the time was that after your jab, if you didn't have your paybook for it to be recorded, the MO shoved the needle back in and took back whatever it was he had just injected.

My fellow troopers in our hut showed the usual human variety. There was Trooper Stark who slept with his eyes open; he was from Glasgow and when I once uttered a 'Damn' he feigned shock and exclaimed 'Och, Alford, that's durrrty talk'; on the whole, there was little bad language in our hut. Trooper Williamson was from Manchester, pleasant and rather good-looking; he would trot along the winding paths between our barrack huts making noises like a truck and changing gear as he went up hills. Trooper Curll somehow always managed to do things differently. He found that when his motorcycle would not start, a quick honk on the electric horn and then it started. The instructor mocked him for this belief, but when the instructor's own motorcycle would not start he was reduced to trying the Curll solution and – it started! And there was Trooper Deadman, a

Welshman, whose name we were careful to pronounce as Dead Man, Trooper Armstrong who was later made a lance corporal and the names of three who with me made up the crew of the Troop Leader's tank on our week's training at Guisborough; but they and the other twenty or so members of our Troop are now only blurred figures in my mind.

For our technical training we wore grey-green denim overalls and discipline was relatively relaxed, but in drill and on parade it was enforced to a high standard. With black berets, red and yellow Royal Armoured Corps titles and flashes, webbing blancoed a pale sandy colour, yellow lanyards, and everything polishable thoroughly polished, we looked extremely smart; we were proud of our turnout and we behaved accordingly.

Technical Training

The training programme covered three trades: driving and mechanical, wireless operating and gunnery. Excluding the commander, the four crew members of a Sherman tank consisted of Driver Mech (the main driver), Gunner Mech (second driver, who sat next to him and manned the hull machine gun) then in the turret were Gunner Op (who aimed and fired the main 75 mm gun, the co-axial machine gun and shared operation of the No. 19 wireless set) and Driver Op (who acted as loader, was main operator of the wireless and was also a spare driver). I was made a Gunner Mech, generally regarded as the lowest in the crew hierarchy. All of us now learned to drive the standard army 15 cwt truck and the Sherman and to ride a motorcycle, and were trained on the Sten gun, the .38 Smith & Wesson pistol and given a go on the Thompson sub-machine gun.

After reveille and breakfast we had a short parade and roll-call; we already knew the training programme for the day from Part 1 Orders the previous evening, and we were then marched off to the training rooms. Our training day was divided into two sessions in the morning and two in the afternoon. My group started with the 'Mech' side. In the classroom we were given a good grounding in all aspects of the internal combustion engine from the four-stroke Otto cycle to the severe practicalities of the petrol and electrical systems, with much practice in maintenance and fault-finding. For the last of these there were large training bays with 15 cwt truck engines mounted on frames; there would be two of us to an engine with one setting up faults for the other to cure and get the engine running again. This was accompanied by afternoons of driving; we drove 15 cwt trucks for miles round circuits of local roads virtually devoid of any other traffic, initially with an instructor who provided help and encouragement and, when we began get the hang of driving, with the same instructor sleeping peacefully next to us. This all provided useful skills which to me have been of lifelong value.

Then it was on to the tanks, Sherman Mk 2s; here maintenance was the main thing, since with such heavy vehicles (about 25 tons) any significant problem required the fitters. We learned that keeping the engine clean made it possible to see when anything developed a leak or came undone. During this phase I saw a Sherman gearbox – large and heavy – which the fitters had taken apart and inside the heavy, bright steel gear wheels had chewed each other up in an astonishing fashion; fortunately we did not have to deal with such problems. Much of the tank driving (in which rubicund Corporal Sutton was my instructor) was also done on local roads, which was possible because our Shermans had tracks with rubber pads – all-steel tracks would have rapidly torn up the tarmac. Even so, miles of roads had to be given concrete edges to stop them crumbling under our weight and many roads acquired a distinctly polished surface from our passing to and fro. One of our driving sessions took us through the outskirts of Durham where someone complained of rude words written on some of our tanks; we were told that only respectable names were allowed, so I named our tank Astyanax (the son of Hector – impeccably classical). The Sherman was an easy tank to drive and its weight and cross-country capability gave one an agreeable feeling of power. On the driving grounds, muddy and churned up, we all became familiar with the characteristic sensation as it surged over the heavily broken ground with the engine rumbling obediently as we decelerated into great potholes and accelerated out the other side. Here I talk of tanks, but we soon learnt to refer to them only as 'vehicles', since 'tank' was a word strictly forbidden on the wireless for reasons of security and this prohibition quickly became a fixed habit. Training was punctuated by trade tests and a driving test until at last the Mech side was completed. By then we all felt fully able to drive a truck or Sherman, to diagnose and cure any common faults, and so keep them running. One by-product of this and other driving instruction was that I acquired a civilian driving licence which still entitles me to drive a tank as well as an agricultural tractor, mower or vehicle controlled by a pedestrian and even a road roller in addition to the more usual car (with or without trailer), and moped or motorcycle (with or without sidecar). Also, it seems, vehicles in categories l and n which the DVLA prefers not to specify.

For me it was then on to Gunnery. The main weapons we trained on were the 75 mm gun and Browning .300 machine gun which were the armament of the Sherman. Again the training was very thorough, taking us through all aspects of the principles and operation of these weapons together with their different types of ammunition and their use in wafare. In the case of the Browning, we dismantled it (so far as one could) and reassembled it until we could do this almost in our sleep; on the 75 we learned to test and adjust sights, to use the power traverse and the gyro-stabiliser, as well as firing these weapons on the ranges. My diary keeping was very irregular at this stage, but a few entries give some idea of this stage of our training:

Tuesday 3 April 1945

On testing and adjusting sights of 75 mm guns all the morning. Rather hard rain and occasional sunshine. Did Browning .300 stoppages until lunch time, the gun had stopped and we worked on it for an hour but could not clear it. Got *Satires of Juvenal and Persius* out of library. Discussion group tonight at 8.15 at YMCA on 'Housing, Permanent and Prefab'. Trooper Jacobs is the speaker. Misfire drill half the afternoon on the same tank in the field over the railway lines. More Browning stoppages.

Wednesday 4 April 1945

Discussion group was good last night, but quite left in its opinions. On Puff range in afternoon then scrubbed Browning bays with solvent for General's inspection. Spent evening cleaning and polishing. [*The Puff range was a model landscape gunnery range where puffs of smoke showed where your shells would have landed.*]

Thursday 5 April 1945

Gyro-stabiliser all the morning. Lunch at 12 o/c. Stowage bays in first part of afternoon, General Morris and various other officers wandered in. Then Powered traverse. Pay at 18.00 hours, drew £1. Had a shower. Played 'Air on the G String' by J.S. Bach [*probably*

119

on the record player in the Recreation Hut]. Our floor was really smashing this morning, after much labour.

Friday 6 April 1945
On tanks all morning, went over the battle run with Williamson and Stark, giving all sorts of firing orders all the time. We each took turns at Commander, Gunner and Loader. I used Power traverse and Gyro Stabiliser. Then we cleaned the barrel of the 75 on the other tank while others had their turns. Shell drill in the afternoon. Showery all day.

And, of course we devoted much time to cleaning and lightly oiling these weapons. In the end we felt confident in our ability to maintain and use them.

There were other aspects to our training. We had training films at the Aliwal, which was the camp cinema; these sessions were unusually popular because the projectionist always ended them with a cartoon. We also had a number of training exercises one of which consisted of a compass march in groups of three for some five or six miles across very bare moorland to a rendezvous point where there was a truck which would provide us with a meal and then return us to camp. We arrived at the truck feeling very hungry and were given a meal which ended with army fruit pudding which came out of a khaki-coloured tin; enhanced by hunger, it was the most wonderful pudding I had ever tasted.

Dangerous Events

It was during our practice in tracking targets with the 75 that we had an accident. Corporal Barker (kind and elderly – probably about 40) was sitting on the back of the turret while we took turns using the power traverse to track cars and trucks passing obliviously along a suitably distant road. As the turret rotated his ankle got trapped between the wireless recess at the back of the turret and the end of the splash-plate which protected the turret ring. Everything stopped and we helped him off the tank and sent for help; he was taken off to the medical hut and sadly we never saw him again. His place was taken by another instructor whose name I cannot remember.

Then there were days on the ranges, firing high-explosive (HE) shells and armour-piercing shot from the 75 and tracer from the Browning, all at unresisting targets. As always on ranges there were events which stick in the memory. We were firing HE and at one point we were supposed to be supporting a general barrage on an enemy position. All the tanks had to do six rounds in rapid fire; about half way through this, one of the tanks let out a most unusual noise and stopped firing. The barrage finished and we were all looking curiously at the tank concerned. Out of the turret wobbled the loader, glasses askew, cradling something heavy in his arms. It appeared that during the barrage he did the usual thing – he loaded, the gunner fired, the gun recoiled, flipped out the empty shell case, he loaded again and so on. But he had got so carried away with the need for speed that he had grabbed the next round and started to load it before the gun had fired. When it did fire (and all this was occurring in seconds) the breech recoiled and crushed this next round between the breech and the recoil guard. He showed us the heavy object he was carrying – an unfired HE round with the fuse cap and cartridge case completely squashed into accordion-like pleats. At least this confirmed what we had been taught – that our shells were 'bore-safe' and would not explode until they had revolved enough times to take them out of the gun barrel.

On this range we also had problems with sheep that would appear near the targets for the Browning machine guns; we tried to avoid them, but shooting had to go on. We were told that, because of strict rationing, all animals properly slaughtered had to be surrendered to the Ministry of Food; but the farmers could keep sheep killed 'accidentally' on ranges and also received compensation from the army. Many of these sheep casualties were probably not quite as accidental as one might imagine.

There was also small-arms training; we learned about the .38 Smith & Wesson pistol, the utilitarian Sten gun (cheap and rather dangerous) and the Thompson sub-machine gun, all of which we also fired on ranges. Again, it is the exceptional events which stick in the mind – the accidents and near misses which occurred despite rigorous range discipline. We were firing the Sten in a small quarry, with six of us in line firing at six targets, single shots at first, then automatic fire. When the Sten is fired the very hot cartridge case is ejected from the right-hand side of the gun. As we were firing bursts at the targets a hot cartridge case ejected from the Sten of the last-but-one man on the right somehow went down the back of the last man on the right, working its way down between his denims and his bare flesh. With a shriek of pain and still firing he swung round towards the rest of us; fortunately his magazine ran out just as he was about to mow us all down. By now we had got used to such near disasters and we helped him to get the cartridge case out of his denims.

Towards the end of the gunnery course we moved up from the 75 to the larger and much more powerful 17 pounder (76.2 mm) gun. After the invasion in June 1944 each Sherman tank troop consisted of four tanks, one of them a 'Firefly' – a Sherman armed with this 17 pounder gun. We went through the usual training on this weapon, which in its gun kit had a mysterious piece of bent metal called 'tool inserting and removing'. None of us ever found out where it was to be inserted or what it removed. But one thing still sticks in my mind: the recoil oil in this gun had the designation CS.11.17.B. I thought this was an elegantly rhythmic name and it stuck in my mind; when documents asked for a serial number I would enter CS.11.17.B, which looked very official and impressive.

The final part of the course was firing at Warcop, a large gunnery range with a tiny hamlet attached to it, some twenty miles west of Barnard Castle. There we had tanks, drivers and commanders/instructors belonging to the range, our trainee troop providing just the gunners and loaders. The tanks would drive along concrete roadways to successive firing positions where, under the instructor, we fired our ration of ammunition for that particular target. By far the most exciting was firing the 17 pounder. The breech was so big that it hardly left room in the turret for the loader and the rounds were very large and heavy, like enormously overgrown rifle rounds. When the gun was fired there was a terrific flash and bang with the brilliant yellow trace going so fast that it was very difficult to observe. The tank rocked back on its tracks and the recoiling breech block slammed back, ejecting the extremely hot shot casing onto the turret floor, where it bounced and continued to pour out choking white smoke from the remains of the charge. The gunner now had to wrestle another round into the gun. The displacement of air by the recoil meant that the first shot on each occasion led to the loader's black beret flying out of the turret and up into the air, while the flash, diverted by the muzzle-brake, came back through the empty co-ax machine gun mounting and removed the eyebrows of some loaders. I watched one round from another tank hit the target, an old tank, and ricochet straight up and up into a clear sky until it disappeared from view.

Altogether, firing the 17 pounder made one feel that here was a weapon which could do some real damage to the enemy.

As so often, there were near-accidents. When firing the co-axial machine gun in the turret, after perhaps fifty rounds had been fired and the gun was very hot, it was liable to 'cook-off', the round up the breech getting so hot that it fired spontaneously. Since we were being driven from one firing point to another, this round could go almost anywhere. Between firing points the driver would have his head out of the driver's hatch, and our Browning machine gun, facing forward, chose this moment to cook-off. The bullet went close enough to tear a 'V' shape in the top of our driver's beret – about an eighth of an inch from his skull; with admirable *sang-froid* he turned and shouted to us to be more careful.

Parades: Auction, Jankers, Blood and Bull

Quite apart from all this training we had a full squadron parade every Saturday morning where we were inspected by our squadron leader. During our course one trooper was killed, his tank rolling over on a slope and crushing him. At the end of one of these parades his kit was auctioned off on the square – a military custom of venerable antiquity.

On another parade I made the foolish mistake of trying to remove an uncomfortable stone from under my boot by pushing it away: .

Saturday 7 April 1945
CO's parade. Trying to move stone from under my boot before 2.I.C. [*the Second in Command*] came to our troop, when Lt Scaife had me shoved on a fizzer for moving. Went up before the O.C. and got 7 days CB. Pretty stiff because the charge was preferred by an officer.

Lt Scaife had shouted: 'That man moved on parade – take his name'. My name was taken by the troop sergeant and after the parade I was up before the squadron leader, my belt and hat removed. I received seven days CB – 'Confined to Barracks', 'jankers' to us. On jankers I had to report for fatigues after tea each day and had to report, polished and blancoed, at the guardroom when the guard was mounted each evening. It was all my own fault; I knew that if I needed to remove a stone under my boot I should have come to attention, stepped forward out of the ranks, removed the stone, stepped back into the ranks and then stood at ease again. Foolishly I hoped no one would notice my amateurish effort to remove it, but they did and the result was a short sharp lesson. At one stage these parades were unusually colourful; some of our Sherman tanks had diesel engines and one result was an outbreak of diesel dermatitis. The treatment for this was a gentian violet dressing and there were lavish patches of this rich colour on many hands and faces along the ranks.

On the 9th of April, while I was on jankers, a blood transfusion unit visited the regiment, and for this a large contingent of us were marched up to the very large gymnasium at Streatlam camp (occupied by the other half of our training regiment) perhaps a mile up the road. The regiment's drill adjutant, a large and imposing captain, was in charge of the proceedings and ordered us, perhaps a hundred for this session, to break ranks and gather round him. He then asked if any of us did not wish to give blood; half a dozen hangdog figures ventured to put up their hands. In the friendliest way he called them forward and said: 'Now don't you worry, everything will be quite all right', and with this he shepherded them into the gym to be the first to give blood. The rest of us then slowly filed in, each having our blood group tested and then being escorted by gentle and charming middle-aged ladies of the Women's Voluntary Service to the couch, where each of us would donate our pint of blood ('an armful'). A rather more professional nurse inserted the needle into my arm, inserted the tube into a bottle and then thoughtfully placed the bottle under the couch so that I would not be distressed at seeing my very own lifeblood pouring out of me and into the bottle. However, there were other soldiers all round me giving blood at the same time, and I could see their blood surging into *their* bottles, so this sensitive treatment was not very effective. Further, one nurse dropped a full bottle of blood nearby and a pint seemed an awful lot as it spread over the floor. At last my bottle was full, I was unplugged, and a WVS helped me off the couch and with warm solicitude supported me out of the gym to where other ladies were providing a sympathetic cup of tea and a biscuit for each weakened donor, and a military clerk entered in my paybook my blood group (B) and the date of my donation in appropriate blood-red ink. When this was finished it was outside and back to the harsher military world. There we fell in, were unsympathetically called to attention and marched at the double back to our camp; only a few collapsed on the way.

But I was on jankers, which meant extra fatigues, and I was not yet finished with blood. Only two hours later, less my pint of blood, I was on fatigues with a party which was marched back up to the gymnasium. The blood transfusion unit and the WVS ladies had all gone, and we moved in to clean the place up. The sight that met our eyes was not one for the squeamish; there was blood everywhere, spilt on the floor, smeared and splashed up the walls, as if some terrible war crime had been committed rather than an errand of mercy. We spent the next two hours cleaning the place up with mops and buckets; the water in our buckets having first run red, then pink, at last ran clear, and we were finished. Then a march back to camp, but for me, on jankers, it was a quick clean-up and then off to report at the guardroom as the guard was mounted. Altogether quite a full day.

In addition to the Saturday morning parade there were regular hut inspections with all our kit set out in regulation pattern on our beds, with our best boots as the centrepiece. This was why every trooper tried his hardest to acquire an extra pair of boots; these would never be worn but were polished up and kept just to be set out for inspections. At these times our beautiful floor, looked after by us with such care, fulfilled its role by drawing favourable comment from the inspecting officer. There was also a strict inspection on the guard mounting parade when we were on guard duty, which came round every few weeks; this was of some significance because there was always one man too many in the guard detail, and the smartest one 'got the stick' – was excused guard duty that night. This was a very real incentive to be really well turned out.

There were also occasional and much more important inspections by visiting generals. Then there were extra fatigues and the whole camp was made even tidier and things that couldn't be moved were whitewashed yet again. (There is an old army dictum: if it moves, salute it; if it doesn't move, whitewash it.) But preparations went further than this. One such inspection was in the middle of winter and trucks were sent out on to the moors to gather clean snow to cover up dirty snow in the camp. Another in high summer had the fitters spraying green paint on any brown patches of grass. At the time (and now, looking back) giving these final touches to an already wonderfully clean and tidy camp seemed to me entirely reasonable.

Time Off

NAAFI is the initials of the Navy, Army & Air Force Institute, but to us it was 'the Naafi' and an important part of our lives. There you could buy cups of char (tea) or coffee, other soft drinks (no alcohol) sweets, cakes, meat pies and baked beans on toast; we all spent a regular part of our leisure hours sitting round tables in the Naafi eating, drinking and chatting with friends. Conversation ranged widely if not very deeply, and one learnt many less conventional things about the army: that the Royal Army Medical Corps' initials RAMC really stood for 'Rob All My Comrades' and that Certe Cito, the motto of the Royal Corps of Signals, was to be translated as 'Its Quicker by Post'. We learnt that the Life Guards wore red jackets so that the blood would not show when they were wounded in battle; and that the snootier Royal Horse Guards wore blue jackets for same reason. (Later I was to learn that while one could refer to the latter as the Blues, one should never refer to the former as the Reds, and also that the role of the cavalry in war was to lend tone to what would otherwise be a mere vulgar brawl. Later still I discovered that the latter was a venerable witticism which had appeared in *Punch* on 10 December 1892.)

We talked about each other's daily experiences with our equipment or our NCOs – generally minor mishaps which we found amusing; and we showed each other our latest prized possessions, such things as a neat electrical screwdriver useful for the wireless course, or our own personal goggles for tank driving, sometimes with yellow glass that made even dull days seem sunlit. We absorbed some practical wisdom: don't wear a ring if you are on a tank as it may get crushed onto your finger, or if it catches on one of the many sharp edges as you jump off the tank it may pull your finger off. And some less reliable information: if you rotated the turret of a Sherman twice round to the left it became unscrewed and would fall off; you would then be put on a charge for damaging army property.

We also learnt some strange litanies:

> Over the bridge you must go...
> But I'm in the family way
> You're in everybody's way
> But I can't swim
> That doesn't matter, it's a railway bridge.

But I've got a tin trunk
I don't care if you've got a brass belly,
over the bridge you must go.

To the woods...
But I appeal to you on bended knee.
You appeal to me in any position
But what about my mother?
Her turn comes later.

And the occasional quip:

And the Lord said unto Moses come forth,
but Moses came fifth and missed his beer money.

Altogether, time passed very pleasantly in the Naafi.

When the Saturday morning parade ended we were free for the rest of the day and there was a minor exodus to the pleasures of Barnard Castle or Darlington. My choice was always Darlington, about twelve miles away, which meant going by bus. This was always crammed full at such times, so full that when we reached a particular short but steep hill the overloaded bus could not manage it and many of us had to get out, walk up the hill and then get back on the bus after it had revved its way to the top. In Darlington there was a W.H. Smith book and stationery shop which to me presented a most appealing atmosphere of calm and civilisation. It had oak panelled walls and was filled with every sort of desirable object which spoke of the desk and the library, echoing some of the pleasures of the stationery shop at Wellington College. There I bought a brass holder for used razor blades; they slotted in safely, could be pushed out a little way to cut anything that needed cutting, and provided a most satisfying combination of utility and pride of possession, to be displayed to friends over a cup of tea in our Naafi. There were at least two cinemas, and I regularly went to one of them for a bit of escapism, although I can remember one newsreel showing the Allied attack on the Japanese at Balikpapan in Eastern Borneo which had grim pictures of flame-throwers in action which were hardly escapist. This would be followed by a visit to Darlington's very superior NAAFI club. Then, when it was time to make for an early bus back to camp, there was another bookshop, down a back street and rather decrepit, but with very cheap second-hand books, and in particular a large pile of art magazines such as *The Connoisseur* and *The Burlington Magazine*. One of these for threepence was my last piece of escapism (rather than any deep commitment to high artistic culture), and it was then back to camp.

I can remember going with some friends into the Information Hut, run by Trooper Jacobs, and full of pamphlets with such names as 'British Way and Purpose', mostly designed to remind us of what we were fighting for. Also in the hut was a wall map with coloured pins showing where the Allied and Russian armies had advanced to. We were shocked to see that the area held by the German army had been reduced to a surprisingly small area covering less than half of Germany. We knew that the war was going well, but we had lived with it for so much of our lives that it had never really occurred to us that it might actually come to an end. And in due course it did so, and on VE Day there was much decorous rejoicing and a large bonfire at the edge of the camp; the only casualty was small wooden handcart which some reckless trooper pushed too close to the flames.

The most noticeable effect of this momentous event was that our sand tables, designed for training in gunnery on the rolling landscape of Western Europe, suddenly blossomed out into green foliage and became jungle tables to provide gunnery training for Burma and other places on the way to Japan. It was after lunch and I was walking back to my hut when I heard the news of the dropping of the atom bomb on Japan. There was much excited discussion of this new development, and although we had little idea of its full import, what was bad for Japan certainly seemed good for us. And in due course there was further rejoicing on VJ Day. We noted what had occurred, but we carried on training in just the same way and in just the same spirit as before, really as if nothing had changed.

Dismounted Training – Slate Ledge

Our training culminated in two week-long courses which reminded us of what all our training was for: Dismounted Training and Collective Training. In Dismounted we had the role of tank crews whose tanks had been knocked out, but who as heroic amateur infantry continued to fight the enemy with our pistols, Sten guns and hand grenades. The course, under Corporal

Stannard, began in a tiny village with us lined up along one side of the road, fully armed and ready to go. On the other side of the road was a low wall and over fields beyond this was a copse. We were to start by charging over to the copse, seizing it and preparing to defend it. Corporal Stannard, unencumbered by any weapons, gave the order and leaping over the wall, led the charge. Nobly we all followed him only to find that on our side the wall was low but on the further side was a drop of about six feet, and our charge began with men and weapons all falling in a heap, after which we limped off doggedly towards the copse.

Usually in the army we never knew the names of the places we went to; we were taken there by truck, did what ever was to be done, and were then taken back to camp by truck. The name of the place didn't really matter. The last day of Dismounted was spent at Slate Ledge, one of the few names we ever did know and one that we had some reason to remember. It was a few miles west of Barnard Castle and the name was an exact description of the place. There was a fairly narrow V-shaped valley with a little stream running along its bottom; on one side the slope was interrupted by a level ledge – Slate Ledge – about 30 yards wide of which a stretch some 200 or 300 yards in length was set out for our exercise. We were gathered at one end of this stretch and briefed on what we were going to do. Along the ledge in front of us could be seen signs of slit trenches. These, we were told, were Japanese bunkers (the war in Europe was over and our training was now refocussed on the Japanese); our tanks having been knocked out, our role was still to go forward, but now on foot, to attack and destroy these bunkers one after the other. For this we were divided into crews of five and, since this was a live-firing exercise, we were armed with Sten guns, plenty of ammunition and live hand grenades. On the other side of the small valley and some 40 yards from the lip of the ledge were a firing party of half a dozen officers and NCOs with Bren guns and a large pile of ammunition boxes, who would simulate live fire supposed to be coming from the bunkers as we attacked them. We were only allowed to fire at the bunkers, *not* at the firing party, and we were to shout *Grenade* when we threw one to allow the firing party to get their heads down.

My group moved up to the start line, a whistle blew and we started forward in line abreast. There was a brief pause and then a burst of fire – all trace – from the firing party and fairly close to some of us. Someone, mindful of his training, started firing back at where the trace had come from – a blast on the whistle, everything stopped – *You must not fire at the firing party* – another blast and our attack resumed. We fired our Stens at the first bunker, the firing party now began to fire more and more and nearer and nearer, and a .303 tracer coming close to you streaks along like a glowing red football and slams into the ground with a sledgehammer blow. One technique they used was to start firing a few yards in front of you and then come closer and closer to try and drive you back; I soon found that if you took no notice they didn't actually hit you, so firing our Stens we continued forward with tracers flying all around. We then mounted our attack on the first bunker. For this one of us crept over to the right, below the lip of the natural ledge, worked his way forward under this cover till he was level with the bunker, then up towards the lip to throw his grenade hopefully into the bunker. The grenade went off, the base plate whining into the distance (*You must shout grenade* – but in the excitement we always forgot), the firing stopped and the bunker was counted as destroyed. We regrouped, reloaded and started our attack on the next bunker; the firing party also reloaded and again tried to drive us back with a hail of tracer. And so on till we had attacked and destroyed all the bunkers and arrived at the finish line. There a sergeant appeared from under cover and asked if anyone had been hit; with bullets hitting rocky ground bits flew about and two had pieces of bullet casing in their arms or legs. The sergeant had his army clasp knife ready, and using the spike (for getting stones out of horses' hoofs) he levered the pieces out; this we appreciated as a thoughtful and kindly act. We then moved back to behind the start line to watch the next tank crew mount their attack on the bunkers.

In such an exercise there was plenty of scope for things to go wrong. Throwing a grenade up over the lip of the ledge to get it into a bunker was tricky; some (mine in fact) hit the lip and rolled back towards the thrower, but apart from a bit of a fright nobody was hurt, and the friendly umpire counted these as destroying the bunker. Meanwhile, fooling around with his Sten gun as he waited a few minutes for his turn, Trooper Curll shot himself in the foot. There was so much firing going on that only those nearest to him were aware of what he had done. Trooper Curll may have been an idiot but he was no fool – he said nothing and went forward with his crew. As they neared the first bunker and the 'enemy' fire increased, he flung up his arms, cried 'I've been hit', and collapsed on the ground. Whistles blew, the firing stopped and tenderly he was carried from the field. This incident was not much of an advertisment for the lethality of the Sten gun, as he was back with the troop after a few days, showing little sign of his injury. Altogether it was a dangerous but very exciting day and everybody enjoyed it. This was evident when towards the end there were only two troopers left to make up the final crew; the sergeant asked for two more to make up the number and everyone volunteered to go over the course again. In the truck back to camp there was little conversation; our minds were filled with the excitements of the day.

Collective Training – Guisborough

The final week of our course was devoted to Collective Training, where we were formed into actual tank crews, each taking over our own tank which we now had to maintain and keep running. We then set off for a week of mainly off-road practice attacks – no live ammunition – on various notional enemy tanks and gun positions.

Monday 11 June 1945
Started out to Guisborough on Collective. Cohen drove for first half, I drove second half.

Our crew:	
Commander	Lt Pates
Driver/Op	Whitehorne
Gunner/Op	Lomax
Driver/Mech	Cohen
Gunner/Mech	Alford

We drove in a convoy of two troops each of four tanks, and this first phase had its own minor incidents. One driver fell asleep and as the convoy went round a gentle bend his tank went straight on, until the bumping over rough ground woke him up and he pulled back into the column; another missed his gear on a steep hill, and cannoned into the tank in front which in turn hit the tank in front of him and so on; our tank got a bit behind and I was told to speed up, with the result that I collided with another tank which had stopped just out of sight round a corner, knocking its commander from the top of the turret down to the bottom. One advantage of tanks was that they were rugged and not affected by such treatment. There was no live firing and our days were spent practising fire and movement attacks on various objectives, reading the lie of the land and taking up hull-down and turret-down firing positions. One thing I remember was our tank commander standing on the top of the turret and getting the driver to go cautiously up a hillside until he could just see the imagined anti-tank gun in the edge of a wood on the next hill; all that the anti-tank gun would have seen was the commander's head just showing over the crest of the hill in front of him. A few yards further up and the gunner would be able to see to fire, then reverse down again before the target would have had time to reply. Guisborough was the nearest small town, but all our exercises were done on the Cleveland Hills. The only problem we had was some, probably RAF, interference with our wireless communications. This was a woman's voice passing short technical messages, until she suddenly said, 'Oh, hello darling', and went off the air never to return.

At the end of each day we formed a laager (pronounced 'leaguer', a defensive formation for the night) where our own supply column brought up food for us and petrol for the tanks. When they had finished supplying us they were free to get back to camp and go off duty, which gave them an incentive to be as quick as possible. In particular they did much of the refuelling, which was just as well because a tank's engine compartment gets very hot after a day's driving around; on two occasions tanks caught fire as they were being filled up. The fitters doing it were very experienced at dealing coolly and quickly with such common mishaps. After maintenance on the tanks we cooked our supper on desert stoves, a petrol can cut in half and then half filled with petrol – effective but, as we shall see, rather dangerous. Then we set guards, got into our blankets next to each other, covered ourselves with the tank sheet and went to sleep.

Accident

At last the week's exercises ended and we formed a convoy of tanks to go back to Barnard Castle, on the way stopping for the night at the Dent House Harbour (exactly where this was I cannot recall), where we just pulled in and parked instead of forming our usual laager. The next morning as our crew were making tea our desert stove somehow got knocked over and I was doused in burning petrol. There were moments of panic as I realised I was burning but a quick-witted corporal put the tank sheet over me and extinguished the flames. I recall panic rather than pain, and when the flames were put out my left leg just felt numb. But others acted quickly – a scout car and driver suddenly appeared, I was put into it and driven off. As we drove on it was as if very distant drums began throbbing in my burnt leg; the throbbing got steadily worse. Then at last we arrived somewhere and I was helped out of the scout car and was being looked at by a medical orderly. By now the pain was severe; he gave me a small glass of something yellow to drink and I woke up in Barnard Castle Hospital.

I was in a fairly small ward filled with similar training casualties; the only one of these I can remember was a chap next to me whose scalp had been torn off when his Bren carrier overturned. It had been sewn back on and by the time I arrived it looked as good as new. A woman doctor and a sister now came to the foot of my bed, talked to each other briefly and went away. Then came a very pleasant nurse who announced she was going to clean-up my burnt leg, which was just feeling very tender until she uncovered it and began to dab it with a cotton wool saline swab; this felt as if she was scrubbing it with barbed wire. I now had a chance to see my left leg, which was a rich plum colour for much of the area from my knee down to my ankle. She then covered it with a dressing and went away. This painful procedure continued for several days, getting somewhat less painful each day. But then the hairs on my leg, which had been burnt off, began growing through again and they itched terribly. After twelve days I was discharged back to my unit. There, when I went into the showers, my leg, still fairly plum-coloured, attracted mild interest. My diary records all this very briefly:

Monday 11 June 1945
Collective was smashing fun. On the last day, Friday, I got petrol burns at the Dent House Harbour and spent twelve days in Hospital.

A Time of Fatigues

Back at the regiment, much had changed. My troop had completed its training and all its members had been posted to their regiments. I never saw any of them again, but in the army one got used to making and breaking friendships in this way. I was now transferred to a new troop at Streatlam Camp a mile up the road from Stainton Camp, but all part of the 61st Training Regiment. There I soon found a new set of friends. Then they too finished their training and were posted away to their regiments. I and a few others were now left 'holding out' – waiting for something to happen to us, but meanwhile doing fatigues of various kinds around the camp and living in a barrack hut with the semi-permanent staff of soldiers, mostly many years older than us, who did all sorts of regular duties around the camp. They, like many of our officers, came from many different units; I can remember individuals from the XXIInd Hussars, the Fife and Forfar Yeomanry, the Lothian and Border Horse, the 17th/21st Lancers and many from the Royal Tank Regiment. The hut I was in had a stove in the middle, and often in the evenings we would all sit round it talking. Periodically one of us would go out to the NAAFI near by, get one of our large mugs refilled with tea, and pass it round the group as conversation went on. It must have been here that I heard my first 'shaggy dog' story – why so-called I have no idea. The essence of such a story was that it was very long, being intended to entertain the listeners over the many long hours which soldiers had to spend with nothing much to do, usually while waiting for something to happen. It would have a wandering but definite central thread with many side episodes giving scope for much descriptive detail (note that in the example below, every segment between semi-colons is such an extendable episode). In this way a good storyteller could spread it out over many nights if necessary, but it often had a sudden clinching end which could be called upon at almost any stage when at last something did happen and the telling had to be quickly brought to an end.

The only shaggy dog story that I can remember was about a man who one day begins to feel unwell – as if he had a weight pressing down on his head and with a feeling of pressure in his ears; he goes to see his doctor who gives him some tablets, no improvement; sees a specialist, recommended to have a holiday; chooses a holiday; goes on holiday, still no better; doctor recommends a cruise, he buys (extensive) outfit from a famous shop e.g. Harrods; goes on cruise; back home again, still no better, decides to cheer himself up by doing some shopping and goes to e.g. Thomas Pink, Shirtmaker, just behind Fortnum & Mason to buy some shirts – greeted by urbane shop assistant, clearly an expert in high-class shirt business – decides on material, length of sleeve, links or buttons (one or two); Now, Sir, I think you will require a 16^1/$_2$ collar – No, no I always take 16 – I really would recommend 16^1/$_2$, Sir – No, I'll have size 16 – As you wish, Sir, but if you have size 16 you will feel as if you have a weight pressing down on your head and a feeling of pressure in your ears.

The reason why our small group was holding out in this way was because we had been marked out as potential officers. Meanwhile we were building up experience of being at the bottom of the pile. Our fatigues were varied; one of them was being sent off with a 3 ton truck to collect three tons of coal from an army coal depot. No problem – off we went, found the depot, were shown a large heap of coal and told to take our three tons from it. We started shovelling it into our 3 tonner; only then did it strike us that we had no idea of how to measure three tons of coal, or what it might look like. Finally we reasoned that three tons of coal should fill a 3 ton truck, so we filled it up level with the side boards. We could not help noticing that the leaf springs on our truck now had a rather strange inverted shape, and as we drove back to our camp it seemed very sluggish and swayed alarmingly on corners. However we pressed on and finally announced our return to the corporal in charge of our own coal dump. He seemed surprised but quite pleased at our efforts, as well he might, because we found later that we had inadvertently collected nearer six tons than three. The 3 ton truck seemed to recover from its ordeal.

For a time we worked in the cookhouse, surrounded by ATS girls with a gift of colourful language, who were bullied into submission by a large and bosomy ATS staff sergeant using even more colourful language. We fetched and carried, we cleaned out the fat traps (ugh!); we tried to get rid of wasps using some new wasp killer which did not seem to work, and we resorted to knocking them down and while they were on their backs dropping the stuff into their mandibles – but they simply ate it and flew away. More fun were camp deliveries, where we took great trays of freshly baked bread and buns to various places around the camp, often being given small rewards from these same trays by their recipients.

At last after many weeks something happened. I was sent off to a War Office Selection Board (WOSB) for testing to see if I would make an officer. There about twenty of us did a battery of psychological and intelligence tests and were interviewed by various panels. (In one of the instant–response psychological tests a surprising large number of my answers came out as 'books'.) We did assault courses and finally did what can only be called practical problem-solving. This consisted of a group of five of us being faced with a wall perhaps 12 feet high; we were given a coil of rope, three short planks and told to get our group over this wall. Or we were faced with a hole 12 feet across, of allegedly infinite depth, and told to get our group across it using the same rope and planks. Some of these tasks could be done, others could not, but we were anxious to please and we did our best. Of course one now sees that what they were looking for was officer-like qualities: who took the lead in suggesting what to do, and in organising the (usually unsuccessful) efforts to actually do it.

More Training

Then it was back to my unit and a further round of fatigues until I was ordered to take my paybook to the Squadron Office; there it had inscribed in it: 'Approved by an Interviewing Board on 28 Sep 45 as a candidated for training at an OCTU' (Officer Cadet Training Unit) – I had passed! Now someone looked at my training record, saw that I had not done a wireless course, and decided that I needed to do one. I spent most of the next six weeks doing the normal wireless course focussed on the Number 19 Set, the standard wireless set for tanks. In appearance it was a pale grey box about 2 feet wide by 1 foot high and rather deeper than that, with the usual dials, switches and knobs, and a red pilot light which I always found warm and friendly (I once had one with a green pilot light which made the inside of a tank feel uncomfortably like a morgue). The two main aspects of the course were actually operating the set – tuning and netting – and wireless procedure and discipline, which were strictly enforced. Soon we were searching for our control station on a given frequency and call sign, netting onto him, reporting signal strength, changing frequency, sending and receiving messages, relaying messages, seeing how long we could keep in touch with control when this was in a distant truck and moving away (which required delicate adjustment and total concentration). Doing it over many weeks soon made all this almost second nature. This wireless training was to prove very useful to me later. There was continuing emphasis on physical fitness with regular PT and cross-country runs; I was also given more experience on motorcycles.

Saturday 2 November 1945

... Did seven mile cross-country run in afternoon. Swine of a course, hills, tank driving grounds, mud etc. I came 42nd out of 60 but I felt quite OK. Capt. Morgan, Col. Byron, SSMs Brett and Murray there, also various other officers etc. Sgt Morris came in first & L/Cpl Jolly second.

Sunday 4 November 1945

Stayed in bed till 10 o/c. Then got up and had a wash. Went down to stores and ordered new beret. Had break in NAAFI. Spent afternoon mending 2nd trousers & braces. I am reading *Pickwick Papers* by Dickens. I have recently read *Nicholas Nickleby*, *Pictures from Italy* and *Uncommercial Traveller*. All v. good.

Friday 9 November 1945

Out on wireless scheme all day to Durham. Call sign YUY. We were No 6, I and Duggan. There were 9 outstations, on 3 centrelines. Net OK second time, but the slow motion control on my 19 Mk. 3 was faulty. Kept up quite good communication up to 6–8 miles. Tried to net B set with Chiswell and Elliot in Y5 but could only hear him strength 1. We got to Durham at 12.30 and had sandwiches and cocoa, then to YMCA. Started back at 1.45. I was commander on the way back as I had been operator all the morning. On the way back Y 1, 2 and 3 got nearly out of communication with control, and Y 4 5 6 7 8 & 9 could not hear them at all; back at 4.30. Spent quiet evening. Jig Lawson came back off leave.

Saturday 10 November 1945

O.C.s parade at 7.50, and a march past with 17/21st Lancers band. Got through OK. Spent next hour with Jig at Other Denominations (*i.e. other than Church of England*) Padre's hour. Very good. Discussed the churches attitude to the working man. Went to Darlington on 12.20 bus. Went to Arcade Cinema. Bought *Oxford Book of Greek Verse in Translation* from bookshop for 10/-. Now I have got beside the Greek verse, *Herodotus* (Bohn), *Marcus Aurelius*, *Cory's Ancient Fragments*, all waiting to go home. Back to camp early.

Then at last my posting arrived. I was summoned to the Squadron Office and given a movement order taking me on to the next phase in my military service – training to be an officer at an Officer Cadet Training Unit (OCTU). Looking back, the 61st Training Regiment, Royal Armoured Corps, had been a very smart and efficient regiment; it had given me an excellent training and I had enjoyed my time with it.

8

OCTU

Wrotham

At this time the process of training to be an officer consisted of three stages: Pre-OCTU at Wrotham, Basic OCTU at Aldershot and the Royal Armoured Corps OCTU at Bovingdon in Dorset. So for several of us from the 61st it was off together to 148 Pre-OCTU at Wrotham Camp in Kent. Wrotham (pronounced 'Rootum') compared poorly with the Stainton and Streatlam camps of the 61st; much of it was unkempt woodland and we lived in very basic Nissen huts. Our latrines were particularly basic, although at that time we just accepted such things. They consisted of a long pipe, about 12 inches in diameter with half a dozen holes in the top, where one's necessary moments could be accompanied by conversation (rather as in ancient Rome, where the latrines were in groups of three). Periodically the system flushed, sending a miniature tidal wave surging down the pipe; then it was advisable to leap off till it had subsided. My part of the camp was run by the Leicestershire regiment and there we mainly did more advanced infantry training. The camp was on the edge of a considerable escarpment, and we seemed to spend much of the day rushing up and down it to our various training sessions.

Monday 31 December 1945
Was in bed early last night at 8 o/c, read the *Iliad*. Leave train from London was held up last night and got in at 02.00 hrs. Reveille 06.15, but we were woken at 06.45. No inspection. Map reading and battle drill all morning, Bren gun [*light machine gun, LMG*] lecture and film. Went to NAAFI with Kingham and Boydell.

139

Tuesday 1 January 1946
Very cold. Morning LMG, Gas. Afternoon Drill, LMG, grenades, Hygiene. We did rifle drill under Sgt Stokes without gloves, and our hands were practically frozen when we finished. Tea was OK but Kingham and I had NAAFI suppers. Wrote to Julian. Still freezing cold this evening; read *Iliad*

The training itself was quite good; I recall a very effective demonstration of how infantry should *not* do it. We watched a section advancing cautiously, but every man had something that rattled or clinked as he went forward. They came under fire, all squealed and ran around in all directions and so on until finally having attacked the enemy with their 2 inch mortar, the order was given 'Stop – Unload', whereupon *two* mortar bombs were emptied from the barrel – if it had been fired the lower bomb would have exploded in the barrel. Here also we were introduced to two of the army's least successful weapons: the Projector, Infantry, Anti-Tank (PIAT) and the sticky bomb. The PIAT was an anti-tank weapon with a relatively short range, firing a 'shaped charge' bomb with powerful armour penetration. It was fired from a heavy and awkward projector and had a strong kick, requiring a large shoulder pad. Unfortunately when fired at short range the explosion of the bomb in effect fired the propelling cartridge in its base straight back at the the person who had just fired the PIAT. Because of this there had to be a corporal to drag us down the instant we fired. We only had one shot each and this was quite enough; a very poor weapon. The sticky bomb also was an anti-tank weapon. It was a spherical bomb covered with sticky material which would stick to a tank (if you were close enough to hit it) and explode in contact with the armour, allegedly doing great damage. The sticky sphere had two hemispherical cardboard covers and a handle by which to hold it. To use it you discarded the covers, arming the bomb, and threw it; unfortunately experience revealed that as the thrower put his arm back to throw, the bomb was liable to touch his back and stick to him. Thank goodness we were only introduced to dummy sticky bombs.

As part of the course we did more motorcycling, which always managed to stop at a transport 'caff' which served fried egg sandwiches and chip sandwiches. One of our instructors looked back at his flock of trainees as he went over the brow of a hill, ran straight into a car coming the other way and was killed. Drill and PT continued to be regular parts of the course and we had a day of shooting on the ranges somewhere near Gravesend. We did a night exercise in the grounds of a castle (was it Leeds Castle?); one company was defending a small wood and I was ordered to be the (Japanese) enemy. It was a beautiful moonlight night but I worked my way unseen quite close to the wood where I could hear the defenders talking. Then I let out a blood-curdling scream and shouted 'You are surrounded!' There was a stunned silence, then the click of safety catches being taken off. They fired Very lights but I continued telling them to surrender. Finally I allowed myself to be captured, since I was getting very cold.

More demanding was the assault course in our final week at Wrotham. Our group of about twenty four marched off, decorously singing 'Green Grow the Rushes Oh!' We arrived at a large chalk quarry, one of a pair joined by a tunnel under the road. Going past a boiler full of hot water, we went down a long steep stairway to the bottom for the briefing on what lay ahead. The actual assault course was in the other quarry, reached by the tunnel; it was a live firing course and each of us would be accompanied over it by an NCO. After the assault course was finished we would come back through the tunnel into the first quarry, climb to the top, clean our rifles (using the hot water from the boiler we had passed) and only then would our time be taken. We were told to stand easy and wait for our name to be called. This was done in alphabetical order, so I was called first. Through the tunnel, and there was a sergeant waiting for me – it turned out that he was Southern Command cross-country champion. A few words and we were off, with the sergeant sometimes behind me urging me on, sometimes ahead telling me to go faster. I ran about 50 yards, then down on the wet chalky ground to fire five shots from my rifle at a target, then up again and a bayonet attack up a steep slope and more running and firing; suddenly a man stepped out of a cave in the side of the quarry, took my rifle, handed me a Bren gun, and we were off again, down, firing, up and on again over heaps of chalk or lying flat in chalky puddles; my rifle was given back to me and so it went on until by the end of the assault course, even though I was very fit, I was utterly exhausted and covered with chalky mud. I was then told to go back through the tunnel, up to the boiler to clean my rifle and then have my time taken. I staggered back through the tunnel; in front of me stood the rest of our group, talking cheerfully together – until they saw this mud-covered apparition stumble out of the tunnel, obviously on his last legs. There was stunned silence as they suddenly realised what they were in for. After it was all over we marched back to camp in silence.

Mons Barracks, Aldershot

Finally the Pre-OCTU course finished and on 8 February 1946 we were posted to the Basic OCTU at Mons Barracks in Aldershot, a rather ugly red brick camp with a large drill square. Now we became cadets with a white disc behind our cap badges and white flashes on our shoulder straps with a red or green stripe across them according to our Company. Here the general military training programme continued, but there were also elementary courses on military law and various administrative aspects of the army. Our platoon now included some older cadets who were going into such things as the Royal Army Ordnance Corps and who would be commissioned directly from Basic OCTU. We took turns in acting for a day as Company Sergeant Major, Platoon Commander and Platoon Sergeant to start building up our experience of command. There were large parades, particularly when a Company ended its course and Passed-out, with the drill taken by RSM Brittain, the senior RSM (Regimental Sergeant Major) in the British army and a very tall, robust and impressive figure. He had a curiously sympathetic air, as if he was rather fond of the soldiers he was drilling. His orders were given very clearly in a wonderful baritone voice – drilling under him was a positive pleasure.

Saturday 9 February 1946
Parade in morning and lectures by Colonel and Company Commander. Had photograph taken. Watched Rugger match in afternoon. Went to Aldershot with Derek Wheatley. Went to tea at Ritz & to Theatre Royal.

Sunday 10 February 1946
Cadet Sergeant Major today. Helped mount guard. Spent whole day doing bull [*cleaning, polishing etc*] and Sergeant Major's duties. Asked for early call at guard room and stayed there until 24.00 hours booking people in. Wrote home.

Saturday 16 February 1946
Platoon Sergeant all day. Did practice church parade twice on square. Spent most of day bulling for tomorrow's guard. Talked to Kingham. Had shower. Several people on Restrictions for not having kitbags out by beds on Friday.

Sunday 17 February 1946
On Guard [*all day*] with Didden, Bulgin, Boydell, Fair, Creese and Bacon. Officer did not turn up to inspect us and mount us so Company Sergeant Major did it. I was awarded Guard Orderly for best turnout on parade. My Bulled-up boots helped a lot. Spent most of day running about getting things for people on guard. Wrote home.

Thursday 21 February 1946
Passing-out parade. Got my name taken on Regimental Sergeant Major's parade before lunch for having no white tabs. Passing-out parade [*in afternoon*] quite good, nice band of Royal Military School of Music. Bulled up in evening. Read in Ante room with Bawden.

Friday 22 February 1946
… Platoon stopped by Colonel for not marching smartly enough. I think the Company Sergeant Major must have 'forgotten' my name was taken yesterday or I should have been before the OC today.

Tuesday 26 February 1946
Out to training area at Long Valley. It was raining when we started but after we had been there a short while it started to snow. Had demonstration on sentries, then did TEWTS [*Tactical Exercises Without Troops*]. Miserably cold. Had lunch in sheds at race course. Marched back, and when we arrived we were all soaked. Took rifle to armourer.

Friday 8 March 1946
By train up to Bangor. Weather very nice. Arrived about 5.30.

The week of field firing exercises up at Bryn Hall near Bangor in North Wales marked the end of the course at Mons. Ten days before we were due to go I developed a problem with my left Achilles tendon – it began to make quite a noticeable creaking noise. In to see the Medical Officer, given 'excused boots' and ordered to return a few days later. No improvement, M.O. gave further 'excused boots'; I was now getting worried in case I missed the week at Bryn Hall. Final visit to M.O. – reported no improvement so I am put back into boots and told to creak my way through the week in North Wales.

Field Firing – Bryn Hall

The day after we got to Bangor we had a long march up to Bryn Hall which was to be our base; this was quite a demanding march and was followed by demonstrations for the rest of the day. The next day we began the live firing exercises which lasted for the rest of the week – a series of platoon attacks on imaginary enemy strongpoints in derelict buildings or behind rocky outcrops with everyone taking turns in commanding the platoon or the fire or assault sections. We carried the usual infantry weapons – rifles, Bren guns, 2 inch mortar plus a load of ammunition for these as well as grenades, food and water. These exercises took us over a large area of hills and streams which made up the field firing ranges. It was tough going, but in this our physical fitness became evident; after climbing up a steep hillside with our loads we would need a rest, but after quite a short recovery time we were ready to go on again, and we did this throughout the week. It was cold and had just snowed as we started, so the first time we went down to take cover our denims got very wet with melted snow; in the event this hardly mattered since we were so active throughout the week that even in poor weather it was getting too hot rather than too cold that was the problem. Typically we would be briefed on a situation facing us – an enemy strongpoint in a ruined farm building – by a member of the range staff; then the platoon commander organised the attack, usually a fire section to fire at the target building to keep the enemy's heads down, while an assault section worked its way round a flank and got very close to the building before the fire section ceased firing and the assault went in with grenades, bayonets and firing from the hip. Then a brief pause and off over a hill to the next enemy strongpoint. This went on all day, but thank goodness it was back to camp as darkness fell, so that the week was very active but at least our nights were warm and dry and we were well fed.

For the first two days I was always in the assault section, which meant that I used very little of my ammunition and continued to carry most of it. The first time I was in the fire section I fired off quite a lot to lighten my load, so much indeed that oil began to bubble out from under the wooden casing of my rifle. There were various unexpected problems, one of which was the Welsh hill ponies. When we were firing at some derelict building they became very interested in the noise of our bullets hitting the walls, coming up closer and closer to have a look. There were strict rules about not hitting ponies (unlike sheep on our earlier ranges) and on at least one occasion an attack had to be called off because the ponies would not go away. A different problem happened to me when we were attacking a strongpoint in a narrow valley with a rocky stream at the bottom. I went forward and threw a grenade – up it went and down into the valley where it hit a rock and broke in half leaving the fuse to go off on its own with a weak pop – not a very good start to an assault. At one of these attacks the directing staff organised a thunderflash cluster which went off producing a mushroom-shaped cloud, just to remind us of the new possibilities in warfare. We all enjoyed our week of field firing; it was very hard work but our morale was high and we all enjoyed the feeling that we had risen to all the challenges which they had thrown at us. Everybody revealed strengths and abilities and we showed ourselves to be an effective platoon. Then it was back to Mons and our own Passing-Out Parade. Those going to more technical arms such as the Royal Ordnance Corps now received their commissions.

Bovingdon

For us Royal Armoured Corps cadets it was off to the Royal Armoured Corps OCTU at Bovingdon in Dorset for our final six months of armoured training, now as officer cadets with a white diamond behind our cap badges and plain white shoulder flashes. We were now addressed as 'Sir' by the OCTU staff; but that word could be expressed with a wealth of overtones, from rage through merely neutral to despair.

We must have arrived at Bovingdon RAC OCTU early in April 1946. There we became 5 Troop and were housed in a 'Sandhurst' block which contained a series of barrack-rooms, each for about eight officer cadets, and each with their own good facilities. Behind these blocks were a large drill square, tank hard standings and driving grounds. Beyond these were the quiet country lanes of Dorset, and villages with deeply English names like Sturminster Newton and Minterne Magna.

At Bovingdon discipline was tighter and the training more demanding than before. At our first address by the commanding officer he made clear to us the standard that was expected, with an emphasis on the example which an officer must set for the men under his command. This meant that he had know as much, and to be as good as any of them, on technical aspects – wireless, gunnery and the mechanical side as well as being an effective leader and commander. We were given a handout of several pages setting out in some detail these and other qualities that were required of an officer.

On Saturday morning CO's Parades we had the band of a Hussar regiment which added another dimension to these occasions. The band used to play a delightful soft and lilting piece of music as the inspecting officer passed along the straight ranks of well-turned-out and soldierly officer cadets; there were the shouted orders and the crunch of our boots on the gravel square as we went through our now near-perfect parade drill, with the final slow march off the parade by the next Passing-Out Troop to the solemn music of the march from Scipio, by Handel.

For these parades I had one particularly precious item – a bayonet (we had real 12 inch ones, not the wartime utilitarian spike bayonets) with scabbard, which previous owners had treasured, burnished and polished. I carried on the good work to such a degree that our squadron sergeant major (SSM) (Welsh Guards, hat down over his eyes and a sharp disciplinarian – but no fool and with a well-concealed sense of humour) even suggested that it should be paraded before the whole OCTU. Before big parades we would have a squadron inspection by our squadron leader and the SSM. On one such inspection an officer cadet was found to have a mark on his black beret: 'Take this cadet's name, Sergeant Major', with the SSM announcing to the cadet, 'You've lost your name, Sir' – and now 'dirty' berets became the focus of attention. Both the squadron leader and the SSM were of moderate height, but the next cadet was very tall and the squadron leader could not see most of his beret. 'Is this cadet's beret clean, Sergeant Major?' The SSM could not see it any more than the squadron leader could, but he moved up very close to the cadet and said loudly 'Is your beret clean, Sir?' 'Yes, Sergeant Major.' Then back to the squadron leader: 'His beret is clean, Sir.' All done with perfect protocol and a perfectly straight face.

We now trained on Comet tanks which we practised driving over the battered training grounds, my instructor being the same Corporal Sutton who had instructed me on Shermans up at Barnard Castle, except that he was now Sergeant Sutton. One part of this section of the course was 'unditching', a necessary skill in a tank crew. In this, one group of cadets would drive a tank into the most awkward predicament they could devise – for example sideways on a steep slope with one track right down in a muddy ditch – and the other group had two or three tanks which in various configurations could be used to tow it out. This often required one or two tanks shackled up to pull, with a third shackled to it side by side to stop it from turning over. We did more motorcycling, including very rough cross-country trials riding; this was most enjoyable and it was astonishing where you could go on a motorcycle.

In wireless we were already competent operators, but now we had netting exercises and competitions over impossible distances where we still managed to keep up communications. Wireless and tactical schemes always required map reading, a vital skill, sometimes using maps without any names but only roads and contours. In these schemes our wireless trucks took us all over this area of Dorset – beautiful countryside with virtually no other traffic – with carefully contrived tactical bounds at which one had to pause, fortunately always in villages with pleasant cafés. Later some of these tactical exercises were done in Matador armoured cars, large and heavy vehicles but much less damaging to the roads than tanks. My experience with these was varied; on one occasion in Middle Wallop a midwife ran her car almost under our Matador. She explained tearfully that she had just attended a difficult delivery and she was very sorry. This impact made no impression on the Matador and we left the fitters mending her car while we pressed on. Later in that scheme we had to move on in a hurry and our route took us along by a railway line, up a long slope with a sharp turn left onto a bridge across the line and then a sharp turn right down onto the other side of the line. As we went fast up the slope I felt we would only just get round the first corner, and as we were crossing the bridge it was clear to me that we would never manage to get round the second corner at our speed. The bridge was quite high, perhaps 25 feet, and I was about 8 feet up in the turret of the Matador, so there seemed a very long way to crash down. With a curious fatalism – a numb feeling as if I was encased in cotton wool and was watching events from some distance away – I awaited an inglorious end. But somehow, I shall never know how, my driver managed to wrench the brute of a Matador round the second corner. Expectation of imminent death evaporated and it was back to the concerns of our tactical exercise.

In gunnery we had new guns and new munitions to master – the Comet had a 77 mm main armament (actually a slightly modified 17 pounder) and Besa machine guns. Under Sgt Hunt, a first rate instructor, we did all the usual learning about the mechanism and maintenance of these guns in gunnery bays and on the tanks themselves. Our live firing was done on the nearby Lulworth range, a pleasant area and full of bird life, which did not seem concerned about shot and shell, but flourished because the shot and shell kept humans away.

Time Off

We normally had Saturday afternoon and Sunday off, although as usual quite a lot of this time was spent in bulling up our equipment or getting some extra sleep. On Saturday afternoon I often used to go into Dorchester, a comfortable country town with quite good shops, a small Roman arena and the enormous Iron Age earthwork of Maiden Castle just to the south, all of which I visited. After tea at a typical Olde Tea Shoppe it was back to camp with the Camp Cinema and the NAAFI to pass the rest of Saturday. This cinema was on the other side of the road that ran next to Bovingdon camp, the road along which Lawrence of Arabia was riding his motorcycle to his cottage at Clouds Hill when in 1935 he crashed and was killed.

Saturday 29 June 1946
On leave from RAC OCTU at Bovington. Home via Southampton. Arrived at 5.30. Everyone fine. Went to Dazzle variety show with Mother, Auntie Bertha & cousin Elizabeth.

Next day I went to the tennis club and it was there that I met Rosemary Harris; she was my partner in a game against June Sharp and Ken Keeling (who during the war had provided us with some tennis balls he had 'rescued' from Rangoon as it fell to the Japanese). My diary tells me that she and I played tennis again the next day and there followed several visits to the cinema together and one to Dazzle, a trip to look round Brighton with tea at Fullers (renowned for its walnut cake) and a trip to Chichester to look round the cathedral with tea at the rather upmarket Kimbell's. These were interspersed with my meetings with Dennis Wood and Roy Chiverton, riding with cousin Elizabeth at the Newburgh Stables up on the Downs, and various family activities. On the last day of my leave I had the excuse of returning a tennis ball to Rosemary at the house in Barnham where she was living with two charming elderly aunts; she asked me in and we drank orangeade and talked. Then it was the 17.55 to London and a train down to Wool, the tiny rail halt close to Bovingdon Camp. Clearly I was much taken with Rosemary Harris and, indeed, was to see her frequently in a later leave in October.

At Last

Back at Bovingdon, as our course went on it became clear that all of our troop were likely to be commissioned. This raised the question of choice of regiment; for many of us this was a shot in the dark. We now had a guest night where officers on the staff of the OCTU came to dinner with us individually as our guests; in each case our guest was an officer from the regiment we had hopefully chosen. I had chosen the 7th Queen's Own Hussars, the regiment which Mike had served in as it moved from Dhond in India in 1942 to Iraq and then to Italy. This meant that my dinner guest would be Major George Murray-Smith of the 7th Hussars. For me (as for all of us) this was a tense occasion. Murray-Smith seemed to me a man of contradictions; he was a big man, but with a slightly effeminate face and manner. I was told much later that in Italy the local women sometimes referred to him in terms rather like 'that lady soldier'. However, he had the Military Cross with two bars and was clearly a fine soldier; I heard that in Italy, as leader of B Squadron, when some particularly dangerous operation was coming up, at the O Group (briefing) he would turn to the commanding officer and ask, 'Colonel, may B Squadron go first?' He was also remembered for throwing stones at his tanks when he felt they were not going forward fast enough. (In similar circumstances another squadron leader, Major Congreve, used to threaten to beat his crews with bootlaces.) I can remember nothing of my conversation with Murray-Smith at the guest night; I am sure I played things very cautiously and responded warmly to any enthusiasms that he revealed. These might have included hunting, for he was a great huntsman and later Master of Foxhounds of one of the famous Midlands hunts. At least I managed not to blot my copybook, and in due course was accepted for the 7th Hussars.

About a month before we were due to pass out we all had a short leave to visit our tailors in London to have our service dress fitted. For this I stayed at the Royal Armoured Corps Club in its elegant house in Grosvenor Square, later demolished to make way for the US Embassy, where I had previously stayed as a trooper. Murray-Smith told me that the regimental tailor was Dege of Conduit Street, a most upmarket concern, and there, hovered over by several respectful tailors, I was measured up. Later I was to go back for a fitting; I put on what seemed to me a perfectly tailored service dress, but this was marked up with chalk for further adjustment, and then as I stood there the sleeves were unceremoniously torn off for yet further changes.

Saturday 31 August 1946

Left RAC Club early. Went to Midland Bank and opened a current A/C. Then to Dege and had my Service Dress fitted. Got a set of pips and 7Hs [*the regimental designation was 7H*] for my battle dress. Bought a Beret Badge from Herberts [*Herbert Johnson, upmarket hatters*], V pukka. In evening went for a walk in Hyde Park. Listened to the band, they played the slow march we have in our Passing out parades. Walked round Serpentine and across bridge. Very pleasant indeed.

My service dress was certainly the most beautiful piece of tailoring that I ever possessed. Its only weakness was that it fitted me perfectly when I was rather lean after so much active training; as life got less active a certain amount of adjustment became necessary.

But the OCTU had one final sting in its tail. Almost our last training session consisted of a forced march, carrying rifles and light haversacks. But it was twenty miles, to be completed as a troop in four hours by alternately marching 100 yards then doubling for 100 yards. We were all fit, but this really was a killer; however, somehow we all came through it. Then it was our Passing-Out Parade before Field Marshal Montgomery, the leading British General of the Second World War.

Saturday 5 October 1946

Passed out before Montgomery. Parade was best ever according to Sgt Hunt. Mike Harari won the belt, I was runner-up. People on parade were Bacon, Alford, Boydell, Harari, Richards, Walton, Hopland, Walden, Stock, Taylor, Haslip, Bulgin, Stopford, Lang. Richardson was sick and watched it. Left soon after parade. Home by 5.30.

9

The 7th Queen's Own Hussars

Life in the Regiment – Soltau

Up to this point my life in the army had consisted entirely of training. This had been well focussed and efficiently organised, and all of it suffused with the wartime spirit which carried on well after VE Day and VJ Day. In my case this training got steadily more demanding, but the prize to be won – gaining a commission and becoming an officer – also became clearer and nearer. Then suddenly I had won through – with our Passing-Out Parade I had now become Second Lieutenant RFG Alford, 7th Queen's Own Hussars; all the continuous demands of training ceased and their tensions fell away. I felt proud of my achievement, which really had demanded a lot of effort, and greatly relieved that at last I was safely through. I was now to be faced with the quite different demands of showing that I was a good regimental officer.

Retrospective Notes from my Diary
Had ten days leave after Passing-Out Parade, saw Rosemary Harris a lot. Reported to 57th Training Regiment Royal Armoured Corps at Catterick in Yorkshire with Harari and Walton on Tuesday 15 October 1946.

Was at 57 TR RAC for 14 days, then had 7 days embarkation leave. Commanded draft of Boydell and 18 Other Ranks from Catterick to Hull on 15 November 1946. Then to Cuxhaven where I commanded a train to Bad Oeyenhausen. Spent night at 53 Royal Horse Artillery at Bielefelt, went to Celle then Soltau on Tuesday 25 November 1946 when I joined 7th Queen's Own Hussars.

The 7th Hussars had been in Italy in the latter part of the war and some time after it ended they had been moved to Germany where they became part of 4th Armoured Brigade whose sign was a black jerboa (a kind of desert rodent like a miniature kangaroo) on a white square. In Germany they inherited the German cavalry barracks at Soltau from the 7th Royal Tank Regiment together with the Churchill Crocodile flame-thrower tanks which they had used during the war. These were cumbersome vehicles which towed a heavy armoured trailer containing what was in effect napalm together with nitrogen cylinders as propellant. Their task was to crawl up to stubborn enemy strongpoints and fire their 'rods' of blazing napalm into them to burn them out; they were really rather a ghastly weapon and as tanks went, these were probably the least appealing type. The regiment had three squadrons of these, about forty of them altogether, along with the related Churchill Armoured Recovery Vehicles (ARVs), as well as American White scout cars, White half-tracks and Humber scout cars. In addition to these A vehicles we had a full complement of B vehicles (or soft vehicles): jeeps and trucks of a range of sizes – altogether a large number of vehicles so that the whole regiment was fully mobile. All the A vehicles and quite a lot of B vehicles were equipped with the standard Number 19 wireless set. An important part of our routine was ensuring that all of these vehicles and equipment were kept clean, fully maintained and ready for immediate use if necessary.

Our barracks was on the outskirts of the very small town of Soltau, which in turn was halfway between Hamburg and Hanover and about forty miles from each. The camp had all the usual military buildings, drill square and tank standings plus large covered riding schools and a very well-appointed Officers Mess; it was not quite big enough to take the whole regiment and B Squadron had to be accommodated about half a mile up the road to Bispingen. When I arrived I reported to the adjutant (Pat Howard-Dobson) who was very friendly; he told me I would be joining B Squadron, directed me to my quarters, which was a ground floor flat just across the road from the Officers Mess, and told me that there would be a regimental dinner that night. Then I unpacked my things and started to settle into my new home. That evening I began to meet my fellow officers in the ante room of the Mess; everyone was very friendly and the President of the Regimental Institute, a very senior major, quietly filled me in on Mess protocol – always Christian names except for the commanding officer, who should be addressed as Colonel. The dinner was impressive, in a fine dining-room with regimental silver on the table, excellent food and service. I was placed next to Colonel Jayne at the head of the table – a gesture of welcome into the regiment, although rather a tense position for me on my first night.

I had never really considered what life would be like in a regiment which was well trained but did not have a war to fight. This I now found out. Weekday life started with a squadron parade at about 07.30 hrs; then quite a lot of the morning was spent on looking after all our vehicles and equipment, together with PT sessions for some groups and further training to ensure that all our soldiers were technically up to the mark. Then for the troops the afternoons were devoted largely to sport, with many inter-unit matches, together with more PT and other outdoor activities. In the evenings for all of us there was a cinema in Soltau which also had occasional live variety shows. After that, for the troops there was a NAAFI Club (of which more later) and for us there was the Mess where we could talk, play cards – and drink. On Saturday morning there would be a larger parade and then the afternoon and Sunday were free. For all of us this routine would give way to a variety of other military demands, particularly roadblocks aimed mainly at catching people who had stolen army equipment, particularly tyres and petrol. Part I orders came out each evening setting out such duties for the following day together with longer notice for bigger commitments, such as brigade or higher formation exercises.

Life in the Mess raised a delicate question; I did not drink and after I had declined a few friendly urgings 'to have one' this became accepted by my fellow officers. I made things easier by drinking unidentifiable soft drinks and always asking to have few drops of Angostura bitters added to them, so that I did not stand out in the crowd. Later my quaint habit came to be regarded as rather useful, because on guest nights and other such occasions I was quite willing to be Orderly Officer, who was supposed to remain sober.

Christmas came and was celebrated with some verve including a party for the children of Soltau. Some officers went carol singing – after a fashion – on Christmas Eve, but the adjutant saw the rowdy singers coming and good-humouredly fired his shotgun in their direction, while his wife enjoyed defending her home by drenching them with a jug of cold water from an upstairs window. There was a Christmas morning football match on a snow-covered pitch, its only rule being that the teams should wear the most unlikely clothing for a game. Robin Carnegie, wearing skis, was in goal for one team and other members managed to rustle up other strange costumes. Some Germans watched and appeared puzzled. The football was not distinguished but a good time was had by all.

Regimental Signals Officer

When I first arived at the regiment I was posted to B Squadron under Major 'Darkie' Palmer, where I took over No 2 Troop. I assumed that, like most subalterns, I would be a troop leader for some time to come. However, after six weeks I was summoned by the adjutant, told that the regimental signals officer (RSO) would be away from the regiment for some time and meanwhile I was to take over his job. As RSO I was responsible for the whole signals side of the regiment which was central to its military operation; this promised more interest and variety than being a troop leader.

As RSO I was suddenly asked by Brigade to account for our regimental establishment of Number 19 wireless sets (these were the standard sets in all armoured vehicles) which should have been about 150. I put two corporals to work to make a list of all our sets, starting with all vehicles which should have them. This total came out to about 100. We then started looking further; vehicles which were not supposed to have sets yielded a whole lot more, and when we looked into barrack-rooms, squadron offices and other similar places we found even more, until we comfortably exceeded our proper number. It was only later that I realised that this was the beginning of the move from the very loose wartime accounting for equipment to the much more rigorous peacetime accounting. Just to be on the safe side I simply reported to Brigade that we had our full establishment of Number 19 sets, keeping the extra ones as a reserve. As RSO I was responsible for the regimental-level code, a simple tactical one called Slidex, which I had to update and revise. I was also responsible for the whole regimental signals net; somewhere along the way we seemed to have lost a regimental command vehicle, so I had a White scout car, which already had a full-sized metal rear compartment, converted to take two sets with operators. I also had a set put up what we called the Crow's Nest at the very top of the Officers' Mess, which was the highest building around. Despite much juggling with aerials, neither of these efforts gave me the wireless range I was hoping for.

Monday 17 February 1947

Went out in Dingo [*Humber armoured scout car*] to test communication between it and Crow's nest station. Ran out of Communication at six miles. Something wrong with aerial in base. Got through on M.C.W. [*a wireless channel*] Out again in afternoon. Spoke through remote control unit to Seagull [*standard code for an adjutant*] (Pat Howard-Dobson). We are not using Dingos for raid tomorrow.

Bitter Winter, 1946–47

As winter came on it was decided that we would shoot some of the deer which abounded on the Luneburg Heath around Soltau, not just for sport but for food. It was all properly organised and under the control of German foresters. About a dozen officers took part and the same number of other ranks; the weapons were army rifles (and allegedly some Bren guns). The bag was good, and the foresters were pleased to have a cull at that time of year. One of our captains over dinner explained that a stag he had shot turned out to have only one ball, and the forester was glad to have it culled. Another captain chimed in that a forester was also pleased with the stag he had shot. I could not resist saying 'I suppose your stag had no balls at all?' But raising a laugh at the expense of one of your seniors is not to be recommended.

The weather had been very cold but was now becoming colder; the Germans were saying that this was nothing – it would get colder yet; and so it did, but then it went on to become colder still until we were only too aware that this was an unusually bitter winter. Our anti-freeze liquid now arrived in solid blue lumps. Vehicles had to be drained off every night and restarted without coolant, which could only be safely put in when the engine was warm. Even so, smaller vehicles on occasions froze up while running. The regiment had a small coach – the Married Families Bus – which often went to Hamburg in the afternoons, with room for other passengers also. Several of us made use of this to go to the Officers' Shop in Hamburg to get extra items of warm clothing – their heavy white wool submarine socks were particularly good. On the way back the road became covered with black ice; the bus slid to the side of the road and could not move any further and the first officer to dismount to see what could be done slipped and fell flat on his back. Luckily we were near a small unit of obscure name and purpose, and apparently run entirely by elderly majors supported by a generous number of German staff. After phoning back to the regiment to explain rather carefully that several officers and the wives of several troopers could not get home that night, we were kindly looked after by the majors, well fed and comfortably bedded. I believe this was the unit whose (commandeered) stately home contained a bathroom with a silver bathtub; this sounded luxurious but was apparently extremely uncomfortable because the silver transferred its heat excessively into anyone taking a bath. By lunchtime the next day the roads were usable again; we thanked the majors warmly and made our way back to the regiment.

The road to Hamburg took us past a large German ammunition dump, at that time open and unguarded, with very many well-spaced large sheds. We visited one of these and found that it was filled with boxes of fuses and booby traps, some of them opened and their contents scattered over the floor – it was a truly deadly place, a real devil's playground. From another part of this dump I acquired two German 'jumping mines'; they were designed so that when any of their three curving prongs at the top were touched, they would jump up a metre or so and then explode – very nasty things. My two had never been filled with explosive or fused, and I used them as bookends. It was around this time that I went off in a scout car across a frozen white landscape on some minor duty; I was not on net and I used my 19 set to look for some music. I happened upon Ravel's *Bolero*, sounding far away and slightly distorted, with a radio beacon behind it, a combination which was eerie and strangely compelling. Several years later I heard *Bolero* in more normal circumstances conducted by Basil Cameron, whose tempo got slower and slower until one wondered if he would ever manage to get to the end. Much later still I found that Ravel himself regarded it as consisting wholly of orchestral tissue without music – one very long, gradual crescendo.

Horses, Dogs and Sports

Several of the senior officers in the regiment were countrymen at heart; they had the use of horses, all taken over from the German army and now on the regimental establishment. One incident will show their robust attitude. The second in command, Major John Congreve, and his wife had been out riding, he on a horse, she on a mare. They had dismounted for a rest when the horse started trying to mount the mare:

'Oh John, stop him, stop him!'

'Don't be ridiculous, woman, that is what horses are meant to do.'

They also went shooting when the opportunity arose and one winter morning several of them went out with shotguns to a nearby area around Bergen-Belsen (a name with terrible overtones) to walk-up partridges; I and a few others went along with them. There were no partridges there, but the trip was worthwhile because the countryside was striking – fields and copses heavily frosted and utterly silent.

Several officers had dogs; Pat Howard-Dobson, our adjutant, and his wife had a charming long-haired miniature dachshund named Sheba, which I looked after for a while when they were away. She chewed up some of my clothing so I had to tick her off; as I did so she sat still but lowered her nose and looked so offended that I had to laugh; she didn't like being laughed at and her nose went down further and her expression became positively mutinous; in the end I laughed so much that I had to go away and leave her. Major Fox had a dachshund which I once looked after, and one of the squadron leaders had a large dachshund, Baron, who was a real working dog; he tried to dig out an imaginary badger next to the Officers' Block in which I had my room. In the end he dug such a deep hole that one night John Harding, one of our captains, fell into it while walking over to the Mess. And there was Polly, an unassuming and amiable animal belonging to Basil Young, another captain; at one point she surprised us all by producing a litter of puppies. She was black and white, smooth-haired and from her well-rounded rear she tapered smoothly and evenly up to a pointed nose – an unusually streamlined shape for a dog. Then there were what one might call the regimental dogs, who were always around and appeared to belong to somebody although it was never clear who this was. This contingent included Garda (slightly rusty black and with uneven back legs), who adopted the regiment at the Italian lake of that name; Diesel (rather fluffy and off-white) who also joined up in Italy; he developed a carnal interest in Sheba and was caught, as one might say, red-handed by the adjutant's wife outside her front door; and finally Killer (a large and morose brown dog) who evidently felt that he had few friends – which was true, although somebody fed him. Both Garda and Diesel would occasionally join us on peaceful missions but Killer always remained behind doing his regular patrols round the camp. (None of these dogs had quite the eye-catching figure of the well-developed bull terrier belonging to the gunnery range staff at Lulworth in Dorset; this showed much pink skin under sparse white hair with a few smudges of dirty grease and bore the highly descriptive name of Body.) A brief visitor to the regiment, no one seemed to know where from, was a large St Bernard; he was getting in the way of drill in one of the riding schools and to get rid of him I attracted his attention and ran out of the double doors. This was not altogether wise because he took the hint and came after me looking large, fast and keenly carnivorous. I escaped by racing through another door, hiding behind it, and then as he thundered past doubling back and closing the door behind me. I began to give more credence to the rumour that St Bernards saved three stranded Alpine travellers out of four but, being kept hungry, ate the fourth.

To keep the troops fit and occupied there were many inter-unit sports competitions. In the winter season it was mainly football matches, followed by rugby. On one cold and foggy day the 7th Hussars went to play rugby against 4 RHA (Royal Horse Artillery) and several of us went as supporters. The fog was so bad that half our team got lost and I was one of the supporters hastily commandeered to make up our number. It was a game memorable for many uncomfortable features: the RHA team was led by a threatening forward of quite unnatural size and speed, the commandeered members of our team were hopelessly out of practice, and the fog made it hard to see what was going on (which at least offered us some protection from the attentions of the RHA giant). We managed a draw of 3–3. In the summer there were cricket and athletics meetings which were well attended, and there were also swimming and diving competitions. One of the latter was held at the baths in Hamburg where to my surprise Jim Astley-Rushton, a rather sedate senior major, beat the Rhine Army plunging record with a plunge of 58 feet.

Everyone attending these competitions came in their own military vehicles, which allowed another kind of competition: a vehicle would be chosen at random from each of the units at the meeting, to be thoroughly inspected by independent fitters, often from Brigade, to see which was the best maintained. Many soldiers took pride in their vehicles both mechanically and in appearance; most of our trucks had wheels where one ring of nuts had to be painted red as a warning because undoing them could lead to the wheel sections separating explosively, which was very dangerous. This led some drivers to paint the other wheel nuts white to emphasise the distinction, but in the hands of enthusiastic drivers this could lead to further decoration beyond the call of necessity and this had to be discouraged before our vehicles, from their official dull army green, began to blossom out like highly decorated gipsy caravans. The army arranged other sports; this included a week of skiing instruction in February, which was very popular with my fellow officers and was over-subscribed. Another was gliding, held in the summer on an ex-Luftwaffe airfield not far from Soltau, where the perimeter track was a graveyard of wrecked German fighter planes. Our very basic glider was launched by a towing truck and I had a few preliminary sessions, but it didn't really appeal to me. Garda came with us to this airfield and raced up and down the runway at great speed. I had seen a tennis court at a house near our barracks, and Major Fairhurst had seen it also – our descriptions agreed exactly. This meant the opportunity to play some tennis, and Tony Reynolds our Quartermaster got our Royal Engineers to go over there and do it up. They came back and said they couldn't find it. Tony Reynolds said nonsense and went off to show it to them – but he could not find it either. We never did solve the mystery of the disappearing tennis court. The army also arranged a lottery for cameras; this was open to all ranks and the winners could buy excellent new German cameras for only a few pounds. Through this I was able to buy a Rolleicord which took pictures excellently, although my pictures themselves could certainly not be called excellent.

Orderly Officer

One of the duties of the orderly officer was to go down to the NAAFI in Soltau to see that closing time was properly observed and all troops left promptly. The problem was the Woodpeckers from Fallingbostel; these were troops from various units, most of them apparently Scots, who were working in forestry camps some way from Soltau. I believe that they all had bad army records and were put on to this heavy work to tire them out, keep them away from temptation and out of further trouble. This was important, because if they did get into trouble their demob would be put off yet again and the army felt it would never get rid of them. On a Saturday evening these Woodpeckers filled up the NAAFI, drinking, being rowdy and often fighting amongst themselves, on one occasion with razors in a toilet cubicle. They would load their tables with pints of beer which they then felt it their duty to drink up before closing time. Clearing them out of the NAAFI called for a delicate mixture of good humour, diplomacy, firm orders and finally force. When I was Orderly Officer, on bad nights I left the guard corporal outside to gather the 7th Hussars as they left and keep them for a while in case I needed reinforcements. In the event I never had to resort to force, although it was sometimes a close run thing, but other orderly officers were not so lucky; several times I went down to the NAAFI to assist them in clearing it. One evening the RSM was there and he whispered to me that it was better to take my hat off in the NAAFI. I found that he was quite right. The troops were off duty and out to have a good time; with my hat under my arm there was less of a gulf between them and me, and the initial stage of persuasion and jollying them along was more effective. One curious thing was that I never felt the slightest qualm about going alone into the middle of this disorderly throng; I was always confident that as an officer I would be perfectly safe amongst our own troops, even the turbulent Woodpeckers.

Within the regiment disciplinary problems were rare. Trooper W (who in my view was mentally unbalanced) had already missed one demob date for some offence. He was currently confined in the guardroom, and given the way he behaved we would never get rid of him. The solution was to release him at the end of his current sentence, promptly rearrest him (for which there were plenty of good reasons), and keep him confined till his deferred demob date was reached. Meanwhile a Court of Enquiry, conducted by Tony Barber-Fleming and myself, looked into his alleged misdemeanours; then on the morning of his demob date he was put in front of a board of discipline, found not guilty and escorted to the train taking him to his demob centre. In my view an eminently practical solution. The only other case I can recall was that of Trooper X; he had signed up as a regular when the regiment was in Italy, evidently under the impression that he would remain in Italy. Somehow being in Northern Germany was not the same and he was constantly in trouble. Venereal disease was then a problem and catching a dose was an offence which could put off your demob date. On the American Forces Network (favoured listening for many, with its trademark music of a close harmony version of 'On the Sunny Side of the Street' by the Modernaires) one of the regular messages was: 'If she's got it, you get it and if you get it, you've had it.' In the regiment there was an immediate treatment room where those who thought they might have caught a dose could give themselves simple preventive treatment before seeing the medical officer next day. In a book they signed to show that they had used the room's facilities, and there they also had to detail how it had happened; making such entries was a mitigating circumstance. Trooper X duly filled in the book:

Where did it happen?
    'End of platform 3, Hamburg Main Station'.
Do you know the name of the woman?
    'No'.
Was a contraceptive used?
    'Yes (it burst)'.

In the end Trooper X deserted and presumably headed back to Italy; we were glad to see him go, and the regiment would certainly make no effort to get him back. However regulations required that we should hold a Court of Enquiry into his desertion and this also was conducted by Tony Barber-Fleming and myself.

One person I knew in the army at this time got drunk one night, fell into bed with a German woman clerk employed by his unit and caught syphilis from her; this came as a nasty shock to him and to those who knew him. Several years later I unexpectedly found myself face to face with him – and his wife – on their honeymoon. It was an agonising moment, knowing that at such a time I would have revived in his mind what must have been a haunting memory. After she had infected him the woman had been fired from her job, but only a short time later I saw her with two sergeants as they were driving away from a petrol point. There was no time to warn them about their passenger.

Repatriating Prisoners

After a couple of months as RSO I felt I had the regimental signals side broadly under control and it was considered that I could be used occasionally for other duties. One of these was to be responsible for a train taking about 200 German prisoners of war back to Austria, where they would be released and demobbed. I had a corporal with me, a substantial supply of foodstuffs (much of which required cooking, although there were tins of bully beef and a bag of sultanas), a stove for cooking together with three jerrycans of petrol, and pistols and ammunition for both of us. On 8 March 1947 we were taken to Munster Lager station where the RTO (Rail Transport Officer) briefed me on our task. This was to guard our train of six coaches (for the prisoners) and a van (for us). Apparently when we got anywhere near the Russian sector they were liable to steal any rolling stock and we were there to prevent this. What about the prisoners? Yes, yes, we could guard them as well and look after the large sack containing their documents, but our duty was to make sure the Russians didn't steal our train on its way to Villach in Austria. Then on Monday 9 March at 08.10 we started off, living in our rail van as the train stopped and started on its slow journey, pulled by an ever-changing cast of engines. Luckily I had brought a *Philips School Atlas* with me, and this and the names of the large stations were our only guide as to where we were. It seemed a good idea to note down the names of the stations, many of them very small, that we stopped at and the time we were at each. I also made a few ill-written notes on flimsy message forms of some of the events on our journey. Our van had a large sliding door; this we kept open and sat with our legs hanging out, watching the countryside go by. Whenever it stopped one of us would walk up and down the stationary train and count the axles.

At Munster Truderling a train drew up next to us containing Polish refugees being sent back to Russian-occupied Poland; they appeared very quiet and depressed. Our Austrian prisoners and later some Jugoslav repatriates covered their trains with festive greenery; there was none of this on the Polish train. The Jugoslav train which we saw at Freilassing also had flags and slogans and was commanded by an American sergeant with some very young GIs; the Jugoslavs were quite jolly and had a man on the platform playing the accordion and surrounded by a crowd. We crossed a bridge at Salzburg late at night and a number of civilians asked if they could have a lift on our train; they had various reasons and tales – one woman claiming to be a Viennese doctor – none of which I really believed, but I turned a blind eye to such extra passengers. We were up much of the night at Salzburg because we were warned that this was where the Russians were most likely to try stealing some of our carriages. We moved off at 03.15 and several hours later arrived at a tiny station named Kleinmunchen; there our prisoners and their documents were collected from the train, our engine left us and we found ourselves and our carriages apparently abandoned in the middle of nowhere. Despite an unhelpful stationmaster I somehow managed to get someone to promise me an engine to take us to Villach, and after waiting most of the day it finally came. I spent part of the day in the stationmaster's office filling in railway forms and stamping them in red and black so that I could wave them imperiously at any other unhelpful railway official. At last, in a freezing dawn, we crossed the mountains over the pass not far from the late Fuhrer's Eagle's Nest at Berchtesgarten; the scenery was magnificent. We arrived at Villach at 10.15 on Thursday 12 March 1947.

I now went off to report to the RTO. His first question was where were the prisoners. I had to admit that I didn't know, but I pointed out that the train which was my primary responsibility was here with its proper number of axles intact. He went off darkly to make telephone calls and returned mollified but not pleased, signed for the train and arranged for the two of us to be taken to the large transit camp in Villach – 316 Medloc 'C', Alamein Camp. There we had first to surrender our weapons at the guardroom; this was in a wired compound guarded by Alsatian dogs, trained by the German army, who at the sight of our pistols went berserk and tried to bite their way through the wire to get at us. They were hustled away, we surrendered our guns and then went off to report to the officer in charge of the camp. That was the last I saw of my corporal, because we were both then under orders from the transit camp which made separate arrangements for us to return to the regiment. The weather was warm and I had two very pleasant days walking around the local lakes and doing some shopping in Klagenfurt. Then my movement order arrived; I joined a train to Calais full of soldiers going on 'Python' leave to the UK from Italy and the Middle East. On this train I made the usual temporary friends and it was a reasonable if rather crowded journey, except that we stopped at 02.00 hours for breakfast in what appeared to be a nightclub whose merrymakers had only just left and where the handbasins were inverted German helmets. Lunch at Traunstein was at a more civilised hour and there was another meal stop in France.

At last we arrived at Calais on Tuesday 17 March; there the RTO told me that I was the only person out of that whole trainful who was not going on to the UK. Instead I was to be locked in as the sole passenger on a train going to Hamburg via Bielefelt, which meant plenty of space but apparently nothing to eat or drink. At last on Thursday 19 March I arrived at Hamburg and a truck took me back to the regiment. There I reported to the Adjutant, returned to the Quartermaster most of the food and our untouched jerrycans of petrol (we had been in no mood for cooking), and returned to normal regimental life.

Exercise Ashtray

At the end of April and the beginning of May there was a major Corps-level exercise with the code name Ashtray. This was mainly a signals exercise involving only the HQs of regiments and above, and as RSO I took part in it. To prepare for it we had a one-day brigade rehearsal exercise called Prelude; of this I can only remember that at the end of the day I arrived back dirty and tired, to the surprise of those who thought such exercises were tame affairs. Then came Ashtray itself, preceded by all the detailed orders, organisation charts, signals diagrams etc. I was a Liaison Officer on the net which linked 4th Armoured Brigade HQ to its armoured regiments: Royal Scots Greys, 7th Hussars, 2nd Royal Tanks, together with supporting arms (Artillery, Royal Engineers, REME etc). The callsign on this net was Baker Nan Baker (BNB), the armoured regiments had callsign numbers 1, 2 and 3, the supporting arms each had their standard number (such as Artillery, 25; Engineers, 27 – all such two-figure numbers pronounced as two five etc) and the liaison officers were 18 with suffixes A, B and C denoting the three regiments. From all this I emerged as Baker Nan Baker One Eight Baker; as the net settled down and we became familiar with each other the codesign was often shortened to just Baker and at times of several interchanges between the same stations to just the codesign number. At last the CO, his HQ operational staff, the regimental command vehicle and supporting vehicles were ready, together with my driver and myself in the signals officer's Dingo (Humber armoured scout car). We moved on to the start line and Exercise Ashtray began.

As all the units moved forward bound by bound they often got further apart, which tested the competence of the wireless operators to keep in communication, and also their wireless procedure, which is essential to keep order on the air. Operating my own 19 set, at first I just listened in to all the traffic; but before long some units had moved out of range from brigade control, and as I was in touch with both stations (although each tended to become fainter as the exercise progressed) I started intervening to pass messages, for example: 'Baker Nan Baker One Eight Baker message for Baker Two Five, through me, Over' – offering to pass on to Brigade Control a message from Two Five who had moved out of touch. In the end I spent most of the three days of Ashtray in the cramped interior of my Dingo, looking fixedly at my 19 set, but without seeing it, living entirely through my ears, totally taken up with my inner vision of the net and all its stations, the traffic passing between them and my own role in helping to keep it going. At last Ashtray came to an end and it seemed strange to close down all those stations that to me had developed characters of their own. From my point of view it had all been a success; our own regimental operators had performed well and I had played a minor but constructive role. Then from the scattered bounds across North Germany where our vehicles had ended the exercise, we formed into a convoy and moved back to Soltau.

Firing and Other Activities

As summer came, regimental life continued on its congenial way. I went to the B Squadron shoot on number 8 range at Belbe; this was done using Comet tanks with their 77 mm guns (a very similar gun to the 17 pounder I fired as a trooper at the Warcop range) rather than the much smaller guns on our elderly Crocodiles. The shooting went well but one of the tanks had an unusual misfire. The propellant charge in the cartridge of an HE shell was evidently faulty and when it was fired there was a feeble bang and the shell went halfway up the barrel and stuck there. The question was, what to do now? We couldn't do the usual misfire drill: 'Misfire, re-cock, fire. Second misfire, wait one minute', which assumed the cartridge had not gone off at all. We tried to push the shell out of the gun with a cleaning rod, but it was stuck fast. The only thing to do was to blow it out and hope that this did not detonate the shell while it was still in the barrel, in which case we would have to explain to the range commander why their gun now had a bulge in it, like a boa constrictor that had swallowed a pig. This shouldn't happen because we had always been told that these shells were bore-safe and could not explode till they had rotated enough times for them to have left the barrel, so we decided to give it a try. The shell was removed from another round and the fully charged cartridge case was loaded into the gun. We all stood back at a respectful distance and the order was given to fire. The result was a strange mixture of a bang and a belch, and we could see the previously stuck shell tumbling through the air as it went up the range. It was an interesting day's shooting. On a few other occasions we did some flaming with our Crocodile flame-throwers to make sure that they and their crews were in good operational order. Filling the armoured trailers with napalm and pressuring up took time, but since their flaming range was only about 100 yards we could test them in a local field. The flaming was quite impressive and I took several photographs.

For a time the regiment was host to General Damyanovic, an unwilling guest who was a semi-prisoner. He was a Yugoslav and the reason for his detention was never explained to us. One of the duties of the orderly officer was to escort the general if he moved outside the camp.

Thursday 31 July 1947
Orderly Officer. Took General Damyanovic for a walk. Talked about Jugoslavia etc. He told me his wife and daughter were still in Belgrade. This proves that woman who came about a month ago was a fraud. She wanted permission for General's wife to come and see him. I told her to come back next day, she never appeared again; she said his wife was in Deipholz camp.

When we escorted him we had to carry a loaded pistol. When he realised this he was rather offended. A few weeks later he was removed from our care.

Every armoured regiment had a technical adjutant, who had responsibility for the whole of its military hardware, including indenting for (ordering) new equipment and spares. In July I was sent on a technical adjutant's course at Lippstadt. There were about twenty of us on the course, which was frankly dull, being devoted mainly to learning how to fill in a variety of army forms to indent for new items of equipment. The only pleasure I could find was from filling in my forms for imaginary and bizarre units (1st NAAFI Parachute Brigade Training Battalion, Dessert Company, Advanced Pastry Platoon) and following this with a long technical description for a very small item (Bolt, 10 mm, Stainless Steel, Heat Treated, Whitworth thread, Hex Head, chamfered, Mark 1*). The course was run by a major and had its own mess which was run by a staff of German women, led by a particularly busty one. At dinner she would stand behind the major's seat at the head of the table, so close to him that his head seemed enveloped between her ample bosoms. One of the officers on the course was from a guards regiment; he caused some surprise by having breakfast with his hat on, which he claimed was a regimental tradition. There was an infantry subaltern from 2 Div with whom I used to play liar dice to while away the time. I discovered how to cheat undetectably and outrageously; in a serious afternoon's play I won more than a whole boxful of matches from him. The most interesting thing about Lippstadt was that we were able to visit the nearby site of the Mohne Dam, breached by the RAF Dambusters raid in May 1943. It had been restored, but the repair showed where the large hole had been blown and below the dam there were still scars from the surge of water that poured through the breach. Around the edge of the reservoir was the wreckage of the German anti-aircraft defences.

The instructors on this course were officers from various units, and the army was keen that those giving such courses had suitable training. The regiment was visited by a Methods of Instruction Team which provided such training, and many of us attended their sessions. They were full of sound practical advice on how to give an effective lecture or talk and I thought they were very well done. Many of the points made in the course stuck in my mind and were to be very useful to me later.

Road Blocks

Back with the regiment we now came to a period of activity in our anti-black-market operations:

Friday 1 August 1947
In morning went on recce with Robin Carnegie in Colonel's jeep over ground near Autobahn for tonight's check up to try and catch

169

people who are stealing tyres etc. Had lunch in Sittensen with RAOC unit, back at 15.00 hrs. We found tyre tracks leading through Sothel. Briefing at 17.00 hrs. Assembled at 22.30. I had L/Cpl Trott's truck. Arrived at RV south of Rotenburg 15 mins late. I led second half of convoy through Rotenburg to Scheessel in Maj. Fairhurst's jeep. Dropped Malcolm Thomas and Cranley Onslow there. Took Fairhurst & John Stanier to Westeresch road, left them, and took rest to Witkopbostel turning. Left L/Cpl Trott there and took others to their posts by scout car. Returned, took over main block myself, sent Trott & scout car to cover Herzwege. Stayed till 05.30. Only 1 truck containing nothing. Driver v. scared when I pulled door open and forced him out at revolver point. Two civilians on foot, both innocent. 05.30 went to Rotenburg. Had tea & bar of chocolate. Back to camp by 07.50.

Saturday 2 August 1947
V. tired. Checked arms, got petrol for Maj. Astley-Rushton in Noel Fairhurst's jeep. Slept on bed till 1.45. Had lunch. Bed 14.30 till 09.30 Sunday morning.

Friday 8 August 1947
Out on scout car patrol. Only myself, Tpr Charity & German policeman. Route out: Harber – Suroide – Wietzendorf – Celle to Hamburg road. Did an hour's check, caught a black marketeer Baruch Krzepicki, a stateless Displaced Person. He had a radio etc and 12,700 marks in notes (£317. 10s.). German policeman took him into custody. One car going from Soltau – Celle did not stop, so I fired two shots on to the road in front of it. It stopped. In afternoon went Bispingen – Luneburg road and did a road block 1/2 mile west of Harber. A car coming from Luneburg turned off up a track before it came to us, but we chased it. It was quite innocent.

I fired two shots during this road check but I pulled the trigger three times – what should have been my second shot was a misfire; these two shots were the only ones I ever fired with anything resembling evil intent.

Tuesday 12 August 1947

Normal day. The 24 hour road check has been very successful. 2 DP black marketeers brought in today. I saw them searched in Guard Room. Had chocolate, sweets, 5 grams gold, 44,000 marks etc. Went to cinema with Bryan – *Canyon Passage*. Not bad. Came back, another Displaced Person had been found with all sorts of kit including gold teeth & diamonds. Took photos of flame-throwing in afternoon.

The Berlin Tattoo

In the middle of August there was the Berlin Tattoo, arranged by the British army to impress the American, Russian and French forces with whom we shared the occupation of Berlin. The first any of us heard about this was when a signal came from Brigade notifying the regiment that it was to send six troopers on a six-week equitation course to learn to ride well enough to take part in a cavalry display – which in the event they did.

Thursday 14 August 1947

Started for Berlin at 07.30 in Married Families bus. Arrived Celle at 08.30, train at 08.45. Very third class accommodation, hard seats, few cups in NAAFI van. Went via Lehrte – Peine – Braunschweig East – Frellenstedt – Helmstedt – Marienborn – Magdeburg – Genthin – Brandenburg – Werder – Potsdam – Grunwald – Charlottenburg. Dull countryside. When we arrived we were taken by Troop Carrying Vehicle to tented camp at north of Maifeld. Quite comfortable. Had tea etc and walked round Maifeld and looked at Olympic Stadium. Wonderful place. At 18.15 went on tour of Berlin with German guide in TCV. Saw Alexanderplatz, Kurfurstendamm, Tiergarten, Russian war memorial, Charlottenburg and air raid shelter [*This was Hitler's Bunker, where we saw the hole outside the entrance at the point where the bodies of Hitler and Eva Braun had been burned*], Kaiserdamm. Very interesting. Berlin is in a terrible state, very smashed up. In evening changed into Service Dress, used Robin's Crossbelt, Robin

Carnegie and John Stanier in Overalls [*dress uniforms*] with red hats, spurs, chain epaulettes etc. [*Both looked most impressive*]. I played the role of ADC, and told everyone they were Equerries. Tattoo started at 22.00 hrs. Excellent show. Lots of Germans there, they seemed very impressed. Americans sitting below me were impressed too. Back at 00.30. Robin and John started on champagne, I went to bed.

The audience was impressed but also puzzled. The military items they could understand; these included a display of battalion drill done in silence – no orders – by an infantry regiment (something like the 2nd Staffords) which was most impressive, and a cavalry ride followed by a charge across the arena. What puzzled them was a very amusing item by a vehicle apparently without a driver which backfired and swerved around the arena as people tried to stop it, and a parade by an English hunt with horses, hounds and hunting pink. They couldn't help enjoying these, but I think they expected everything to be more sternly military.

Going back to the tour we did before the Tattoo, I wrote down the following impression a few weeks later:

Berlin is a mass of ruins, although when I was there it was an August evening and the setting sun bathed everything in a lovely shade of pink, and the weeds growing in the ruins were brilliant green. Everything was quiet and even the few buildings that were undamaged by bombs or fighting seemed stunned. The great avenues and streets were almost deserted and the tranquillity was unnatural. There were no more victorious hordes marching through the city now, bearing their Swastikas and shouting their Heils, only a few pathetic looking figures in the tattered remains of uniforms.

The next day we had a slow journey back to the regiment. The crowds of Germans on Magdeburg station – as when we came – looked as if they had been waiting for days. Arriving at Celle the transport back to camp was delayed and we spent some time in the Ratskeller talking about patrols, internal security, and anti-black-market measures.

Food from Denmark

On 4 September the regiment had to provide a contingent for Exercise Oasis. This was the landing at Hamburg of a boatload of Jews who had been caught trying to enter Israel; this made headlines at the time. When they came back our chaps were scathing about the American press, who had been urging some Jews to cringe against barbed wire so that they could take photographs showing the brutality of the British.

In Germany we had to depend on army transport for nearly everything; 15 cwt trucks were used for many purposes and all the squadron leaders and many other senior officers had jeeps; they had first claim on these but would often make them available for others to use. With so much regimental motor transport and the rather dangerous German roads and drivers, there were inevitably accidents.

Monday 4 August 1947
Bank Holiday. Heard that Ian Wheldon smashed up Jim's jeep last night. John Stanier cut a bit but not bad. Played bridge in afternoon.

Thursday 7 August 1947
Went to Hamburg in Trooper Butcher's Dingo. Rained on and off all day. Saw Cochran at 94 General Hospital, took statement from him about his Matador smash. Saw Robin Carnegie there. Lunch at the Atlantic Hotel. Very cosmopolitan atmosphere. Went to Officers Shop, no brown shoes size 9. Back by 16.10 hrs.

Monday 8 September 1947
Normal day. I am looking after Simon, Maj. Fox's dachshund. CID say Pole's death was an accident. He was killed by our 15 cwt as he got out of a ditch.

Saturday 11 October 1947
[*Coming back from leave in UK*] Caught train from Hook to Rotenburg. Waited in club for transport. Driver told me 4 chaps had been killed in a Passion Wagon smash [*Passion Wagon – any vehicle used for recreation – excluding the Married Families Bus!*] Arrived at Regt at approx 10.45.

It was felt that rather more variety in the food in our Mess would be welcome and at that time it was permissible to send a truck up into Denmark to collect some minor luxuries. I volunteered for what seemed likely to be an interesting trip.

Sunday 14 September 1947
Final arrangements for Denmark. Cpl Ball is coming with me.

Monday 15 September 1947
Started for Denmark at 08.30. Driver on a charge for being late with detail. Hamburg, where I met Robert and got Kroner; chap in Customs Office, told us we would only be allowed in in civvies. (Turned out to be wrong.) Cpl Ball went back with Robert as he had only uniform [*Trooper Curtis now became driver of our 15cwt*]. Continued via Neumunster, Kiel (lunched at Yacht Club), Evenforde, Schleswig and Flensburg. Got to frontier at Krusaa. Control chap told me that today was last day to bring food across, so I pushed on to Kollund, 3 km across border and bought 1,440 eggs, 100 tins caviar, 10 tins smoked salmon costing 340, 180 & 35 kroner respectively. Managed to get them across. Danish control chap asked me only how many eggs, so I told him 1,440. Left stuff with 3rd Tanks in Flensburg then went back and managed to cross border again. Bashed on to Kolding. Curtis stayed at leave camp, I stayed at hotel. Spent 2 hours in Palmhavn night spot. Great fun, lots of portly old men & v. few not bad women dancing on tiny floor. Some quite nice looking girls at next table. Very good band and singer. Tried to tell night porter I wished to be called at 08.00 hrs.

Tuesday 16 September 1947
Evidently successful last night as I was woken at 08.00. However I woke at 06.00 of my own accord and did not sleep much after. Breakfasted on coffee and cakes. Old woman at table opposite wearing 'Bowler hat' & smoking a cigar normally associated with American big businessmen. Lots of Sholevagn (driving instruction cars) driving around Kolding. Street organ has started up, rather good. Every now and then it starts playing 'Auld Lang Syne' in the

middle of other tunes, I do not know why. Bought photo corners for Pip Coddington, and bulb for Cranley Onslow. Then to Middlefart, Fredericia, Vejle and back to Kolding. Near Middlefart we stopped at a village named Snoghoj pronounced Snoggage [*in fact, Snorhoy*]. Took photos of Middlefart Bridge, lots of big jellyfish in sea. Found a starfish.

It was then back to Flensburg to spend the night with 3rd Tanks before returning to Soltau with my booty. That evening I and some subalterns from 3rd Tanks went out to a restaurant for dinner. We went in an old Volkswagen with a defective accelerator so that the driver had to use a hand throttle which meant that the gear changing had to be done by the front passenger. This made our ride rather alarming, particularly as Flensburg is a port and many poorly lit roads seemed to end on a quay with a straight drop into the Baltic. Back at the regiment I delivered my goods to the Mess. These now included several cheeses rather like Camembert which I had picked up somewhere and these were the first of my purchases which we sampled at dinner the next night. When we cut into them, tiny maggots slowly emerged; but we were not going to be put off by this, which we decided was a sign of the maturity of these cheeses, so we pushed the maggots back in and ate the lot.

College of the Rhine Army – Gottingen

I was now due for leave in the UK and was given nineteen days plus four days for travelling, lasting altogether from 18 September to 11 October. This I spent largely at home in Aldwick. Already change was coming over the horizon. My demob group was 64 C which indicated a date early in January 1948, and this made me eligible to attend a month's course at the College of the Rhine Army (CORA) at Gottingen. There I chose courses in economics, business organisation, company law, government and politics; in the evenings I went to extra lectures on subjects of general interest or to debates. The course was attended by perhaps sixty people – a complete mixture of units and ranks, including a number of ATS girls. We lived very comfortably in an Officers Mess which included Captain Mendelsohn who was in charge of the course. An additional pleasure was that we could get very cheap tickets for the Gottingen Opera, where the first two rows were reserved for us. The Opera seemed to run a repertory system which allowed me to see half a dozen different operas. This course was my first experience of academic work as an adult and my first introduction to economics – taught by Sergeant Smith, who had been at the London School of Economics. I found the whole course most enjoyable.

Return to the UK

We were now notified of another major change – the regiment was going to move back to the UK, in fact to Streatlam Camp at Barnard Castle where I had finished my training as a trooper two years previously. For our own kit we were now issued with German munition boxes; what they had contained was not clear, but mine had a distictly chemical smell. The regiment was taking a few White scout cars and half-tracks with it, but most of our armoured vehicles had to be prepared to go into storage on Ordnance Parks. They were moved by rail on flat trucks and my role in this was to act as train guard and commander of a small group of two Honeys (light tanks) three Churchill Armoured Recovery Vehicles (Churchill tanks adapted for the recovery of other Churchills which had been disabled) and two Slaves (light tracked vehicles containing an auxiliary engine for charging up the batteries of any other vehicles that might require their services). These were all going to the Ordnance Park at Varrelbusch. I supervised them being driven on to the flats at Soltau and then with Sergeant Fowler as second in command we started at 20.00 hrs on 19 November.

We then ran into a problem – one of the flats developed a 'hot box', a bearing on one of the axles began to fail and run hot; it had to be replaced, which took time and threw out our timetable.

Wednesday 19 November
Hot box on one of ARV flats. Had to halt at Bremen Schalbusch at 01.00 hrs. Passed message to Regt via RTO. Got to Hamburg at 10.00 approx. German engineers saw the flat at 11.00; decided to move train to Werkstat at Bremen. Moved at 14.00 hrs. Started mending at 15.30, finished 18.00 hrs. They jacked up flat and

ARV together, placed new wheels in bogey section. Stayed in Goods yard all night. Very cold indeed.

Thursday 20 November 1947
Moved at 10.40 to Oldenburg. Arrived at 13.05 hrs near Stellwerk VI verscheiter bahnhof. Went to RTO on local train. Tried to get food in Oldenburg, no go. OC Varrelbusch said he would have some at Cloppenburg station at 21.30 for us. Bought cakes for chaps. Back on local [*train*] at 18.00 hrs. Raining. Left goods yard at 19.10 hrs.

Friday 21 November 1947
Arrived Cloppenburg 03.00 on 21 Nov. Food was waiting for us. It was spoiled as we were 5 1/2 hrs late. Moved to Varrelbusch at 11.00. Unloaded vehicles by 15.00. Stayed at Officers Mess at Ahlhorn. Remembered at 20.00 hrs that ARVs were not drained off. Went back to Varrelbusch with two fitters & drained them. Back at 21.00 hrs; used our truck which had arrived.

Saturday 22 November 1947
Back to Varrelbusch, collected documents etc, back to Soltau via Delmenhorst (had break), Bremen & Rotenburg. Arrived at 15.00 hrs. Missed big party held on Friday night.

In tanks, burns are a common injury; they can be agonising and someone screaming with pain is bad for the morale of those around. For this reason tanks have at their rear an external first aid kit, containing amongst other things treatments for burns – chloroform capsules (which could be crushed under the nose of the victim to make him unconscious) and morphine. When I returned to Varrelbusch for the last time to collect documents etc I found that all the external first aid kits on my Honeys and ARVs had been opened and the morphine stolen.

During 1947 various war crimes trials were being conducted in Germany, and Basil Young, one of our captains, was called to be a member of the tribunal in one of these trials. He was away for a few days and when he returned he told us that the accused men in this trial had been found guilty and sentenced to death. Some time later Basil was ordered to go to the prison at Hamelin to witness their execution by hanging; this he had not expected. My only contact with these trials was a brief visit to one of them:

Thursday 4 December 1947
Went to Hamburg in morning with Sam Scott in Personal Utility vehicle. Went to War Crimes trial. Heard defence counsel of a Col Muller of SS. Had lunch at Four Seasons. Went to Officers Shop, bought gloves & blanket. Back by P.U. Large explosion with vivid orange glow at explosives trial ground as we passed. Had Orders Group with Capt Wetherall & all advance party at 15.45. Went to Sgt's mess party in evening. Left early.

Friday 5 December 1947
Finished packing etc. We left at 16.30 & went to Hannover Transit Camp. Food dreadful. Went to club and had dinner. Convoy consisted of 7 x 3 tonners, 1 x 15 cwt, 1 Jeep.

Saturday 6 December 1947
Up at 04.30, moved to Hannover Stn. Put baggage (6 tons) on train. Arrived Hook at 17.00 hrs. Shifted baggage on to boat, embarked at 21.30. Drunken Captain caused trouble.

Sunday 7 December 1947
Up at 05.00. Baggage off boat and on to quay and then to van. Went through Customs, paid £2. 6s. 5d on my stuff. Moved at 10.10 to York. Had tea at hotel. Then to Darlington, then Broomielaw. V. cold.

Broomielaw was a tiny halt on the little-used railway line running just by the south boundary of Streatlam Camp which was about three miles from Barnard Castle. We were told that the halt was built for a wealthy old lady who lived at a local mansion named Broomielaw; when she invited someone to stay she used to enclose a first class return ticket to Broomielaw Halt. But times had changed and I assume that it now had only military traffic for the nearby Stainton and Streatlam camps.

I was now back at Streatlam Camp where I had completed my tank crew training over two years previously. The camp was not as crisp and orderly as when I had been there, but at least I was in comfortable officers' quarters. Now one of my duties was to dip the regimental petrol tanks using a long rod to measure the level of the fuel, as part of the monitoring of the regiment's use of petrol. I soon found that dipping them several times one after the other produced levels which differed significantly. When the time had come to leave Germany, we were taking only our White scout cars and half-tracks and I had been responsible for these. Understanding that back in the UK there would be peacetime accounting for petrol, I took the precaution of having their capacious petrol tanks filled right to the top so that we had a reserve in case of need. My experience in dipping the tanks showed me that this reserve would be useful.

But there was now a definite change in the tone of life in the regiment; when we were in Germany some feeling of the wartime army remained, but now it was real peace-time soldiering, with all its restrictions and lack of any immediate purpose. At this time a number of ex-Indian Army captains and majors were drafted into the regiment, and I was not impressed by them (although one made a brief name for himself on television as he was filmed coping ruggedly with a lonely old age). In addition the weather was very cold and miserable, and with my demob now coming up, it suddenly seemed time to move on. This made leaving the army, which had been my life for over three years, which had taught me a great deal and which I had greatly enjoyed, easier and indeed welcome. I left the regiment on 10 January 1948 and was demobbed at York the same day, receiving the usual grey pinstripe suit, green pork pie hat and other items of civilian gear. I was back home at Aldwick by seven o'clock that evening.

A Retrospective Note:

In my diary I mention three of my fellow officers in the 7th Queen's Own Hussars: Robin Carnegie and John Stanier, who were subalterns with me, and Pat Howard-Dobson who was a captain and our adjutant. I have to admit that I did not at the time appreciate their military potential, but in due course Robin Carnegie became a Lieutenant General while John Stanier and Pat Howard-Dobson both became Field Marshals. This seems to me an extraordinary record for a single generation of officers in a single cavalry regiment.

10

Back to the City

Demob Leave

I now had three weeks' demob leave which I spent at home at Aldwick, relaxing with the family and renewing my contacts with old friends. Roy Chiverton was now up at Cambridge reading modern languages and Dennis Wood was at Queen Mary College, London, reading chemistry. A more recent friend at Bognor was Mark Fairclough who was training to be an accountant and lived with his jolly and rather theatrical mother in a flat in a large old house in Norfolk Square, near the Royal Norfolk Hotel. He was a great fan of the French singer Charles Trénet and sometimes we would listen to his collection of records. On one occasion I called to see him and was rather surprised to be greeted enthusiastically by his mother – 'DO come in, dear'. Mark was out but there in the sitting room was an elderly and also faintly theatrical lady and her most stunningly attractive daughter. I was introduced: 'This is my dear friend and this is her daughter Vicki Emra – Vicki dances at the Windmill Theatre, you know, and she is engaged to an American general.' (The Windmill Theatre was at that time well known for its beautiful and underclad showgirls.) It turned out that Vicki wanted to go to the variety show that was on at the Pavilion that evening because one of her friends was performing there. 'Her mother and I have so much to talk about; WOULD you, darling, take her to the performance at the Pavilion this evening?' I could hardly refuse, so with this vision of beauty in my care it was off to the Pavilion only some ten minutes walk away. We applauded her friend's act and after the show I treated her to a cup of coffee at a local café. I then duly delivered her safely back to her mother. Going out with a girl from the Windmill could be made to sound very impressive to one's friends. This was my only connection with the racier end of show business.

At the more sober end was Rosemary Harris, whom I had first met at the Nyewood Lane Tennis Club when I was on leave from OCTU; she was by now a struggling aspirant in the Bognor Repertory Theatre (and protégée of June Flavell, an established member of the company) but destined to become a well-known actress. (June Flavell had a cousin, Toni Stephenson, who will appear later in this book.) Getting into the theatre was clearly a tough business and when I once met her on the bus she could hardly talk, having been screaming as noises off in the scene of a shipwreck. She was living with two charming old aunts at a house called Red Gables in Barnham. I visited her there on one occasion and her elder sister, equally attractive, had just arrived to stay; sadly her husband, an officer in the RAF, had recently been killed in a plane crash. My visit proved to be ill-timed and I could only murmur a few inadequate words of sympathy and escape.

Later I saw Rosemary a few more times when she was playing the lead in *The Seven Year Itch* at the Aldwych Theatre just round the corner from LSE; I saw the play, collected her from the stage door and we went out somewhere. A few other meetings and finally we had a vague arrangement to meet outside Swan & Edgar, a store fronting onto Piccadilly Circus, to have lunch – if she could manage it. But she couldn't and we never met again. However I was not going to allow this to deprive me of a planned lunch at the Cathay Chinese restaurant, which was on the first floor where Glasshouse Street runs into Piccadilly Circus and to which I had been introduced by Michael Rowe during the war. It served a wonderful dish of lobster with noodles – generous and excellent value – which I had already decided upon. But lunch on my own required something to read so I stopped at the newspaper stall on the edge of Piccadilly Circus close to the restaurant and asked the hoarse-voiced paper-seller if he had the *New Scientist*; his reply was 'NUDE WOT?' Over all the years that I knew it nothing seemed to change in the Cathay restaurant and even the elderly waiters remained the same. It had some tables by large windows which looked down over the bustling life of Piccadilly Circus, and having one of these tables added greatly to the pleasure of eating there. The restaurant itself has long since disappeared, and although those same windows still look down over the busy street scene, when I last saw them they appeared empty and lifeless.

Back to Avenue Road

While I was still in the army my brother Michael had been demobbed and had started at Portsmouth Poly pursuing his long-standing ambition to become an architect. For this he could live at home, but I was due to return to a job in the City (at that time all demobbed men had a right to return to a job with their previous civilian employer), so when my own demob leave was finally over, I went back to 20 Avenue Road which was the obvious place for me to live. The house had been partly let for most of the war and still had a tenant on the ground floor. It had no bomb damage but the whole place was in a rather dilapidated condition after some eight years of neglect. I took over the first floor using what had been my parents' bedroom as a bed-sitting room, and went through all the things that had been roughly stored away, recognising many items I could remember from my childhood, selecting and cleaning the things needed to make my new home comfortable. I had to restore a kitchen in what had become a rear bedroom and for this I found a diminutive and elderly gas-fitter who arrived cycling very slowly on an ancient bicycle. He gave me an estimate of the items he would require and added rather defensively 'and then, of course, there's the labour'. The whole cost came to something over two pounds, which seemed cheap even to me; a few days later, after testing the gas pressure with an ancient instrument, he declared the job done. With my 'new' kitchen in working order I now had a fully-fledged place of my own. The more so because the ground-floor tenant, Miss Hancock, accustomed to having the house to herself, was not pleased at my arrival and soon left.

Back to the City

Getting 20 Avenue Road into a suitable state took about four weeks in all, and I returned to Gerald Hodgson & Co, Stockbrokers, on 1 March 1948. With people coming back from the forces there were many new faces and the firm already had its Blue Buttons in place so I was put into their Statistics Department. This consisted of Peter Raleigh (ex-Navy) who was in charge, Hamish Orr-Ewing (ex-Army) and me. We shared a rather small room, and as junior member of the team I had the daily, and tedious, task of filing away the Exchange Telegraph and Moodies cards for each quoted company. Between us we valued deceased estates, passed judgement on trust portfolios and tried to advise clients on investments. These were all done to the best of our ability but, looking back, it was all very amateurish. One of my tasks was to look at trust files from a bank in Guildford. I designed a form which brought out the salient features of a trust portfolio, but some portfolios seemed to me very odd. In the end I developed a formula for my reports: 'If the purpose of this trust is [*followed by the improbable objectives implied by the holdings*] then we have no suggestions for any changes in the portfolio; if there are other objectives we shall be pleased to advise.' In our little department my two colleagues were congenial but the work was not very exciting.

I now had a new daily train journey to work, from Isleworth Station to Waterloo, then by the Drain (the Waterloo and City Railway) to Bank and a short walk to the office. I soon made friends on the train, particularly Mr Pleeth, a petroleum chemist and an expert on alcohol as a fuel. There was also Joan Unwin who worked at the National Institute for Economic and Social Research and often travelled with us; what struck me were her neat and elegant Brevitt shoes in a summery sandy colour – it was as if for me they marked a final transition to peacetime. And on the train I met again some childhood acquaintances, in one case an ordinary youth who had suddenly metamorphosed into a surgeon. I joined the St Mary's Tennis Club where I had first learnt to play some ten years earlier, its pavilion unchanged and with the same warm, woody scent on summer afternoons. Also there was Mr Pleeth, a strong and fast player against whom I had many singles and doubles matches, most of which he won. There was also a contingent of pleasant young men training to be teachers at the nearby Borough Road College, led by one with the unlikely name of Guffog, who added verve to our games.

Visits to Aldwick

Back in the City and living in the family house at Isleworth, I continued to go down to Aldwick for many weekends, catching the familiar train at Victoria Station. If I was early I used to keep my seat by putting something on it together with a copy of the *Church Times*; mother quite liked to read this and no one would think of taking over a seat so obviously reserved by a clergyman. Arriving at Bognor after one of these journeys I was approached rather apologetically by a pleasant lady. She explained that she had often seen me on the train and wondered if I could help her. She lived with her parents in Gossamer Lane at Aldwick and they had an au pair girl who knew nobody locally and was finding life very dull. Would I be an angel and take this poor deprived girl out perhaps to a cinema, or indeed anything to give her a little social life. Ever helpful, I agreed that I would sacrifice some of my time in this noble cause, and it was arranged that I would call at their house the coming Saturday to take her out.

I duly arrived there to be faced with Sylvana Lindhé – half Italian and half Swedish, with the best parts of each. She was tall, blonde, slightly suntanned, really beautiful. At that moment I realised that she was something quite out of my league, but I fulfilled my social duty on that and several further occasions. My doubts were strengthened when she appeared driving (rather erratically) a large Austin Princess car lent to her for a few days by an undefined friend she had met in London. She was always very charming to me but our lives and interests clearly were going in very different directions. At a party I introduced her to Brian Johnson, a local estate agent, who took her over from there – to his enthusiastic pleasure and my relief. It was many years later that he and I next met at a local party and he thanked me warmly for introducing him to such a heavenly creature.

In 1949 Roy Chiverton invited me up to Cambridge to stay with him for the last weekend in February. I remember watching the rowing crews – white sweaters and coloured scarves and caps – launching their boats, and having dinner with him in hall. I enjoyed the visit very much, but somehow I could never see myself in those surroundings. Later I can remember having lunch with Dennis Wood at Queen Mary College, London, where by then he was devoting himself to research on olefines for his PhD; there was much talk of the mishaps of his fellow research students, of experimental rigs which instead of blowing things out, sucked them in and clogged everything up.

Life at Isleworth

But increasingly my life focussed on Isleworth, and still in pursuit of finding some congenial friends I joined the local Young Conservatives. This branch was run by a chap I can only recall as Peter who had been a Dakota pilot towards the end of the war. One of his tales was of the plan for an attack on an airfield on the coast of Burma. He was to fly one of about sixty Dakotas whose role was to drop paratroops who would gain control of the airfield so that the Dakotas (which would then have little fuel left) could land. What if the paratroops could not drive out the Japanese and gain control? Why then the Dakotas were to fly out to sea and all sixty were to ditch near some destroyers which would be waiting to pick up the crews – or at least the ones that survived. Luckily this operation was cancelled at the last moment, but even planning it showed the risks and expenditure of aircraft that could be seriously considered at that late stage of the war.

I think it was at the Young Conservatives that I met Jeanie-Puss, who lived not far from me and worked in an advertising agency in the West End. She had a charming face and a figure to match and I spent many cinema tickets and cups of coffee on her. My particular memory of her was one warm summer's afternoon when we caught the number 37 bus over to Richmond (no car at that time) and walked along the river to Petersham Meadows where we joined a throng of people on the grass enjoying the sun. As she lay sunning herself I made some gently teasing remark about her eyes being two beautiful limpid pools, but added 'Oh dear, some crows seem to have been walking round these pools.' At this unexpected twist she burst into laughter so warm and spontaneous that I suddenly saw her in quite a new light. We had many pleasant times together, but at a deeper level our interests did not really coincide and we drifted amicably apart.

As a more serious activity, I decided to read the whole of our multi-volume set of Gibbon's *Decline and Fall of the Roman Empire*. My memory tells me that I succeeded in doing this with the exception of one chapter on, I believe, the development of Roman law after Justinian. This I gave up after the first two pages. But reading the book made me a great admirer of Gibbon's style, with its felicity of expression, majestic flow and gentle irony.

The Territorial Army

Beneath this account of my return to living in Isleworth and working in the City for most of 1948 and 1949 there was another layer of activity which took up quite a lot of my spare time. When I was demobbed in January 1948 I still wished to keep some links with the army, and on 6 February 1948 I joined the Territorial Army as a lieutenant in one of its armoured regiments, the 3rd/4th County of London Yeomanry (3/4 CLY). There I found some twenty officers, including Cranley Onslow who had been a subaltern with me in the 7th Hussars, and Mike Harari who had been with me in 5 Troop at the RAC OCTU, together with about sixty men. 3/4 CLY had its headquarters and drill hall in leafy and affluent St John's Wood, London NW8. Our colonel was Lord Onslow who lived in Temple Court, a handsome house on the Onslow estate at Clandon near Guildford, and our second in command lived in a flat at the top of Clandon House, a National Trust property, which was nearby. The regiment's location in St John's Wood was quite good for recruiting the weekend soldiers required by the TA, but it had no tanks at its drill hall because a less suitable location for heavy tracked vehicles it would be hard to find. This group of around twenty officers and sixty other ranks provided a nucleus around which a full regiment could be formed without delay. Indeed we were to see this happen.

It is easy to forget that at this time the Cold War was gathering momentum, leading to the Berlin Blockade between June 1948 and May 1949. With a belligerent Soviet Union, war was very much in the air and the weekend soldiering of the TA had very serious overtones. My diary reminds me of how active we were, going out at weekends in trucks or Daimler armoured scout cars on various exercises in the greener areas around London, all aimed at keeping up our military skills. On some weekends we went down to the Onslow estate at Clandon where we drove Honey light tanks around a track marked out for us. On one occasion, going round a corner, there in front of me suspended from a branch of a tree was a plump trooper swept out of the turret of the tank in front. On some of these weekends I and another subaltern drove down in a Daimler scout car. Coming back in the evening it felt rather strange driving round Hyde Park Corner all equipped as if for battle, but surrounded by peaceful red London buses and interested passengers.

On one weekend we went down to the Lulworth ranges in Dorset for firing practice, using tanks maintained by the range staff who were always accompanied by their bull terrier. We all fired our allocation of rounds for the Comet's 77 mm gun and enjoyed the chance to use tanks in their proper role of delivering firepower. It was there that we were given a brief demonstration on night vision; we went into a room which was then plunged into darkness except for a light source so faint that initially it was entirely imperceptible; we were told that as visual purple accumulated in our eyes we would find our night vision improving, and sure enough after several minutes we began to perceive faint images thrown by the light source. It was a very effective demonstration and I have retained a deep respect for visual purple ever since.

A visit to the Royal Aircraft Establishment at Farnborough took up another weekend. This was aimed at strengthening inter-service understanding, and for this we were all given a flight, some twenty at a time, in a transport aircraft. This plane was entirely empty; there were no seats and we all sat on the floor, sliding towards the rear as we took off. Fortunately none of us had heard the dictum that the important thing about flying was knowing how to crash safely. We also saw a De Havilland Vampire practice a belly landing on a large rubber mat; it was flown by a naval test pilot and we were told that his heart was thrown forward by some alarming amount due to the sharp deceleration every time he landed.

On another weekend a small group of us went on an Aerial Photographic Interpretation course at Medmenham (close to where I had been at school at Colet Court in 1940). There we were given a day of concentrated instruction and then set to practise interpreting wonderfully detailed, and in effect three-dimensional, aerial photos – 'vertical pinpoints' – of northern France taken by Allied reconnaissance aircraft at the time of the invasion in 1944. We soon learned the rudiments of interpretation, picking out bomb damage, defences and one particular give-away of German army headquarters, the figure-of-eight riding tracks used for exercising officers' horses. We were each given a selection of such photos to take away with us for practice. These simple skills had been important in the war, when such photos were often taken on one day and delivered to front-line units the next; in our battlefield tour of Operation Goodwood in Normandy we had been told that such was the dust and smoke that the colonel of one tank regiment had to go on foot using such photos to lead his regiment forward. One part of the Medmenham unit at that time was strictly secret. We later learned that there the aerial photos of Russia taken by the Luftwaffe were being examined for any information which might be useful to us in the developing Cold War.

The culmination of all this activity was the annual two-week summer camp. As the summer of 1949 drew nearer, with Berlin blockaded and the air bridge supplying the city in full swing (it peaked at 800 flights per day), the government decided that the Territorial Army was to be made up to full strength for the summer camp. Although the Russians called off their unsuccessful Blockade in May the situation was still tense and these arrangements went ahead, so that our fortnight's camp at the large training area of Thetford/Dereham in Suffolk found the regiment suddenly made up to full strength by officers and men, many of them with battle experience, called back from civil life together with a full complement of Comet tanks. Then for a fortnight we practiced tank tactics at troop and squadron level

Out of these days of training, two incidents stay in my memory. The first was when we were starting up early in the morning with orders to move off at a given time. The driver of my tank then reported that the petrol filter had leaked during the night and the bottom of the tank was flooded with petrol. We had to move off shortly and I reasoned that as the air intake for the engine compartment, which was quite a blast, could be directed through the driver's compartment and the fighting compartment (the turret), this should evaporate the excess petrol quite quickly – provided it did not catch fire. I told the driver to get into his seat, and stationed two other crew members on the outside of the tank to pull him out quickly if it did catch fire. I then told him to start up. The engine roared into life and out of the back of the tank came a great plume of petrol vapour stretching for a couple of hundred yards, turning our view of the countryside into a wobbling mirage. There were a few backfires from the engine but luckily nothing to set the whole lot off. After only a couple of minutes the driver reported that all the petrol had gone, so the rest of us mounted and we were off. It was an episode not without its worrying moments, given my own experience of early-morning petrol fires. Back on the tank park one evening, a tank did catch fire as it was being refuelled. I remarked on this to one wartime subaltern, but he replied: 'I only turn round if there are two tanks on fire.' The second incident was towards the end of our fortnight when all the sixty tanks in the regiment were set out in parade formation in a shallow valley. It was an impressive sight, and with all their engines rumbling, it gave a real sense of the weight and power of an armoured regiment.

11

Student Days at LSE 1949–52

Thoughts of University

One day in the office Peter Raleigh suggested that I should think of going to a university as he felt it would suit me. This, combined with my experience at the College of the Rhine Army in Gottingen, awoke new prospects in my mind and I began to make enquiries. The nearest and most obvious place was the London School of Economics; I learned that as an ex-serviceman I could be admitted if I passed the Forces Special Entry Exam (a highly diluted version of Higher School Certificate, which was the A level of its day). I now looked around to find evening classes as preparation for this exam. In Hounslow I found Major Drake-Brockman's tutorial establishment where I took several short and rather elementary courses, although what sticks in my mind is the Major's analysis of the advantages of the old-fashioned conventionally shaped wooden barrel over the modern cylindrical steel variety (from standing on end, the wooden barrel could be easily rocked over onto its bowed side; there it could be easily rolled and turned in any direction, and it could be rocked back on to its end again; none of these could be done with its steel counterpart). I also went to a course at Isleworth Polytechnic (now West Thames College) housed in Spring Grove House, Sir Joseph Banks' fine mansion which was only a few hundred yards from our house. I had never been into it before although as a child I had passed it many times. (Walking past it one summer afternoon, a cricket match was going on in front of the mansion and as I watched the bowler took a wicket, breaking a stump in two; the wicketkeeper held the two pieces up in the air in triumph to show the onlookers.) In retrospect, my preparations for Forces Special Entry were ill-organised and rather feeble, but in due course I sat the exam and was notified in December 1948 that I had passed and had become a matriculated student.

I now had to apply to LSE for entry and my diary reminded me that my application form had to be in by 23 February 1949; it required two references and I wrote to Walter Oakeshott (who had been High Master of St Paul's when I was there but was now headmaster of Winchester) who agreed to be one, while the other was the Earl of Onslow who was my colonel in the 3rd/4th County of London Yeomanry. Passing Forces Special Entry was regarded by LSE, quite rightly, as a very moderate achievement and I knew I would have to take the School's entrance examination and this required more academic preparation on my part. The only economics I had done was in the four week demob course at Gottingen; it was already January 1949 and with the entrance exam for LSE coming up on 21 April I did not have much time. Looking for a tutor, I found Michael Kaser who lived in Richmond, was then at the Foreign Office and much later was to be a professor at St Antony's College, Oxford. As a good Cambridge economist he advised me to buy Marshall's *Principles of Economics* (which I did on 27 January) ready for our first meeting which was in his room at the Foreign Office on 3 February. I then had a series of very useful sessions with him, sometimes at the FO, sometimes at his home in Richmond. I also felt that my French required help and I found Michel Prot, a student from France who lived locally and was taking some educational course in London. The work with him that I remember was in spoken French; he had a book of sermons by the seventeenth-century Bishop Bossuet, renowned as an orator and stylist, and I would read these aloud, with helpful corrections from him. The bishop's sentences (ordered, lucid, magnificent) and his style (broad, massive, luminous) – six epithets used by Lytton Strachey in his *Landmarks in French Literature* – were such that it was hard not to recite his sermons in a suitably solemn and episcopal voice, and when I was trying to speak French this soon became a habit. In an oral exam, commonplace questions answered in imperfect French but in a sonorous and stately manner would have caused some surprise. My LSE exam number arrived on 15 April and on 29 April I sat the entrance exam, 10.00 to 5.30, at the Imperial Institute in west London. On 14 June I was delighted and relieved to receive a letter saying that I had passed and been accepted for the BSc Econ degree, but with the condition that, since

I did not have any A levels, I would have to show satisfactory progress in my first year to allow me to move on and complete the degree. Then on 6 July I noted in my diary that I had posted to LSE my completed registration form, two photos of myself, proof that I had passed Forces Special Entry and had therefore matriculated, and a fee of 1 guinea. In due course I was called for an interview at the School with David Solomons, Reader in Accounting, at which we discussed the particular courses I would be taking; looking back, I still was not at all clear about the nature of most of these courses. My final piece of preparation, noted in my diary for 15 August 1949, was to start reading Boulding, then the recommended first-year economics textbook. And so it was that on 2 September 1949, after a year and a half back in the City, I left Gerald Hodgson & Co – with much goodwill on both sides – to go to university, inspired by the advice of Peter Raleigh.

LSE

There were only a few weeks before term began when through the post came a document from the School announcing that the BSc Econ degree had been reformed and setting out the new structure. In my mind's eye I can still see clearly this sheet of paper; the subjects I would be studying suddenly leapt into focus, their very names now shone with thrilling intellectual promise. Part I then covered the first two years of the three year degree course and the subjects taken by all of us under this new structure were:

> Principles of Economics
> Applied Economics
> Political History
> Economic History
> Elements of Government
> History of Political Ideas
> Elementary Statistical Methods and Sources

together with two alternative subjects from a list of ten from which I was to choose:

193

Logic and Scientific Method
Elements of English Law

I can remember my sense of elation at the prospect of studying all these subjects, but at this stage I was quite unaware of just how demanding it was going to be.

Then on Wednesday 5 October 1949 term started and with a frisson of nervous excitement I made my way through LSE's arched main doorway in Houghton Street into an entrance hall buzzing with other Freshers. I found myself surrounded by people of around my own age, who were eager for endless discussion over endless cups of coffee. It is difficult to convey the excited anticipation that all of us felt; the School then, as later, bubbled with intellectual vitality.

The School at that time really consisted of just one building, later known as the Old Building; the library took up a considerable portion of this with everything else crammed into the remainder, and despite much smaller numbers than later, it was all very crowded. There were many things we had to do in those first few days: registration, learning our way around the School's rabbit warren of corridors, getting our timetables of lectures and classes, finding the rooms in which they would be held. At the same time we were making our first tentative friendships and fending off or joining student societies which were trying hard to recruit new members. Altogether they were a rather frantic first few days, but soon all of us had settled down when on the following Monday teaching began and we entered the more regular pattern of life in term-time. For me this included my daily journey to LSE, the largest part of which was the same as when I was working on the London Stock Exchange (also with the initials LSE) – the train from Isleworth Station to Waterloo, but then instead of the Drain to the City, I now walked across Waterloo Bridge and up Aldwych to the School in Houghton Street (incidentally, not an easy name if you were one of the many overseas students).

There must have been something over 300 undergraduates in my year, and 200 of them were, like me, taking the revised BSc Econ degree and in the first two years taking most of the same Part I courses. This gave us a certain community of interest. The rest were doing other degrees such as law and history and we mixed rather less with them. One group were those doing sociology, who seemed to me nicely spoken young ladies preparing themselves rather elegantly to do social work amongst the disadvantaged. Some of these added tone to the circle in which I found my friends.

I soon became aware that the London School of Economics was an institution with a worldwide reputation for scholarship but a British reputation of being a hotbed of Harold Laski and socialism. Certainly when I mentioned that I was at LSE there were sometimes raised eyebrows, pursed lips and a sharp intake of breath. But while the active student radicals – Communists, Leninists, Trotskyites, far left-wing socialists and other varieties – were the most vocal and most noticed, they were a very much a minority. Going to only a few meetings of the Students' Union and watching their machinations provided me with some education in practical politics. There, they regularly tabled motions criticising the government and supporting the Soviet Union and its various front organisations. Their endless points of order made typical union meetings so tedious that before long only the few active radicals would remain at the meeting and their motions were then easily passed in the name of the whole Students' Union, to make headlines the next morning which would outrage so many older readers. I found no pleasure in these meetings and I soon ceased to attend them.

It was only towards the end of my first year that I discovered that most of my fellow students were on local authority grants, which I had never even heard of, and that I too would be eligible for one. I had been able to attend the School only because my father agreed to pay the bills on 20 Avenue Road and provide me with just enough – in fact about £3 per week – to live on (of course, the pounds were much larger in those days). I was duly awarded a local authority grant for my second and third years, and this relieved my father of part of the expense of supporting me.

Names, Faces and Occasions

The two fellow students that I was closest to were Maurice Peston and Jack Pulman. Maurice I must have met in my first term because his telephone number – CLIssold 1499 – is noted at the end of my diary for 1949. Jack Pulman I met somewhat later and one rather tenuous link between us was that we had both served in cavalry/tank regiments – he had been in the

4th/7th Dragoon Guards. As well as much discussion of academic work, which was the main focus for all three of us, we founded the Rationalist Society which aimed at rational and unbiassed discussion of, well, everything really. A number of like-minded friends joined and the Students' Union even gave us space on an official noticeboard to advertise our activities. Unfortunately my memories of exactly what we discussed have faded away. Maurice Peston in due course was to become a professor of economics at Queen Mary College and later still Lord Peston, while Jack Pulman reached a peak in quite a different field. He became a very successful writer and adapter of works for television and wrote, amongst many other things, the screenplay for the highly regarded television series *I, Claudius*; he died at a sadly early age.

I was once having coffee with Maurice and two girls, Anne Hetherington (who dressed unusually well for a student, favouring checks by Burberry – 'a distinctive luxury brand with distinctive British sensibility') and Ruth Mansur (who was Turkish and very mature) in the tiny coffee shop, next to the main entrance to the School, known to us as Smokey Joe's (though I think that its real name at that time was Wright's Bar). Ruth suddenly said to me 'Roger, you know you don't have to win every argument; why not try just being polite and friendly?' This was something of a surprise but on consideration it seemed good advice and I took it to heart; but perhaps not sufficiently so because much later, Anne Robbins, Lionel Robbins' daughter, told me that she had regarded myself and Maurice as the two most arrogant and argumentative students she had ever met. I would like to think that she was unduly sensitive, but she may well have been right; Maurice and I were both reflecting growing confidence in our intellectual abilities and could not resist exercising them.

Over the following three years there were a multitude of other students in our year with whom I came in regular contact and for quite a number I can still remember a face and a name, even some trivial incident. I used to sit next to Jackie Clarke in our demography lectures given by David Glass; she was lively company and lent me a biro with ink of a memorably strong cyclamen colour which has left its unmistakeable traces in my records. Jill Crewdson I remember because she arranged a play-reading at her home in Kensington where I was given the role of a mathematician, speaking in a clipped and precise voice. Very different from the rest of us was Margot Naylor who took the BCom in her fifties and was running a small hotel in west London where several of us were invited to drinks parties; she was a very kind and mature figure on the outskirts of our circle and was later to become a noted financial journalist. Hilda Jefferson was a very pleasant companion and we drank much coffee together; I was to see her and her husband at reunion meetings and later found that they were friends of Dennis Wood whom I had known from our days at Aldwick. Edward Horesh I knew at Colet Court (while we were evacuated he received a letter addressed to Mr Housh and this provided a convenient nickname) but he was also the first person I spoke to in LSE's entrance hall on my very first day, together with Tony Isaacs who was to graduate a year later than us, the same year as Ron Higgins who even as an undergraduate was becoming world-weary and needing a walking stick to help him through life. As I now look through a list of the Class of 1952, most names just drift past me, but some suddenly and clearly summon up a face: Graham Bindon, Gerry Egerer, Helen Karger, David Philips, Monty Tubb and a dozen others; but in what particular circumstances I knew most of them I can no longer recall. All of these were in my own year, and it was with them that I had most in common; but in the year ahead of us (the Class of 1951 whom, when we were Freshers, we respected as veterans of learning and survivors of exams) there are also some names which summon up faces: Neville Beale, Gordon Downey and Graeme Nichols, all of whom I was to come across later in life. In addition to these there were a surprising number whom I didn't know then but were later to become colleagues at the School: Chris Archibald, Percy Cohen, Bernard Corry, Leonard Joy, Jack Kitchen and Kurt Klappholz. All of these helped to form the bustling crowd of students who were a part of my three undergraduate years at the School.

Academic Work

The memories of many ex-LSE students seem to focus on their activities in the Students' Union and its meetings, on the gyrations of the School's political societies, on the amateur journalism of *Beaver* and the *Clare Market Review*, on somewhat alcoholic jollifications in halls of residence and the Three Tuns, and on the Saturday night 'hops' in the refectory. But I had already tasted enough adolescent freedom and none of these activities had any appeal for me. Early on I discovered that I enjoyed academic work and found it very rewarding; increasingly I developed an ambition to do well. However, I found it tricky to keep work on my nine different Part I subjects in balance and to help with this I started keeping a work diary, subject by subject, day by day, to the nearest quarter of an hour, recording all my effective academic work; it was purely for my own eyes and was honest and unbiassed. But what it mainly revealed was that after some ten hours a week of lectures and classes I was only doing about another twelve hours of reading and writing essays. Too much time was being spent on discussions over coffee, which were stimulating but did not deliver the work that courses required. Instinctively I felt that well-organised hard work was quite a good substitute for brains and that success in academic work was therefore going to require a greater and more systematic effort on my part. I began consciously to organise my time more effectively and to drive up my hours of academic work; they were well up by the end of my first year but I think it was not until sometime in my second year that they reached a sustainable average of about thirty five hours a week. This proved to be my ceiling and it seemed to me quite a heavy academic load. It had required real self-discipline and the harsh truthfulness of my work diary, but this same work diary gave great encouragement by showing how my hours of effective academic work were cumulating over time.

Lectures (in which I took rough notes which I wrote up later) and classes gave structure to our daily lives. The main lecture courses in our first two years had large audiences and were held in the Old Theatre; there I favoured a seat in the middle of the front row of the balcony. My memory of these lectures has been overlaid by many later ones so that only some highlights remain. Radomysler's lectures on economics were excellent and we began to catch up with the year ahead. I particularly remember Harold Laski lecturing on government (it must have been in the last year before he died); he was a charismatic lecturer and on the podium seemed to us to be a physically towering figure although he was in fact quite short. His charisma never led me to have any sympathy with his left wing views. Amongst other lectures we had in the Old Theatre was a series by Sir Arnold Plant on the economics of industry; in talking about the problems of the cotton industry he alluded to its lack of technical progress quoting, with a sly look at his audience, 'We must get rid of this redundant old plant' – a well-worn joke, but new to us and we all enjoyed it. I also remember a lecture on geography by Dudley Stamp in which he illustrated the daily rainfall pattern in the tropics by slowly raising a carafe of water, emulating slow evaporation in the hot mornings, and then pouring it down into a glass showing the ensuing rainfall in the afternoon. Next to me on the balcony of the Old Theatre was often a friend who, in writing his lecture notes, would get to the bottom of the page, turn the paper through 90 degrees and then write another side of notes across the first lot. The curious thing was that both sets were quite legible.

Smaller lectures were held in various rooms and of these I remember chiefly our lectures by Karl Popper (held in an underground room) on logic and scientific method. He introduced us, amongst many other things, to the distinction between the mind seen as a bucket to be filled up with information and the mind seen as a tool for solving problems, and to the difference between 'knowledge that' and 'knowledge how'. One oddity in his delivery was that he always pronounced 'subtraction' as 'substraction'. I also remember a tale that Popper told us in one of his more informal moments. When he was a young philosopher in Vienna he was a member of an intellectual circle which included Arnold Schoenberg. They used to hold evening meetings in each other's apartments and one of these meetings, to hear a new piece of music by Schoenberg, was held in an apartment on a fourth floor accessed by a very small lift. Schoenberg insisted that his piece required a double bass and after a great struggle this instrument was got into the lift, taken up and struggled out again. Then in Schoenberg's composition the expectant audience heard it play one solitary note. Popper was much amused by such demanding musical integrity.

All these lecture courses were complemented by classes of some twelve students taken by a member of the teaching staff (I do not recall any being taken by postgraduate students). These were normally held once a week, providing further systematic discussion of topics raised in the lectures and dealing with our various difficulties. In addition class teachers set essays as part of the programme of class work. These lectures and classes were supplemented by our own reading and note-taking on books and articles recommended by our lecturers.

Finally, we each had a tutor, usually a different one each year. However, over my three years I had only two, first Loudon Ryan who was very helpful on micro-theory (he was particularly keen on oligopoly); he once confided to me that his ambition was to own a Morris Minor pick-up and a pleasant house. Since he later became Governor of the Irish Central Bank I guess that he comfortably exceeded these modest early ambitions. The second was Ralph Turvey, at that time the youngest Reader in Economics by far. He was just about my own age but again was very helpful. He also took some of our economic theory classes, and Maurice and I devoted some time to producing particularly twisty questions in unsuccessful efforts to catch him out. Both of my tutors required essays in addition to those done as part of class work. Together all of these – lectures, classes, essays, your own reading and help from your tutor – formed a balanced and effective teaching structure, and these were the dominating features of my student life at the School. A dull, nerdy and pedestrian existence? Not in the least; every subject I was studying was revealing new vistas, new insights and demanding active thinking. To me it was an enthralling and challenging engagement with a vast new intellectual world and my own feeling of growing understanding gave me a tremendous sense of satisfaction. And while work came first, even when I was doing my maximum of 35 hours a week there remained many hours for conversation with friends over coffee or lunch in the refectory and other necessarily inexpensive pleasures. To me it was student life at its best – a wonderful combination of freedom and self-discipline, of the serious and the lighthearted.

Our first year was not without incident; the revised BSc Econ had teething problems and our worries reached the ear of Lionel Robbins who called a meeting in the Old Theatre for all first year students to hear our complaints. In the Senior Common Room many years later Lionel teased me by maintaining that I had been a ringleader of this early student revolt, as he called it, and quoted me – correctly – as standing up at the meeting and saying: 'It's not that we don't want to work, it's that we don't know what work we should be doing.' The problems were quickly resolved and our discontents died away.

At the end of the first year we had exams, at that time called Collections. My increased work paid off and I passed all of them, which allowed me to go on to the second and third years of the BSc Econ. However, these were not as important as the second year exams, then called Part I, the results of which helped to determine the class of degree. These exams also I managed to pass; indeed to my surprise I won the Allyn Young Prize, which came in the form of £10 worth of books, for the best performance in the economics and statistics papers. The Director of the School at this time was Sir Alexander Carr-Saunders – on the outside vulture-faced and forbidding but on later and closer acquaintance, cultivated and kindly. I teased my friends by saying that I was going to ask for his collected works as my prize; in fact that amount of money allowed me to choose Ricardo's *Principles of Political Economy*, Harrod's *Life of Keynes*, one or two LSE reprints and the two-volume *Shorter Oxford English Dictionary* which I continue to use. In due course I was called to the Director's office where I received from him my chosen books, each with a neat coat of arms in gold stamped on the cover and the prize inscription on the inside, together with some of his own encouraging words.

It must have been in our second year that I and some others were asked to be paid interviewers in some fieldwork for a research project. Using questionnaires I had to interview six specific persons, names and addresses supplied, some on their saving habits and some on other topics which I cannot recall. In my mind sticks the name of Miss Montmorency with what seemed a very upmarket address in Putney. In my mind's eye I could see an elegant and charming young woman with exotically interesting saving habits. When I got there Miss Montmorency had been transformed into a Mrs, and I interviewed her in a tall and gloomy kitchen festooned with wet nappies; I cannot remember her saving habits but they were certainly not exotic. Only later did we discover that the researchers were not interested in saving or any other topics; what they were interested in was our performance relative to that of professional interviewers. A very different extramural activity was a student weekend at Cumberland Lodge in Windsor Great Park, and going down there by rail in a group with Martin Wight from the International Relations Department. He was adored by his students but to me he was a very pleasant man who seemed rather too soft-left. What we discussed over that weekend I cannot remember, but I am sure it was anxiously worthy.

I come from a hoarding family and up in our loft I recently uncovered a box containing some of my notes and essays written while I was an undergraduate at the School. This included over 100 sides in my then small neat writing (long since degraded) of notes on Radomysler's lectures on economics and a selection of class and tutorial essays. For Arthur John there was a class essay of four and a half sides (which at 450–500 words per page amounted to about 2000 words) on 'How far is it true to say that a "world economy" existed in the third quarter of the nineteenth century?' for which I got a B. An essay of six sides for Jack Wiseman on 'Cost, price

and profit under imperfect competition' was graded B+/A–. On five sides
I accounted for the failure of the 1848 revolution in Germany for Matthew
Anderson; only B and the comment that it was quite good but unoriginal
(!). In the history of political ideas I produced five sides comparing the
Greek and Roman ideas of law for John Watkins who gave me B++ and
commented that it was a good clear analysis with the significant factors
kept continuously in view, adding a further 23 lines of detailed points –
really conscientious marking. For John Watkins again, this time for
government, I produced four sides on the origins and consequences of
centralisation in France; B++. For Mr De Smith only two sides on the
concept of *mens rea* in criminal law, awarded a B. This rather random
selection of essays amounted to 71 sides of essays in economics, and 61
sides of essays on other subjects. The former includes a third year essay on
demand theory and rationing for Ralph Turvey which covered eleven and
a half pages plus three pages of very neat diagrams; I can remember
discussing it with him, but there is no mark on it – perhaps after ploughing
through it he was too exhausted to write one down. Further rummaging
in our loft turned some 70 pages of notes and class essays on Popper's
course on logic (some of it looking quite formidable) and about four times
that amount of third year notes on macro and monetary theory. The overall
impression given by this selection is that I was doing quite a lot of work.
In my second year at the School, with work becoming ever more demanding,
it became clear to me that I could no longer afford the time required by
the Territorial Army and after more than three enjoyable years I felt I had
to resign.

Finals – and After

When we moved into our third years of the BSc Econ our courses became
more concentrated and specialised. For our particular group of about twelve
students doing Economics Analytical and Descriptive (always referred to
as A & D, the specialist economics group) they were:

> History of Economic Thought
> Economic Theory
> Applied Economics

One from a list of three alternative subjects
(Public Finance was my choice)
And in Finals there was an essay on
one of the above fields.

Our classes in economic theory were then taken by Professor Lionel Robbins, head of the Economics Department; he was tall, distinguished and an impressive speaker who for emphasis sometimes adopted a good-humoured orotund style which was eminently imitable. He conducted these classes in his large study, lounging on a sofa, comfortable but alert, while we sat on chairs in a semicircle round the room. One class topic I remember particularly. It was on money, and Robbins began by pointing out that the names of most coins were in fact weights of some monetary metal – pound was an example. Suddenly my years of interest in coins paid off. I cautiously pointed out that many coins in fact got their names in rather different ways: guinea (from the source of the gold – Guinea in Africa) and thaler/dollar (from the source of the silver – Joachimsthal in Bohemia); florin, crown, escudo (taking their names from the emblem on the coin); and there were also groat, shilling, franc, ducat, denarius, drachma... My list of exceptions got longer and longer while Robbins (who fortunately had a nice sense of humour) tried hard to suppress his amusement as his leading assertion was steadily demolished.

There was so much going on at the School that we seldom had occasion to visit other colleges, but on one occasion Maurice and I went up to University College to hear a lecture by Tarski, a noted Polish logician favourably mentioned by Popper in his lectures, and by then at an American university. The medium-sized lecture room was full and onto the podium came Tarski – dressed in a very smart suit, looking very American – together with the chairman. A few words of introduction, then Tarski stepped up to the lectern, took a quick look at the audience, picked up a piece of chalk, turned to the blackboard and wrote on it: 0 1 2 3. He turned back to the audience and began: 'Consider the number series zero, one, two, three.' Immediately in the middle of the front row a very short Middle European man stood up and said loudly: 'Zero iss not a nomber.' There was a moment of frozen silence; Tarski turned to the blackboard, rubbed out the zero and calmly began again: 'Consider the number series one, two, three...' The rest of the lecture I cannot remember, but obviously I paid attention because in my cache of undergraduate work I found five and a half sides of notes on this lecture which was entitled: 'Meta-mathematics, the general theory of mathematical science'. Much of it consists of symbolic mathematical logic (although I record Tarski as saying that symbolism was a very superficial part of logic) before going on to completeness and decidability. Tough but interesting. Maurice remembers going up to him, I think with me, after the lecture and saying that we came because Popper had told us what a great man he was. He was more than pleased. I have faint memories of Maurice and myself going to a lecture by Professor Joad, a popular philosopher and member of the BBC's *Brains Trust*. I feel we were not impressed.

In our final year, to strengthen our work in economics, Maurice, Jack Pulman and I used to spend Wednesday afternoons (kept free from lectures and classes to allow other students to play games) in a classroom going through Economics Finals papers. While this was very helpful, it could also be rather worrying, as one of us might suddenly see what a question was getting at and start suggesting how it might be answered while the other two were still groping in the dark. Luckily such flashes of insight were fairly evenly spread between us. As we worked together in this way I can remember Jack, who was more interested in politics than Maurice and myself, wondering whether he should have specialised in government rather in economics.

Our third year was at last drawing to a close and Final Exams loomed over us. Even though we were by then seasoned examinees, these were particularly stressful because of their importance for our class of degree. They will have started like all the earlier ones: waiting outside the examination hall, butterflies in the stomach, cold sweaty palms and muted nervous conversation; then ranks of students spaced out at desks, each with a green covered answer book in front of them together with the question paper; 'You may now begin' from the invigilator; then reading the paper through twice to get its full flavour before choosing the first of four questions to answer and setting out rough notes for it; a palpable decline in tension as the whole room of silent students, heads down, now geared their nervous energy to writing their answers; then 'Your time is up, please stop writing'; flooding out of the examination hall, relieved and anxious to hear how your friends had found the paper, but not in too much detail because at that moment you did not want to be told that you had missed some vital aspect in Question 5; finally leaving the strains of this examination behind and briefly relaxing before final preparation for the next paper. I still have the Economic Theory paper that we sat in Finals. We had to answer four questions out of twelve and I had marked three of these: on the demand curve, on saving and investment, and on wage cuts and employment. The fourth one evidently involved Say's Law, because I have an uncomfortable memory that Say's name escaped me at the crucial moment and I had to leave a blank and hope that the examiner would see that the rest of the analysis was correct and that it had to be Say's Law.

Then there was the long wait until the results came out, during which there were processes of which we knew nothing: initial markings, reconciliation, completion of the mark frame and the final examiners' meeting to decide degree classification. At last the results were pinned up on a board on the ground floor of the Old Building and there was a nervous rush to see how we – the Class of 1952 – had all done; Maurice and I both got Firsts and Jack got an Upper Second. All that effort and work had been worthwhile; there was vast relief and mutual congratulation. There was also an undercurrent of sadness, for our time as undergraduates at the School was now over, three years which had seen us all change and develop in ways we could never have foreseen, three years which we would never forget.

It is hard to put into words the importance to me of these three years at the School. It was a strange mixture of a wonderful student world free of adult responsibilities, and a tough intellectual world, stimulating but very demanding, which I know enhanced my understanding and intellectual effectiveness in ways which for me were truly life changing.

* * *

I have made no mention of my parents over these years, mainly because they were simply always there; they were providing me with a home at 20 Avenue Road and another at Aldwick, now their own permanent home, where I was always welcome when I came down for a break. They gave a warm atmosphere of support as well as modest but vital financial help when I needed it, but both of them had artistic backgrounds and never had anything to do with universities. I cannot recall any occasion when we discussed what I was studying at the School, but we had plenty of family and other topics to talk about and communication was never a problem. They just accepted that I seemed to be doing something worthwhile and they found their pleasure in my pleasure at what I had accomplished. Many years later my mother remarked teasingly 'He can't be doing anything very important, after all, he's just our Roger.'

12

Life at LSE in the 1950s

Onto the Staff

I cannot now remember the circumstances in which I was offered a one year assistant lectureship at the School, but Lionel Robbins must have been responsible. I still have the two letters from the Director (Sir Alexander Carr-Saunders) that I received in August 1952, the first rather official and offering me a one year assistant lectureship, the second a very kind one congratulating me on getting a First and on being appointed an assistant lecturer in economics for 1952–53. Inwardly I felt a wonderful glow of achievement. Then it was home to Aldwick to relax and forget about work for a while. A few weeks later I had a letter from Maurice Peston, making his final preparations to go to Princeton, to which he had won a University Fellowship; his luggage had been collected by Cunard, but 'I cannot remember whether I locked one of the suitcases. Don't laugh!' He then went on to give me a list of books he was leaving for me in David Knox's room, some of which 'you can present to any of your students next year who appear to be poor and deserving'.

A few weeks, and then in October 1952 the academic year began again. There was the usual jostling crowd, second and third year students greeting their friends after the long summer vacation and excited at moving up a year, new students – freshers – trying to find the Registry or the Refectory and slightly bewildered just as we had been three years before. But there were none of the familiar faces of my year; all had moved on and although I would meet a few of them later as visitors to the School or at the ten-yearly Class reunions, most I would never see again. But the School itself was the same as ever; as I entered it now

I had a frisson of pride and pleasure – for me a new life was about to begin.

As a temporary assistant lecturer I had, not quite a room of my own, but one which I shared with a congenial young lawyer named Gunther Treitel; there I could hang my coat, keep some of my books, see my students and work in peace. I was now a member of the Senior Common Room, newly built and handsome with its barrel-vaulted ceiling, and in the winter a large open fire which made it very comfortable. As you entered the Common Room, you were served by a pleasant waitress who would greet each of us by name and knew just how we liked our tea or coffee; to the left of the fireplace Lionel Robbins could usually be found, chatting with other members of the Economics Department, while around in the easy chairs would be many faces that were already familiar from lectures or classes. In the Common Room the atmosphere was relaxed and first names were the rule (the one exception being Sir Alexander Carr-Saunders who was always addressed as Director). However I could not help feeling that it would be presumptuous for me as the most junior member to address Lionel Robbins as Lionel. Instead I ensured that my conversations in his circle were carefully crafted to avoid any need for his first name; after a few years this inhibition gradually faded away. Towards the end of the Michaelmas term Lionel Robbins invited Maurice and myself to dinner at his home in Hampstead. Originally this was to have been on Saturday 6 December, but the great London fog of 1952 came down on the Friday and our dinner was postponed until Sunday 14 December.

Unfortunately I cannot remember anything about this occasion, but I can remember the fog and its three successors (December 1956, January 1959 and December 1962) which were the last examples of what Dickens had termed 'a London particular', before clean air legislation brought them to an end. Their most striking feature was the blanket of silence they laid over London and the possibility of getting lost even in what should have been familiar places. This led most people to stay at home so that suburban areas seemed almost uninhabited as well as silent. Later when I had my first car I ventured out in one of these fogs only to find that the glow-back from the fog meant that headlights were worse than useless, and I can recall having to get out and search for the kerb to find where I was on the road. There were many instances of buses being able to move only if they had someone on foot to lead them. The railways also were greatly affected and

I can remember hearing the bang of the small explosive capsules they laid on the line behind trains brought to a halt to warn following trains that there was a hazard ahead of them. When these fogs came down, it was a pleasure to be safe and comfortable at home with books and the BBC for company.

Move now to the middle of 1953; I had greatly enjoyed my first year teaching at the School and I have a copy of my letter of application for a (non-temporary) assistant lectureship in Economics as advertised in *The Times*. According to the list of the Selection Committee, which I still have, I was interviewed on 18 June 1953 by the Director, and professors Robbins, Phelps-Brown, Edwards, Plant, Baxter, Paish, Sayers and Ashton. I was then offered an assistant lectureship in Economics which I eagerly accepted. A fortnight earlier London had celebrated the Coronation, but of this I have only one memory: it caused the lamp-posts in Aldwych to blossom out in a pleasantly festive shade of pale blue.

Academic Activity

Since my interests inclined towards monetary economics and financial institutions, I was attached to the Money and Banking group under Professor Richard Sayers which at that time included Stewart Wilson and Alan Day. Richard himself was mainly a historian of money and banking and was the most stiff and withdrawn of all my colleagues – not an easy person to get to know. However I shall have more, and more sympathetic, things to say about him later on.

My first year teaching programme was fairly light, consisting of five first year Economics class groups, each of which met weekly, and being tutor to perhaps a dozen first year students, which meant seeing them generally twice a term and marking their essays. I now had to prepare for my class teaching which was due to start shortly; from my own experience at the School I had a clear idea of how to organise these classes, and after some consultation with the lecturer I soon had a programme of class topics ready. I then had to give some thought on how best to put these topics across to students and the problems they were likely to have. Again, having been through these same classes as a student was a great help. At that time my own way of running them was to give two students each the task of introducing that week's topic in the form of an essay (which they had to be prepared to speak from, rather than read out). At the class I would choose one to open and the other to comment and raise issues. I then had to encourage participation in the discussion by the other students – not always easy, and requiring a mixture of encouragement and pressure. At the end of the class I collected and marked the two essays. I felt that my classes went quite well and that I was a reasonably competent teacher.

At each class I had to tick off on the class register the names of those present and take some action on the habitual absentees. This was of more importance than it might seem; most of our students at that time were on local authority grants and since there was no check on attendance at lectures, class attendance was the only evidence the School could offer that they were actually present and doing some academic work. At the end of term I had to enter on the register my assessment of each student's performance in class together with their essay marks, and return it to the registry. The same process was done by class teachers in each of their subjects and all these results then went onto a student's record card. I would be sent these record cards for my own tutees and could discuss with them any problems which might be emerging. At the end of the academic year such a record card – if properly filled in – would give a reasonable overview of a student's progress, and material on which to base future references. Class teaching of this kind was a major component of the teaching duties of all junior members of the Economics Department. In due course I was also given second or third year classes and later still, Master's course classes and seminars. In addition one would be allocated a lecture course; in my case after two years or so I was given responsibility for a macro-economics course. This meant thinking carefully about how the subject could best be developed for that particular audience, preparing the lectures and organising the reading list. I greatly enjoyed all this teaching and I found it very rewarding to see the sudden dawning of comprehension as I delivered yet another example or analogy to help students with one of the more difficult bits of analysis.

Apart from teaching within the Department several of us had to do some economics teaching for other Departments; in my case this consisted of trying to bridge the yawning gulf between micro-economics and the young ladies in their first year reading sociology. Less welcome was evening teaching; I found that I was expected to take one or two evening classes in economics, attended by people who were taking the BSc Econ part-time. They came to these classes after a full day's work; they were often jaded, but they worked as hard as they could and I had to admire their tenacity. There were also the students, some to whom I was tutor and others that I taught in classes, who required help of various kinds. One of these, a rather pale and refined young man, was a sociologist whom I taught in one of my non-specialist economics classes. Military service was still in effect and he was a conscientious objector; after several discussions of his beliefs he asked me for a testimonial to go to the tribunal which would consider his case. Our discussions convinced me that he was genuine and I wrote a testimonial to that effect, adding that I disagreed profoundly with his views; this both eased my conscience and strengthened my plea on his behalf. I received a letter of thanks from him with a promise to tell me what had happened about his court-martial, but at this point my records come to an end. Many years later, at some meeting his name was mentioned and he was pointed out to me – by then he bore little resemblance to the willowy youth of my memory.

Beyond teaching there was research. I attended Richard Sayers' Money and Banking seminars and Lionel Robbins' graduate seminars in economics. The pressure to publish was then much lower and I was expected to produce at least an article acceptable to a respectable journal to show that I was suitable for promotion to lecturer at the end of my four year period as an assistant lecturer. I already had an interest in demand theory, and reading Milton Friedman's article *The Marshallian Demand Curve*, which seemed to me entirely un-Marshallian, led me to look more closely at Marshall's analysis. I made some progress and an early draft was read by Lionel Robbins who later told me that it had played a considerable part in gaining my full assistant lectureship in June 1953. At a later stage I sent a copy to Milton Friedman himself, who was visiting Cambridge at the time; I felt it was very considerate of him to reply with several pages of comment although needless to say he did not agree with my interpretation. It was at this point that I showed my draft to Richard Sayers, who was editor of *Economica* at the time, and he responded by saying that when finished he would accept it for *Economica*. This was a tremendous boost to my morale and my article *Marshall's Demand Curve* duly appeared there in 1956.

In addition to this I was working to develop my understanding of the British monetary system, building on my early experience of markets on the floor of the Stock Exchange and on my more recent time in the London Discount Market. These strands of teaching and research formed the basic pattern of my academic work at the School throughout the 1950s. There were also the usual administrative activities: occasional Departmental meetings, meetings of the Academic Board of which all teaching staff were members (although without a vote for their first year), some interviewing of prospective students and other occasional activities. Soon I felt fully engaged in the work and life of the School.

The Phillips Machine in Action

In August 1953 London University held a summer course at the School and I was asked to be a tutor together with Bill Phillips and Jack Wiseman. Bill had already built what became known as the Phillips Machine (which modelled the working of the economy using coloured water to represent money) and he used it in teaching the macro-economics course in this summer school. I don't think the students really took to it, because at the end of the course we had a party and they put on several sketches. One of the sketches was of Bill teaching his course using the machine. On the stage 'Bill' would say a few sentences, elaborating by pointing to their mock-up of his machine and then suggest some discussion – complete silence; he would try again and again, but always no response. The students in the audience laughed and clapped appreciatively. At the end of the course each of us was presented with a book token by the students; I used mine to buy *Roget's Thesaurus*, 1938 edition, which I still use in preference to its later editions.

The members of the summer school were given some recreational visits and I accompanied one of these to see Battersea Power Station, then in full operation. When we were shown the great furnaces we were told that the Bank of England, faced with problem of destroying old banknotes, had tried tying them tightly into bundles and stoking them into the furnaces. However they found that the compact bundles were scorched at the outer edges but not destroyed. They then tried avoiding this by tying them up in loose bundles but the string burned through and the notes blew out of the power station chimneys all over Battersea. The notes had been defaced but it was still something of an embarrassment to the Bank.

Later the Phillips Machine lived in a large cupboard in a room later incorporated in the Robinson Room restaurant. (For several years a group of us used this room after lunch for table tennis. Frank Paish, Ken Minogue, myself, Kingsley Smellie – despite his artificial legs – and several others were regular players.) On occasion the machine was wheeled out of its cupboard, filled up with pale pink water and demonstrated to various people. I can remember Bill muttering something about the need to have striped water to make the flows show up more clearly. In fact I tried putting extra pink dye into the M2 tank and found that this allowed one to see the darker colour percolate through the system in quite an instructive way. One important feature of the machine related to its behaviour as the tank which modelled national income approached full employment; elementary text-book models had rising real income with constant prices up to full employment and then changed abruptly through 90 degrees to constant real income and rising prices. Clearly realism required that prices should begin to rise before full employment, replacing this right-angled relationship with a smooth curve. Bill incorporated this more realistic feature in his machine which required some rather careful design of the water-flow slot concerned. It was this relationship of prices beginning to rise as the economy approached full employment, incorporated in his machine, which inspired him to seek and quantify it in the real world, giving rise to the Phillips curve. His results and their policy implications raised much controversy and made the Phillips curve famous. Later a second machine was constructed so that there could be 'international' interactions between them, requiring various wires linking the two. Both machines were prone to leaks and I can remember Bill and James Meade busily splashing around them in pools of pink water as they tried to adjust these wires to give sensible results. The Phillips Machine was becoming sufficiently well known for *Punch* (13 August 1953) to have a one-page spoof on it under the name of the Financephalograph, with a full-page cartoon by Emmett.

With Bill and some others at lunch one day discussion turned to footnotes in articles and it was suggested that someone should try writing the limiting case of an article with a title and then just superscript numbers indicating footnotes, for example: *A Hypogenic Note on Price Theory*[1,2,3,4,5,6]. This zero-text article would have trumped the alleged book *Of Owls in Iceland,* in which the text consisted of one chapter containing one sentence: 'There are no owls in Iceland.'

213

The Library

In the Library there was Room Q, a pleasant room in which a range of recent acquisitions was displayed. Both as a student and later as a member of the staff I found it a pleasant room to work in and I would also visit it to glance over these new arrivals. Looking at them idly one day I came across a book in a plain rather bright blue utilitarian binding which turned out to be Heinrich Schliemann's *Briefwechsel,* a volume of his letters. I knew of Schliemann as the excavator of Troy from a book I had found in a second-hand shop many years before: Walter Leaf's *Troy – a Study in Homeric Geography* (1912) with its wonderful colour-coded map of the successive cities of Troy. I could not resist dipping into these letters and I still remember two of the episodes in Schliemann's earlier and enterprising life as a Baltic merchant which are recorded there. In the first he had invested heavily in a cargo of indigo which he had just imported into the port of St Petersburg. There was a great fire at the docks and all the warehouses were burnt to the ground, and as he walked away from the scene of devastation convinced that he was now a ruined man, one of the dockworkers called to him. The warehouses had been full and they had to put his cargo of indigo in that old shed over there, one of the few buildings that had survived the fire. The second episode occurred when he was travelling by train from Warsaw to Hamburg. In the middle of the night the train stopped and the passengers found themselves looking at a red glow in the sky which they learned was the Baltic port of Memel, timber-built and now on fire. At the next station Schliemann went to the stationmaster's office and was able to cable an order to Hamburg to buy up all the available stocks of timber, which he had immediately foreseen would be in great demand for the rebuilding of Memel before the winter set in.

Another and very different book which I found there and dipped into was *Meaning in the Visual Arts,* a volume of philosophical essays on art history by Erwin Panofsky. The essay I remember particularly was entitled 'Et in Arcadia Ego', taken from the title of a painting by Poussin of a group of Arcadian shepherds and damsels contemplating a tomb which had this phrase inscribed upon it. To my untutored eye this phrase – 'I, too, once lived in Arcadia' – was a reminder from the occupant of the tomb to those now looking at it that for them also the pleasures of life would end in the tomb and a handful of dust. But perhaps it was Death who was warning them, and the essay explored the literary and cultural background of this warning, and its significance and development, with great erudition and in voluminous detail. I enjoyed following his analysis in a field very different from my own.

At this time the nearby Parish Hall (subsequently the School's building PH) was used on certain evenings by Sea Cadets for band practice and in some rooms of the Library one could hear them thumping and tootling away. There were plans to use this space in the daytime as a crèche for the School's staff, this led to much discussion in the Academic Board which then used to meet in what later became the Vera Anstey Room. I can remember suggesting that discussion had gone on for long enough and that what was needed now was a decision.

Some Colleagues

I enjoyed all my academic activities but added to them were the pleasures of having such congenial colleagues; they provided a veritable feast of excellent conversation over lunch in the Senior Dining Room or round the large open fire in the Common Room. Lionel was undoubtedly the dominant figure in the group of economists usually to be found to the left of the fireplace. He was tall and, appropriately, rather 'lion-faced' with a shock of grey hair and a mouth which turned easily into a smile. He was dominant but never dominating and conversation flowed easily in his presence, much of it on the economic and political events of the day and the affairs of the School. Economics in itself had only a small share of the talk beside the fire, after all this took up most the rest of our time; but I can recall one occasion when talk did turn to price theory, leading Lionel in his most orotund, even Churchillian, manner to observe: 'Surely, anyone wishing truly to understand price theory would go first to von Stackelburg's *Marktform und Gleichgeweicht*, would they not?' Yes, yes, agreed our little group round him, sycophants all on this occasion, that is exactly the book we would go to. In fact I am perfectly certain none of us had even heard of it, let alone read it in the original German. And this, as I discovered later, for a very good reason. I had been looking up some work by Professor G.L.S. Shackle and, with the serendipity which was possible with the old card catalogues, I stumbled across a nearby card for von Shackleburg [*sic*], *Marktform und Glelchgewelcht (1934)*. There was only one copy in the Library of this book which Lionel had praised so highly, and here it was, incorrectly catalogued through a misspelled name, so no one could even have found it through the catalogue, let alone have read it. They could, of course, have gone to Alan Peacock's translation of it which had recently been published, but I think that none of us were aware of this either and no one mentioned it at the time.

Lionel had a nice sense of humour; I remember him telling us of one of his lectures where a woman sat in the front row knitting. He crushingly suggested that if she wished to knit, perhaps she would do so at the back of the room. Instead of stopping knitting and paying attention, the woman moved slowly to the back and carried on knitting. Lionel could not help smiling ruefully as he admitted that she had won this encounter. I can also remember him being very amused when he had been marking an examination script and had come across the words 'as Robbins sagaciously observes'. Not long after I arrived in the Senior Common Room Lionel decided that the Economics Department ought to develop relations with French economists (quite a significant move at a time when such links with the continent were only slight). A French professor was invited over to give a lecture and Lionel made it clear that all members of the Department were expected to attend. The lecture was in French and the only thing I can remember were its first few words: 'Les économistes Francaises sont toutes individualistes...' The lecture revealed little common ground from which to start and Lionel's initiative did not progress any further.

These conversations round the fire brought out many tales from my colleagues; one of these was Frank Paish who as a gunner had won the Military Cross in the First World War and who introduced me to the useful piece of information that the weight of a projectile in pounds was equal to the square of the bore of the gun in inches. I remember his tale of seeing a battered shelter of timber and corrugated iron behind the front line, the very thing his battery needed. He got there only to find it had just been occupied by another unit. Some quick thinking, and he claimed that he had just come to collect the shelter which belonged to his battery, but as a gesture of goodwill he would leave half of it to its newly arrived occupants. They were so touched by his generosity that they even helped him to make off with the other half of *their* shelter. He was a non-drinker and a non-smoker but he used to carry matches in his pocket; this, he claimed, was to help other people to smoke and in this way to pay a larger share of indirect taxes (this was long before smoking was seen as a health hazard). He had also paid Lionel Robbins £1 for the right to borrow such small sums as he might need from time to time over the indefinite future. One of the many things that I picked up from Frank was the difference between insurance and gambling: insurance covers those risks which in the nature of life are unavoidable and have to be borne by someone, while gambling creates risks for those who find pleasure in bearing them. Another was that in financial documents, the more important the substance, the smaller the print. He regarded the public as very gullible in financial matters, and felt that a scheme for insurance against the end of the world could be very profitable. One of his dicta was that since you are unlikely to get what you like, a sound policy would be to learn to like what you can get. I wrote an article with Frank for *The Banker* in 1956 and I have always remembered, and tried to emulate, his care in getting what he termed the 'carpentry' of the wording just right so that it was a smooth and exact fit with the intended meaning. In writing for the *London and Cambridge Economic Bulletin* revisions to the data often required late radical changes in the text of an article; in those days typesetting was expensive and Frank observed how fortunate it was that the words 'rise' and 'fall' both had four letters so that the not infrequent revisions from one to the other caused no difficulty.

And there was James Meade, most pleasant, looking every inch the scholar that he was and with a rather diffident manner, who was then responsible for the International Trade group of third year economics specialists. I still have a letter from him dated December 1955 apologising for being remiss on talking to Dick Liprey about a student who wished to change his special subject – the writing in black ink is clear, well formed and somewhat calligraphic. At one time he was supervisor to a Japanese graduate student who asked if he might take a photograph of James. This was agreed and in due course James seated himself behind his desk while the Japanese organised his camera on a tripod. At last everything was ready; James composed himself, the Japanese pressed the button, then dashed round behind James' desk, seated himself on James' lap and off went the flash. I never saw the photo but I like to imagine a beaming Japanese and a very surprised James.

Surprising things also happened to Bill Phillips; apart from being the owner of the Phillips Machine, Bill also had an old car which in those days he could park outside International Hall in Bloomsbury where he was then living. One day the car was missing, but the next day it was back again, and Bill soon realised that some other person was also using his car. He was never able to discover the identity of his fellow driver and was finally reduced to leaving notes for him on the seat – that the car needed more oil or needed its tyres pumping up. At one departmental teatime meeting Bill attempted to adjust a loaded multilevel cake stand, only to collapse the whole lot into a squashy mass; this caused much amusement but was not quite what we had expected from someone who was, after all, a very practical electrical engineer who had laid mains all over Finchley. The only unkind words I heard from Bill were directed towards one Senator Brewster, whose aircraft company produced the Brewster Buffalo, a fighter aircraft of very poor performance which, according to Bill, at above 10,000 feet lived up to its name by wallowing like a buffalo. Bill was an armaments officer in the RAF trying to defend Singapore (where he was captured by the Japanese) and he still remembered with distaste these inferior aircraft. A few years later I called on Eli Devons in his room, to find him and Bill deep in discussion, planning the new MSc. I prepared to withdraw but Eli suggested I should stay and join in; I cannot remember any details, except that to me it was a very interesting meeting.

Within the Department there were others whom I now met and was to continue to see and talk to for more than half a century; in particular there was Ralph Turvey, who had been my tutor, and Basil Yamey who was a colleague for all this time. Basil had been in the Air Force helping to train pilots in South Africa during the war, and he told me of trainees concentrating so hard on landing that they forgot to lower the undercarriage and crash-landed; to cure this a loud klaxon was installed close to the pilot to warn that the undercarriage was not down, but some were concentrating so hard on landing that they didn't even hear the klaxon and still crash-landed. Basil produced an article for *The Times Review of Industry* which ended up with a really clinching sentence which he was rather pleased with; the editors agreed, but took it from the end and made it the first sentence, which Basil had to admit was a great improvement and something of a lesson.

There were many colleagues in other Departments whom I remember with pleasure. One of these was Michael Oakeshott who had just erupted onto the LSE scene, replacing Laski's managerial socialism with the concept of government's role being simply to keep the ship of state from running onto the rocks. I attended his inaugural lecture and remember him using the phrase. Here was something new indeed; furthermore a professor of government who was joint author of *A Guide to the Classics*, a book about horse racing. He was witty and urbane, and an excellent chairman of the BSc Econ Examining Board. I remember his tale of the deeply scholarly historian who was just about to take up the chair of Naval History at Cambridge when it was discovered that he had never seen the sea; the University Chest had to be persuaded to pay for a day trip to Hunstanton so that he would be suitably qualified for his new post. Donald Watt later claimed this was a canard, but many of us felt it deserved to be true.

Michael Wise, a geographer, led our team of non-professorial teachers in its meeting with the University Grants Committee (UGC) during their visitation of the School in 1955. His opening statement emphasised our high morale, collegiate spirit and pride in the School; it made a visibly good impression on the UGC members, indeed our whole team found it inspiring. My role in this meeting was the humble one of drawing attention to the shortage of rooms for academics, illustrated by figures for the rising number who were having to share. Only some fifty years later did I squeeze out of Michael that the UGC had said in their report how impressed they had been by this meeting, and that he was called in by the Director to be congratulated on his leading role in its success.

And there was Vera Anstey, elderly and kindly, who had been at the School nearly as long as Lionel Robbins. She remembered the time in the 1930s when the School was much smaller, and recalled an end-of-term party organised by the Students' Union in what was then the Barley Sugar Room (so-called from the twisted wooden columns on either side of the fireplace); it was a wet day and the fire was surrounded by drying stockings and Lionel, already a professor, was dancing with a girl who was an officer in the Students' Union. This indeed was an image from a different world. It was with Vera Anstey that I first spent a day interviewing students, and she confessed that she found it very hard to turn down charming young ladies whom she felt would be a social asset to the School. In my mind's eye I can still see her, unfashionably dressed, arriving at the School carrying her books in a drooping knapsack on her back.

After I arrived the Monetary Group consisted of Richard Sayers, Stuart

Wilson, Alan Day and myself, then came Roger Opie in 1954 and Tony Cramp in 1958, with Stuart leaving in 1959 for a chair at Hull. Elsewhere in the Department there were the usual changes including the arrival of two who bore marks of the Second World War: Andrew Ozga (in 1953) had lost an eye through an RAF attack on a train on which he was being transported as a prisoner, and Kurt Klappholz (in 1955) still had his concentration camp number tattooed on his arm; but the most significant was the arrival in 1958 of Eli Devons from Manchester. I liked Eli, but looking back I feel he was not the right man for the Department; several of my younger colleagues thought that his chair should have gone to Harry Johnson, but his time was to come later and for the moment he went to a chair at Chicago. Another arrival, after working with the Army Operations Research Group as a scientific officer, was Maurice Peston (in 1958) who from having once been a fellow student now became a colleague. Maurice was a guest at one of the Director's dinners and was placed next to the Archbishop of Canterbury who, to Maurice's surprise, leaned over and asked him what he was giving up for Lent.

There were two people whom I spoke to only a few times, both of them close to retirement: Eleanora Carus-Wilson (mediaeval economic history) was interested to see our family copy of Lindsay Fleming's three-volume *History of Pagham in Sussex*; she saw such local histories as the basic sources for her subject. The second was T S Ashton (economic history) who, when he retired in 1954, gave me a number of his books on economics including several by Marshall and Keynes; this was very kind of him and was much appreciated. And then there were the administrators. Anne Bohm, later secretary to the Graduate School, was the one I best remember from these early years; she was ever-present, devoted to the School, most sociable and already building up her wonderful store of memories of the School and its graduate students. But there were several others, and I soon found that they were all unfailingly helpful and that a few words with them at lunchtime in the Senior Dining Room could clarify and solve many problems for myself and my students.

One factor supporting the collegiate feeling at the School was its physical compactness. Everything then was in the Old Building, which meant that nearly all of us had rooms which were quite close to the newly built and handsome Senior Dining Room and barrel-vaulted Senior Common Room, which encouraged us all to make full use of them. When I arrived on the staff in October 1952 our numbers, though well up from the 1930s, were still low by later standards. There were approximately 1,500 undergraduates, 300 graduate students and 180 teachers, all concentrated – or overcrowded – in the Old Building. This also contained the Library, taking up much space on the lower floors, and filling the bowels of the building with its reserve stacks, tended by sub-librarians working underground like troglodytes. Also in the basement was the large vertical photocopying camera, predecessor to our xerox machines, tended by Mr Copelin, which produced a negative (white on black) image of a page which then had to be re-photographed to produce a black on white copy – not very convenient. Elsewhere in the building a few corridors were lined with elegant pale fawn Ashburton marble, while some of the smaller staircases at that time had fawn and red detailing to the steps which added cheer to these areas. However in most places the Old Building was undistinguished within its sturdy but darkly stained exterior of Portland stone. It was without the many accretions of later years when the School was sometimes referred to as the empire on which the cement never sets. Within this rather dour physical structure the atmosphere of the School glowed with great intellectual liveliness and, for me, social warmth.

More Activities

In July 1953 I received a letter from Ursula Hicks inviting me to become a Consultative member of the Editorial Board of the *Review of Economic Studies*. In the letter she gave some background: 'As you probably know, the *Review* was started in 1933 by a group of us who were then young research students, and it has been our plan to try to have some of the youngest generation of economists always on the Board. In fact, it is an inexorable rule that on becoming a Reader or Professor members of the Consultative Board must retire, although this does not apply to the Managing Editors'. I accepted and the Board met twice a year, usually at the School, to decide on the contents of the coming issues of the journal and to keep an eye on its financial condition. The editorial board consisted of Nicky Kaldor (Cambridge) who acted as chairman, Harry Johnson (Cambridge) who did most of the actual editing, Ursula Hicks (Oxford), and then about four Consultative members including Bryan Hopkin

(Treasury) and myself although our names never appeared on the cover of the *Review*. As we went through the accounts at one meeting Bryan became agitated and at last burst out: 'Mr Chairman, I must point out that the Balance Sheet is headed Profit and Loss Account and the Profit and Loss Account is headed Balance Sheet!' Nicky just smiled enigmatically and said that such a thing need not concern us unduly and we carried on with the meeting, leaving the *Review's* quirky accounting in place.

The most important business was the new articles which had been submitted for the *Review*. There Harry took over and starting with the first one, he read out the name of the author, his university and the title of the paper. At this point Nicky intervened in his slow but unstoppable way – I felt he was like a tank rolling forward, crushing all obstacles – saying that the author would be saying such and such, that for several reasons he was wrong and that the article would therefore be unsuitable for the *Review*. Harry smiled tolerantly during this intervention, then said that he would now tell the Board what the article was actually about and after some discussion there was generally agreement to accept or reject it. Each article was dealt with in this same way, including Nicky's view on its probable contents and their obvious errors. Most of our meetings were of this kind except one, when before the meeting Harry (who was Canadian) felt a need for a Canadian drink called Red Eye (a pint of beer with a tot of tomato juice in it); I and two other economists went along with him to a pub, but there Harry's eye was caught by a pinball machine and he insisted on trying it out. The result was that we were late and missed most of the financial part of the agenda. The kind of articles published in the *Review* were not really central to my interests and in due course I retired from the editorial board.

More in my line was the London & Cambridge Economic Service (LCES). It published a *Quarterly Bulletin* which contained one or two articles on particular aspects of the economy and regular features reviewing recent economic developments and making some forecasts. Every quarter the editorial committee had to suppress an urge to say that forecasting was particularly difficult at that time, because it was clear that forecasting was difficult at any time. (Much later Charles Goodhart told me that when he was in the Bank of England, forecasting at every particular time was regarded as 'uniquely' difficult.) The person on the editorial board that I remember most clearly at these early meetings was Brian Reddaway (Cambridge); he had some very clear economic insights but otherwise tended to be slightly querulous, and openly incredulous that others could hold the views that they did.

At this time the Radcliffe Committee had been set up to look into the British monetary system and particularly into monetary policy. Richard Sayers was the leading figure on the committee and in due course there emerged many volumes of evidence and the Radcliffe Report itself, which mainly reflected Richard's views. The Report was not well received; it was widely felt to lack a clear and workable framework for monetary policy and this criticism was a great disappointment to Richard. I can remember Lionel Robbins' seminars in the Graham Wallas Room at which the Report was discussed; Richard sat at the back and at every effort to clarify what the Report was really saying, he pursed his lips and shook his head gloomily, implying that yet another speaker had missed the point. Harold Rose remembers Richard saying that his critics should have 'read between the lines' and that my response (though not made to Richard himself) was that 'the Committee should have written between the lines'.

The London and Cambridge Economic Service had an editorial board drawn equally from London and Cambridge, each of these choosing their own membership. In each quarterly *Bulletin* there was an article on Home Finance. Harold Edey and I took this over from Frank Paish and wrote it from June 1957 to June 1958, after which it was written by myself and Harold Rose, who came to the School in 1958. In the middle of 1959 the Cambridge half of the editorial board invited Richard Kahn, King's College, Cambridge (inventor of the multiplier and a hard-core Keynesian) to join the board and he accepted. He had read our Home Finance articles and was worried about the general tenor of them (which he regarded as based on the quantity theory and hence showing us to be twenty five years out of date) but he swallowed his scruples and accepted the invitation. As regular contributors Harold Rose and I normally attended the quarterly editorial board meetings, but we were neither of us present at the first meeting attended by Kahn; this gave him no opportunity to confront us with his objections to our Home Finance articles but it was the plan for us to review the Radcliffe Report that so incensed him that he resigned from the board after attending only this one meeting ('. . . when a Report of this kind appears, which is regarded as a quarter century milestone, it should be reviewed by economists whose ideas are not a quarter of a century out of date'). In his resignation letter to Harold Edey (secretary of the London half of the committee) he added: 'My own personal feeling is that Cambridge ought to withdraw from its association with the [*London and Cambridge Economic*] Service ... I do not wish my name to be mixed up in any way in it.' The sourness of this letter led several of us at the London end to feel that board was better off without him. Harold Rose then wrote asking Kahn to clarify his objections to our Home Finance articles. He sent me a copy of Kahn's reply with the covering note: 'I am enclosing stanza II of the Genghis Kahn saga. I shall spend a very pleasant half hour this weekend drafting a reply to the peril from the East...' This led to further correspondence and a conciliatory letter from Kahn conceding that he may have misinterpreted our approach but still revealing doubts, while Harold and I conceded that enforced brevity might have caused obscurity and possibly misled some readers as to our views. Our review of the Radcliffe Report went ahead and looking back, both Harold and I felt that we did quite a respectable job on a rather unclear Report; the only difference between us over this piece of work being that each of us was sure that the other was responsible for whatever merit it may have had.

As the dust settled it became clear that Kahn, as a hard-core Keynesian, could see the quantity of money as affecting income and prices only through the rate of interest; we took the same view in general, although at first Kahn did not seem to recognise this, but we did also have an uneasy feeling that persistent excessive growth of money could pose some more direct longer-term inflationary dangers. All this had led Kahn to regard us as pre-Keynesian quantity theorists and twenty five years out of date; in retrospect it would be truer to say that we were a decade ahead of our time in suspecting some influence of the kind which later was to be central to the view of the Monetarists.

Harold Rose proved to be a very pleasant colleague with a nice sense of humour; it was he who provided a classic Freudian slip: 'Well, that's life with a capital F.'; and *very* much later the wistful comment, 'Oh, to be eighty again'. In his retirement he produced a biography which revealed facets of his life which to me were entirely unexpected. This was a striking example of something I was to become aware of over the years, namely that I knew only a few of the facets of the lives of my colleagues, mainly those academic facets which had brought them to the School. It was this shared harmony which helped to make academic life at the School so congenial. Sometimes this harmony did receive a small shock, as when husbands and wives attended the Director's annual party and I was sometimes left wondering how *he*, whom I thought I knew quite well, could be comfortably married to such an unlikely person as *her*. There were also to be occasions when I regretted not knowing more facets of my colleagues' lives; Dennis Sargan, an econometrician, was a colleague whom I talked to occasionally over twenty years, but only in his obituary did I discover that he, like myself, had been keenly interested in gardening.

Shortly after I came on the staff I was approached by Michael Peacock, whom I had known as a student at the School and who had joined the BBC. He invited me to become the economist on a small team who were working on a new project – a monthly programme of economic commentary to be called *Almanac*. This team consisted of Grace Wyndham Goldie, Donald Baverstock, Michael Peacock, a statistician whose name I cannot remember and myself, together with Alfred Wormser who was to do the graphics. There was one big problem; graphics then were a matter of cardboard and ingenuity (which Alfred had in abundance) but filming technology was still very undeveloped and we had to film and time my commentary and Alfred's graphics (columns rising and falling to illustrate such things as Britain's changing trade balance) so that the two could be fitted together for the broadcast late in the evening; this was never satisfactory and was probably the reason why the programme was broadcast only on four occasions between January and May 1954. I came to the conclusion that I was not really the person for this kind of work, which needed an experienced economic journalist. While we were working on these programmes there was a very unfortunate event. Michael Peacock had been involved in asking Chester Wilmot, a very well-regarded journalist of the time and author of the influential book *The Struggle for Europe*, to return to London on some matter not connected with *Almanac*; he had been on the De Havilland Comet which went down into the Mediterranean on 10 January 1954 killing all on board. Michael was understandably distressed by this.

Only much later was I to realise the amount of BBC talent that we had in our small team: Grace Wyndham Goldie was a senior and influential figure in the BBC, who played a major role in developing its current affairs programming; Donald Baverstock became Controller of BBC 1 before moving to Yorkshire Television; Michael Peacock became Controller of

BBC 2 and then of BBC 1 until he also moved to commercial television. He was later to become a substantial benefactor to the School – the Peacock Theatre and the Peacock Atrium in the Library are named after him.

As the 1950s wore on I took on some other outside activities; these brought in some welcome income and it is the appearance of these earnings in my tax records which reminds me of them. For several years I gave a lecture course to trainee Scottish accountants as well as occasional lectures to other colleges and institutions; I published a few articles in periodicals dealing with banking and finance as well as in some newspapers, particularly one for the Paris office of the *New York Herald Tribune* for which I was paid the then handsome sum of £50, and a contribution on the London Money Market for *Encyclopaedia Britannica*. But what promised to be the most interesting task was an invitation to join Paul Bareau, then a leading financial journalist, in writing the proposed history of Schroders, the merchant bank. To build up our knowledge of the firm we visited its offices, talked to various members of the staff and were given copies of several documents; the firm then arranged for Paul to visit New York to speak to their American offshoot while I had a rather less glamorous trip to Cornwall to interview their oldest surviving employee. We also talked to two elderly Schroder ladies at their house near Windsor. By now we had been provided with a research assistant, a person I had known when we were both students, and he and I began to analyse the firm's Conditions Book which named all their trading contacts up to about the 1870s and the terms agreed for the business between them. Paul then produced a draft first chapter. I thought it was a masterly effort considering that so far we had little definitive information on the firm's earlier years. Suddenly trouble erupted. It seemed to Paul that the firm was run by two competing families, the Schroders and the Tiarks, and he had mentioned this in a way which the senior Tiarks did not like. We each suddenly received a letter telling us that the senior Tiarks would deal with this topic himself and would we please return all documents relating to the firm. At this point the project ended and we were paid off. It was not until some forty years later that the history of Schroders appeared, written by Richard Roberts, son of Ben Roberts whom I knew well as a colleague at the School. On the current Schroder website the name Tiarks does not appear in the company history.

For me life at the School had now become a well-ordered annual cycle. Each autumn the academic year started with a new intake of students, new faces in my classes and lecture courses, new tutees to interview and assist with their choice of subjects and other problems. My class teaching and lectures always needed developing and updating, the Robbins and Sayers seminars continued, and my own research and understanding slowly cumulated. Promoted to lecturer in 1956 and now a settled member of the Economics Department, I took a growing interest in the affairs of the School and was a regular attender at the Academic Board. I greatly enjoyed my work and my colleagues, and I always felt that same frisson of pride and pleasure as I entered the School.

13

The London Discount Market

For his seminars Richard Sayers used to invite speakers from financial institutions to talk about their work and one of these was Ronnie Gillett, Chairman of Gillett Brothers Discount Co Ltd, who talked to us about the London discount market. It must have been with Richard's help that he agreed that after I graduated I could work for seven weeks – Monday 7 July to Friday 22 August 1952 – in Gilletts in order to get some first-hand experience of its operations. The company was in the process of producing a book on the commercial bill market, *The Bill on London*, and I was able to give them some assistance with its editing and in suggesting journals which might review it. I still have the copy of this book that they gave me, and two letters with their kind acknowledgement of my help.

From the start I was put into the dealing room; this contained six desks, three on each side facing towards one end. Beyond the dealing room in that direction was the directors' dining-room and, I think, the directors' offices. I sat at the rear desk on the left and the rooms behind me contained the administrative offices of the firm where most of the staff worked. One of the senior clerks there spent much of his time writing out cheques for large sums – hundreds of thousands of pounds – and these amounts became habitual; he then had to pay a utility bill of £20 which he did at the office. He received a puzzled letter from the company thanking him for his cheque for £20,000 but...

I now found myself dealing in call money. The situation in a discount house was that it borrowed very short term money, most of it overnight or at call, from a wide range of banks. In the morning these banks would call back some of these loans and the afternoon was spent phoning round the market trying to borrow enough money by three o'clock to cover the loans recalled in the morning. The amounts were large – at present-day values perhaps 40 to 50 million pounds would be our afternoon target to meet the morning calls. There would be two or three directors and myself ringing round banks to borrow this money, a million here, half a million there, the director in charge announcing changes in the rate we should offer in order to keep the money coming in. Every new loan received was called out, entered by the person in charge of the daybook on a lectern which stood behind me in the dealing room, and repeated aloud by him as confirmation. With the large amounts involved and the three o'clock deadline, it was all rather exciting. And supposing the money simply didn't come in fast enough? Then there was an earlier deadline of 2.30 p.m. for borrowing from the Bank of England – the lender of last resort. The directors had to make an estimate of how much money they could expect to come in after 2.30 and then, if they anticipated a shortfall, borrow enough money from the Bank to balance their book. In the dealing room there was a glass-fronted cupboard with a glossy top hat for each director and close to it a very accurate clock. If they felt it was likely that they would have to borrow from the Bank, one of the directors would have taken out his top hat and would be ready with an eye on the clock so that the decision to borrow could be made with just enough time for him to walk down to the Bank and into the office of the Principal of the Discount Office to do the borrowing at exactly 2.30.

The top hat was more than just a quaint hangover from the past; it ensured that the Bank's doorkeepers (themselves handsomely dressed in pink-coated livery and their own gold-braided top hats) would always allow the wearer to pass through without delay. I can remember visiting the Discount Office at 2.30 on a bad day for the market. There was a queue of perhaps four directors of discount houses, all wearing top hats, waiting at the door of Hilton Clarke, the Principal of the Discount Office, while inside, standing behind his desk stood Hilton himself, a tall and commanding figure, wearing his usual black jacket and dark striped trousers, agreeing a loan with the director of the first discount house to arrive.

Each morning the directors and senior managers of all the discount houses went out on rounds visiting the money managers of the major banks; these visits allowed discussion of anything happening in the market and maintained their personal connexion. Then, wearing a top hat had the same function – it would allow the wearer straight through to talk to the money manager. On one occasion the rather imperious chairman of a discount house neglected to wear one when visiting the money manager at a bank and was courteously intercepted:

'Can I help you, Sir?'

'I am here to see Mr...'

'Of course Sir, and who are you from?'

'I am not *from*, I *am*.'

Gilletts also did a large business in bank and commercial bills and their in-house expert was Mr Parry. One day Ronnie Gillett suggested that I would find it interesting to sit by him when he went through the bills that Gilletts had discounted (bought) that morning. Mr Parry welcomed me to his desk and explained that he had been in the commercial bill business all his life, having started with the Yokohama Specie Bank in (I think) 1905. He then pulled forward the pile of bills bought that day and picked up the top one.

'Ah yes, a Brown Shipley acceptance; pin holes in the corner – a good sign, shipping documents have been attached to it – a genuine trading transaction. Signed by old so-and-so, an excellent man, I know him well. But, oh dear, he's put on the wrong amount of bill stamps. Never mind.' He opened a drawer and in it was a whole selection of bill stamps; he selected the extra stamp that was needed and stuck it on the bill.

'There now, that's all right. I have known all the people in the London bill market for years, you know, and we all understand each other.'

To me this was something of a surprise, because bills of exchange are important documents which legally are supposed to be correct in every detail. More surprises were to come.

'Now here we have a Schroder bill – excellent people, I've known George there for many years – now that's right and that's right, but oh dear, he's forgotten to sign it.' And Mr Parry picked up a pen and with a flourish signed the bill. 'There now, that's all right – we are all friends in the bill market, you know, and we all help each other.' And so it went on until every bill in the day's purchases was gently massaged to be 'correct' in every detail. For me it was an educational afternoon. But it is worth remembering that Mr Parry was right – all the bill market people in London really did know and trust each other, and there was a long experience of fair dealing between them. If a bill had been drawn on a bank newly arrived in London, without an international reputation and with a quite unknown London bill manager, I would guess that Mr Parry would have been much stricter. But, of course, such a bank newly arrived in London would have taken care to employ someone already experienced and well known in the market.

Some time later I wrote a very brief account (only some twenty column inches or so) of the operations of the discount houses for the *Sunday Times*. Shortly after it appeared I happened to call upon Hilton Clarke, Principal of the Discount Office, to whom I had been introduced by Ronnie Gillett. Someone was with him so I waited outside his door, but he saw me, quickly invited me in and introduced me to the person who was with him, the chairman of one of the discount houses. The latter was most complimentary about my short article, the only one he had ever seen which really explained the work of the discount houses. A very agreeable encounter for me.

The rank of Principal was not one of the highest in the Bank and it disguised the fact that the Principal of the Discount Office was in fact the Governors' eyes and ears in the market. He was the father confessor to the banks with dealings in the money and bill markets, which really meant all of them, but particularly the merchant banks and the discount houses; as such he was the recipient of every kind of highly confidential information and questions about these participants in the money market, as well as any wider rumours which were going around. Often someone would mention to him that they had heard something about a particular bank and look at Hilton questioningly; if Hilton did not want to be drawn into a discussion he would just reply, 'So rumour hath it', and pass on to another topic.

Through Ronnie Gillett I was able to visit some other money market firms. One of these was the only remaining running broker, a partnership which operated from a bare basement room under one of the large overseas banks. There I found four brokers in top hats, in a room containing only a cupboard, a table and some chairs. The senior broker was a Mr Hartley (father of the actress Vivien Leigh). We talked briefly about their business, which seemed little changed from a running broker's business in the early nineteenth century: they bought bank bills mainly from accepting houses, parcelled them to suit the particular requirements of other banks and sold them on to the latter, taking a turn (a small profit margin) on the way. Being purely brokers, they had little need for capital and they certainly hadn't spent any on their office.

I also spent a day with Gerrard & Reid, who were in effect a discount house but without re-discount facilities at the Bank, so that unlike Gilletts, for example, if they were short of money near the end of the day they couldn't go to the Bank and borrow at Bank Rate against the security of eligible paper (prime bank bills, Treasury bills or short dated government bonds) but had to find it at somewhere in the market – at a price. This seemed a hazardous operation to me, but they had survived for many decades and obviously knew their business. Talking to Theodore Reid was very interesting; he told me that his father had discovered bond-washing (a way of making money from bond operations cum- and ex-interest) in the 1930s and had made a steady £20,000 a year from it until others began to copy him and overdid it. This led the Inland Revenue to crack down on the practice and it had to stop.

I had become interested in the money brokers, firms which borrowed and lent gilt-edged stock and money to banks and stock jobbers. One of these was Sheppards & Chase and I visited their offices and talked with Mr Sheppard about their business. They had very dowdy offices, which indicated to me that they were a partnership and unwilling to waste their own money on smart offices, whereas companies were only too willing to do so with their shareholders' money. Cazenove also had a money broking arm at that time and David Cazenove, who ran it, was very helpful when I wrote an article on the money brokers for *The Banker*, June 1959. The money brokers did not have re-discount facilities at the Bank and had to get all their money in the market. However, on one occasion Cazenove were having such difficulty that David had no option but to go to the Bank for help (amongst some teasing from those who knew where he was going and why). The Bank was unwilling to let a money broker fail, but as Cazenove had no re-discount facility the Bank offered David a (more expensive) commercial loan, which he took gratefully.

When I was in the Bank I often went to see Jasper Hollom about the gilt-edged market in connexion with the *Quarterly Bulletin*. On one occasion, there on a nearby desk was *The Banker*, open at my article on the money brokers. When Hollom was appointed Chief Cashier *The Banker* published a photograph of him at his new desk, looking rather grim; in the market this was jocularly given the title 'Hard times ahead'. I sometimes exchanged a few words with Hollom when we met on the Waterloo Station concourse when he was living at Selbourne (of Gilbert White fame); there he had the misfortune to cut off one of his toes with a lawnmower.

Watching the discount houses and others ringing round for money led me to wonder what would happen if something really disrupted this process. I was told that this had happened. On one occasion Martins Bank temporarily lost the whole of their in-clearing, so that they faced all the claims of other banks on themselves but none of their (normally largely offsetting) claims on other banks. On another occasion rain flooded the cable ducts in the City and all the telephones were cut off just as the discount houses were phoning round in the early afternoon to get in the money to balance their books. These tales didn't include how the problems were resolved; I imagine that in the first case the Bank would have provided overnight help, and in the second would have declared a temporary moratorium, carrying the interrupted day's business over to the following day. In an international centre like London with so many overseas links, this would still have left hard cases to be resolved by negotiation between the parties concerned, but in such circumstances most banks would be very cooperative. After all, you never knew when such a problem might hit your own bank and require some help from your competitors.

Another participant in the money market was the Special Buyer, who at one time was Peter Baring, a director of the smallest discount house, Seccombe, Marshall and Campion. The Bank of England liked to buy a steady trickle of bank bills to keep itself informed of the quality of the paper in the market, and it did this through the Special Buyer. He had another role also. Banks called money from the discount houses in the morning in order to make payments to other banks; in the afternoon these other banks would have this money available to lend back to the discount houses. The main discrepancies between this ebb and flow were the net payments to or from the government's account held with the Bank of England. If the Bank wished to maintain the existing level of short-term interest rates it had to neutralise any such net payments by offsetting operations in the market, since otherwise the surpluses or shortages of money would lead to undesired movements in these rates. In the afternoon the discount houses would sometimes find money unusually short; had the Bank managed to smooth out the shortage or should the discount houses prepare to borrow from the Bank? The person to ring was the Special Buyer because it was through him that the Bank would tell the market how it saw the situation. The answers from the Special Buyer which I heard were typically that the Bank had done its operations as usual and 'the money is there somewhere, you just have to look for it'.

For a long time the discount houses dominated the weekly Treasury bill tender, and indeed they were looked upon favourably by the Bank because they agreed that between them they would always, if necessary, take up all the Treasury bills on offer, so that the government could always be sure of meeting its requirement for money. Typically the discount houses tendered for much more than the offer and expected to receive anything around a 50–70% allocation. But then, rather than buying Treasury bills from the discount houses, some banks began tendering for themselves and receiving the same proportionate level of allocation; the discount houses felt that while they accepted the duty of covering the tender, others without such a duty were taking business away from them. The largest discount house, Union Discount, decided to take action. At the next tender it did not put in a any bid, with the result that the outside tenderers, and in particular the banks, received unexpectedly high and undesired allocations. This tactic was referred to by Trinder, the manager of Union Discount, as 'choking them with cream'. It was a warning to outside tenderers that they now faced more risk than they had thought.

On a later occasion when I was at Gillett's I felt it would be interesting for students to see what a Treasury bill looked like, and I asked Ronnie Gillett if I might borrow one to have a photocopy taken. He was quite willing, but felt he should clear it with the Bank of England first. He phoned the Bank and after a pause he was told that there would be no problem with this. Accordingly a £100,000 Treasury bill was put into a messenger's pouch and he and I went off to catch a number 11 bus to the School; we got there, the Treasury bill was photographed (with its serial number carefully obscured) by the Library's large vertical camera in the bowels of the Old Building. The bill then went back into the messenger's pouch and he took it back to Gillett's. It was then about tea-time so I took my photocopy up to the Senior Common Room to show Frank Paish, who had in the past done a lot of work on Treasury bills. There by the fire were Frank, Lionel Robbins and some others; I showed Frank the photo and he started out of his chair with excitement – he had never actually seen a Treasury bill before. Lionel was very amused and said that Frank was like a writer of erotic poetry who had just seen a woman for the first time. It was only some days later that Ronnie Gillett told me that after we had already left with the Treasury bill there was a frantic phone call from the Bank of England to say that in no circumstance could a photocopy be taken of a Treasury bill. Recently I looked at my copy of *The Bill on London* and slipped into it I found my photocopy of the Treasury bill, but also a photocopy of a 'Z' account certificate for £625 of 2¼% Exchequer Stock 1955 (which was in effect a 'bearer' form of this stock) which must have been taken at the same time. The two were in a clearly identifiable Gillett paper sleeve with a red bar and 'Gillett' in white, keeping them together; this would have been a typical parcel of security and cover (together worth just over £100,000) which would have been deposited with a bank which had lent Gilletts £100,000 of call money. The Treasury bill would mature after 91 days but the 'Z' account certificate would be valid until 1955, and the photocopy was so convincing that Ronnie Gillett wrote to me suggesting that I should write 'Specimen' on it, which I did. Later I lent this parcel to Mr Chalkley, one of the directors of Gilletts, to illustrate a lecture he was giving to an Australian bank.

In a discount house, ringing round for money in the afternoon was always rather exciting, with occasional unexpected events. One afternoon at Gilletts we had a call from Czarnikow, a major sugar trader, asking if they could have an immediate loan of £2 million. They should have known that for a discount house such a request, reasonable in the morning, could in the afternoon cause problems by abruptly increasing the amount of money we had to look for when there was not much time before the books had to be balanced at three o'clock. The phone was put on mute and the directors held a hurried discussion, some for, some against. However the money position was fairly easy and it was decided to take the risk. Back on the phone, with a beatific smile in his voice, Ronnie Gillett said 'Delighted to be able to help you', and the business was done. Some of the banks lending call money were not well regarded; one was a consistent caller in the morning, but always lent very late in the afternoon, expecting a higher rate; of this bank's money market manager it was said that, 'He is so sharp one of these days he will cut himself', and we made a point of only taking his money at a normal rate. On other occasions there had to be personal entreaties to some of the largest banks to lend us a bit more; I can remember Ronnie Gillett looking forward to the day when we would have video phones so that the dealers could see each other. Then, behind himself he would arrange a backdrop of weeping women and children to try and soften the hearts of reluctant lenders. One safeguard for a discount house was privilege money; this was an overnight money facility extended by the largest banks that a discount house could draw on if necessary; it was included in the expected post–2.30 inflow which helped decide whether or not to borrow from the Bank.

As I have said, it was standard practice for the directors of discount houses to do rounds of visits to the money managers of the main banks each morning. If privilege money had been taken overnight, it was on these visits that the rate would be negotiated and this would sometimes be above the closing market rate. It was then that Ronnie Gillett would refer to these banks as 'our nearest and <u>dearest</u> friends'.

All call money borrowed by a discount house had to be secured, and the messenger going to the lending bank to collect the banker's payment (in effect a cheque) for the loan would have with him a parcel of Treasury bills, bank bills and short bonds worth slightly more. This, in the discount house's own clearly identifiable sleeve, he handed over in exchange for the banker's payment. The discount houses made the market in such bills. A discount house would typically be buying bank and commercial bills every day as well as taking up Treasury bills from the tender. At the same time they would be selling such bills to banks which would specify maturity dates and types that they wanted. One of the arts of the person on the security desk was to have the bills most likely to be sold, held as security by banks which were nearby and from which they could be quickly recovered in exchange for comparable parcels; there was a constant shuffling of all this paper around the banks, as dealing and this kind of repositioning went on, but with the security and cover always being maintained for each loan.

Sitting at a dealing desk in Gilletts and borrowing large amounts of money overnight from banks I found exhilarating and it seemed quite a responsible task. However, a moment's thought would reveal that this money could not go astray, and the only risk I posed to Gilletts was that I would take in some money at too high a rate. Typically those of us on the dealing desks agreed a rate at the start of the borrowing session and as the position became clearer the senior dealer, usually a director, would say out loud, 'Things are slow, offer a quarter more' or some such instruction. There was sometimes badinage over the phones ('We can offer you a special $4^{1}/2\%$ because you are our favourite bank' – when in fact this was the going rate) and there were times when I could have paid perhaps $^{1}/4\%$ too much for some money. But these were all annual rates of interest and on quite a large loan of $£^{1}/2$ million this $^{1}/4\%$ would amount to interest of £12,500 per annum; but I was dealing with overnight money and overnight it would be 1/365th of this, or just over £34. This would really be the upper limit of the amount at risk from any deal I did in money, and a true measure of my responsibility.

On one occasion this difference between the annual and overnight cost of a given rate arose in a very different context. An overseas bank made a very large error in managing its money position and was forced to go late in the day to one of the clearing banks, cap in hand, to borrow this amount overnight. After a quick telephone consultation with the Bank of England (because such a loan would significantly affect the clearer's own balance at the Bank) the loan was agreed to, for a lump sum payment of, allegedly, £750,000. Calculating this on an overnight basis gave an equivalent annual interest rate of 700% and this was the rate reported in the *Financial Times* the next morning. This was indeed an exceptional spike in the overnight rate.

My time in and around the discount market was most interesting and enjoyable; it was Ronnie Gillett's kindness and support which made it so because this opened the way to many other visits to Gilletts and to other institutions later on. But I also owe a debt of gratitude to many other members of Gilletts, and to the members of other firms I visited, who were all endlessly patient in answering my questions.

14

Life at Home in the 1950s

Avenue Road

Back home at 20 Avenue Road, Isleworth, my younger brother J moved in for a while (he had a job at Power Jets, the company set up by Whittle who was a leading pioneer of the jet engine) until he disappeared into the RAF to do his National Service. For part of this he was stationed at Tangmere, which we had watched being dive-bombed by Stukas in August 1940. My older brother Michael, now qualified as an architect, also moved in when he got a job with a firm of architects just off the Strand and quite near the London School of Economics. We sometimes travelled back from Waterloo to Isleworth Station together in the evening, chatting all the way, often each with our legs crossed. Then suddenly we were at Isleworth Station; out we got, each with a numb leg, and the two of us obviously suffering from a family disability would limp painfully down the platform together. It was while Michael was living with me that we resuscitated the coke-fired central heating system which my father had installed before the war. The work was done by a heating engineer who bore an uncanny resemblance to Harry Johnson, and I had to hold myself back from asking him how his work in international trade theory was progressing. We also had the electrical system overhauled; it was in a very poor state, having originally been in one of the few areas on DC and then clumsily converted to AC. When let during the war it had been provided with two meters, for upstairs and downstairs. During the overhaul they put in a new meter and then somehow managed to read our electricity consumption for the latest quarter as the difference between the new meter reading (zero) and the old one (about twenty years of consumption). The result

239

was an electricity bill of extraordinary size, accompanied by a letter admitting that there appeared to be some mistake and arranging to come and investigate.

Mike and I devoted some time and several cans of Cuprinol to holding back wood beetle in our floors, one of which had to be completely renewed. We also had the front step redone in white terrazzo and the encaustic tiled hall floor covered with a pale fawn linoleum. The ground-floor back living room was papered in a rusty red wallpaper with a cartouche pattern in white, and finally we repainted the green front door in a rather fetching shade of lilac. We felt that we had greatly improved our rather fusty old house; but now as I write them down I have severe qualms about some of the things we did. By this time Mike had bought a car, a rather elderly but reliable Singer saloon; I made a contribution towards its purchase and had limited user rights over it. Sometimes late in the evening hunger would overcome us and we would drive several miles (but at that time a pleasurable drive in our very own car along roads with very little traffic) to Chiswick High Street where there was a real transport caff which all through the night sold wonderful hot steak pies. In due course Mike was promoted to run his firm's office in Malvern and he moved down there, coming back only for occasional weekends. After he had gone I put the final touches to the hallway – two simple Scandinavian brass wall lights from Liberty's and a D-shaped wall table in black with a gilded carved edge which I made myself. I had discovered the pleasure of shopping for items to decorate my part of the house in what I felt was a tasteful and pleasing manner.

When Michael left, my mother found an elderly housekeeper, Mrs Baker, who was given her own bed-sitting room and kitchen on the first floor while I moved downstairs, using what had been our main reception room as a generous bed-sitting room and study. She kept the house clean (helped by one, and sometimes two, cleaning ladies who came more for coffee and conversation than for cleaning), did the shopping and cooked one meal a day for me. She was a good plain cook but her Yorkshire puddings were quite exceptional – as light as love – and made with a few apparently careless whips of the mixture with a wooden spoon in a white bowl. Mother and Dad occasionally drove up from Bognor in the Land Rover, to which my father was devoted and which had an extra high-powered spotlight which at night would illuminate about a mile of the straight road across the flood plain south of Pulborough. With available bedrooms, for a time I had paying guests, first two trainee BOAC pilots on the Britannia fleet and later a physicist who was working on guided missiles. The only thing I can remember about him was that his team had mounted the guidance mechanism the wrong way round in an expensive test missile which, after it was launched, turned round and headed belligerently back at those who had just fired it. But in due course I was able to dispense with paying guests and Mrs Baker and I enjoyed the house in comfort on our own.

At this time we had a burglary, a very inefficient one leading to no identifiable loss. I discovered the break-in when I came home one evening and promptly phoned the police. Obviously it was a quiet evening for crime because several police cars, with nothing better to do, came to join in. Then came a police van with a large Alsatian dog and handler. As soon as it was out of the van the dog bounded through the front door and up the stairs, dragging its handler who called out 'Don't go near him, he's dangerous!' In a second incident I was awakened in my ground floor bed-sitting room by someone shining a torch through the window. I got up stealthily, put on my dressing gown and slippers, picked up the poker and slipped out of the front door and, as it were, confronted the would-be intruder from behind, shouting as loudly as I could, 'What are doing?' Instant panic from him as I tried to corner him in the front garden, but he broke away and ran off down Avenue Road. Wearing slippers, I couldn't chase him effectively but I flung the poker in his direction and it clanged past him striking sparks from the road. I hope I frightened him out of a life of crime.

Social life

My colleagues at the School made life very pleasant; our academic inclinations and the affairs of the School gave us a strong common bond and over lunch or around the fire in the Senior Common Room conversation covered a wide and most enjoyable range of topics. Indeed, life at the School suffered from only one weakness – there were very few young women of my age. Students did not count because *in statu pupillari* ruled them out and for this side of my social life I had to look elsewhere. By the mid-1950s I was approaching thirty years of age, I had a comfortable home and Mrs Baker to look after me. Like all the young men I knew, I enjoyed taking girls out but I was becoming conscious that something was missing. Recently I read of a survey that showed over seventy per cent of both men and women rated being married to the right person as the most important thing in life. Within me there had stirred some awareness of this. The army had imbued me with the principles that 'time spent in reconnaissance is seldom wasted, and in wireless communications, when searching for a new frequency, 'search boldly'. My leisure time now included bold reconnaissance looking for the right girl. On the surface this was the pursuit of pleasure; deep down it was serious business involving an important part of my own – and someone else's – future happiness.

One girl that I did not need to seek out was Jenny Tregear; she was really a family friend because she shared a Jewel class dinghy named *Trio* with my brother Michael and Peter Cooper, our family solicitor. They sailed from the Bognor Regis Yacht Club, usually, it seemed to me, in rough grey weather, getting very wet and cold in the process. She was very easy to get on with and since she worked in London we sometimes met for evenings of entertainment, which had to be low-cost since I had only just emerged from being a student. She had a cousin Jane who was a fashion journalist, and I particularly remember her coy response to some compliment: 'Oh, you're only saying that because it's true.'

Meanwhile my social circle had begun to widen. Someone introduced me to the English Speaking Union (the ESU to us), of which the younger members' branch was essentially a social club, centrally located in Charles Street just off Berkeley Square. There I found a whole new range of contacts: a strong contingent from the advertising agency J Walter Thompson which was just around the corner; Jill Lloyd, the Younger Members' secretary and participant in many social activities; Cyril Wallworth, a higher civil servant, keen diner-out and man-about-town; John Masterton, large and muscular, and Bob Teodorini, an American and about half the size of John, who together claimed to be writing a musical using the piano in the ESU's ballroom; a tall and rather cadaverous man who claimed to be a devil-worshipper and many others. Through someone at the ESU I was introduced to a small social group known as The Samovar. This was organised by a pleasant elderly woman who felt that when young men and women graduated from Cambridge they lost touch with each other, the very people with whom they had most in common (which to her meant potential marriage partners); she set up a club called The Coffee Pot, limited to thirty members, to help remedy this. The Coffee Pot filled up immediately and she then started up a second one – The Samovar – on the same lines, but less oriented towards Cambridge. Through the ESU, The Samovar and some parties I met quite a number of very pleasant young women; bold reconnaissance was proving really rather agreeable.

In getting to know a girl, the standard first move was to invite her out to dinner, and this was greatly helped by the emergence around that time of some relatively inexpensive restaurants. One of these was Luba's Bistro which was in two or three converted garages just off the Old Brompton Road, a few hundred yards from Harrod's. It was run by Luba herself – large, fat, Russian and very much in evidence all the time. It had red and white check tablecloths, candles in bottles and was very much geared to a young, less affluent and less demanding clientele. Its menu consisted of only a few main dishes and of these I can only remember Blanquette de Veau and Boeuf Bourguinon. It was cheerful, unpretentious, full of atmosphere and in a very good location, just the place for taking a girl out to dinner. Another was El Cubano, also in the Old Brompton Road, and even closer to Harrods. This was the first place at which I had Chicken in a Basket – beautifully rotisseried chicken served in a woven basket and eaten with your fingers; it was accompanied by their own special barbecue sauce, which the proprietor later revealed to us was simply a half-and-half mixture of mayonnaise and tomato sauce. I tried a few other restaurants, but Luba's and El Cubano were my preferred ones.

Nightlife

One evening when a group of us were having supper at the English Speaking Union a friend joined us and announced that she had discovered a new nightclub which had just opened in a cellar in Berkeley Street, just off Berkeley Square, and only a short walk from the ESU. This sounded interesting, so after supper she led us to the Blue Angel. It was a very pleasant private club, small, really quite cheap, freshly decorated, with a bar and a number of tables some in alcoves. On the rear wall was an enormously enlarged photo of Marlene Dietrich, sitting on a bar stool dressed as a chorus girl, from the film *The Blue Angel*. There was a small dance floor and in one corner a grand piano played by a West Indian musician named George Brown, who on some nights was backed up by two or three other instruments. The membership was entirely young and good-humoured, there with friends to enjoy the atmosphere, the music, and to dance in nightclub fashion – cheek to cheek from head to foot. This was all gently aided by a few drinks, but there was no binge drinking, no drunkenness and never a sign of drugs. I used to take girls there on Saturday nights; very often there was a contingent of beefy rugby players from Richmond, but they like everyone else were there to enjoy themselves and there was never any hint of trouble.

Later I used to take girls to another night-club called Le Condor in Soho. It was much like the Blue Angel but rather larger, with a similar young membership and not expensive. It too was very well behaved. I still have an image of it in my mind: after midnight, low lights and soft music, a dozen couples dancing slowly, close together, their eyes closed, sharing a warm and intimate contentment, each in a world of their own.

Although one could normally expect to be invited to the occasional party, giving a party ensured a more reliable return flow of invitations; but this required a suitable venue. It was through Jill Lloyd that I met Ann Holloway, whose father was a maxillary surgeon. As well as becoming a congenial friend of both Michael and myself, and remaining so for all these years, she had two things which set her apart from most other girls – a white Morgan sports car and a tiny mews house at the very end of Cheval Place, a stone's throw from Harrods and only just over the road from Luba's. Her house had just one large room on the first floor and a bedroom which was virtually an eyrie up under the roof and reached by a ladder. On the ground floor was a tiny bathroom with black fittings and a tiny kitchen with a large piece of biltong on the wall, maturing steadily over the years; but most of it was devoted to a garage containing her beloved white Morgan. If ever there was a house designed more for entertaining than for living in, this was it; Mike and I always joined together in giving parties and we gave a number at which we provided the drink, Ann provided the very pleasant venue and we shared the guest list.

For a time we had a similar arrangement with a colleague of mine, an Irish economist named Don Walsh, who had a suitable flat somewhere near Thurloe Place. I remember once walking with him from the School to a wine merchant he knew in Jermyn Street to order the drink for one of our parties. We entered what was more like a drawing room than a shop and were greeted by a rather effete young man who offered Don a glass of wine; then with much knowledgeable talk about drink he took down our order. It was from him that I received a recipe for a punch with something of a kick in it, which we used at the start of our parties to ensure that they got going to the point where we could divert our guests onto the various bottles which they had brought with them – 'Run out of punch? My God, do you mean we've got to start drinking that stuff we brought with us?' These parties were social occasions full of pleasure and good humour – I cannot remember anyone getting drunk, becoming obstreperous or being sick over the carpet. I played the role of attentive host and as usual I never drank but always had an enjoyable time. After a few such parties I found that for a room of a given size, with its ordinary furniture pushed back to the walls, allowing six and a half square feet per person gave the optimal number of people for that room. I kept records of the drink and food consumed, and all the various accessories required, from glasses and ice to napkins and Twiglets, which made later party planning much easier. To put matters in perspective, Michael and I probably gave one or two parties each winter and were invited to perhaps half a dozen others – altogether rather more than one a month over the winter. I still have the guest list of a party we gave on Saturday 6 November 1954; there are 34 names on it, 19 girls and 15 men, amongst them Michael Oakeshott, Ernest Gellner, Ralph Turvey and Jim Durbin, all colleagues from the School. These parties were an agreeable way of meeting people and at every party where I was on my own I made a point of inviting a new girl out to dinner, all in the cause of bold reconnaissance.

One point needs to be made here. At that time relations between young men and women, certainly in my circle and indeed generally, were much more circumspect than they became later. The main factor behind this was fear by the girls of unmarried pregnancy. This meant that kissing, cuddling and even some warm-hearted fumblings were permissible, but beyond that, certainly not. It followed that only marriage could offer young men and women the ultimate intimacy and emotional security that all of us were really looking for, a special status it has often lost today. The great change was to arise from the contraceptive pill which was to have social consequences far beyond those foreseen by its inventors, who apparently thought it would simply allow married couples to plan their families more effectively.

Cars

All this social life required a car; initially I shared one with Mike, but when he went off to run his firm's office in Malvern I bought one of my own, a very basic green Standard 8. I paid £300 for it and went home, ready to call and collect it the following day. That night I was haunted by dreams in which this car turned out to have no engine or to suffer from strange and indefinable faults. Daylight was a relief, and when I collected the car it did have an engine and ran as well as could be expected from such a utilitarian vehicle. Its seats were thin, rather hard, and upholstered in an improbable orange tartan. It had lockable doors but no ignition key, just a knob, and it had been fitted with an disproportionately expensive Motorola radio. Its demister consisted of an electric filament, poorly protected, along the bottom of the windscreen in front of the driver; this filament twanged musically at exactly 55 miles per hour. When the engine idled it gave out a slow tock-tock-tock sound; a mechanic listened to this with pursed lips and diagnosed big-end problems. After a few years I sold this car to my younger brother J and several years later the engine was still emitting this same sound, just as healthily as ever. My next car was a white Austin A35, a great improvement. Driving at night I could imagine that it was an Aston Martin DB6, but daylight expelled such comforting fantasies. A car was essential and meant that on a date I could collect a girl from her flat, drive to Luba's, with parking nearby, then after dinner it would be on to the Blue Angel, plenty of parking in Berkeley Square, and then as the night drew on drive her home again. Independent of public transport and with plenty of parking, this marked a real step up in my social status. I only had one real contretemps with this A35; once I was driving fast along a virtually empty Great West Road at night when its windscreen shattered and turned opaque. As I had been told, I thrust my fist through it and although I could see enough to stop safely I was surprised at the blast of air that came through the hole and the amount of non-lethal glass fragments which fell into my lap. However, I had one or two lesser incidents. Again on the Great West Road, once as a traffic light changed I obediently screeched to a halt; a lorry driver behind me got out and came up to me: 'Look, mate, you may be able to stop like that but I have a load of iron rods and I can't – you're lucky not to have them up your backside.' I have remembered this ever since. I also bumped lightly into the Indian High

Commissioner's car just by the bottom of Kensington Church Street. I got out and apologised to him, but his only response was a silent and world-weary gesture implying that nothing mattered any more.

Fossils

At this time I usually spent part of the Easter and summer vacations with my family down at Aldwick (as well as always being there for Christmas). One interest I had there was fossil hunting on the foreshore with Edmund Venables, a first-rate local naturalist, and his friend Mr Taylor, a retired schoolmaster. The London Clay, some 60 million years old, came to the surface around the low-water mark and in one area it contained pyritised fossil shark and other teeth, bird bones, seeds still with their carbonised coating and various other things, but what particularly interested us was fossilised beetles. All these fossils were washed out of the clay and deposited around the rocks, often in drifts of pyritic grit. Searching for them down at the low-water mark on a still evening was a pleasure in itself, the world seemed to consist of just a wide deserted beach, calm sea and vast sky, and you could hear a subtle change as the tide turned. A sharp eye and a little experience could soon find larger items like shark's teeth and I got a lot of pleasure from finding these – many shark's teeth were up to an inch long, some pin-sharp and with exquisite natural curves. But the real challenge was the beetles (mainly weevils, which are a sub-family) which were very small, the size of a match head, and could only be found by sorting through pyritic grit with a magnifying glass after it had been taken home and dried out. My part-time and amateur efforts found eight of them, while the much more dedicated Venables and Taylor had between them collected over two hundred. I gave my beetles to Mr Venables and all these finds were deposited in the Natural History Museum in South Kensington as the Venable–Taylor collection from Bognor. Each of these names is commemorated in the long scientific names of three of the tiny finds: *Venablesia colluvium*, *Taylorlus littoralis* and *Erirrhinites bognorensis*. (There being three of them here rules out the venerable joke about the lesser of two weevils.) Years later Venables told me that when construction work at the museum required deep piling into the London Clay, under their very own building they found – fossil beetles. My wife was once at the hairdressers when the girl doing her hair let slip that she liked beetles. 'Why how strange, my husband is interested in beetles as well.' But, of course, it turned out that there are beetles and The Beatles.

Apart from the usual fossils I found one of the much larger shark's teeth – nearly three inches long – and later part of the carapace of a turtle and one of its leg bones. I showed these to Venables and he and Taylor went straight down to the beach and found further pieces. In due course all these parts of our turtle went to the Natural History Museum and I received a letter from the Keeper of Palaeontology and one of the Curators thanking me for donating my share of the 'beautiful partial carapace of a Leathery Turtle' which was an 'important and interesting gift' to the national collection. The leg bone was of less significance and they returned it to me with its identification: '?Euchelys' – '?good/true turtle'. My fossil hunting turned up other things as well, particularly bullets and parts of aircraft left over from the war, but also on one occasion a heavy gold ring. This went to the police and in due course was claimed. I also found a name disc belonging to a friend's dog, giving the impression that it had gone down to the beach and then simply dematerialised, leaving only its disc behind.

More Social Life

All of the girls I took out were pleasant enough to attract my attention in the first place but, as one might expect, with most of them the chemistry failed to develop and our acquaintance was short; and, after all, I had no reason to expect any of them to find me particularly appealing. Only a few of them remain in my memory. One was very charming with an attractive lisp, and strikingly well-dressed; she was secretary to a well-known journalist and did tend to be rather fixated upon him; also her brother was training to be an embalmer... Another was sweet but not very conversational; an interesting thing about her was that her brother drove around East Africa monitoring locust swarms. The one that I most remember was yet another Anne whom I met at The Samovar. She taught art at a school in south London and was very good company. At one time she and another girl shared a flat just off the King's Road which on one of its walls had a very large and striking paper mosaic, Byzantine in style, made by her pupils (I would guess with very close supervision from her). Later she moved into

248

a house in Walton Street with several other girls, again not far from Luba's. One feature of this house was that the District underground line appeared to run only a few inches beneath the floorboards, a loud rumbling frequently reminding one of its presence. I particularly remember going with Anne to watch the polo at King's Lawn near Windsor. This was in the days before terrorism and we just drove in and parked on one side of the ground; on the other side was the Royal family with a few other spectators. There were no police in evidence and at one point the Duke of Edinburgh said, 'Come on, sausage' to the Queen. It was a beautiful day and somehow thoroughly English.

For more than a year Anne and I must have seen each other quite frequently, often for dinner on Saturday evening, usually at Luba's or El Cubano, followed by Le Condor, which she preferred to the Blue Angel. On a few occasions we went to other restaurants; on one particular occasion we decided to go to a Chinese restaurant in the King's Road. Anne was rather elegantly dressed and as we walked along to the restaurant, there ahead of us, clearly dressed for a dowdy evening at home, was a mutual friend walking her rather unwholesome dog. We stopped, exchanged a few friendly words, then Anne said, 'What a nice dog', and bending down made refined stroking motions, carefully keeping her hand several inches above the unappealing animal – a brilliant compromise between cordiality and distaste. My friendship with Anne was essentially casual, enjoyable and mutually convenient. I still took other girls out, as bold reconnaissance required.

... until I find her

It was while I was down at Aldwick in the spring of 1959 doing some fossil hunting that I was invited to tea by Sonia Bech (mainly a friend of Michael's, and sister of Barbara Bech with whom I had travelled on the train during the war). She lived at The Farmhouse, near the duck pond and only a few hundred yards from my parents' bungalow. There also was Toni, Sonia's best friend and now a health visitor in Portsmouth, whom I had barely noticed at the same house some six years earlier when she was a young nurse, slightly spotty and on her way to do nursing in Kenya. But now she seemed rather different; well practised, I asked her out to dinner, in fact for that very evening, and she accepted. Shortly afterwards Derek Bech, Sonia's brother, also asked her out; on hearing that she had already agreed to have dinner with me, he remarked 'Roger's rather fast isn't he?' I felt a touch of pride that my man-about-town image had at last been appreciated. I now started to see Toni fairly often. A few months later Sonia threw a party with dancing in the dining room. Toni's brother, also a Michael, was there with a girl. She was pleasant and I chatted with her and danced with her several times during the evening. During one of these dances I found the lights rather clinical, and under the influence of Le Condor, I turned them off. This certainly appealed to most of the dancers, but Sonia was rather put out as it was no longer *her* sort of party. Only later did I find out that Toni was cast into gloom by the thought that I was showing increasing interest in another girl; at home tears had rolled down her cheeks and dropped into the pastry she was making.

I now started seeing more of Toni – dinner at local restaurants, visits to the cinema, walks along the beach, a drive up onto the Downs to see the glow worms, then up in town I introduced her to Blanquette de Veau at Luba's and Chicken in a Basket at El Cubano. I found her very easy to get on with, warm and entertaining; as we got to know each other better we found more areas of harmony. She met some of my friends and, indeed, was put up by Anne for one night at the Walton Street house which by that time Anne was sharing with a galaxy of other young women. It was there that we all sat around chatting one evening when the conversation turned to the then new fabric Terylene; I had with me a Terylene shirt I had just bought and they were interested to hear how this new material should be treated, so I read out the detailed washing instructions. At the end I added 'Now take off the shirt...'

I was finding an increasing glow of a quite new pleasure in Toni's company; she was playing a growing part in my life and I gently detached myself from Anne and from other girls, although they may not have really noticed and they showed no lustrous-eyed regret. On one occasion I was driving mother into Bognor when we passed Toni cycling in the same direction, dressed in a pleated white nylon dress and looking really very attractive. We stopped and I introduced her to my mother. As we drove on, mother said what a charming girl she was; it was good to have her approval. Now came true courtship, suffusing life with a warmth and excitement which, as every romantic novelist knows, it is impossible to describe adequately. It had to be conducted on a small budget. I never bought Toni gifts of any consequence, but I did notice on my night drives between Bognor and Isleworth that that there were often catseyes displaced from the centre of the road, lying shining in the gutter. I took to stopping and collecting these, but they were disappointingly dead when out of the headlights and as a tentative offering they were regarded by Toni as a curiosity rather than a heart-softening gift.

Closer and closer; then confident that I had found the right girl at last, I asked Toni to marry me. To be truthful, this emerged as a rather low-key and tentative suggestion; clearly she accepted me although neither of us can remember the details. I had already acquired an engagement ring – just in case – from Fenn's, the jewellers in our local row of shops at Isleworth. It was a secondhand solitaire ring, platinum with a diamond of just about one carat, costing what seemed to me the large sum of £85. I had first reserved it with a deposit of £5 (I still have the receipt, dated 14 September 1959) and then had it on approval. I took it up to Hatton Garden, went into one of the diamond merchants there – a room with a single bare bulb hanging over the counter – and explained to a rather hard-faced man that I was thinking of buying an engagement ring costing £85 but that I had no knowledge of the value of diamonds, could he help. Perhaps he was softened by the sight of (fairly) young love, because with a grunt he took the ring, pulled out a lens and looked closely at it. Then with another grunt he handed it back to me, said 'You should buy it', and disappeared into a back room. Shortly after I had placed the ring on her finger, Toni came to lunch with me in the Senior Dining Room at the School; to avoid any unseemly congratulations she agreed to wear her engagement ring on another finger.

Now matters rolled inexorably forward; on Monday 26 March 1960 a notice appeared in *The Times*: 'A marriage has been arranged and will take place shortly between . . .' And shortly indeed, for on that same wet Monday morning we were married at the church of St Richard in Aldwick, with family and only a few friends present, followed by lunch at a local hotel. Toni accepted all these arrangements without demur; it was only much later that she revealed that she would really have liked something rather more upmarket. But that was how it was, and the only photographic record of the event was a slide of Toni and myself outside the church which faithfully recorded both us and the grey and rainy day; it was taken by Toni's best friend Sonia, and subsequently we lost it. To me, at any rate, the trappings of the event were of much less importance than the fact that we were married and that a wonderful change had occurred in both our lives. Later we would sometimes recall the fragile chain of events which had allowed us to find each other. The thought of how easily this chain might have been broken was chilling, and we had to hold each other very closely to banish it from our minds. And whenever we passed St Richard's church, I would repeat my grandfather's witticism: 'The church I went into once too often'; but we both knew it wasn't true.

We spent our honeymoon in Paris. In my A35, cleaned and maintained for the occasion, we drove down to the unpronounceable and obscure Lympne micro-airport near the Kent coast. On the way Toni regaled me with tales about her fellow nurses in Oxford, particularly one named Marietta; it proved a most entertaining drive. Lympne seemed to consist of a very small building in a very large field. There our car was loaded with two or three others into a Bristol Freighter, we and the other passengers got into seats behind the pilot – I cannot remember any doors – and off we went across the Channel at very low altitude, arriving at Le Touquet after a flight of some twenty minutes. Then it was off to Paris, making our way there by easy stages and staying at the Chateau de Montreuil in Montreuil-sur-Mer, and at the Pavillon Henri Quatre at St Germain-en-Laye. These had both been recommended by Cyril Wallworth at the ESU, but at the first we had a bedroom decorated with a motif of monkeys and filled with the sound of a large party on the floor below; the latter we found suffocatingly upmarket and the renowned view from the terrace towards Paris shrouded in mist, so we left after only one night. In Paris we found a small hotel, Le Chariot d'Or in the Rue de Serbie which promised parking (after the manager had moved his car) and from this base we drove around the city – exciting but risky – and ate at a selection of starred restaurants selected from our *Guide Michelin*, of which we found the one and two starred ones best suited us. After a week of this enjoyable indulgence it was back home to Isleworth, and converting my bachelor pad into a home for two. Mrs Baker was now relieved of the task of looking after me. Toni, rescued from health visiting in Portsmouth, was happy not to start thinking about a job.

15

The Bank of England and After

Into the Bank

In late November 1959 I received a letter from Maurice Allen (Adviser to the Governors) inviting me to lunch at the Bank and suggesting a temporary appointment for two years as the first outside economist seconded to the Bank of England. With the approval of Richard Sayers and the School I accepted this offer and in the middle of April 1960 I walked through the main entrance of the Bank as a temporary employee. I was politely asked by one of the attendants – in the Bank's handsome livery of pink tailcoat, black trousers and top hat with a band of gold braid round it – whether I required any assistance. I was directed to the Central Banking Information Department (CBID) where I was welcomed by John Fforde, head of the General Office, the section of the CBID which was to be responsible for the Bank's *Quarterly Bulletin*, and introduced to the other members of the team with whom I was to work for most of the next two years.

On the outside the Bank was all stone, pillared and nicely detailed, but windowless. On the inside it was a magnificent building with everything expressing the highest quality, from the mosaic floors to the handsome long-case clocks in the Governors' corridor, whose measured tick-tock spoke of two hundred years of loving care. I never ceased to enjoy the pleasure of all this quality as I moved around the Bank, and there was the additional pleasure of the garden court at its centre.

For a start I had a brief interview with the Deputy Governor, Mr H.C.B. Mynors; the only thing I can remember about this is that he told me of one old director of the Bank, during a discussion of the position to be taken up by someone, saying: 'It doesn't matter what you pay him, the question is, where will he eat, and where will he wash his hands.' At that time it was often these visible things which determined status, rather than income, which was never talked about.

Then my first week was spent being shown some of the more interesting aspects of the Bank. I was taken down and shown the bullion in the deep vault, pallet after pallet each carrying an orderly structure of 400 oz gold bars, all of the same highest purity, some of it belonging to the Bank, some held to the account of foreign central banks. What most struck me was the very different shades of gold: some light and bright, some with a redder hue and some, from the Congo, looking rather muddy. When I had visited Hilton Clarke on, I believe, a Thursday afternoon, I could hear the noise from the bullion yard just outside his window where they were breaking open boxes containing the latest gold consignment; now I could see where all these new bars ended up. I was also shown the finely engineered weighing scales on which the weight of the bars was checked and I was introduced to one of those responsible for them, a Mr Cornwell who happened to live in Guildford.

My next visit was to the Bank's collection of forged banknotes, then mainly the old green £1 notes, which were held in filing boxes. I would guess that the number I saw was well under one thousand and most of them seemed to me forgeries which would be taken as genuine by a busy cashier. All of these came from the notes returned to the Bank as no longer fit for circulation; such notes were sorted through by girls and I was told that, as an incentive in what must have been a wearisome task, a girl who detected a forgery received a day off.

This was followed by a visit to a very sensitive area – the Bank's foreign currency dealing room where they monitored the performance of sterling in the foreign exchange market and dealt as required. The basic problem was Britain's weak position; there were large sterling balances which could be sold if confidence in sterling began to weaken; this would tend to drive down the sterling exchange rate. Preserving the fixed exchange rate would then require the use of our limited gold and currency reserves to buy sterling, offsetting the selling. If the loss of confidence and hence the selling grew, we would ultimately be faced with an unacceptable loss of reserves. Then the next stage would be to raise Bank Rate (by 2% if necessary) to show the Bank's determination to defend the sterling exchange rate and to slow down the outflows and induce inflows into sterling; and if that didn't work sterling would have to be devalued, which would at that time have been regarded as the ultimate failure. The Bank's first line of defence was small-scale tactical operations in the foreign exchange market to try and forestall any cumulating sales of sterling. That was what I saw while I was in the dealing room; there were reports of sales of sterling coming out of Frankfurt, and the chief dealer's response was to arrange offsetting purchases apparently also from Frankfurt so that the potential speculators against sterling did not see any cumulating stream of sales which might tempt them to join in. The Bank's day-to-day management of sterling at this time was really psychological warfare against speculators.

Down to Work

Initially I shared a room with Christopher Wiles and there my in-tray was periodically replenished by one of the pink-coated messengers. Most of these papers seemed to come from people in the Overseas Department reporting on the work they were doing; while this might have been in case I had some comment to make (highly unlikely), I suspected that it was mainly to show that they were doing something. Through these papers I became acquainted with complex issues relating to a tiny savings bank in a truly remote corner of the Pacific Ocean, whose joint status and some currency problems seemed to me to involve complications quite out of proportion to the size of the institution concerned. I also received quite perceptive commentaries on the macro-economic problems of one of the larger Latin American countries. I thought of the advice I had read somewhere that the best way to deal with such papers was just to write on them 'Noted and Returned' and put them in the out-tray. However all of this was peripheral, and my real work with the group was helping in the preparation of the forthcoming *Bank of England Quarterly Bulletin*, acting as rapporteur for the Committee on Internal Statistics (CIS), and doing research on various topics which came down to me from John Fforde.

Some of the research was short-term investigation of some topic which came to our group from further up the hierarchy, but some of it was more fundamental. For example, we spent much time exploring the possible ramifications through the monetary system of inflows and outflows of foreign currency. In another project I had my first acquaintance with the flow-of-funds framework and indeed was asked by John Fforde if I would like to go to Iceland for a week or two to help them set up their flow-of-funds accounts. This I declined as my concern was rather with the conceptual framework while they seemed to be more interested in data problems.

The Committee on Internal Statistics, often referred to as the Home Figures Committee, was chaired by the Chief Cashier, Leslie O'Brien, and attended by a Director, Heads of Departments and Advisers to the Governors, and should have been of some significance in policy-making; at its monthly meetings the latest figures on the monetary side of the economy were gone through and comments made upon them, to be sent up to the Governors (always referred to in the plural). In particular they went to Humphrey Mynors, the Deputy Governor, who had chief responsibility for the home side, the Governor having chief responsibility for the overseas side. One of the members of the Home Figures Committee was Maurice Allen, Adviser to the Governors, and it was to him that I as rapporteur submitted my draft of the committee's conclusions. He was slight in person, enigmatic and pernickety, with a dry academic manner. I would take my draft, on green paper, like all drafts in the Bank, to him and wait as he read it through, usually with an expression of distaste. He would then begin redrafting it. To me he seemed to specialise in long and tortured sentences, which wound their way in convolutions rich with subjunctives, subclauses and sub-subclauses, loaded with possibilities, hints and allusions, all obscured by misty qualifications. I often suggested that his redrafted sections were not entirely clear. His response was 'D-D-Don't worry, *they* will understand, *they* will understand', referring to the Governors. Only occasionally did I manage to get him to change anything in his version.

So far as I could judge, despite being a high-level committee of the Bank, the monthly reports of the Home Figures Committee had little discernible influence on policy. Indeed, on one occasion the committee did appear to make some tentative suggestion in this direction, only to receive a very brusque reply from the Deputy Governor: 'When I want advice on policy I shall ask for it.' This was read out very flatly to the committee by its chairman. But I soon came to realise that the Bank was chiefly concerned with tactical operational problems: managing sterling so as to maintain the fixed exchange rate and managing the money market and gilt-edged market. To this, the summary of the proceedings of the Committee on Internal Statistics did not contribute anything of immediate operational interest.

BEQB

The Radcliffe Committee had recommended that the Bank should produce a *Bank of England Quarterly Bulletin* (*BEQB*) to make its views known and to help educate public opinion. The time was now coming for the General Office to produce Volume 0, No. 0 as our dry run, and then go on to Volume 1, No. 1. Our team for this was led by John Fforde who had a DPhil in Economics from Oxford. He was rather reserved but was good to work for. I sometimes exasperated him by declining to work on some topics I felt were outside my field of interest or competence. After one such occasion he finally said: 'Well, what *are* you interested in?' The true answer to this was that I wanted to sit on a committee with the Governors as they discussed monetary policy, but I had already sensed that any such discussion would be confined to a tiny group of the Governors and their closest advisers in conjunction with the Treasury. I think John Fforde also regarded my attempts to understand the influences shaping monetary policy as getting perilously near a potential leak, since I was only in the Bank for two years and would then carry everything I had learned outside its walls. He need not have worried; I had already willingly accepted that secrecy had to seriously limit any communication with those outside the Bank, and that even within the Bank secrecy sometimes had to apply to the exchange of information between working groups. This wall of secrecy around the Bank was very effective and on several occasion I was amazed at the discrepancy between what the press and banking commentators were regarding as currently important and the quite different issues which were exercising us within the Bank. The Bank did not have the problem which faced the Treasury and other ministries: leaky politicians who could not always be excluded from the inner thoughts of the senior civil servants.

We were all made acutely conscious that the *Bulletin* had to be absolutely correct in its facts and that its comments must not arouse fears or doubts which might embarrass the Bank's management of markets. The main commentary of the early issues was first drafted by John Fforde, and then gone over individually and collectively by all of our team: myself, Buckingham, Jackson, Wiles and others. The revised second draft, together with two or three articles on particular topics, usually drawn from outside our group, went out to other interested parties such as Heads of Departments. When their comments came in our team went through every word again and a third draft was prepared and this process went on for about twelve drafts until almost everything that might have been original, interesting or informative had been carefully smoothed away. What remained often seemed to me defensively banal and simply left readers to worry over what the Bank could possibly mean by some of its Delphic comments. At last the final draft went before the Governors and I can remember only one occasion when a draft came back from Mynors, the Deputy Governor, with an amendment. He had deleted a two-letter word and in the margin had replaced it by 'of'. We all puzzled over this new amended sentence; what did it now mean? We read it to ourselves and to each other. It seemed to have some distant and mystic significance, but exactly what? In the end we gave up and that issue of the *Bulletin* went out with the Deputy Governor's amendment. Two days later I happened to glance over the change and suddenly it struck me – what Mynors had written in the margin was not the word 'of' but the proofreader's delete sign; he just wanted the original short word deleted. I hastened into Bill Jackson who had been in charge of the final editing and told him; he just put his head in his hands and groaned 'Why couldn't you leave things alone?'

But in the end nobody seemed to notice the oddity of this sentence. Indeed, so far as I can now remember only once was there any question or feedback on any of the issues of the *Bulletin* which I worked on. This arose from an article on bill finance for which I had the main responsibility. I had to clear this article with Hilton Clarke but the deadline was getting near and Hilton was due to go off on a visit to Southampton. However we both travelled up to Waterloo station each day, Hilton from Clandon near Guildford and myself at that time from Isleworth, so we arranged to discuss changes to the article over a cup of tea at one of the buffets on the Waterloo concourse. Hilton then went off on his visit and I carried the now tea-stained version on to the Bank. When this article duly appeared Hilton received a very diplomatic communication from someone in the market pointing out that one of the calculations in the article was wrong. Hilton shared this with me but decided that the best policy was to say and do nothing and I don't think anyone else in the Bank knew of the error. It was some time after this that Mynors startled us with the statement that he was looking forward to us making a serious error in the *Bulletin,* because then our readers would recognise that the Bank was only human and the burden of perfection would be lifted from our shoulders. But we were sceptical. His statement seemed to us simply to reveal his pleasure in paradox and we carried on pursuing perfection; we had no desire to test out his actual response to a serious error.

Visits

While I was in the Bank I joined in two official visits. One was with Mynors when he attended a conference at Oxford of the Association of University Teachers of Economics to give a short speech on some banking matter. I and another person, I cannot remember who, but call him Smith, formed a small entourage to go with him. After he had made his speech there were questions and someone asked about policy in the gilt-edged market. Mynors carefully parried it, regretting that he could not comment on such a sensitive matter although he was fortunate in having two of the Bank's experts with him. At the word 'experts' all eyes swivelled respectfully onto myself and Smith, and I could feel the audience thinking 'These are two men who are filled to the brim with the secrets of the gilt-edged market.' I looked enigmatic while my body language replied: 'Yes, we are experts who really do know all these secrets'. But it was all play-acting in support of Mynors, since both Smith and myself had only a basic awareness of the Bank's general attitude and guidelines in its management of the gilt market. Indeed this was all there was to know.

The second visit was to Birmingham where the then new Governor, Lord Cromer, was to meet local businessmen and make a speech at a dinner in the evening. I travelled up to Birmingham by car with Sir Cyril Hawker, one of the Directors of the Bank. At that time he and I travelled on the same train from Isleworth and Putney respectively to Waterloo. At first when he got on, there was I in his favourite compartment, difficult to ignore and unrewarding to talk to, but as time went on our travelling relationship thawed somewhat and in the Bank we had several interesting conversations. But now he had me at very close quarters for three hours in the back of a Daimler; this was a long time and our conversation was sporadic and not altogether easy. In the evening after the dinner and speech I joined Hawker and the Governor in the latter's room at the hotel and we had a long and very free discussion. On the way back to London Hawker and the Governor talked privately in the back of the Rolls-Royce while I travelled next to the chauffeur.

Around the Bank

As I moved around the Bank I met many people from other departments and heard many, possibly apocryphal, tales such as that of the clerk who marked his place in one of the Bank's ledgers with a kipper and of the entry in the attendance book that 'Mr ... did not attend the Bank today, having been hanged for murder'. And there was the Bank Picket, a body of guardsmen who, since the Gordon Riots in 1780, had marched from Chelsea Barracks each evening to guard the Bank. There was a room for the subaltern in command and by tradition the Bank left a gold sovereign on the mantelpiece as a tip. The tale was that one wealthy and arrogant guards subaltern saw the sovereign, wrapped it in a £10 note and put it back as a tip for the Bank.

One person I remember was George Blunden, later Deputy Governor, who proved to be remarkably well informed about all the internal goings-on in the Bank. At that time it was his responsibility to take the day's bill purchases in to Hawker for him, as a director, to endorse on behalf of the Bank. On one occasion, instead of explaining what had to be done, he placed the bills on Hawker's desk and then stepped back and waited. Hawker, who was very good at dealing with businessmen but was not a technical banker, looked at the bills, fiddled with the top one and was finally reduced to asking George what he was supposed to do with them.

Another Bank man was John Guiseppi who was in the Secretary's Office; he had written a history of the Bank and was a very pleasant lunch companion (and lunches at the Bank's club were really very good and excellent value); he and I were often joined by a man named Humphreys, also good company. I never met the Governor, Mr Cobbold, as I moved round the Bank, but at Christmas he came round on brief visits to all our offices, an uneasy occasion of mixed goodwill and embarrassment on both sides. One tale about him was that, coming up to town in his chauffeur-driven Rolls-Royce on his way to give evidence to the Radcliffe Committee, his car broke down. It turned out that neither he nor his chauffeur had any money on them, and he had to go to the nearest station and try to get a ticket to London. One can imagine his tall and distinguished figure bending down to speak to the clerk in the ticket office: 'My man, I am the Governor of the Bank of England but I have no money; would you be so kind...' Later, confirmation of this event came from someone at that meeting of the Radcliffe Committee when the Governor finally arrived, together with the additional detail that the Governor had offered the ticket clerk a Bank of England cheque for ten shillings and sixpence to pay for his ticket, only to have it taken away and shown to some superior who refused to accept such a dubious-looking piece of paper. Later the Governor became Lord Cobbold; protocol required that certain consequences should be clarified, and round came an official notice to all staff stating 'The, Governor does not wish to be addressed as My Lord Governor.'

I met James Selwyn because he was Deputy Chief of the CBID; he had been at the LSE in the 1930s, graduating with a First in statistics. Despite his position in the Bank, I got the impression that he felt undervalued and dissatisfied; after he retired, however, his career took a sharp turn for the better. He became Commissioner for Securities in Hong Kong, a job which he enjoyed enormously and which I felt gave him the most rewarding period of his professional life. By the time he had fully retired we were living not far from him in Guildford and we met for coffee and talk on many occasions. When he died we attended his funeral service at Guildford Crematorium; as it came to an end we all started to file out of the chapel, expecting the usual final piece of solemn music. But someone put on the wrong tape and out of the loudspeakers came a burst of pop music and a bright and upbeat voice: 'Here in Hong Kong it is a beautiful morning and we are all going to have another wonderful day. Here is some music to speed you all to work...' It was as if the chapel had suddenly filled with sunshine, and in recalling James's happiest years it seemed entirely appropriate.

I met many other people in the corridors of the Bank and several of them are mentioned elsewhere, but looking at the forty or so names on the book token which was their farewell present when I left I am particularly reminded of Coleby, Luce, Spicer (excellent with figures and much relied upon for the *Bulletin*), Preston (who invited me back to lunch two years after I had left the Bank) and the tall figure of Guy de Moubray, who sent me a kind letter of congratulations on the birth of our first son.

After the Bank

I left the Bank at the end of May 1962 and after we had moved down to Guildford in July 1963 I used to travel up from Guildford's London Road station with two people in the Bank of England, Claude Loombe (an expert on the Middle East, Adviser to the Governors and later Chairman of the British Bank of the Middle East) and Roy Clifford (then in the Overseas Department and later the Bank's agent in Birmingham) both of whom lived near me. They were very congenial travelling companions and the affairs of Abu Dhabi and the Bank bulked large in our conversations. One day Roy told us that there had been some upset in the Bank because one of the girl clerks had appeared in Mayfair. This I couldn't quite follow and with confused thoughts of Queen Charlotte's Ball I asked 'Do you mean she was presented at Court?' Certainly not; she had appeared in the nude in a magazine called Mayfair. This gave the Bank the problem of maintaining its own respectability while not firing her unfairly. I believe that it was George Blunden who had to negotiate the Bank's way through this delicate affair.

Onto this same train at Clandon station would come Hilton Clarke and also Frank Paish (one of my close colleagues at the School). The two of them didn't know each other and as far as I am aware never spoke on the train, but there was a certain piquancy in their proximity. In the 1930s Frank had developed a way of estimating changes in the Bank's foreign exchange reserves from the weekly changes in the tap Treasury bill issue. Evidently his estimates had got rather close to the truth, because Hilton confided to me that one of his early tasks in the Bank had been to manipulate these tap Treasury bill figures so that Frank's estimates would always come out wrong.

Over the coming years there were a number of echoes from my time in the Bank. The first was when I received a call from a bank in the United States asking if one of their people could come over to London to see me. I had no idea what this was about but I agreed to see him. A few days later a tall and distinguished American appeared and we talked in my room at the School. He told me that he was General Counsel to the bank concerned and they were very worried about their London branch. There had been some problem (I imagine fraud of some sort) and their London manager, who was British, had reported this to Head Office in the States. They were very concerned and had asked if he had reported this to the Bank of England. The gist of his reply was that he had been looking in a shop in Threadneedle Street opposite the Bank when Keogh, then Principal of the Discount Office, had passed by. They had exchanged a few words and Keogh had said 'I understand you have had a spot of bother'; the manager had replied yes, but that everything was now under control. Keogh had replied 'That's good to know' and walked on back to the Bank. The manager said that this meant that the Bank knew about the problem and would ask if it wanted to know more, but meanwhile nothing further need be done. The American Head Office simply could not believe this story and immediately feared that something must be even more seriously wrong in their London operation. My visitor had come to ask me my opinion on the manager's story: could it conceivably be true? I was able to assure him that what the manager had said was entirely in line with the way the Principal of the Discount Office would approach such a situation. We went over it several times with me explaining how such things were done in London at that time. Finally my visitor accepted that their London manager's account was to be believed. How the American bank got hold of my name I have no idea, and I heard nothing further.

The second echo was when two Turks, a man and a woman, came to see me. They explained that they were from a Turkish bank (they never revealed its name) which wished to open a branch in London. They didn't want this to become known until they were sure that their application would be approved by the Bank; would I give them my considered opinion of the likelihood of such approval. This was quite outside my experience in the Bank and all I could do was give them my own thoughts on the kind of things that the Bank could be expected to take into account in judging their application: was their bank sound and well thought of in Turkey? What was its position in the pecking order of Turkish banks? This was significant, because if it did gain approval for a London Branch, banks above it in the pecking order could argue that this strengthened their case for such approval, when the Bank might have other reasons for being doubtful about them. And there were various other points, but I was in no position to give them the solid assurance they sought. I suggested other places they might try – one or two of the large firms of accountants who made a business of helping foreign banks into London. They thanked me politely, but I don't think I was as helpful to them as they had hoped.

A tutor does not usually have to assist students who have come into conflict with the Bank of England, but one of my own postgraduates came to me one day very worried and carrying a letter he had just received from the Bank threatening him with dire penalties for breaking the Exchange Control Regulations. He was Swiss and he had noticed that in London large, crown-sized, continental silver coins of the eighteenth and early nineteenth century were not popular with British collectors and were considerably cheaper here than they were on the continent. To help pay for his stay at the School he began a small arbitrage business, buying such coins, taking them back with him to Switzerland and selling them at a profit. He then remitted these funds to his account in the UK and I think that it must have been at this point that he broke the Exchange Control Regulations by not declaring his foreign currency earnings. I suggested to him the commonsense solution: that he should write a contrite, even grovelling, letter to the Bank explaining that he was only a Swiss student who knew nothing of these regulations, and was deeply sorry for breaking them inadvertently. He should go on to ask if the Bank would be kind enough to tell him exactly what he should do to rectify his position because he was anxious to be on the right side of the law. I explained that the Exchange Control experts in the Bank would enjoy exercising their deep understanding of their own intricate regulations in telling him what he should do. In due course he received a letter back which in a kindly way told him how to put everything right. Sometimes a tutor can be useful.

The final echo also concerned Exchange Control. I had met Douglas Dawkins when I was in the Bank and as he lived near Guildford I sometimes talked to him on the train going home in the evening. By now he had become the Head of Exchange Control, and one of these conversations was particularly illuminating; I asked him quite casually about the rules governing their operations, and he responded by immediately quoting about ten of these and their sources. Most of these sources were to me unexpected, obscure or unknown. They included subsections in long-forgotten budgets and brief statements in Parliament. It was a most illuminating example of what was everyday working knowledge to a Bank insider but, I would guess, quite unknown to most outsiders, even those in commercial banks who were concerned with exchange control. Not long after this I had a more practical question to ask him. A friend approached me with an unusual problem; the firm of which he was a director had discovered a cellar full of Exchange Control forms, extending over several past years, which should have been returned to Exchange Control at the Bank. Could I make any suggestion on what they should do about them now? I said that I would put out a sensitive feeler next time I saw Douglas on the train, and this I did. My suitably hypothetical questions met with calm, good-humoured and almost equally hypothetical replies. I became more concrete, he still did not seem unduly concerned, and then we arrived at Guildford and our conversation had to end. Before I could contact my friend who had raised the question, the end of Exchange Control Regulations was announced. No wonder Douglas could be calm and not too concerned. But there was another angle to this matter. Some of Britain's balance of payments figures were constructed on the basis of these Exchange Control returns (indeed it was rumoured that the forms were simply weighed to give initial estimates) and here was a cellarful of errors in these balance of payments figures. A sobering thought for those who had to use such figures in the formation of policy.

Early in 1970 Maurice Allen retired from the Bank and Kit McMahon invited me to his farewell dinner which was held at Chez Solange in Cranbourn Street. Our earlier tensions were long forgotten and it was a most pleasant evening. Just over a year later, in May 1971, the Bank issued a consultative document, *Competition and Credit Control.* I felt it was essential that there should be a proper occasion to allow the many economists interested in the field of monetary policy to discuss it. I think it was Brian Quinn whom I approached with this proposal (and I am sure others must have had the same idea). The Bank agreed to provide all the facilities for such a seminar, including coffee from 09.45 to sherry at 18.00 hours, and arranged for the Money Study Group to organise it. I have a letter from Brian enclosing the Bank's press briefing on the seminar for my information and enclosing the Money Study Group notice over the name of Bob Nobay. It was a most interesting meeting although I am not sure that all the questions raised were fully answered.

Later Visits

In 1971 Allen Harvey and Ross, one of the discount houses, invited me to join a team they were sending out to hold two presentations, one in

Basle and one in Geneva in an effort to drum up business from the continent. Each presentation consisted of a short description of the various facilities this discount house could provide, followed by a panel for a question and answer session. In the latter my fellow panel members revealed little of the skills of chairing such a meeting that one had to learn for the many classes and seminars at the School. The result was that I tended to take over the managing of these sessions, bringing in the other panel members who would know the answers but myself doing a good deal of clarifying of both questions and answers; my fellow panellists seemed quite happy to leave this to me. It was well organised and in Geneva we received transcripts of the proceedings, but in English translated back from the French translation (given out to the locals) of the original English. The result was disheartening – there was much confusion, particularly between interest rates and exchange rates. Whether any business arose from all this I never knew.

The trip itself was luxurious; Toni had been invited to come with me and she greatly enjoyed herself going on visits by car with other wives while we men had to sit through the meetings. In Geneva Toni steeled herself to pay what seemed a very high price for a short coat with a fluffy lining, but in general everything was so expensive that we didn't buy anything for the children and instead purchased their 'presents from Switzerland' back in Britain. They were suitably pleased and never saw through our mild deception. Shortly after we came back Toni, wearing her new coat, went to our local butcher's shop to buy something. The pleasant lady cashier, seated in her glass prison, noticed the coat and asked Toni where it came from. Toni replied that she bought it in Switzerland. Wide-eyed and in a hushed voice the cashier asked 'Do you buy *all* your clothes in Switzerland?'

Over these years I continued to see Hilton Clarke, now chairman of Charterhouse Japhet, on the train and on one occasion early in 1974 we had a long talk about City affairs. He blamed many accepting houses for lending to the fringe banks via the inter-bank market without adequate attention to their soundness. He said that Gerrard & Reid were now larger than Union Discount and I told him about my week with Gerrard before they became a fully fledged discount house and Theodore Reid's tale that his father invented bond washing in the 1930s, making a steady income out of it till the boys who took over Ionian Bank joined in and overdid it, leading to it being stopped. He told me about the takeover of Gerrard & Reid by National Discount when the latter were in trouble – their bond man seems to have been rather a gambler. I said that bonds seem to have been the problem for many discount houses – they seemed to find it hard to cut their losses, compare Union Discount recently. He agreed but pointed out that discount houses did take on the duty of making a market in (short) bonds after the war, and Union took this duty seriously. One reason for the growth of the now combined firms of Gerrard & National was their lack of any feeling in this direction. Also, apparently, they gained a lot of fixture money from Barclays (Peter Forrester of Barclays knew Whittaker of Gerrard & National very well) which helped them.

I think it was partly because of my, now distant, Bank of England background that in the early 1990s I was invited to join a small team to go to Romania and advise them on the creation of a Treasury bill market. There were three of us, one ex-Bank man, one who had worked on the bill side of a commercial bank, and myself. We ran almost immediately into a problem. We felt that an introductory issue of Treasury bills should be made so that the local banks could get some experience of the role these could usefully play in their balance sheet management. An extremely bureaucratic civil servant from the Romanian Treasury was adamant that this was impossible as legally the Treasury could only issue bills if it needed the money and had no other way of raising it. We discussed various aspects of a bill market and tried to contrive ways round this ban, but in the end it meant that practical progress was impossible, and we left without achieving anything. We had stayed in the Bucharesti Hotel which previously housed Communist apparatchiks visiting the city for Party occasions and to have a good time as a reward for service to the Party. There was a bar on the ground floor filled with high-class tarts, making it clear what had constituted a good time for loyal Communists. Bucharest seemed rather run-down except for the truly enormous and magnificent Ceaçescu palace and conference centre with its pillared hall, great corridors, multiple massive reception/conference rooms and a balcony looking down a wide boulevard from which Ceacescu evidently intended to address his adoring countrymen. It did not quite work out like that as they executed him before his palace was finished.

The final echo of my time in the Bank only emerged some forty-four years after I had left it. I had been acquainted with Forrest Capie (Professor of Economic History, Cass Business School, City University), meeting him at various conferences and seminars over many years. In 2005 I heard that he had been commissioned to write the fourth instalment of the Bank of England's official history, covering the years 1958–79. Since he was one of the few monetary historians that I knew, and because I wanted now to dispose of quite a large quantity of books and miscellaneous papers on banking in Britain (which by now had themselves become monetary history), it seemed a good idea to offer them to him. These included a full run of the *Bank of England Quarterly Bulletin* from Volume 1 No. 1 up to the 1990s, which covered the period he was concerned with (but I kept my copy of Volume 0 No. 0 which was our initial dummy run). I think it was the temptation of the set of the *Quarterly Bulletin* which led Forrest to relieve my bookshelves of quite a lot of other material as well. He invited me to meet him at the Bank and we discussed my memories of my time there (1960–62) which was in the period he was concerned with; it was a pleasure for me to recall this period of my life and I hope it would be of some use to him. While in the Bank I had kept a diary, but I had completely forgotten about it and it was only by coincidence that a few days later I uncovered it while going through various other papers. Most of the entries reveal my, sometimes critical, interest in the structure and objectives of policy making as seen from within the Bank, the views and personalities of some of those involved, and operational aspects of the Bank's management of money markets and the gilt-edged market. It seemed to Forrest that some of this might indeed be of some use in his work. Because of the rather specialised material as well as the many contractions and initials which I used, it was clear that I would have to transcribe and mildly edit its eighty five pages, some 42,000 words. It would be pleasing if this final echo of my time in the Bank were to prove of some value for the Bank's own history. As well as being a reflection of its time, such a diary can give a sense of immediacy, and for this reason the next chapter gives a selection of its entries.

16

Diary: The Bank of England 1960–62

Even after I had left the Bank there remained with me for many years a feeling of secrecy over much of what I had learnt of its affairs. Any use that Forrest Capie might make of the Diary in the official history of the Bank kept it still, as it were, within the walls of the Bank of England. But quoting extracts from the Diary for this book did raise questions in my mind, if no longer quite of secrecy then at least of its diluted aspects – confidentiality and discretion. But more than forty five years have passed, the Bank has changed radically, and nearly all of those mentioned by name are no longer living. I have therefore suppressed any qualms I might have had and below I give extracts from the Diary covering much of my two years in the Bank of England spent working on the *Quarterly Bulletin*, on various research projects and acting as rapporteur for the Committee on Internal Statistics (CIS). These extracts have been chosen to give examples of the main threads running through the Diary: policy-making in the Bank, the views and personalities of some of those involved, and the Bank's management of the gilt-edged and money markets. The latter were important because we had to deal with them in the Commentary in every *Quarterly Bulletin* and at every meeting of the CIS, but they were also of particular interest to me.

The original Diary entries were sometimes written on the day, sometimes written up a day or two later from rough notes jotted down on the day and sometimes retrospectively. For speed they often omitted 'the' and 'a' and first names; they also often used just people's initials. To make the Diary more easily readable my transcript often restored or expanded these but otherwise I did minimal editing in order to retain its authenticity.

Friday 28 October 1960

Short talk by the Deputy Governor [*Humphrey Mynors*] to Assistants, Advisers etc explaining background to Bank Rate cut [*of ¹/₂%*] yesterday.

1. Governor's neutrality in Mansion House speech in present circumstances really pointed to a fall. Betting on one of the next two Thursdays almost a certainty. Did it when expected – no desire to fool market over timing – its expectations could be sound. Tradition of fooling it could therefore be dangerous and was certainly not Bank of England policy.

2. Discount houses reduced tender rate on previous Friday; no sharp reaction by the Bank did point strongly to a reduction* as the Bank does not without reason swing its action around. Therefore when no heavy borrowing at the Bank (apart from a small accidental borrowing on Tuesday) the Bank line was clear.**

* cf 6 Sept 1961. [*This Note was added to the Diary later.*]

** This shows that the Bank's views can be read clearly by those in the business, without the need for explicit policy statements – Deputy Governor.

But this does point to the fact that close control over tender rates may in fact be a disadvantage because then the Bank's action tends to reveal what is coming next. More flexibility for the market could give more freedom over timing to the Bank. [*Note added a few days later.*] (Sharp borrowing on Saturday [*presumably 29 October*] by the discount houses was partly a mistake.)

Monday 14 November 1960

... Also had a long talk with John Fforde. I said it would be nice to know what impact, if any, the home figures committee [*the Committee on Internal Statistics, CIS*] had on the Governors. He said he thought it had some effect. He explained that the way the Governors worked was to ask for the opinions of Advisers, the Chief Cashier's Office and full time directors on a topic, consider them, and then decide for themselves, perhaps asking Advisers [*etc*] to comment on their [*the Governors'*] view. There appears to be no big debate or discussion at the Governors' level at all. What there is occurs at the Adviser and Chief Cashier's level and below. In Fforde's own case, he only has contact with the Governors on Home Industry and Exchequer forecasts, none at all on the balance of payments and only a little on internal finance. The whole arrangement he agrees is autocratic. He said that the Governors essentially took their own decisions, bearing in mind many considerations, particularly of timing vis-a-vis external, the Treasury etc, which they alone knew about. He agreed that much would depend upon the new Governor [*Lord Cromer*] (about whom no one I have talked to knows anything) and how he worked. They felt that when the tour of duty of HCBM [*Mynors, the Deputy Governor*] ran out three years after CFC [*Cobbold, the Governor*] retired, the former would leave.

Fforde's own view was that fundamental work was needed on growth and the balance of payments. At present the ministerial and Treasury view seemed entirely short term and non-fundamental. If something was wrong their only remedy was to put on more short term measures and for longer.

Friday 9 December 1960

In the last few days the final revisions to the *Quarterly Bulletin* commentary have raised some problems. Comments on events in the gold market in October have been altered extensively, and it is still not revealed to me what did in fact occur. It seems likely that the US views on the legitimate monetary use of gold caused the Bank to let the price rise, and the US then got cold feet and changed its view. But no one who knows is willing to reveal what occurred. Also troubles over the principle of commenting on action in the foreign exchange and gold market – never done before, but it is now done with the gilt-edged market, and why not some comment on the others. The technicians appear to be very much against it.

The Deputy Governor's foreword to the Commentary stresses the Bank as banker to the government. This fits with the view in the

[*Bank's*] Radcliffe evidence, which shows this view to be held in a rather naive way – or is this a smokescreen?

Thursday 5 January 1961

Talked to Maurice Allen [*Adviser to the Governors*] late yesterday. He mentioned the many tactical factors affecting the timing and announcement effect of Bank Rate. He quoted examples of government/Bank of England disagreement which had affected timing – back bench pressure on the Chancellor had caused it in one case, basic disagreement on the outlook and the balance of monetary/fiscal measures in others. These sort of factors had given rise to the impression that the Bank always tries to fool the market over timing. He pointed out the difficulty of being frank about such matters in the Bulletin. I agreed but stressed the importance of the *Quarterly Bulletin* for giving a better understanding of the general lines of Bank thinking, and he agreed. (He quoted as an example the rise in Bank Rate in June – one factor was to make the government take budgetary action later in the year, if further action was called for. The rate was moved then to stop the government relying upon Bank Rate later.) He stressed the role of personal relations in overcoming some of these disagreements between the Bank and the Treasury. He quoted a case of the Governor, the Prime Minister and the Chancellor settling an apparent Treasury/Bank impasse by a chance meeting at a cocktail party. It seems to me as if some airing of the matters in dispute would be a good thing. He also stressed the effect on foreigners' views of changes in Bank Rate as showing the UK authorities' state of mind (a very expensive way).

Sunday 29 January 1961

Some time ago, talking to Thornton, I was saying how the Bank seemed determined to be a weak central bank in many directions. He thought that this was so. He said that (in his view) this was because the Bank had no faith in its ability to manage the system with any precision so that it deliberately tried to avoid getting firm control over, and thus in its own view becoming responsible for, such things as deposits. In addition this would mean a different approach to the gilt-edged market, and some very radical changes.

(Implication is that the system is better on its own and implies judgements about outcomes.) He agreed that obscurantism had prevented any informed alternative view from emerging. Thornton described the Bank's view as being that 'monetary policy is psychological warfare'. He stressed that Special Deposits were voluntary; this seems to be a typical piece of Bank psychological warfare – keeping everyone guessing what the real situation is, and what the Bank will do next.

Tuesday 7 February 1961

Talked to Jasper Hollom [*Deputy Chief Cashier, responsible for the management of the gilt-edged market*]. The Bank does not like to sell a tap stock below a recent issue price, otherwise holders who applied find it falling under them; if this happens consistently, fewer applications. (In my view this is all irrelevant really, but the Bank action is based on this.) Since there are few holders of such a stock and therefore few sellers, such a stock can be 'stranded' as the market falls. Sometimes an institution will approach the authorities (via broker, jobber) and suggest a switch into such a tap stock if the authorities will reduce the differential between it and the stock the institution is prepared to sell. The proposition may involve quite a large fall from the 'stranded' price, but only a small one from a realistic price; a further result will be a refloating of the tap stock. This happened recently with the longest tap stock, when a switch [*by an institution*] from War $3^{1}/_{2}$% [*into the stranded top*] was proposed and was done with a step down from a stranded price. The Bank likes to keep a line of War $3^{1}/_{2}$% as it is widely held, a bit speculative and free of tax to overseas residents. If anything is going on, it always reflects in War $3^{1}/_{2}$%, and with a line of stock the Bank has some control. Average holding [*by the Bank*] used to be £10m plus or minus, but is now more. A lot was taken in (on a falling market helped down by the authorities) from Egyptians a year ago, for compensation payments. Then the authorities were pressing prices down unobserved, or so they hoped!

Holding the price of the long tap steady means that with a high coupon such as the present $5^{1}/_{2}$% stock, this is equivalent to a falling net price because of accruing interest. The long end is the one related to equity investment. Recent weakness at the long end has been related to the medium 'hump' in turn due to a now expired tap. Investors preferred to get a good yield for ten years rather than go long and get a worse yield and greater uncertainty. Over ten years, blue chip equity investment gives better prospect of yield, under ten years medium [*term*] stocks look better. Medium stocks for income therefore give good returns and are hedged by redemption. Recent loss of medium tap does not worry the Bank – a new one can be organised in 3–4 days if necessary.

Friday 24 February 1961

Had a long and very frank talk with John Fforde. I told him that I felt there was no real leadership for the General Office (and myself in particular) to respond to. Apart from the *Bulletin* and other regular work, there was no guidance on what topics could usefully be thought and written about; in particular, there was no indication of the direction of policy thinking higher up. This was the main weakness which left us with no sense of direction to follow. (Altogether I let off a large scale complaint.) The timing was stimulated in part by Roger Opie's telling me about the organisation of the Economic Section, its active internal life, and the leadership it receives from its heads.

He agreed that from many points of view the internal organisation of the Bank was defective. He pointed out that the Bank did not work on a committee system (as did the Civil Service), and that the Governors are highly operational. They did not exert any leadership in ideas partly because of this, and because in part they were not always mulling over new ideas. (I got a strong flavour of the Bank's unwillingness to extend its area of responsibility if it could possibly avoid it.) He did not feel that much of the statistical work was lacking in direction because of ignorance of policy (as I had said). He felt it was interesting in its own right (I denied this, for myself). He felt that the General Office could think up and write up subjects on its own. (I denied this on the grounds that policy was the fixed arbiter of relevance, and we knew nothing of it.) He rejected my suggestion of weekly meetings – he would either have nothing to say or it would be too secret to reveal.

We covered many other topics – he asked me what I *was* interested in – I didn't seem to like anything. I replied that I was an economist and not a statistician; I was interested in policy and what was significant for it. He said that when he entered the Bank he had no illusions what it was like. I replied that I had a lot of illusions, because no one had given me any hint of what it was really like. He also said that I had not concealed my poor view of much that went on in the Bank. Altogether an active morning with no holds barred and a good deal of acrimony on both sides. (Fforde revealed a fair amount of quick and bad tempered reaction.) However we finished up on quite good terms. The next thing I am going to do is look at Maurice Allen's model of the financial system; as I pointed out to Fforde, this was my sort of subject (but it had not been mentioned before to me).

Wednesday 15 March 1961
Last week Fforde was alarmed that [*the*] Sayers seminar was to discuss the view of the National Institute of Economic and Social Research (NIESR) on devaluation. As a result I saw the Deputy Governor on Thursday. Pleasant and cordial talk. He said that being from LSE he did not doubt that my views would be taken as personal, but that I should take reasonable care not to say anything appearing to commit the Bank in any direction. He said he welcomed the National Institute's expression of its view! (Typical subtle paradox of Deputy Governor type.) This because it showed that National Institute's following of the Treasury line was weakening – greater independence. We also discussed the teaching of applied economics which we agreed needed improvement.

Finally he asked me how I was enjoying being in the Bank; I said that it was a love–hate relationship, with varying proportions of each. My main feeling was that we got insufficient leadership in our thinking from the top, not enough awareness of policy. This he thought was an interesting view, which he would like to discuss further at some later date. I said I hoped for the opportunity.

Friday 21 July 1961
Talked to Stevens [*one of the four full-time directors of the Bank*]. Told him that considering the General Office wrote the *Quarterly Bulletin* and the *Annual Report* for the Governors and wrote assessments and papers for them, they (and Stevens and Watson [*Head of Overseas Department*]) showed little if any interest in its members. No one came to see it, there was no attempt to educate it to do its job better; Stevens accepted the criticisms and said he would think about them. But he did not quite see how we could be educated as there was little to educate us in – the Bank was an operating institution and most of its actions were really reactions to situations facing it. I suggested there must be ground rules – general principles etc. Stevens said that these were so simple as to be platitudinous and any more active policy was liable to run into a political quagmire. He kept his cars open in Books [*the daily morning meeting with the Governors*] to learn all he could and tried to get the Committee on Internal Statistics to think about and discuss relevant topics. He agreed that its [*CIS's*] operation was still constipated. The impression I got was that the ruling few are very few – the Governors, Parsons (all on the Committee of Treasury) with others (Maurice Allen etc) ad hoc. Stevens seems nearly as much outside as we are.

Tuesday 25 July 1961
After Selwyn Lloyd's [*the Chancellor's*] statement [*which included a rise by 2% in Bank Rate*] Alan Whittome, John Page and I were summoned to a meeting in the ground floor committee room at which the Deputy Governor gave a briefing talk on the new measures. Room very full, most Advisers there and Principals etc.

The Deputy Governor appeared rather depressed. He had not heard the statement, but spoke from the meeting he had with Selwyn

Lloyd on Sunday at which he was given the details. He felt that government expenditure should have borne more of the brunt – hard to believe nothing more could be done. The Payroll tax had no friends: it might release labour but probably unskilled, and not skilled (which was the real shortage); might stiffen employers in wage negotiations – but unlikely; might have been used simply because it had been fought through the House of Commons. But apparently regarded now as a mistake. Bank Rate has some (undefined) internal effects; apparently stock accumulation and 'Speculation' are expected to be affected. Also a 1% rise would not end uncertainty in the gilt-edged market, whereas 2% would, and would set the scene for a recovery of confidence (in gilt-edged). Overseas central banks assumed that the Bank would act to halt any large resulting hot money inflow. (Apparently external not so important! When he spoke of internal effects he had a very 'inward' faith-based look and seemed unlikely to take any disagreement kindly.) The announcement in the House of Commons was very carefully preceded by the 'announcement' at the Bank – the board [*which showed Bank Rate*] was put up a minute or two before Selwyn Lloyd reached this point [*in his speech*]. Several people came round to ~~see if the Selwyn Lloyd was right (!)~~ [*sic*] confirm his statement.

Tuesday 1 August 1961
Someone said today that Darby said that Mynors [*the Deputy Governor*] was utterly conventional in his approach to any action. Bearing in mind that he was once Secretary of the Bank, this does not seem surprising, for Secretaryship somehow seems to exalt form above content. When running the Statistics office, he was said to be able to do everything himself – someone said that this shows in the utterly negative approach of all who were ever under him – they just had to do what they were told and ask no questions. His interest in genealogy and cosy trivia (the holding of Bank of England stock by the professors of divinity in the University of Utrecht) all point to a very limited outlook; but to great capability within those limits. The limits seem to exclude any willingness to really search for the truth or for sound opinions; if it is familiar and satisfies appearances, this is enough.

Sunday 20 August 1961

Have travelled on the Drain or up the Travelator (the Waterloo
and City Railway) with the Deputy Governor a few times recently.
[*He lived just outside Guildford and travelled up to Waterloo and on
to the Bank each day.*] On one occasion he found me talking to
Paul Bareau [*a highly regarded financial journalist*] and Manning
Dacey [*Economic Adviser to Lloyds Bank*] at the top of the Travelator.
As he went past he said 'What a thing to see on a Wednesday' (the
Committee of Treasury day). I walked on with him. He said that
he used to fear that Manning Dacey was going to burst, but now
he has slimmed a bit.

I met the Deputy Governor coming out of the Bank one evening.
He said that we seemed to work the same hours (Whittome
suggested that I should have replied 'Yes, but I take work home
with me'.) We talked about stockbrokers, whom the DG said lived
in very sordid offices. He agreed that this was in part because they
were spending their own money on these, not shareholders money.
He also said that a stockbroker had told him that switching following
the Trustee Act was being held up by legal uncertainties – many
Counsels' Opinions were being sought, as insurance if nothing else.
Obviously rich legal feeding in all this.

On last Friday (18th [*August 1961*]) I saw the draft of the article
on Bank Notes for the *Quarterly Bulletin* on which the Deputy
Governor had queried the 'volume' of notes – weight? Cubic
volume? and added 'Once I compared the surface area of notes in
circulation with the area of Hyde Park and Kensington Gardens.
The result was astonishing but not very useful'.

Wednesday 23 August 1961

Whittome has prepared an article [*for the Quarterly Bulletin*] on
Basle help [*cooperation over the recycling of funds leaving the UK*]
but Parsons apparently turned it down because it gave all the broad
figures – and we had not told the IMF these details or even the
total! It seems incredible that the IMF should have made the loan
to the UK with[*out*] knowing the true position of the borrower.

Apparently P.J. [*Per Jacobsson, Chairman Managing Director of the IMF*] was told personally, that was all. Very irksome for Whittome. Parsons, Watson and Rootham simply decide this sort of thing without him [*Whittome*] even present to defend what he has written or the reasons for writing it. One problem has been explaining the channels through which it came; currency deposits with the Bank of England Banking Department were not in the Bank Return – was the Bank only the agent, selling currency to the EEA [*Exchange Equalisation Account*] and holding bills on account? Or was it acting as a banker? The latter seems true, but the figures follow the former. (Not all; some was apparently shown in Other Accounts.) Apart from that, help appears to have gone into OO [*Overseas Official account*] if the Treasury bills were held by the central bank direct or ONO [*Overseas non-Official account*] if invested via a commercial bank in London.

Thursday 31 August 1961

Basle cooperation article has been reconsidered. Big fight in committee. Watson, Parsons, Rootham, Fforde, Maurice Allen for it (now!), Bridge, O'Brien and Hawker strongly against. The operators fear it may prejudice their freedom of action in the future and may increase instability by preventing a blanket of silence falling over events. (What if future cooperation, kept secret, and not ended by an IMF loan? Also will have to reveal quarterly the later changes in the remaining borrowing.) Others feel that since figures are published, known special factors must be revealed, otherwise liable to charges of cooking the figures. Also concealment is already difficult, changes in sector debt holdings do require some explaining. Also concealment did not stop the outflow in the second quarter of 1961.

Revealing the magnitude of the deception also worries some of the anti's; another factor is that O'Brien [*the Chief Cashier*] appears to fear what this may lead to in revealing gilt-edged operations, although no suggestion now of less than quarterly revelation, and this has not seemed to harm Bank operations. (Some questions also of the Banking Department treatment of cooperation money?) No agreement at the meeting. A statement of the two sides' views is to go to the Governor for him to decide.

Wednesday 6 September 1961

Alan Whittome (+ John Fforde) has at last actually dealt with the Governor [*Lord Cromer, who had become Governor on 1 July 1961*] face to face. Following the meeting at which the Governor was told that no agreement could be reached on the Basle article, he [*the Governor*] tried to find some compromise, rewriting parts and reducing the hard figure content. He also rewrote part of the Commentary. In general his drafting is not very good; really needs considerable tightening up, but no one seems willing to tell him flatly that this is so. At present the situation is that the Governor's redraft plus amendments has now gone to the Chancellor. It now remains to see what happens to it at that end.

Thursday 5 October 1961

John Fforde is really an exceptionally keen worker. He is capable of terrific attention to detail. When dealing e.g. with a document he pays tremendous attention to:

terms of reference (or committee framework)
the Bank's role in relation to the document
date of writing and subsequent events
reasonableness of every figure and assumption
their detailed implications
(money and real, forecasts and figures)
exactly how each aspect links up with other
information, papers etc

In fact, preparation for a full-scale and searching examination on the field in question. Altogether, very impressive.

Monday 23 October 1961

Talked to John Fforde. Extended credit controls under consideration once more. The history as Fforde saw it (but did not necessarily approve) was that in the early 1950s the Bank dismantled the nearest thing it had to a real weapon – Treasury Deposit Receipts, which in any case it had a moral unwillingness to use ([*because of the*] terms of introduction) and no clear recognition of need to use – and relied upon requests etc in large part directional. This allowed tactical manoeuvre against the Treasury, pleading the need for persuading the banks, and therefore need for appropriate policies at the Whitehall end. Neither the Bank nor the Treasury were keen on a direct Treasury/banks connexion (overseas confidence aspect here) and the Bank was not keen on having, or trying to have, full control over the banks: a) the banks then had ample gilt-edged and imposing Special Deposit type control could look difficult (no thought of education and persuasion of opinion in support of this) b) banks might withdraw cooperation on selective controls and require exchange control type of guidance case by case. This in turn could create responsibilities for the clearing banks, to be borne by the Bank. On control of other institutions, the Bank was not anxious to extend title of 'bank' as defined, to other institutions (Companies Act privileges on hidden reserves) and Whitehall was not keen on putting all financial institutions into the Bank's field – Board of Trade interests in hire purchase for example. But some views in the Bank that there should be complete control or nothing over outsiders (Maurice Allen). Abortive bill in ... [*sic*]

Monday 13 November 1961

At the Committee on Internal Statistics meeting Hilton Clarke said that after the 6¹/₂% Bank Rate the discount houses were not looking for a lower Treasury bill rate – they simply felt they had to keep in business. Feeling that 6¹/₂ would not be for long – a silly rate – not low enough to keep out foreign money etc. Expectation of a further fall and a terrific overseas and outside demand for Treasury bills. Outsiders (Keyser quoted) could sell off hot bills [*profitably*] to the clearing banks on account of customers [*to be held by customers not the clearers themselves*]. The market felt it had to keep in this [*Treasury bill*] business and therefore had to keep competitive bids. The market cannot force Bank Rate down – e.g. early 1959: convertibility going well – the market saw Bank Rate going down but [*it*] stayed put throughout the year – couldn't force it down. So long as the authorities can keep money rates up this puts an effective ceiling to the discount houses' bid* (but outsiders could get all the bills – what of Hilton Clarke's inside tender then?). In fact the real danger point seems to be the Treasury bill/commercial bill rate link and the Bank Rate/advances rate [*link*]. If the Treasury bill rate falls unduly, then strains on the bank bill/advances rate link.

* But if a fall in rates is expected, they [*the discount houses*] can get [*the Treasury bill rate*] right up [*i.e. down*] against the (average money rate) floor as earlier this year; and if absolutely certain of a fall in rates they could take the Treasury bill rate down below the average money rate for a little while.

Jasper Hollom [*now Chief Cashier*] pointed out that the shortest bond is never available to the market – the Issue Department is a large buyer-in (it may hold a quarter or more at maturity) – only the next but one [*maturity*]. Some problems seem to have arisen because the next shortest bond is not attractive relative to the shortest one. Overseas Official [OO] holders therefore cannot be advised by the Bank to do this switch in their [*OO's*] own interest. Apparently asked to do so to help the Bank – quite exceptional – usually customer's interest [*is used*] as a facade at least. (The expected fall [*in Bank Rate*] has pushed the rate on the next but one bond out of line.)

I gather there has been a £10 million mistake in the published Basle figures between Official Overseas and Overseas Non-Official. Information kept so close by Roy Bridge that no one in Balance of Payments [*Office*] knew about it! Going to be left. Someone said that the only true figure in the balance of payments is the gold reserve – too optimistic?

Sunday 17 December 1961
Quite frantic work over the last two to three weeks on the commercial bills article for the *Quarterly Bulletin*. Original draft by Hilton Clarke, rewritten by Alan Whittome. This was then discussed by myself, John Fforde, Bill Jackson and Whittome. I had a lot of comments, and as Whittome was then getting busier on the commentary, I took over the article. Substantial redraft by myself put the article into final form. Several sessions with Hilton Clarke – the first in the buffet at Waterloo station where, coming from my train, I met Hilton as he was on his way to Southampton. We did a brief bit of work amid the puddles of tea before he had

to catch his train. Met Menzies – head of Export Credit Guarantee Department and Adviser to the Governors designate. (Met Gibson Jarvie on the Drain on the same day.)

All sorts of difficulties arose [*with the article on commercial bills*] – poor figures, 'self-liquidating', endless drafting points. But eventually it went to the Deputy Governor and was passed (O'Brien [*now a full-time director of the Bank*] liked it) and to the Governor (who wanted two introductory paragraphs). Also to MacKinnon of Brown Shipley, who didn't know the difference between the rate of discount and the rate of interest. Really very hard work, but interesting. Hilton Clarke and Dudley in the Discount Office kept on disagreeing on the Bank's quality control over commercial bills.

One reason why quite a lot fell to me was because Alan Whittome was having a very difficult time with the Commentary. The Treasury was very difficult over the Basle figures; wanted all reference to figures excluded for third quarter of 1961. Ridiculous, and the Bank presented an almost united front in favour of giving more [*figures*] than the Treasury wanted to. Frank Lee [*Permanent Secretary of the Treasury*] not really very cooperative. Difficulty over third quarter of 1961 balance of payments announcement which omitted Basle completely. Eventually the Governor saw the Chancellor of the Exchequer and settled it largely in our favour. But *Quarterly Bulletin* seriously held up due to this, though publication is likely to be on time. In all this the Bank is in favour of educating public opinion, the Treasury obscurantist.

Saturday 13 January 1962
Had a talk with Fforde a few days ago. Subject of devaluation came up (I had mentioned an aspect in the CIS assessment) – clearly a very delicate one. Fforde was very uncommunicative, but clearly thought has been going on at the top. His message to me was that it was more expedient for us in conversation etc to stress things like export incentives. He also reminded me of my own views that if we really get down to doing things which would be necessary for effective improvement of the balance of payments by devaluation

(efficiency generally, keep down wages costs, keep up slack in the economy – and high elasticity of supply of exports) then devaluation might not prove necessary. In other words, as far as possible avoid touching the subject directly.

(Maurice Allen said that Bank Rate seldom changes in the period immediately before the budget (sterling is seasonally strong). The record does not really bear him out but the point is obvious enough). Another thing that Maurice Allen told me was the Governor's saying that he believed in having a look under every stone.

Saturday 20 January 1962

Talked to Jasper Hollom about the effect of the conversion offer for the February maturity (offer on 8 December for application on 18 December, 6% 1972 and another tranche of 5½% 1983/84). In the market there was talk about this reducing the amount of stock in the market – all nonsense in fact – and a rise in market optimism (and official net sales) due to this. Hollom said that the terms did imply a slightly less determined suppression of the market by the authorities – a less aggressive posture. It all went back to the Chancellor's speech (Budget?) when he said that there would be no need to raise new money in the stock market in this financial year, and added some implication that this might help the long market. This latter came from Maurice Allen and was rejected by John Fforde and myself as not really following. According to Hollom, even though the Bank had good reason to think that the outcome of the budget was likely to be less favourable than the estimate, let alone the July estimate, they did not feel forced to reverse the Chancellor's stated view by their actions – instead they indulged in a little opportunistic salesmanship, allowing the market to delude itself and gaining some net long sales by doing so. The fact that undateds are now much freer with the end of the 08/12 tap is really illusory – a new tap stock could be produced at only 3–4 days' notice if really necessary. Interesting example of short term management of market expectations.

In the Committee on Internal Statistics I objected to statements about a rise in gilt-edged followed by a fall 'damaging the gilt-edged market', on the grounds that people still held gilt-edged stocks despite an almost continuous fall over more than a decade. Hollom seemed to take the same view as myself here – letting them be wrong does not necessarily do any harm.

Tuesday 23 January 1962

Suggestion that total Bank lending to the discount houses each banking month should be shown in *Quarterly Bulletin* table 6 had been agreed by the London Discount Market Association who think it would improve the table. The first explicit evidence that those contributing statistics also find them useful, or at least interesting.

Maurice Allen once described monetary policy to me as 'psychological warfare'. The emphasis in the Bank on psychological effects of measures, from Bank Rate to Special Deposits, is easier to understand when it is recognised that those [*outsiders*] involved are in constant close contact with the Bank through one channel or another and, crucially, via market operations, so that people in the Bank are very conscious of their reactions in outlook. The use of Special Deposits in July was regarded as having psychological effects in making the banks concerned over liquidity – to keep it in the forefront of their minds; also affected would-be borrowers. Level of gilt-edged also became more of a matter for the banks' concern and thought. Apparently a feeling (by Chief Cashier?) that if Special Deposits were not used in July this would be interpreted as a lack of faith in the weapon. In fact the Bank has got faith in Special Deposits, although not as a total answer. In July there was pressure on the pattern as well as on the total of bank lending; also apparently there was a warning [*to the banks*] not to resort to gilt-edged sales to maintain liquidity or not to rely upon the Bank helping the banks to offload stocks, and not to try to escape via commercial bills.

Sunday 18 February 1962

Saw Chalkley [*a director of Gillett Bros, the discount house*] on the train about three weeks ago. He said that Ronnie Gillett found the Governor and Deputy Governor very gloomy about the budget prospects – presumably the fear that Government expenditure will not be held down sufficiently; last time I saw the Deputy Governor, I felt he had aged and really looked rather ill.

Talked to Hilton Clarke a little while ago. He gave the impression that the Bank was waiting for Whitehall to make up its mind about the reduction in Bank Rate. Meanwhile there have been savage tactics in the money market; the market is very confused because all reasonable pointers point to a fall which has been held up for semi-political reasons (fear of a green light over wages; July rise was on psychological grounds – the same grounds are now hindering a fall). (I noticed that the rise in sterling seemed to begin before 25 July – Bank Rate up to consolidate the movement? Indications of psychological effect seem to turn not on the level of the rate, but on the rate of change of the rate, hence the asymmetry between +2% and [*its reversal by*] a succession of −1/2%'s.) Hilton Clarke was expecting the market to tell the government that they were going to swing round to a view of 6% for the year ahead if Bank Rate was not down by the next tender and push up Treasury bill rates accordingly. This has happened, and will now make a cut in Bank Rate difficult without showing up differences in view and raising questions of who was out of line. Another problem that Hilton Clarke saw before this was that holding rates up via action in the money market meant that prior indications of a fall in Bank Rate would be [*made*] too obvious by the easing of tactics (unless as above the outlook swung round).

A position of technical strength: when things cannot get any worse.

Last weekend I started a trip to Birmingham [*where the Governor, Lord Cromer, was to make a speech*] with Sir Cyril Hawker. Enjoyed it enormously. Met Governor and had a long conversation with him and Hawker on Tuesday evening late in his hotel suite, on government expenditure. I felt that their attack was rather weak – no hint of rate of return approach – simply desired less of it. No distinction between possible economies given policy and changes in expenditure via changes in policy; also refused to see difficulties in quick changes to get quick effects on expenditure. Also refused to see monetary limits as implying policy changes if [*they are to be*] effective. [*The Governor*] revealed one strong principle – honest money, but here also no evidence of underlying thought on relative costs and returns etc of such a policy. He speaks very sloppily, is a bit effete and a shade supercilious, but occasional touches of quite nice humour. No signs of [*other*] deeply seated principles. Not well equipped intellectually, but no fool (his writings perhaps show more strength). Difficult to see any real leadership on any central banking issue, but probably no obstruction to general progress. He takes his position pretty easily and seems a typical scion of a merchant banking peerage family; he can be quite tough when his own decisions or views are opposed. I feel the Bank could/should have done better.

In our discussion I said that John Fforde's draft of the Governor's speech was better than the one [*the Governor*] delivered. I stressed the advantage of appearing technically in command of the subject as against aiming at the lowest level (TV scientists example). Better to win over the more informed public and let views percolate from there. I quoted the general view of informed public opinion as the only sound foundation for sound policy, and it was not opposed. I also said that one technique in his speeches could be to draw out the implications of government policy, perhaps asking if this was what the country really wanted. He said before this that one couldn't keep on at the government over expenditure, in speeches at least. On the way back in the Governor's Rolls (which did 115 mph on the M1) [*the chauffeur told me that its tyre pressures had been specially increased for this speed*] he and Hawker talked about City (= merchant bank) candidates for his previous Washington job (where he found the work hard).

Sunday 25 February 1962
Talked to Hawker last week about the burden on full-time directors. He agreed that it was very heavy, but in his view the Bank's solution was more likely to be through Assistants to directors rather than through more directors (which would involve statutory questions

because of the Bank of England Act). I felt that such an arrangement could be an excellent training facility also.

Talked to John Fforde about the Governor. Ff said that he felt he was a typical product of his environment – he has their moral outlook and prejudices. His stress on honest money is one of these, and (with plenty of inflationists about) probably a good thing. At Birmingham he stressed that those putting money into the Post Office Savings Bank ought to be able to withdraw the same real value later. (What are the others [*other principles*]? Supremacy of London as a financial centre? Growing role for merchant banks/accepting houses? Independence of the Bank of England? Certainly restraint of government expenditure.) But Fforde agreed with me that the moral basis of such assertions is unsophisticated and not strong – it can always be discomfited by the reply: would you prefer honest money and 10% unemployed to 1% p.a. dishonest money and 2½% unemployed? A governor of the Bank of England must have at least this degree of sophistication surely? Also Fforde agreed that since it is hard to pinpoint any substantial amount of individual hardship due to inflation, such moral fervour may be ineffective.

Friday 16 March 1962
Blackler said that the BIS was a very useful central banking organisation. It performs a number of useful services, including directing attention to problems, and beyond that it operates in the Euro-dollar market* (it used to operate in the gold market in gold deposits) and it makes a profit to help pay its costs. As chief operator MacD [*full name not recorded*] is pure 'economic man'. If any arbitrage in Euro-dollars is worth doing, he will be operating. His activity is a better guide than arbitrage calculations!

*The Bank of England does put a small amount of dollars on deposit with the BIS, but it is chiefly continental central banks which do this.

In his talk to Sayers' seminar MacD showed just that little reserve/neutrality of spirit which is typical of Bank and civil service people talking to outsiders.

Thursday 17 May 1962

Before starting the Commentary for the June Bulletin Fforde and Thornton saw the Governors; one object was to avoid any clash between the content of the Commentary and any policy measures which might occur before its publication or immediately afterwards. No lead whatever from the Governors. They only said they would bear in mind the tone of the Commentary and timing of publication as a consideration in the timing of policy. This seems to raise the question of the Governors' view of policy – a full forward programme? or a few main aims and otherwise opportunist on other possibilities and timing? Probably the latter. I also got the impression that the *Annual Report,* while a Parliamentary commitment and thus unavoidable, was to be scaled down as far as possible.

* * *

This last extract is from the final entry in the Diary. My secondment to the Bank of England ended on 31 May 1962 and I returned to the London School of Economics.

17

Life at Home in the 1960s and 1970s – with Children

Life Together

We had only been married for a fortnight when the time came for me to move to the Bank of England, coming home each evening and telling Toni about my day in the City. Several other friends were now married and provided us with a social circle and occasional small dinner parties, but mostly we were happy going to the cinema together or with friends, or just being on our own. We paid occasional visits to my parents and to Toni's mother, widowed many years before, who lived within a mile of each other at Bognor. However, their backgrounds and interests were very different and after meeting at our wedding they really had little incentive to see each other and relations between them were slight though in no way strained. We did some redecorating of our part of 20 Avenue Road – the ground floor – but already there were thoughts of a house of our own, and some window-shopping at estate agents with this vaguely in mind.

At weekends we would often go out for walks or visits, and one place we visited several times was the Natural History Museum in South Kensington. When buying Toni her diamond engagement ring, I had borrowed a book on diamonds from the local library and was soon able to differentiate between the modern brilliant cut and the earlier cut with a smaller top face or table; I concluded that many of these older stones, which came from Brazil, had superior fire to the more recent ones from South Africa. This, and the fact that Toni's father had once been a diamond merchant, gave both of us a mild interest in diamonds, and when visiting the Natural History Museum we always went to one gallery where there was a display case containing a collection of rather small but rare and exotic coloured diamonds – one or two of the usual yellows, but also green, blue and red ones. Then one day it wasn't there, and it turned out that it had been stolen. In due course it was replaced by another similar collection until many years later that too was stolen. It was as if someone had taken *our* diamonds.

Toni had passed her driving test at Chichester and going on a visit one afternoon I suggested that she should drive. This lasted for only a few minutes; it was clear that she must have had an remarkably sympathetic driving tester since her skill at that time is indicated by the fact that on her way to the test she had gone round a roundabout the wrong way. Further, around Chichester there were no hills, only one mild humpbacked bridge, and as a result her hill-starts were alarming and unsuccessful. Clearly she needed more practice; up onto Richmond Hill and with gentle instruction she became able to move off uphill with less and less over-revving and roaring. She practised her driving while I was at work, going over to Richmond to do some shopping, but nervously choosing the middle of lunchtime when she reasoned there would be fewer other cars on the road. She soon developed into a competent driver.

We continued to see some of my friends from the English Speaking Union, amongst them Cyril Wallworth still a keen diner-out and man-about-town. At one time he was engaged to a very pretty, rather pale and fragile-looking girl with red hair and green eyes. Allegedly it was called off because they could not agree about the central heating temperature they were to have in their intended home, she wanting it cool for her complexion and he wanting it warm for comfort. She then went off and married an elderly American millionaire who very considerately died shortly afterwards. Suddenly Cyril began to look very pleased with himself and after some pressure he revealed that he was again seeing his ex-fiancée who was still pretty, pale and fragile but now also wealthy. Perhaps the temperature still wasn't right because nothing came of it. It was Cyril who gave Toni a copy of *Real French Cooking* by Savarin (whom we both confused with Brillat-Savarin, quite a different person); her cookery skills were then at an early stage and she felt its recipes were altogether too advanced for her. For example, how do you cook a rabbit? 'Place in your rabbit two truffle-stuffed pigs trotters … cook on the spit, basting with a little brandy'; she refused to read any further. Later Cyril came to supper with us at Avenue Road, this time with a pretty and fragile ballet dancer who felt unwell halfway through the meal and had to withdraw. Despite this second blow to her cookery, Toni forgave Cyril. Even she would admit that some of her early attempts using recipes from less advanced cookery books were not entirely successful, particularly poached white fish with grated chocolate. A test that she passed triumphantly was cooking jugged hare, although leaving out the jugged bit. This animal, just a leveret really, was one of my brother Michael's road victims on his drive down from Malvern and he produced it from the back of his car when he arrived. Toni felt trapped into cooking it but left our local butcher to do the messy business of gutting and skinning.

A House and a Family

Our next move was to do some casual house-hunting. Our search area was the arc south of London from Brasted in the east (where we had gone to dinner with Alan Whittome from the Bank and his wife) to Guildford in the west. While we could not say exactly what we were looking for, we felt we would recognise it when we saw it; what we could say was that we could afford a price of up to £5,000. A few visits produced some salutary shocks; anything near that price was not the sort of house we were looking for. Our expectations were scaled down, our price limit was painfully raised and our search became more serious and focussed on the Guildford area, conveniently between London and Bognor. James Selwyn at the Bank of England lived in Guildford and he provided us with a copy of the *Surrey Advertiser* from which we gleaned the names of the main local estate agents.

Soon particulars of houses for sale would arrive by post, glowing with promise. Quite early on we received the particulars of Peony Cottage – price £5,000 – in Wonersh, a village just south of Guildford, and we viewed it the next weekend. It was an old end-of-terrace cottage, right on the village street, with no parking and only a small garden. We took the key (from under the watering can by the back door) and let ourselves in; it was charming, of cosy proportions, with wide old floorboards and a brick bread oven. We loved it, but it was quite impractical; however we did not abandon it entirely, for on many of our later house-hunting trips to Guildford we stopped at Peony Cottage, still unsold, let ourselves in and ate our picnic lunch there, enjoying its atmosphere. Other properties we viewed were less uplifting. One Saturday particulars arrived of a Surrey farmhouse – it sounded most appealing and urged on by Toni we were soon on our way. It was approached down a tatty road lined by unpromising 1930s bungalows, but the farmhouse itself was even worse – it was of indeterminate style, in a poor state, charmless, with depressing surroundings and a sitting room with a chimney breast which was tile-hung with roof tiles. Further, we discovered that nearby was a back-garden factory devoted to recovering used fat from fish and chip shops. This was our worst viewing, but there were many others which were not so objectionable but were certainly not what we were looking for.

House-hunting was interrupted by a traumatic journey – taking Auntie Bertha home. Auntie Bertha (whom we met in Chapter 1, where she was instrumental in finding the house at 20 Avenue Road for my parents) was a continuing and kindly presence throughout our childhood. In early May 1963, then in her eighties, she had been spending a short holiday with my mother at Aldwick when she was taken ill. Mother became deeply concerned and it was arranged that Bertha should be taken home as soon as possible. Michael would drive her from Aldwick up to a halfway point where he and I would meet and I would then take her on to Oxford and there deliver her to her daughter and son-in-law, Joan and the Revd Harry Wilkinson, with whom she was living at Kingham. It was only when I met Michael and transferred her to my car that it became clear just how unwell Auntie Bertha was. Driving on my own, there was little I could do to help her; she was groaning and clearly in distress and it became uncomfortably clear to me that she might die en route; thoughts of what I should do then loomed alarmingly in my mind. If I drove slowly it would take longer and increase the chances that she would die before we got to Oxford, but when I tried driving faster poor Auntie Bertha was swayed around in the back of my small Austin A35, showed increasing distress and wanted get out of the car. Then my car started running out of coolant and emitting clouds of steam; I stopped at a large house and asked for some water, fearful that the lady would come out with a jug of water for a strange young man only to find that he had a dead woman in the back of his car. So our nightmare journey continued, with me on tenterhooks, driving as fast as I dared without precipitating the death of my passenger. At last we reached Oxford with Auntie Bertha still alive and, greatly relieved, I handed her over to the Wilkinsons. My worries had not been unfounded; poor Auntie Bertha died shortly after she arrived home and I was left feeling uncomfortable at the role that I had played.

A house and a family seemed to us to go together, and both were slow in showing up. The family part was so slow that Toni attended a fertility clinic; mere preliminary examination proved remarkably effective and at the next visit she was found to be pregnant. Many weekends were now spent driving around looking at houses; and as Toni slowly bulged we also had to look around for ladies' loos. I went down one Saturday on my own and saw a house – 13 Aldersey Road in Guildford – which I liked; the elderly owner, Miss Edge, told me that it was under offer but allowed me to look around. It was in excellent order and was the best prospect so far, but its price at £8,500 was well beyond our limit; however we liked Aldersey Road which was quiet, well-tree'd, some 12 minutes' walk from London Road Station leading to Waterloo, and surrounded by good schools. We told the estate agent to let us know if any other properties there came on to the market. Slowly our expectations were further scaled down and our price limit further raised. In July 1962 Mark was born and our search party then consisted of myself, a slimmed-down Toni, and Mark in a carrycot on the back seat. There were interruptions from family affairs (of which more later), but our search now became more serious and reached its peak during the freezing winter of January and February 1963, when on one long run the small engine of our Austin A35 did not even warm up properly and on occasions I had to use the choke to keep it going at all. Along some roads the high banks of frozen snow made it impossible to park in order to see properties; for some this did not matter, as Toni declared firmly that she was not going to live in that sort of road.

Then as the thaw began our luck changed too; particulars of another house in Aldersey Road – number 7 – arrived through the post. It too was priced at £8,500, but we went to see it anyway. We rang the doorbell and it was answered by Miss Violet King, small, elderly, short-sighted and nervous. She was not expecting any viewers and was rather flustered by our arrival, particularly when we told her that we had received the particulars from an agent she had not heard of. She allowed us into the hall while she phoned her agent to clarify matters. When he answered, we still remember her words: 'You are a very naughty man. . .'; but this was evidently followed by a reasonable explanation – the house had not sold and as was customary it had been circulated to other agents, hence our arrival. Mollified, Miss

King now allowed us to put Mark and his carrycot in the sitting room and look round the house. It was somewhat run-down, but with a generous garden; at last we had found the house we were looking for. We expressed our interest and parted on good terms with Violet and her equally elderly companion, 'Nibby', a woman of some character who had passed the Advanced Driving Test in her late seventies. My older brother Michael, who was an architect, did a survey for us, noted some bomb damage and pronounced it free from any alarming problems; negotiations then began. The house had not sold at £8,500 and through her agent she came down to £8,000 and then £7,750; we forced ourselves up to £7,500. And there matters stalled for several weeks – it was a time when the property market was leisurely compared with the mad scramble it turned into much later. Then the agent contacted us and suggested that we and Miss King should split the £250 difference which separated us. Even at £7,500 we felt we were dangerously overstretching ourselves, but we were so close and had invested so much time in searching that we agreed, though with misgivings. I was driving up to Cambridge for a meeting of the London and Cambridge Economic Service, and had arrived at Harold Rose's house in Letchworth to pick him up where he greeted me with the news that Toni had phoned to say that Miss King had agreed and the house was ours for £7,625. There was a wonderful sense of relief that at last we had a house, even though our financial position – a mortgage of £4,250 – to us seemed perilous. The legal arrangements were completed (with some fine-tuning which saved us a few pounds in stamp duty) and at last number 7 Aldersey Road, Guildford, Surrey, was well and truly our very own house. (For more on the history of this house see Chapter 27.)

On Friday 5 July 1963 a great green Bentalls removal van drew up outside our new house. The large rear doors were opened and there, dwarfed by its vast emptiness, were our few worldly possessions: two beds, a cot, a desk, a few chairs and a tea chest containing everything else. It took the removal men about ten minutes to unload and carry our belongings into the house, then off they went leaving us with not just a sparsely furnished house, but with a home of our very own.

Toni was now pregnant again so only vital work on the house could be done immediately, primarily the installation of a new central heating system before the cold weather came. This was done by a local firm, D H Bryant Ltd, who prided themselves on leaving the house at the end of each day perfectly tidy with no sign of all the work they were doing, and when Annabel was born they presented Toni with a bouquet of flowers. The company has looked after our central heating ever since with apprentices who worked on our system in 1963 coming back as mature engineers many years later to maintain it. Other improvements were then done over the following years, as time allowed between what then became our main domestic task of looking after two, then three, young children: Mark (born 3 July 1962), Annabel (7 October 1963) and Richard (15 May 1966). But life was good – Toni and I had each other, we had a house and family and I was enjoying my work at the School; the Swinging Sixties came and went entirely unnoticed by us.

We had only sporadic contact with our very Scottish Cousin Arthur but he visited us just before Annabel was born. One look at Toni's bulging figure and 'Och, your baby's not due yet, you're too high.' He was not quite right as Annabel was born only a day or two later. He also provided us with a family phrase; he regaled us with tales of his car which had achieved a quite improbably high mileage and when I ventured to suggest that our car was proving quite reliable his only comment was, 'Och, they're *soft metal*', a generally dismissive phrase which we adopted and used in many contexts. Poor Arthur; he had been in the merchant navy and after having been twice torpedoed in the North Atlantic and surviving one of the notorious wartime Arctic Convoys, he was drowned while sailing alone off Abersoch in 1965.

Some months after Mark was born a turn in the generations was brought home to us by the death of my father. While I was still in the Bank of England he had been diagnosed with lung cancer, but it had become evident that radiotherapy was not working and that he had not long to live. I and my brothers now found ourselves precipitated into a new world of Estate Duty, lawyers, surveyors, estate agents and property negotiations which was to have important implications for our future. The events which ensued are set out below in Chapter 28, 'Alford Financial History'.

Help Around the House

With three young children to look after, Toni now needed some help in the house and we had a succession of dailies, all of them very good, one of whom was Mrs Washington. Her main point of interest was that when her daughter needed a stair carpet, Mrs Washington knitted one for her. But it became clear that Toni deserved more help than just the few hours a week from a daily. Through friends we acquired Inger, a Scandinavian au pair girl; she was round-faced and bosomy, and on one occasion, seeing her coming down stairs, a carpet-layer could only stare and say '*Cor!*' We soon found that she was only sixteen, younger than we had expected; her aim in coming to England was to get away from her family and school; her English was already very good and her interest in children was nil.

Most of Inger's first week's wages were spent on 'ladies' intimate apparel' – pairs of peach-coloured knickers – and the second week's wages went on sunglasses with mirror lenses. These she was very pleased with and she wore them all the time so that, disconcertingly, I could see myself in them at breakfast. Soon when we went out to dinner with friends we were well placed to contribute our au pair experiences to the conversation ('I don't have time to bath Mark, I have to get ready to go out'). We also found that she did not like babysitting: 'I don't like being on my own'. More to her taste than babysitting was 'Dutch Bob' (in fact some perfectly ordinary English youth) who was staying two doors up the road. Inger would go out into the road and casually bounce a red ball, hoping that he might emerge and be decoyed into conversation with her; but Dutch Bob was never ensnared.

She was only too willing to share her interests and enthusiasms with us; as she talked to Toni in the kitchen, to emphasise her view, she would come closer and closer, and Toni would back away until finally she became trapped in the larder with no further means of escape. On one occasion Inger rested her hand on the pram and inadvertently rocked it as she expressed her opinion on some subject. In the pram Annabel fell asleep. This was one of the few occasions that she did anything directly for our children.

Inger used to go to Guildford's All Nations Club and we once asked her what she did there. She met friends; yes, but what else?

> 'I tell them about Mr Alford painting the radiator.'
> 'Surely that is not very interesting?'
> 'The way I tell it, it is *very amusing*.'

So not only were we keeping our friends entertained with tales about Inger, but Inger was keeping her friends entertained with tales about us.

At the All Nations Club she met AI Sabah, a well-heeled Arab youth. We were not at all sure that we approved of this, and late one evening, after they had spent a good deal of time parked in his Mini outside our house as they said their goodbyes, I felt that I had to intervene. I went out to the car, opened the door, and Inger nearly fell out. I told her to go upstairs to her room, and as she flounced off crossly, I told AI Sabah to follow me into our sitting room. Once there I told him that Inger was a member of our household, and he would fully understand that I therefore felt responsible for her. Yes, yes, he fully understood. But, I told him, women are weak and foolish creatures; Inger would tell my wife everything that occurred when she went out with him, and my wife – also a weak and foolish creature – would tell me everything, so that whenever he was out with Inger it was as if I was there too. Oh yes, sir, he fully understood. This I felt should cool his ardour down to a reasonable level.

As an au pair Inger was both exasperating and entertaining, but not at all the help that we had hoped for. Finally, we managed to pass her on to another household while being careful not to mislead them about her usefulness, which made it a delicate operation. From her new employer we heard later that one evening she had come home somewhat distraught and declaring dramatically that AI Sabah had tried to strangle her in the drive. Her new employer said that she would phone the police.

'No, no, I may want to go out with him again tomorrow.'

With all the ups and downs of our relationship, Inger evidently felt some attachment to us, perhaps as a little corner of stability in her world of change; for several decades she kept us informed of her activities by an annual letter and also visited us on several occasions. Her letters were utterly straightforward and in excellent English with some very colourful phrases of her own: when she was a courier taking tourists round sites such as Troy, her boss was a Turk – 'He sits at his desk and I gaze adoringly at him, he is such sweet poison!' And we did at least have some small influence on her – I insisted that when washing up she must thoroughly rinse all the detergent off plates before drying them; this made a lasting impression upon her and she told us that she had done this conscientiously ever since.

After Inger we had Elizabeth, a properly trained Violet Melchett nursery nurse, who was very good with the children and full of energy, doing far more than just being a nursery nurse. Next to help with the children was Micheline (soggy and needing help rather than giving it), then Jenny, untrained, but at least another pair of hands. At the same time, to help with the housework for a few hours each week came Mrs Phillips, who kindly gave us a clump of her Bachelor's Buttons (*Kerria japonica* 'Pleniflora') which proceeded to grow ten feet high and invade our neighbour's garden. Then came Mrs Fay who had been in service since her youth; she gave our morale a lift when she answered the telephone by announcing: 'Mr Alford's residence'.

Our Children when Young

Looking back over these years, they were dominated by our three children – Mark, Annabel and Richard – because we knew instinctively that they needed all our love and attention. Most of the detail of those years has long since faded, but here I have set out a few particular recollections together with a number of my diary entries; all of these are for the years when the children were twelve years of age or under. It should be noted that at this time Annabel was always called Lulu; this arose from Mark's early attempts to say Annabel, which emerged as Abbalulu and which we then adopted and shortened to Lulu.

Recollections – late 60s

Mark [*aged 6*] had been playing in the garden with some friends. He told us that they had been playing at cowboys, running up and down the garden shouting YIPPOO! The other day he asked Toni 'Who was on the phone?' Toni replied that she was; 'No, no, who was IN the phone?'

We spent the afternoon at a friend's farm near Aldwick; Richard went off exploring and suddenly reappeared spouting tears and pursued by a very small but aggressive Bantam – 'He pecked me and he banged me with his wing.' Much consolation required.

We influence our children in unexpected ways. Lulu has a red plastic toy telephone. She has just made an imaginary phone call, producing an uncannily accurate imitation of Toni's manner on the phone – charming voice, sparkling little laughs – with body language to match. In Mark's case, we were going out shopping when he emerged from the breakfast room and cried out 'Where my list?' – which is Toni's perennial cry. Mark may have found a new gardening technique – as he came up the garden he saw a beautiful peony just coming into flower, stopped and gave it a kiss.

Monday 29 November 1971
At home, played Happy Families in my study this evening. Lulu plays with no holds barred. She was thinking of stacking the cards (in her favour) till I stopped her; she revokes, looks at other people's hands, asks for Mr Bun the Baker's Daughter (to maximise her chance of success). Toni won. Went in to tuck up Mark and found that he had half pulled out the bed that fits under his own and was sleeping perilously on its narrow width, wrapped in his eiderdown. He used to do this more often – obviously he finds its adventurous to sleep like this. He is now really quite a weight to lift back into his own bed.

Saturday 10 June 1972
Took Mark into town [*Guildford*], dropped him in North Street to go and buy himself a cricket ball; played cricket with it – much more dangerous than our usual tennis ball game. Lulu batted as 'Evonne Cricketgong' – after Evonne Goolagong the Australian tennis star. When the latter was playing at Pit Farm, our local tennis club, a few weeks ago Lulu asked 'Are they tennising against each other's countries?'.

Friday 16 June 1972
Had a bath prior to going out. First Richard joined me in the bath (he loves doing this); discussion of my umbilicus and more intimate details in comparison with his. Then Lulu came and joined us, despite feeble protests from me; finally Mark got in as well. Extremely crowded and uncomfortable, but much enjoyed by them.

Thursday 17 June 1972
The children had their first try at badminton, with a cheap set I had bought; very erratic, but enjoyed knocking about. Took Richard to the Library; he talked to the budgerigar, straightened up books and slid under bookshelves while I chose something to read.

Monday 19 June 1972
Richard woke early and when told it was not time to get up, dissolved into a storm of tears. Complete recovery after breakfast, and left for school at his usual early hour – he still insists on going early, apparently worried that he will be late unless he gets there twenty minutes early; and school is only two minutes down the road. [*A little while ago the school had delicately suggested to us that it would be better if he did not arrive forty minutes early.*] Walked to the station leaving Lulu at her school on the way; we played a word game as we walked along, and practised the six-times table.

Thursday 29 June 1972
As Toni and I were sitting in my study having coffee after supper, Richard (whose bedroom is next door) announced 'Robert Price bit Simon Lodge at school today'. What happened? we asked, with visions of the headmaster avenging poor Simon Lodge. 'Just teeth-marks, that's all.'

Friday 30 June 1972
First thing in the morning from Richard, still cosily tucked up in bed:

> 'Mummy, if I tell you something, you won't be cross and say "OH RICHARD!" will you?'
> 'What is it, darling?'
> 'I've got chewing gum on my feet'
> 'OH RICHARD!'

Toni and I were sitting in my study after supper. Richard suddenly remarked from his bed 'I can smell a strong smell of fruit cake'.

With a shriek Toni flung down the paper and fled downstairs. The cake, for Mark's birthday, seemed to be unharmed.

More Recollections

A large Edwardian house only a few streets away caught fire when it was being demolished. Clearly there was no reason to try to save it and the fire was allowed to burn. Seeing this house in the evening with fire glowing at its windows, Toni thought it looked as if some great entertainment was taking place inside, to me it looked like some indefinable tragedy. The scene was certainly dramatic; this, the strong smell of burning and no one doing anything about it made an impression on all of us, particularly Mark who wrote a poem about it.

Huckle, the grey and white cat who lives opposite, spends a good deal of time with us. He is a cat of some character, but not always of good character; when he is under Lulu's bed, trying to get him out and downstairs is fraught. In the downstairs bath he has discovered the pleasure of sliding around on his side patting and chasing a marble; on most mornings he devotes several minutes to this quite noisy exercise. Then out into the hall where a children's wall hanging has a bell on the bottom; half a dozen leaps up to ring the bell and he feels set up for the day. He enjoys being with the children in the garden. As they straggle down to play in 'Catkin Cottage' (a rough play house hidden away by the shed at the bottom of the garden) Huckle goes too. Once when they were playing cricket he tried to join in; Lulu shoo'ed him away, Huckle went away a few feet, bounced back, then up on to his hind legs to deliver a two-pawed retaliation on Lulu's leg, and then off with tail up in triumph. Much wailing by Lulu from surprise rather than injury.

On Christmas Day (the only day I am forced to go to church) Mark did a reading from the Old Testament; he read it clearly and beautifully, and Toni and I were agreeably surprised. The content of the lesson seemed to me most unsuitable – full of killing and taking spoils.

My older brother Michael regularly spent Christmas with us and our Christmas puddings had the traditional coins hidden in them (by now one pound coins rather than sixpences). Michael seemed extraordinarily lucky in finding these coins in his helping of pudding, and our children complained at the unfairness of his success. It was only later revealed to them that Michael had been surreptitiously adding his own coins to his helping of Christmas pudding to tease them.

Our children very much enjoyed the annual LSE children's party. At one of these I was one of four summoned up onto the stage to help a conjuror with a trick. We each extended our right hand and he placed some prop upon it, then as he turned to the audience to explain what he was going to do, I put my right hand, with prop, behind my back and extended my empty left hand. The conjuror turned back to us and was astonished to find my hand empty. This simple manoeuvre was much appreciated by the audience and gained me some kudos with our three, but I had to come clean and the trick proceeded.

Lulu went to a party at a house off the A31, the Hog's Back; she looked very sweet dressed in a dark blue velvet dress with white lace at the wrists and neck. I, on the other hand, looked very scruffy when I stopped working in the garden to go and collect her. Coming home along the Hog's Back I started to pass a Rover with a well-dressed couple inside. As I drew level my car's engine cut out completely. The Rover slowed, encouraging me to overtake, but with a dead engine I was slowing also, and steadily we slowed down next to each other. The couple in the Rover were now looking rigidly ahead and clearly thinking that they had some lunatic driver next to them; with the Rover right beside me and having to keep my eyes on the road, I was unable to make any conciliatory gesture and was left wondering what to do next. Slower and slower, with the couple in the Rover looking even more rigidly ahead and determined not to catch the eye of anyone so unbalanced and so close. We were now going so slowly that the Rover decided to make a break for freedom. Tentatively it drew ahead a little and then quickly accelerated away, greatly relieved to have escaped from the Hog's Back maniac. My car now came to rest on the verge; Lulu and I got out and the only way to get home and summon the AA (no mobile phones then) was to thumb a lift. So this ill-assorted couple – a little girl, sweet in a charming party frock, her hand held tightly by a scruffy man, obviously up to no good, tried to get a lift. No wonder most cars were careful not to notice us. At last a man in a little old van took pity on us; it turned out that he had done work in Aldersey Road and he drove us home. I think Lulu just found the van an exciting new way to travel.

In a note book – Lulu's version of the highest mountain in Britain: 'Ben Nellie'.

Sunday 27 Jan 1974
In the afternoon collected Richard from a party; he had fallen into a stream and was rather pale and wet. Later Lulu opened Mark's door too far and wrenched the hinges; myself cross and Lulu tearful, but allowed her to listen to David Copperfield at 8 p.m. on the radio: 'You are letting me have luxury, and I have been so naughty'.

Wednesday 30 January 1974
At about 4 a.m. Lulu suddenly arrived at my bedside and announced rather tearfully that she had swallowed a marble. I told her that it would come out at the other end, and not to worry; in any case how did she come to have a marble in her bedroom at that time in the morning? Suggested she must have dreamt it. Somewhat consoled she went back to bed. Returned a little later to announce that it had been a dream. Richard then appeared – he had a pain in his tummy. Came into my bed and we slept till morning.

Thursday 31 January 1974
4 a.m. again. Pussy, a black cat whose real name was Coalie, and who lived over the road until we adopted each other, was wandering around growling – I had forgotten to shut her in the breakfast

room, and if she is left to wander this is what she gets up to. Lulu woke up, woke me, and together we went down to shut Pussy up – she looking very self-satisfied as if she was particularly popular. Then took Lulu back to bed, kissed her goodnight, into bed myself and back to sleep.

Sunday 3 February 1974

Toni in bed with flu. Children very good – I produced very basic meals. Lulu cleaned the oven and swept etc and obviously enjoyed being helpful. We all listened to David Copperfield 8–9 on the radio – excellent.

Monday 4 February 1974

Lulu at home because 11+ [*exam*] papers are being marked by her teachers; she continued yesterday's good work, scraping nasty things out of crevices in the oven. She and I then went shopping, back for lunch – very simple. After his bath Richard put on Toni's sheepskin coat and crawled around being an animal – looked exactly like a charming baby orang-utang.

Monday 11 February 1974

Very blustery gale last night. At about 3 a.m. Richard came into our room – he didn't like the wind. I didn't like it either and had been kept awake by it. He came into bed with me, we had a very cosy little talk and then both fell asleep.

Tuesday 12 February 1974

On my way to the station this morning, I was passing Lanesborough School playground when a ball flew into the road. Found myself talking to Richard and other members of his form – all crowded against the wire [*netting*] like inquisitive little calves. Richard pink and pleased at our encounter.

Wednesday 13 February 1974

When I arrived home Richard and Lulu were in the bath; we had a little talk and I left them discussing the naughtiest boys in Richard's form – pleasurable horror at their evil deeds as recounted by Richard, and the number of debits they have got. Also discussed Richard's credits, (and his occasional debits) which are of considerable interest to us – not, I might say, because of their great number, although he does fairly well, but because they make a useful entry point for hearing about what goes on at school. In bed he told me who had got most, who least. He is very interested in them but not obsessed. Before I kissed Richard goodnight I asked him a few simple sums. Lulu insisted on being asked some too – a man has 3 sheep, buys 10, sells 6 etc. Then we had one with ponies – one of Lulu's enthusiasms; a horseshoe on each hoof and a spare one on each tail – Lulu helpless with laughter. Then snakes with 20 ribs, bought 6, 3 died etc. Mark was in the bath and listening. He pointed out that the the ribs remained even if the snakes died – had to drop that one. Then Mark's turn – gave him a few and he replied with 51 apes each with 21 teeth etc – he couldn't finish because he was laughing so much.

Friday 15 March 1974
Home early and Toni collected me from the main station. Toni went out to evening meeting of Appeal Committee for the Church Hall. Lulu and Mark came into the study before they went to bed and I asked them quick-fire questions on multiplication tables. They enjoyed this so much that Mark had to rush off to the loo.

Saturday 16 March 1974
Lovely day; finished pruning the roses and then had a bonfire which the children enjoyed. After dark Lulu and Richard kept it going and took their supper down to it; not a success, Lulu trod in her soup and Richard spilt his on his knee – retreat to the house in disorder.

Sunday 17 March 1974
Mark [*unwell and*] in bed for much of the day. After tea I did (at his request) my imitations of Terrifying Criminal, Tree Sloth and Educationally sub-Normal Boy Scout. Usual great success with Mark, but Toni less impressed – she feels it may be revealing the true me.

Tuesday 2 April 1974

I rang Toni from the School today and also spoke to Richard; he sounded very grown up and sensible; he is eight in May. Saying goodnight to the children is tending to grow longer again. A cuddle for Richard, kisses for Lulu (both accompanied by sums, general knowledge questions etc) and a talk with Mark, take quite a time. But they do enjoy it so.

Sunday 7 April 1974

[*In the evening took some plants to friends.*] Lovely red sunset low in the west, Richard very impressed. On the way back we stopped at the top of Harvey Road and looked [*down*] over Guildford with the sun sinking to the horizon – watched it disappear – really a very striking sight. Richard liked this and we discussed it earnestly on our way home.

Tuesday 16 April 1974

Busy week with Holiday Fun. Mark doing Cycling Proficiency and Lulu and Richard both doing roller skating in the morning. In the afternoon Judith Banton took Mark and Lulu to Beekeeping. The children all went into town by bus on their own and were allowed to have an ice cream each. [*Toni was one of the group of mothers running Holiday Fun; this organised a whole range of activities for children in the holidays.*]

Monday 3 June 1974

Mr Pilkington [*was at our house*] when I arrived, after his [*maths*] coaching session with Lulu. We had a drink on the terrace and talked – very congenial. Mark was with us and casually dropped items of educational news – he has most credits in his form; he got 95% in a Common Entrance maths test paper; came top in hardest Common Entrance English paper that his teacher had come across. Very encouraging, rather appealing and all done very innocently.

Recollection – 1975

Annabel [*aged twelve*] went with a school party to France. Going over, the weather in the channel was very rough and most of the

20 Avenue Road, Isleworth, circa 1928, with Auntie Kate and mother (holding her cat); our family home from 1922 until the Second World War.

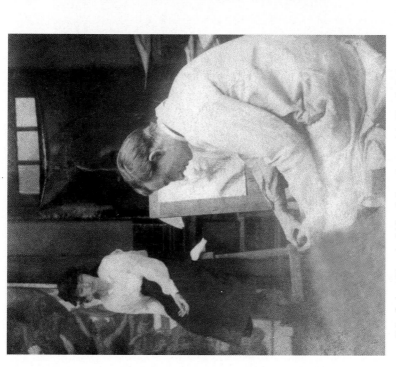

My father Frank Alford drawing, with Doris Mary Davey (later his wife and my mother) in the background. Probably at Lime Grove School of Art, circa 1919.

My older brother Michael, right, and myself (aged 8) rather inelegantly posed; Aldwick 1934.

Phyllis was our maid at Avenue Road, but here she is looking after me (aged four) at Aldwick.

3 South Avenue, Aldwick Gardens, our holiday home in the 1930s and
later our parents' permanent home; taken in 1954.

7 Aldersey Road, Guildford, rear view in 1934, two years after it was built.
A house quite unknown to us at that time, but destined to play a large part
in our lives many years later.

In Civil Defence uniform as a member of a Rescue Party: 1944.

Cartoon by Mr Pasfield, drawn in the House, teasingly picturing me as a Bevin Boy; 1944.

Mother feeding Raucus, our very intelligent pet rook; Aldwick 1944.

Damage at Shelley Road, Bognor Regis, by a flying bomb, 27 August 1944; this incident is described in my diary.

Crocodile flame-thrower tank practising; 7th Hussars, Soltau 1947.

From a group photo of the 3rd/4th County of London Yeomanry, Territorial Army, 1949; I am in the middle of the back row.

Just de-mobbed from the 7th Hussars but loyally wearing the regimental tie; 1948.

Myself on the left, commanding a Comet tank, Thetford - Dereham training area; summer 1949.

Leading my troop of four tanks at Thetford - Dereham with a Daimler scout car in front; 1949.

Myself, my older brother Michael and my younger brother Julian - always J to us; Aldwick, 1955.

Myself and Bill Phillips when tutors to a Vacation Course, LSE 1953.

My mother and father relaxing on the loggia at Aldwick; mid 1950s.

The garden at Aldwick in spring, with mother standing by the fountain; mid 1950s.

Richard, Annabel, myself, Toni and Mark; Guildford, 1981.

Richard, Annabel and Mark; 2000.

Myself giving a lecture, 1981.

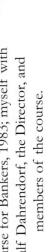

Course for Bankers, 1983; myself with Ralf Dahrendorf, the Director, and members of the course.

At home together; 2002.

Toni on our gravel drive; Guildford 1996.

With members of one of our Russian courses on their graduation day; I have already put on the Financial Times tie they have just presented to me; 1995.

7 Aldersey Road, Guildford, our house and home since 1963; rear view in 2004.

7 Aldersey Road, view down the back garden, early spring 2006.

party were sick; Lulu was not, and gained many brownie points by ministering to the afflicted. In Boulogne one of Lulu's friends was still unwell and had to be led round the town bent double; the highlight of the trip seems to have been a funeral at Boulogne Cathedral. After a meal (unwise, surely?) the return trip was just as rough and Lulu again had the opportunity to distinguish herself. At the school a cluster of increasingly anxious parents had to wait some two hours before the coach finally arrived at 10 p.m. with its load of pale and wobbly children – except for Lulu, who had flourished in these dire circumstances.

Household Activities

Toni's infrequent appearance in these memories is very misleading. She played the central role at home, and her ability to do all her multifarious tasks and keep everything running smoothly meant that most of the time there was little of interest to report – except that everything was running smoothly. But there is also the fact that most of the quotes have to come from my diaries, as Toni only had time to keep very sparse ones over those years – mainly dates of appointments, and school terms; if she had kept more extensive ones the entries would have given a much more balanced picture of her role. We did have one way of sharing family duties more fairly; by the time the children had been tucked up, Toni would be feeling pretty tired and would go to bed quite early. Then, working in my study or after I had gone to bed, I was the one on night duty. Soon I developed a capacity for instant response; at the first sound of distress I would be out of bed, fully alert, and beside a whimpering child, ready with a bowl to deal with the unwelcome reappearance of last evening's supper. A few more heaves, a little comforting – 'Better out than in' – a quick wipe of the mouth, a sip of water, a final kiss and I was back to bed and asleep again. These short interruptions seemed to have little effect on my night's rest.

We took a reasonably rugged view on the ability of our children to survive the everyday hazards of life, but occasionally a new risk did emerge which seemed to require further exploration. One of these was the rinse-aid recommended for our dishwasher. I had some qualms about this ('gives you sparkling shiny dishes') being ingested by children over a long period so I rang up the the company's Customer Service number. My call was answered by Smooth Silky Voice; I tell her that I have a question about Rinse Aid and she launches into a glowing tribute to their product. I politely interrupt her to say that I wish to ask someone a technical question. Reproachfully Smooth Silky Voice asked me to wait a moment, and she would put me on to the supervisor. There was a brief pause, then Harsh Continental Voice comes on: Nothing wrong with our Rinse Aid, why you cause trouble? I have a technical question about its safety, please can I speak to one of your technical people? They very busy (then unwillingly) will ask them ring you if they have time. Next day the phone rings and Soft Scottish Voice announces that it is one of their scientists: I expect you have read these reports about children drinking rinse-aid and dying. Well, no, I had never heard of this new hazard, but what about long-term effect of ingestion of the residues? The amount is too small to matter. But how do you know? Because it's too small to measure. Have you tried measuring it? No. Why not? Because it's too small to matter. We went round this litany several times before I gave up and we never bought any rinse-aid. In fact with a double sink, ample hot water, an ergonomically arranged kitchen (stack, wash, rinse, drip dry, put away, all in a smooth progression) we have tended to use our dishwasher only when we have several friends for a meal or a larger family group at Christmas. And on these occasions our dishes seem to emerge from it sparkling and shiny without any additional help.

Another expert was more helpful. When going on a week's holiday, Christian Williams, one of our neighbours, accidentally switched off their freezer. On their return there was panic and a vast amount of food was condemned to be thrown away by his very safety-conscious (Finnish) wife Riitta. It all looked OK to us and a horrible waste so we took quite a lot of ex-frozen vegetables; I was in favour of eating some expensive packs of ex-frozen meat, but Toni drew the line at this and they ended up inside a very contented dog. This left us with the vegetables; just to be sure I rang up a frozen food company and talked to their technical man. He said that he would eat them – except for carrots, something less safe about them – without a qualm, and indeed did so; all the talk about not refreezing was because it could affect their physical structure (mushy peas?) and people might then complain. If one did not mind this possibility, then refreeze several times – he would. So we did, and in due course ate up all the refrozen vegetable casualties from our neighbour's freezer without any ill effects.

Education

While all this was going on, we taught our children the alphabet and a few simple words so that they had some grounding when they went to school. Both Lulu and Richard started at Drayton House nursery school, but Mark went straight into Lanesborough Prep School. On the first day he went in without any trouble, but by the second day he had realised what school was really like and had to be carried in by Mrs Helm, head of the junior Department, spouting tears and leaving Toni to wobble home needing a glass of sherry. None of them had any difficulty in learning to read, using the method by which we ourselves had learnt to read and which we must now call 'synthetic phonics', namely learning letters and their sounds which could then be built up into words. And it also allows written words to be broken down into letters and sounds – even many adults find it useful when coming across words like 'predestination' or 'Neanderthal'. (How the teaching profession could fail for decades to see the undoubted effectiveness of this method is quite beyond me. It makes me feel that too many of them cannot have any real teaching instinct.) The children learnt some basic arithmetic using Cusenaire rods at home and then multiplication tables at school (reinforced at home by a gramophone record of these tables). Spelling and tables then provided an enjoyable form of quiz at bedtime or at mealtimes; but the latter did not always have much scope for such activities, because many of our meals seem at that time to have consisted of mince followed by semolina. These were not dishes to be lingered over appreciatively – our speed record for lunch at home was eleven minutes from start to finish.

With school came homework; this faced little distraction, since we did not have television until many years later. Much worse was the annual hobbies day when children like ours, who seemed to have no displayable hobbies, had to be persuaded to do something – usually at the last moment; and indeed they did a little, while we parents, in showing them how to proceed, did most of it – cardboard sculpture, paper mosaics, wooden fort or whatever. Luckily we did these things sufficiently badly to pass as our children's own work. There were, of course, some objectionable children who carved out chess sets or collected and labelled bird and animal skulls, and they would be awarded the 'First Class' stickers; we concealed our jealousy of their success behind tight-lipped congratulations. Toni and I regarded music, like hobbies, as fine for those with the relevant talent, but none of our children were musical; only Lulu managed to make progress, if minimal, with the recorder and less with the violin. Not for us the pride of parents with children who were learning two instruments and playing in the school orchestra. Games were another weak spot; Annabel quite liked them but neither of the boys showed any enthusiasm; Mark's high point was being scorer to the first eleven at Lanesborough and Richard had no high point at all. But Toni and I felt that there were plenty of other activities that they could enjoy and we gave them general encouragement but did not try to push them in any particular direction. On one occasion Richard's form were each asked to write a description of themselves; Richard reported that his friend David's description began: 'I am a kind and handsome boy...'. We never knew what Richard had written.

While Lulu could stay at the High School from 5 till 18, the boys had to move on from Lanesborough at the age of thirteen. Right at the start we decided upon Charterhouse – only some six miles away – as the school for them to move on to, and we put their names down not long after birth. Then came the next hurdle of choosing a House for them to join. The school suggested a particular House, and I went there to look round it and meet the Housemaster. I did not take to this easy-going young man or the tone of the recently built House and wrote to the Headmaster, van Oss, telling him this. He responded sympathetically and said that he fully understood what I was looking for and would himself select for me a suitable House and Housemaster. In due course I was introduced to Mr Marriott, the Housemaster of Girdlestonites, a House normally referred to by its alternative name of Duckites. He was much more what I was looking for: mature, sensible and firm (and, incidentally, the part-time curator of the Royal Collection of postage stamps). The house itself was an Edwardian structure and evidently well run; later, when I met his wife, I could see more clearly who played the major role in this. Duckites was a 'tight ship' and that was what I wanted; Mark's name went down for Duckites. Now fast forward to Mark coming up to thirteen and due to enter Charterhouse next year. A note from the school: Mr Marriott was retiring as Housemaster;

his place would be taken by Mr Balkwill and we were invited to tea to meet him and his wife. At this point I should say that both Mark and Richard settled in quickly at Duckites, got on well with Balkwill, enjoyed their time at Charterhouse and look back on it with pleasure. But for me, meeting him for the first time, he was the very replica of the easy-going, rather untidy young Housemaster that I had rejected all those years before. Our conversation strengthened my view, but by now it was too late to change House; fate was against me and I accepted the inevitable, the outcome of which was much more successful than I dared hope. Duckites under Balkwill seemed to me a very loose ship; physically it now became untidy, with a heap of sand on the floor of one of the reception rooms for his children to play in. He had a large fawn and hairy dog, Rupert by name, who appeared to have two tails and regarded anyone entering the house as an intruder to be seen off with a snarl. On one occasion another master drove past in his Land Rover, his own dog with its head out of the window enjoying the passing scents; Rupert launched himself at this apparent intruder, seized him by the throat and the Land Rover drove on with Rupert dangling over the side still hanging on to his victim.

At that time Charterhouse took day boys as well as boarders and we put Mark and Richard down as day boys initially with the option to board. This allowed both of them to adjust to the school in their own ways. Mark cautiously remained a day boy until he entered the sixth form; Richard after one year as a day boy was eager to become a boarder. For us it was a successful adaptation of courses for horses. Both were to play a small part in the physical changes in Duckites. Mark was one of the sixth-formers who were invited to join in the design of a new extension to the house to provide studies for the senior boys; Richard's contribution was rather different.

Having overlapped with Mark for one year Richard now moved into Lower Cubes. Most of the houses at Charterhouse had by this time moved into well-equipped new buildings; Duckites was an exception, remaining in its solid Edwardian edifice, where Lower Cubes was a large dormitory divided into individual cubicles by six foot somewhat cracked asbestos partitions. But each resident was keen to decorate and improve his space. Richard, like some others, turned his cube into something like a pavilion by suspending a striped sheet over it and persuaded me to buy him two plants, an *Asparagus sprengeri,* and a large and showy *Dieffenbachia picta* for decoration; the former was tough, thrived on neglect and survived its time with Richard; the latter was much more delicate and lasted only a year before going to meet its propagator. Most boys had extra lights; unfortunately there were very few electrical sockets and soon each of these had a whole series of plug-in extensions giving off a faint smell of scorching Bakelite; wires trailed everywhere. Other boys brought in all sorts of well-intentioned items to 'improve' their cube, including flattened cardboard boxes to extend the partitions and add privacy or to line the floor. Richard felt that his improvements had produced a comfortable and distinctive space of his own; when I went to see it, I was dismayed by what I found. The boys were clean, well fed/and pleased with their first efforts at home-making, but Lower Cubes looked rather like one of the cardboard-box shanty towns created by down-and-outs. This strange mixture of expensive education and squalor was suddenly brought to an end by the arrival of a Fire Officer to inspect the whole house. I don't know what he felt about the high-cost slum that he found in Lower Cubes, but the electrical system was instantly marked down as a fire hazard, compounded by the surrounding combustible decorative home furnishings. All the 'improvements' in Lower Cubes had to be hastily removed, although the cracked asbestos panels were only taken down some considerable time later.

By the time Richard had arrived in the sixth form Balkwill felt that some of his older charges deserved an introduction to the finer things of life. This consisted of driving them in his elderly Renault car to Folkestone and then travelling by hovercraft over to France for some real haute cuisine helped down by plenty of wine, and then back again very late on the same day. Fortunately I never knew at the time about this and other 'official' escapades.

Annabel continued at Guildford High School for Girls (she was to stay there from five years of age to eighteen); having her at home meant we saw rather more of her minor school emergencies and had to transport her around for coaching in maths. We stoically put up with her efforts on the violin – fortunately short-lived – and the vagaries of some of the dishes which emerged from her Home Economics course. On the morning of her A level in art we helped her to recover her project from the dustbin where it had been inadvertently dumped, but generally this stage of her life at home did not provide quite the same scope for memorable events as did Mark's and Richard's life at boarding school.

Our Children Growing Up

Our children were growing up and the burden on Toni was relaxing. Mark left Charterhouse at the end of 1980; he then spent eight months working in the Computer Unit at the University of Surrey, just on the other side of Guildford, where he was encouraged to take various short courses in computing. At the same time he did some programming of a Data Inspection Package for me. He then went up to Exeter College Oxford as a Scholar to read physics, with us (particularly Toni) ferrying him and his luggage to and fro. One memorable journey was on a bitter snow-bound winter's day when we drove and slid cautiously the whole way and the screen-wash froze on the windscreen. Of his daily life at university we now heard very little. He graduated with a First in 1984 and then went to Harvard to do a PhD in physics. It was there that the computing courses he had taken when at the University of Surrey Computer Unit proved so useful, because at Harvard there was no advisory service or help and postgraduates were expected to find out for themselves how to use the computer system. He completed his PhD in 1990 and then had the usual post-doc appointments, including two years at Cornell where he met and married Mari Watanabe, a Japanese doctor specialising in the electro-physiology of the heart. Then after two years teaching at Glasgow they returned to the States with Mark as a tenured Associate Professor of Physics at Washington University, St Louis.

When Annabel left Guildford High School for Girls in 1984 she went to Oxford Poly (later Oxford Brookes University) to study hotel and catering management. Once again we were ferrying a child to and from Oxford. She graduated in 1987 and was offered the choice between a BA and a BSc; she chose the latter as looking more businesslike. After jobs in public relations firms, she and a girl friend together set up a PR company specialising in the field of food and catering. This proved very successful and in the late 1990s they sold out on very good terms and Annabel went off to Australia with her Australian partner and their daughter.

In 1985 Richard went to Southampton University to read English and another programme of ferrying began. Toni did more than her fair share of all this driving. My own main memory of our route to Southampton was its particularly hazardous merge into the fast traffic of the M3. We did not hear very much about the student life of Mark and Annabel at their different Oxford institutions, but in Richard's case we did hear of one episode. Advertising was a career that appealed to him and, encouraged by me, as a first step he started a Communications Society for those with career interests in the media generally. Richard, as the founder, was the chairman of what became a very successful student society. In his final year job applications began, but entry into advertising proved difficult. For one of the society's meetings Richard approached Grey, an advertising agency, who agreed to send someone to speak to the society on careers in advertising. In due course an account executive and two supporters arrived for the scheduled meeting, which was very well attended. Richard opened the proceedings, introduced the visitors, and went on to say that that the audience looked forward to hearing their talk as many would like a career in advertising and hoped that they would not receive a letter like the one he himself had received only the previous day, and he then read out his letter of rejection from Grey. After the meeting closed, the account executive quietly suggested to Richard that he should apply again to Grey; he did so and this time was offered a job. Even describing this episode makes a parent cringe, but it started Richard on a career which led him to becoming a managing director of M&C Saatchi.

Toni was a wonderful mother, there all the time to provide our children with love, support, food and clean clothes. We saw them make the usual progression from demanding and messy babies into real little children who often said and did charming things and began to reveal the first traces of their own distinctive characters. Then came adolescence and their characters began to emerge more clearly: Mark, very academic, hard-working, and cautious; Annabel, more outward-going, more self-willed and entre-preneurial; Richard, good-humoured, an organiser who always got on well with those around him. As they moved into their careers we felt we had given them a good start. But although they were now independent and self-supporting, we could never lose our slightly anxious concern for their welfare.

18

Life at LSE in the 1960s and The Troubles

Library Reforms

Early in 1960, just before I went into the Bank of England, I had become dissatisfied with two aspects of the School's Library. First, I had found that when I looked in the catalogue for ordinary government statistical material under its normal name – National Income Blue Book, for example – there was no guide entry directing me to the proper title, which in this case was: *UK CSO National Income and Expenditure*... There were some guide entries of this sort and I suggested that the Main Library catalogues should be made more user-friendly by having many more of them. An extreme example of unhelpfulness which I told the Library about but did not include in the memorandum was the entry for GATT which appeared only under: *[The] High Contracting Parties to [the] General Agreement on Tariffs and Trade*. The second aspect was that library facilities for undergraduates needed to be greatly improved. These two suggestions went as two memoranda to the Library Committee and I received in reply a letter from the Director which was constructive in tone.

I left the Bank of England at the end of May 1962; back at the School I found expansion plans were in the air and this led the Academic Board on Saturday (!) 23 November 1963 to agree that at last something had to be done to improve what was then the (undergraduate) Lending Library, something I had urged nearly four years earlier. With the support of Eli Devons I sent a paper round the Department urging that we should organise ourselves to help with this improvement. I was made a member of the Teaching Library Sub-Committee of the Library Committee, then I became our Departmental Teaching Library Representative and finally Convenor

317

of all such Departmental Representatives. This put me in a position through meetings, papers and private persuasion, and with the support of many others, particularly Harold Edey, to help shape the new undergraduate library and push matters forward insistently if slowly. By about the middle of 1966 the Lending Library had become the Teaching Library; it had been rationalised and extended; a short-loan/offprint collection had been added, the whole being clearly focussed on reading material to support courses taught at the School, and with arrangements intended to make it responsive to student demand. In 1978 the Teaching Library was to become a separate collection within the Main Library and I managed to stop it being renamed the General Collection – the one thing which it was not – and instead to be named the Teaching Collection, which continued to clearly indicate its role; this was finally changed to its now equally appropriate name of the Course Collection.

A New Building and New Colleagues

There had been physical changes in the School as well. Clare Market was a short street which ran along the north side of the School. On the other side was a long narrow building occupied by the St Clement's Press, a printing works, and another smaller building occupied by an obscure laboratory belonging to the Royal Navy. Periodically dark blue vans would arrive there and things would be delivered in boxes; we sometimes speculated on what they could be – parts of dead sailors? Or specimens of the food that had killed them? We had no idea, and not enough interest to go and ask. But now both buildings had been taken over by the School, renovated, and turned into teachers' rooms, teaching rooms and the computer unit, and renamed the St Clement's Building. Its main entrance now had glass doors with tasteful supply and demand curves etched upon them; more controversially, the large clock at its west end had been replaced by a mosaic, predominantly in pale blue with symbols of progress in aluminium attached to it (these included the Comet airliner and a factory with a tall chimney, neither of which proved to be fortunate or durable symbols). There was quite a lot of feeling that this was less attractive and less useful than the clock, and in the Academic Board there was a reactionary, but unsuccessful, campaign to 'put back the clock'.

The Economics Department took over a part of the St Clement's Building and Leslie Pressnell, a monetary historian who joined the Monetary Group in 1960, was allocated a pleasantly spacious room on the third floor, S.378. When Leslie left in 1970 to go to a chair at the University of Kent, I inherited this room. Several doors down the corridor there was a ladies' loo, and in due course its door developed a loud and annoying squeak. Eventually I brought up from home a small oilcan, but as a safeguard I approached Jan Stockdale, a social psychologist who at that time was Advisor to Women Students, to whom women students could go with complaints about such things as sexual harassment. She agreed to help and in due course we met at the offending ladies' loo; she kept watch while I sneaked guiltily inside, oiled the hinges and then we both hurried back to our rooms. Sometime later I passed her in Houghton Street and before I could stop myself I had greeted her with, 'Hi, babe, fancy a bit of sexual harassment?' She smiled and continued on her way. I hoped she hadn't heard.

There were also changes amongst my colleagues: Leslie Pressnell has already been mentioned, Roger Opic had left for Oxford in 1962 (although we continued to see him around the Common Room as he had taken over the editorship of the *Bankers Magazine* which required his regular visits to London) and Tony Cramp was to go to Cambridge in the following year. We were joined in 1964 by Laurence Harris and a year later by Brian Griffiths (both our own graduates).

Another person who had arrived in the Economics Department in 1960, though not in the Monetary Group, was Diana Oldershaw. She liked dogs, particularly Weimaraners – large, greyish and smooth haired. Her room often contained two of these and she could be seen striding along the corridors of the School on her way to take them out for a walk. She tried her hand at breeding these dogs and over lunch one day gave us an account of her efforts. Diana with her well-bred bitch and another breeder with her equally well-bred dog met in Diana's garage and the two animals were introduced. They showed little interest in each other and these two respectable ladies were finally reduced to trying to push them into close proximity to demonstrate what they were supposed to do. What little libido the animals may have had now evaporated, and the more they were urged the more mournful they looked. At last Diana's bitch looked at her so reproachfully that she felt guilty and gave up. Later Diana gained some notoriety because she refused to have her Weimaraners' tails docked as the Kennel Club rules required. But history proved to be on her side and docking was increasingly called into question until in 2006 it was made illegal except for working dogs.

Another arrival in the early 1960s was Lionel Needleman, whose main field was the economics of housing. He had a wide range of interests and I found him a most congenial colleague. These interests included gardening, particularly plant propagation, and he gave me many unusual plants for our garden. One of his favourite books was Cecil Torr's *Small Talk at Wreyland* (Wreyland is a tiny hamlet close to Lustleigh in Devon). It is a delightful book of meandering reminiscences and quotations from extensive family diaries, by a man of wide cultural interests; Lionel sought out a copy which he gave to me with a very kind inscription. I found it not only a relaxing pleasure to read, but also a book one could dip into and usually find something interesting. Where else would one learn that when Darwin received his Doctorate in the Senate House at Cambridge in 1877, some wags had suspended two stuffed monkeys, one containing a musical box, from the galleries so that they dangled over Darwin's head. When Lionel arrived at the School he had to find a local doctor; having no information to help him choose the best one, he went to see the school's medical officer and asked him for the name of *his* doctor! To my regret Lionel moved on to the University of Leicester in 1968, but we were to meet on a number of later occasions.

Conversations

I wish my diary had given more detail of some of the many enjoyable conversations I had with colleagues over lunch or in the Common Room, but only occasional and fallible recollections remain. I can remember having lunch with Theodore Plucknett, Professor of Legal History, who explained why the claims to the oil believed at that time to lie under the English Channel were definitively in favour of Britain because of legal rights clearly established in mediaeval times. Later it appeared that the French shadily trumped his learning by securing agreement that precedents established so long ago should be ignored.

Estate Duty brought me into contact with Ash Wheatcroft, Professor of

English Law and an expert on the subject, and we often had lunch together. He would try out on me various of the Christmas puzzles he used to set for tax lawyers: convoluted arrangements to avoid what was then Estate Duty, using very obscure legal provisions – but would they really stand up in court? Sometimes he had the pleasure of himself revealing even more obscure legal provisions which would defeat them. Hence insulting your heir, him suing you and getting heavy damages, thereby passing over a large sum and avoiding Estate Duty, he judged would fail because of the offence of the Misuse of the Machinery of justice. And the deathbed ploy of placing your wealth in a building surrounded by land over which there was no right of way would fail to reduce the value of your estate to zero because of the provision for Access of Necessity. If you give your heir a Treasury Bill, when it matures can it really be deemed to have evaporated, turning into a gift of no value? Or how about putting a large sum of money in a suitcase and 'losing it' just where your heir would happen to 'find it'? Or the use of the provision that a specific gift could only be given once: a multimillionaire (MM), in front of witnesses, gives his heir (H) a clearly identifiable parcel of bank notes – for example tied up in gold and green ribbon. H uses it to buy a block of MM's other assets, handing it back to MM in payment; MM gives it back to H as a second gift and then H uses it to buy a second block of assets and so on. Would this clearly identifiable gift be counted only once no matter how many times it was actually given or how much value it had transferred away from the Estate Duty net? But Ash would warn that some blatant schemes would provoke the Inland Revenue into finding unforeseen means of defeating them. Most of these schemes were swept away by the later move to Inheritance Tax.

Another discussion which extended over several lunches was with some younger lawyers and revolved around whether in criminal cases the jury should have the maximum amount of information about the accused, as any economist would suggest, or whether the information should be strictly limited to only what was immediately relevant to the case in hand, as the lawyers asserted. We reached no agreement but I gather that the change has been towards the economists' view. Mortgage lending was a subject which interested Jim Durbin; he had several suggestions for reform which I discussed with him. He was a statistician and half protagonist of the Durbin–Watson figure which is central to the analysis of time series. He was a keen mountaineer and used to walk up the six storeys of the St

Clement's Building to keep in trim. One conversation which I didn't have was when I went to Alan Day's room to ask him something; instead of Alan, I unexpectedly found two strangers seated behind his desk. Seeing my surprise one of them announced brightly: 'The cell has divided!' This was Andrew Shonfield, a distinguished financial journalist, who was doing some work with Alan at the time.

It is said that everyone remembers where they were when the news came through of President Kennedy's assassination on 22 November 1963. I was in the Senior Common Room with Eli Devons and two recent arrivals in the department (I think they were Reddy and Banerjee) at around 7 p.m., discussing some departmental teaching matter. We were sitting to the right of the fire when in came Helen, the very pleasant waitress who usually served our coffee and tea, looking very tearful and bearing the shocking news. After that the memory fades, but another one emerges. The previous year Toni and I, still living in my parent's house in Isleworth, had walked up to the Great West Road to see the Kennedy entourage driving from Heathrow into London. Bronzed and smiling, Kennedy seemed to us, as to so many, the right man to lead the free world and to promise hope for the future. We waved as he passed, something that neither of us had ever done before for any political figure.

My own teaching programme at the School had now settled back into its familiar pattern of lectures, classes and seminars for the third year Monetary Group, MSc Monetary Economics seminars and the Money Workshop together with a suitable number of second year macro classes. The usual proportion of my time was taken up with my tutees, discussing their class reports, giving advice and dealing with a range of fortunately minor problems. One student I had was a Vietnamese postgraduate who gave me a small plastic 'Product of Vietnamese Village Industry' Catholic statuette showing Jesus holding open his chest to reveal his Sacred Heart. When I told my colleagues about this rather grisly gift I was told that I was fortunate not to have been given the more advanced electronic version where the Sacred Heart lit up in red and pulsated. Richard Sayers continued his monetary seminars until he retired in 1968; when John Hicks delivered a public lecture on liquidity he attended one of these seminars for discussion of his lecture. It was well attended and so far as I can remember Hicks sat comfortably puffing his pipe, listening but saying nothing, leaving the meeting to discuss matters amongst themselves. But some comments evoked eloquent body language from him. One observation raised his eyebrows, another led him to nod appreciatively and make notes on a piece of paper. When the lecture was finally published we could see no sign of any changes arising from this meeting.

In 1964 I was promoted to a senior lectureship and then in 1965 to the Cassel Readership in Economics. It did seem to me that in the Economics Department relatively few Readers ever achieved promotion to Chairs; however, for the moment I was pleased to have moved up a step.

Retirements

My most senior colleagues were now beginning to retire. Frank Paish went in 1965; we had been close colleagues and had taught together as well as often travelling together on the train. He was very down-to-earth and straightforward; I can remember Lionel Robbins saying that Frank's mind was so clean you could eat your dinner off it. He could also be lighthearted – if specially requested he would pull his face into that of a mediaeval gargoyle, something he had perfected when at school at Winchester. Personally we had an army background in common, although our experiences could hardly have been more different, and it was only when I read his brief biography that I really learned of his experiences in the First World War, in which he won the Military Cross. Then in 1966 Lionel Robbins retired; he was a big man in every sense and a powerful figure in the affairs of the School. He was cultured and had a very nice sense of humour; although I had known him for many years, I really saw only the LSE facet of a man whose activities and interests covered many fields, but I liked and respected him. It was he who was the centre of the small group of economists who for many years used to entertain each other with conversation over coffee or tea on the left-hand side of the fireplace in the Senior Common Room. I remember him causing much amusement amongst his colleagues when he chaired a lecture in the Old Theatre by a distinguished visitor, either Hicks or Harrod; Lionel started by introducing Hicks as Harrod or Harrod as Hicks and then fell fast asleep on the platform for the whole of the lecture. To mark Lionel's retirement Ronnie Edwards gave a private dinner party to which I was invited and in due course a Festschrift was published in his honour to which I contributed an article on direct credit controls in the UK. This volume was edited by Bernard Corry and Maurice Peston, both his students and for a time my colleagues at the School before both moved on to chairs at Queen Mary College. Lionel continued to give some lectures after his retirement and I used to see him around the School; my last memory of him is seeing him squeezing his large frame into the Austin Mini which he had chosen as the ideal car for a crowded city. In due course our new library building was to be named after him, a tribute to his major role in achieving such a significant step forward for the School.

In 1967 Eli Devons died; he had been ill for some time and I visited him at his home in Cobham (I believe Max Steuer also visited him) but poor Eli was a shadow of his former self and despite my efforts to cheer him up it was a sad occasion. In 1968 Richard Sayers retired and there was the customary retirement dinner for him; it was felt that, in his withdrawn way, he might decline to attend, so his wife guaranteed to get him there on time without him knowing what was coming. It was not a very cheerful occasion. Many of us felt that he was retiring as a disappointed man; the Radcliffe Report, of which he was the leading figure, had not been well received and had failed to make an impact on monetary thinking and monetary policy. Some of the younger economists present did not have even the good manners to conceal their dismissal of his work and one or two others revealed hints of ancient grudges. It was not quite the occasion one would have wished for. In due course a Festschrift was published in his honour, edited by CR Whittlesey and JSG Wilson, to which I contributed an article on the relationship between Bank Rate and other short term interest rates.

Richard's later life seemed to me very sad; he left his wife and set up home with the woman who had been his research assistant when working on the history of Gillett Brothers, the discount house and this alienated his whole family. I heard much later that he was finally living in a rather chaotic and down-at-heel house, presumably the house in Clacton-on-Sea from which he wrote to me in 1981 when he agreed to be my referee when I applied for the Cassel Chair in Money and Banking against the formidable competition of Willem Buiter, who naturally got it. It was a sad letter; he felt out of touch and he was keenly aware of the breach '...accidental or deliberate, or what was the reasoning if the latter...' with the tradition of historical and institutional monetary scholarship which he had built up at the School. He promised to send me three of his papers from 1978–79:

'...these are of course my final publications. I am now quite incapable of writing even a paragraph fit for publication.' He was hoping still to have lunch with Theo Barker (then in the Economic History Department) 'when there is any stable evidence of my being able to sustain reasonable conversation (even if only small talk!) for more than five minutes'. It was an unhappy decline for a man who was a true scholar in his chosen field. Face to face he was not an easy person, but he was a great help to me at a number of points in my career, amongst them assisting the publication of my first article and with my secondment to the Bank of England. Looking back over a number of letters I received from him, I am struck by their kindness, in particular one he wrote to me when he saw my engagement to Toni in *The Times* in 1960: 'I should like to give you something [*in the event this was to be a very upmarket fountain pen gold-banded and with my initials*] to mark the occasion, at the same time marking my appreciation of the tremendous help you have been in these last years... And the other purpose of this letter is to wish you well in your new work [*at the Bank of England*]. You carry a great responsibility in being the first of what I hope will be a long and distinguished line... So, on all fronts, all the best!' On paper he was able express a warmth that so often eluded him in personal meetings. However, on one occasion he did unbend enough to tell me that on the way to his christening – in a carriage – his parents suddenly realised that Arthur Sidney, the forenames they had chosen for him, would give him the initials ASS; hastily he became Richard Sidney Sayers. On another occasion he told us of his experiences early in the war when he was in the Ministry of Supply and concerned with the import of various exotic materials such as uranium and mica. In the case of the latter (a natural glass, transparent, fireproof and used in oil stoves) he found that the only importer was a solitary man in a tiny office up a dismal staircase somewhere in the London Docklands. It clearly gave him pleasure to discover this and other tiny but finely tuned channels of trade. Two final glimpses: many years later Paul Volcker told me that when he came to the School as a postgraduate student in 1951, his interest in banking led him to introduce himself to Richard, whose first words to him were 'Are you here to work or to play?' When in his retirement Richard was at the Bank of England writing his volumes of the history of the Bank, Paul Volcker was again in London and enquired if he might visit his old supervisor, only to receive the brusque reply – No.

The Troubles

Around us the annual cycle of the academic year rolled on and life at the School continued comfortably on its way, oblivious of what was to come. When I look back at the troubled years of 1966–67 and 1968–69 they are a haze of student demands, demonstrations, sit-ins, occupations, meetings, and a few clearly remembered incidents. I was not a member of any of the committees of the School which were directly engaged in dealing with the student dissidents and was seldom close to the main actors in these events. But I was present and active on the ground throughout, doing all I could to oppose the ideas and actions of the trouble-making student leaders and their naive followers. I was entirely confident in my own grasp of the ethos and importance of the School and I was sure throughout that in causing these troubles students were abusing their position. They were here to learn and their behaviour was wasting their own opportunities, damaging those of other students and harming the reputation of the School, an institution which had a role and importance far greater than the distant or trivial issues that they were focussing upon. They made demands, but they had neither the maturity nor the experience to lend any real weight to those demands.

Early on I formed the view that it was essential for everyone really concerned for the School to hold on to the central principles that the School was an academic institution and that irresponsible interference with this role was not to be tolerated; youth, immaturity and personal neuroses were no excuse. As I walked up Aldwych to the School each morning, instead of the pleasant anticipation I usually experienced, I now had a sense of exasperation at the prospect of the latest student sit-in or occupation, but at the same time a determination to take every opportunity to argue with the dissident students, emphasising the irresponsibility of their actions, making clear my strong disapproval of their behaviour and standing up for what I knew to be the true values of the School.

In the first phase, culminating in 1967, the student at the centre of the trouble was Adelstein, President of the Students' Union, but in my view a young man who had brought with him to the School feelings about apartheid which seem to have developed from opposition to neurosis; I was told that he had compared the position of students at the School with the suffering of the Bantu under the South African regime. Joining him was Marshall Bloom, an American postgraduate who brought to the School his experience of civil rights campaigning in the States. Their objections to Walter Adams as Director of the School seemed to be that he had been head of a university in Rhodesia, a country with a regime of apartheid. All the evidence was that Adams did not approve of apartheid and had been doing his best for education in difficult circumstances. The case against him therefore appeared entirely misplaced. Whether Adams was a suitable director in other respects was something that students were in no way qualified to judge. After many convolutions and sit-ins, Adelstein and Bloom were suspended; then their suspension was itself suspended and this phase of the troubles died away.

Adelstein himself I barely saw; but I was in the Senior Common Room one day when a stranger was brought in by a porter – when I asked if I could help him he turned out to be Adelstein's father, presumably present in the School in connexion with disciplinary proceedings against his son. I gave him a cup of tea, we talked briefly and he seemed bemused by his son's activities and their consequences. He was then called away. I also barely saw Marshall Bloom; but when everything had blown over I came across him photocopying his press cuttings in the Library before going back to the States where he later committed suicide.

It was in the middle of these confusions that I began to feel that my colleagues who were of the same mind as myself should make our views publicly clear. After some consultation, I composed a brief statement condemning the troublemakers:

> We, the undersigned members of the teaching staff of the London School of Economics and Political Science, condemn the attacks made upon the Director designate by some students of the School, and the violence to which they have led, as entirely contrary to the spirit in which the affairs of the School should be conducted and a potential threat to academic freedom.

I called a meeting of my colleagues on 2 February 1967 in what is now the Vera Anstey Room. It was very well attended, my statement was approved, I signed it first and was followed by all those present; ultimately 125 members of the academic staff signed it. I sent copies of the signed document to the Director and to the press. It is the document referred to by Harry Kidd on page 55 of his book *The Trouble at LSE*. The most cheering thing about these troubles was the firm sense of shared values and commitment to the long-term interests of the School that I found in so many of my colleagues across all Departments.

The second phase of trouble in 1968–69 was altogether nastier, involving the row over internal gates in the School – perfectly normal security precautions turned by the activists into an excuse for causing trouble – and the behaviour of two junior members of the academic staff, Blackburn and Bateson. The former I had seen around, but at no time did I ever knowingly set eyes on the latter. At the beginning of term I had gone to the students' refectory for a cup of coffee and found myself behind an American student. We exchanged a few words and I did not take to him; he proved to be Hoch, who together with Schoenbach, another American postgraduate student, were the leading activists in the affair of the gates and their forcible removal. Many of us regarded them (and some others) as being bitter and neurotic over what they saw as the American government's betrayal of their generation through the Vietnam War and the draft for military service. This led them to a rejection of any authority and to behaviour which had a very nasty and destructive tone, involving occupations and sit-ins, physical damage to the School, verbal and written personal attacks and the disruption of teaching. It also led to some positively paranoid accusations, for example that the teachers at the School were deliberately holding back knowledge from students. It was around this time that I saw one British student behaving in a very wild manner, and I think it was he who was photographed gesticulating beside Walter Adams at the main entrance. On a later occasion I noted that some other students seemed to cluster round this student when he was behaving wildly, evidently trying to hold him back. At one stage students (and one of our female research assistants in the Economics Department) picketed the entrances to the School and I then made it my business to go through every picket line as often as I could, making clear my disapproval of their behaviour. I can remember moving up and down behind the picket line in front of the main entrance and warning the pickets that they must not obstruct people entering the School and could only engage them in discussion. At the height of these troubles, in order to remain close to events, I stayed one night at Charles Goodhart's comfortable London flat and another in considerable discomfort on a sofa in Harold Edey's room at the School. I made a point of being present as often as I could at demonstrations and at student meetings in the Old Theatre. At

328

one of these meetings I can remember Leslie Pressnell, then secretary of the Graduate School Committee, standing up to rebut some paranoid accusations. With Lionel Needleman I attended another of these meetings and could see an opportunity where, with perceptive leadership from the School, the troubles might have been brought to an end without betraying any matters of principle.

Confusion and disorder in the School was often made worse by the presence of many people who had nothing to do with the School but who seemed to be attracted by the scent of trouble and who in practice could not be kept out. These included Tariq Ali as well as a group of anarchists I met in the entrance lobby who claimed to be there to give organised (!) support to the dissident students; also a man who I thought said he was from *Police News*; I found this rather surprising, but in fact he turned out to be from *Peace News* which I assumed was some left-wing front organisation. And there was Danny the Red who came over from Paris and spoke at the School. The press were around the School all the time and in one newspaper there appeared a picture of me taken from behind and facing a yelling student (the same student who appeared in the photo with Walter Adams at the main entrance mentioned above). It was around this time that a reporter asked me what I was doing in the midst of some disorderly demonstration, and I replied that I was there to exercise a sedative effect upon the students. In the Bank of England someone drew this to the attention of Maurice Allen; his comment was 'How strange, he never had that effect upon me.' On one occasion Matthew Anderson, a professor of history, and I were having coffee in Smokey Joe's next door to the School's main entrance when there was some altercation outside. We immediately went out and found that a student had tried to stop a delivery of some sort to the main entrance; the deliveryman did not like this and had chased him up Houghton Street where the student was tackled and brought to the ground by a police student (we had some of them at that time). As we arrived the two of them were on the ground surrounded by a circle of students who seemed intent on rescuing their comrade. Matthew and I stood over the pair and ordered the other students to stand back. Meanwhile a girl student activist, short and plump, whom we had already nicknamed Mother Earth, appeared on the scene, threw herself down, cradled the troublemaker's head on her lap and looked romantic defiance at Matthew and me. It would have been funny had it not been yet another annoying piece of student nonsense.

329

Another incident occurred during the visitation by the Parliamentary Committee. They held a meeting in the Founder's Room, seated behind a large table, to try and find out what the trouble was all about. The students became very rowdy and began to surge towards the MPs. Frank Land (our computer services manager) and I stationed ourselves between the two sides, and told the students in no uncertain terms that they must stand back from the MPs, who by then were in full retreat through a door behind us. The students, as was a common tactic, were shouting 'Don't you touch me' – the object being to make it appear that we were the aggressors. As the MPs withdrew Robin Blackburn leapt onto the committee's table and declaimed in a ludicrously dramatic way: 'This is our meeting now.' He was later dismissed from the School for misbehaviour, as was Bateson.

None of my teaching was disrupted; only on one occasion did an unknown older student come into a class but he just sat at the back and did nothing. Alan Day was less fortunate and had a glass of water thrown over him at a lecture. I can remember being invited to address the crowd of students sitting-in in the main entrance hall; my message to them was that they were behaving disgracefully. Later I saw one of my own students in a group going in to occupy the area round the Director's office; I grabbed him by the arm, pulled him out of the group and pushed him off towards the stairs, telling him not to behave like a fool. I was disappointed to see a person who had been one of our own Monetary Group students taking part in one demonstration, and as with so many others I left him in no doubt of my strong disapproval. Eventually the troubles faded away as the summer term finished and the ringleaders left the School as their time here came to an end. In my view this fade-out was itself evidence of the shallowness and lack of any real substance behind the arguments and actions of the dissident students. One sad aspect of the troubles was seeing how willingly many students responded to the spurious arguments of the troublemakers. This revealed only too clearly that while these students had a lot of potential, they had as yet no experience and little judgement.

In my view, two of my senior colleagues played an unexpected role in these troubles. Ralph Miliband, a political scientist, I knew only a little; I was aware of his left-wing views although at that time I did not know how radical they were. At one stage, on the main staircase looking down into the entrance lobby filled with sitters-in, he urged a group of colleagues, including myself, to join these students; I argued strongly against this and our group dispersed without doing anything. John Griffiths, a constitutional lawyer, I knew much better. I had always found him witty and engaging; he had been a Gurkha and we had shared reminiscences about the army. I attended one quite large meeting that he arranged, and I was greatly surprised to find him arguing for action by his colleagues on the side of the students. I argued very strongly against this and helped to stop anything from being agreed. I am glad to say that after the Troubles had become just an annoying memory cordial relations between us were restored.

Faint and futile echoes of the Troubles appeared at intervals down the following years – so faint and futile that they had no significant effect on the School and made no lasting impression on my mind. The last of these, however, left its mark in a letter to the School Secretary, Christine Challis, which she copied on to me. It was from Tom Bulman, general secretary of the Students' Union, dated 16 February 1990 and was headed: 'Post "Occupation!" thanks'. It apologised for any disruption arising from the Students' Union's occupation of the Old Building over the night of Wednesday/Thursday 14/15 February and asked her to 'pass on special thanks to Roger Alford, Iain Crawford, Neil Plevy [*the latter two both administrators*] and, in particular, Clive Shorthouse and George Burman [*two senior porters*] for their cooperation and understanding under difficult circumstances'. But still nothing stirs in my memory.

19

The Money Workshop and Harry Johnson

Starting the Workshop

When in the middle of 1962 I came back to the School from the Bank of England, Richard Sayers' banking seminars and Lionel Robbins' economics seminars were still going strong, but there was nothing focussing on money and macro-economics. I consulted Richard Sayers and Alan Day, both of whom agreed that there was a need for such a seminar and were happy to see me organise one; but both were very busy and did not feel they had time to participate. In this way the Money and Macro-economics Workshop was born in 1963. At first I got together a small group of younger economists: myself, Jim Thomas (who had arrived on the staff in 1961), Vicky Chick from University College and a few others, to discuss topics in the field. Soon visitors began to attend and give papers, and the Workshop flourished.

One of these 'others' at the first meetings was Stan Fischer (later a professor of economics at MIT, First Deputy Manager of the IMF and Governor of the Bank of Israel) who I think was at that time doing the MSc; the Workshop meetings were post-MSc and strictly speaking he was not eligible. I had taught him in a third-year macro-economics class where he asked one of the best questions I ever faced in such a class. We were going through ISLM analysis, and I postulated the usual change in expectations which shifted just the IS curve; his question was that surely the LM curve depended upon the same body of expectations as those behind the IS curve, so shouldn't such a change affect both curves? Years of teaching equipped me to deal with this: yes, that could be true but the expectations behind the two curves were looking at rather different aspects of the economy, so that it was legitimate to partition these expectations and allow the two curves to be independent and one to shift with the other unchanged. But his question was better than my answer and I was pleased to have him attend the Workshop.

I first met Harry Johnson at an editorial meeting of the *Review of Economic Studies* in 1953. By 1966 he was recognised as one of the world's leading economists and when he arrived at the School in that year I went to see him, told him about the Workshop and in effect invited him to take it over. His response was that he would certainly become a regular member, but that he wanted me to continue to organise the programme and chair the meetings, and this was how the Workshop was run for the eight years that Harry was at the School. His regular presence raised its profile and its performance to an entirely new level and attracted academic visitors to the School who, together with our own colleagues and PhD students, generally provided a flow of very good papers for the programme. Although to us it was usually referred to as the Workshop, it appeared in the School's Calendar as a one and a half hour seminar on Wednesdays at 4.30 to 6.00. It was named Statistical Testing in Monetary Economics (1965–66) over the names of Alford, Chick and Thomas, and then from 1966–67 onwards as Monetary Economics: Theory and Testing over the names of Alford and Johnson – a truly penny-farthing (or rather farthing-penny) combination. I am glad to say that Vicky Chick and Jim Thomas both remained regular attenders.

Meetings of Friedman's seminar at the University of Chicago, of which Harry had been a member, were rumoured to be stressful and bloodstained affairs, and at first we wondered if Harry would bring some of this carnivorous spirit with him; but in the Workshop we were all relieved to find that, if it ever existed, he had left it all behind in Chicago. We held our meetings in Room S.419, which had four large tables pushed together in the middle with about twenty five chairs round them, and a long blackboard. Harry usually sat facing the blackboard near the left corner of the long side of the tables. I sat in the middle of the short side to his left, both of us near the door. During the meetings Harry used to whittle away at pieces of wood, carving small animals and leaving a little heap of wood chippings to mark where he had been sitting. Sometimes he seemed absorbed in his carving, sometimes he seemed somnolent, but both were very misleading because he was listening all the time and at the first false step by the speaker he was instantly all attention, pinpointing a weakness (usually one the rest of us had not seen) and asking to have any doubtful statement clarified or justified. One of his characteristics was that he always seemed to have a relevant theoretical model immediately in his mind; this served to orient him when others were losing their way in the middle of some convoluted argument. His instant grasp and critical insight were very impressive. The speaker would sometimes elaborate a point by putting yet another equation on the board; I noticed that the less confidence he had in his new equation, the sooner he would start to rub it out. But before he could do so Harry would intervene: 'No, don't rub it out, let's have a good look at it' and something which seemed a good idea at the time would have all its weaknesses exposed. I always felt that his criticisms were acute and unsparing but fair – for him it was the accuracy of the theorising which mattered and I cannot remember him being unduly harsh.

Diary Entries 1971–74

My diary keeping was always patchy, but during 1971 to 1974 I did keep one for quite a lot of the time. Selected entries from this diary will give some flavour of the Money Workshop.

Monday 29 November 1971
Harry Johnson performed at the seminar, speaking on Dutch methods of monetary analysis. Not at his best – a rather jaded delivery*; I had to work hard to keep the discussion going. It livened up towards the end, but even so ended 5 minutes early. The main conclusion was that the Holtrop model was crude and we did not know how effective it had been as a guide to monetary management in the Netherlands.

* Markedly different from his performance when Don Nichols presented his paper. Then Harry started by saying that for reasons of his own research he was going to be rather critical of the paper (which he certainly was). He picked on point after point, bringing out really brilliant summaries of large areas of the subject and their development – producing these like a string of sausages from

almost invisible cracks in the paper's arguments. A really bravura performance, ending with an offer to take the paper for the *Journal of Political Economy* if it were revised in the light of his (and other) criticisms.

Had lunch with Alex Swoboda and organised him to give a paper next term. This session it is not proving as easy as usual to recruit contributions from within the School.

I must intervene here to retract the above simile of a string of sausages. I was obviously feeling for the idea of things being produced out of thin air in the way a conjuror produces strings of sausages from an apparently empty top hat; but what Harry was producing was not soft dull sausages but a string of sharp and illuminating insights.

Wednesday 1 November 1972

Morris Perlman's paper at the Seminar; very well delivered but not altogether clear or cogent. His final equation (on the board at ten past six!) did shed some light. At 7 p.m. I passed Ostroy's room; he and Paquin (who is finishing a PhD in maths etc) were sitting down still discussing the Seminar. I joined them for a few minutes – suggested that the question was the existence of a set of assumptions which would give Morris's results – did such a set in fact exist? Simultaneously Ostroy said Yes and Paquin said No; I left them to it. An hour later I went past Ostroy's room on my way to the Director's Reception. They were both still there, but now both scribbling all over the blackboard and both talking at the same time. Obviously a stimulating paper.

Wednesday 17 January 1973

Very good seminar. Paper by Ostroy – Informational efficiency of monetary exchange. Very abstract but very good and clear presentation – he kept the members of the seminar right up with the argument. At five to six both Charles Goodhart and myself pointed out that we had only five minutes left and had not yet got to the monetary part. We got to money at last and ended at about 10 past 6.

Wednesday 6 February 1974

... Lunch with Alan Day; John Watkins and Basil Yamey talked with us for a few minutes. Ron Jones and Bob Mundell then joined us. Bob is on his way to a conference somewhere ... we had a very interesting conversation on world trade and politics, continuing over coffee in the Senior Common Room ...

... Money Workshop started a little uncertainly and then went well; Ross Starr (who gave the paper) was a little nervous. Afterwards talked for half an hour to Nick Barr about our wealth tax models ...

Wednesday 13 February 1974

... 3rd year seminar went well. Talked with Ed Mishan at lunch, chiefly about present problems which we agreed are largely political and for which economists can offer only economic, i.e. irrelevant, solutions. Talked with Marcus Miller and Ralph Turvey over coffee afterwards. Collegiate examiner's meeting; chatted with Ilersic, whom I haven't seen for some time. Then tea with Michael Beenstock (Treasury) and David Gowland (York and ex-Bank of England) who gave the paper at the Money Workshop. Good meeting (23 present), good discussion but ended up discussing spectral analysis, pre-whitening filters, four types of window etc. Kept my end more or less up – luckily I was not the only ignoramus. Many of those present were not known to me as this was a joint meeting with the Treasury's Workshop in Applied Economics.

Wednesday 20 February 1974

Good Money Workshop – Case Sprenkel (Illinois) gave a good paper – very interesting on demand for money by US corporations – very pleasantly delivered.

Wednesday 13 March 1974

... Various tasks in the afternoon, then Money Workshop – paper by Marcus Miller and Bill Allen (Bank of England). Good attendance, very good paper and good discussion.

Friday 15 March 1974

... Coffee and long talk with Marcus Miller about Bill Allen's paper. He sees it as an attack on the price mechanism optimists – particularly Friedman, as it implies that speculators can make profits but still not iron out fluctuations in prices (or rates of exchange); and their rational expectations model gives the same result. We agreed that Friedman is fixed in a long run equilibrium model and spends a lot of time showing how the world can be adapted to fit his model so that his policy views derived from it will be 'correct'. But which version of F's view can we rely upon? What crucial adaptations are going to be recommended next which, if omitted, might mean that his prescriptions will not work, and what are the side effects of his various amendments of the world e.g. full indexation of wages, particularly if the authorities are not willing to pay the (unknown) short run price of entry to his long-run nirvana...

My role in all this was to organise the Workshop and keep it running smoothly, recruiting people to give papers, arranging the distribution of the programme, and chairing the meetings. Being chairman really consisted only of introducing the speaker, keeping some order in the interventions and discussion, trying to ensure that everyone had their say on one topic before a question was allowed to move discussion on to another topic, delicately winding up the proceedings at a hopefully well chosen moment and thanking the speaker. All this allowed Harry to devote his talents to joining in the discussion as he wished. But I did not allow my role as chairman to stop me from actively joining in as well. Apart from those mentioned above a number of other colleagues attended the Workshop at various times; amongst them I remember Frank Hahn, John Sutton, Cliff Wymer (who brought with him some unfamiliar mathematics in which the Greek delta required a bite out of its base), Megnad Desai and Oliver Hart.

Seminar Topics and Broader Aspects

Within the field of money there was a considerable variety of topics discussed in the Workshop at this time, but two of them took up many meetings.

338

The first was the book *Money in a Theory of Finance* by Gurley and Shaw. I can remember mentioning the authors when we were talking with Lionel Robbins in the Senior Common Room; he raised a surprised eyebrow and said 'Girlie?'. We spent many seminars discussing their concepts of inside and outside money. The second topic was much more important – monetarism, as expounded by Friedman and supported by many others; this had implications for policy which gave it a much wider interest, and many of these meetings were attended by people from the City, the Bank of England and the Treasury. They were very crowded and we managed to get up to forty participants into our room intended for twenty five. All our seminars had a sense of expectation, but in some of these the atmosphere was unusually tense and with a certain feeling of drama. There were keen arguments between pro- and anti-monetarists, but I cannot recall Harry ever committing himself one way or the other on its practicality for policy.

The sharpness of Harry's mind would not have been obvious to anyone just seeing him around the School. He was of medium height, somewhat plump and with a very smooth complexion (later partly concealed by a beard). He had rather a soft voice with (not surprisingly) an equally soft Canadian accent. For someone relatively bulky he walked with rather small steps, and I always remember him in an unsmart grey suit. Often when I went to talk to him in his room he seemed to be writing standing up, with the paper on top of a filing cabinet. His handwriting was not well-formed but was reasonably readable; I wrote a paper on direct credit controls for the Robbins Festschrift (1972) and showed him a late draft. His response came in seven pages, some of it written in rather pale green biro; it began: 'This is a useful paper but it seems to me that you could be more imaginative with it, in the following ways...', and there followed not just comments but also elaborations and theoretical extensions with formulae which would develop the usefulness of the rather turgid indicators I was setting out. His intellectual vitality shone through these seven pages.

Harry was quite prepared to participate in some of the wider affairs of the School. The Civil Service Commission paid us a visit to talk about recruitment – in particular they felt they should be getting more graduates from the School, something nearer the numbers they got from Oxford and Cambridge. Harry and I attended the meeting for the Economics Department and it was Harry who pointed out how much smaller the School was than either Oxford or Cambridge, how many of our students were from overseas and therefore not eligible for the Civil Service and that our subject mix gave many of our graduates attractive careers elsewhere. In the end it seemed that the Civil Service was in fact getting a fair share of our relatively small eligible output. Possibly because of this meeting I was later invited to sit on a Civil Service selection board. I found it rather dispiriting, interviewing quite good candidates for deadly jobs with the Ministry of Labour on Tyneside. One of my own students appeared for interview and I declared my interest, but he was good and the board agreed that he should be offered one of these glum jobs. As soon as I got back to the School I urged him to refuse the offer and look for something more in line with his talents. Sitting on this board introduced me to a number of Civil Service forms which seemed to have been designed in a truly contrarian spirit, with large spaces for very short answers and tiny spaces for long ones. I pointed out this elementary design fault and someone somewhere said they had noted my points, but I withdrew from this dismal interviewing and heard no more.

The Department periodically took a look at the structure of its undergraduate teaching and in 1969 Frank Hahn, who had only come to the School in 1967, was asked to conduct such an enquiry. The idea was that being a new arrival he would see our arrangements with fresh eyes. Harry took much more interest in such teaching arrangements and content than most of the big names who came into the Department and I sent him a copy of my criticisms of the proposals that had emerged from Hahn's enquiry. His reply from Chicago gives his view on the structure of undergraduate teaching:

May 12, 1970

Dear Roger:

Thank you for sending me your criticisms of the Hahn proposals. While I have not thought anywhere nearly as long about the problem as you and they have, it seems to me that your emphasis on (1) possible future changes, like the course unit system, (2) viability in terms of our experience so far, (3) the balance between lectures, classes and seminars, and (4) flexibility in providing for the different streams, should be very useful.

I like particularly the suggestion of Principles I and Principles II. Most course structures I know are weak on the central core and long on the specialities. This is OK if the speciality teachers always have the central core in mind, but often they treat it only as a source of propositions to which they provide a confusing number of exceptions.

Yours sincerely,
Harry
Harry G. Johnson

I heard Harry on a later occasion express this last view about our own MSc; he felt that at this level also there should be more concentration on the core and less on the specialities.

On the wider stage Harry was one of the movers in setting up the Money Study Group which was to hold very successful annual conferences. The first of these was held at Hove in October 1969 to celebrate the tenth anniversary of the Radcliffe Report. The keynote speaker was Richard Sayers (who had retired two years earlier) and just before the proceedings opened I realised that his talk ought to be recorded; Harry agreed, but we could not find any recording equipment at such short notice, so the opportunity was lost. The volume which emerged from the conference was *Money in Britain 1959–69*, edited by David Croome and Harry Johnson; in its introduction it mentioned that Richard Sayers had given an informal talk, but that is all. I played a small role in these proceedings with a discussion paper on the operation of monetary policy since Radcliffe. Kit McMahon was at the conference; his coming appointment as a Director of the Bank of England had been announced, but he had then made some unwise public statement and some people at the conference wondered if his appointment might therefore be put in doubt; in fact his career went forward unscathed.

In 1970 there was a similar conference at the University of Sheffield which resulted in the volume *Monetary Theory and Monetary Policy in the 1970s*, edited by George Clayton; my minor contribution was a discussion paper on bank liquidity. I can recall on that occasion a cheerful group visit to the gardens of Chatsworth; equally memorable to me was the fact that on either side of the entrance to the university building in which we were meeting were particularly fine specimens of the golden-leafed *Aucuba japonica* 'Crotonifolia'. I took several cuttings from these and in a damp tissue they survived the journey home and in the following years produced several beautiful specimens for our garden. There followed conferences at the School in 1971: *Current Inflation*, and then at Bournemouth in 1972: *Issues in Monetary Economics*, these last two volumes edited by Harry Johnson and Bob Nobay (a protégé of Harry's, then at Liverpool) and there was a series of further conferences after that. Bob was always a very helpful presence at these meetings and I remember Harry presenting him with one of his carved animals.

The Human Cost of High Productivity

Harry was also responsible for getting some corporate well-wisher to finance the visit of a group of British economists to the University of Paris IX – Dauphine. There the meetings were held in a building previously used by NATO and presumably filled with Russian bugs; if they were still at work, the Russian intelligence officers must have had a very dull and perplexing time. For me there was one very unhappy incident on this visit. We were invited to drinks by one of the French economists at his flat, which was decorated with some beautiful mediaeval painted church carvings in wood. Harry quickly drank himself into a stupor and had to be almost carried back to our hotel by some of our group. To me it was totally unexpected and appalling to see Harry's powerful mind completely switched off and his body reduced to an inert lump. I had known, as had so many others, that Harry seemed driven to work at a quite abnormal pace, and that flying to conferences and drinking seemed to be his only escape from this internal pressure; but I was not one of his drinking companions and never imagined that his drinking could be so extreme. Many younger economists admired Harry, but I had already seen that some of them had tended to admire not just his work but also his hard drinking. In this Harry set a most unfortunate example and I felt that those foolish enough to follow it showed a high degree of immaturity.

I always had the highest regard for Harry but now I also felt desperately sorry for him; for the first time I had seen for myself how he was caught between the terrible pressures of intensive work and destructive relaxation. Harry left the School in 1974 to return to Chicago; he died in 1977 at the age of only fifty-four.

20

Diary: The Early 1970s

These diary entries (together with those in the previous chapter) cover only some three years but they are a contemporary record and give a fair picture of some of the major threads of my life at the School from the 1960s to the 1980s.

Tuesday 6 June 1972
Went up to the School; travelled with Roy Clifford and Claude Loombe [*Roy was in the Bank of England, and Claude had recently retired from it*]. Interested to hear that the Sheik of Abu Dhabi (a place which looms large in both their lives) had been awarded a Papal Knighthood for services to Christianity in Abu Dhabi. Called at the School to deal with mail etc and deliver my scripts to [*my colleague*] Brian Griffiths for second marking, then on to the Bank of England/University of Bradford Conference on strategic planning for financial institutions. This was at Draper's Hall – entered through a large doorway in Throgmorton Street which I had passed hundreds of times when I was in the City, had but never seen open before. Corridors, great halls with paintings and decorated ceilings – much of it dull, but quite impressive. Sat with Frank Cassel and saw many Bank of England people. Generally interesting papers.

Many years later, after Draper's Hall had been refurbished, I was invited to several dinners there by Christian Williams, a Guildford friend who was a member and later Master of the Draper's Company. The Hall by then was bright, clean and gilded, altogether large and very striking. Its entrance

345

in Throgmorton Street has two large flanking stone statues of Persians but is rather squashed between two shops and gives no hint to the passer-by of the magnificence within. I saw these statues every day when I was working on the floor of the Stock Exchange in 1943–44, but it never occurred to me to wonder what lay behind the entrance they guarded. It was on the other side of the street from these statues that I and our two dealers were standing when the flying bomb went off behind Moorgate Tube in July 1944.

Tuesday 6 June 1972 – cont
Dinner at the School in the evening – one of the Library Appeal public relations dinners. Guests were G.S. Bishop, M. Littmann, A.W. Pearce, Sir Edward Playfair, S.J. Pears and Geoffrey Bell (whom I had seen only last Friday at his party, where I saw Frank Cassel, Kit McMahon, Bruno Schroder etc). From the School were the Director, Lionel Robbins, Alan Prest, Lady Serota, myself, Ash Wheatcroft, Maurice Freedman and John Morgan (Governor). Quite congenial; discussion of LSE's image – not altogether satisfactory. Travelled home with Alan Prest; coming down in the lift, I suggested that if we really want to improve our image in the City and industry, we should set out to recruit the sons of chairmen of leading companies. Alan replied that this was what Cambridge did.

Thursday 8 June 1972
Miss Foo (3rd year Monetary Group) rang at lunch time; her party for next Thursday is in fact today – if I couldn't come we must have lunch etc. Easier to go. Uncrowded drive up. In fact really rather pleasant small party; several students and ex-students of the School, a chap called Baker from the BBC, a journalist from the *Guardian* etc, also Marcus Miller and wife (plus baby in the passage outside).

Miss Foo (small, very vivacious, 'call me Louise') is going to Rowe and Pitman as an investment analyst. Miss Burton (who graduated last year) was there and is an investment analyst with Warburgs, and there was an American girl who was an investment analyst with Robert Fleming – obviously it is *the* career for girls. Gave Marcus, Marty and baby a lift back to Latymer Court, Hammersmith. Marty says their daughter looks like Marcus, I tell them Lulu looks like me, and we commiserate.

Monday 12 June 1972

Up to LSE. Roger Pownall (one of our MSc monetary students) has had a letter published in *The Times Business Review.* He called in at my room and we talked; I didn't agree with his letter, but pleasant discussion. Talked with Vicky Chick on her teaching for us next year – agreed on what should be done; conversation flowed on over other topics – Keynes, Myrdal, Leijonhufvud, where she feels she is having fundamental thoughts. Lunched with Christopher Foster, Marcus Miller; pleasant conversation. Talked with Kurt Klappholz at tea – he has given me 9 third year tutees for next year; I remonstrate gently, equally gently he explains the inevitability. Basil Yamey says that Robbins Festschrift has been put back again; all concerned are getting bored to death waiting for it to appear. Xeroxed three articles; the other machine in the room went wrong and poured smoke everywhere as I copied away. Train home crowded and delayed.

Thursday 15 June 1972

Went up to the School. Agreed marks with Brian Griffiths and held meeting with 2nd year students to brief them about next year's work. Later, undergraduates summer party. Really very pleasant – quite keen discussion on students' rights and duties with a group of the second year.

Monday 19 June 1972

At the School, saw Harry Johnson briefly; he agreed to the Monetary Seminar switching its time to 4.30–6.00 on Wednesday. London and Cambridge Economic Service meeting in the afternoon. Peter Oppenheimer very lively, Robert Nield rather politically conscious, Frank Paish very sure of his views and Brian Reddaway slightly plaintive. Not very inspiring altogether. Saw a student and said goodbye to Professor Izzo, who is returning to Siena.

Tuesday 20 June 1972
Something wrong in the new regulations for the Bsc Econ. Rang Alan Walters, who agreed with my view, and Dennis Sargan who also agreed but felt we might not be able to alter things at the Academic Board on Wednesday. Basil Yamey said he had ceased to feel strongly about anything and would take what came.

Wednesday 21 June 1972
Due to go to the Guildford Society lunch, but felt I should go up to the School to the Academic Board, where the new degree arrangements are to be finally approved. The draft does not fit with the Economics Department view of 4 exams at the end of the second year; much consulting etc. However the handout for students implies what we want, so let it go. Board rather boring. Strawberry Tea at 4 p.m.; watched Alan Stuart [*Chairman of the Senior Common Room*] make a very short speech and presentations to retiring colleagues. It will be my turn to do this next year.

Thursday 22 June 1972
George Clayton [*Sheffield*] rang and agreed marks. Addressed post-Part I monetary students. Urged them to work hard in their second year – so many regret not doing so. Saw some of them afterwards – I am their stop-gap tutor till a chap called Shorrocks comes next year. Monetary Group examiner's meeting. Farewell dinner to Harry Townsend and Frank Hahn. Quite a high-powered gathering, pleasant atmosphere. They both talked about their time at the School – much anecdote.

Tuesday 27 June 1972
Up to School. Wrote letters and cleared up odds and ends all day. Lunched with David Martin and John Peel; apparently [*name omitted*] the currently leading (but not very active) dissident student has done no work in his three years and has a very high ratio of chip to shoulder.

Monday 3 July 1972
Up to School. Spent the morning writing letters and tidying up.

At coffee talked with Ben Roberts about gardens – he has 3 acres in S. Berks or N. Hants, I can't remember which. Tried to get hold of Mike Parkin about the MSc scripts I finished marking over the weekend, but he is out to conferences much of this week. Final BSc Econ Examiners Committee meeting at Senate House; went up by taxi with Margaret Sharpe and Jack Fisher. Not very inspiring proceedings, but everything affecting the Monetary Group went off without any problems.

Tuesday 4 July 1972
Up early to drive to Oxford for the Money Study Group seminar in honour of Sir John Hicks. Listened to a rather ill-humoured paper by Courakis, blaming the Bank of England – but not clear what they were being blamed for; also too long and lacking in focus. Sat next to Ursula Hicks – I always find her very kind and homely. Paper by Soskice was well-delivered but did not enthral me. Lunch with Meltzer and Hicks. I never cease to marvel at the woolliness of Hicks in conversation and lectures, and his depths and strength in most of his writings. He showed signs of agitation at Meltzer's monetarism. After lunch walked round the meadows with Charles Goodhart and Alan Meltzer. Afternoon lecture by Franco Modigliani; he attributed most of his good points to what he referred to as his really first class graduate students. A good performance. Harry Johnson summed up; his beard is thickening up, but he himself seems more tense and less at ease than in the past.

Gave Mike Thornton [*Bank of England*] a lift home, and as we got into the car found I had acquired a £2 parking fine for parking without a disc in a (very badly signed) disc parking area. Pleasant talk as we drove back. Stopped off at home and talked over a drink; Toni looking very charming in trouser suit, and cooking Oeufs Mornay for supper – the very picture of an elegant housewife. Not perhaps typical, we agreed, but made a good impression!

Wednesday 12 July 1972
Up to town with Roy Clifford. MSc examiners meeting at 10.30; all went off satisfactorily. Saw Lionel Needleman lunching with

Kurt Klappholz and they joined myself and McNaught-Davis – more talk of gardens. Lionel had spent the morning arbitrating on a minor industrial dispute in a firm. Dealt with mail etc in the afternoon. Bought some books. Home by fairly early train; saw Claude Loombe and joined him at Claygate; he has been told that with the new sterling area arrangements, he must declare his bank account in Kuwait! Arrived home to find that Toni had been strawberry picking; they were almost the same price as in town, but fresher, and by mistake she had bought 12 pounds! Strawberries truly ad lib.

Friday 21 July 1972
Lionel Needleman arrived in the morning, bringing about 15 plants for me and a bottle of wine. Walked round the garden, with him taking any cuttings he fancied. Lunch and then pleasant afternoon walking round Wisley [*the Royal Horticultural Society gardens*].

Very pleasant evening at the [*School*] Reception. Talked to lots of people – our new Medical Officer, Pitt-Rivers, Ernest Gellner, various visitors and new members (Ellen [*de Kadt*] and a Social Anthropology research officer who was analysing Sepik River art). Very pleasant discussion particularly with the last two.

Wednesday 18 November 1972
Good Workshop; paper not very well developed, but discussion went well.

Thursday 19 November 1972
Graham Jones. Charterhouse. He will ring to confirm. [*He did confirm and I talked to his sixth-formers taking Economics A Level, mainly about macro; I took them through IS-LM.*]

1973

Wednesday 24 January 1973
Up on the train with Claude Loombe (Chairman of the British Bank of the Middle East), tried to get him to contribute to our

350

Library Appeal. He may weaken. Very good Workshop – Richard Jackman on Leijonhufvud and Keynes; very well presented and interesting. Came back on the main line with Ken Clucas (First Civil Service Commissioner); interesting talk with him – he has the problem of staffing a prices and a wages board (two boards, to show they were right to scrap the single Prices and Incomes Board).

Tuesday 30 January 1973
…7.15 Library Appeal dinner. Dinner was very pleasant. Mrs Thatcher agreeable and fairly keen. Sat next to Norman Biggs (Chairman, Williams and Glyns Bank); very pleasant conversation on Bank of England (where we knew many of the same people – he was there 1927–46) and on Proust. Then next to Earle [*London Business School*], who raised some slightly ill-natured questions about the MSc (which were misconceived, and which I rebutted), and Sidney Rolph.

Tuesday 6 March 1973
Senior Common Room dinner. Very successful; Sparrow [*All Souls, Oxford*] talked quite well, but younger members not in sympathy. Excellent food, good conversation.

As Chairman of the Senior Common Room Committee I received a warm letter of thanks from John Sparrow a few days later.

Friday 13 April 1973
Visit of Chinese Ambassador to LSE. Michael Wise and myself (as teachers) plus Ashley etc [*as administrators*] escorted him around. Saw several things I have never seen before.

On the mezzanine floor of the Old Building were two anonymous doors which in all my years at the School I had never seen open. One of them was specially opened for our tour and behind it was the School's telephone exchange.

1974

Monday 14 January 1974

Up to town. Morning taken up with meeting about University Superannuation Scheme; addressed by Logan [*Principal of London University*]. I made the point that no fundamental questions had been asked about the lifetime distribution of incomes and consumption. Pleasant talk with Case Sprenkel (Illinois) then to Government Bookshop in Holborn and looked at other shops also.

Rail strike is on for tomorrow, so confirmed with Mrs Stephenson [*Toni's mother, whom I always called Mrs S*] that I would be spending the night at her flat in Lonsdale Square [*in Islington*]. Harold Edey is staying up also, and we had dinner at the Cathay Chinese Restaurant overlooking Piccadilly Circus. Slept at Lonsdale Square. All very welcoming.

Tuesday 15 January 1974

MSc seminar with Alan Walters in morning – quite active. Talked with Lowe (graduate student on leave from IBRD [*International Bank for Reconstruction and Development*]) in afternoon. He had spent time at the White House before returning from his Xmas vacation in the West Indies. He said that the impression he got was that the US government as a constructive force had simply ceased to work. Many unimpressive characters around there also. Good 2nd year class – it went on till six. To Mrs S for supper; long talk with Nookie Gonzales [*second cousin of Toni*] who is staying with her. He is intellectually completely undeveloped – no reasonable University could accept him.

Tuesday 22 January 1974

Travelled up with Laurie Martin (Professor of War Studies at King's College, London), Peter Lyon (Institute of Commonwealth Studies) and Claude Loombe; pleasant conversation on the way up, then Laurie, Peter and I walked over Waterloo Bridge to the School, dropping Laurie off at Bush House where he was to broadcast on some defence subject.

Met my new temporary secretary, Miss Jones – seems pleasant and helpful. Talked for a while to Woodward (US) and Periyielotis (Greece) both MSc students. Then to coffee in the Senior Common Room and to the MSc seminar with Alan Walters. Paper was on demand for money, given by Peter Jonson (Australia) who in fact is doing a PhD. Well presented and very active discussion between Jonson, Alan and me – no danger that the students will think the subject is cut and dried. Gave my view and discovered that Jonson has come to similar conclusion and is going to do his PhD thesis work on that basis. Lunch in Senior Dining Room with Jim Thomas, Nick Barr etc. Alan Day came and joined us; both he and Nick have been writing (in *The Observer* and *The Guardian* respectively) on wealth distribution. Talked with John Pike (the School's Financial Secretary), who told me about the financial arrangements of the Strand House completion. At coffee afterwards C.G. Allen (one of the Librarians) showed me the *Daily Telegraph* parliamentary column – Labour members crying 'Who is Alan Day?'. Back to my room and xeroxed some reading lists for students; Woodward and Periyielotis came back as arranged, also Miss Tabassi (UK). Talked about MSc seminar topics and reading. Then Ramcher (Swiss) came in to consult about his courses, followed by Peter Jonson for further talk about demand for money. Also saw De Gannes (West Indies) and Ruchpaul (India) briefly. Call from Bill Letwin who sent Everett Hagen (just retired from Massachusetts Institute of Technology) over to see me; I was able to suggest some names for a project he has in mind. He wanted to phone someone outside, but we have been incommunicado all day because a fire at the Holborn telephone exchange has cut off all our outside lines. Walked with him to Aldwych to get a taxi, and he told me about his job as part-time adviser to Saudi Arabia – very interesting – development with money no object! He said that their government machine was patchy – much of it efficient, some very poor – because of need to maintain tribal/regional balance. Business stops over Christmas while they organise Mecca for the pilgrimage.

Cup of tea in the Senior Common Room and brief talk with John Alcock ('Our beloved Academic Secretary' 'Did you say bloody

Academic Secretary?'). Also spoke to Michael Oakeshott – told him we would be on holiday near him in the summer (at Beaminster in Dorset); he said we must visit him, and I threatened that we would. Then off to 2nd year macro class down in the basement. Good paper on integration of labour market with IS-LM, and everyone very attentive. Class went on half an hour extra; then talked briefly to several students afterwards. Back to my room talking to Mr Guh (Pakistan) who appears to be about 45 years old and some sort of muslim religious leader. He is really 3rd year, but comes to my class because he finds talking and listening more useful than reading. He has a marked hesitation in his speech – not at all common amongst the students I have come in contact with. Thought I had lost some bank notes – couldn't find them anywhere in my jacket pockets – then found I had put them in my overcoat inside breast pocket. I keep them loose as I long ago gave up carrying a wallet, which I found bulky, expensive and tending to accumulate rubbish.

Over to Waterloo by bus; trains all awry because of ASLEF [*a trade union*] work to rule, with large crowd on the concourse and few trains. Caught train to Woking and another one on to Guildford. Saw John Hancock (Cabinet Office/Central Statistical Office – one of Claus Moser's assistants) but he was not going straight home, so had a taxi to myself from the bottom of North Street – too much of a queue at the station. Saw Gordon Bridger (Overseas Development Agency and Chairman of Guildford Society) there who told me that Geoffrey Maynard (University of Reading) had joined First National City Bank – not clear on what basis, but evidently very remunerative.

Wednesday 23 January 1974
11.30 3rd year seminar: The Importance of Money.

Busy day at the School; Jim Thomas's paper [*at the Workshop*] went down quite well. Trains chaotic; travelled home with Gordon Bridger, Radford and Stevens, all in ODA. Stevens attends our MSc seminar – strange to see him on the train; also saw Guy Gammell. Walked home from London Road station with John Twining.

Sunday 27 January 1974

Worked at home on flysheet concerning student entry to the Senior Dining Room. Talked to Alan Stuart (who is on leave from the School) on the phone about it.

Tuesday 29 January 1974

Up to School. Excellent MSc seminar – very good paper by Miss Carver. In afternoon long phone call from Bill White (ex-Bank of England) from Bank of Canada in Ottawa about a student. Then saw other students and long talk with Kantor, visiting teacher from South Africa; he is on Research Fee, and I am his supervisor. Very good macro class which went on for two hours; contains some very good people, particularly Delap (ex-Sqn Ldr [*and bomber pilot*], RAF) and Zucconi [*?ex-taxi driver*].

Wednesday 30 January 1974

Up to town with Claude Loombe and Horner (who is with Zwanenberg and deals with dog oil amongst many other things) and his daughter. Talked with Lionel Robbins and Anne Bohm at coffee. Saw various people during the afternoon, then tea with Alan Coddington (LSE) and Richard Jackman followed by Money Workshop. Active discussion, but Leijonhufvud's ideas seem to get cloudier rather than clearer. Talked for an hour with Nick Barr afterwards chiefly about our interest in wealth taxation. Talked with Marcus Miller as I left the building; he had come from a meeting with Harry Johnson concerning his international monetary project – he said that Harry was in good form, very much on the ball, but seemed to tire towards the end.

Trains very bad at Waterloo and announcer advised catching a train to Woking. Met John Pike (Financial Secretary of the School) and travelled with him, talking pleasantly of Strand House (our new library building to be) etc. Off at Woking. A lift got myself and John Pike to my house. John rang home for his son to drive over and fetch him. A drink and further talk till his younger son arrived – all very congenial. Toni had had her hair done this afternoon and looked – and was – very charming (as always, of course). Then some supper at about 10 p.m. and to bed. Worked on wealth tax in bed.

Monday 4 February 1974

Talked to Geoffrey Wood (Warwick). I am due to talk about Flow of Funds there on 14 February; Bain's *Economic Journal* survey rather scoops my field, and I discover Alan Roe is now at Warwick also. I suggest we make it a Colloquium and Geoffrey agrees. A midland rail strike is scheduled for 14 February, so it may never come off anyway, but meanwhile I have to prepare.

Tuesday 5 February 1974

Up to town with Claude Loombe. Good MSc seminar. At lunch heard that Imre Lakatos had died on Saturday. I recently had quite a lot to do with him. It started with my efforts to raise contributions to the Library Appeal from members of the Senior Common Room (the effort was chiefly walking, talking and phoning – on the whole people were very willing to give). I had just succeeded in persuading a young Philosophy lecturer to give a token amount (he had philosophical doubts at first, which my now considerable practice, and a small knowledge of the facts, had managed to overcome) when in came Imre. I asked him to contribute also (previously he had methodological doubts and had declined). He asserted that the Library was so bad that it did not deserve any money – he would write to *The Times* and expose the Appeal etc. I deployed my well-used arguments and finally he burst into good humour and also made a contribution.

A few days later Imre's rage with the Library and particularly with Mrs Nowicki (the Acquisitions Officer) boiled up again [*when he was cross dear Imre looked just like an angry chicken*] and over lunch one day we had further discussion, punctuated with rage. I found that he had no idea of the role of the Teaching Library, which had caused him to misunderstand the role of the Main Library. He had some sharp resentments about poor Mrs Nowicki which he did not conceal – on the contrary he broadcast them, which nearly reduced her to tears. As I simply could not believe the perfidy he attributed to poor Mrs N, I began conciliation. Cases were examined, goodwill alleged, misunderstandings blamed, subtle difficulties expounded. We agreed that Mrs N would answer in detail every case Imre considered unjust (chiefly refusal to buy expensive books in German). With a few diminishing spasms of rage, peace was restored. Imre said at one stage 'Its all right for you – they will listen to you. They just say I am a funny bloody foreigner.' The final spasm was a half-hearted burst of rage against the Teaching Library. But I primed Goddard (the librarian) to pre-empt this by checking the Teaching Library holdings of Philosophy items against the Calendar entries [*of recommended reading*], and writing to Imre showing that the holdings were in fact quite good, but suggesting that the remaining items should be acquired. Peace had been restored, at least temporarily; in poor Imre's case it is now permanent.

After lunch talked to John Alcock. We have had four deaths of serving teachers since I started teaching at the School in 1952: Arthur Fox, Eli Devons, Richard Titmuss and now Imre. Earlier poor Radomysler had committed suicide; I came on to the staff really as a replacement for him.

After a reasonably good 2nd year macro class (with some complaints registered against their Economic Statistics course), I caught the train to London Road and walked home in quite heavy rain.

As a student, I found Radomysler a very good teacher; his first year macro lectures carried us forward to the point at which we were beginning to catch up with the second year. I heard that he had a rather hard time at one of Lionel Robbins' seminars, but he seems to have been a troubled man. I met his brother who came over from Brazil for the funeral.

Wednesday 6 February 1974
Up to town with Claude Loombe – train late. Talked to Marcus Miller at coffee. He has rather changed his mind about the miners, whom he previously felt were justified in their overtime ban and wage demands – he now feels that if a company behaved in this

way he would have to condemn it, therefore consistency requires him to condemn the miners. 3rd year monetary seminar rather better than usual. Lunch with Alan Day; John Watkins and Basil Yamey talked with us for a few minutes. Imre died apparently from a coronary. The cremation is tomorrow and Peter Bauer and John Watkins himself will say a few words. John wrote the very good obituary in today's *Times*; the excellent detail was possible because of the detailed curriculum vitae which Imre wrote when he came to the School, together with other records written in Hungarian relating to Polya etc.

Monday 11 February 1974

Up to School – trains rather late. Took a class for Brian Griffiths, who has gone up to Blythe to fight the general election as a Conservative. Lecture 4–6 on macro-management, with coffee at 5 and casual discussion till 6.20. Home by fast train to Guildford and then taxi.

Tuesday 12 February 1974

Up to town via Guildford main station; met Peter Lyon (Institute of Commonwealth Studies) and a young solicitor, very pleasant. Hilton Clarke (Charterhouse Japhet) joined us and we went up on a slow train via Woking. . . . Lunch with Partha Dasgupta, Amartya Sen, Alan Day and Ray Richardson. Discussed Amartya's scheme to buy a house in Mornington Crescent, and warned him about dry rot, new road schemes and Camden Council's Third Part Accommodation [*for indigent families*] next door!

On another occasion I was having lunch with Charles Goodhart and some others when Frank Hahn joined us; he looked very pleased and announced that he had just bought a house. Charles joined in and said that he too had just bought one. Frank then suddenly said: 'My house cost £300,000, how much did yours cost?' There were moments of frozen silence, Charles struggled with his conscience but then felt that he had to tell the truth and admitted to a figure many times larger than Frank's. Tableau!

Wednesday 13 February 1974

Up with Claude Loombe... At coffee talked with Donald MacRae and Basil Yamey about the difficulty of writing references when one doesn't really know the standards of the receiving institution or how it will interpret one's own standards. Both Donald and I had noticed Oscar Browning's letter of application for the Regius Chair, quoted in the *Times Literary Supplement* article on Acton's appointment. We agreed that it was very urbane – well worth cutting out for future reference.

That cutting is pasted in my diary, and is reproduced here by kind permission of the *TLS*:

There was sorrow in Cambridge at the death of Seeley on January 13, 1895. But regret soon turned to panic when it was realised that the Prime Minister, an Etonian of standing, might be disposed to favour Oscar Browning, an Etonian of notoriety and a Liberal to boot. The historians of Cambridge rose almost to a man to warn Downing Street about the OB. 'As to the most notorious candidate', Sir Frederick Pollock wrote from Oxford, 'well, I need not tell a fellow Etonian that O.B. is about the only person who takes himself seriously.' So he did. Browning had sent Rosebery a long letter written the day after the Vice-Chancellor's notification of the vacancy:

'The post [Seeley] held should be occupied by a man of genius, and I know of no man of genius to fill it. Having been, as you are probably aware, engaged in the College and University teaching of history for many years back, it has been suggested to me that I might have some claim to succeed to the Regius Professorship which is in your gift, and that I have also been told that if I wished to be considered a candidate I ought to write to you to say so.'

He warned Rosebery that 'upon enquiry you may hear that my appointment would not be acceptable to a certain section at Cambridge', and explained the anti-Liberal prejudices which had 'injuriously affected' his position. Rosebery was as bland as Browning had been prompt: 'I . . . take note of the wish you express in so modest and friendly a spirit', he replied, but Rosebery was too good an Etonian to take much notice of it, and Gwatkin, Creighton, Maitland and other influential objectors had nothing to fear. (*The Times Literary Supplement*, 8 February 1974)

Although there may have been sorrow when Seeley died, at an earlier time he had not been without his critics. Cambridge tradition records that when, in 1869, he succeeded Charles Kingsley as Professor of Modern History, a don coming away from Seeley's inaugural lecture remarked: 'I never thought we should miss poor Kingsley so soon.'

I had many pleasant talks with Donald MacRae (Professor of Sociology) who admitted to being a compulsive reader; he once told me that if there was no newspaper at breakfast he would rather read the Cornflakes packet than nothing at all. He was a person of great erudition and when in his reading he came upon some unfamiliar word or usage he would note this on a postcard and send it to the *Oxford English Dictionary*. This led me much later to follow his example, though only once and by email rather than postcard. I was certain that the indentation in the top of a brick was called a 'frog' but the only dictionary I could find that recorded this was the *Shorter Oxford English Dictionary*. Unfortunately the first and only example of the term that it provided was a quotation which actually threw doubt upon it. I then found the term was regularly used in brick-centred circles and sent my email to the *OED* gently suggesting that a quotation drawn from them would be better than their existing one. I received a most courteous reply accepting my criticism and promising revision in due course. I also took the opportunity to point out that in their recommended usage of the term 'century' they suggested that, as an example, the years 1200–1300 should be referred to as the thirteenth century and 1300–1400 as the fourteenth century, which meant that the year 1300 was in both the thirteenth century and the fourteenth century. This was clearly regarded as much more serious matter than one of brick terminology and I was told that it would have to be referred to the higher echelons of the *OED*, after which I heard no more.

Thursday 14 February 1974
Morning at the School going over my paper on Flow of Funds, then up to University of Warwick to deliver it to a select (= small!) seminar run by Geoffrey Wood; Alan Roe the only one who really knew anything about the subject. Dinner with Geoffrey and a pleasant chap named Round, then train from Coventry to Euston, arriving 9.50; taxi to Waterloo in time to catch 10.02 to Guildford – good going. Wet walk home from London Road [*Station*].

Sunday 17 February 1974
Long telephone conversation with Marcus Miller about estimation of bank profits (which he feels are quite unjustifiable), efficient markets and do brokers misuse quantity (as opposed to price) information, all part of his concern about Gowland's paper upon which he is going to be a commentator at some conference. In my view it all turns upon the efficient markets hypothesis and reconciliation of ideal type with real time/operational aspect.

Monday 18 February 1974
Up to town. When I got to our two hour 2nd year session on macro-management they told me that Marcus Miller was giving a public lecture on monetary policy in a series organised by Peter Wiles, and suggested that we used the first hour to go to it and the second to discuss it. This we did, and had a very good discussion – they concluded that Marcus and I were not very far apart in our views.

Tuesday 19 February 1974
Fair MSc seminar, quite an entertaining account of Michael Parkin's work on a model of CCC [*Competition and Credit Control, the Bank of England policy statement*]. We concluded that he had omitted stability considerations in getting his ambiguous results.

Wednesday 20 February 1974
Good 3rd year seminar on 'Structure and efficiency in the UK financial system before CCC'. Lunch with Alan Day, Megnad Desai and David Hendry. Talked with David about the Central Statistical

Office data bank – he told me a very tangled tale of an access program from Southampton University needed for it which had arrived through odd channels. The main thing is that we should fairly shortly have the data bank in operation.

... After the Workshop I talked with Christopher Foster till Parkinson from Central Office of Information arrived at my room bringing Le Fournier, a French journalist from *L'Expansion.* We adjourned upstairs to the Senior Common Room bar and then to Rules [*an expensive restaurant in Covent Garden*] for dinner. We chatted very actively – a new audience for my various elderly bon mots. I enjoyed it; we found plenty to discuss and a good deal of common ground. He is writing an in-depth piece for his journal on the UK and its future. Parkinson is an ex-clergyman who had doubts. He is a relative of John Fforde [*in the Bank of England*].

Thursday 23 February 1974
Supper with Geoffrey Bell [*once one of my students and later with Schroders*] and his wife Joan, to meet Ira Scott. Long talk with Peter Jay – interesting.

Monday 11 March 1974
Up with Peter Lyon. Excellent lecture/class on macro-management – very responsive group of students. Had lunch with Bob Orr (Department of Government) and lamented the country's political problems. In afternoon saw Mr Bonet, a Brazilian refugee from the right wing Chilean regime, whom Peter Wiles asked me to advise about graduate work. Rather a floppy and forlorn man of about thirty. Home with John Patterson (Treasury) who also sees good reasons for gloom, except in departure of Barber from political life at the next election – he is not very popular.

Tuesday 12 March 1974
Up with Claude Loombe and Hilton Clarke (Charterhouse Japhet) who gets on at Clandon. At the School long conversation with Mr Lowe (MPhil, on leave from International Bank for Reconstruction and Development) discussing whether he should go back to IBRD

at the end of the year (he is going to). Good MSc seminar. Lunch with Ed Kuska, Ed Mishan and Marcus Miller. Saw Mr Lowe again in the afternoon and pushed him into doing MSc test questions as a check on his progress. Anthony Saunders (PhD student) also called and left me an essay.

On the way to tea in the Senior Common Room I found myself coming up behind Michael Oakeshott on the small staircase by the Graham Wallas Room; I declaimed 'Make way for blazing, ardent youth – we are reaching for the stars and must not be held back by old and outworn people and ideas...' [*He took this with great good humour*]. He and I then talked over tea about the problems of having at least having some idea of what one's colleagues are discussing in their seminars. I recalled the abortive multi-disciplinary seminars on Slavery – particularly one speaker who was there to lay down the [*Islamic*] law on slavery and was not interested in listening to anyone else. We agreed that we were fortunate in having no colleagues like him.

Last macro class for this term; cup of coffee with Marcus and discussion of Nield model on macro-management, then a non-specialist revision class from 6 o'clock. Room had been double booked and some Social Anthropologists were waiting – first time I can remember such a double booking. Very efficient porter found us another room so that the Anthropologists could use the room with the projector.

Home with Ken Clucas who has just become Permanent Secretary in the Department of Prices and Consumer Affairs (or some such title). He likes Shirley Williams, his minister, but is very busy. We lamented the inflationary outlook and had a most enjoyable talk about his and the country's problems.

Wednesday 13 March 1974
Up to town with Claude Loombe and Hilton Clarke. Saw students and made telephone calls then coffee in Senior Common Room and 3rd year seminar – quite good. Quick lunch talking to Peter

Wiles about Bonet, our Brazilian/Chilean refugee student whom I saw on Monday. Then to Senior Common Room AGM in Graham Wallas Room – very sparse attendance and all went through without difficulties. Talked with Ken Wallis afterwards about car parking. Various tasks in the afternoon, then Money Workshop – paper by Marcus Miller and Bill Allen (Bank of England). Good attendance, very good paper and good discussion. Mainline train to Guildford and home by taxi.

... Lunch with John Alcock [*Academic Secretary of the School*] and Bill Letwin [*Government*]. Bill thought that as holder of an endowed readership I should be paid more – John said that the endowment was now probably worth about 20p, which led on to the idea of mutual endowment of posts at this figure so that we could all have named posts. Bill said that there were some colleagues whose names he would rather *not* have to his endowed post. This led us to think of the least desirable endowed positions – Hitler Chair of International Relations, Stalin Chair of Government.

Tuesday 19 March 1974
Gave paper 'Introduction to Flow of Funds' at Surrey University – just round the corner. Went quite well; sherry afterwards with some staff and students. Asher Tropp and Kate Evans also present. Then off to dinner with Colin Robinson (Professor of Economics) and Stephen Frowen at The Withies, Compton. Very pleasant evening – good food and good conversation. Home before 10 p.m.

Sunday 31 March 1974
Worked on an article for *Encyclopaedia Britannica* – 'London Money Market' – heavy revision of an earlier one.

I had written this earlier one in 1965 and it certainly needed revision; through this I was invited to the dinner for British contributors to the new edition of the *Encyclopaedia* which was held at Claridges on 22 April 1974. There we were seated at tables of six or so and I still have the list of the contributors and their subjects marked with some of those at my table. On my right was the contributor on 'Tanks and Armoured Fighting Vehicles';

my background made conversation with him very easy although he was a mechanical engineer and an expert in designing them to actually work rather than in their operation as weapons. On my left was 'Human Eye and Vision', an expert on good eyes, while opposite him was 'Eye Diseases and Visual Disorder', an expert on bad eyes. Further round the table was 'Theories of Pain' who seemed reasonably cheerful despite his rather grim subject. It appeared that in his hospital when people were in agony, he was called in to study them. I like to think that he also alleviated their pain, but I don't remember him emphasising that. Also on our table was a lady whose subject escapes me; was she 'Human Liver'? Or 'Choreography and Dance Notation'? Or 'Frederic Chopin'? What they made of 'London Money Market' I cannot imagine; I suspect that to them the idea of a market in money would have seemed bizarre. Elsewhere in the room were two other people from the School: Willie Robson (City Government) and H.S. Morris (Minorities and Ethnic Groups); there should have been three but Brian Abel-Smith (Economics of Health and Disease) was unable to come. I regretted not meeting 'History of Egypt' and 'Evolution of Man' and I might even have had had genial conversations with 'Branchiopoda', 'Meteorites' and 'House of Bourbon', but there were some sixty persons present and one could not meet all of them. One entry on the guest list surprised me: Arthur Koestler – 'Wit and Humour'. As the evening wore on the conversation flowed and all of us had a most enjoyable time.

Monday 1 April 1974
Surrey Schools Conference at University of Surrey. Talked about economics. Then back to work on *Encyclopaedia Britannica* article. Almost immediately I received a telephone cable from Chicago saying they could handle my copy if it got there this week, so quickly finished it and into the post.

Tuesday 2 April 1974
Up to School with Peter Lyon. Admin and talking with colleagues – long talk with Harold Edey over coffee. Went to Bank of England to collect some statistical publications from Randle (Librarian) – very affable but he talks so hard that he is difficult to get away from. Saw Geoffrey Wood in the [*Bank*] Library. Lunch with Case

Sprenkel (University of Illinois), Philip Klein (Pennsylvania State University) and Nick Barr.

The Bank of England let me have quite a lot of their recently discarded statistical and other publications which I thought would be of interest to our Monetary Group students. When I collected them they were so heavy that I had to take them to the School by taxi. Close to my room was the stairwell with a long window sill where I used to put these publications with a notice inviting anyone to help themselves. They would disappear quite quickly.

Friday 19 April 1974

Addressed Malaysian Students group on world inflation etc. They obviously looked at the Arab oil price and wanted to do the same thing with rubber and tin. Some straight talking on both sides – in general good-humoured and constructive. Their secretary, Mr Hussein, is an older student doing a PhD at Imperial College. He took me to lunch at a Chinese (SE Asia variety) restaurant in Edgware Road. I had Singapore laxa – absolutely delicious. I found Hussein a very nice chap.

Monday 3 June 1974

Up to town. Met Rev Sam Ebo [*a West African cleric visiting Toni's church*] at station and travelled with him. At Clandon Frank Paish got on and joined us; he and I talked pleasantly while Sam read the paper. Had my eyes tested at the School; I may need reading glasses, but my long sight is good (still no difficulty in reading the bottom row of letters [*on the test card*]). Call from Alan Day; went to talk with him – he wanted me to take over part of Kurt Klappholz's admin duties in the Department, mainly concerned with allocating teaching duties etc. Alan also confirmed that Harry Johnson had resigned – not really a surprise. Long talk with Mr Lowe (IBRD) who will be going back to Washington at the end of the month. Lunched with Margaret Sharp [*later Baroness Sharpe*] (she used to be a colleague at the School, but is now in Washington with her husband, who is in the Embassy – she is doing some work at the Brookings Institution). Also with us were David Metcalf and his research officer named Smith. They have a project involving internal labour allocation/ promotion within Midland Bank. Saw Alan Day at coffee after lunch and agreed to take on the admin work. Saw Charles Braybrooke about a decent cover for the Money Workshop papers; he passed me on to Lewis who can do what I want for about £5 per 1,000 – if the Department will pay.

Call from David Martin [*Sociology*]; his son is taking Economics at A level and David wanted some advice on reading in order to help him – his school does not seem very good. Talked to Richard Caves [*Harvard*], who is at the School for about a month; a very cultivated and congenial person. Also talked with David Hendry about his multipurpose multiple regression – should be usable by amateurs by September; at coffee this had arisen when I spoke to one of the Statistics research officers about data bank material. At tea talked with Jim Durbin about his Building Society mortgage scheme; explained my doubts to him and we discussed these and other things for about an hour. Took four scripts to David Metcalf, who is going to adjudicate on them, as Tim Josling and I are some way apart in our marks. Home by train to [*Guildford*] main station and then by taxi.

21

Life at LSE – More on the 1970s

Allocating Teaching

In 1975 I was asked by Alan Day, then Convenor of the Department of Economics, to take over the duty of teaching allocation for the mainstream courses in the Department (the teaching allocation for the smaller quantitative group – maths/econometrics – was done by that group for itself). My role now was to ensure that all our teaching commitments were met for the next academic year 1975–76, which meant that I had to begin work immediately, while all my colleagues were around for the summer term and I could easily talk to them. Fortunately there was a considerable degree of continuity from one year to the next; taking on a lecture course meant a considerable investment in preparation – lecture notes, reading list, class programmes and other handouts – so that the lecturer would normally expect to stay with a course for three or more years. Classes had less continuity as all of us could take first or second year classes (although most of us had quite strong preferences between macro- and micro-economics classes) and changes in allocation of these classes was the usual means of adjusting teaching burdens between teachers.

My activity now became focussed on creating a large matrix table with some 35 rows, one for each teacher (full-time and part-time), and 75 columns, one for each course. These varied from large first year lectures with around 200 students or more and perhaps 15 class groups, to small courses, sometimes done for other Departments, with only one class group. I was able to make many cell entries in actual contact hours of teaching for teachers and courses which I already knew about. At the foot of each column was the total of contact hours of lectures and classes required (demand) and the number so far provided (supply). I also showed exports and imports of contact hours to or from other Departments. For each teacher/row there was on the right the total in contact hours of teaching analysed into lectures, classes and seminars. At that time there was a presumption that all members of the Department should do roughly the same equivalent hours (e.h.) of teaching; these were weighted hours, the weights being: 1.5 for lectures, 1 for undergraduate classes, 1.1 for MSc classes; weights for a seminar varied, depending roughly upon how many people shared the running of it. For each teacher, at the end of his row in the matrix table the details of his contact hours were then weighted to give a total in equivalent hours. It was recognised that while lectures and classes were pure production, seminars usually contained an element of consumption for those running them. There were also allowances for those carrying out administrative activities; for example, I was given a credit of 30 hours for doing the teaching allocation.

The demand side – how many class groups we had to provide for each course – required much liaison with Miss Boas who was in charge of timetables and received student registrations for each course. She was stern and efficient, always taking a grim view of the timetabling problems she had to face (but which in the end she always managed to overcome); the chief of these was fitting all the School's teaching into our limited number of class and lecture rooms. I used to approach her with a sunny smile in the hope that some of it would rub off on her, but it never did. Then came the supply side. The main problem here was people leaving the Department or going on sabbatical leave, followed by people wanting a change in their teaching and finally newcomers to the staff whose preferences were not fully known. All of these affected the rows in my matrix table which in turn would show up any problem areas where course requirements might come up against a shortage of suitable teachers. In the case of newcomers, who were often at universities overseas, I started to fit them in by suggesting to them some teaching duties which seemed consistent with their apparent interests (using correspondence or phone – no e-mail then) to see how they responded. But in most cases it came down to face-to-face negotiation, often done in the Senior Common Room after lunch where many of my colleagues would be having coffee. When I approached them – in my usual friendly way, of course – they would now display a certain understandable wariness because they suspected, often correctly, that I would be coming to persuade them to take on some new teaching. However, it was all conducted very amicably because they knew that they would have to accept a roughly average burden and my powers were only those of gentle persuasion, supplemented by one effective ploy. This was to start by suggesting to a colleague some teaching which I knew he would *not* like and quickly follow his protestations by suggesting that the only real alternative was the teaching I actually wanted him to do. Without exception he would hastily agree to what I wanted. These negotiations extended to a number of part-time teachers, who were sometimes retired colleagues, sometimes postgraduates or research workers at the School, sometimes people doing private research whom we had found to be good and reliable teachers in the past, as well as some new part-timers recommended by members of the Department. Visiting scholars would often volunteer a certain amount of teaching and Tibor Scitovsky was such a visitor in 1976–77. I remember him particularly because to me he was an important name in welfare economics; when I suggested some lectures in that field he looked shifty and claimed, rather unconvincingly, that he really didn't know very much about the subject, and volunteered instead to take on some quite different lectures and seminars.

When someone agreed to take one or two class groups in a particular course I would report this to Miss Boas who would add their names to her list of class teachers on that course, and the teacher himself would contact her to see what time slots were available for his classes and to choose those which he found most convenient. By the end of the summer term my matrix table would show only a few teaching commitments unfulfilled. In the middle of the vacation I would take a reduced photocopy of the matrix and colour the unresolved cells, making it easier to focus on the remaining problems. Apart from a few negotiations over the phone, these things generally had to wait until near the beginning of the new session in October when my colleagues were again around the School and when Miss Boas would tell me of any alterations arising from students changing courses. Then in the week or two before the end of the vacation, the final teaching allocations would be agreed and everything would be ready for the coming Michaelmas Term. Even during term the occasional problem would arise requiring further persuasion of one or two colleagues.

My first report to the Professors of Economics was written in about May 1975 and looked briefly at the allocation outcome for the then current year 1974–75 (in which the Department as a whole delivered 7,524 equivalent hours of teaching) and then looked forward to 1975–76. The prospect was uncomfortable because we were going to lose a larger than usual number of teachers who in 1974–75 had produced 1,331 equivalent hours (e.h.) of teaching and with financial stringency, the prospect for replacements was unpromising. Most of my six page report was therefore devoted to a detailed look at ways in which we could economise on teaching hours to help meet our expected shortfall in staff. But my first year's work on teaching allocation also proved useful when there was a visitation by the University Grants Committee in 1975 and I was one of the team from the Economics Department to face them (I seem to recall that Max Steuer was also a member of the team). There were a number of questions about staffing and teaching arrangements, and because of my work on teaching allocation I found myself the only one fully briefed to answer them.

The BSc Econ degree covered many different subjects and Departments were supposed to work to the 'Oakeshott norm' of 50 contact hours per course, which was intended to preserve equity between students, between teachers and between Departments. But within this guideline multiple class groups for our large courses took up a lot of contact hours and the number of classes for some courses seemed unduly generous. Limiting this class content of courses to 20 contact hours (which on the previous year's figures would save 650 e.h.) was one of many detailed proposals in my report. Others included: taking full account of cancelled, curtailed or unexpectedly shared courses (saving 159 e.h.); undergraduate seminars to be treated as classes (45 e.h.); adjustment of weights for more than one person taking a seminar (92 e.h.); no credit for attending seminars in other Departments (88 e.h.); raising class sizes from 12 to 15 (500 e.h.), but a reduction in MSc class size had already been agreed (–40 e.h.); and several other minor suggestions. Finally I mentioned some cost-effective ways of offsetting the effects of any reduction in contact hours per course: some programmed instruction for maths and statistics (looked at earlier, but which if deemed satisfactory could yield further significant saving in e.h.); improvement in feedback on shortages in the Teaching Library (now the Course Collection); reviewing our assumptions and guidelines on the scale of reading lists and their priority indications, as well as on the level of textbook provision that students should make for themselves and its implications for the Teaching Library. I was invited to attend the meeting of the Professors of Economics at which my report was discussed. Some of my suggestions were accepted, as well as some others which I raised during the meeting; there was a very full and fair discussion and I was thanked for my work on a difficult task.

Over the next two years the pressure on the Department's teaching staff continued and these same possible solutions, and others, continued to be discussed and in some cases implemented. In the final year of my allocation duties, 1977–78, a new issue arose from a visiting Social Science Research Council team who thought that our MSc mainstream macro and micro courses received insufficient class teaching. I did a detailed investigation of this, ending up with tables and regressions which confirmed the view of the SSRC team. At this time there were no fewer than 17 MSc optional/ specialist papers, some with only very few students, and reducing this number was one way of releasing contact hours for the MSc mainstream courses. Some papers suggested for extinction were fiercely defended by their proprietors, showing that a scholarly awareness of social welfare did not exclude a more pressing awareness of private interest. My reports gave me the opportunity to raise some sensitive matters: my concern that recruitment to the Department gave undue weight to research potential and did not pay sufficient attention to our teaching needs; and that all new staff should be made clearly aware that they were expected to join in mainstream first and second year theory and applied class teaching (I had sensed a danger of unhealthy specialisation in order to avoid this).

As my three years of responsibility for teaching allocation neared its end, Alan Prest, who had then become Convenor, asked if I would continue for another three year stint. This I declined as I was now becoming more engaged in my own research. But in my letter I felt bound to point out that administrative work like teaching allocation, and indeed teaching itself, no matter how well done, seemed to have no influence on promotions, which appeared to be determined entirely by research performance or potential. This same point had been made earlier by Harry Kidd in his book *The Trouble at LSE*, pp. 1–2, 15, 130.

The Monetary Group

Behind these administrative activities the usual academic round continued. When Richard Sayers took early, but planned, retirement in 1967 he was succeeded by Alan Walters but it was Leslie Pressnell who took over responsibility for the third year undergraduate Monetary Group; and when he left in 1970 for the University of Kent I took it over. Alan and I ran the MSc monetary seminars together; his room was next door to mine and we had much amicable talk, but he was a monetarist and I was not, which meant that there was no lack of active discussion in our seminars. He also had an interest in transport economics and was much involved with the question of developing Foulness as a third London airport; my brother Michael suggested that as a compromise we should instead further develop Heathrow but rename it Foulrow. Brian Griffiths was a helpful backup in the teaching of monetary institutions but in 1977 both he and Alan Walters moved on. Alan Day now had more interests elsewhere, and in 1979 he became Pro-Director which took up much more of his time which left me as effectively the only survivor of the Monetary Group built up by Richard Sayers. The next arrival was George Akerlof, he joined in the Money Workshop but he never seemed to settle down at the School and he stayed for only two years. His wife, Janet Yellen, was also at the School for those two years and although I spoke with her on only a few occasions, I found her very pleasant and with real intellectual horsepower.

The Monetary Economics Group of undergraduates for which I was now responsible took two core courses in their final year. The first was Monetary Theory for which there were a number of people in the Department who could do the teaching; the second was British Monetary System and this was the course which I taught throughout the 1970s and 80s. It consisted of twenty lectures, usually fifteen classes for each of three or four groups (all nominally of one hour, but having to allow some time for changeover) and ten or fifteen undergraduate seminars of $1\frac{1}{2}$ hours. Richard Sayers had always aimed to give our Monetary Group students some sense of the realities of financial institutions by having these seminars given by people from the City who were experienced in banking and financial markets, and after he retired this practice was continued by Leslie Pressnell and then by myself. We had good connexions with the City and the School's name helped to bring in very good speakers. The aim of the British Monetary System course was to introduce students to the structure, characteristics, main operations and regulation mainly of banks, and but also of other financial institutions in Britain, together with monetary policy. The seminars brought us close to the current operations in the financial system and were highly instructive not only for the students but also for me. (These were very different from the MSc seminars in monetary economics which I used to take jointly with Alan Walters while he was at the school; in those the papers were largely theoretical and were given by the students in turn.) Over these years my teaching programme consisted of the British Monetary System course and the Money Workshop, for which I had to organise the programme and chair the meetings, together with my allocation of second year macro-economics classes to take me up to the roughly equal teaching burden across all members of the Economics Department. The following account of my experience with lectures, classes and tutorials, although in this chapter on the later 1970s, can be regarded as broadly true of both my earlier and later years.

In the 1970s the pace of change in British financial institutions was already growing significantly, and keeping up to date required an increasing amount of institutional research. The results were fed into my teaching of the British Monetary System course, which was designed to present a clear and up-to-date account of the subject set out in a way which would be most helpful to students. To support the lectures they needed a lecture plan, a reading list structured by topics and starred for importance, a set of handouts on certain key aspects and a programme of topics for class discussion, all of these fully updated. For myself this required very clear and fully updated lecture notes. My aim was to go into a lecture well enough prepared to speak directly to my audience but with very well-structured lecture notes which were clear to my cursory glances, so ensuring proper order and coverage of the topics concerned. These were also an insurance against any sudden blankness of mind. The revision of these notes each year I used as a rehearsal for the lectures themselves, talking them through to myself (and sometimes aloud where no one could hear me and start having doubts about my sanity) all of which helped towards an effective presentation. However, at one stage I became conscious of too many um's and er's as well as occasional fluffing and concluded that my lecturing style required some attention. This led me to record some of my lectures to get a better idea of how they seemed to my audience. The results revealed too many shortcomings. I tightened my presentation, and made it slightly slower and more deliberate; this led, I like to think, to a marked improvement.

I greatly enjoyed teaching; holding the attention of an audience was a challenge and lecturing to an interested and attentive audience I found most rewarding, particularly seeing their understanding light up as some less easy point suddenly became clear to them through examples and analogies. I found that one great advantage of lectures, compared to written material, in my field of financial institutions was that I could start a topic with a carefully simplified case which would allow students to grasp a clear basic framework into which the complications of the real world could then be gradually fitted and their significance made clear. In all sorts of ways – reminders that this was a starting point, hints that there was more to come, tone of voice, the whole attitude of my exposition – I could persuade them to stick with my development of the topic and recognise that my simplifications would in due course be removed to reveal a more complex and realistic picture. And if their own thinking was to run into confusions later, this also gave them a basic framework to fall back on and then to start from again. It always seemed to me very difficult to develop such an institutional subject in a written account where one knew that other specialists would immediately leap in and point out that almost all simple statements required considerable qualification. Just so, but to add in all the qualifications at each initial mention of some aspect would simply blur the picture for students. Helping students in this way to develop their understanding always seemed to me a thoroughly worthwhile activity. The fringe bank crisis of 1973 occurred while I was teaching my usual course on the British Monetary System. At one lecture I was able to show the students an attractively coloured leaflet that I had just received by post; it was from Cedar Trust and was offering a range of gifts – I particularly remember the picture of a small dinghy with a delighted family around it – to those who would deposit various not very large sums of money, but by the time I received it Cedar had collapsed. A graphic lesson on desperation, risk and reward.

From my own experience I was always conscious of the difference between teaching economic theory, where the object is typically the exposition and exploration of a particular model in which realism is sacrificed for clarity, and on the other hand the difficulties in explaining the real world – in my case the British banking and financial system – where multiple influences are always simultaneously at work and where there is never any clear starting point for exposition. Some theoretical framework is essential in order to organise what would otherwise be a haphazard assemblage of facts, and this also helps to develop rigour in reasoning. It is then a question of the balance between fact and theory, their fruitful interaction and the success of the combination in helping students into the subject. For undergraduate courses in general, I would have opted for rather more applied economics, partly to make the subject more relevant to the world around them and partly to place greater emphasis on helping students both to appreciate the complexity of the world and to develop the judgement necessary to deal with it.

Class arrangements differed between subjects; in macro-economics, for example, the topics were largely determined by the lecturer running that course, as was their form. Sometimes these classes would go through pre-set exercises which the students had just done on their own, and deal with problems arising from them. Classes in my own British Monetary System course were on the lines already described for economics classes I took when I started teaching, with a list of topics for each meeting handed out at the beginning of term and two class members allocated to each topic. At the class I would then ask one of them to open on the topic (speaking to the class and not just reading from their paper) and the other to comment and raise issues. Class discussion was then determined by the particular aspect of the topic or its problems which emerged, and sometimes by the evident need for some aspects of the topic to be briefly gone through again by myself. I would then collect the two papers and mark them, with these marks going into their class report. In my experience British students tended to be reticent in class and at first had to be cajoled into open discussion; their attitude often seemed to be 'Better to be thought a fool than to open your mouth and remove all possible doubt.' More understandably, the same was true of many foreign students, particularly those whose mother tongue was not English; American students tended to be the most open and willing to speak out. One way or another a reasonable degree of discussion was generally achieved and participation was another of the things that was recorded in each student's class report at the end of term.

Perhaps it was getting older that led me to have more paternal feelings towards my students. In classes I would sometimes look around these young people and wonder what the future held for them, hoping that they would do well, marry the right person, have satisfying and fulfilling lives. I felt that seeing them as students was seeing them at their best, with their youthful energies geared to really worthwhile and absorbing intellectual effort. In most cases when a series of classes came to an end the students either moved on a year or graduated and most of them I would never see again. But there were a few exceptions. Two students in one of my British Monetary System classes got married not long after finals; they shared the good news with me, and Toni and I sent them a wedding present with our warmest good wishes. At the end of one term we went off to the States for a holiday. Going into Boston and visiting Faneuil Hall – a great temple of food and drink – the first person we saw as we entered was an American girl who had recently been in one of my classes and now had a vacation job in one of the food boutiques. And in Moscow, walking near Red Square I met a student from the Monetary Group some ten years earlier, and only a few days later, and less surprisingly, I met a member of our first Russian Course. Around the School, and particularly in the Senior Common Room, over the years I have many times been greeted by visitors who had been in my classes or lectures many years, some times decades, earlier. I am still in touch with one person who was in the very first economics class I took in 1952, helped by the fact that he is a fellow resident of Guildford; this is Peter Lyon, later a colleague at the School in the International Relations Department, then for many years at the Institute of Commonwealth Studies.

Seeing my tutees was a regular task which took up more time as the number of my tutees rose; although I had all their details and photos, it was not always easy to remember who was who. When a tutee appeared unexpectedly I found one convenient solution was to tell him that I just wanted to make sure that I had his initials right; when he gave them to me a glance down my list would reveal to me his surname and then his details would come flooding back. In the last resort I adopted the technique used, I believe, by Louis XIV; this consisted of saying in the most gracious way 'Now just remind me of your name', as if I had already been thinking about him. In addition to particular appointments with tutees I wished to see, each of us in the Department had a well-publicised 'Office Hour' advertised on our door to ensure that we were regularly available to see tutees or other students who might want to talk to us. Tutorial meetings were mainly pastoral rather than for teaching, because the different subjects taken by students meant that no tutor could adequately deal with all of their courses; teaching in support of lectures, and dealing with problems, was the role of the classes in each subject. In tutorial meetings we would discuss the tutee's class reports (not always complete and occasionally missing) from class teachers in each of the four subjects which they took each year and these would sometimes reveal problems requiring help. Their choice of courses for the next year was a regular topic; there was always discussion of how they felt they were getting on generally, which opened up further aspects of their work and allowed them to raise any other concerns such as careers and personal matters. The latter produced a trickle of minor problems with only very occasional difficulties which were more serious, typically to do with their family or health. For most of these one could only express sympathy, give commonsense advice and help them to get in touch with those professionals who had the skill to deal with such problems. In due course my tutees would need references; over my career at the School I must have written hundreds of these, striving to be helpful and truthful, and always getting pleasure from writing a really good reference for a really good student. Looking back over all the undergraduates I have taught, I see a receding crowd of increasingly blurred faces from which a fair number, but a tiny proportion, stand out more clearly; but looking at the references I have written (and I still have a sizeable box full of them), the stimulus of just a name is often sufficient to summon up a face and often some reminder of the person.

Quite early as a tutor I had found that there were a number of issues about academic work which arose regularly and this led me in the late 1970s to produce a four-page handout, *Academic Work at University*, which addressed them. It was written in a very direct tutor-to-student manner with an emphasis on intelligent self-management. It urged students to work hard (perhaps keeping a work diary to pace themselves); suggested how they could organise their time and their work effectively; gave them advice about various aspects of academic work and exams, and finally gave them the consolation that many problems in studying are very common and can be overcome. It was adopted for distribution across the Economics Department. It developed over time and continued to be distributed for many years after I retired, its core advice remaining unchanged because students and their problems remained unchanged; the final version is reproduced below in Appendix 1. A later generation of teachers decided that such humane advice was no longer needed in an increasingly technological world, and it was allowed to fall out of use.

At this time quite a number of applicants for the BSc Econ degree were interviewed, often because they were not straightforward cases; a few times a year myself and a colleague from some other department would spend most of a day doing our share of these interviews. We had the applicants' details on their UCCA (application) forms and our object was to find out more about them to see if they were good enough to be offered a place. The applicants were usually rather nervous and we were sympathetic in our efforts to find out how good they were, but there were sometimes cases where applicants had been badly advised or seemed to me to be going in the wrong academic direction. In these cases I would tell them that we were switching off the interview for a few minutes and I would then give them what helpful advice I could before switching the interview back on again. This made the interview helpful to the applicant and a more constructive activity for us.

In the case of one of my first year tutees, our initial tutorial meeting was filmed for the first LSE public relations film. He was surprised to find my room filled with a film crew to record his first meeting with me and I think he went away with a very strange idea of what a tutorial meeting involved. There were occasional surprises in the other direction. I was once talking to a group of five new first year tutees, when my phone rang. I answered it, said that I was seeing students and would ring back, and as I replaced the phone one of the girls leant forward wide-eyed and said: 'I do admire your telephone manner.' At university, unlike school, parents are normally never seen. I did have one case where a tutee came to see me accompanied by his mother, and this revealed where his problems lay; another tutee brought his grandmother to meet me, but such cases were very rare. Sometimes we had an unexpected view of a student. When Walter Stern (Economic History) retired in 1979 he told us that he had been looking through his records and had found that one of his tutees, Jagger M, had asked if he could have permission to join a pop group in his spare time; Walter's reply was yes, provided it did not affect his academic work. It evidently did affect his academic work. It was Walter who under the title 'Memorable Words' had collected examples of the strange things that students sometimes wrote down under the stress of the examination room, for example:

It must be remembered that at this time England was covered by circumstances.

In England in the 19th century, the population showed a sharp increase due to the development of scientific methods.

The railway age also witnessed the urbanisation of towns.

Hargreaves spinning jelly...

Roger Holmes (Industrial and Social Psychology) on the other hand produced aperçus (I think that is the word) for example:

Bureaucracy: method before matter

Irony: having it both ways.

Also the occasional play on words:

(Of a seminar visitor, less controversial than expected): He came, he saw, he concurred.

Letters to the Press

On 17 June 1976 I had a letter published in *The Times* on immigration, expressing my view that the social strains of immigration and the anxieties of white Britons were being dangerously neglected. This elicited a letter in reply from three of my colleagues, Richard Layard, Morris Perlman and Alisdair Smith; in my view they missed most of the points I was making and objected to points I had not made. I had a number of favourable comments on my letter from outside the School and one from Ed Mishan (also in the Economics Department) who had asked to see a copy of it:

22 June 76

Roger,

Thanks. Am keeping tabs on *The Times* correspondence, and will intervene if and when the tide seems to be flowing the wrong way.

So far I reckon you're on top.

Ed [*Mishan*]

I composed a reply to my three critics but, not unreasonably, *The Times* was unwilling to devote any more space to a difference of opinion within the Department of Economics at the School. Subsequent experience confirms in my own mind the validity of my argument, and shows the damage that has been done to democracy by political cowardice and political correctness over immigration. In 1978 I returned to the subject of immigration with another letter in *The Times*, replying to a letter from Bernard Levin and one from Sir Alfred Ayer and others; I noted the widespread concern about immigration and its effects upon Britain, and ended by saying that British democracy was on trial. In my view it failed this trial.

Over the years I have written many letters to the press of which thirty have been published, twenty-one in *The Times* and nine in the *Financial Times*, the last one appearing in 2007 in the *FT Online*. There is a checklist of these letters in Appendix 2. Only the very first of these letters would I now withdraw. It was critical of the public schools at a time when I was greatly impressed by the academic standard of the grammar schools. When so many of the latter were destroyed – an act of unbelievable educational vandalism – I came to feel that it was essential to support the public schools for their high educational standards. If I were asked to choose one of my letters as being of longer term relevance it would be that published in *The Times* of 3 September 2002. This identified poverty with low productivity per head and (with Africa in mind) went on: 'Every story and picture of the hungry and deprived should be greeted not with guilt and anguish but with the practical question: "Why do these people have such low productivity per head?"' It then listed the main causes: lack of democracy; governments with no concern for their own poor; corruption; lack of education; a mindset obstructing the growth of productivity; and population growth. It viewed the prospects of overcoming these obstacles as unpromising. My opinion on these matters has not changed.

Other Activities

John Pike was Financial Secretary, a most pleasant colleague and a very efficient administrator. There were two matters which came up, small in themselves, but which let me see him in action. When the library was still in the main building one of the new Xerox machines was installed in one of its rooms on the second floor with a hatch through which material could be handed to a girl for xeroxing. I pointed out to him that if this hatch was made into a door people could go in and do the xeroxing themselves and that locking the door of this room into the rest of the library would keep the library secure. We looked at the room together and he agreed. Two days later there was a door in place of the hatch. Similarly when the library had moved into the Robbins Building, a barrier had been installed to keep cars out of its forecourt but it was so positioned that it also obstructed people going to the library. I drew this to John's attention and the next day the barrier had been repositioned. It was most refreshing to have such an immediate response to a clear problem.

For many years pension arrangements for academics had been done through life insurance policies, with Mr Scriven, the School's Assistant Secretary and Accountant, urging us all to take out with-profits policies with Equitable Life. This was very good advice for the time (much better than some academics were given in other institutions); it was only thirty years later that an – in my view – economically illiterate judgement was responsible for nearly bankrupting the 'Old Equitable'. But in 1973 there were proposals for changes in the pension arrangements to a scheme called USS and the Principal of the University of London came and explained these to the Academic Board. The School then asked Alan Stuart, Harold Edey and myself to look into these proposals. This we did and after a good deal of discussion and consultation we raised a number of points. Only when we were ready to report were we told that since the proposed arrangements had been approved by the Treasury, any comments were superfluous. One thing which emerged from our work on the USS proposals was that the great majority of our colleagues had only very faint ideas of their pension arrangements, and indeed of anything to do with saving and investment beyond the most elementary level. They simply believed that the School would ensure that academic pension arrangements would somehow be fair and reasonable.

Alan Stuart was a statistician and author with Maurice Kendall of the *Advanced Theory of Statistics* (in three volumes!) and at that time he was taking an interest in the price movements of securities. I can remember a long and interesting conversation with him and Maurice (who had his arm in plaster, having fallen out of an apple tree) about whether such price movements were a random walk. Maurice was one of the originators of operations research – the application of scientific thinking to practical problems thrown up during the Second World War; one of these was how to optimise the loading of scarce shipping by combining cargoes of, for example, dried egg (light but bulky) and ammunition (heavy and compact) so as to fully use all the space and all the weight-carrying capacity of a vessel. Alan, in some later work, was to find a cubic relationship between votes cast and MPs elected for any party, but this relationship turned out not to be robust. I can remember him telling me that he once gave some statistical advice to Lord Rothschild (who was a scientist) and received in return several bottles of wine – one a vintage Pouilly Fuissé; enquiry revealed that this could be expected to fetch over £1,000 at auction, but after some thought Alan and his wife drank it, on the grounds that such an opportunity would never occur again.

It was around this time that L B Schapiro and Ellen de Kadt (both Soviet specialists) and myself were asked to meet three heads of provincial Russian universities when they visited the School accompanied by their Embassy/KGB minder – a snappily-dressed and rather effete young man, very western in appearance, and clearly totally bored by his charges. My role was to talk about the teaching of economics and our visitors told us that all such teaching in Russian universities was based on the writings of Lenin. I replied with our case for freedom in such teaching. Hearing their doctrinaire view was interesting but deeply unappealing and I felt that there was no meeting of minds. The meeting ended with them giving each of us a close-fitting embroidered hat of vaguely central Asian appearance. Looking back after the meeting I felt that I should have been more outspoken.

Students

For some time I was the School's staff representative on the local committee of AIESEC, which arranged international exchanges and internships for students of economics. The undergraduates involved were very keen and active in running its affairs. If the need had arisen I would have used my own contacts on their behalf but in the event my role was an honorary one. I also took a general interest in postgraduate affairs and in 1972 I put forward to the Scholarships and Prizes Committee a proposal for a loan scheme to allow postgraduates to finance their way through a higher degree. Later, in 1978 the Graduate School Committee was considering proposals for a new structure of the PhD and amongst my papers I have found a detailed flow diagram which I had produced to clarify these proposals, together with many comments upon them, all of which I sent to the committee.

At a rather different level, when *Beaver*, the LSE student newspaper, ran a poetry competition I felt that as a communal gesture I would enter it. Temporarily suffused with literary spirit I wrote my poem with taste and care, adding four *haiku* to appeal to any Japanese judge. By the time my inspiration was exhausted the competition had closed, been judged and a winner announced. I had been so engaged with my own entry that I never noticed this. However, it would be wrong to waste my deathless words so here is my entry in full. To influence the judges in my favour I included notes for the many university teachers who would surely wish to give full attention to such path-breaking works in their more advanced courses on English literature – if only to brand me as the author of an unusually unspeakable poem and an ass of assonance.

Poem

In Portugal the northern chalk
supports the cork-oak and the cork-oak auk
whose hoarse coarse squawk attracts the cork-oak hawk.

The hawk will lurk, and stalk the cork-oak auk
and jerk it from its arc of cork bark in a cork-oak fork
and grasp its dark marked egg as portly walkers gawp.

After much talk, a stark chalk baulk and plaque
mark out a cork-oak auk park where swarthy wardens work,
the awkward auk-wards of the northern chalk.

Within the chalk baulk with the cork-oak auk
there lives Hark! Hark! the cautious cork-oak lark,
also, alas, the avid raucous gawky cork-oak stork...

[NOTE: It has been suggested that, rather than the work of a gifted amateur, this could well be an unpublished poem by Elizabeth

Barrett Browning originally intended to be included in a later edition of her *Sonnets from the Portuguese*; if so, it would appear to be the only known example of her 'plastic scansion'. The 'unclosed' ending of the poem would be characteristic of her onward-reaching sensitivity.]

*   *   *

Modest three line verse
    Short, uneven metre, terse
Longer would be worse

Just five, seven, five
    That is all; *Haiku* its name
Simple but alive

Sprouts, grows, flowers,
    Slowly withers, seeds, then dies
Sprouts, grows, flowers

Out my papers go
    Records from so long ago
Now it must be so

[NOTE: These four pregnant *oeuvrettes* are striking examples of western-style free-verse-form *haiku*. The self-referential character of the first two is noteworthy for creating *meta-haiku*.]

There followed a less good-humoured engagement with students. From my diary:

Friday 15 March 1974
Someone told me that there was an attack on me in '*Beaver*' [the School's student newspaper] for 14 March. Found a copy in the foyer of the St Clements Building. They reprint (quite accurately) the two flysheets about the opening of the Senior Dining Room to all members of the School. As usual Beaver lacks talent and argues wildly. Another item attacks 'men only' jobs being registered by our Careers Advisory Service (of which I become Chairman next term).

This came about because of a proposal in 1971 by thirty-nine of my colleagues that the Senior Common Room (SCR) should be opened to students as well as staff. I regarded this as an absurd example of romantic political correctness; I was active in opposing it and the motion was heavily defeated. Later seventeen of the earlier signatories put forward an amended proposal that just the Senior Dining Room (SDR) should be opened to students as well as staff. The SCR Committee finally accepted this motion and requested that it should be accompanied by two statements, one for and one against. The statement in favour was written by Mike Reddin and Jonathan Rosenhead, and I wrote the statement against. Both papers were circulated and were published side by side on the front page of Beaver for 14 March 1974 with the subheading: 'Roger Alford illustrates staff elitism at LSE'. The case in favour was that opening the SDR would improve contacts between students and staff, would reduce the disparity between the facilities for the two groups and would remove a sense of injustice which was a bar to a sense of community. I accepted that student refectory facilities needed improvement, but my case against opening the SDR was that 'it is simply a fact that staff and students are significantly different populations in terms of age, duration of stay at the School, academic attainment, income, responsibility for others etc ... to pretend that they are the same, and that therefore the same refectory and social facilities will be equally appropriate and acceptable to both groups is simply unrealistic'. The accompanying editorial in *Beaver* was in favour of the motion and was mainly an attack on myself, I didn't mind but I did wish that it had been better argued and better written. When put to the members of the Senior Common Room, the motion was defeated by 226 votes to 71 and was never revived.

It must have been in the following year that a group of students made a rather hangdog attempt to invade the Senior Dining Room, apparently to stage some sort of street-theatre; I was Chairman of the SCR Committee at the time and I placed myself between the coffee annex and the main dining-room and would not let them through. They then sat down in the annex apparently discussing their street-theatre ambitions before drifting off. I have vague memories of another occasion when the SCR was closed for a few days with sitters-in inviting alleged members of the IRA to address them, but I cannot remember any details.

22

Life at LSE in the 1980s

Flow of Funds

I had first started looking at the UK Flow of Funds accounts when I was in the Bank of England; I had retained an interest in them after I returned to the School and had worked on them at various times. Indeed I had used them as a framework in my British Monetary System course in the mid-1960s, as I was reminded decades later by David Llewellyn (then at Loughborough) who had attended those lectures as a student. I had now begun serious work aimed at exploring and clarifying the structure of these accounts and its implications. The need for such clarification was brought home to me when a friend who was a senior economist in the City told me that he found it very difficult to develop an intuitive grasp of the signs of the entries in these accounts and always had to go to an item he was familiar with to reorient himself.

I was mainly concerned with the conceptual aspects of Flow of Funds (FoF) and the focus of my work was the zero-sum FoF matrix table. This records financial flows between sectors, covering domestic sectors and the overseas, or rest of the world sector so that in principle it covers the whole world and all possible transactors. In this format a transaction is recorded by a zero-sum double entry for each sector/transactor, and since the matrix table includes both parties to a transaction this produces a quadruple entry system where each individual quadruple entry sums to zero down each column and along each row. Summing all such transaction quadruple entries cell by cell over a period would in principle produce the zero-sum FoF matrix table recording that period's financial flows. In practice entries are estimated for each cell individually from the available data and putting

389

them into such a format immediately reveals inconsistencies in this flow data, shown by the error entries required to maintain the zero-sum condition of the matrix table. From this starting point I was able to explore many of the implications of this matrix table format and the behaviour of the error entries.

One thing I had developed in some earlier work and included here was a concept which I rather unimaginatively termed 'purchasing power' (a form of meta-money) which provided an intuitive basis for understanding the signs in the flow of funds matrix table. I had sent a draft of my first chapter in which I set out the characteristics of the zero sum matrix table and explained my concept of 'purchasing power' to Roy Allen, who had designed the presentation of official statistics in the related area of the balance of payments, a presentation I followed in my work. He, of course, had no difficulty with the signs of entries which puzzled so many people. In his reply he said 'Since I deal (somehow or other!) with the <u>flow of funds</u> table in the B. of P. [*Balance of Payments*] lectures I welcome a nice clear statement to which I can refer students. Where and when do you plan to publish?' Later he added 'The use of "purchasing power" helps – but don't over do it!' My work was sadly slow and Roy Allen died in 1982, four years before it finally appeared.

Another conceptual idea which emerged from my work related to seasonal adjustment. The FoF matrix table for a period consisted of cell entries which were estimates of the cell-by-cell sums of the quadruple entries generated by all the transactions in the period. For policy, such a quarterly matrix table would need to be seasonally adjusted and this was normally done by adjusting each cell individually and then by some arbitrary process constraining the results to meet the zero-sum requirement. I reasoned that one is really trying to seasonally adjust the underlying transactions and therefore their quadruple entries. This suggested a procedure for seeking out some best-fit form of seasonal adjustment by manipulation of the data by means of quadruple entries. I mentioned this to some of the people concerned in the Bank of England, but nothing further came of it.

All of the text (draft and final) of my book on FoF I typed on my Bluebird portable typewriter at home late at night when I could work undisturbed. (I only took to word processing when it was too late to use it for this piece of work.) I also had to draft many tables and diagrams, and these were properly drawn for me by the School's Drawing Office under the supervision of Jane Pugh who was both charming and efficient. (She continued the admirable practice of her predecessor, Eunice Bicknell, in using Baskerville, a distinguished English typeface, for the School's letterheads and invitations.) The graphs were produced by my own Data Inspection Package (DIP). This package (which was announced in ESRC *Data Archive Bulletin*, January 1985) made it very easy to import series from official databases, to manipulate them in many ways and to plot them. DIP was designed by myself from the user's point of view and programmed by my eldest son Mark who at the time was waiting to go to Oxford to read physics, having spent eight most instructive months working in the Computer Unit of the University of Surrey in Guildford. His work on DIP was financed very economically from two research programmes called MIME and DEMEIC (I never found out what these initials stood for) managed by Megnad Desai who was very helpful. Part of my research led me to Hadamard matrices and to investigate a form of these which I called obstruction matrices. When Mark was still working in the Computer Unit of the University of Surrey he produced a program for this and did the calculations for these matrices up to order 60 using their Prime computer system.

As my work progressed it was a matter of typing, cutting and pasting; my typescript grew and suffered many layers of revision, ending up with a series of patchwork sheets often several feet long; these at last were cut into A4 lengths and xeroxed, resulting in quite a respectable final typescript. This at long last went to Gower who agreed to publish it in association with LSE. They specialised in publishing short runs of books on obscure subjects and were conveniently located in Aldershot, less than half an hour's drive from home. There I had many meetings with my copy-editor, a pleasant young woman who had an eagle eye for my errors and was an unrelenting guardian of Gower's house style. The book finally appeared in 1986, chastely entitled *Flow of Funds* on its cover with the added subtitle *A Conceptual Framework and Some Applications* on the inside title page. It contained 185 pages of research, including 44 footnotes, 9 appendices and a three page glossary of abbreviations giving the location of the first use of each, as well as many matrix tables, layouts and graphs. At the time it was published I reckoned that there were about thirteen people worldwide who might be interested in it. The book received one mild review, one or two of the thirteen got in touch with me about it, Richard Layard sent me a kindly note, Harold Edey made a comment, and that was that. At least I had got Flow of Funds out of my system.

Other Activities

One day over lunch Anne Bohm, Secretary of the Graduate School, told me that on her trips abroad on behalf of the School she received a number of enquiries about whether the School ran any courses for bankers. In 1981 the financial situation of the School was worsening and I put forward a detailed proposal for a 'Course for Bankers' which would aim to make money for the School, noting that such a course would need to have positive support from the School and from the Economics Department. I received this verbal support, but all the organisation had to be done by myself. Fortunately Graham Dorrance (who many years earlier had been a part-time lecturer at the School before going to the International Monetary Fund) was visiting the School and he was willing to join in and do some of the teaching. After a few teething troubles the course went well but in the end I ran it for only two years; it entailed an excessive amount of work for me and although its total net earnings for the School came to some £22,000 in the first year there was no response when I reported this to the School's Secretary and to the Director. A very different course was run by Mike Burrage (Sociology) and Bob Orr (Government) explaining a range of British institutions for senior overseas businessmen and others who were working in London. It was held in the evenings and I gave a session on the British financial system and London as a world financial centre. This was an interesting exercise in explaining our system in a concentrated form to a very different audience. Bob took a rather cynical view of life and one of his dicta was that 'public money is for wasting'.

I was invited on several occasions to give some lectures on the London capital market at the Wirtschaftsuniversitat in Vienna. My host there was Professor Hugh Purcell, a most engaging and cultivated man who made my visits a real pleasure. He and some of his colleagues were excellent hosts and I was taken to several operas, some excellent restaurants and, as the guest of a group of diplomatic and business wives, on an all-day visit (by the ex-Royal Train) to a large casino outside Vienna. I also had the opportunity to walk all around the central area of the city enjoying its sights and atmosphere. On one occasion there was a music competition in progress and bands were to be seen from all over Austria, each in its particular quasi-military uniform. Near the Cathedral I watched one of these bands playing as it marched along, and was surprised to see a number of men and women, mostly middle-aged, fall in behind it, obviously enjoying marching to the music. On another occasion I was told that on the steps of one public building in Vienna they filmed a sequence in which an actor in full SS uniform had to escort a woman to a car and salute as it drove away. The director was afraid that the actor might be lynched by the crowd and prepared a quick exit for him, but when the sequence ended, so far from trying to lynch him, the crowd burst into applause. Such hints of underlying militarism I found rather surprising given Austria's disastrous experience in wars. Vienna has a wealth of galleries and museums, and it was in one of the latter that I came across a display of Chinese bronze drums; this interested me because there are several Chinese – or Karen – drums in Toni's family, arising from their connexions with Burma. We have one of them at home – a sizeable object 27 inches across by 20 inches high. The display showed that in use a drum would be suspended rather awkwardly from one of the bronze loops on its side; exactly how these loops were used had puzzled us. It didn't clarify the matter of the small frogs, of which Toni's drum has four sets evenly spaced round the top edge, each set consisting of three frogs one on top of the other; allegedly the number of frogs is an indicator of the status of the drum's owner. I greatly enjoyed these visits to Vienna.

For a number of years I gave two or three lectures on Study Skills at the beginning of the academic year. These were held in the Old Theatre and were well attended by undergraduates as well as a range of other students and they gave plenty of opportunity for questions. All these students were given a copy of *Academic Work at University* which spread its influence beyond the Economics Department. Patrick Dunleavy in the Department of Government also gave some lectures on study skills from the slightly different perspective of his own subject. When he was away and unable to give his lectures I took over and combined the two courses; my last lectures on study skills were in March 1999. Urging and helping students to get the very best out of the wonderful opportunity of three years at the School always seemed to me a thoroughly worthwhile activity.

Each year the School held two or three Visit Days, when prospective applicants could come to the School, be shown round by current students and given a talk for an hour or so by a member of the Department that they were hoping to enter. These days were organised by Mary Whitty, our most pleasant and efficient expert on undergraduate admissions, and for many years both before and after my retirement I was asked by our Departmental Tutor to talk to these groups of students about the Economics Department; latterly our Department Tutor was Ed Kuska, who gently persuaded me to continue giving these talks until April 2002. I always told my audience that they would have a wonderful time at university but that I would concentrate on the real reason for coming – *WORK.* I would then take them through the structure of the degree year by year, giving them serious information, putting in all the points that I felt would be helpful in choosing courses, while trying to keep up their interest. Then there was tea and biscuits followed by questions; fortunately Mary Whitty was always present, because there were frequently questions about the School's evaluation of A level marks and about student accommodation on both of which she had the answers at her fingertips. All students were given a copy of *Academic Work at University* as they left. I think that these visits were useful to our would-be students; quite often parents would be present and several expressed their appreciation of our arrangements.

One topic which concerned me at this time was an aspect of our method of classifying degree results at the final meeting of examiners. This concern had arisen at first because our rules had always been that a marginal mark could be dragged up by strength in other papers to allow a higher class of degree, but it was not permissible to raise a degree class by pushing up a marginal mark by sympathy from below, when such strength elsewhere was absent. I felt that there was sometimes pressure from new colleagues unfamiliar with our system to raise marginal marks in the latter cases and I circulated a note to my fellow examiners restating our long-standing practice. I was confident that our system (based on the classes of papers not on summing of marks) was both fair and reasonable, but no one had attempted to reduce it to an entirely objective algorithm. I happened to talk to Tony Wrigley, a demographer, about this and in due course he produced an algorithm in the form of a detailed flow chart which incorporated the process we used. This must have taken quite a lot of work but in clarifying the process it really revealed that such an explicit algorithm would not really add, anything useful to our existing more intuitive method.

Academic Governor

In 1985 I was elected an Academic Governor of the School for four years, a member of the Standing Committee of the Court of Governors and the Academic Governor member of the Information Technology (IT) Panel, as well as now an ex-officio member of the IT Committee. This kept me actively interested in the development of the School's IT facilities until I stepped down as an Academic Governor when my term ended in 1989.

The meetings of the Standing Committee were interesting and one might have expected it to be a place where power resided. But in an institution like the School where consensus is the rule, the power of the Standing Committee seemed much more diluted when one became a member of it. The committee had six academic governors, six other governors, some student governors and a chairman. Sometimes the chairman would open by saying that the meeting need not take long; I did not like this, and nor did Ros Higgins, an international lawyer, who often sat next to me. We both felt that the meeting should go on as long as was required for full discussion of the items on the agenda. After a while I noticed that the outside, non-academic, governors in their dealings with the student governors were not merely polite but almost deferential, while the academic governors treated them much more as equals and viewed them with a degree of cynicism. I wrote a note to my fellow academic governors drawing attention to this and contrasting (1) students in their normal role of pursuing understanding, where academics do indeed feel that they have a special responsibility and a special attitude towards them best summed up in the phrase in *statu pupillari* with (2) students as governors at the Standing Committee or the Court of Governors, where they appear in quite a different role – as student politicians seeking influence, and in that role they were not *in statu pupillari*. They were then all too often interested in harnessing the School's name to the latest outside campaign which had taken their fancy and in asking for more welfare services without taking account of where the resources were to come from. The interests of the School as an academic institution and a centre of excellence, its strategy for survival to give the same opportunities to future generations of students as the present student governors were enjoying – these were conspicuous by their absence. Further, student generations turned over very rapidly and each new generation was liable to bring with it some new political enthusiasms and new welfare demands, often quite unrelated to the real purposes of the School. Each wished to make its mark in its short term of office and was only too happy to use the School as a convenient arena in which to flex its infant political muscles. My feeling was that the respectful attitude of the non-academic governors to the student governors did not help free discussion and mutual education.

One of the student governors had an enthusiasm for ethical investment which I did not share. He was able to engender much discussion in the Standing Committee and the Academic Board and I seem to remember that the School eventually agreed to some degree of ethical investment of the School's funds. Exactly whose ethical standards were to be applied, and to what level of purity, was never clear.

Teaching

Earlier I had recorded some of my lectures as a form of quality control. Now an increasing number of students, particularly foreign ones, would come into the lecture room and immediately place a small tape recorder on a desk in front of me ready to record my lecture. I used to tell my audience that I could see some reason for overseas students doing this, in case they got lost at some points in the lecture and wanted to go over it again, but I urged all of them to be active and participative listeners, fully engaged with my delivery of the subject. I could see the danger of students feeling they could allow their minds to wander if they knew they were recording a lecture, and having it on tape could make them feel that it could be stored away (and listened to again?) rather than actively getting to grips with the material here and now. With this trend for recording I could not help foreseeing its final phase: a recorded lecture being played and being re-recorded by a whole roomful of student tape recorders, with no one present at all.

For the classes in the British Monetary System course I introduced a new series of handouts headed 'True or False – and explain'. Each consisted of up to twenty carefully constructed short (usually one-line) statements about financial institutions which were subtly wrong or misleading, or in a few cases true but in a rather tortured way. They provided exercise in very close reading, requiring students to analyse exactly what a statement was saying and whether, or in what circumstances, it was true or false. In some classes we would start going through one of these handouts; I would begin by picking out a particular statement, asking one of the students to read it out, give his view on whether it was true or false and explain why. I would then ask the rest of the class to vote on whether his answer was correct or not and ask a dissenter to give his reasons for disagreeing. The students responded with interest to these teasing and tricky statements and their voting often led to heated arguments breaking out between the students, and an unusually high degree of active participation, so much so that we usually managed to deal with only a few statements in a class. It was left to me to finally give my own answer – which often led to further arguments. Altogether the result was classes which for all of us were not only instructive but lively and enjoyable as well. Later, such classes were to appeal particularly to our Russian students.

To my teaching programme I now added a ten lecture postgraduate course on Euro-markets – those large and growing bond and banking markets in London where the main currency used was the US dollar. Such dollars, outside the regulation of the US financial authorities, were termed Euro-dollars and had no connexion with the Euro as a currency which was to emerge much later. The main topics in this course were Eurobonds, syndicated credits and loan agreements, and country risk assessment. It attracted a regular audience of about fifteen, most of them with City experience; lecturing on such a subject to such an audience was both enjoyable and stimulating.

For many years there had been formal arrangements for student feedback on all our courses and these and any other problems were discussed once a year with student representatives at staff-student meetings. I remember one meeting when Charles Goodhart was Departmental Convenor because he started by going through the feedback forms which were always returned by only a proportion of students. He reported to the meeting that one course had a 100% Excellent rating; he then revealed that it was my course on Euro-markets, but that only one student had filled in a response form. Having good-humouredly inflated and deflated me in the same sentence he went on through the other responses, ending up by revealing that in one of his own courses there had been criticism of his use of the blackboard. I felt these meetings were of some value. A few students felt that they should make full use of such occasions, but they usually had to scrape around to find something to complain about which could reasonably be rectified. One complaint that often arose was about a compulsory course on statistics; the course was there as a necessary skill and for their own good, but some students simply did not like statistics and therefore complained. All we could do in this case was to point out its importance and tell them that they had to tough it out. These meetings were good-humoured and a useful additional contact with students.

The changes emerging in the financial system included increasing competition in banking and financial markets generally, and growing emphasis on each employee's contribution to his institution's 'bottom line' – profits – and the resulting bonuses. This meant that in many institutions, practitioners were becoming more pressured and less willing to give time to addressing our undergraduate seminars. I now often had to go to further up the management of an institution (where the name of the School always elicited a positive response) to get support which could then be used as a mild lever of persuasion on those at the operational level. This allowed the seminars, started by Richard Sayers all those years ago, to maintain their high standard.

Whatever Next?

Near us in Guildford is Tormead School for girls and I was once (and only once) asked to talk to the sixth formers about macroeconomic policy. I carefully tailored my talk to this audience and it was followed by questions; one girl asked what was the role of God in these matters. After a moment's surprise, and taking account of the audience, I gently replied that this had to be a matter of personal belief. But it was immediately borne in upon me that in all my years at the School the role of God in economic matters had never arisen at any point in lectures, classes or seminars, or even in conversation with my colleagues. Considering things carefully I conclude that I am an atheist; but I am also deeply influenced by the Christian values of the English society in which I grew up and have lived all my life. I believe that life in society is only possible if there is a shared moral core of practical ideals about how we should behave towards our fellow men, towards our families and, indeed, towards ourselves. I follow the view that the concept of God is a projection of human needs with its roots in childhood when we are entirely dependent upon our parents, who to the child seem so powerful. But it is this moral core which really matters. I would like to see much more emphasis on this in Christianity, with its imaginative embroidery of miracles, Three-in-One and an afterlife relegated to their true status as venerable fairy tales aimed originally at the uneducated peasants of the ancient Middle East. But I would be very careful not to attack a simple belief in God which can be such a help and consolation to so many people and which seems to have no undesirable consequences.

I seldom attended seminars given by other Departments, but I did go to several meetings of one of them. Various newspaper reports had drawn attention to satanic or ritual child abuse, at that time mostly emanating from the USA; I felt instinctively that there was an element of hysteria in these claims and I didn't really believe them. I then noticed that Eileen Barker's Sociology of Religion seminars were going to include several meetings on this topic and she said that I was very welcome to attend. At these seminars one speaker pointed out that in their research they had never found any two cases of such ritual abuse leading back to one alleged abusing group, as if such groups only ever abused one child, which seemed unlikely (if, indeed, there had ever been any such groups, which to me also seemed unlikely). The statements by children in several cases were filled with fantasy, sometimes evidently drawn from horror videos; and there was the Californian case of children saying they were abused in an underground tunnel or room at their pre-school; there was no such tunnel or room. In one seminar the speaker read out to us a transcript of a child being questioned; it was full of leading and suggestive questions calculated to get the admissions the questioners clearly wanted. In a television programme many years later I heard one of the people who had been engaged in this kind of questioning say that if the required admission was not forthcoming, then clearly it was being more deeply concealed and further questioning was needed until at last it was brought out. The clear implication was that, in effect, the person being questioned *could not* be innocent but must be guilty; Stalin's inquisitors would have been proud to have such a colleague. One seminar covered ritual animal abuse, which appeared to occur only in the USA. Forensic veterinary surgeons were employed to investigate every such report appearing in the press over a period of six months; they turned up plenty of evidence of natural scavengers at work but no evidence of ritual abuse. Altogether I found that my scepticism on ritual abuse was amply justified and in particular that the evidence drawn from the questioning of children was utterly unreliable. Indeed such questioning was likely, sometimes calculated, to implant ideas and fantasies into the minds of suggestible children, and the questioners themselves seemed to be the prey of extraordinary ideas and fantasies. Later cases in the UK confirmed me in my view. I also found the views of another colleague, Jean La Fontaine, illuminating. Altogether a most interesting series of seminars on a subject populated with a caste of naive fantasists who created a great deal of suffering and unhappiness. One member of the seminar sitting in front of me was interesting in a different way: he had a wire leading from under his shirt collar up into the top of his head.

Postgraduates

Although over the years I had contact with many PhD students at the Money Workshop, I had only a small number of PhD students in my own institutional field, mostly in the form of a half-share in ones who were working on the banking institutions of their home country in which I provided the banking side of their supervision while someone from another department provided the depth of knowledge of the country concerned. But I was adviser to a number of senior visitors from overseas banks, universities and governments who came to the School for various periods of time, not to take a higher degree but as what we termed Research Fee students, to attend courses and learn about the institutions which made London a major international financial centre.

The last PhD student of my own was Don Roth; he had been a noted sportsman and scholar at Princeton, had an MSc from Chicago and an MSc in International Monetary Economics from the School, but by the time I became his supervisor he was Chairman and Chief Executive Officer of Merrill Lynch Europe. Although his life was very busy he still had a hankering after academic study and was certainly ideally placed to work in his favoured field of Euro-markets and international finance. Not many supervisors have a car sent to whisk them silently and swiftly to lunch with their postgraduate student. For another luncheon I met him at the office of one of their subsidiaries in the heart of the West End – it was called Merrill Lynch Private Capital and he told me that it would accept only clients who had $200 million in freely investable capital. Its offices were in a charming Georgian town house, with the thickest carpets, a range of magazines like *The London Gentleman* and *International Polo*, a delightful view through to a walled garden edged with red geraniums and the most elegant receptionist; the whole place was filled with the air of calm luxury required to attract these super-wealthy. The only external sign of all this was the name of the company on a polished brass plate about four inches by three inches. I teased Don that this was a bit blatant, surely something more discreet – say three inches by two inches – would be more suitable.

When in due course he became Treasurer of the World Bank, Don told me that wherever he went bankers and financiers of all kinds were so keen to talk to him that to avoid them he had to keep a very low profile; this led to positively clandestine meetings between us before he finally felt that due to pressure of work he had to give up his PhD registration at the School. A few years later we were on a family holiday in the States where our eldest son Mark was doing a PhD in physics at Harvard; he and I and our youngest son Richard (who was reading English at Southampton University) drove down from Cohasset on Boston Bay where we were staying to have a look at Rutgers University where Richard was due to spend a semester as an exchange student. Don lived in a handsome house nearby and he invited us over to lunch with him and his wife; he then took us round Princeton with much insider commentary. Regrettably I never had another PhD student anything like Don Roth.

I had many meetings with Max Fry (who had been in our Monetary Group as an undergraduate in the 1960s) when he was doing his PhD on a flow of funds analysis of the Turkish economy. It was rather like being his supervisor, but I don't think I had any formal responsibility for him. When we were on holiday in California many years later he was teaching at the University of California, Irvine and we visited him and his family. They were living in a neat house on the edge of the desert and had problems with rattlesnakes; we sympathised, but I couldn't help feeling that the snakes had been there first. He was a keen violinist and collector of stringed instruments; on one of his later visits to me at the School he told me he had just bought a very expensive instrument and this led him to tell me about his collection. It was very sad that he died when only in his mid-fifties.

One unusual contact with a PhD student arose through a friend in Guildford who was a professor of civil engineering at the University of Surrey. One of his PhD students had run into a problem and he asked me if this student could come and talk to me about it. The student duly called on me at home and over a cup of coffee he explained that he was dealing with very long-lived civil engineering structures and (although he didn't use the term) trying to do cost-benefit studies of them; his problem was that when he added up the benefits over, in the limiting case, an infinite period, the benefits approached infinity and his exercise collapsed. I explained the concept of discounting future benefits at a rate of interest and suddenly his infinite benefit problem was solved. His relief was a pleasure to see.

One day I was doing some work in our front garden when a young man with a clipboard stopped and asked me if I would be kind enough to answer a questionnaire. It turned out that he was a PhD student at the School working on the geography of friendship. I invited him in and over tea we talked about his project and he took down my answers to his questionnaire. I came out rather badly – on his definition I seemed to have no friends. With further clarification I was relieved to find that after all I did have a few. I never saw him at the School and I never knew what happened to his work.

Colleagues

In the Economics Department the early 1980s saw a number of retirements of colleagues whom I had known for many years. One of these was Peter Bauer who had been at the School for some 37 years and was notable for his opposition to central planning as the means of helping Third World countries to develop. Arriving at the School one day I was gleefully told that on the previous evening he had been a member of a panel of speakers on television discussing this topic; the chairman had asked another member to make a brief opening statement and he then asked Peter to reply. As the camera swivelled on to Peter, there he was, busily writing, and without lifting his head he said 'Just a minute, I am writing down some of the errors of the previous speaker.' Another retirement was Basil Yamey who had been at the School for 34 years and who had joined with Peter in exposing the weaknesses of development planning, but his work on competition policy meant that we continued to meet around the School for many more years. Hal Myint also retired, another specialist in economic development; I can remember talking with him about the problem of population growth in so many Third World countries. His attitude was that these were well known to development economists but no one was willing or courageous enough to do anything effective to focus attention upon it. Another leaver was Alan Day, who had been a stalwart member of the Monetary Group until he became a very efficient Pro-Director under Ralf Dahrendorf in 1979; but his retirement in 1983 was sadly due to ill-health. The Director asked me to write an appreciation of Alan's career for the *LSE Magazine*, which I did; he asked for just one minor amendment but otherwise said that he liked it. Fortunately Alan recovered in due course and went on to create a fine garden round his manor house in Kent. Dennis Sargan was an econometrician and now he too retired after 21 years at the School; I had known him, though never closely, and it was only after his death that I learnt that he had been a keen gardener. It was sad that I had missed the opportunity to talk with him about our shared interest.

Looking back, conversation with colleagues over lunch or in the Senior Common Room normally revolved around academic matters, public affairs or general topics where discussion would flow easily. This was understandable because these drew upon matters and attitudes which had brought each of us to academic life at the School and meant that we had much common ground. Only occasionally did conversation move to a colleague's specialist field, and it was sometimes easy to overlook his importance in his subject and instead to see him mainly as congenial companion in the Senior Common Room. Indeed it was sometimes only their obituaries which revealed to the rest of us the full intellectual stature of our colleagues. Only occasionally did conversation move over to the domestic field of our families and home interests. Indeed I must have known some colleagues for many years, even decades, without knowing anything of their family life or where they lived, and my own family life would have been equally obscure to them. In many ways this was no bad thing, because I knew them through their qualities which brought them to the School; when I did occasionally meet their wives at the annual Director's parties these did not always seem as congenial as their husbands. Another retirement at this time was Peter Wiles who was renowned for his efforts to fillet-out meaning from Soviet economic statistics; I can remember Terence Gorman, who was primarily a theorist, saying how much he admired Peter for pursuing applied economics in such an intractable field. (Terence was Irish, burly and humorous; he came to the School at the same time as Frank Hahn and moved to Oxford in 1979 after being at the School for twelve years.) Many years later Peter was still to be met around the School when, in the *Financial Times*, I came across an astonishing item: the First Annual Report of the Russian KGB. I showed it to Peter who was equally astonished. I seem to remember that this was followed later by another news item to the effect that they now had women doctors at the Lubyanka, with the implication of gentle, cool and healing hands. Evidently the public relations industry was very active in Moscow. Later it also became evident that it was active in the Vatican. It had been found that the Roman Catholic doctrine of Limbo (where the souls of unbaptised children are condemned to linger on the edge of Hell for all eternity) did not go down well in many Third World countries. Good public relations required that this doctrine should be dropped and so it was. How many would have suspected that in such a rigorous faith there was such responsive flexibility to the demands of PR?

Peter once told me that the Academic Board provided some of the best committee meetings he had ever attended. Certainly discussion was constructive and to the point, with none of the annoyances of pernickety and wrecking points of order. This was because there were no formal rules of debate in the Academic Board; at one time some new members made an attempt to introduce such rules, but after due consideration at one of its meetings the Board turned this down, maintaining our long-standing preference for free and constructive discussion. I was a regular attender at the Board for most of my time at the School, because I felt committed to the School and wanted to play my small part in shaping the way it developed in its academic arrangements while maintaining its own particular academic ethos. Few of the 'big names' brought to the School for their research abilities ever attended.

These losses to the Department were balanced by arrivals, amongst them Charles Goodhart (returning to the School after having gone to the Bank of England in 1970) and also Charlie Bean and Mervyn King, both of whom would much later reverse the flow and leave the School to go to the Bank of England. There was also Nick Stern (born in Brentford, next door to my own birthplace of Isleworth, as I discovered when we walked across Waterloo Bridge together on one occasion) and Ken Binmore who transferred to the Maths and Statistics Department after only a year. Ken was a game theorist who, I felt, did not really take to me; however, he was a colleague, so I responded with carefully engineered good humour: I simply declined to notice any reservations he might have about me and often went over to talk with him in the Common Room. The result, I felt, was a tense rather than any warm relationship between us. Someone I saw around but talked to only occasionally was Ernest Thorpe in the Department of Government. I had come across a quotation from the works of Francis Bacon, Lord Verulam, which seemed to me profoundly true and showing great insight; the version I knew was:

Truth emerges more easily from error than from confusion.

I mentioned this to Ernest and said that I wished I knew exactly where it came from. He said that he would find out, and sure enough a little later I received a note in his tiny but clear writing giving me the reference: *Novum Organon*, Book II Aphorism 20, together with the original Latin and the Spedding translation. How helpful colleagues can be. And, indeed, in other ways; most academics will know how, at conferences or informal meetings, so much work can be saved by a short conversation: 'Well, the main point of my book is that...' and there in a few sentences you have the kernel of an argument which is often diluted over many chapters and footnotes as well as being obscured by elaboration and defensive arguments.

Amongst the senior administrative staff there were also changes; John Alcock, the Academic Secretary, and John Pike, the Financial Secretary – the two Johns – retired in 1983. I found both of them very congenial as well as being most efficient administrators, and this was the general feeling amongst the academics. They had succeeded Harry Kidd, whom I also liked, and were in turn succeeded by one person who took over both duties: Christine Challis, who came with the reputation of being a bundle of energy which soon proved to be correct. Much later I worked closely with her on certain projects and found her also most pleasant and efficient. I believe that the School has been most fortunate in its senior administrators and indeed in its administrators generally. In the early 1980s one of these was an assistant registrar named Wood. I found that he was very interested in

Roman magic and ritual, and I was able to lend him a 1929 British Museum guide book which had a section on this field. The thing that particularly interested him was the illustration of a bronze right hand with ritual objects – a pine cone, snake with a cock's comb, winged caduceus, a frog etc – attached to it. Such hands were often dedicated to Sabazius and were intended to ward off the evil eye. We had several interesting conversations, but regrettably he did not remain at the School for very long.

Only a few colleagues lived in the Guildford direction; David Martin, whose subject was Sociology of Religion, lived in Woking and I once travelled back from Waterloo with him and a distinguished American sociologist with much interesting conversation on the way. Later when I used to be blackmailed by my wife into attending the Christmas morning service at Guildford Cathedral ('No Christmas dinner otherwise!'), there was David in handsome clerical robes. I remember him once telling me that at a conference on some religious subject he came to the conclusion that he, an academic sociologist, had more belief in religion than most of the clerics present. For a time Rob Farr, a social psychologist, lived not far from us and again a train journey home provided the opportunity for a particularly interesting conversation.

Ian Nish (Japanese Diplomatic History, and a fluent Japanese speaker) lived a few miles away at Oxshott; with him and his wife Rona we had many pleasant lunches, sometimes at our house but more often Toni and I seemed to visit them. There we met a number of Japanese, since Rona also had Japanese connexions, in her case with the wives of Japanese businessmen and academics living in London. I was able to perform two minor services for Ian. The first concerned one of his newly arrived postgraduate students – a Korean, I believe – whose bank would not release the funds that he needed for living expenses in London. Ian asked me, as someone who was supposed to know something about banking, if I could help. He and his student came to my room at the School and gave me the details of the case; I then rang up the bank which produced several layers of bad excuses which I had to knock down increasingly harshly until they finally had to admit that they were in the wrong, and the money was released. The second arose from Ian's interest in the Lytton Commission of 1931 which enquired into the Japanese occupation of Manchuria. A significant role was played in this enquiry by a consul named Moss who left, for his family's eyes only, an illuminating inside account of these events.

Quite fortuitously it turned out that the latter's son lived in Guildford and that I had a slight acquaintance with him; I was able to invite him and Ian to coffee, and this meeting allowed Ian to get permission to quote from this family document for his research.

I had several casual conversations over the years with David McKnight, one of our social anthropologists who specialised in the aborigines, and was a blood brother of a tribe in Australia's Northern Territory. At a jumble sale I found a book by Daisy Bates on her life with the Australian aborigines and this led to a number of enjoyable conversations with him over lunch. By his account their alleged sense of harmony with nature was contradicted by their willingness to burn a thicket to get some animal out of it and then to walk off, leaving a bush fire to rage off into the distance. David, bushy bearded, retired early and went to live in Rome; later he told me how refreshing it was to be able to get on with his work without interruption. Sadly he died in 2006.

Another conversation over lunch led Tony Atkinson, in the Economics Department, to lend me a book *False French Friends* on the pitfalls of assuming that a French word appearing similar to an English word would mean something similar. To us 'cabinet' makes one think of government, while in French it can mean 'toilet'; this was the basis of an elderly joke about a British minister's wife trying to explain in French that her husband was not available because he had gone to the cabinet with much paper. Things may appear to happen at a different speed in France because 'décade' can mean ten days rather than our ten years. Talk over lunch was certainly not all serious. I remember once at lunch joining a group in which Adam Roberts (International Relations) was giving a most amusing account of a paraplegic holiday – a visit with some friends to Switzerland which was plagued by accidents. This stirred a memory; in the 1950s I went by car to collect my brother Michael from Victoria Station on his return from a skiing holiday in Switzerland. His train looked like part of the retreat from Dunkirk; there were stretcher cases, plastered limbs and crutches everywhere. Mike, not the sportiest of persons, was fortunately intact.

23

Towards Retirement

The Train to Waterloo

Travelling regularly to London, and the friends I travelled with, meant that the train journey played a significant role in my life. There are two rail lines from Guildford to Waterloo: the fast line via Woking and the 'little line' via Cobham which had many stops, making it rather slow. I normally travelled up to the School by the little line, catching the train at Guildford London Road station, a comfortable twelve minutes walk from home and its first stop after leaving Guildford main station, so that the train had not yet become crowded. At London Road the 'up' platform for Waterloo had an asphalt surface and when stiletto heels arrived it developed a pock-marked appearance, but as they went out of fashion the asphalt, warmed by the summer sun, very slowly flowed back and became smooth again; in the mid-1960s it had a paper stall catering for the morning commuters but this soon closed down. In those days as we waited for the train the stationmaster would sometimes appear, look at his watch, and then at the right moment open a wicker hamper full of homing pigeons which clattered noisily off into the air, competing to get back home as quickly as possible.

Many years later my older brother Michael, an architect living on the seafront at Brighton, arrived home to find one such homing pigeon, lost and exhausted, on his doorstep. He took it in, got special pigeon food for it (of which it ate half and scattered the rest all over his flat) and nursed it back to health. He tried to identify its owner but failed and in the end he took it, now fit and well fed, deep into the Sussex countryside and let it go. He arrived back home and was astonished to find – What! *another* pigeon on his door step? But no, it was the same homing pigeon which now regarded his flat as its home; it was like trying to throw away an unwanted boomerang. But now salvation appeared in the form of a real expert, and from marks under its wing he was able to identify its owner; the pigeon then had the indignity of being sent home by post – in a special pigeon box – to be reindoctrinated with its true home address. I see plenty of pigeons in London and recently, as I went down the stairs into the underpass outside Waterloo, there a few feet away was a pigeon confidently making its way up the stairs. And once, when I was on a tube train, it stopped at Earl's Court, the doors opened and in hopped a pigeon. The doors closed and the pigeon pecked about until at the next station the doors opened and it hopped out again.

When free from his pigeon Michael regularly came over from his flat in Brighton to spend the weekend with mother at Aldwick. While there he would often work on his current architectural project, which on one occasion was the design of Basingstoke Sewage Works. There was a convenient plan-copying service in Bognor and he sent these plans there to be printed off. Later he collected the prints and back in Brighton he unrolled them only to find that he had been given prints of a map of the Downs just north of Chichester. Meanwhile up on the Downs just north of Chichester, at the start of a day's fieldwork, a group of earnest students of geography from Bognor Regis Teacher Training College each unrolled a plan of Basingstoke Sewage Works.

The passing scene on our rail journey to Waterloo became very familiar – fields and greenery at first, then increasing urbanisation. Around Clandon, our first stop, one of the landowners at that time raised pheasants, and we used to go past fields filled with them and their feeding pens. These pheasants spread themselves around the countryside, and even as far as our own garden. At one point in our journey there was a bluebell wood which in spring was a wonderful sea of blue, but in due course the M25 was built straight over it. In some places you could look down into people's gardens; one house was crowded up against the high embankment and its owners had defiantly named it 'Bank View'. (In Martyr Road in Guildford there was a row of squeezed-in houses; a similarly defiant housewife named one of them 'Little Martyr'.) At some point before Clapham junction there was a brickwork bridge; normally the train went fast under it, but passing slowly under it one day I could only wonder at the craftsmanship of the courses of brickwork curving in two dimensions, which carried a road across the railway lines at an angle but produced an arch aligned with the railway track. Then from Clapham Junction (at one time said to be the busiest railway junction in the world) we were just one of half a dozen other railway lines running onto the long and high Victorian viaduct into Waterloo. While reading *The Times* on my journeys I began to notice that they were making the print smaller and greyer; but a pair of reading glasses, with half-moon lenses, revealed the distasteful truth. After constantly mislaying them during the first few days I took to wearing them on a thin black ribbon round my neck. Since then I have never mislaid them, but as they hang on my chest when not in use they do tend to accumulate crumbs.

By now some regular travelling companions of many years had left me. Claude Loombe retired and Roy Clifford was promoted to be the Bank of England's Agent in Birmingham, while Hilton Clarke retired somewhat later. Peter Lyon and Laurie Martin have already been mentioned as occasional travelling companions, but Peter's work at the Institute of Commonwealth Studies took him on to different trains, and Laurie left the Department of War Studies at King's College in the Strand to become Vice-Chancellor of the University of Newcastle and then Sir Laurence.

The timing of my journey home in the evenings was variable and I therefore nearly always travelled alone. I would walk over Waterloo Bridge and up into Waterloo Station, past the two war memorial plaques from which I always read a few names. As it left Waterloo the train would descend into silence (this was before mobile phones and their noisy users), some passengers reading, others already dozing after a hard day. On occasion I too found that it was wonderfully pleasant to doze off, rising into consciousness just to check each station and sinking exquisitely back again. For those who were awake there was sometimes a different pleasure: spectacular sunsets with extravagant colour and clouds across the wide spread of western sky revealed from the high level of the viaduct outside Waterloo; some were so striking that one almost expected them to produce thunderous tones like a great celestial organ. Sometimes, instead of the slow line, I would go home on the fast train via Woking and Toni would pick me up from Guildford's main station, altogether quicker and more comfortable. One slightly annoying feature of this fast route home was that the train used to halt for a while just outside Guildford station for no discernible reason; apparently some passengers complained about this, it was found to be unnecessary, changes were made, and from then on the train ran uninterruptedly into the station. One evening in 1976 I went home this way later than usual; my carriage was only sparsely filled and those people all got out at Woking. It was a year of drought and of heath fires which could no longer be controlled and had to be left to burn, spreading their acrid smoke for miles around. As the train left Woking it entered a dense cloud of smoke from the heath fires and from the fires along the sides of the line; these flickering fires, the smoke, the darkened sky, the strong smell of burning and myself in an empty carriage, I felt like a character in a modern dress dramatic version of a mythical descent into Hell.

A person with whom I travelled up to town occasionally was Philip Wood, a partner in Allen & Overy and an authoritative international financial lawyer; he had lived in the next road to us before moving out to a large house south of Shere where he constructed an extensive bluebell walk. When I was working on my lectures on Euro-markets we had one particular conversation in which he set out with wonderful clarity his insights into the problems then arising from the restructuring of certain international syndicated credits. Afterwards I could not help wondering how much his expertise would have cost if I had been a client rather than a friend.

Waterloo Bridge

Two of my colleagues at the School, Ian Nish and Michael Leifer, now also travelled on my line but we travelled on different parts of the train, and it was at Waterloo Station that we generally came together to walk over Waterloo Bridge to the School. Michael's expertise was on South East Asian politics and Ian's was on Japanese diplomatic history. A recurring question which I discussed with Ian as we walked over the bridge was how historians reconciled their accounts of the apparently orderly evolving of events with the acute uncertainty which the decision-takers had to face at every stage. This seemed entirely absent from most historical writing, as if the historians' knowledge of what actually happened next dulled their sense of this inherent uncertainty.

Our walk across Waterloo Bridge presented a panoramic view from the Houses of Parliament on the left past the dome of St Paul's and the City to the great tower blocks of the Docklands on the right. As the water of the Thames became cleaner we would see occasional cormorants flying up and down the river, and more recently I saw one diving and bobbing up as it fished in the grey-green water. Walking over the bridge was very pleasant in the summer but it could be bitterly cold in the winter and warm hats then became the order of the day; mine was a black furry Kruschev-style hat while Ian's was an equally foreign-looking grey affair. Our route took us past the bus stop where in 1978 the Bulgarian defector Georgi Markov was murdered by a tiny ball-bearing laced with ricin, fired into him from an umbrella on the orders of the Bulgarian government with the assistance of the Russian KGB. We then went past the point where our eldest son Mark had a disconcerting experience. At the time he was programming my data inspection package (DIP) for time series when, walking over the bridge to the School, he was suddenly confronted by three villainous looking characters, one of whom drew his hand menacingly across his throat. After the initial surprise it transpired that they were Italian tourists (over here with a Mafia tour group?) who were looking for Blackfriars Bridge to see where Roberto Calvi, the Italian banker, had been found hanged in June 1982.

From Waterloo Bridge you could at one time see on the river just below Somerset House a pontoon carrying a miniature floating police station for the River Police. One day it sank gently into the river, and it was interesting to speculate what would have happened next. The River Police could hardly phone the River Police for help, and what could the Metropolitan Police or the Fire Service do, except see the funny side of such a slow motion and miniature catastrophe? However, somebody came to the rescue and the embarrassed little police station was refloated. It was later replaced by a larger and much more impressive RNLI Lifeboat Station. Above it for many years there was a large gap in the facade of Somerset House caused by a wartime bomb. Eventually I was to watch this injury being slowly healed by a team of builders, so successfully that I can now see no sign that there was ever any damage. It was over the side of Waterloo Bridge that Frank Paish was occasionally seen furtively to drop something. It turned out that these were packets of used razor blades, and to Frank the bottom of the Thames seemed the safest place to dispose of them.

Church and School, Waterloo, 1880–1901

In really bad weather I would catch a bus over a blustery Waterloo Bridge to the School. Waiting for such a bus nowadays I find myself facing the church of St John the Evangelist on the other side of the Waterloo Road. It is a handsome neo-classical building, light and spacious inside, dating from the early 1820s. As soon as the church was completed, a school – St John's Boys' School, Waterloo – was built in Exton Street next door. In 1880 my maternal grandfather, Arthur James Davey, was appointed headmaster of this school at the early age of 26. Family tales give us glimpses of his life and character as headmaster, most of them coming down through his wife Alice (Nana to us as children) and his younger daughter Doris Mary Davey, later Alford, our mother, who died in 1985. Here, with some editing, I give them in my mother's own words.

Arthur James Davey

My father loved his work as headmaster, which was his hobby as well as his job. The term 'youth leader' was not known in those days, but it would have described him. He was full of enthusiasm, persuading the manager to let him use the nearby Royal Victoria Hall and Coffee Tavern for the School minstrel show; his wife Alice – my mother – always attended these events, sitting in a box. [*The manager concerned was Emma Cons; she was joined by her niece Lilian Baylis in 1898, under whom it was later to become famous as the Old Vic.*] He took a party of boys that he had chosen himself up to Olympia, winning a shield for a drill display. He got Doulton's China Factory near the School to let him have examples of their work for a china exhibition held at the School. Amongst other things he started the School library which included the works of Kipling, Richard Jeffries and other great and popular writers of the time.

I seem to remember being told that there were about forty pupils when my father became headmaster of St John's Boys' School and about four hundred when he died. Small fees were charged, varying according to the pupil's capacity to pay. There were a certain number of charity boys who had to wear coats with the name of the donor charity inscribed on the buttons. One of the first things my father did was to get this humiliating state of affairs altered. He was unable to persuade the Governors to do away with the inscriptions altogether but managed to get the inscriptions put on the back of the buttons.

He had a beautiful tenor voice, trained at the Guildhall School of Music, and in turn he would bring home boys with promising voices and give them lessons in the evening so that they would be a credit to the choir on Sundays. The Guildhall School of Music advised him to give up teaching and make a career of his singing, something it was possible to do in those days, but he could not bear the thought of leaving the School, which to him was like a family. He was a great admirer of Gilbert and Sullivan and both played and sang their operas; he sang a good deal for charity at the Foundling Hospital and at the Home for Incurables at Putney and everything connected with the church. On one occasion he sang a duet with Lloyd Chandos, a famous singer of those days. He had what was known as a sympathetic tenor voice, and this often made people wipe away a tear or two; he himself used to deplore the fact that tenor songs were so sentimental. He was very humorous and could tell a joke briefly and wittily. This with his singing meant he was greatly in demand at dinners and festive occasions. I think it was his kindly wit that endeared him to all who knew him.

His own father, Walter Davey, was headmaster of St Peter's National School in King Street, Hammersmith where he lived on the premises. [*He became headmaster of St Peter's before 1871 and retired some time after 1891, so that for many years father and son were both headmasters.*] He was a very clever man and [*it is said*] won a Balliol Scholarship when he was young [*though it appears that he was unable to take it up*]; but he was singularly free from any ambition and was quite content to settle down at St Peter's School with his garden and greenhouse and dally the time away with a few pupils. [*I remember my mother telling me that when her father came across something interesting or had a question to ask, he would say 'I shall just go over and have a word with my father about this.'*]

My father made a point, where possible, of interviewing the employers of the boys when they left school and would call to see how they were getting on. He liked to see them apprenticed to jobs in which there was some future. A large number of the employees at Waterloo Station had been his pupils, and on the rare occasions when he was late for his train home there was consternation. The driver would be looking anxiously from his cab while a couple of porters would wait to hurry my father on as soon as he appeared. His bag would be taken by one and his arm taken by the other and with cries of 'Here you are, Sir, we've waited for you' he would be helped into a compartment and off would go the train just a little late.

He was very particular about his appearance, always looking immaculate in a top hat and striped trousers. He believed in cold baths and physical exercises, cycle rides before breakfast and always walked through the park and chatted to the gardeners on his way to Ravenscourt Park Station. He never had an illness until the last one, pneumonia, which caused his death in a matter of days. The sudden death of one who was so alive was a great shock to all who knew and loved him. 'He came into a room like a fresh breeze!' was often said of him. He was not a teetotaller, but he drank very little, smoked a pipe, played cricket and tennis. He took in *Punch* as his father did before him [*and these, bound into volumes, are still in the family together with many of his other books*].

When he died from pneumonia in 1901, aged only 47, his friends formed a Committee to raise money for a stained glass window to his memory in St John's Church. The leaders in this were the Vicar of St John's Church, and three members of Morley College with whom my father had been associated. The Committee stated that Arthur Davey 'has won the affection and esteem of all who have come into contact with him' and later of the 'widespread esteem in which Mr Davey was held'. The money was raised and the window was installed in the south side of the church with the inscription:

IN MEMORY OF ARTHUR JAMES DAVEY
FOR 21 YEARS HEADMASTER OF ST JOHN'S BOYS' SCHOOL
DIED 30TH OCTOBER 1901 AGED FORTY SEVEN YEARS

On 8 December 1940 the church was badly damaged by a bomb and the window was destroyed, but after ten years of being left exposed to the elements, the church was restored, together with an exact replica of my father's window [*which at that time was moved to the Lady Chapel*], and rededicated in 1951 as the church for the Festival of Britain. I attended by invitation the rededication service, which was honoured by the presence of Princess Elizabeth, shortly to become Queen Elizabeth II.

Doris Mary Alford

With the sudden death of Arthur Davey a pall of sorrow and many tears descended upon his family. His widow was devastated by her loss. Relatives were able to ease the worst of the material consequences and her younger daughter Doris – my mother – although only seven years old at the time, was a great emotional support in the years that followed. And she in turn was very fortunate in having three cousins of her own age to whom she became very close and who restored liveliness and pleasure to her childhood.

At the time when Arthur Davey was headmaster many of those living in the area around Waterloo were very poor. But there were glimmers of hope from the efforts by some to improve these people's living conditions through charity and by others, like my grandfather, who devoted their lives to helping children born into a life threatened by poverty.

Towards Retirement

Frank Paish, who had been a close colleague and travelling companion until he retired in 1965, died in late 1987 and at the School a memorial meeting was held for him in the Founders' Room on 17 January 1988 at which I was one of the opening speakers. Frank was a buoyant, responsive and witty man and with so many of us recalling our memories of him it became an occasion of warm-hearted good humour. I told the meeting some of the entertaining tales about him and of the things I had learned from him, all mentioned in an earlier chapter. Before coming to the School as a lecturer he worked in a bank in South Africa and it was there that he observed fire insurance claims rising as business turned down. And it was he who noted that as incomes fell, imports fell – the income effect – which solved the problem faced by Taussig, who looked only for price effects and could not find them. My last memory was of him surging across Waterloo Bridge in a voluminous dark overcoat while I pattered along beside him trying to keep up with his pace and his conversation. At the meeting many others joined in with their affectionate memories of Frank and there was much laughter, making it a very fitting, indeed uplifting, memorial meeting.

With his observation of insurance claims rising as business turned down, Frank would have appreciated a joke which I only heard later:

San Francisco; a property developer is telling a friend, also in the business, about his largest property:
Developer: 'Now this building of mine is insured for 50 million dollars against fire and earthquake.'
Friend, after a pause: 'But how would you start an earthquake?'

Not long before I retired the Students' Union decided to have a lunchtime debate in the Old Theatre on 'Should LSE be Alcohol Free?' I don't know how they came to know that I never touched alcohol (a habit I shared with Frank Paish) but they clearly regarded this as making me a suitable person to open in support of 'Alcohol-Free' (as I preferred it) and I accepted their invitation. At the meeting I opened by pointing out that the temperance side of such a debate often put forward a reformed alcoholic to make their case. Indeed if they looked at me they would see baggy bloodshot eyes, a red-veined nose, blotchy complexion, a drooping double chin and a general air of deterioration. However in my case this was not due to drink but to having spent so many years dealing with students. I then went on to draw a much grimmer picture of the effects of alcohol – jolly vomiting students, drink dissolving the civilised veneer and leading people to do violent and terrible things. I allowed one bright spot – the widespread approval on not drinking if you are driving. It was a very decorous debate and there was no drunken bottle-throwing or brawling that might have strengthened my case, and my side lost heavily. But it was an enjoyable occasion.

The momentous event outside the School at around this time was the collapse of communism in the USSR which had a specific effect within the School. It was announced that the Russian people were desperate for donations of books in English, and Waterstones, the booksellers, announced that they would arrange and pay for the transport of these books to Russia. The School set aside a room where such books could be placed. I managed to put in quite a number from my own room, but by the end of the first day the room was full to bursting point. In the event I transferred a whole lot more books, mostly from home, which I delivered by car to a rather ramshackle warehouse somewhere behind King's Cross Station. In all I donated about 800 books.

The End?

I was due to retire at the end of September 1992 but some time before that I received a letter from Charles Goodhart, who was Convenor at the time, proposing a farewell dinner to mark my retirement. But I suspect that the moving spirit behind this was Vicky Chick who was one of the original members of the Money Workshop and whom I had met at so many seminars and other meetings over the preceding thirty years. The dinner was held in the Director's Dining Room at the School, and both Charles and Vicky were present together with Alan Day, Roger Opie and Stewart Wilson, who had at some time been my colleagues in the Monetary Group, and Max Fry, Laurence Harris, Peter Spencer and John Trueman who had all been students in the Monetary Group. Present also were Richard Jackman, Morris Perlman, Max Steuer, Jim Thomas and David Webb, all current colleagues in the Economics Department, together with Gordon Pepper from the City who had been so active at meetings of the Money Workshop. Finally there were some ten letters of well-wishing apology from others. With so many friends that I had known for so many years it was a most relaxed and heart-warming occasion, with all of us sharing our recollections of past years. I still have the menu with its many signatures, and in the following years there bloomed in our garden the fine shrub rose 'Frau Dagmar Hastrup' which was their retirement gift to me. Then in due course there was the usual Senior Common Room summer Strawberry Tea with a few words on behalf of our group of retiring members, and kindly small gifts to see us all on our way. As my retirement date approached I started giving my remaining books and journals to colleagues. The end appeared to be nigh.

A Digression on Exotic Languages

Polynesian etc

In earlier years one person I often travelled with on the train was Jasper Buse, Reader in General Linguistics at the School of Oriental and African Studies. He was an congenial travelling companion and our conversations were wide-ranging. His specialism was two Polynesian languages – Samoan and Rarotongan. He was engaged in the long-term project of compiling a dictionary of these, and he shared with me a curious problem he had come up against. The missionaries, who provided the earliest information about these languages (as they did for so many others in the Third World), reported a particular number system. Such systems are normally very stable and slow to alter, but the modern Polynesian number system was quite different, and it was difficult to account for the change. One possibility was that the missionaries had been told some ritual number system rather than that in daily use, but so far he could provide no convincing explanation.

Samoan and Rarotongan were not the only exotic languages that I brushed up against. Jasper introduced me briefly to an elderly lady whom I had seen occasionally on the train. She, I found, was a world authority on Vietnamese, and in particular on its root language Old Mon. And I had a fleeting glimpse of another exotic language on a particularly rainy day when I caught a bus over Waterloo Bridge. As our bus slowly made its way forward I found myself standing next to a pleasant young man who turned out to be the British Museum's expert on Aramaic, who explained to me that it was really intermediate between Hebrew and Arabic. Many years later my wife and I went on a tour to Syria where we visited Maaloula, the only place where Aramaic is still spoken. There in the church a girl read for us the Lord's Prayer in Aramaic; despite the difference in language there was a curious sense of familiarity in the rhythm of the words. Aramaic is often said to have been the native language of Jesus, but I can remember one lunchtime at the School when I joined two historians who were discussing whether Jesus would have spoken Greek.

Another expert in linguistics was Jean Aitchison who was a lecturer in linguistics at the School. I sometimes had lunch with her and what first impressed me was her approach to word processing, in which we were then both beginners. She told me that every day she tried out some new command or facility, whereas at that time I tended to stick to the operations I understood and required, rather concerned that if I strayed too far I might never find my way back. In our interesting conversations one topic emerged on which I was never able really to engage her. It seemed to me a matter of genuine interest to consider the relative efficiency with which different languages were able to transmit information. This would cover both the linguistic structure which would allow this to be done with different degrees of directness; or by seeing how long it took for an average non-native speaker to learn a language to a given standard of information-transfer; or whether the same information took more or fewer words/syllables/letters in different languages (multi-language instructions for much electronic equipment were an obvious starting point). I was never able to engage her interest in this topic; it was as if from the perspective of linguistics, each language was to be considered in its own right and such comparisons of efficiency would be odious.

Ancient Egyptian

I have already described my first steps in trying to learn Ancient Egyptian – sitting at my child's desk up in the loft at Avenue Road copying out lists of Pharaohs and hieroglyphs. I already had Renouf's *Ancient Egyptian Grammar* to which I later added the *Hieroglyphic Dictionary of the Book of the Dead* by Wallis Budge and, by the same author, *The Nile* with its excellent dynastic lists of the hieroglyphic names of the Pharaohs. I soon learnt that hieroglyphs are mostly a form of rebus – where one thing is pictured but another thing is meant. They are pictures of things, often stylised, but used to indicate the sounds – letters or syllables – of the Ancient Egyptian language (just as '4' indicates the syllable 'for' in text messaging); thus a picture of a basket, *neb*, indicates the syllable *neb* (which is often found with its meaning of *lord*; I have a faience bead with the inscription reading *Amen Re neb* – Amen Re is Lord), while the hieroglyph of a goose, *sa*, indicates the syllable *sa* (which also means 'son of' and is frequently used in royal titles). A proportion of the hieroglyphs are determinatives, which are not pronounced and do indeed indicate the thing pictured; these are used to clarify the type of thing referred to by the word. Further, in formal inscriptions there was always attention to balance and decorative effect, and to the magical significance inherent in many of the hieroglyphs themselves.

But the challenge was not the transliteration of the hieroglyphs, but what these sounds meant in the language of Ancient Egypt; this meant vocabulary and grammar, and here my early efforts ran out of steam. I continued to maintain a casual interest in the subject, but I was later overtaken by my brother Michael who, many years after his wartime service in Egypt with the 7th Hussars, became deeply interested in Ancient Egyptian and took a three year evening course taught by Vivian Raisman at the City University. After he died in 2000 she and her husband, a research biologist, came and had lunch with us at Guildford so that she could take back with her many of Mike's more technical books on Ancient Egyptian, to give out to her current students. Amongst the volumes that I kept was Barbara Watterson's excellent but demanding little book *Introducing Egyptian Hieroglyphs*. This had the added interest of revealing that the words ebony, gum, sack, chemistry, ammonia and the name Susanna/Susan all had their roots in Ancient Egyptian. That such names as pharaoh, Memphis, Thebes and oasis are derived from Ancient Egyptian would not seem surprising, except that the names of other such quintessentially Egyptian things as obelisk, sphinx, mummy and Nile have names which have no connexion at all with the language of Ancient Egypt, the first two being from ancient Greek, the last two from other Semitic languages (Nile is from *nahal* meaning river). I had always assumed that the name Ozymandias was just Shelley's romantic invention, but I now found that it was in fact a passable version of *usr maat re* (the power and truth of Re), the shortened prenomen of Rameses II, one of whose ruined colossi was the subject of Shelley's magnificent sonnet. However I feel that he is unfair in referring to that Pharaoh's 'sneer of cold command'; the upper half of his great statue in the British Museum gives him a rather benevolent expression. It is the trio of statues of Sesostris III which are more deserving of Shelley's description, although I would describe them as expressing a grim tight-lipped authority.

Black Athena

The first two volumes of Black Athena by Martin Bernal appeared in 1987 and 1991, putting forward the thesis that Ancient Egypt and the ancient

422

Semitic cultures of the Levant had a much greater and more vital influence on Greece in the second millennium BC than was generally recognised. He saw Ancient Egypt as essentially an African culture, and the subtitle of the volumes puts his view very succinctly: *The Afroastatic Roots of Classical Civilisation*. They are substantial volumes of great erudition, wide scope and fascinating detail, moving easily between these cultures and languages. As well as history, Bernal is deeply concerned with historiography, attacking as anti-Semitic the Aryanisation of Greek studies and its deliberate overlooking of the influences from the cultures of Ancient Egypt and the Levant. And he pursues a further objective – the reduction of European (i.e. white) cultural arrogance. This is done by asserting that there were four Ancient Egyptian dynasties which 'one can usefully call black' and that one of these, the twelfth, had particular influence on early Greece. These were the Hyksos, the invaders who ruled lower Egypt for about one hundred and fifty years in the second millennium BC and, led by Sesostris, were said also to have ruled early Greece and to be the carriers of this influence. (Sesostris is the Greek version of Senwosret, the name of three pharaohs of the twelfth Dynasty of whom I and III are the leading candidates for the connexion with Greece although the latter, from his statues mentioned above, had no black African facial features.) These views were starkly emphasised by the title *Black Athena*, although later I read somewhere that this title was the publisher's rather than the author's, and was aimed at raising controversial interest in the book and extending its market.

Our eldest son Mark bought me a copy of the first volume of *Black Athena* as a Christmas present in 1991 and we both read it, and in due course the second volume also. We found Bernal's views most intriguing and these have cropped up as a topic of conversation between us on many subsequent occasions. However, like others, we remained sceptical of his view that the Hyksos were the carriers of this influence on early Greece, or indeed that this influence was significant for those aspects of much later Greek civilisation which we so value today.

The two volumes present Bernal's interesting suggestions on etymologies, of both persons and places, which link Ancient Greece and Ancient Egypt; a leading example of these is his derivation of the name *Athens* (which appears to have no root in Greek) from the Ancient Egyptian *het Neit* (the House of Neit, an Egyptian goddess). He also reminds us of the accepted view that the name *Egypt*, through the Greek *Aigyptios*, is derived from *het ka Ptah*, meaning the House of the Soul of Ptah, the ancient name of the great temple at Memphis (from *men nefer* meaning established, beautiful), the capital of Lower Egypt. (I can still remember Mr Berry, a history master at Colet Court, explaining to our class of twelve year olds that Lower Egypt was at the top of the map and Upper Egypt at the bottom). It is a potent thought that Ptah, the name of the great creator god of Ancient Egypt, still echoes in the modern world through the letters *pt* in Egypt (and in its corrupt form Copt). It also echoes, though less clearly, in *gypsy* (derived from the mistaken belief that these people came from Egypt), and more speculatively and even less clearly in *ghetto* which some have derived from *egitto*, a corruption of Egypt. The word 'pyramid' is a case of some interest; it has often been said that it was derived from the Greek *pyramis*, a cake of that shape; but now Bernal supports the view that it is derived from the Ancient Egyptian *pa mr*, meaning tomb, pyramid, which would imply that the Greek cakes got their name from the Ancient Egyptian, exactly reversing the earlier view. He makes a number of other interesting suggestions: that the word *martyr* came to us through the Greek from the Ancient Egyptian *mtrw* meaning witness, as did myth from the Ancient Egyptian *md.t* meaning speech or discourse; that *Asia* came to us through the Anatolian *assuwa* from the Ancient Egyptian *isy* which referred to some area around Crete and the Levant; that *labyrinth*, rather than being derived from the Lydian *labrys*, meaning double axe – a symbol of royal power – may instead be derived from the great 'labyrinthine' palace of Amenemes III, another twelfth Dynasty pharaoh, through his praenomen *maat en Re* which under surprising transformations emerged in Greek as *Labares* and hence *labyrinth*. To this he adds the suggestion that the pre-Greek *-inthos* may have come from the Ancient Egyptian *ntr* meaning divine. On a different level he reminds us that the name *Europe* has its roots in the Semitic *'rb* meaning west or evening, and he refers to the spice cumin as appearing under this name in the Linear A syllabary. At one School dinner I found myself seated next to Auriol Stevens who worked for the Committee of Vice-Chancellors and Principals of the Universities of the United Kingdom and was the wife of our Director, John Ashworth. She too had just read the first volume of *Black Athena* (apart from Mark, the only other person I ever came across who had done so; no one else I knew had even heard of it) and this provided us with a topic of quite absorbing interest over dinner.

Basque

In the Senior Common Room I sometimes talked to Geoffry [*sic*] Allen, one of our librarians; he once told me that he had just completed a manual to help librarians identify which of the European languages a book had been written in. It sounded interesting, and glancing at it later I came across the pages on Basque (which, in Basque, is Euskara). I knew that it appeared to have no affinity with any other European language and certainly to Indo-European eyes the names of the numbers alone were enough to reveal its alien character:

1	Bat
2	Biga
3	Hiru
4	Lau
5	Bost
6	Sei
7	Zazpi
8	Zortzi
9	Bederatzi
10	Hamar
20	Hogei
50	Berrogeitahamar
100	Ehun

His manual says that Basque shows signs of a few borrowings or influences from two other nearby tongues, French and Spanish; the numbers 2, Biga and 6, Sei might show evidence of this, but the rest are from a different world – that of Europe before the coming of the Indo-European-speaking Celts who were to push the ancestors of the Basques into their present corner at the western end of the Pyrenees. I concluded that, even though Basque had the merit, perhaps even the tiny usefulness, of being a living language, I would stick with the thoroughly dead but to me much more interesting Ancient Egyptian.

Recently, wanting to check something, I typed 'Basque' into Google and was rewarded with:

'Seriously Sexy Basques
Gorgeous Sensual & Feminine'

Thank you, samantha.lingerie.com, but not quite what I was looking for. It was only later that I found buber.net/Basque/Euskara, which is a treasure-house of information on the Basque language.

Body Language

A very different, indeed hardly exotic, language is body language (and I do not mean mime, its conscious and theatrical form) which can indeed speak volumes. I was once sitting in our car in Chichester's South Street waiting for Toni. A few yards further along on the other side of the road was a cinema. A mother and her daughter, aged about eight, were walking hand in hand and as they passed the cinema the little girl suddenly saw that it was showing some ballet film and, without being able to hear a thing, I saw the child's body language express a whole battery of yearnings: 'It's a ballet film – could we see it? – I really want to see it – please, please let me see it – Oh, mummy, I really, really want to see it – why can't I see it – Oh, mummy…' It was a brilliant and touching performance. On another occasion we were on holiday in Brittany and walking along a small street lined with parked cars. Two young French women met face to face as they tried to walk through the same narrow space between the two parked cars. Their silent exchange of blame, disapproval, hauteur and dismissal – all in some two seconds – was eloquence itself.

Baby Talk

This is an exotic language of a kind, but it is one with deeper roots than one might expect. *The Times, Body and Soul* Supplement, Saturday, 30 August 2008, p. 3, reports research by the University of British Columbia published in the *Proceedings of the National Academy of Sciences* which shows that newborn babies are much more stimulated by repeat syllables rather than single ones. This would appear to provide some fundamental basis for the widely noted reduplications in baby talk such as: *Ma-Ma, Da-Da, Na-na* and *din-din.*

426

24

Affairs of the School

Over the years, like so many of my colleagues, I had been engaged in my share of matters of administration and policy as a member of various School committees, of the Academic Board and as an Academic Governor. Some have already been mentioned and others in earlier years have passed beyond recall. But particularly in the years before my retirement these 'affairs of the School' took up an increasing amount of my time and attention, and to give a balanced account of my life at the School I set out here a summary of them.

Fees for overseas students

Until the late 1970s overseas students did not pay fees for their education at British universities. When the government proposed charging them fees there was discussion in the Academic Board and a substantial majority were against this change. Arguments against fees then came from many directions which led me to set out my own refutation of them in a six page paper in November 1979. I sent this to the Pro-Director, Alan Day, to give to the Director. Some of the points made in my paper were as follows.

Some have argued against such fees on the grounds that the keen overseas demand for British university education showed their need for it and that it should therefore be free. My response was that this demand was keen *because* this education was free; the demand came not from the needy but from overseas elites whose children have already had their earlier education conducted in English. Why should we subsidise these elites? British taxpayers were clearly becoming unwilling to do so. The countries from which most of these students came charge Britain a market price for their exports of goods and commodities, and it was only reasonable that Britain should charge them the market price for our exports of services. We were frequently told that the world did not owe us a living; similarly, we did not owe the world a living.

Another group of arguments expressed the belief that overseas students were valuable to Britain. Many would be trained on UK technology and would retain a preference for it when they returned home, thus helping UK exports. But much of UK industry used overseas technology, and in any case, if well educated, such students would always look for best value, whether from the UK or elsewhere. To suggest that they would still be inclined to give preference to UK goods and services was a dangerous argument, telling overseas countries that those educated in the UK would be sympathetic to UK rather than act solely in the interests of their own country – an economic fifth column. But such education in Britain would surely generate goodwill towards Britain? Bitter experience seems to show only too well that, while it may create goodwill towards individual academics, a country cannot buy any lasting or practically useful goodwill by subsidies, aid or any other such method. A related argument was that overseas students know about their own countries and this can help to educate and inform us. But such students would have lived in their homeland only as children and dependants and they know relatively little about their own countries – as little as most British students know about Britain.

There were many more arguments on both sides. A few days after I sent him my paper I received through Alan Day a response from Ralf Dahrendorf, the Director:

> I enjoyed reading this – it helped to clear my mind. Since I have always been opposed to phoney arguments, I liked some of RA's refutations.
>
> Ralf
>
> 5/11/11 [?1979]

I cannot remember what other circulation my paper had, but I feel that it was not large. I know one person outside the School who received it in 1981, because in his reply he said:

We come out, to a surprising extent, with the same answers, which I credit to your sound intuition and my sound research.

Mark Blaug

On this subject I was one of those going with the flow of events, and soon overseas students had to pay fees.

Scholarships

In September 1954 the Director invited nine members of the Economics Association, all from grammar schools, for a meeting at the School with himself, Henry Phelps-Brown, Frank Paish and Bill Phillips, myself and possibly some others. I was to open our discussions and the first topic was to be the lack of Open/Entrance scholarships to the School. Nearly thirty years later I returned to this subject. Although the School had a number of sponsored scholarships for those who were already undergraduates, I had the impression that we were not attracting our fair share of AAA grade entrants and to help rectify this situation I produced a paper (9 November 1981) proposing that the School should have its own undergraduate scholarship scheme which I hoped would compete with the Oxbridge scholarships. There should be twenty entrance scholarships in the first year and the same number of (senior) scholarships in each of the second and third years, building up to a steady level of sixty in all. This proposal went to the Academic Studies Sub-Committee of the Academic Policy Committee and after further discussion with me it was recommended to the Academic Board which approved it at its meeting of 1 December 1982. It then went to the Admissions Committee in February 1983 and I sent a note to this Committee with some further comments on the proposal including the fact that in 1980–81 no fewer than 26% of entrants to Cambridge gained entrance scholarships or exhibitions; in that year the School offered no entrance scholarships at all. The scholarship scheme was then put into effect by the Admissions Committee at its meeting on 15 March 1983 to begin in the following October. By December 1986 the scheme had begun to build up and the Director held a tea party for School scholars, twelve entrance scholars and ten (second year) senior scholars. In due course

Oxbridge ended their scholarship schemes and the LSE scheme was then discontinued as well.

Word Processing

It was only after the greater part of my book on flow of funds was completed that I moved over to word processing. Alma Gibbons introduced me to the School's Word-11 system shortly after it was installed; it had the disadvantage of being a wired-in system which could only be used at the School, while I preferred to do much of my work at home. I found the menus not very convenient and produced for myself a large sheet with them all set out in hard copy; I showed it to Alma who felt it was useful and I gave it to her for her training course. Then and later she was very helpful to me over word processing.

The first computer that I used at home was lent to me by the Economics Department; it was a BBC B with the basic word-processing program VIEW and I had my own very slow EPSON 9-pin dot matrix printer. Being able to do simple word processing and printing-off at home in the evenings and at weekends was a revelation. I soon acquired a BBC B of my own for use at home and then a second one with printer for my room at the School so that I could transfer working documents between the two by floppy disc. My interest now being aroused, I volunteered to become a member of the School's Information Technology (IT) Committee and later I also became a member of the IT Panel. I produced four papers for the IT Committee. In November 1984 I wrote a very critical note on a report it received on the future of word processing at the School. My objections were that it only considered upgrading our wired-in Word-11 system (which had many critics) and restricted itself to equipment compatible with it instead of looking at other possible systems; it made no projection of future demand; it did not adequately consider the word-processing requirements of academics, particularly for working at home, which pointed to stand-alone desktop PCs (laptops were yet to come); the number of these in the School could grow with demand. I concluded that we needed a thorough and constructive discussion of the IT options facing the School from which an entirely new start could be made. The second paper put forward a proposal for a statement of objectives for the IT Committee – virtually a permanent background agenda for our meetings. It covered in brief detail: the assessment of demand for IT by different groups within the School; on the supply side, the cost-effectiveness of equipment; in the light of these and the financing possibilities to decide upon the range of equipment which would best meet the School's requirements; it suggested detailing the School's existing stock of IT equipment and its likely growth (and its need for accommodation) and consideration of our arrangements for training and encouragement in the use of IT facilities. In January 1986 I put forward the third paper, *Some Aspects of Word-Processing Systems*. This started with a schematic history of word-processing from typing in program lines using high-level languages such as Fortran which typically required a lot of correction, done originally by line editing and later by screen editing in which entries and corrections could be made at any point of the several lines on the screen. It was then immediately apparent that text could be entered and edited in the same way – the discovery of a new use for an existing facility – and this was the beginning of word processing. The paper then went on to suggest a systematic way of assessing the 'cost'/convenience of word-processing operations to assist the choice of new stand-alone computers/word-processing packages for the School. It finished with very brief critical reviews of three then current systems: Wordstar–2000 on IBM PC, Word–11 and VIEW on BBC B. In October 1986 my last paper for the IT Committee was an attempt to assess systematically the appropriate level of terminals per student at the School, taking account of the UGC's guidelines for 1990. It ended by asking 'whether we, as teachers, consider that the resulting level and ratio of student terminal hours [*per week*] is in some sense [*educationally*] justified or satisfactory'. This concern has recently resurfaced.

As word processing spread amongst my colleagues I noted one interesting feature: people became fierce supporters of the word-processing package they first learned to use. I saw a long battle between supporters of Microsoft Word and those of WordPerfect over which should be the School's standard package as the PC finally became our standard equipment. In my own case, a similar conservative attachment led me to move from the BBC B to its successor, the Archimedes, only to find myself out of the PC mainstream with its increasing power and range of facilities. The time then came when I had to make the painful transition to a PC, helped by the School's IT unit which gave me initial help and continuing support.

The next phase after word processing was e-mail and the Internet, or rather the first version I used – ARPANET. This was the US defence net which they opened to other users to help keep it in active use; then the US Congress decided this was giving away a valuable service and we were expelled from it and on to BITNET, then JANET and finally the Internet as we now know it. My first experience of these systems was with a 75/300 baud modem lent to me by Ailsa Land who was in the Department of Operational Research. It was slow, but having it working at all was a thrill. Our eldest son Mark went to Harvard in September 1984 to do a PhD in physics and much of our subsequent written communication with him there was done by e-mail over whichever of these nets was the current one. There were occasional hiccups, and on one occasion I was advised to consult someone at Abingdon who was supposed to be the guardian of the current protocol of the system. My problem puzzled him and he was reduced to suggesting that I could try adding a comma at some point in the address; so much for the rigour of protocol.

The Role of Secretaries

The spread of computers and word processing through the School saw more academics producing their own documents. I was struck by the great difference between a typist uncritically typing from a handwritten draft, and an academic entering his own document directly into a word processor, which allowed typing, initial editing and correction all to be done at the same time, as well as making subsequent editing much easier. This raised the question of the future role of secretaries and in 1985 I sent a paper to Christine Challis which looked very critically into several aspects of this. I was aware of its sensitivities so this paper was headed *Secretarial Services – further points PRIVATE DRAFT*. I concluded that the School got poor value for money from secretaries because working for four or five academics (as most of them did), there was no one person to see that they were putting in an appropriate effort. I saw many of them spending a long time over coffee and lunch, and they were often underemployed during vacations when most of their academics were away. What they did then I was not sure, but one did sometimes have the impression that the School was staffed largely by telephone answering machines. When I went to see Christine

432

about this paper she held up her hands in mock horror (but perhaps some real horror also). She promised that she would take note of what I said in the paper but added that it must be kept strictly private between us, as otherwise she could see much trouble from outraged secretaries. The second paper a few months later was subtitled *Some sources of dissatisfaction with current secretarial arrangements*, and looked more constructively at the same problem, suggesting that academics should each be given a budget to be spent on any of a specified amount of in-house secretarial services (full-time or term-time-only); outside contract typing; services for maintaining contact with students; or on IT and word processing equipment for their own use. This four page paper gave detailed estimates of how such a scheme could work, with gains to academics and the School. In a final paragraph I pointed out that I had produced the document myself at home on the BBC B using VIEW and my own printer, mostly working late in the evening, and that I now did virtually all my own typing on such equipment. This whole subject came up again later and I sent Christine Challis a further one page note elaborating various points from my previous paper.

The Environmental Code

As the 1980s moved on most of us became increasingly aware of the generally run-down appearance of the School, and particularly the poor state of so many of its teaching rooms. I had earlier been a member of the Accommodation Committee when it conducted a survey of teaching rooms which confirmed how much needed to be done. As we looked into one classroom with its chairs awry and the board still covered with writing from an earlier class, Michael Wise recalled that when he first came to the School in 1951, as a class finished there would be a porter outside waiting to clean the blackboard ready for the next one, but those days were long gone. After this survey matters had come to a halt. I now decided that more determined action was needed and I proceeded on three fronts: first, to make teachers play their part in keeping classrooms tidy; second, to set up a specification for teaching rooms and third, to help keep the School free of rubbish, outdated notices and general grottiness. For the first of these I started in May 1986 with a letter to Bob Pinker, who was Pro-Director, suggesting he should write to all our colleagues urging them to leave a teaching room in the state they would wish to find it – clean blackboard and chairs in order – as a matter of natural courtesy between colleagues. Clearly this was not enough, and at the next stage I drafted an explicit code for class teachers which in effect said that they and their students should leave a classroom as they would wish to find it: the board cleaned, plastic cups and discarded paper put into the rubbish bin, and chairs properly replaced. This again went to Bob Pinker who was very much in favour of it, and he got the Committee on Accommodation to recommend it to the Academic Board where it was approved on 24 June 1987. In leaflet form it was then distributed around the School.

We already had a scheme of environmental stewards, student volunteers who were supposed to keep an eye open for the more obvious untidiness, but the scheme needed revivifying and I volunteered to take it over for a while to try and make it more effective. I met the stewards regularly and they worked hard, but they could only have a limited effect. The steward I remember most clearly was an American student who worried about discarded batteries polluting landfill; he urged me to do something, but there were then no facilities for segregating dead batteries and I had the difficult task of evading his urgings without discouraging his perfectly sensible concerns. The experience of working with the Stewards led me to set out the objectives of the scheme in the form of a two page document *An Environmental Code for the School* in October 1989, which incorporated the code for class teachers. This was widely circulated and later was able to state in its first paragraph that it had the support of the Director, Pro-Director, the Secretary and the Bursar (and, in due course, the Secretary General of the Students' Union). Christine Challis, the School Secretary, proposed some mild redrafting, most of which I turned down ('I have accepted a <u>few</u> of your redrafts') on the grounds that they were too bureaucratic, while my version was more forceful as 'a direct, personal and persuasive statement from someone directly concerned with the environment (myself, in charge of Environmental Stewards)'. I urged Christine to put the Code before the Academic Board on 22 November 1989 and added: 'We should talk soonest – even if only to quarrel.' In fact Christine was the most reasonable and pleasant administrator one could wish for; she accepted my final version and the Code went before the Academic Board. It was approved and was then widely circulated, at first in the form of the original document over my name, but later as a School document. It was subject to later revisions as new problems came to light and was given further publicity in the *LSE Circular* of 29 January 1990.

Teaching Rooms

The third part of my campaign was propelled by my view that teaching was a primary aim of a university, which had to be much more than just a research unit or a think-tank. The School had been short of teaching rooms for many years and there were complaints about a number of those that we did have. I was a member of the Committee on Accommodation when we carried out an inspection of teaching rooms in 1985, led by Michael Wise, who was Chairman. I believe that the Committee made some recommendations but progress was painfully slow. Both Michael and the next Chairman, Bob Pinker, were very supportive when I then went on to do my own survey of teaching rooms and set out a Specification for Teaching Rooms. This went through all aspects of these rooms which affected teaching and proposed standards for each of them. It started with the Teaching Wall – the one behind the teacher – and specified non-distracting decoration, ample boards (increasingly whiteboards), markers, cleaners, facilities for hanging maps, suitable lecterns (with dimensions) and so on to chairs, tables, layout, even the position of the clock (at the back of the room where the teacher could see it) and all the other aspects of a teaching room. I also invited colleagues to nominate the worst teaching room; this achieved a response which in other circumstances might have been called enthusiastic, as well as a number of expressions of support for my efforts. After discussions with her, I sent Christine Challis a paper *Teaching Rooms – A Plan for Action* ('bowdlerised, purified and de-odorised'). Following this, my *Specification for Teaching Rooms* went to the Standing Committee on 7 March 1989, before the Academic Board on 8 March and then to the Committee on Accommodation which included it in their draft Terms of Reference which at my urging explicitly included the duty of overseeing its implementation. In due course all this came into effect – on paper at least.

As my retirement (September 1992) began to loom, all these matters were taken over by others; but two concerns remained with me. The first was that without some person taking a real interest in such matters and pressing them forward, little gets done; and the second was that all too often the successors don't read the files (if there are any) of what has been learned or decided in the past, such as the now approved *Specification for Teaching Rooms*. Such problems of institutional memory affect all, organisations, and in my view there should be specific arrangements to maintain it. I often asked senior bank executives what they did to maintain their bank's institutional memory; did they ask all managers above a certain level to write down on one side of A4 the main lessons that they had learnt from the past year's business? The brief answer I received was that they did not, but in my view they most certainly should, and so should chief executives in most organisations. Such a process would provide an important and condensed body of recorded experience of great value to the next generation of managers or administrators, part of whose remit should include reading these records.

The *Calendar*

The School's *Calendar* is a key source of information on courses and has always required considerable annual updating. It is highly structured but not always easy for the outsider to use. In 1963 I suggested that it would be useful to have a keyword index to subjects and courses. I felt the case was persuasive but it did not persuade. I was a member of the Academic Studies Committee in the mid-1980s when there was discussion of what material about each undergraduate course should be in the Course Guides. This turned on two elements: (1) the Syllabus, felt by some to be a quasi-contractual definition of the coverage of a Course, but to others raising the danger that some disaffected student who did badly in an exam might claim that the course did not conform to its Syllabus; (2) the Course Content, a statement of what a Course would actually cover in that particular year. In my view Course Content was the element relevant for students and Syllabus was relevant for giving the Department some broad control over course coverage. In March 1988 I put my view to the Academic Studies Committee in a one page note, *The Calendar: Course Guide, Course Content and Syllabus*, arguing that our committee and then the Academic Board had made a mistake, and urging that we should drop the Syllabus from the *Calendar* and have just the Course Content; but again my persuasion failed and we continued to have what became Core Syllabus and Course Content. For my own British Monetary Systems course I always added to the Core Syllabus entry 'Other relevant topics', just to ensure that I could cover events which might arise in unexpected corners of the subject and could not have been foreseen when the Core Syllabus was written, but which seemed to me to deserve some attention in this course. I was approached by Arthur John who delicately suggested that this blew a hole in the limitation intended by the Core Syllabus. Equally delicately I explained my reasons; he tried again, but I held firm and heard nothing further. However, for many courses the Core Syllabus tended to become so general as to provide little restriction on the teaching and no advantage to the students, which supported my original argument for excluding it from the *Calendar*.

Later it was found that students in the Economics Department were being allowed an unintended and educationally unsatisfactory choice of certain papers in their second and third years. In May 1989 I sent to the Professors of Economics a short paper, *Proposed Changes in Calendar Entries*, explaining the problem and showing how it could be overcome by revised versions, which I attached, of the selection lists for each of the then six Economics special subjects. This was approved without alteration and I was asked to take my proposal forward to the Academic Studies Committee. In my paper I noted that 'although we believe that only a few students would be foolish enough to make bizarre and unsuitable choices ... nevertheless we feel it is better to remove the temptation'. The proposal was approved by the committee and the changes appeared in the next edition of the *Calendar*.

A Logo for the School

In the 1980s it seemed that every organisation was acquiring a logo, and in about 1988 from somewhere came the proposal that the School should consider having one. A public relations firm was commissioned to work on it and I was one of the group, led by Christine Challis, to whom they made their presentation. The meeting was not a success for the PR firm. Their proposed logo was supposed to encapsulate the essence and strengths of the School, but it was very similar to the wobbly flame already used by a large gas company. To me it seemed to symbolise a weak argument petering out before it got anywhere. All those on the School's side heartily disliked it and after the meeting nothing further was heard of the proposal. I personally was very glad that instead we retained the School's letterheads in Baskerville typeface which we had used for so many years, together with our coat of arms. These, in black, seem to me to have an elegant and powerful simplicity.

In the end we did acquire a (home-grown?) logo, a red rectangle with the letters LSE which appeared on various School documents and envelopes, and as a lapel badge. My criticism of it was that its design and colour were very ordinary and had little flavour of the School. In my view, if we were going to have it at all, it should have had Baskerville lettering, or some variant of it, together with the handsome and solid maroon colour which, starting in 1958–59, has been used for the binding of the School's *Calendar*, both would have a real association with the School.

Teaching, Research and the Future of the School

I was not the first person to feel a growing concern over three matters: (1) the balance between teaching and research; (2) support from academics for academic administration in the School; and (3) the career prospects and status of the non-professorial majority of academics. The Director had started a series of one hour seminars (sometimes called School Seminars, sometimes Director's Seminars) to look at the many issues affecting the School; for the seminar on 29 November 1989 I was invited to open discussion of a six page paper I had written entitled *Teaching, Research and the Future of the School*, which aired my concerns. Quoting selectively and paraphrasing from this paper:

(1) **On the balance between teaching and research:** The growing emphasis on research means that we have to recognise that there are important points of conflict between teaching and research. Both make demands upon an academic's time and attention; successful research often requires ruthless dedication and this may mean equally ruthless relegation of teaching and students into a poor second place. We cannot allow undergraduate teaching to drift into a situation where it depends upon the crumbs of time and attention left over from research. Some degree [*sic*] of

specialisation between these two activities is necessary, and both should carry appropriate rewards and provide satisfactory career prospects.

(2) **On the support from academics for academic administration in the School:** The School depends upon many academics being willing to give time and effort to a whole range of the School's administrative activities – attendance at the Academic Board, membership of the many committees, talking to potential students on Visit Days, visiting schools – all requiring a commitment to the School and often a detailed knowledge of its administrative and teaching arrangements. Currently teaching staff are appraised under three headings: teaching, research and administration; I believe that this is seriously misleading. Most younger academics believe, correctly, that research publication is the overwhelming consideration for promotion, which gives them a powerful incentive to concentrate on their research and avoid any involvement in these broader activities which are essential to the well-being of the School.

(3) **On the career prospects for the majority of academics:** The School claims to be a great international academic institution. But any non-professor going abroad for academic reasons will soon discover (if he comes clean) that he has to explain why he is not a professor. After all, *every* US academic is a professor (and, if he is a visitor to the School, will be called and respectfully treated as such even though he may in fact be an assistant professor, equivalent to a lecturer). If the School really values its long-staying and senior non-professorial staff (most of whom will never get chairs) it must offer them more recognition and status, and in this way provide a more satisfactory career.

My proposed solution to these three problems was based on my observation that at Oxbridge, being a Fellow conferred status in the eyes of the world far beyond that of lecturer, senior lecturer or reader. I suggested that this title should be given to those long serving non-professors who are good teachers and play a full role in the wider affairs of the School, and that ultimately they could become Professorial Fellows of the School and referred to as professors for all School purposes. The emphasis on Fellowship would not be simply cosmetic; it would signify a commitment to the School, its teaching role, its concern for undergraduates and its academic administration. Promotion for research activity is initiated by Departments; promotion to Fellowship or Professorial Fellowship should be in the hands of the Director who could take a broader view of value of these teachers to the School. One advantage of my suggestion was that it would cost the School nothing as it had no effect on pay scales but was purely the conferment of local titles.

This gives the gist of my paper to the School Seminar. In effect it was urging a rebalancing of the incentives for research on the one hand and for teaching and academic administration on the other. In the event the seminar recognised the problems I had diagnosed but showed little enthusiasm for my solution.

Looking at some other points raised in my paper, I noted that the relative structure of salaries (taking the top of each scale) at that time was professors 100, senior lecturers/ readers 84, lecturers 71, much less than the differences in status as seen from outside the School. But the British public knows of only one academic rank, and that is Professor; in their eyes if you are not a professor then clearly you are second-rate. I would also add here that the difference in status which was so evident to outsiders was in my own experience singularly absent from relations between colleagues within the School. With my own solution not really a runner, I favoured moving over to the US university system of assistant/associate/full professors with everyone being referred to as Professor. Later Richard Layard put this suggestion to the Academic Board but nothing came of it. The School remained content to belittle the status of its own non-professorial staff relative to their American equivalents with whom they most commonly faced comparison, and to maintain their rather low status in the eyes of the British public. Really rather strange for an institution focussed upon the social sciences, but where its man-management of most of its own academics was singularly lacking in insight and sensitivity.

I might add that the reason for my pressing the matter of status for non-professorial staff was that most professors showed no concern about it and the non-professorial staff were unwilling to raise an issue which would appear so self-serving. But I was a senior non-professor, nearing retirement and with nothing personal to gain from the case I was putting forward; I felt it was my duty to speak out for those who were understandably inhibited from pressing their own case.

Teaching and Tutoring

I now passed on to problems facing undergraduates with a two page paper *Undergraduate Teaching and Tutoring* (Feb 1990) to which was attached my handout for undergraduates in the Economics Department, *Academic Work at University*. Its main proposals were:

1. The Dean of Undergraduate Studies should take on the role of managing the BSc Econ degree, to ensure that: the School's teaching ethos is maintained; teaching commitments are to be seen as a positive and primary claim on the time and attention of all teachers and that they are scrupulously fulfilled; that class registers (the only evidence we have of any kind that an undergraduate is actually in attendance at the School) are properly completed; that new teachers are properly briefed on what we expect from our teaching staff.

2. We should develop an explicit Code of Conduct for all concerned with undergraduate teaching and tutoring, making clear that these activities are properly and responsibly carried out to clearly stated standards. There were elements of such a Code in our booklet *Information for Undergraduates and their Tutors* but this needed to be developed much further. The Economics Department's Handout: *Academic Work at University* verges on a Code of Conduct for our undergraduates in their academic work. Currently unsatisfactory features are: 'In the School's Calendar there is bizarre disorder in the numbering of Course Guides ... and their constituent lecture and class series.'; breadth of choice in courses is leading to congestion of timetables.

3. The responsibility for ensuring that reports for all undergraduates in all classes must be placed clearly on Convenors of Departments. At present our most pressing problem is that the class reporting system is insufficiently effective – I had recently received report cards for my tutees, only 76% had class reports, of these one third lacked any comments and one third contained no grades. 'It is only at Departmental level that suitable pressure can be placed by academics on other academics and teachers to produce proper reports on all undergraduates ... The Registry

should be required to notify the Director of any missing or late reports.' In short, I was urging that Convenors should be doing more focussed academic administration.

This paper had a wide circulation and the next step was a letter from the Academic Registrar on 7 March 1990, with an equally wide circulation:

Undergraduate Teaching and Tutoring

The Director has asked that the recommendation contained in the attached paper from Mr Alford on undergraduate teaching and tutoring should be examined. The paper follows up a number of points made at the Director's seminar held in December 1989 [*actually 29 November 1989*], and the issues it raises are of importance for undergraduate students and for the School as a whole, especially in the light of the increased attention being given nationally to academic standards and the assessment of teaching in universities.

It then went on to ask for comments by 27 April. The comments on my three recommendations were reported to the Academic Board on 6 June 1990. There were nine comments altogether, seven from conveners; four of these responses welcomed my paper as initiating a broader discussion of the matter. On the specific recommendations the comments were:

1. The role of the Dean of Undergraduate Studies: two gave unqualified supported, two qualified agreement, three no comment.
2. Code of Conduct: three unqualified support, two neutral, two no comment.
3. Convenors to have responsibility for Class Reports: two supported, four not in favour, one no comment.

The Dean of Undergraduate Studies was sceptical.

The responses included a number of further points: the role of departmental tutors to be enhanced; teaching should be put in a much more positive light, not just seen as an impediment to one's own research;

the lack of incentives or sanctions to encourage good teaching or administration; teaching should be a real rather than a ritual criterion for promotions.

From these results it seemed to me that many Convenors were unwilling to take on demanding administrative tasks (just the kind of tasks that my paper for the Director's seminar had envisaged being done by Professorial Fellows). Otherwise I felt that there was a significant tide of support for the view I was putting forward.

The decision of the Academic Board was to set up a working party to look further into all these issues, now covering also teaching and tutoring at the taught postgraduate level, and to report early in 1991; I was thanked for my work in this area. Meanwhile in December 1990 I revised and extended to eight pages my September 1989 paper, *Undergraduate Teaching and Tutoring at LSE*, which was my proposed Code of Practice in these fields, and this went to the working party which by now had generated several subsidiary working parties, including one on teaching. Looking back on my efforts to improve teaching I can remember at the time a feeling of mild optimism that something might be achieved. In the event all my efforts were to come to nothing; the final reports of the Working parties were a comprehensive victory for research over teaching.

The reports of the Working Party on Teaching and Tutoring and its offshoot, the Working Party on Teaching, duly emerged and here I just quote some highlights from the two, with my own comments in italics within square brackets.

1. 'The School's mission statement lays equal emphasis on excellence in teaching, research and scholarship.'
2. 'LSE ... will never give priority to good teaching when promotion is under consideration ... poor teaching should be one of the factors taken into account during the promotion process.'

   [*Since the School does not give equal promotion and rewards for teaching and research, the equal emphasis on the two in its mission statement is seriously misleading.*]

3. 'A two tier system of academic staff ... teachers and researchers

443

... would be disastrous ... and likely to reduce the quality of *both* [*sic*] teaching and research.'

[*My proposal was not for a two tier system but for some degree of specialisation; in general specialisation is regarded as beneficial because it leads to people doing more of what they are best at, and therefore producing a better outcome overall.*]

4. 'This is not the time to relegate teaching to an inferior activity.'

   [*My proposals emphasised its importance and were aimed at encouraging good teaching by improving its rewards and status.*]

5. The School should occupy 'a high quality niche in the mass higher education system...'

   [*Yes indeed, but can it seriously claim to be pursuing this objective when it explicitly refuses to reward good teaching?*]

6. 'There is ... genuine symbiosis between research and teaching.'

   [*There is even more genuine conflict between the two in their claims upon an academic's time and attention.*]

7. 'One of the recommendations in the "Alford paper" ... was that the School should develop an explicit Code of Conduct on undergraduate teaching and tutoring on the lines of a document produced for undergraduates in the Economics Department.' [*This was my handout Academic Work at University.*] 'A prerequisite for any improvement in the quality ... of teaching is the introduction of a Code of Conduct...'

I was glad that they accepted my recommendation for a Code of Conduct, but in sporting terms the result was a 6–1 win for research over teaching. Not surprisingly, I was left with the feeling that the two working parties were so obsessed with the School's place in the world pecking order of research that they had not been able or willing to reorient themselves sufficiently to consider with care much of what I had said in my papers.

Looking back, in my concerns about teaching I contrasted it with the other major academic activity – research. I wish I had made more use of the term scholarship as a bridge between the two, because this seems to me to combine devotion to one's subject, a humane urge to pass on one's understanding by teaching both undergraduates and graduates, and a desire to deepen one's understanding by research, with all three being in balance. Indeed, teaching at university level cannot be done without the significant research component required for keeping up with one's own field, although this kind of research does not usually result in publications. But what concerned me was the increasing amount of hi-tech research which seemed to require its own special and secluded environment, well away from undergraduates, and which was so all-consuming, and so vital for promotion and reputation, that this balance was being distorted and the teaching was liable to suffer. I am sceptical of the School's attempt to bridge this gap by an emphasis on 'research-led teaching'. The two are conducted at entirely different levels; undergraduates deserve a range of courses carefully designed for their level to help them absorb the received body of the subject; a few exciting hints of new thinking can enthuse them, but the object is to give them a sound basic knowledge of the subject. For this many things have to be carefully prepared and monitored: for each course, the organisation of content and presentation, appropriate handouts, suitable class programmes and briefing of class teachers, and careful examining, all entirely focussed upon the needs of undergraduates. However, there is no certainty that someone recruited for their talent in hi-tech, high publication research in the deep recesses of a subject will be able or willing to provide these, although they will typically produce good supervision for PhD students. Perhaps it would require a different approach to be sure of recruiting the necessary number of academics who are very good at undergraduate teaching – the core activity of a university – and regard it as an important and rewarding part of their career.

Looking now not just at the School but at universities generally, we know that if people are well taught at university, they carry the intellectual benefits for themselves and value for the economy over their career and beyond. But what has been the value produced by the large amount of hi-tech, typically mathematical/quantitative, research in economics which we could compare with the value produced by teaching? There are certainly many private benefits of such research (as indeed of all research): the pleasure of being left alone to get on with something you enjoy doing; advancing your technical expertise and keeping it in good working order; enhancing your own, your department's and your university's position in the pecking order of your subject. But where are the public benefits – the robust and useful functional relationships in the economy which such research in economics might be expected to uncover? In the physical sciences research has uncovered a vast range of such relationships, and it is this achievement that has given the word research so much kudos; is it right to accord such kudos to hi-tech research in economics which has been unable to produce any such body of robust and useful results? And are there fundamental reasons why such research in economics can deliver only meagre public benefits? Having raised this question about the value of research, I am led to the paradoxical conclusion that what is needed now is more research into the value of research in economics.

The Offprint Collection

The Library contained the Course Collection, geared to support taught courses, within which was the Offprint Collection which held usually multiple copies of those articles recommended in reading lists and which were subject to heavy demand at particular times. These items were on short loan (three hours), long enough for them to be read, while maximising their availability. (I preferred the name Short Loan Collection because that was exactly what it was and because it contained more than just offprints.) My own students made a lot of use of the Offprint Collection and I, like many other teachers, provided items for it. But the librarian concerned began to raise difficulties about accepting some items on grounds of copyright, and after making enquiries I came to the conclusion that the Offprint Collection was applying an unduly restrictive interpretation of copyright, but that there were also genuine copyright constraints that needed to be overcome. In a rather technical four page paper, *The Offprint Collection and its Current Problems* (October 1990), I set out the problems and possible solutions, amongst which were that the Library should: recognise and make full use of the existing flexibility under our licence from the Copyright Licensing Agency; seek permission from certain journals to go beyond the copying already licensed; agree mutual and broader copyright permission between the School's journals and others journals; look at chapterisation of some books (splitting them into individual chapters which could be lent out separately – already considered as far back as the 1960s) and other possibilities. I attached to my paper proposed letters to the two journals of particular interest to my own students, which asked in very precise terms for wider permission to copy items for the Offprint Collection. This paper was discussed in the Library Committee, of which I was a member at that time; the main issue – the restrictive interpretation of existing copyright conditions – was resolved, the proposed letters were sent and the requested permissions were received. In the end a satisfactory accommodation was reached on some of the other issues and the usefulness of the Offprint Collection to our students was maintained.

Class Reports and Grading

Early in 1991 I returned to the matter of our system of reporting on student progress and sent the Academic Registrar a note again setting out its weaknesses. Our system envisaged that at the end of each term a tutor would receive a complete set of class reports on each tutee, that his tutees would then come to him to discuss these reports and the tutor would make his comments in the light of these discussions. All of this would be recorded on the tutee's tutorial card for that academic year, the tutorial cards for each of the student's three academic years would provide a full view of the student's progress at the School and together with results in Finals would be the basis for future references. This system was also important for other reasons: it was not practical to record attendance at lectures so that class attendance provided the only record that a student was academically active (and bodies giving grants to students sometimes wished to be assured of this); such progress reporting could throw up early warning signs of problems; and it provided evidence that a student was properly prepared to enter for exams. In my view the system was sound in principle but was not working efficiently: class reports were sometimes inadequate or late so that the comments by tutors were sometimes less well informed and less helpful to tutees than they should have been, and tutees were often lax in seeing their tutors. I had earlier proposed improvements which placed on Convenors of Departments the responsibility for making the system work effectively; they were evidently not keen to take this on, although they were the people with the status which would allow them to do this.

In May, with help from Jim Thomas, who was Departmental Tutor in the Economics Department, I proposed a more tightly organised system which would have placed greater responsibility on students and tutors and which should have improved the operation of the system. In November 1991 I set this out in detail in a six page paper, *Tutors, Tutees and Class Reports*. This proposal I circulated to the Academic Registrar and others concerned; some looked upon it with favour, but it would have involved significant changes in documentation and organisation, as well as more work and commitment from all concerned. But at that time such a system had to be paper-based which made it relatively clumsy, and I was not surprised (even slightly relieved) when my suggestions were quietly shelved.

Later, when the spread of computer technology made it possible, the School introduced *LSE for You* which was a much more efficient electronic implementation of the information flow set out above. I was given a demonstration of this system in 2007 and it seemed to me in principle to provide exactly what was required. My only doubts were over who would manage the system and provide the discipline to ensure that all concerned fulfilled their roles effectively.

I attached to my November 1991 paper a related but independent paper: *The Need for Consistency and Comparability in Grading*. Such consistency and comparability were essential if the information flow set out above was to be reliable. In this paper I set out explicitly the practice which in my experience had always been followed in the Economics Department (and I believe most other departments). With an increasing number of teachers coming from diverse backgrounds I felt this practice needed to be made explicit.

The ultimate benchmark of academic quality that all experienced teachers kept in mind was the final degree classification: First, Upper Second, Lower Second, Third, Pass (these last two being proportionately very small) and Fail (I can remember coming across only one, and that was an evening student many years ago). In any year an essay or class work grade should indicate that the quality of such work, if maintained, would lead to a particular class in Finals; in effect it seasonally adjusted marking across undergraduate years but anchored these marks to Finals classes. Typical grades would be A for work pointing to a First, B+ to an Upper Second, B– to a Lower Second, often with liberal additions of further ++, +, –, – –, to add nuances of quality.

*   *   *

Such were my efforts, in the years before my retirement in 1992, to help improve various aspects of the School's arrangements. But since then much time has passed and much has changed.

25

Still Around LSE: 1992 and After

Japanese Bankers

Anne Bohm, for so long Secretary of the Graduate School, had a phrase, 'Gone today and here tomorrow', to describe our colleagues who retired on one day and then reappeared the next having been persuaded to take on some role to help relieve the pressure on the full-time teaching staff. In my own case this reappearance arose from a call I received from Peter Dawson, who was in the Department of Government but was also responsible for the School's Executive and Professional Education unit, asking me if I would be interested in running some short courses for promising young Japanese bankers. My role would be to give them several sessions each week on Banking and Capital Markets in London and conduct them on some visits around the City. This appealed to me as I would keep me active in my main field of interest, it would maintain my connexion with the School and it was reasonably well paid. I agreed and ran a number of these courses each lasting some six weeks for groups of about twelve participants. We would have several meetings a week, part lecture, part discussion; their understanding of English was good, they were keen to learn and these meetings went well. They each had their own copy of the *Financial Times* and as part of our meetings I took them through the structure of the paper and we would discuss one or two of the items of financial news. At that time the proposals for the Eurofighter were in doubt and I had to explain that the heading 'Eurofighter nosedives' was a typical case of the joking allusion often contained in such headings; to them this was an entirely new aspect of British newspapers.

I took them on visits to one or two banks in the City but mainly to the major markets; at each they would be given a presentation explaining the function of the market before viewing it in operation. The visit to Lloyds insurance market was mainly of interest for the architecture of its building, since men in grey suits walking purposefully around did little to illuminate the real role of that market. The London Metal Exchange was much more impressive, with dealers seated in the ring, their clerks and telephones close behind them, shouting at each other in a rising crescendo as the end of one of the short dealing periods approached and the immediate deflation into talk and movement when it arrived; to the casual observer such a market appears chaotic though it is in fact highly structured. LIFFE, the London International Financial Futures Exchange, was at that time something to behold; we looked down on a dealing room which seemed the size of a football field covered with men in jackets of every colour, gesturing and shouting like rioting football fans; the sheer scale, noise and activity were astonishing, with the chaos appearing even greater because the structure was even less obvious. Later the business was to move on to computers where the scale and activity continued, but unobtrusively and in silence.

Our Japanese also visited the local branch of Nat West Bank on the corner of Houghton Street, less exciting but of considerable interest to them. There they were taken in detail through all aspects of the branch and its work. When they were being shown the stock of banknotes in the vault one of the Japanese asked if he might hold some; he was given a small wad of new notes and with one flick of his fingers he turned them into a perfect fan where they could be counted easily. As far as I could judge, they all enjoyed their weeks in London. One of the groups invited myself and Toni to a farewell dinner at a nearby Japanese restaurant; the food was delicious and it was a most genial occasion. We invited another group to our house in Guildford. After a suitably fishy lunch, for those keen on golf we provided putting on the lawn, some played ball, some lounged around talking and all walked round the garden. It was then tea and with much thanks they went off back to town in their minibus. It was a most enjoyable occasion, but one which we came to feel might be the explanation of a strange event which occurred a year or two later. There was a ring at our front door; outside was a group of about eight Japanese, obviously expecting to be asked in. None of them spoke a word of English. It seemed only polite and hospitable to motion them in, through to the conservatory and out into the garden. There they made gestures of pleasure and spent some time looking around it with interest. When that was over they made many gestures of thanks and departed, leaving us baffled as to who they were and how they had come to visit us, but feeling that we had done our bit for good international relations.

Helping Russia

Meanwhile communism in Russia had collapsed; Richard Layard was advising the Russian government and he and Charles Goodhart had perceived that there was a virtual vacuum in the financial skills that would be required by the new emerging Russia. They were instrumental in securing a substantial amount of money from the Foreign and Commonwealth Office Know-How Fund and from George Soros (who had been a student at the School at the same time as myself, but whose friendship I had foolishly failed to cultivate) to provide economic and financial education for promising young Russians. The intention was that in 1994–95 and each of the following three years there would be a six-month course for thirty participants (usually plus two from the Far East). They now asked me if I would take on responsibility for the academic side of these courses which would come under the Executive and Professional Education (EPE) unit of the School. The head of EPE was Anne Brown and a meeting with her further clarified what was involved. She and her group would arrange my trips to Moscow to select the participants, and deal with their visas, travel, accommodation, subsistence allowances, payments etc leaving me to deal with the whole of the academic side. A significant element in the programme was the Chancellor's Scheme which offered the students a period of attachment to British financial institutions after the end of the course. The key people responsible for all this non-academic side were Anne herself, Adam Austerfield, Janice Jordan who was Anne's secretary and personal assistant, and Tamara Lomidze, a junior assistant who was from Georgia, ex-USSR, and spoke Russian; they were to prove a very efficient team. Each of the four annual courses had the official title 'LSE Course in Banking and Finance'; but for convenience we usually referred to them as the 'Russian Courses' which, because their six months ran from October in one year to March in the next, in many documents were dated by their starting year as RC94 and so on. I was designated as Academic Director of these courses although I sometimes forgot and signed myself as Academic Tutor.

Preliminary planning of the academic side had already started before I had agreed to take on this responsibility but there were many details still to be arranged, in particular negotiating with colleagues to do the teaching. All the people I wanted to use were already heavily burdened, but a combination of sweet-talking and money brought agreement to take on the courses which were required. Then in July 1994 came my first visit to Moscow to interview sixty young Russian applicants and select the thirty to come on the course. On the flight to Moscow I had a window seat, which I always prefer, and several times I saw other aircraft; it reminded me that I was flying through one of the great battlefields of the Second World War, and how many had spotted other aircraft in much more dangerous circumstances. Arriving at Sheremetyevo 2, Moscow's main international airport, there were long slow queues at the passport desks, where eventually a hard-faced Russian looked suspiciously at me and my passport and reluctantly let me through. There was a car waiting for me and I was driven off to my hotel. On most of my visits this was the Baltschug Kempinski, which looked across Moscow River at St Basil's Cathedral and Red Square. There, outside the hotel, was a doorman in a pale grey frock coat, two guards in uniform each with a sub-machine gun, and in the foyer two rather heavily-built and watchful men with bulges under their jackets.

Interviewing in Moscow

I now had to contact the British Council who were acting as the School's agent in Moscow for the Russian Courses. It was they who did the advertising, received the applications, and did the preliminary sifting to produce the sixty candidates whom I was to interview in one of their committee rooms. Then for the next week or more I made my way each morning to the British Council offices, sometimes by the Metro but usually walking. At the interviews I was normally supported by two or three other people who had some interest in the course; at different times there was one from the Soros Foundation (which was partly funding the course) and one or two from other organisations concerned with financial education in Russia – one from an accounting institution with a growing number of trainees in Russia and one a publisher of financial textbooks. I was in favour of having them there to see the selection process but, not surprisingly, they had no experience in this kind of interviewing, and although I encouraged them to ask questions and shared with them my opinion of each candidate, in the end the interviewing and selection were left almost entirely to me.

The interviews were all conducted in English which allowed us to judge whether the applicants had an adequate grasp of the language, which most of them did and several proved to be fluent. Many of the applicants had science backgrounds and several had worked in military research institutes. My scraps of knowledge of science together with gently interested questioning led them to explain the work they had been doing, and from there to open up further and give me some idea of their general quality and responsiveness. A few topics that emerged remain in my memory; one girl explained that she had been doing dynamic analysis of explosions. Another had been dealing with attractor theory to explain the meandering of rivers, and there was a colonel from the KGB who at the KGB 'university' had achieved an A+ grade in the paper on Weapons of Mass Destruction. His Turkish was graded as perfect and he claimed in the interview that one of his ultimate ambitions was to do a PhD on the comparative structure of Turkish and the major European languages. My faint memory that Turkish was an agglutinative language helped things along. Altogether I enjoyed the interviewing and our last day would be devoted to a review of all the provisional decisions and then the final selection of the successful candidates. Over the four courses we interviewed 240 candidates and selected 120.

Around Central Moscow

The Baltschug was very well placed for walking round central Moscow which I soon came to know quite well. In the evenings and at weekends I visited many of Moscow's attractions. I walked across Red Square and visited the Kremlin; it was exhilarating to find myself so close to the heart of what had once been one of the world's most brutal and secretive regimes. Once as I walked along the path round the Kremlin gardens I was surprised to come across a Russian in uniform who had on his fist a very large hawk. Later enquiry revealed that the Moscow crows had taken to sliding down the golden domes of the cathedrals in the Kremlin and scratching them; this hawk was Moscow's ultimate crow-deterrent. On the other side of Red Square from the Kremlin was the massive GUM store, already blossoming out with boutiques selling Western luxury goods and in some cases flaunting advertisements for them at Lenin's tomb across Red Square. Further on, round the corner of the Kremlin, was the Russian War Memorial, all at ground level and lacking in grandeur, but with its central perpetual flame a powerful focus of remembrance of the Soviet Union's horrific losses in the Second World War. At weekends newly married young couples, the brides in white wedding dresses, congregated there to be photographed in front of the War Memorial. Many then went on to the Sparrow Hills overlooking Moscow where I saw these couples being toasted by their friends and the brides being photographed mounted on the docile horses kept there for the purpose, their new husbands holding the horses' heads. It was all very simple and good humoured.

Beyond Red Square was Tverskaya Ulitsa, a wide street in which was the Intourist Hotel, with a poor reputation as a hotel but with a public foyer where I could have a cup of coffee and watch a corner of Russian hotel life go on around me; in an alcove there was a television set on which I was once able to watch some of Wimbledon. The street outside revealed more fashion-consciousness than elsewhere in Moscow; one year it was full of elegant young women all wearing similar palest fawn floaty summer dresses. Up against the hotel in what appeared to be a large conservatory was a pizza restaurant where I often had supper in the evening, as it was more interesting and much cheaper than eating at the Baltschug. Turning right after leaving Red Square one came to the Bolshoi. On my first visit to Moscow I was fortunate in meeting up with Amos Witztum, who spoke Russian and whom I often used to see round the School; he was very helpful in knowing where in Moscow one could buy such simple Western things as aspirin or sticking plaster, and how to buy tickets from an 'official' ticket tout when we went to one of the Bolshoi's ballets together. Further on were the contrasting Detsky Mir – Children's World – an enormous toy shop, but also the Lubyanka, headquarters of the OGPU/NKVD/KGB. I walked slowly round the Lubyanka in memory of the thousands who had been tortured and murdered in its cellars. Behind it was the KGB Museum and I tried to visit it, but was refused entry by one of the guards. He then had second thoughts and asked me 'KGB?' Since I was wearing a business suit and must have looked as Western as possible, that he might think that I could be a member of the KGB gave me cause for thought. I later learnt that the Museum took only group tours and I went on one of these. It was conducted in a most sanitised way by two suave and civilised KGB officers who spoke perfect English and explained that documents forged in the West were often given away by the staples they used. I asked a few pointed questions and later wished I had asked more, and more pointed, ones.

A few streets from the hotel and away from Red Square was a park, long but not very broad, with a wide central path running its length and at the far end a fountain which blew plumes of water high in the air. Beyond that was a large and rather grim block of flats, conveniently just across the Moscow river from the Kremlin, where many of the top Soviet apparatchiks had lived. On its wall there were a number of memorial plaques, most of them probably post-Stalin. This was certainly so with the plaque to Marshal Tukachevsky, the head of the Russian army who was executed by Stalin during the great purges of 1938–39. Halfway along this park was a statue of a Russian painter named Repin and from this statue it was only a short distance over the Moscow Canal footbridge to the Tretyakov Gallery with its large collection of Russian paintings. Entering the Gallery was easy but the multitude of rooms made it less easy to find the way out. There I saw groups of hapless army conscripts being introduced to their artistic heritage and being thoroughly bored by it. Just past the gallery there was a door in a wall which revealed a very small café where I sometimes had a cup of coffee; by my last visit it had expanded and outgrown the intimate character which to me had been its main attraction. Not far away was an Irish Bar, filled each evening with Englishmen trying to brighten up their time in Moscow. Further away was the Pushkin Museum which I visited on many occasions; on one visit there was an exhibition of the treasures discovered at Troy by Schliemann. The gold necklaces and beads attracted most attention, but to me much more interesting were the half-dozen curved and decorated 'batons' carved from very hard stone and of unknown significance. I have often seen the photo of Schliemann's wife Sophie wearing some of the gold ornaments, but I had never seen any reference to these batons. I liked the Pushkin Museum with its collection of paintings and its small but interesting Ancient Egyptian collection, the whole thing being on a much more humane scale than the enormous Hermitage in St Petersburg. Not far from the Pushkin there was supposed to be the (Moscow)

Lenin Museum which had a reproduction of Karl Marx's study when he lived in Soho in London. My enquiries met with evasion, and I was finally told that the museum had been closed and dismantled.

In Moscow the larger local food shops still used the Soviet system of choosing your goods, queueing for a docket for these goods, queueing with the docket to pay, and then queueing again to collect the goods. But in a number of places there were groups of market stalls selling foodstuffs, particularly fruit (at one time they overflowed with bananas) and large kiosks with windows crammed with drink and sweets and just a small opening where the shopkeeper would serve you. During my visits I was very conscious of run-down central areas already being improved and property development going ahead, sometimes on a very large scale. Just behind the Baltschug there was even a development being managed by an Italian firm from Udine – to me a curious echo from the past because this was the very small town where some of the 7th Hussars had ended up when the fighting in Italy ended. And there was abundant evidence of the loosening of the bonds of the Soviet past; not far from the Russian War Memorial there appeared a small park with a narrow winding lake scattered with statues of characters from Russian fairy tales; out of fashion were such things as the heroic statues of Lenin and Stalin, as well as those of such people as Stakhanov, the unbelievably productive Russian miner, and other characters from the Soviet era's propaganda fairy tales. Further along the river there also appeared a large statue of Peter the Great in a sailing ship; and across Red Square I once saw a crowd of soldiers emerging from a parade, at their centre some senior officers together with priests of the Russian Orthodox Church. Upriver towards the Pushkin Museum the Cathedral of Christ the Saviour, blown up by Stalin, had been rebuilt with its onion domes clothed in gold allegedly provided by the Moscow crime bosses; but they did not compare well with the Kremlin domes, these new ones having a more sagging shape and darker, duller gold.

Outside Moscow

My experience of Russia on these visits was concentrated on central Moscow and I only made two excursions outside the city. The first was a one-day cultural tour to Pushkin's house and museum, led by a Russian who was obsessed with the poet and his works. But I was able to see the unexciting town of Tver and various rather dismal villages and roadside wooden hovels. The other was a trip I made with a very pleasant chap on the cultural side of the British Embassy; he met me at the airport on one trip and it was wonderful to be ushered by him out of the queue and smoothly through the diplomatic channel to his waiting car. Later he took me to visit one of the fortified monastries outside Moscow; there on his advice I crossed myself (the only time I had ever done this) as we entered the church where a service was in progress. Inside I stood behind a small and crumpled old woman; she looked so downtrodden that I took her hand as we went out and slipped some money into it – perhaps equivalent to fifty pence; she took it but did not look at it or turn round. Outside I felt a warm glow of having done a very small good deed. As always, the male voices were impressive and as the service ended two doors opened behind the altar to reveal a very brief vision of gold and light, evidently a promise to the congregation of what awaited them in heaven. On this trip we also visited a Russian country house of the kind which in Britain would be looked after by the National Trust. There we were warned to take care in the grounds as there were ticks and Lyme disease around. Later he invited me to spend an afternoon at the Embassy dacha with himself and his family. There I met his mother, a keen gardener with whom I had much interesting conversation. I also met the Russian mosquito, much larger and hungrier than the British variety but rather slow and quite easy to swat. My companion from the Embassy was a most helpful guide and he made this visit to Moscow particularly enjoyable. The time came to return to London and it was back to Sheremetyevo 2 by car, past the rickety wooden houses and people selling goods by the roadside – all sorts of things from electric cables to sacks of goodness knows what – and past the memorial marking the point closest to Moscow reached by the German armies in December 1941. There were the usual security checks at the airport, and at one of these a woman security officer asked me something which I could not understand and I replied that I did not speak Russian; she looked at me coldly and said 'I was speaking English.' Although I very much enjoyed my visits to Moscow I always felt a sense of relief when I was safely through the various security checks and on the plane home.

Teaching Russians

During all my years of teaching at the School I can recall only one or two minor hitches in the allocation of teaching rooms and the provision of class registers. For the Russian Courses the academic administration had to be of the same high standard and with the number of teachers involved this required quite a lot of organising, consulting, negotiating and confirming. The courses covered basic economics and accounting, for which we could draw on existing LSE courses, though sometimes with our own classes, and then new courses in corporate finance (John Board), banking and financial institutions (myself), central banking (Charles Goodhart), securities markets (Chris Thomas, from London Guildhall University) and weekly seminars which I chaired and for which I had to organise the speakers. Each year the academic planning was completed in the period of calm while we awaited the arrival of our thirty Russians, a few days before term began in October. When they arrived Anne Brown and her team, fully prepared, would swing into action, collecting them from the airport, checking them, briefing them and placing them in their halls of residence, as well as dealing with the multiplicity of minor questions and problems that arose (on one occasion discovering that one hall had no bedding available for half a dozen of the new arrivals, and having to go out and buy it). Next day I had a meeting with them to explain the course arrangements and to hand out the timetable for the first week; each Friday from then on they, and each of their teachers, would get a timetable for the following week. Next they were given a tour of the School by some of our undergraduates and shown the rooms where their courses would be held; everything was then ready for the teaching to begin on the following Monday. By then each teacher would have received a mosaic with photos and names of all the students. One year some wag added to the mosaic a photo of Adam Austerfield, touched up to look like Hitler and with the name Austerblitz; the students enjoyed this touch of irreverence.

I enjoyed teaching the Russians; they were keen and attentive students, clearly aware of their good fortune in coming on the course, with the likelihood of very good career opportunities afterwards. I saw them several times each week in my own lectures and classes and in seminars; at the end of these teaching sessions some would come up to me with a whole range of questions and comments which allowed me to get some idea of how the course in general was going. In addition I saw many of the other teachers around the School and they too kept me informed. This feedback from both students and teachers, and careful progressing during the course to ensure that the academic side ran smoothly, allowed me to see where a few helpful adjustments could be made to the current course, but more particularly where changes could usefully be made to the course in the following year. One improvement was the increase in the number of seminars, some given by the School's own experts, for example on Russian economic history, but most given by experienced practitioners from the City on such subjects as lending assessment by banks, trade finance, investment banking and debt recovery. I chaired all these seminars and was impressed by the standard of presentation and expertise.

I enjoyed organising the academic side of the Russian Courses but at one stage my duties expanded in a very unexpected way. For RC94, the first of the courses, the teaching rooms we used were organised by the School's administration as for any other teaching, which meant that we used a variety of rooms. Then suddenly I was told that the Russian Courses were to be allocated rooms of their own, or rather a very large room, on the fifth floor of the Robbins Building – the Library – which I was invited to divide up and furnish to suit these courses. In a place like the School, where space was always scarce, and to me, who in the past had urged improvements in teaching rooms and had produced the specification for them, this was almost a miracle. Then much measuring and squared paper with cardboard cut-outs showing chairs and tables to scale, much rearranging and checking, and there finally emerged plans for a teaching suite consisting of a lecture room with chairs and tables for thirty two, a classroom which would take twenty, a common room area and a very small room for the course director. All this was approved by the School's building officer. The two teaching rooms were to be equipped according to the specification I had set out, and the Committee on Accommodation had approved, some five years earlier. Then to the furnishing officer who had catalogues of furniture, furnishing fabrics and carpets; I chose light beech tables, matching chairs upholstered in dusky pink fabric and dusky pink carpets, and these were all ordered. Then work started on the conversion and promptly came to a halt; they had discovered asbestos in the roof and specialist asbestos removers in space suits had to be brought in to remove it. After what seemed an interminable delay, work on the conversion started again and

461

then suddenly it was finished, the carpets and furniture were installed and our Russian Course could begin to use our new teaching suite consisting of rooms R.505a, b, c and d. These were probably the only rooms in the School designed by a teacher, for teaching, and conforming to the approved specification for teaching rooms. They were warm and welcoming, and fulfilled their purpose admirably; they were the best teaching accommodation I had ever used in all my years at the School. In the common room area there were some easy chairs, a coffee machine, a notice board with its own copy of the timetable and other notices and a 'good delivery' shelf (taken from the concept in some financial and commodity markets): items placed there were deemed to have been delivered to the addressee. This placed responsibility for checking out his mail firmly on the addressee. An unforeseen facility was an emergency exit door opening onto the rest of the large flat roof of the Robbins Building, where in good weather we could go out into the sunshine and enjoy the local roofscape and a more distant vista towards the City. Several unexpected things emerged during the Russian Courses. The most surprising one was that nearly half of the students had never taken written exams and a further third had taken ten per cent or less of their exams in written form, so that altogether some eighty per cent of them had effectively no experience of our standard type of invigilated, written exams with an unseen question paper and anonymous scripts for marking. Some of our students were already using the Language Laboratory but this discovery led me to lay on additional classes in written English and a programme of take-home tests to be done alone under broadly examination conditions to get them used to our system. Some of the students told us that their exams had all been vivas where the candidate would choose two face-down cards at the start; on the face of each card was a question and after a pause for thought they would be called in for their viva exam on just these two questions. To us it seemed a strange and unreliable method of judging students' performance. Some of our women students emphasised, not entirely jokingly, how important it was for them to look their best and to wear short skirts at these vivas.

I emphasised to the students at the start that it was to their advantage to immerse themselves in English and try to avoid falling back into Russian amongst themselves. However the cohesiveness of the group and the relief of using their native language proved too great. Indeed, although their comprehension of spoken English clearly improved greatly during the course, I felt that for some their spoken English was no better than when I interviewed them in Moscow, and in some ways was worse. I felt that they were not mixing enough with other students and to this extent were missing out on the 'LSE experience' which several of us felt was a desirable feature of their time at the School. As the course drew to a close there were exams to be organised: question papers, random numbering of candidates and their places (which had to be well spaced), answer books and invigilators; and at the end of the exam the collection of answer books, distribution to markers, collection of marks and the final classification of the results. All the markers used our own familiar system of marking with a pass mark of 34; I felt that to outsiders this would look unnaturally low, so that these marks were rescaled to a more normal pass mark of 50 on student transcripts. Unlike our own system these marks were then added up over all papers and the top ten per cent or so were awarded our Certificate in Banking and Finance with Merit, most were awarded the Certificate and the bottom group with poor performance in one or two papers were simply said to have attended the Course. By now those on the Chancellor's Scheme would know the financial institution they would be placed with, and we conducted a detailed feedback exercise to gauge their opinions on all aspects of the course. Then at last there was our final meeting; with a few well-chosen words the presiding figure (on one occasion it was Richard Layard, who with Charles Goodhart had been instrumental in starting these courses) would present the certificates, richly embossed with the School's coat of arms. At this point one of the groups then presented me with a tie patterned after a page of the *Financial Times*, which as a gesture of thanks I promptly put on, to warm applause. Then with much mutual congratulation and promises that they would keep in touch with each other, the course ended. Since the Russian Courses were being financed by the Foreign and Commonwealth Office (FCO) Know-How Fund and by George Soros, after each one I wrote a full final report to give them the confidence that their money had been well spent. In fact the FCO at one stage asked two outside economists to give an unbiassed judgement on one course; I knew nothing about this, but we apparently emerged from it with credit. In September 1995 Anne Brown and I had a short visit to Moscow to meet the students from the first of these courses, RC94, and to get further feedback on the value of the course. We met them at a reception, together with other people of local influence, and the feedback was overwhelmingly positive.

Epilogue

The intention had been to have four or even more, of these Russian Courses with the finance starting to come in part from Russian banks, who were regarded as the immediate beneficiaries of these courses. In September 1996 Christine Challis, the School Secretary, together with myself and Adam Austerfield, went on a fund-raising mission to banks first in St Petersburg and then in Moscow. It soon became clear that Russian banks were out to make money here and now, and that building up their human resources and looking forward to management succession was at the very bottom of their agenda; clearly they were not going to provide any funding for these courses. And in Moscow we saw that Russian banking had a character of its own; in one bank you entered by going one at a time through a narrow door into a very confined chamber; that door closed behind you and only then did another one open in front, allowing you into a lobby; there facing you was a table with a shallow bowl on it with the notice: 'Leave your guns here'. Adam reminded me of a further episode; we were talking to a senior figure in another bank and I put to him that suppose their boss (the proper word at that time) were to be run over by a bus and killed, what were they doing about management succession? His answer missed the point but was revealing: 'Ho! Ho! he could not be run over by a bus, he goes everywhere in an armoured limousine with armed guards in front and behind.'

We also visited some universities and institutes to see if they would be willing to pay for places on the course for their staff. Perhaps the most striking feature in St Petersburg was the downtrodden state of the university, which had no money for even, basic maintenance and barely enough for heating, let alone any to pay for places on our courses; and although less downtrodden, the same was true of the universities and institutes we contacted in Moscow.

In St Petersburg we stayed in the Grand Hotel which was very comfortable, although there was bottled water in the bathrooms with a warning that the local water was too dangerous even for cleaning your teeth. Food at the hotel was expensive and we usually ate at a Chinese restaurant just along the street. We were in St Petersburg for a weekend which allowed us a few visits. One was to the Hermitage – an enormous and impressive collection, including a vast imperial reception hall, though I preferred a charming columned entresol, delicately decorated in white and gold. Another was to a concert of what I suppose was avant garde music – tuneless and aggressively applauded by intellectuals with straggly beards. Christine and I took a tour round the St Petersburg canals and we all went to a chilly but enjoyable evening display of fireworks over the river Neva. On my own I walked past the cruiser *Aurora* – famed for its role in the Revolution – to the Lenin Museum; in its entrance hall was a heroic stained-glass window of Lenin, but with the end of Communism there was no other vestige of him. His museum had been transformed into the Museum of Russian Political History, filled with photos of bearded nineteenth-century ministers and town councillors. The only people I saw in there were the grim and unwelcoming women attendants in each room. As I was entering, a mother and young child were emerging, and as I was emerging another mother and young child were entering. It was unbelievably dull and I could only suppose that these children were being taken there as a punishment.

Then there was our flight to Moscow. Anne Brown had taken care to book us on an airline which used Western aircraft maintained by British Airways engineers. Needless to say something went wrong and instead we found ourselves in a Russian aircraft, apparently a converted light bomber, its interior narrow, grubby, with holes in its carpets and some seats which had become detached from the floor. When we arrived at Moscow it seemed to me that we were going to crash short of the runway, but the plane just managed to reach it; we learned later that the pilot had to land in this way as there was no reverse thrust and he needed every inch of runway to slow down.

We all three got on very well and had much agreeable conversation during our visit, but this and other fund-raising efforts were in vain. There was simply not enough money to finance the intended fourth Russian Course, but only enough to run it as a six-week summer course which was then held in August–September 1997, RC96 having finished in March. The originally planned six-month RC97 had already been advertised in Russia and had attracted a shortlist of some 60 applicants. These were now all informed that the course had been changed, but virtually all still wished to apply and these I duly interviewed in Moscow, selecting 31 who came on the course. The shorter time for this course led to large changes in the content (in particular more corporate finance) and a change in the teaching structure. The course produced favourable opinions in the feedback exercise, although the students found the second half rather a strain.

Looking back over the Russian Courses, particularly the first three, I very much enjoyed managing the academic side and had a certain pride and relief that each one had gone off without a hitch. Meeting each group at their interviews in Moscow, teaching them three times a week during the course, encouraging them through their (unfamiliar) exams and being present at the final award of their certificates, sharing their pleasure and sense of achievement, all of this gave me a most rewarding sense of constructive involvement with these young Russians. This led me to donate my copies of the *Economic Journal* to the International College of Economics and Finance in Moscow which has been very short of such journals; these are regularly taken to Moscow by Richard Jackman who is the School's representative on its Management Committee.

At the end of the last Russian Course there was a final irony. Our teaching suite was the only set of rooms in the School designed by a teacher for teaching, and conforming to the Specification for Teaching Rooms which I had produced, and the Accommodation Committee had adopted, in 1989. This suite had proved highly satisfactory for teaching but now, after only two years, it was to be handed over to a research unit: the Centre for the Analysis of Social Exclusion (CASE) under John Hills (with whom, despite this takeover, I had some interesting and friendly conversation). But further change was to come; in 2000–01 the Robbins Building which contained the Library was remodelled. The whole of what had been our Teaching Suite was swept away and the Robbins Building was given an entirely new, much more extensive, and very impressive fifth floor devoted to research and occupied by CASE and the Suntory-Toyota Centre (STICERD).

A Central Asian Problem

At the same time as one of the courses was being held for the Russians, a quite separate small group from ex-Soviet Central Asian states, some six men and one woman, came to the School for a six-month course organised by the School's Executive and Professional Education section (EPE) who also organised the Russian Courses. I had no responsibility for this group and had only seen them briefly at one of the receptions. When they came the group had little English, but they all spoke Russian so that a main link with them was through Tamara Lomidze, the junior member of Anne Brown's management team. One day the woman in the group came to Tamara, the only person she could really communicate with, in deep distress. She said that the men on the course were bullying her, telling her that as a woman she should sit at the back of the class, keep quiet and not ask questions. Tamara immediately reported this to me. Such a problem had never arisen in all my time at the School and clearly something had to be done about it and quickly. I felt that there was no alternative but to take action myself. With Tamara I went straight up to our teaching suite where the group were in the classroom with the woman sitting pathetically at the back. I asked them if what I had heard was true; sullen silence was answer enough, and I then launched into a scathing attack on their behaviour; I am afraid they may have missed the finer points of my invective but I made sure that they could not mistake my anger. I finally demanded that they should each stand up in turn, apologise and say that they would never behave in this way again. Very reluctantly, one after another they did so, but one refused. I threatened that if he did not do as I demanded I would have him removed from the course and sent home. I was getting near the door to carry out my threat when he finally rose with black looks and apologised. With one last demand that this should never occur again I left the room with Tamara behind me, looking rather shaken by the whole highly charged episode. At least the woman now knew that she had Tamara to go to and that I would be firmly on her side. This left the question of what to do next. Nobody else knew about the whole episode; the men had not been humiliated in front of any of their regular teachers and it seemed to me better for relations all round to leave it at that. As far as I was concerned the matter was allowed to fade away – provided they never behaved like that again.

Courses for Indians

Even while the current Russian Course was still running, Anne Brown was in the process of arranging some courses at the School for Indians. These courses were connected with the fiftieth anniversary of Indian independence and the first of them was the British Chevening Scholarships Programme for Young Indian Bankers ('Chevening', from the official country residence of the Foreign Secretary, being the label given by the FCO which was financing the course). It was a six week course for twelve participants and would be held from the end of April to early in June, between the Russian Course RC96 ending in March 1997 and the next Russian Course then planned to start in October. I had agreed to take on responsibility for the academic side of this course, which Anne Brown hoped would be the first of many. In March 1997, to give it a good send-off, she and I and Crispin Lyden-Cowan flew to India for a week to publicise the course, to persuade a number of influential Indians of its importance and to meet the scholars who would be coming. We had a daylight flight to New Delhi and from my window seat I watched the fawn and arid deserts of the Middle East drifting past for hours; on the flight I met Amartya Sen whom I had known at the School in the 1970s. In New Delhi we attended various receptions and Anne and Crispin drummed up interest in our courses and produced press releases. We were taken on some tours of the city, visiting a Hindu temple, seeing the Red Fort and driving through the incredibly spacious New City, but we were dissuaded from entering the Old City which harboured a generous selection of diseases. Our hotel was very good and its restaurants, where we mostly ate, were also good; but I could not help noticing groups of aircrew all eating the same food. Given the various tummy bugs in India this did not seem a good idea, and reminded me of an incident that happened to my friend Christian Williams. After a business meeting in Constantinople he and a few others were offered a flight home in a private jet. A short while after take-off the pilot came back into the cabin to talk to his passengers, only to collapse vomiting on the floor. His passengers looked at him in pale-faced consternation until they were assured that there was a second pilot up front; what if they had then been told that the two pilots had eaten together before the flight? But our own flight home was uneventful. It was a night flight and the great desert areas of the Middle East showed the merest scatter of lights, but on our starboard side we had a fine view of the comet Hale-Bopp.

This course for Young Indian Bankers went very well and for me it was an interesting change to teach people who already had quite a good practical knowledge of banking; but before this course finished it had become clear that the final Russian Course would now be only a six-week summer course, although I would still have to fly to Moscow to interview the candidates. But Anne Brown had another, and very different, Indian course coming up: the Chevening Gurukul Scholarships in Leadership and Excellence. This was a course for outstanding young Indian business men and women in their thirties, each with a proven record of success. (One of them was in the business of women's underwear, or as he delicately put it, 'Ladies' intimate apparel'.) Their course was very different from the previous ones; it combined short attachments to British businesses with an eight week programme from October 1997 to early January 1998 at the School for seminars on mainly business topics, together with some City visits. It seemed appropriate that for these participants Meghnad (Lord Desai) should be Academic Director while I agreed to be Academic Coordinator; but tacitly Meghnad and I agreed on a division of labour – he provided the status and I did the work. This consisted mainly of finding appropriate speakers for the quite heavy and wide-ranging programme of seminars, and chairing most of them.

For me 1997 had proved to be a busy year but a very satisfying one. However, the Indians on these courses had minds that moved quickly and this as well as habit led them to speak in a rapid, almost machine-gun-like, manner. All too often I found myself having to ask them to slow down or repeat what they had just said, and this tended to interrupt the flow of discussion and was not fair to the audience. It was this as much as anything that led me to review my future with these courses. I had greatly enjoyed all of my work for the School's Executive and Professional Education section: the organising, the teaching and the trips to Moscow. The administrators I had worked with – Anne Brown, Adam Austerfield and latterly Christine Challis, as well as a number of others – had all been very congenial and efficient; but, with much regret, I felt it was now time to retire from these courses.

Helping with Bankruptcy

The five years following my retirement had been largely spent in running courses for EPE. Another and very different activity arose from an article on bankruptcy written by Aghion, Hart and Moore (AHM). As I explain

469

in Chapter 28 below, I had some direct concern with commercial bankruptcy. In addition a close friend had been looking at a bankrupt firm with the thought of purchasing it and in the process getting a close-up and disturbing view of how a bankrupt firm was treated; the two of us had long discussions about the practical aspects of bankruptcy and the cavalier way in which the assets of bankrupt firms were often handled. In trying to learn more I even contrived an invitation to a short play put on by one of the larger insolvency firms to illustrate their work; it was interesting and instructive – and quite entertaining. All of this gave me a real interest in AHM's article, which although presented with much technicality, had at its heart what I regarded as important suggestions for the improvement of bankruptcy procedure in Britain. Although I never met Aghion, I discussed the article with John Moore, who was at the School, and with Oliver Hart who had been at the School in the early 1980s before he went to Harvard; he had attended the Money Workshop and was still an occasional visitor to the School. All I could do was express my support for their work and provide some useful contacts to help it forward. The first of these was Philip Wood, a friend from Guildford with whom I sometimes travelled on the train; he was a lawyer with Allen & Overy in the City and an authority on international financial law. I invited him to lunch at the School on 2 March 1993 for a first meeting with Oliver and John and afterwards he wrote them what I thought was a brilliant two-page letter setting out his insights into bankruptcy and its problems, with a copy to me. A few weeks later I had another lunch with Oliver. Then in May Philip invited Oliver, John and myself to a lecture with the title 'Bankruptcy in 156 Jurisdictions' which he was giving to the Master's degree insolvency course at the Institute of Advanced Legal Studies in Russell Square. The three of us attended it and afterwards retired with him to the bar of the Russell Hotel nearby for further discussion. In July John wrote to me (and I am sure many others) enclosing a write-up of the AHM work focussing upon the UK, and designed to be easily understood, asking for any suggestions on how it might be helped to reach a wider audience. I wanted to help and was able to provide further contacts in the Bank of England and the Treasury. One result was that I received from the Insolvency Service a consultative document which included the AHM proposals and asked for my comments. My reply on 18 January 1994 was as follows:

The Insolvency Act 1986 – CVAs and AOs

Thank you for sending me the above consultative document. I wish to restrict my comments here to the proposal put forward in Appendix E by Aghion/Hart/Moore.

In my view these proposals represent a quite new and carefully structured approach to bankruptcy which deserves careful consideration. However, the proposals do require a very different stance from the current one, and my fear is that few of the practitioners in the field will have had the time or the natural inclination to go into them as thoroughly as they deserve and instead will find it easier to ignore or dismiss them. What is needed is a further stage of development which would require a meeting of both practitioners and academics to put a range of representative real-life cases through the proposed procedure; this would educate both sides and would allow the practitioners to make much more soundly based judgements upon the proposals.

I am greatly struck by the way in which investment in development and testing is lavished upon the most trivial of consumer goods and upon obscure corners of research in the natural sciences. Here we have bankruptcy, involving hundreds of millions worth of resources and of correspondingly great importance to the economy; it would be singularly unfortunate if such a relevant and promising proposal were to be dismissed before a necessary further stage of development has been undertaken.

The final stage of my efforts to help led to a letter dated 11 October 1994 from the Treasury:

Insolvency Reform

Thank you for your letter of 18 September. Your support and encouragement is appreciated.

I have copied your reply to Professor John Moore and Professor Oliver Hart.

Regrettably, I do not have a copy of my letter but its general drift can be seen from the Treasury's response. At this point there was really nothing more that I could do to further the AHM proposals, which in my view did not in the end have the influence on bankruptcy procedure that they deserved. I felt that AHM's work was an example of top theoreticians working fruitfully on a significant problem in the real world.

Mondays at the School

Although time has passed alarmingly quickly, my links with the School continue. For many years I have been a regular attender at Charles Goodhart's Financial Regulation Seminar which meets at 17.45 to 19.15 hours on several Mondays each term and there I see familiar faces, one of them Geoffrey Wood (of the Cass Business School), who for many years was an excellent external Examiner for our Monetary Systems paper. On our way home after the seminar we discuss its proceedings as we walk over Waterloo Bridge together, finding much to agree upon, and on a clear winter evening both enjoying the striking array of lights from the City to Canary Wharf which is revealed by the curve of the Thames. This late timing of the Seminar is to allow people from the City to attend, but to me it has another advantage. I travel up to Waterloo on a late morning (and low cost) train to arrive at the School around midday; then in the Senior Dining Room it is all too evident that time has moved on; amongst all the new faces there are now only a few familiar ones to have lunch with. But there are usually some – particularly Basil Yamey, and recently I had a pleasant lunch with him, Charles Goodhart and Ken Minogue, while I often see Ray Richardson around. I then have an afternoon free before the seminar and this allows me to visit a museum or an art gallery, or to have some time in the Library to clarify some details in the course of writing this book. If I go to the Royal Academy I also visit Fortnum & Mason on the other side of Piccadilly, which is like an on-going exhibition of high living. To me the ground floor is now a death trap of sugary pleasures, but the delicatessen is full of interesting things, particularly an intriguing range of cheeses. On the other floors are many other upmarket delights; one that recently caught my eye was a small display of individual Victorian teacups and saucers in charming designs at astonishingly high prices. I find it all rather stimulating, although I have no desire to join in as a purchaser. This was not so in the distant past, when Fortnum's marron cakes were a great attraction. And on one occasion I went in there to buy – of all humble things – a tin of Heinz Vegetable Soup; there were very few customers around and the floorwalker, in morning dress, intercepted me helpfully; I explained my need, he led me to the counter, summoned an assistant, told him what I wanted, and when it arrived carried it in a bag to the exit, handed it to me and inclined his head politely as I left. These were his duties as a floorwalker and he took them seriously; equally seriously I appreciated his attentiveness, thanked him, and departed in a faint glow of well-being.

On one Monday it occurred to me that I had last visited St Paul's Cathedral – only a moderate walk away from the School – when I was a child, so I visited it on one of my afternoons before the seminar. By chance Harrow School was holding a choir practice before an evening performance and their fine singing greatly enhanced my enjoyment of the visit. Westminster Abbey I had also neglected and when a little later I went there on a Monday afternoon visit, Westminster School was holding a choir practice, again a wonderful accompaniment to my visit. Toni and I both know Chichester Cathedral well, but we happened to visit it again recently and, to our pleasurable surprise, John Rutter, the London Philharmonic and a choir were holding a rehearsal. In all, three visits made memorable by the unexpected pleasure of fine choral music.

Although my diary-keeping had now become very lax, I do on occasion keep a fairly full account of the events of a single day:

Monday 21 February 2006

Up to the School for Charles Goodhart's Financial Regulation seminar this evening. Bumped into Christopher Foster in Senior Common Room, he had come for lunch with Julian le Grand but had arrived early, so we had quite a long and very interesting chat. We seem to agree on a wide range of things: the ineffectiveness of so much government activity; the totally disproportionate costs of the crash (!) programme of rail improvements after the death of a few people in a rail accident – compare value of human life saved in what is already one of the safest rail systems in the world; failure of economic aid to address the population problem and instead exacerbating it; desirability of nuclear power, and [*the unfortunate*]

473

breaking up of research group on dealing with high energy waste in the 90s for fear of environmentalists' views etc.

Lunch with Ken Minogue; recalled life at the School when we used to play table tennis after lunch and the generally more comfortable existence for us then. Joined by Nick Barr and Charles Goodhart; gave Nick my short memoir on Bill Phillips together with 1953 Summer School photo with Bill and myself. Talked about pension problems and all agreed on main lines of a solution: end means-tested state pension, raise retirement age and create safe small-savings media. Several other topics also. David de Meza came over and talked to me; he was once in one of my economics classes but is now back at the School and is bearded like Karl Marx, but very good-humoured. Mike Bromwich also came over and asked if I would like an invitation to Will Baxter's 100th birthday celebration in July; yes, I would. In coffee queue talked to Richard Jackman and gave him latest copy of *Economic Journal* to go to Moscow – he bought me a cup of coffee. Also there was Saul Estrin who is coming back to the School from the London Business School. In SCR read a review of book of Lytton Strachey's letters in *NY Review of Books*. Interesting; briefest mention of his book on French literature *Landmarks in French Literature* which am just finishing and which I regard as wonderfully well-written.

Then into Library to look at early copies of LSE *Calendar* to get some information for my memoir. Also looked at von Stackelberg's book and Alan Peacock's translation of it; looked at Gurley and Shaw also. Coffee in student refectory and then to Charles' seminar; reasonable attendance; several sceptical of his quantitative work on a metric for financial stability. I made several points. Interesting continuation afterwards over wine and crisps. Forrest Capie brought back my [*Bank of England*] diaries, as I shall have to transcribe them myself. Walked over bridge to Waterloo with Geoffrey Wood – windy and cold, then home to Guildford, met by Toni in the car.

A recent innovation at the School has been an annual meeting and lunch for retired members of staff, these have been organised by Kate Barker,

Secretary for the Senior Common Room Committee, with support from Celia Phillips and others, and are very pleasant occasions for meeting old colleagues. There I see Derek Diamond with whom I have discussed problems of town planning over the years (and in whose family villa in Spain we once spent a memorable summer holiday); Bob Pinker, who was a most sympathetic and helpful Pro-Director; also John Carrier and Jonathan Rosenhead whose political opinions I may not entirely share but with whom conversation proved most congenial, and Susan Dev whom I have known for many years. Amongst the administrators I have seen Mary Whitty and Janetta Futerman whose helpful good humour made it a pleasure to deal with them over many matters relating to students, and John Pike whose merits I have extolled elsewhere and who seems unchanged after twenty five years. Just being around the School means that I see other familiar faces: John Macve, once an undergraduate in the Monetary Group, Lucien Foldes, Julian Fulbrook, Ian Nish, Jan Stockdale and, when he is visiting from Madrid, Adam Austerfield. As my mind looks back I am conscious of many more names and faces, far more than I can mention here; to all of these I can only say that if they remember me, I will assuredly remember them and always with pleasure.

The Financial Regulation Seminar is now a major reason for my coming to the School. Its meetings and related conferences allow academics and practitioners to combine their insights and experience, and this helps to drive forward high-quality institutional research, not only on Financial Regulation but also on other aspects of banking and financial markets both in the UK and in other countries. With the financial world changing and my own intellectual capital eroding, I have to be increasingly an interested listener, although on occasion the recollection of some lesson from history, institutional detail or point of principle allows me to make a brief contribution. Attending the Seminar is an important part of the thread still linking me to the School and to the remaining colleagues whom I still see there. This thread is now thin but still very strong.

I came to the School as an undergraduate in October 1949, graduated in the Class of 1952 and was taken on to the teaching staff. Setting aside my two year secondment to the Bank of England, which, in my mind, never really separated me from the School, there I remained until my retirement in 1992. I continued teaching courses for a further five years, and then performed a few further minor duties; these, together with my many years of regular attendance at the Financial Regulation Seminar, my continuing use of the Senior Common Room and, in the last few years, my use also of the Library while writing this book, mean that in January 2009 I can reasonably feel that I am in my sixtieth year of connexion with the School, years which I can look back on as having been wonderfully stimulating, fulfilling and enjoyable.

26

Life at Home – on Our Own

More about Toni

This is a suitable place to say more about Toni – Antoinette Beatrix Alford née Stephenson. Her father, Robert William Lightfoot Stephenson, had been a diamond merchant before going out to Burma in a similar line of business. On one of his leaves in Britain he met and married Beatrice Malvine Richardson, a nurse at St George's Hospital (which has since moved upmarket to become the Lanesborough Hotel, overlooking Hyde Park Corner). Toni had a sister, Jacqueline, and a brother, Michael. Jacqueline lived partly in South Africa and partly in Britain; she died in 2002. Michael now lives in Spain but still keeps in touch. (What inspired my mother-in-law's name Malvine is not known – possibly the heroine in some novel – and although it is rare it does appear as a first name in various countries; it seems to be derived from St Malo in Brittany, whose fishermen first occupied what we call the Falkland Islands, giving them their French name Malouines and hence their Spanish name, Malvinas. I am afraid that it is only by chance that the name Malvine has recently been given to the access system for modern manuscripts and letters in European libraries.)

Robert Stephenson (usually called Rupert) died when Toni was only five and in due course her family moved to Bognor Regis; she attended Chichester High School for Girls before following in her mother's footsteps by training to be a nurse, in her case at the Middlesex Hospital in London. She then went out to Kenya as a nurse during the Mau Mau troubles, returning in 1958 to train as a midwife, a Queen's District Nurse and then as a Health Visitor. This training endowed her with a practical medical background, dismissive of mystical cures and fringe fads. Her first job as a health visitor was in an insalubrious quarter of Portsmouth and from this she was rescued by an unlikely white knight – one Roger Alford, Lecturer in Economics at the London School of Economics, who perceived that under this severely medical education and grim occupation lay a person of wit, charm and loving kindness whom he persuaded to marry him. She devoted herself to bringing up their three children and as these began to grow up she was able to become locally active in a number of good causes, starting with the National Association for the Welfare of Children in Hospital, and then Holiday Fun, which organised activities for children in the holidays. She became a member of the Wives Fellowship in which she has remained active ever since and was for several years a committee member and programme secretary of the Guildford Society. As her children became older she felt the need for a minor occupation and for several years took a part-time job as a doctor's receptionist for which she was quite unusually well qualified and which she enjoyed. For many years she was a member of the management committee of a nearby old people's home. On one occasion she received a desperate call for help from the matron – one very elderly resident had suddenly died in their telephone kiosk. Toni and the matron together had to get the poor old thing's body out of this cramped situation, into a wheelchair, squeezed into the small lift and back up to her room, always keeping a slightly guilty lookout to ensure that the other residents didn't notice anything; this was nothing exceptional for someone with Toni's nursing background. She is an active Conservative and supporter of our local church, Christchurch, helping to run regular group activities for elderly parishioners (many younger than herself) and serving coffee after some Sunday services. She is a member of our local branch of the National Association of Decorative and Fine Arts (NADFAS) and has now become a steward and guide conducting parties round Watts Gallery in nearby Compton. This she combines with running the home and looking after her white knight, now elderly but still active though showing rust in places.

Wit?

It is fortunate that Toni and I have a very similar sense of humour; it is somewhat cynical, and ironic in the sense of saying one thing but using intonation and body language to convey something different, often the very opposite of what is said. Our ironical exchanges (*pace* Roger Holmes' view of irony – having it both ways) are teasing and entirely without unkindness or intention to hurt. This is usually clear because the irony is ridiculously exaggerated, and we treat it as a way of producing what we regard as witty remarks or amusing exchanges; these are always followed by our appreciative laughter at what we feel to be our own wit. To illustrate this kind of irony using the written word is difficult, and this is why some have suggested that such badinage, however entertaining at the time, should be allowed to float away rather than attempt the difficult task of writing it down and simply killing it in the process. But it would be a pity to make no effort to share with others what has given us both so much amusement and pleasure. So risking banality and the lead balloon, here I shall try – but you have to remember that Toni's contributions are suffused with her charming and teasing manner.

I take as my starting point a cartoon which originally appeared in *Punch* February 1888 (but here considerably modified) which appealed to us both. A newly married couple are seated alone in a train compartment:

> He, solicitously: Are you quite comfortable?
> She: Yes, thank you.
> He: No draughts or lumpy springs?
> She: No.
> He: Change places.

In the Victorian world perhaps they did change places. In our world they would have burst into laughter, enjoying the unexpected ending and both knowing that he didn't mean it.

A similar example from home. Toni and myself (R) watching a TV advertisement making extravagant promises for some beauty product:

> Toni: I use that to keep my body looking soft and young.
> R: It's not working.

More generally:

> Toni, pathetically: I am just an ugly old woman.
> R: Darling, you are not *old*.

R: You married me for better or for worse.
Toni: Yes, but I didn't think the worse would be as bad as this.

Sometimes Toni tries sweetness on me:

Toni: Who's a bad boy? And who needs kisses to make him good again?

Toni, wheedling: I have a favour to ask you – you won't say no straight away will you?
R: Well, I shall think for a minute and then say no.

but not always:

Toni: Have you drunk that Yakult yet?
R (crossly): No.
Toni: I see the bad bacteria are getting the upper hand; now drink it up and become nice again.

Many of our witticisms are just one-liners and those I remember are all by Toni. On being asked what she was writing:

I am writing down all the things I don't like about you.

Some are just charmingly apt:

I feel all twangy and fit.

After a reception at which the champagne flowed:

I feel all frisky and uninhabited.

Others are excuses:

I don't need a bath, I'm all clean from yesterday.

Or regretful:

I am sorry I was nasty to you – but I did enjoy it so.

Looking in the mirror after a bath:

> A lump here and a sag there – I shall just have to die with my clothes on.

Or just observations:

> I'm only nasty to you when I am feeling ugly and unhappy.

Although our irony is well understood between us, sometimes it is unilaterally disarmed. On seeing me emerging dirty and bedraggled after some particularly messy gardening in the rain:

> Toni: You really do look a pustule ... but you are *my* pustule.

But not always; in similar circumstances:

> Toni: You look like an awful old tramp – go and look at yourself in the mirror and when you have recovered from the shock, comb your hair.

Just to balance things up, I have a formula for a very versatile and annoying kind of double-edged entendre, which allows a compliment to carry its own antidote:

> R: I think you're intelligent/a good cook/very pleasant/a good driver ... and I don't care what your friends say.

Toni also has a nice turn of phrase. About a country walk with a group of elderly friends:

> The stiles were difficult and walking sticks fell about all over the place.

Laughter and old age can collide:

> Toni: Don't make me laugh too much or I shall fall over.

R (looking in the mirror despondently): Even my eyebrows seem to have lost their vigour.

Toni: I am as fit as a fiddle – a little old worn-out fiddle, of course.

Some are suitable to be told only to other elderly married couples; Toni coming up against me lovingly:

There, I'll push up all close to where your genitals used to be.

The Daily Round

One difference between Toni and myself is that she is a lark and I am an owl. She has always risen early and gone to bed fairly early while I rise later and go to bed later – 3 a.m. has recently become my standard bedtime while writing this book and I get up at around 9 a.m. While we enjoy each other's company we each also enjoy having time on our own, and our lark/owl habits allow Toni to have two early-morning hours to herself, while I still find that life calms down as midnight approaches and in my study I can get on without interruption. Similarly when I go to seminars at the School Toni enjoys having most of a day on her own, and when she is out at meetings or at Watts Gallery I enjoy a period of solitude.

Our daily round is nothing exceptional. Our breakfasts are always separate, Toni having hers before I get up, and then for the rest of the day there is mild activity divided up by coffee at eleven, lunch at one, tea just after four and then supper and washing-up between seven and eight. Mention of washing-up brings to mind cutlery; when we were first married, Kellogs had an offer of 'Moderna' satin-finished stainless steel cutlery – excellent value at £1 a setting with one coupon from a packet of Cornflakes or All-Bran. There was a limit to the amounts of these products we could consume, but we had loyal and self-sacrificing friends who consumed on our behalf and gave us the coupons. (I never did like All-Bran which seemed to me like processed cardboard and for many years we have preferred linseed which has similar merits.) This arrangement allowed us (and my brother Michael) to acquire many place settings, some dozen in our case. We have remained loyal to our 'Moderna' cutlery as have several of our friends, and indeed we inherited Michael's place settings. A large amount of it must have been bought when we bought ours, but in my experience it seldom appears in those boxes of orphaned cutlery you see in jumble sales or car boot sales, implying that those who have it like it enough to keep it in the family.

We have a large Sainsbury's supermarket a short drive away and I quite often do some of the shopping; I enjoy seeing all its evidence of economic activity and this allows me to see and choose things which appeal to me. There is a market in Guildford on Friday and Saturday, mainly for greengroceries and I occasionally walk in to buy things there; over the years the quality of the produce in the market has improved. At weekends in the summer there is a large car boot sale every Sunday on the A3; I go there occasionally and have bought things from ginger jars to tools.

I quite often go to our local dump to dispose of some unwanted items, and I find it difficult not to notice some other person's discards which I would find useful, and this I have often managed to sneak into my car while the attention of the jealous guardians of Guildford's rubbish is turned elsewhere. I once saw a perfect desk chair (rotatable and with five-fold castors) standing by the pile of scrap metal; I asked the guardian in charge if I could have it – 'No, no, nothing is allowed to be taken off the dump, it's more than my job's worth...' I pointed out that the chair was perfect and that it was a terrible waste to destroy it, and asked if I could pay for it; same answer. After we had gone round this litany several times I gave him my ultimatum: if I can't take it or buy it, you turn your back and I shall steal it. After a brief pause he turned away still grumbling his instructions that nothing was to be taken off the dump. I popped the chair into the boot of my car and drove away feeling simultaneously guilty and exhilarated by my virtuous act of recycling. And it is not only the dump. Skips also often contain useful items – and they have no guardians; many useful things in my shed have come from skips.

A Life Less Sweet

Our main meals, lunch and supper, have always been simple and they now have a pattern: each day one is prepared for both of us by Toni, who is a very good cook, usually just a single dish out of her repertory of recipes.

The other meal is more flexible and do-it-yourself and this suits us both very well. For me these meals now have an additional significance.

A few years ago Toni began to worry about my cholesterol and urged me to have it tested at a mobile unit which at that time used to appear occasionally at the top of Guildford High Street. I dismissed her worries and refused to go for a test. When I got there the tests found that my cholesterol was OK but my blood sugar was high, over 20; I had late onset diabetes. I was given advice by my doctor and others, but I didn't find this particularly helpful because, as I now realise, so many doctors and dieticians tailor their advice to try and avoid scaring patients by emphasising the consequences of neglected diabetes, and to avoid urging a serious change in lifestyle which will discourage patients and lead them to give up making any effort at all.

In my view the result is that many diabetics do not really believe that diabetes (which initially can be symptomless) is really a nasty threat to their health. I feel that the professional pusillanimity of doctors (which is not present in the case of smoking) prevents them from giving straight information of the sort that I had to find out for myself. I decided that I would try to do without any tablets or injections for as long as possible, saving them up for when there might be no alternative, and relying instead upon diet and exercise. My starting point was that the danger was high blood sugar. A little searching around and some basic science made it clear that all carbohydrates (CH) end up as blood sugar, so the obvious answer was to keep down not just sugar itself – refined CH – but also all other CH: potatoes, bread, rice, pasta etc. This I soon found was the Atkins Diet, intended for slimming but also recognised as helpful in the management of diabetes. Being retired and living simply meant that I could follow the kind of diet that the professionals seemed reluctant even to mention to people whom they felt would find it too difficult to follow. What emerged was a regime which would certainly not suit everybody but which does suit me. It is based upon an electronic weighing scale, a copy of McCance and Widdowson's *The Composition of Foods* (fifth edition), careful reading of the labelling of foods, my own tables of the composition of our own usual foodstuffs copied from all of these in the form of a combined ready reckoner and daily record, meal by meal, of my consumption of (a) grams of carbohydrate and (b) the grams of sugar in that carbohydrate, the two denoted by CH/s. My daily target is no more than 60 grams of CH of which under 20 is sugars, which I denote by 60/20. It involves weighing many CH items at mealtimes but this is easy at home and after a while it becomes a habit and a way of life. The reward to me is that it is keeping my blood sugar down to a reasonable level, under 6. I have lost weight under this regime (Toni expresses concern for 'her diminishing boy' and says I look shrivelled). I weigh myself daily and so long as my weight is under 11 stone I am confident that my blood sugar is reasonably OK; I now check it with my blood test kit only once a fortnight or so for confirmation. This regime has led me to a high-protein diet but, to the eater, protein and fats are only limited substitutes for carbohydrate, so limited carbohydrate is not fully offset by eating more proteins and fats, with the result that calorie intake declines in total; this seems to be the basic mechanism of the loss of weight under the Atkins Diet. But I am conscious of frequently feeling slightly hungry and one needs the threat of diabetic complications to make one stick to the regime; living quietly at home makes this much easier. Incidentally, many professionals try to encourage diabetics like myself by telling them that occasional sugary treats are OK. I entirely disagree; I suspect the occasional will become more frequent and the whole seriousness of the effort will begin to drift away. It seems that for those who are healthy but just wish to lose weight, their strength of will is seldom sufficient since it lacks the reinforcing threat which faces diabetics. The final pillar of my regime is regular exercise – some active gardening and/or a brisk walk (thirty to forty-five minutes) each day except in the worst of weather. With my high-protein diet it is a good idea to drink plenty of fluids – 3 litres is my daily minimum; the question of alcohol does not arise since I have never touched it. In the end I can only say that my regime seems to suit me and for the moment I am surviving and my downhill progress does not seem unduly rapid. But I am always told that diabetes is a progressive condition and I shall have to wait and see.

Are all these outpourings an indication of hypochondria or egomania? Neither, I am just passing on the information which I had to ferret out for myself, it has been useful to me and it might be helpful to some of the increasing number of people who will suddenly find themselves with late onset, or Type 2, diabetes.

Relaxations

During lunch I look at the **TV** guide and mark one or two programmes, if any, that may be worth our watching that evening. After supper, snuggled comfortably on the sofa in the playroom we normally watch for a while then I complain about the programmes and Toni dozes off. What she really likes are genteel murder mysteries, with a minimum of blood, well filmed, focussed upon well-spoken people (no foul language, which we both greatly dislike) who live in period houses on the edge of charming villages; *Midsomer Murders* is her favourite series, followed by Morse, Sherlock Holmes and 'Agatha Poirot' (our composite title). In my closing years I am quite prepared to watch some of these with her; many of them are repeats but sufficiently unmemorable for us to have forgotten we have seen them before, perhaps one advantage of old age. I really prefer fact-based programmes: wildlife, science, archaeology and history. Toni's objection to some wildlife programmes is that they just show animals killing other animals; this is often true and reminds me of my mother's description of nature as a great blood machine, which Toni accepts but does not want to watch. David Attenborough's films are honourable exceptions to her objections. One programme that impressed us both was the first series of *Lonesome Dove*, an evocation of the dusty, undeveloped rough and tough old American West with no false glorification and no holds barred. We listen to the radio news at lunchtime, usually an arts programme at supper time, and we watch parts of the television news. I haven't been to the **Cinema** for years but Toni occasionally goes with a friend. The films that stick in my mind are ones we saw together many years ago, *Carmen Jones* and *Black Orpheus*, for example, both of which impressed us greatly at the time. Now we wait idly for films to filter through to television. I have never been a very keen on the **Theatre**, although we do go occasionally, and I have always found Shakespeare more appealing on the page than on the stage. There the actors seem to intrude between me and the text, and I particularly dislike the way in which they sometimes show their familiarity with the text by instant response ('SomersetMyLord') which I find a very annoying kind of Shake-speak.

Music does not play any large part in our lives. Toni has never really moved beyond her childhood exposure to the popular music of the 1940s, and is liable to desert the washing-up and burst into a performance of her very own dance routine when the radio plays some music with a beat or a 1940s hit long forgotten by the rest of the world. I have always been a casual listener, although I regularly tuned into Capital Radio late at night when I was doing rather mechanical statistical work on flow of funds. Now it is Classic FM, or some of the music I have stored most conveniently on my computer. This currently ranges from *Pearl of the Quarter* (Steely Dan), *No Woman No Cry* (Bob Marley) and *Killer Queen* (Queen) to *Dance of the Blessed Spirits* (Gluck), all twenty one *Songs of the Auvergne* (Canteloube) and many pieces by Handel and Schubert. The Eurovision Song Contest is one programme we watch each year with ghoulish glee at the songs (increasingly overshadowed by the excessive visual presentation), which we regard as the musical equivalent of a horror film – compulsive and repellent in equal measure. Something very odd happened in the 2007 contest; obviously Serbia got the wrong end of the stick and instead of a trashy song suitable for clubs or discos it won with a piece of music of operatic quality excellently sung by someone evidently chosen for her voice rather than her figure – Molitva, sung by Marija Serifovic. Since it was sung in Serbian I have no idea what it is about. But you need words for 'voice music' and we now have websites which give the lyrics of pop songs sung in English. They reveal the banality of the words and the oddity of some of the subjects even when the music is at the top of its class: for example, a retired terrorist (?) remembering the good old days and a mother feeling she should spend more time with her daughter (*Fernando* and *Slipping Through my Fingers*, both by ABBA). And some classical lyrics are sometimes even worse: *The Pearl Fishers* duet by Bizet is a case in point. Incidentally one of the two singers is named Nadir – an unusual example of self-criticism by the librettist?

Poetry plays an even less important part in my life than music, but there are certain poems which I like: Keats' *Ode to Autumn* (which I learnt at school) and Tennyson's *Crossing the Bar*. Some years ago I came across a paperback on the critical appreciation of poetry: *Close Readings* by A F Scott. I had never really read anything in this field before. The book is organised into themes – metrical structure, rhythm, imagery etc and as examples of these qualities it brings in a number of poems, either new to me or shown in a new light, and this I enjoyed. Recently I came across a poem by Les Murray, the first two verses of which appealed to me for their grim realism about Aids:

Aphrodite Street

So it's back to window shopping
on Aphrodite Street
for the apples are stacked and juicy
but some are death to eat

For just one generation
the plateglass turned to air
when you look for that generation
Half of it isn't there

It will be clear enough to any reader that I am neither a poet nor poetical by nature, but my mother – Doris Mary Alford – did have some talent in that direction. She had two books of verse published by the Fortune Press: *Snow upon the Hearth* (1966) and *The Kindling Light* (1968) as well as a self-published paperback of light verse, *Rhymes by Dorinda*. One of her poems in the first of these seems to me to have a touch of true poetry; it appears in different draft and final versions, with one of the latter being displayed for many years in the foyer of the Chichester Festival Theatre. Here I give the version I like best:

ON THE BUILDING of the CHICHESTER FESTIVAL THEATRE in OAKLANDS PARK, CHICHESTER, SUSSEX

Rise up – immortal Theatre from the soil
That Saints have trod and pilgrims' prayers have blest
Temple of mime and mirror of the muse, whose dome
Shall breast the drifting sky from sea to Down.

Here shall the actor strip his very soul
To clothe it in another's charactry
Here eloquence, like a flight of doves
Shall circle in the clear expectant air
And inspiration – reaching to the stars
Glean a rich harvest there.

All about – the ghosts of Rome look on
Generals and legionaries – this their camp
Where Stane Street like a shining sword
pointed the way to far Londinium.

Now in the setting sun the Roman eagle blinks
The people wait
Impatient at the slowly moving hours
Till voices vibrant with the players art
Shall shake the dormant echoes and out-sing the birds
In a great spate of Drama and a feast of words.

In 1980 mother wrote the following poem to be hung in the Lady Chapel
of St John's Church, Waterloo:

Here
Let the
Stranger
Kneel in prayer
The young that seek,
The lonely and the old
Within these walls a sanctuary find
With every hope and inner secret told
So rest the burden of their care
And in the silence hear
His will made known
They shall not rise
Without a hand to guide
Nor step into the
Busy street
Alone

*   *   *

Reading for me begins at breakfast each day with a skim through most of *The Times* (excluding the sports pages which do not interest me in the slightest) but I read the letters, perhaps a leading article and a few news items in full; I look at the Deaths to see if any acquaintances have appeared there, read any interesting obituaries and look at the weather page. I used to take the *Financial Times* as well, but doing justice to both papers could be burdensome, and as Toni likes the *Times 2* crossword, I gave up the *FT* and now have access to the online *FT* instead; but it is not quite the same and I still miss my daily *FT* with its serious content and agreeable lack of sex, violence and third-rate celebrities. Toni often looks at *The Times* before I come down to breakfast, but the rest of her reading is chiefly pre-Second World War literature, modern detective stories and anything about the artist G F Watts which would assist her in her duties as a guide at Watts Gallery. Guildford Library is quite good, but I have become more choosy with age, finding fewer books that I feel have something new and interesting to tell me. I use Google and the Internet (and Wikipedia) as a source of information which in other days would generally have come from books if the right book could have been found. Recently my younger brother's cast-off copies of the *New Scientist* have provided some reading of substance which I enjoy.

Pastimes Toni very much enjoys doing her low-level *Times 2* crossword after lunch, with me acting as consultant for some of the tricky clues, followed by mock quarrels over how many points I am allowed for my contributions. Neither of us feels any urge to learn the cryptic code used by the main *Times* crossword. We play an occasional evening of Mah-jongg with some friends. Toni's parents had been in Burma and she played it as a child and has taught our children and me. There is something pleasing about the symbols on the 144 'tiles' in the handsome set which has come down to us through her family; their bamboo backs and ivory fronts are beautifully smooth from long use, adding tactile pleasure to the game. When any of the children were at home we sometimes played Scrabble, rejecting the use of the absurd dictionaries which include far-fetched short words designed to ease up and speed up the game. If we had wanted to do this we would have allowed the use of my copy of *Musical Instruments: A Comprehensive Dictionary* by Sibyl Marcuse. This includes such useful Scrabble words as 'ayi' (a small drum of the West Ewe of Ghana), 'buk' (a friction drum of NW Poland used only at Christmas time) and 'pua' (a globular nose flute of Hawaii); 'qquepa' (a marine shell trumpet of ancient Peru) would seem promising, but unfortunately the Scrabble set contains only one letter Q. We recently returned to Happy Families, an infuriating game with many implicit lessons about negotiation.

When the family was at home for Christmas we would sometimes play well-known word games. In one we had a long list of things from 'Country' through 'author' to 'kitchen item', some twenty in all. Each had a copy of the list, a letter was chosen and then there was a limited time to fill in names of the things on the list beginning with that letter. You scored only for names that no one else had used which put a premium on the unusual. There could be problems: is a parsnip-measure (used for judging in vegetable shows?) a kitchen item? And one beginning with the letter P or the letter M? The other game consisted of one person choosing an obscure word from a dictionary, everybody else then writing down on slips of paper what they imagined its meaning to be, the chooser writing down its true meaning; these slips were exchanged, and read out. Each person then revealed what they believed was its meaning, with the chooser finally revealing its true meaning. It was this game that introduced us to 'ruelle' (the space between a bed and a wall) and 'diaulos' (a Greek footrace, an architectural feature or a double flute). I sometimes found an imagined meaning more appealing than the true one, such as one imagined meaning of 'diaulos' as two islands which are joined at low tide; if this doesn't have a word of its own I think it deserves one.

Another occasion which brings families together is a birthday. I no longer welcome mine and although we are a family which takes all such anniversaries fairly lightly, some very mild celebration usually occurs and this means a birthday cake and candles. At my age some eighty candles on a cake would be ridiculously crowded but I offer a solution to this problem. From now on the number of candles on my birthday cake will represent my average expected years of life (from *Interim Life Tables, England* – available on the Web). On my latest birthday cake there would be just seven candles – a considerable economy; and as one gets older the expected years of life decline, so the number of candles will have a downward trend. But their number will always remain encouragingly positive; even at the age of 100 there would still be two candles on the cake.

Walking is something that Toni and I do together only occasionally, and then mainly when we go to meet old friends down in Sussex. There we usually walk between the beautifully kept paddocks of a stud farm, past elegant and disdainful mares. In Guildford, when it is not the season for active gardening, I take a daily brisk walk on my own. It consists partly of suburban roads on my way to and from Stoke Park, which I enter from Ladymead at its north-east corner. It is spacious – some 35 hectares of rolling parkland, edged with trees, with a spinney, and a pleasure to walk over. On a few days in the year it is devoted to farming shows or pop concerts and at weekends it is host to games of cricket or football and rugby. On a recent Sunday, as I walked past, it was almost filled by a rugby congress for five to twelve-year-olds. There were dozens of teams in a wide range of colourful shirts supported by a large contingent of parents and trainers who had brought with them lines of equally colourful canvas pavilions. Then Stoke Park was indeed a 'fair field full of folk', but most of the time it is calmly empty. Our Parks Department keeps it agreeably neat, sometimes giving it the scent of new-mown grass. (Echoes of my early army training can intrude upon even these peaceful surroundings. As I walk, I can see ahead and to the left a suspicious line of trees – what might lurk there? I am on an exposed forward slope, with dead ground ahead but then a dangerous crest . . .) The only person I meet to talk to on these walks is a rather quirky birdwatcher who lives near us; I know only a few generalities about birds, but by careful attention to his knowledgeable comments, and playing them back to him with gentle variations, I can keep a conversation of good-natured agreement going for several minutes, until he feels the need to get back to his binoculars and serious bird business. Sometimes I take my walk on a winter evening and then the busy traffic on each side of Stoke Park produces red and white lights like moving Christmas decorations. On the other side of Ladymead the glass-covered Sports Centre with its own surrounding lights looks like a fairy palace and the floodlit tower of Guildford Cathedral on Stag Hill looks romantically distant rather than plain and dumpy.

Michael and *The Paradise Rocks*

My older brother Michael died in November 2000 at the age of 78. He lived in Brighton where he had practised as an architect and had been a very active member of the Kemp Town Preservation Society. One of his interests was birdwatching, particularly seabirds, and for this he spent many holidays in the Shetlands where he soon acquired a circle of friends. For photographing birds he had a green moveable hide which he would erect at various bird-frequented places; he discovered later that the locals could not understand why he always took a green portable lavatory around with him.

Mike (as we usually called him) was interested in our family's history and with mother's help had produced a family tree which was extensive rather than distinguished. When our mother died in 1985 he took over her collection of family photographs which, at our urging, she had annotated. This allowed him to build up an organised family archive of photos which came to fill twelve large albums. By the time this was completed he was nearing retirement, and his mind began to turn back to his own early years and our holidays at Aldwick in the 1930s; he started to write down a few reminiscences, did a bit of research to clarify a few details and was hooked. His project began to blossom out into a plan for a full-scale book and this was soon taking up a large part of his time. As his work progressed Mike and I had frequent, long and enjoyable phone conversations late at night in which we shared and stimulated each other's memories of our childhood. Fortunately he had followed me into word processing which now made his work much easier. He always had the same computer and software as myself which meant that I could help him in his early stages, although he soon became fully operational on his own. The draft of his book began to grow and his backup discs began to proliferate. He also collected photographs from friends and cuttings from local papers as illustrations.

He had done several years of work on his book when his health began to show signs of trouble. He had late onset diabetes, lived on his own, was fiercely independent and did not receive the medical help or domestic support that he should have had in these early stages. It now emerged that in addition to his diabetes he was suffering from haemolytic anaemia. As we became aware of his situation Toni and I did all we could for him; he spent some time in a convalescent home near us which he liked very much and then stayed with us for a while. In hospital at Brighton the drugs for his anaemia had side effects which required an operation, and so his downward path became evident to us. Mike rang me from the hospital on one occasion and in the voice I knew so well he told me that everything was very satisfactory. He was on a train to London and at each stop medical staff got on and gave him the necessary treatment – they really were being very good to him. This combination of perfect coherence and total hallucination was really rather worrying; in our next phone conversation a day or two later he was entirely rational again. We visited him in Brighton Hospital as often as we could and he remained cheerful and optimistic until his last few hours.

Our family solicitors dealt with his estate, but the sad duty of clearing his flat and arranging for its sale fell upon Toni and myself supported by J and his wife Audrey. The weather that winter was dreadful, so wet that our usual route into Brighton was flooded, creating additional traffic problems. Along the seafront howling winds and horizontal rain added to the gloom of our visits to the now unheated and desolate flat. Many years earlier Mike, J and I had arranged some coordination of our wills and it was agreed that Mike would leave nothing to J and me but everything in equal shares to our children, his six nieces and nephews. After the contents of the flat had been valued we invited the six to come and choose any items that they wished to have. In the past we had never had any disputes over shares in family assets, and I wished to ensure that none occurred now. It was therefore agreed that any of the six choosing an item of significant value would have that value included as part of their share of Mike's estate, so that equality of shares would always be maintained. In the event there were few such items and none of them were chosen by the six, who went for things with personal associations or household items. J and I took books and various personal things, or bought some more valuable items from the estate at valuation. Everything that remained was given to more distant members of the family or sold to dealers. Finally the flat was sold, and it was a great relief that we no longer had to make frequent visits to Brighton which Toni and I had come to dislike for its sad and uncomfortable associations.

From his computer and his many backup discs I was able to recover a virtually complete but unedited text of Mike's book, together with many folders containing amongst other things the research work he had done for it and a folder containing the originals for the proposed illustrations. With his text loaded onto my own computer I was able to read it for the first time; many parts I had discussed with him in our late night phone conversations but other parts were new to me and I was agreeably surprised by both the book's style and its content. Mike had made some tentative movements towards publication and I now accepted the responsibility of ensuring that it would be published. But first it had to be edited and I did this myself. In its final form it had 21 chapters, 318 pages and 140,000 words, so this was a considerable task. There were the usual crop of minor corrections to be made but relatively few major ones, just some stylistic smoothing and the occasional purple patch to be excised, together with a few obscure and archaic words which Mike rather liked but which were distracting to the reader. This took the greater part of a year and while Mike himself had found an excellent indexer, I had to find a publisher. After some false starts I found Phillimore, publishers specialising in local history, who were conveniently just outside Chichester. When Michael's estate was being wound up his six beneficiaries had agreed that £5,000 should be reserved to help pay for the publication of his book, and that its copyright should be vested in myself and J. This contribution was part of the deal with Phillimore for the production of 1,200 copies, and at last the finished text with all the illustrations and index could be handed over to them. There were some problems. The publisher was concerned about copyright in the many photographs even though these had been given to Mike specifically for the book but for which there was no record of permission to use them. It took me many months to ferret out the owners of something like 100 photos and get such permission; I also had to procure maps for the front and back inside covers. The publisher's editor then proposed changes in the order of topics which were quite unacceptable to me and I had to threaten to withdraw the book to get him to leave it as Mike had intended. At last the book with its title *The Paradise Rocks* appeared in 2002, very well produced and priced at £25. It was a book of particularly local interest which received one or two favourable reviews but a flood of appreciative comments from local readers and, indeed, from some readers who knew nothing of its locality. We were very pleased with the outcome and felt that it was a worthy memorial to Michael.

Sadly my younger brother Julian, but always J to us, died in August 2008, when this book was at a late stage; he was an engineer with an inventive mind and a musical talent. I was in close touch with him and his family in his final years and they always visited us in Guildford at Christmas time; these were occasions filled with eager discussion over a whole range of scientific and other topics. His grown-up children and his wife Audrey remain warm members of our wider family.

Brangwyn in his Studio

One thing that emerged from Michael's flat was the diary kept by my father (with contributions from my mother) when he was assistant to the internationally renowned artist (Sir) Frank Brangwyn in 1918–22, the diary itself covering most of 1921 and 1922. We had vaguely known it was there but it was in several unimpressive notebooks and my father's writing was difficult to read; with it were a number of letters from Brangwyn to my father concerning affairs of the studio. After I had looked at the diary more carefully I got in touch with Dr Libby Horner, the leading expert on Brangwyn and his work; she read it and felt that it should be published. In her view it was of considerable art-historical interest because while there were many accounts of the views of great artists on art and on wider matters, there were few accounts like this of life in a great artist's studio. She took on the task of transcribing it and because of her comprehensive knowledge of Brangwyn's career and work she was able to provide most of the footnotes with their helpful supplementary information. I went carefully through her transcription and between us we were able to clarify most of the remaining uncertain readings. I then did the editing and layout for publication, choosing with Libby's help the illustrations of Brangwyn's works which were related to the diary, together with relevant photographs. I then chose the artwork for the covers and finally the twenty two illustrations of my father's work. These to me were an important aspect of the book because my father never exhibited, and in consequence he did not appear in any reference books of British artists of his time. The inclusion of a selection of his works ensured that his talent as an artist, perceived at an early stage by Brangwyn, would be properly recorded. My next task was to write the Introduction; this described the background to the diary, provide document maps for the diary and letters, and set out the policy on editing. Finally I wrote the Preface.

The book has 174 pages, 66 plates, and is printed on high-quality paper in a fairly large format – 276 cm × 218 cm, this makes it rather heavy. Nearly half of the plates are in colour, which raised the usual problems of colour-matching. I remember sitting round our breakfast-room table under artificial light with our expert printer and his wife (also a printer) and comparing different colour-balanced versions of the same illustrations, all of which looked very different when taken outside and looked at in daylight.

These problems led me to do a little research of my own. At that time the National Gallery was having an exhibition of paintings by El Greco (which left me a little surprised by some of his flesh tones); on sale were postcards of some of these paintings and they allowed me to borrow two or three to compare with the originals. The colour reproduction was, to put it kindly, somewhat lacking in accuracy, but overall the postcards did give a fair reminder of the paintings. I concluded that perfect colour reproduction was unattainable and reasonable reproduction was acceptable. The colour made it an expensive book to produce and the printing cost for 600 copies came to £14,000. *Brangwyn in his Studio* with the sub-title *The Diary of his Assistant Frank Alford*, edited by myself and Libby Horner, was privately published by myself in May 2004. I felt that the printers had produced a handsome volume. The book included a brief biography of Brangwyn by Libby Horner and a brief biography of my father by myself. It was writing this that brought home to me how many gaps remained in my knowledge of my father's life, and this was one influence leading me to write this present book.

Paper etc

In my own writing I now seem to consume a good deal of scrap paper, for which I have stock of elderly sheets which have been used on only one side, allowing me to put the backs to good use. I sometimes imagine excited archaeologists in a distant future uncovering a dump of my used scrap paper – a latter-day Oxyrhynchus; they would ignore my own scribblings and look eagerly at the original writing the other side in their efforts to reconstruct our civilisation. Occasionally I too notice what is on the other side of a piece of my scrap paper. On one such sheet I have just come across a completed feedback page from a student on one of the Russian Courses of the mid-1990s and there I found that in Applied Micro-Economics 'Richardson is very good at taking what is superficially understood much deeper and ensuring in-depths knowledge', in Banking and Financial Institutions 'Roger [*sic*] is very knowledgeable and very patient with us', and in Corporate Finance the seemingly more enigmatic 'John Board is an extraordinary lecturer', but, like the others, it is accompanied by a tick in the 'above average' column. Such are the serendipitous rewards from saving old paper. But in retirement my supply of elderly used sheets is steadily diminishing. I am no William Stanley Jevons, the Victorian economist, who feared a worldwide shortage of paper. As a precaution he accumulated a large stock and on his death his heirs received this ample legacy.

On the other hand I seem to have accumulated a more than generous amount of other office supplies. This started when a local stationer's shop closed down many years ago and finally sold off its remaining stock at such low prices that I could not resist buying much more than I would ever really need. A few years later another such shop closed down and again I was hooked. The result was that I acquired an absurd number of pencils of various unlikely grades from 4B to surely the ultimate deterrent pencil graded 9H, as well as sticky labels of various sizes and colours, rolls of Sellotape, erasers, paper clips, folders, files and much else. On top of this I inherited from my older brother Michael more such office items used by him as an architect. Despite giving things to various good causes I am still grossly overstocked. Looking through all these pencils recently I noticed that a number were old and of unusual brands; thanks to Google I found a pencil collector (!) in the USA who expressed an interest in these and I gave them to him.

As a family we have always been collectors rather than disposers, and on one wall of my study are eight shelves carrying neat and businesslike open-topped black boxes, each 15½ inches by 11¾ inches and 4 inches high. These hold A4 sheets and folders very comfortably, and for holding my own and other family papers I find them more convenient than box files, which always need opening and closing. Altogether there are more than thirty of them and I have more in a large cupboard. They are very strongly constructed and look purpose-made, which they are, except that their original purpose was to hold celery for sale in Sainsbury's, after which the boxes were given to anyone who wanted them or thrown away. A little cutting down to a uniform height with an electric saw and some black paint to cover up the few signs of their origin and they are perfect filing boxes: easy for moving papers in or out, transportable if I wish to work on the more spacious breakfast-room table and, with their clear external labels and pink contents lists at the top, a helpful reminder of what is where.

Like many people, I suffer from the 'Pending' problem – matters which have not yet come to a conclusion, but drag on awaiting an answer or an estimate or further information or... Above my computer I have two shelves with a stack of eighteen labelled dark brown plastic filing trays (again the heavily marked-down products of retail distress). Here I keep these pending papers in flimsy transparent slip cases, again easy to see their contents, and a constant reminder. To keep matters in proportion, quite a few of these trays are empty, each awaiting some new long-drawn-out affair to start filling it up.

Signs of Age

I know that time is passing, but a decade and a half after my retirement I still find it hard to appreciate that I am actually getting old. A little while ago, travelling home by train after an interesting day at the School, I was standing in a crowded carriage. There were a number of women standing, and I could see that even if I had found a seat I would have to give it up to one of them. So, reflecting that I was after all an active, capable, mature and self-confident citizen, I stood there comfortably enough. At that moment I caught the eye of a young woman who was sitting nearby and she silently offered me her seat! Clearly she did not share my robust vision of myself. Declining her kind offer required some advanced body language to deliver a suitable wordless reply: your offer is much appreciated, but I really am quite comfortable standing up, in any case I am getting out shortly but you are most kind and thoughtful. When we arrived at Guildford, Toni was there in the car to meet me, and outside the station was this same young woman looking rather lost. I asked if I could help and we ended up giving her a lift to her destination – an agreeable exchange of kindnesses. More recently, on a crowded Tube train, a middle-aged woman silently offered me her seat...

27

House and Garden

7 Aldersey Road

Our house in Guildford has been the centre of our family life for forty five years and since a picture is worth a thousand words, one of the illustrations in this book is a photo of the back of 7 Aldersey Road in 1936 and another is of a similar view in 2006. There is also a photo of our back garden in 2006; sketch plans of our front and back gardens will be found in Appendix 5.

When we bought 7 Aldersey Road from Miss Violet King in 1963 she gave us two files, the first relating to the construction of the house. In 1931 Mr King, who had been Guildford's town dentist, was living with his family at Rexholme (note the play on words) in Lower Edgeborough Road on the Eastern edge of Guildford; in October of that year he commenced negotiations over the purchase of a plot of land in Aldersey Road, only two streets away. This plot had originally been part of the garden and orchard of Ivor Heath, a large house further up the road originally occupied by a member of the Hornby family of model railway fame. The plot originally had a 60 foot frontage, quickly enlarged to 65 feet and then, to accommodate a garage at the side, to its final 70 feet. The cost of this land was £7 10s (£7.50) a foot frontage with no charge for depth (some 240 feet), making its cost £525 in total for a plot of about 0.4 of an acre. Some of the negotiations have a very modern ring; the estate agents selling the land and the prospective builder both clearly wanted to clinch the deal. They began by offering a package of the land and the new house as specified for £2,175, asking for a £500 deposit, offering bridging finance at 5 per cent p.a. for the balance of £1,675 and setting a date for the occupation of the house.

They then addressed any worries Mr King might have about selling Rexholme when the time came to move. If Rexholme was not sold by the time Mr King moved into the new house (and they expected to sell it for around £3,000), they themselves would then purchase Rexholme at the agreed price of £2,800; a variant on this scheme allowed for limited sharing of any loss or profit when they came to sell it. Another suggestion was for Mr King to sell off 60 feet of the garden of Rexholme (in their view also worth £7.50 a foot frontage), let the house at £150 p.a. ('a very good return') and wait three to five years for the market for such houses to recover and then sell it.

Mr King did not adopt any of these suggestions and instead bought the plot in Aldersey Road (in the name of his twin daughters Violet Minnie and Edith Amy) for £525 and in January 1932 signed a contract with the local builders R. Holford & Co to construct a five-bedroom house for £1,720. Building seems to have started right away; the roof tiling was nearly completed by 5 April and the building was finished and the final account presented on 27 June 1932. There were agreed extras of £36 15s, making the building cost £1,756 15s; with £525 for the land, the total cost came out at £2,281 15s. The customary retention by the client of £100 from this sum to cover any initial defects was paid in full to the builders on 30 December 1932. When Mr King and his family moved into the new house he named it Ivorholme (another, and even worse, play on words – 'I've a home'). The file of papers we received from Miss King included photographs of the rear of the house when it was just finished and in 1936, when a rockery and terrace had been added (with the tiny figure of her or her sister sitting there) together with a greenhouse. Rexholme, however, was not sold but was evidently let, with its garden intact, since Mr King still owned it more than ten years later. It still stands (now without most of its garden, which was sold off probably in the 1970s) in Lower Edgeborough Road, a large and once quite opulent house with its name firmly displayed over a generous front door and up on the wall the date 1900 in rather large romantic figures on a flamboyant plaque.

The last wartime incident in Guildford was a flying bomb which landed on the house Merrydown, 12 Aldersey Road, at 7.25 a.m. on Friday 25 August 1944, the violent explosion reducing the house to rubble. It killed two women and a third died later in hospital. The local paper at the time reported that the explosion caused widespread damage, stripped leaves from the trees and broke shop windows in the town. Our house, number 7, just across the road from number 12, had its share of damage – broken windows, ceilings down, tiles blown off the roof – but worse damage on the north-east corner of the first floor which was nearest to the explosion. This was temporarily repaired with the fifth bedroom losing roughly half its space in the process, presumably to simplify and speed up the work. Some twenty years later, when I first viewed number 7, I had immediately seen in the door of the bathroom (which faced where the flying bomb had fallen) typical signs of blast damage: indentations, some irregular, others sharply linear, depending on whether the smashed window glass had been blown into the woodwork flat or edgeways on. Fortunately the house had been very solidly build with its foundations on a substratum of chalk, and the damage did not lead to any further problems over the decades to come.

The second file Miss King gave us when we bought number 7 was the War Damage claim arising from this incident. During the war all property owners paid War Damage Contribution, in effect a half-yearly insurance premium against war damage. The file started with a letter from the Borough of Guildford saying that all the First Aid Repairs had been completed and if any further work was considered necessary this required the completion of War Damage Commission form C.2. It was not until July 1945 that more permanent repairs (with a proper specification by a firm of architects) were started by Holfords, the firm who originally built the house. Simultaneously this specification was sent to the War Damage Commission for approval. The two Miss Kings (temporarily living at an address two streets away) had to make stage payments as the work progressed with the War Damage payments arriving often a month later. The correspondence engendered by this process, revealing the shortage of some building materials at that time, finally came to a close in 1948. The total cost of reinstatement paid by the War Damage Commission was £1,855 7s 6d, with the Miss Kings evidently paying architect's fees of £128 13s 3d. The damaged first floor north end of the house still lost nearly half of the bedroom involved. This can be seen from the two photos of the house: the left-hand roof line in 2006 is significantly cut back when compared with it in 1936.

The House since 1963

When we arrived in 1963 the house was in a rather run-down state but Miss Violet King, then the surviving twin, did leave various carpets and curtains which would serve for the immediate future. New central heating was installed before winter came, but then for the next few years children and just keeping going had to take priority. Slowly we began to make improvements but to detail these would be tedious. One thing that is worth mentioning is heat insulation, where we were somewhat ahead of the game. Many years ago I got from what was then the Building Research Station a set of data sheets on how to calculate insulation values, and this stimulated me to action. Our cavity walls were infilled with insulating stillite wool, we added a 'warm roof' – the sloping inside of the roof was insulated (rather crudely but effectively) with fibreglass covered with flexible polystyrene sheeting, and we also had 4 inches of fibreglass on the floor of most of the loft. The wall between the sitting room and the garage was only a 9 inch non-cavity wall; to insulate this a layer of fibreglass covered by hardboard was added on the garage side. Our insulated hot water cylinder is in a large airing cupboard, really a very small room, with two sections of outside wall producing a high inside-outside heat gradient and these had additional internal insulation. The location of this cylinder meant that there was a long draw-off to get hot water to the kitchen; this I found inconvenient and wasteful, so many years later I had a pumped hot water circuit installed which reduced the draw-off time to a few seconds. Finally, our kitchen has two quite large windows; on winter nights we cover these with 1 inch expanded polystyrene (EPS) screens (strengthened by two coats of white emulsion paint). These are very cost-effective insulation and greatly add to the comfort of the kitchen on cold nights. This form of EPS window insulation was recommended by the Watt Committee, 1979; I drew this to the attention of the Energy Saving Trust, whose calculations confirmed my own in showing that it was very cost-effective, but surprisingly they showed no interest in publicising it, apparently because it was not permanent like double glazing. After I did a certain amount of nagging they did finally refer to it, but only in an obscure corner of their website.

Just before I retired we had a conservatory added onto the sitting room and next to it the rear half of the garage was converted into a garden room, all three being linked by double doors. The conservatory was made by a company (since defunct) called Room Outside and they nominated a builder to do all the work. His first name was Norman, always Norm, and he worked with one of his sons on the construction, the other son later doing the plastering in the garden room. To have some way of distinguishing the three of them we referred to them as Norm, Abnorm and Subnorm. Working together, Norm and Abnorm appeared to understand each other perfectly without ever speaking. As the conservatory neared completion it became clear that they would welcome further work, so we got them to widen the terrace and extend it round the end of the conservatory to the garden room and some other tasks. They were very good builders and we were very pleased with their work.

Of all our changes to the house, the conservatory is the one that has given us most enjoyment; it is 21 feet by 13 feet and is equally for plants and people – a mixture of indoors and outdoors which gives us the advantages of both. We use it constantly from March to October and it is a continual source of pleasure to us. Heat losses in the winter from such a conservatory would have been so high that rather than attempt insulated glazing we settled for single glazing with safety glass. The roof is of Georgian wired glass with very pale blinds and we keep these fully extended both in summer to keep out the sun and in winter to help keep in the heat. They allow ample light through for the plants. For background low-intensity warmth we installed underfloor off-peak electric heating which keeps the frost out and allows tender plants to stay there all the winter. Then for occasional winter use – if we have a few friends in for drinks – we use its permanent high-level 2 kW radiant heater and two 3 kW blow heaters which warm it up to comfort level in less than half an hour. These blow heaters are placed in appropriately sized plastic plant pots so that their blast of hot air goes upwards rather than along at floor level where it either dries out plants, scorches ankles or threatens to burn the furniture. One of these blow heaters is on a thermostat and comes on occasionally to back up the underfloor heating. Overall, this gives us a heating regime exactly geared to our winter use of the conservatory.

Life in Aldersey Road has not been entirely without stress. In 1972 developers suddenly became active and I found myself drawn into the local opposition to their planning applications; fortunately there were several keen activists, but nevertheless I found myself chairing meetings of 'concerned local residents' to clarify and set out their objections to the latest scheme. There would then be a few years of quiescence followed by another rash of planning applications, and this has gone on ever since. I regard much planning as bureaucratic and ill-conceived, with many towns in the South-East having their character destroyed by 'Town Cramming' induced by a strangling 'Green Belt'. Many years later in a memorandum to the *Barker Review* (2003) I denounced 'Green Belt' as a highly misleading term; this memorandum was on the Web for several years (in Google, search for Barker Review Alford) and it may still be there. Up to now local residents have had a fair degree of success saving this area of Guildford, but developers never give up.

When we first arrived in Aldersey Road we seldom felt it necessary to lock our front or back doors or to lock the car, which normally sat on the drive outside the garage. Now we are part of a Neighbourhood Watch scheme; we have security lights and a burglar alarm, although there is little of portable value in our house to attract burglars; we have crunchy gravel on the drive, access to the rear of the house is blocked, and we lock everything when we are away even for short periods. All of this is due more to general precaution than to any real expectation of crime.

Books and Pictures

Several things would strike a neutral observer coming into our house. First there are a lot of books; they come from various sources – many inherited, many bought at jumble or other sales (at some of which I have been in charge of the book stall) and a minority bought new. My own books on economics are in my study and are just those remaining after selling some (mainly early editions of Marshall's *Principles of Economics* and books by Keynes) and steadily giving away a large number, including journals, to colleagues and friends. I was particularly grateful to Geoffrey Wood for taking some of my material on banking.

Our remaining books cover a wide range. Just looking along the bookshelves, there is quite a lot of biography (I see *Brian Howard, Portrait of a Failure*, by Marie Jacqueline Lancaster, a fascinating account of a downward spiral, and the very different *Period Piece* by Gwen Raverat, a charming account of a Cambridge childhood and one of Toni's favourites). There is quite a lot of classic literature (including many volumes of

Thackeray, Dickens and Henry james) and a scattering of modern fiction which belongs to Toni who also uses Guildford Library to feed her considerable appetite for detective stories. For decades I have read almost no modern novels; I find it difficult to suspend disbelief and I am unwilling to make an effort to surrender my mind into the hands of novelists whom I have no reason to trust or respect. But one novel I did read is *The Leopard* by Giuseppe di Lampedusa, in the revised translation by Archibald Colquhoun (I have the Reprint Society 1961 edition). This impressed me when I read it many years ago. It contains one passage which still sticks in my mind; Tancredi and Angelica, engaged to be married, are dancing at a ball:

> ... The black of his tail-coat, the pink of her interweaving dress, looked like some unusual jewel. They were the most moving sight there, two young people in love, dancing together, blind to each other's defects, deaf to the warnings of fate, deluding themselves that the whole course of their lives would be as smooth as the ballroom floor, unknowing actors set to play the parts of Romeo and Juliet by a director who had concealed the fact that tomb and poison were already in the script. Neither was good, each self-interested, turgid with secret aims; yet there was something sweet and touching about them both; those murky but ingenuous ambitions of theirs were obliterated by the words of jesting tenderness he was murmuring in her ear, by the scent of her hair, by the mutual clasp of those bodies destined to die.

There are quite a number of books on gardening, of which some are useful but many seem to copy their contents from preceding books; a number of books on Ancient Egypt (I see John Romer's *Ancient Lives* which records the lives of the tomb-workers in the Valley of the Kings); many more on Greece and Rome (clustered round the *Oxford Classical Dictionary*) but the six volumes of Gibbon's *Decline and Fall of the Roman Empire* which I read long ago have unaccountably gone missing; and there are the two volumes of *Black Athena* by Martin Bernal which has intrigued me more recently. On the Middle Ages I have *Montaillou* by Le Roy Ladurie, an extraordinary and tragic glimpse of twelfth-century Languedoc; nearer in time is the *Memoirs of the Duc de Saint-Simon* edited by W H Lewis and

Every Day Life in Papal Rome by Maurice Andrieux (who explains that the death of a Pope was rather welcomed as opening up opportunities for a new generation of Papal favourites and placemen). There are some books on religion – particularly on the emergence of Christianity from Judaism which to me is a most interesting subject – and the informative *Opening Up the Bible* by Mary Batchelor. Perhaps as an subconscious hedge against the future, I have a copy of the *Koran*. There are a few books on politics including the English translation of Hitler's *Mein Kampf,* once in the Metropolitan Police Libraries, on the inside rear cover of which I have copied a quotation from Leon Feuchtwanger: 'Hitler's *Mein Kampf* is a collection of 164,000 offences against German grammar and syntax'. Next to this is my copy of the *Communist Manifesto* and I like to think that these two neutralise each other. There are some books on modern history but many more on warfare. There are a few volumes of poetry, including my mother's two slim volumes, but the one which really meant something to me when I bought it in May 1944 was the even slimmer volume *From the Greek* edited by Higham and Bowra (slimmer because it was printed on very thin wartime paper). With all the uncertainties of war, I found it a comforting and inspiring affirmation of our cultural roots. We also have *Cat Poems* by Jacintha Buddicom (a Bognor friend of my mother's) and next to it her book *Eric and Us,* in which her family's friendship with the schoolboy Eric Blair throws light on the person who grew up to become George Orwell.

I have a taste for reference books; apart from the usual English dictionaries I have found that Oxford's *Hart's Rules for Compositors and Readers,* and the *Oxford Dictionary for Writers and Editors* are both interesting and useful for answering recondite questions, such as the meaning of the word 'guillemets' (these are the French quotation marks « »); this word is not in *Chambers Dictionary* or the *Shorter Oxford* but thanks to Google I found that it is in *Merriam-Webster's OnLine Dictionary.* In Microsoft Word, under Symbols, guillemets are called double angles and there they also have single angles < > which *Hart* says can be used as parentheses. On the opposite page in *Hart* is a section on dashes which are also sometimes used as parentheses; there only em and en dashes (or rules) are mentioned while Microsoft has three additional varieties: hyphen minus, soft hyphen and horizontal bar. Where it is desirable to minimise the interruption of the flow of a sentence, I personally favour using dashes as parentheses rather than using the conventional kind. I have a much-used copy of the *Oxford Spelling Dictionary*, a Christmas present from our younger son Richard, which I find particularly useful for its guidance on hyphenation.

I have quite a number of other reference books which can come in useful on occasions – these cover quotations, abbreviations, etymology, Latin phrases, rhymes, machines, the arts, typefaces and Swahili – as well as several editions of the usual *Fowler, Roget* and *Brewer*. It was only when I got to this stage in looking at our books that I realised that I had no idea of how many we had; a quick sample survey showed that 24 inches of shelf contained about 29 books and by measuring the length of filled shelves I arrived at a total of just over 1,400 books around the house, with an uncounted number up in the loft. Have I read them all? Only a proportion, I'm afraid, but the presence of all these books on our shelves I find agreeable and friendly; those I have read and enjoyed are there to remind me of that, those I have not read are a reminder that they are there to be read if I should feel so inclined.

In my reading I have come across many trivial things which have stuck in my mind. Sir James Frazer was the reclusive author of *The Golden Bough: A Study in Magic and Religion*; many people thought his wife was domineering and that he was hen-pecked. When Lady Frazer heard of this her response was immediate and apt: 'He is not hen-pecked, he is hen-protected.' Misprints can carry unexpected truths. Many years ago I saw such a misprint in one newspaper and I wish I had cut it out at the time; the item argued that the wealthy West must be made to lend to the Third World, but the misprint said that they must be mad to do so. Another example urged that the press should be given a strong line on some policy matter, but the misprint converted this into a strong lie. A very different misprint was in the notice of the engagement of some unfortunate young man ... to Violent Jean, daughter of... There was a large political graffito on a hoarding I once saw in Isleworth; its message was clear but its literacy let it down; I give it exactly as it was written:

SMASH ~~TORISM TORRY~~ TOR

And there are some remarks which I feel deserve to be remembered and kept available for reuse, like Noel Coward's comment to the leading man in a rather poor play: 'Good is not the word'. And I would include two reports, the first by Dr Thompson (Master of Trinity College, Cambridge 1866–86): 'The time which Mr Jebb can spare from the adornment of his person, he devotes to the neglect of his duties'. The second by a colonel in the Royal Horse Artillery on one of his subalterns: 'I would not breed from this Officer'. Returning to Noel Coward, I am reminded of his comment during the Queen's Coronation; the very large Queen of Tonga (a kingdom once renowned for its cannibalism) was in the procession in her open carriage, with next to her a very small man. Someone asked who he was and Noel Coward leant across and said: 'That's her dinner'. A relatively recent source of wit is the car sticker; in Houghton Street I saw one with the message: 'Fight Poverty – Marry a Millionaire' and somewhere else 'Give Blood – Play Rugby'.

We have a number of pictures on our walls, oil paintings, red chalk and charcoal drawings and etchings by my father, all reproduced in *Brangwyn in his Studio*. We also have two other family paintings: a portrait of Toni's grandmother's grandfather who was rector of Cavendish in Suffolk from 1808 to 1860 and a portrait of 'Uncle Henry', in fact my great-great-uncle Henry Doré 1829–90, who was a stockbroker; both of these are by unknown artists. Three of my father's oils give some character to our sitting room and elsewhere we have a number of others as well as framed Christmas cards, etchings and drawings, all by Brangwyn. My brother Michael was a competent watercolourist and we have his picture of the 1951 Skylon as seen across the river from his desk in the architect's office just off the Strand where he was working at the time. Also on a wall by the back door we have a long python skin, rescued from being made into handbags by the leather business in Walsall which was in Toni's family until it closed after the war. To many people coming to our house this is of more interest than any of our works of art.

Blue and White

As we gradually got our house into order, we received from Toni's family two pairs of plump blue and white Chinese vases, one pair about 12 inches high, the other about 16 inches. After a period of indifference I began to like them; I would not have liked their cobalt blue colour in paintwork or fabrics, but it seemed to harmonise perfectly with their hard translucent porcelain. I bought a few low-priced blue and white *Prunus*-pattern ginger jars in antique shops which gave me similar pleasure and I was hooked. From then on I bought any reasonably priced piece of Chinese blue and white that I came across. Medium-sized ginger jars were the commonest (although I never bought any of the modern transfer-printed ones) but I also bought a few larger ones, some 'carp' and 'dragon' plates, very small tea bowls, vases and other items. Toni too liked blue and white and was tolerant of my collecting.

At Neal Street East, a shop that used to be in Covent Garden, they sold all kinds of modern decorative orientalia, but at one time they also had a number of antique Chinese plates, about seven inches across or smaller, which I was able to buy in one of their sales. Much blue and white was made for export but these plates, greyer in tone and with two types of design, would have been for use in Chinese homes and some of them had the added interest of 'owner's marks' – Chinese characters cut into the hard glaze (these also appear on many of our very small tea bowls and some experts believe that these are characteristic of pieces which have come from China through Malaya). They also had on their backs either a red or a yellow patch of easily removable paint; these I was told indicated that they had come out through one of the two authorised Chinese export channels for antique items . One common problem is that the covers (lids) of many ginger jars are lost or damaged; where this is so, I have replaced them with suitable inverted Indian small brass bowls (bought very cheaply at car boot sales) which when polished formed a most pleasing complement to the blue and white porcelain. We have ended up with about 150 of these items of Chinese porcelain. None of them are of significant value, they are to me just very appealing decorative objects. But within easy walking distance of the School there used to be something very different. I often visited the Percival David Foundation in Bloomsbury to gaze wistfully at its exquisite blue and white Chinese porcelain and other treasures. The collection has recently been moved to the British Museum, and I shall continue to visit it in its new home which fortunately is also an easy walk from the School.

I am not entirely limited to blue and white; over the years I have also collected some Chinese earthenware, shallow bowls, octagonal or lobed-oval, which are mostly bluish green inside and palest grey outside (although there are other combinations) where they have sparse but bold flower and other motifs in pink, yellow, blue, green and white. Most of my eleven pieces have 'China' on their base, perhaps showing that they date from before 1919, because after that, according to the Victoria and Albert Museum, it is more likely that they would be marked 'Made in China'. They give me pleasure, but being decorative both inside and out, they are difficult to display. Apart from ceramics I have acquired many other things that appealed to me at the time and which now languish in cupboards and drawers. But some are still to be seen around the house: a team of seven small brass acrobats, a most dramatic prancing horse and rider (both on a high shelf in my study), what appears to be a brass sporran and a set of very heavy brass bracelets, all West African; some small Indian brass statuettes, one of a religious triad with much of its detail polished away by devoted hands; and some bells, a set of engraved cupboard locks, and a set of seals, all in brass and all Chinese. Recently we visited some acquaintances who had lived in West Africa and were surprised to find that they had the almost the same brass sporran and prancing horse and rider; but their sporran still had what appeared to be ritual objects suspended from it. I showed photographs of these items to an anthropologist at the British Museum and he was particularly interested in the sporrans but could throw no further light on their significance.

The Garden – Starting Out

When we arrived at 7 Aldersey Road we found ourselves with a sizable garden to look after. Miss King, from whom we bought the house, had employed a part-time gardener whose name – and I am not joking – was Mr Digweed. At that time neither Toni nor I had any gardening skills. I regret to say that at 20 Avenue Road I had simply neglected the garden. Indeed I hardly noticed that it was there, although I did remember as a child hunting through the grimy, acrid privet hedge in the front garden and finding Magpie moths (*Abraxas grossulariata* – thanks to Google) with their handsome white, black and yellow colouring. Now I felt that as a responsible householder I had to do something about our new garden, but we were both very busy, Toni with young children and myself with the School; we needed help. Mr Digweed had retired, but I managed to get a new gardener for a few hours a week. He was a nice enough man who had only one ear. As a start I had our soil tested – it is about 4 feet of sandy soil over chalk, dry and hungry – and the results showed that it was deficient in nearly everything. Our new gardener was sceptical: 'They've got to say something, haven't they?' but the state of the garden told me that they were right. Our inheritance of plants was varied. The front garden had shrubs and small trees – not bursting with health but well established and holding their own; the back garden had a long box hedge running down the right-hand side, some miscellaneous very old apple trees left over from the preceding orchard, a handsome line of eight lime trees at the end, and a very large walnut tree (planted by our Miss King's sister in 1933, given a Tree Preservation Order in 2005 and taken down as diseased in 2008). Against the back of the house was a *Wisteria sinensis*, a vine of unknown variety and a fig tree, all in good health. Altogether we inherited eighteen worthwhile varieties of plants and trees in the garden of which only three were herbaceous – one peony, one iris and a sprinkling of *Lychnis coronaria*; otherwise, golden rod of a very poor form predominated, accompanied by the weed *Euphorbia peplis* which unfortunately proved to be one of our most loyal plants.

Our first gardener left in due course and his successor 'tidied up' my early attempts at planting and I had to recover them from the compost heap. He did not stay long after this, and from then on I did the gardening myself with support from Toni and occasional outside help for tree work and other heavy tasks. I read gardening books, looked at other people's gardens and learnt by doing, encouraged by the odd occasion when something I had planted produced a few flowers. There was a lot to learn and the process was to be spread over many years. We had arrived in 1963 but it was only in 1968, when the earlier pressures of babies and very young children had eased a little, that serious thought and action could be brought to bear on the garden. After the first few years of negligible new planting, that was the year in which I felt I should keep a record of all the plants that I bought for the garden, a record I have kept up ever since (all my figures exclude annuals or bedding plants). This record is now on my computer and shows that in 1968 I bought some 180 plants in nearly 150 varieties, really to see which ones would like our soil and situation. The answer was that most of them liked neither, so that a high proportion of these plants proved to be a very expensive form of compost. But I persevered, getting a better idea of what would do reasonably well and planting about half this amount in each of the following two years and more than this in

1971. These early years of planting were to set the garden up for several future years, during which it required only much more modest additions and replacements but much moving around of plants as I began to perceive the positions they liked best. This was followed by occasional years of major springtime activity as we pursued our changing ideas of what we wanted from the garden. To bring matters up to date, over the forty years to the middle of 2008 I had bought for the garden (or acquired as gifts or exchanges) 2,597 plants in about 1,340 different varieties. The garden as it stands now is populated by the tougher survivors of all these acquisitions, encouraged by generous amounts of compost and fertiliser.

The Front Garden

Neither of us like too much hard landscaping, but some was essential. In the front garden the main central island bed up against the pavement was given a dwarf wall along its inner edge and we had some new soil brought in to raise its level; this soil was not very good and contained several dead baby grass snakes. At the same time we decided to have the front fence repaired. The man who came to do the work started by taking it all down to work on it more easily; we were so pleased with the more open effect that we stopped the repairs and instead got him to take away the old fence. The drive, which had been a mixture of brown gravel and clay-with-flints, we covered with almost white natural gravel from Chichester which had the effect of cheering it up and reflecting light into the hall. In some mysterious way our gravel seemed slowly to disappear, and to top it up we drove down to the same gravel pit, where they were still working on the same stratum. They weighed us in on their weighbridge, we were allowed to go to fill up our sacks and buckets until we felt our car was fairly heavily loaded, then back onto the weighbridge. The cost of our load was tiny, revealing that the cost of gravel is chiefly transport rather than the material itself. (Frank Paish would have corrected me and said that all production is transport.) Later this stratum ran out and we had to depend upon the much more expensive bags of white limestone chippings, but we reduced the cost by buying broken bags or ones discounted in sales.

Now the tallest plants in the front are the original pair of purple-leafed nut trees *Corylus maxima* 'Purpurea', together arching over the end of the drive which leads into the garage together with an 8-foot box hedge concealing our boundary fence. At the other end of the island bed is a white lilac of an unknown but vigorously suckering variety whose ambition is to fill the whole bed and beyond; on the other side of the drive is a narrow bed with a *Trachelospermum asiaticum* climber to cover the fence on that side. The island bed also contains a large silver box *Buxus sempervirens* 'Elegantissima' and a conifer which started out as a charming little thing but has now reached 10 feet (I have to confess that it was one of the few plants which have evaded my record-keeping and its precise variety is not known). Elsewhere in the island bed are some twenty other evergreen shrubs which include varieties of cotoneaster, euonymus, lonicera, nandina, olearia, osmanthus, skimmia and viburnum, as well as a deciduous shade-loving *Philadelphus coronarius* 'Aureus'. These all give us some privacy and a variety of greens. Against the house there are other evergreen shrubs – four pyracanthas, another *Trachelospermum asiaticum*, and various aucuba, euonymus, ligustrum, *Prunus laurocerasus* and other plants, and a deciduous Cotoneaster horizontalis. These all help to soften and humanise the front of the house. The *Aucuba japonica* next to the front door is the best golden female form 'Crotonifolia' of which we have several others in the back garden.

The Back Garden

In the back garden we had to start with some more hard landscaping. When we arrived there was a rough stone terrace some 5 feet wide along part of the back of the house. This was too small to be useful and we decided to replace it; but Toni and I differed over the new terrace. I wanted something generous in size, she hankered for something cosy and small, just a minor upgrade of what we had inherited. With canes and tape I produced various possible layouts (the best tape was that from the Bank of England, which tied up the statistical publications that the Librarian used to pass on to me for my students). Then looking at these from all angles, I eventually persuaded Toni that generosity was the best policy and we decided on one some 12 to 15 feet deep by 50 feet long in York stone with inverted V jointing. Because of the lie of the land it is 1 to 2 feet above garden level with a stone retaining wall and four steps down to the lawn. This small element of height was to give a more flattering view of the garden. The terrace was built for us in 1969 by Mr Yeo (short and solid) and his son (willowy and bespectacled) with a foundation of 'hand-pitched hardcore, blinded with sand'. The day came for the delivery of the York stone; that morning in *The Times* there was a news item about people in a Wandsworth bus queue finding that they were standing on sand and ashes because someone had stolen the York stone pavement. As I was reading this a very large truck arrived filled with our York stone, which looked suspiciously like Wandsworth pavement; it had fragments of yellow lines, oil marks and the flat stains of old chewing gum. I looked away and pretended not to notice. I turned away for another reason also. Some of the slabs were very large and many were up to 6 inches thick; I could not envisage how our father-and-son team were going to unload them, move them, cut them up and lay them without rupture or crushed limbs. But this they did and we were very pleased with the result.

The existing fig tree against the back of the house had to go and later so did the vine, but we wanted to save the large *Wisteria sinensis*; to do this we had a low brick wall built round its vulnerable root area and the terrace was bridged over this enclosure, leaving an opening 4 feet by 1½ feet for its trunk to emerge and for us to feed it if necessary. It has been perfectly happy in its new compound and has now grown right round the house, nearly to the front door. On the other side of the French windows to the breakfast-room (which were added at this time) there is a large *Trachelospermum jasminoides*, and both of these climbers flower profusely and have a lovely scent in spring and summer respectively. To provide a sense of enclosure and a suntrap we had a brick wall built at the north end of the terrace. My brother Michael, who was an architect, recommended that where this wall butted against the house we should link the two with copper wall-ties which would stretch if the terrace were to settle, as was likely over time; steel ones, he told us, would break. This wall supports a pergola over which the wisteria has grown. The conservatory was later built over the south end of the terrace, shortening it down to about 37 feet long, but the terrace was then widened to some 15 feet with a 3-foot wide extension round the conservatory to reach the garden room. There it has a step down to what might be rather grandiloquently called the lower terrace. A *Prunus* 'Accolade' provided just the right amount of shade until it inconveniently died in 2005, and in the height of summer we replaced it with a green fabric gazebo which has proved surprisingly satisfactory. This part of the terrace is large enough to accommodate half a dozen people round a table and on it there are two tubs each with a golden fern *Nephrolepis exaltata* surrounded by trailing *Lysimachia nummularia* 'Aurea', each displaying a totemic-looking fox's skull found in the garden. These contrast with the main terrace where there are three tubs filled with white begonias together with a clump of some further ten pots of salmon-pink geraniums (really pelargoniums) up against the house. To soften the end of the terrace there are a variegated hydrangea 'Tricolor', a spreading dwarf elm *Ulmus elegantissima* 'Jacqueline Hillier' and another aucuba, all in sizeable pots. There is no natural standing water anywhere near us, so we have two birdbaths on the terrace.

Looking down the garden from the terrace, on the right and facing south-east is the main mixed border; this is some 70 feet long, between 9 and 12 feet deep and backed by a 12-foot box hedge. This is not a good arrangement since the box is hungry for moisture and nutriment; we have to keep watering and feeding the bed to keep its plants growing well which means that the hedge does even better. The first plant in the corner of this bed is a *Cupressus sempervirens* 'Stricta', now some 40 feet high and with two main stems, not at all the right thing for the tall and columnar Mediterranean cypress. This arose because Lulu fell on it when both she and the sapling were young; she was unhurt, but not so the cypress, which still bears the scars of the encounter. From there down the garden it is a mixed border with a structure of shrubs interspersed with perennials to give colour. Some of the shrubs are large – a purple-leaved berberis, deutzia, kolkwitzia, philadelphus, ceanothus and choisya; many are smaller – golden-leaved berberis, euphorbia, potentilla and a few of the tougher roses – 'The Fairy', 'Coral' and 'Cornelia', and several clumps of *Erysimum* 'Bowles' Mauve' a sub-shrub which likes our dry and sandy soil. Finally it has self-sowing Aquilegia and quite a number of herbaceous plants – phlox, anemones and also clumps of a small golden bamboo and patches of creeping plants – purple-leaved ajuga and sedums. More recent arrivals are a number of alstroemerias, some tall *ligtu* hybrids, some short Princess varieties. At a rough count this border contains some 130 plants. Altogether it gives colour to the garden but it is a shifting population because each year there are casualties, discards, replants and newcomers. This border finally merges into the rose bed which has roughly 50 roses in it, now chiefly 'The Fairy' with groups of 'English Miss', 'Queen Mother', and a few others together with a back row of four old-fashioned roses there primarily for their scent. Finally behind the rose bed there is a line of *Cornus alba* 'Elegantissima' which helps to lighten the effect of the large clump of 25-foot laurels – *Prunus laurocerasus* 'Rotundifolia' – behind them, and placed there to give a visual stop to this side of the garden.

The left-hand side of the garden is a border of evergreen shrubs, now of some size, and chosen to give a variety of greens, golds and some silver. Next to the lower terrace there is *Aucuba japonica* 'Crotonifolia' and fatsias backed by pyracanthas. Then further along there is a *Philadelphus coronarius* 'Aureus' (the only deciduous shrub), *Buxus sempervirens*, *Lonicera pileata*, silver-edged holly, euonymus, piptanthus, *Prunus laurocerasus* 'Marble', *Aucuba japonica* 'Golden King', griselinia, ordinary laurels at the back, golden and silver privets, a low clump of silver *Senecio laxifolius*, and, again as a visual stop, three very large *Cotoneaster lacteus* edged by a spreading clump of *Hebe* 'Marjorie' and behind them a sizeable yew tree. The *Aucuba japonica* 'Golden King' is the male equivalent of 'Crotonifolia' of which there are several in the back garden. When they are all in flower I cut off some flowering heads from this male and introduce them to the flower heads of the females which later produce much better crops of red berries; our other female forms 'Picturata' and the green 'Longifolia' are also responsive to this introduction service.

These cotoneasters and hebes on one side and the rose bed on the other narrow the lawn down to a width of 7 feet as it leads into a small glade previously occupied by the walnut tree and backed by a 10-foot laurel hedge of 'Rotundifolia' (which goes on nearly to the end of the garden) with clumps of bluebells in season and a *Choisya ternata*. Then, between a pair of large holly bushes, a wooden arch 5 feet wide leads into the last section of lawn which has concave side beds; in the left-hand one is a fine *Viburnum plicatum* 'Lanarth' and a variety of smaller plants. There the large laurel hedge continues across the bottom of the garden, and finally behind that is our row of limes, over 40 feet high when they recover from their recent pollarding. In the right-hand concave bed are two silver privets, another aucuba, a large clump of phlox and some other plants backed by a trellis with two clematis over it. This conceals the usual rather untidy working area and standings for reserve plants (I always like to have a selection

518

of these to fill the gaps which are liable to emerge). Reading through this introduction to our garden makes me feel that I have overstated its merits. It is of modest amateur gardening quality, and all one can really say is that in summer it makes a pleasant impression, and the further away you are from the flower beds, the better they look. It gives me quite a lot of work but a great deal of pleasure.

In the working area we have two sheds, an old one 6 by 9 with a wooden floor on brick supports; it is used for longer-term storage: seldom-used tools, tiles left over from work in the house, sieves, a leaf sweeper and much junk. It cannot be locked, since Mark when about five carefully buried the key. The other is 11 by 14 with a proper concrete base laid by Norm and Abnorm. It has mains electricity and contains garden tools, the lawnmower, household tools, nails and screws of all sizes (except the size you want) in glass jars (so that, unlike boxes, you don't have to open them to see what is inside), pieces of wood and miscellaneous other potentially useful things of all sorts. At one time all the smaller tools were higgledy-piggledy, and I found myself buying a new screwdriver or pair of pliers because I could not find the ones I already had. But one summer I devoted several weeks to radically tidying up my shed with the help of a lot of Sainsbury's boxes like those I have in my study but painted a tasteful forest green (because that was the colour left over from some other task), all neatly labelled and placed on newly erected shelves. This revealed that I had no fewer than 12 screwdrivers, five pairs of pliers and a wide range of other tools, gadgets and oddments. But now I can lay my hands on all of these, and my electrical tools, immediately. Indeed I am now ready for a multitude of jobs around the house; thirty years ago this would have been really useful, but now apart from the occasional shelf there is less of such work to be done and most of these items deliver just a comforting service of availability.

Two elderly apple trees, one half-hidden amongst the laurels, still provide a few apples and our two nut trees in the front garden fruit quite well, but entirely to the advantage of our local squirrels; we have never gone in for growing vegetables, mainly because the only suitable beds for this are those we prefer to use for ornamental plants. We did try growing strawberries in pots but without success. We have some local friends who also tried growing strawberries, but had poor crops. The wife read somewhere that frogs might be eating their strawberries. She reported this to her husband who thought the idea ridiculous and insisted derisively that they go down to the strawberry plants straight away and see if the frogs were at work. When they got there he mockingly lifted up some undergrowth to show the foolishness of the whole idea, and under it was a frog with a strawberry in its mouth.

The Conservatory and the Garden Room

As mentioned earlier, the conservatory is built over what had been one end of the terrace and it is entered from the sitting-room by the original double doors. It has a floor of expensive terracotta tiles, really a mistake, because the instructions expect you to devote much of your life to such a floor, periodically moving all the furniture and plants, cleaning off the tiles with white spirit, reoiling them with boiled linseed oil, repolishing them with Trafficwax, buffing them, replacing the furniture and plants and then repolishing the tiles at intervals until it is soon time to go through the whole major performance again. Our own alternative strategy is based on benign neglect punctuated by the occasional spot of polish. All the plants are in pots, many on low and unobtrusive white benches against the walls, others on individual stands. Many of the plants get changed and moved around, but they currently include eight or more large salmon pink geraniums (which had fifty full blooms out in mid-September), a *Hoya carnosa*, a large golden *Aucuba japonica* 'Crotonifolia', three different Cyperus reeds, a large *Asparagus sprengeri* (which in the summer bears a multitude of tiny white flowers that smell of butterscotch), tall brugmansias brought in from our small greenhouse, via the terrace, for their 6-inch white flowers in season, and some Chlorophytums. As seems suitable in a conservatory, nearly all the furniture is made of bamboo and comfortably cushioned in a gentle green swirling pattern; three small sofas are round a glass-topped table clustered at the far end with two additional chairs ready to pull up if needed, leaving ample circulation space. We thought of having all this furniture recovered using the same fabric, only to discover after much enquiry that our original fabric had a pirated design and could not be purchased. The legitimate fabric that ours had been copied from had only a single colourway that we did not like, so progress on this front has halted. We regard the conservatory as our most successful change to the house and we use it constantly over spring, summer and autumn. We find it gives us most agreeable feeling of being simultaneously inside with some protection and outside because of all the plants. This feeling is heightened when it is windy, and even more so when it is raining.

On one side of the conservatory the double doors lead out onto the main terrace and on the other, double doors flanked by two large *Chlorophylum comosum* 'Variegatum' lead into the garden room. This is a plain white room 18 feet by 10 feet with a very pale fawn tiled floor. It contains a long white dining table and white chairs, and here we often eat in the summer. Along one wall are spaced three tall slim cyperus reeds which act as wall decoration; at the far end is an aspidistra which is nearly 6 feet across and on the other side is another large *Chlorophytum comosum* 'Variegatum' on a high sill cascading down for six feet and there are one or two other plants. The garden room has French windows out onto the lower terrace, another place where we can east in the summer.

But nothing is without its cost; we have to act as mother nature to all these plants in pots, in the conservatory and garden room and on the terrace. Except in the dead of winter they have to be watered, fed, tied up, cut back, and kept not too hot and not too cold: but in retirement this becomes part of our pattern of living and is no real burden. Our holidays are now in warm countries when winter allows us to leave our pot plants for weeks if necessary.

Animals and Birds

When the children were young they were given some guinea pigs which lived in a hutch until they escaped. They then became free-range guinea pigs, grazing rather charmingly on the lawn, making no attempt to leave the garden and living under the old shed. When winter came we put them back into the hutch; on one occasion we couldn't catch one, but we came out late in the evening to find the fugitive snuggled up against the hutch trying to get in. They were with us for several years, but one by one they disappeared. The only other pet we had in these years was a black cat named Coalie; she didn't like the dogs which arrived in her house, number 14 on the other side of the road, so she moved across the road to our number 7. We could hardly claim we owned her, it was rather that she had chosen us. We have a photo of Coalie with a daisy chain round her neck; Lulu is there looking very pleased with her decorative effort, Coalie is not

521

so sure. We cannot count Huckle, the sturdy grey and white cat who later lived opposite; the two children from his home frequently came over to play with our three and he often came too, later becoming a frequent visitor on his own. In due course his family moved and took him with them; poor Huckle, so robust when we knew him, did not like the change, apparently lost the will to live and just died.

My parents had also been adopted by a cat, small, hunched-up and grey; they named her Prudence but the name was not effective and she produced a litter before they could have her spayed. They kept one of the kittens, which Michael named Butchie. Pru must have a hard life before she found us because she was sweet but tough. When she heard a dog bark she would growl, Butchie (who had none of the character of his mother) would retreat under a bed and Pru would go boldly off to make sure the dog was not too close. On one occasion it <u>was</u> too close and my mother went out to investigate terrified howls and yelps to find a dog with Pru, all claws out, hanging angrily onto its back. Later Michael took over Butchie and had a cat flap installed for him in his flat at Brighton; he tried to instruct Butchie on how to use the thing, but as Michael gently pushed Butchie up against it to show him how it worked, Butchie simply oozed away left or right and would have nothing to do with his new amenity.

We must have had foxes around us for a long time before they became less nervous urban foxes and we started to see them in the garden. Suddenly we realised what had happened to our guinea pigs. The first fox that we saw regularly was an old one with a grey muzzle, and relatively tame. He would stretch out on his stomach on the lawn, calm but watchful, and wait to be fed; we could get within a few feet of him and rather liked having our own fox. Since then we have normally had one or two that we see fairly frequently in the back garden. They all follow a path along the box hedge, round the side of the house and out onto the road, setting off our security lights as they go and sometimes giving us a glimpse of their journeyings. Once for a day or two we had a young vixen in the garden, too young to have learnt fear of man. I could stand close to her as she lay in the main border eating something. On one occasion as we sat on the seat at the bottom of the garden this young vixen suddenly appeared in the gloaming and began to nibble my sandal. But she soon grew up and became just another wary urban fox.

For many years we have had a family of crows who regularly visit our garden. Each spring we have an older mated pair and two or three young who are only slightly smaller than their parents; these young poke around the lawn in an ineffective manner, always getting in the way and demanding to be fed. One year a very young one landed in our garden and could not take off again. I caught it in the hope that it might become a pet as intelligent and charming as Raucus had been all those years ago. But Raucus had no family to warn him against humans, while my new captive had two agitated parents cawing out that they wanted him back and would not desert him. It was no contest and I quickly released him. All our vegetable waste goes onto the compost heap behind the large laurel hedge at the bottom of the garden, but all edible scraps go out onto the garden. Some are put out during the day for our crows and other birds, chiefly blackbirds and tits; for the latter we also have a peanut feeder on which we sometimes see a lesser spotted woodpecker or a nuthatch. The rest of our scraps are put out in the evening for the fox. Sometimes we see him find these things and take them away to some quiet spot. Often we put them out and looking only a little time later find that they have already gone. Apart from seeing them we often hear foxes barking, particularly in the winter when they are looking for a mate. It sometimes reminds me of television plays where a few trees and a fox barking indicate deep countryside.

On a much smaller scale we have a family of woodmice which live down by the roots of the wisteria; sometimes we see them trundling along the wisteria branches like little railway trains and on summer evenings we see them on the terrace just outside the breakfast-room, nibbling something and then zipping under cover. The first one we named Cedric, and every successor has inherited the name. At one time one of the Cedrics found his way into the house and Toni was not at all pleased; we bought a humane mousetrap and ultimately caught no fewer than fifty six of Cedric's clan, on several occasions finding two mice at a time in the trap. We released them some way away, but it did occur to us that they might be homing mice, rather like Michael's pigeon, and that our humane trap was no solution. We then adopted a two-track approach, finding and sealing up Cedric's entrance routes into the house and providing a few tastefully arranged blue grains specially designed for him. These were an effective discouragement and since then he has remained outside. Recently I saw the current Cedric pop his head up from a broken joint in the terrace; his shape was that of Mickey Mouse but the sun shone through his ears and turned them pink.

Squirrels are one form of wildlife that is less welcome, and this is chiefly because some go for the bird feeder filled with peanuts, pull it down and try to open it. We bought a squirrel trap and caught the two who had learnt this trick; after a year or so another pair also became troublesome, these also we caught and we have had no trouble since. Because of their depredations on the other local birds we discourage magpies and jays, and the crows join us in this but not from the same benevolent motive but because they regard them as competitors for food.

Looking Back

Toni and I feel that we were very fortunate to find this house all those years ago; we have introduced changes and additions to it in ways which have made it more convenient and comfortable, and for us it has always been well located. Such has been the rise in property prices that few if any of my successors at the School would be able to buy such a house at the stage when we did. It has given us so much in so many ways; in it we enjoy 'winter with its cosy hours' (the phrase is my mother's) and on a summer morning from our bedroom window we enjoy looking down the garden in bloom; then we have the pleasure of walking from the sitting room into the conservatory with its salmon-pink geraniums, into the garden room with its dominant white just softened by a few green plants, and out to sit on the lower terrace with its view over the lawn. In the evenings we often walk down to the end of the garden, sit together on the seat and listen to the birdsong – there are no other houses to be seen and we might be alone in the world. With all this, with each other and with our family, we have much to be grateful for.

28

Alford Financial History

When reading biographies I have often wondered just how people financed the lifestyle I see portrayed. The only book I can recall which addressed this question is *Downhill All The Way* in which Leonard Woolf reveals the income and expenditure of himself and his wife Virginia Woolf over the years 1924 to 1939. As he says, 'the private finances of people seem to me always interesting; indeed they have so great an effect upon people's lives that, if one is writing a truthful biography, it is essential to reveal them'. Economists, of all people, should not be nervous of talking about money, and this is my occasion for such revelation.

Artist, Decorator, Architect, Developer

My father, Frank Alford, was born in Neath, South Wales, in 1896. He had marked artistic talent which took him from his local school to Swansea School of Arts and Crafts and then to the highly regarded St John's Wood Art School in London where in his first year he won the Silver Medal and a scholarship for three years' tuition. During the war he was in the Royal Artillery but while still in England he was kicked by a mule, quite badly injured and left with a recurrent rupture. From 1918 to 1922 his artistic talent took him to the position of assistant to (Sir) Frank Brangwyn RA in his studio at Queen Street, Hammersmith. His keenness led him to take additional evening art courses at Lime Grove School of Art in Shepherd's Bush. There he met a young fashion artist, Doris Mary Davey; they were married in July 1920 and in due course had three sons, Michael, Roger (myself) and Julian (J).

Working with Brangwyn had considerable prestige but not very much money, and when their first child Michael arrived in 1922 my father evidently felt that he had to move on, becoming in turn an independent artist, a muralist and decorative painter and then in 1925 a West End interior decorator working at the top end of the market and with an office at 19 Hanover Square. His business developed well and brought him into contact with the Duke of Newcastle, who reputedly owned 27,000 acres of land at Dorking, and he went on to become architect and developer to the Duke's estate. My father's transition from the fine arts to commercial work drew him to the attention of the Royal Society of Arts which aimed to encourage the applied and industrial arts. The president, Harold Sanderson, wrote to him with an invitation to become a Fellow of the Society and suggesting two distinguished Fellows to nominate him. He was duly elected FRSA in July 1934.

Meanwhile he began building up a property portfolio of his own which by 1939 consisted of a 4,000 sq ft steel framed building designed by himself (originally a billiard hall, much later turned into offices), next to it two shops each with two flats over, and a rear storage building, all of these on the north side of the Great West Road (now the M4) and close to the junction with Ealing Road; he had also built a café/roadhouse on the Kingston Bypass and bought a 5-acre field at Slinfold in Sussex for an intended country cottage.

The first phase of the development of the Duke's estate was Castle Gardens, a mile or so east of Dorking, designed by my father. It was nearing completion and substantial further schemes were being prepared when on 3 September 1939 war broke out and my father's career was fatally disrupted by some ten years of wartime and post-war restrictions. The house in Isleworth was closed up and the family moved to our bungalow in Aldwick. With the fears of invasion in late 1940, it was my mother who insisted that the family should move from Aldwick to Slinfold. Feeling marooned in the heart of Sussex and with nothing else to do, my father, helped by my elder brother Michael until he was called up in November 1941, started to build a smaller country cottage using mainly recovered building materials. But wartime restrictions left the family living like refugees; invasion fears having disappeared, we moved back to Aldwick at the end of 1941.

Starting Again

Back in Aldwick my father wanted some bricks; he came across and later bought the Lion Brickworks which had 6.6 acres of land in Hook Lane at Nyetimber only one and a half miles away. He ran the brickworks for a while, then renamed it Windmill Park, after the nearby and prominent Nyetimber windmill. On the site he designed and built a very pleasant small office building, with some additional commercial space, which looked more like a country house, and a 5,000 sq ft commercial building which at one stage had the distinction of housing Victor Crabbe's collection of sixteen Rolls-Royce cars. The land had development potential but this required additional access and to provide this my father bought off-plan a house in an adjoining development with the intention of knocking it down to give the extra access. The neighbours objected loudly, so my father let it be known that he would instead use it as a holiday home for East End delinquents; the objections immediately ceased. My younger brother J lived in the house for some time and in due course it was indeed demolished to provide the required access. Further up Hook Lane my father bought the 4.1 acre Scott's Field (for some history of this field see Appendix 3). This he bought in the name of my older brother Michael, I believe in recognition of all the work he had put in at Slinfold in 1941. My father then rented it from Michael, renamed it Dukes Meadow (for simplicity it was not given an apostrophe) and turned into an upmarket caravan park. At around this time he sold the cottage at Slinfold and the café/roadhouse on the Kingston Bypass, presumably to help finance these purchases, retaining his other properties on the Great West Road.

While I was still in the Bank of England my father was found to have lung cancer; he had emphysema as a young man and had been a heavy smoker, a lethal combination. He had radiotherapy treatment but shortly after I left the Bank of England it became apparent that he was dying. With the firm support of my mother he accepted the approach of death, saying to me on one occasion 'It's not so bad, really.'

Before he died, I and my two brothers had some difficult decisions to make. The most pressing of these was how to reduce the impact of Estate Duty, the predecessor to today's Inheritance Tax. My father strongly approved of our doing this, but his deteriorating condition meant that he had to leave it to us to arrange and we agreed that I should take the lead, for a very good reason. At the School there had always been a general understanding that members of the Law Department would give a reasonable degree of helpful advice to any colleagues who needed it, and it so happened that in the Law Department we had Ash Wheatcroft, Professor of English Law, first editor of the *British Tax Encyclopaedia*, and the leading expert on Estate Duty. It seemed to me that the only action we could take was to break up Windmill Park (which even before my father's illness had become economically inactive) into three mutually obstructive parts and for our father to give each of his sons one of the three parts. The valuation of each part separately would be much less than the valuation of the whole as a single entity, thus reducing Estate Duty. I went to see Ash, seated benevolently behind his desk smoking his pipe, and explained our problem and my proposal. He agreed with my strategy and only a day or two later we had a meeting of myself, Ash, Peter Cooper our solicitor and John Smith our accountant, at which Ash gave us valuable advice on how the break-up should be done to make it legally watertight; for example, that it should be done not just notionally, but that the separate parcels of land should be identifiably pegged out on the ground. Having his expertise behind us was a great relief, and I arranged for the break-up and gifts to be put into effect as Ash advised and for this to be done very quickly. Everything was completed by 14 November; my father was now sinking and he died twelve days later, on 26 November 1962.

Alford Joint Assets

We now faced the matter of my father's will, which had been less pressing because with the consent of all interested parties it could effectively be rewritten after my father's death. Most of my father's estate had originally been left to my mother; however, she was essentially an artist and poet, and it was clear to her as well as to us that she was simply not the person to manage properties. Her general attitude can be seen from a later event. Following the fringe bank crisis of 1973 the equity market declined to near the 1913 level. I was sure that at this level it was grossly oversold and I tried to persuade my mother to put some of her £20,000 deposit with Abbey National into the market. Her response was to say that it was very nice of me to think of her, but her Abbey National branch was very convenient, there was a chair so that she could sit down when she talked to the very pleasant girl behind the counter, so she preferred not to change anything.

We therefore all agreed that the will should be rewritten to leave everything to us three brothers in equal shares, with a separate undertaking by us to provide mother with an appropriate income for the rest of her life. The valuation of the estate was another matter requiring some care, particularly the choice of valuers. We appointed a small local valuer, an earthy north-countryman, who took a very sober, even pessimistic, view of values. Indeed I think he believed that the whole of the increase in values since the end of the war was essentially unrealistic and would shortly be reversed.

We had to wait two years for the break-up of Windmill Park to become effective in saving Estate Duty. Meanwhile I had to negotiate with adjoining owners the purchase of another acre of land and a number of detailed boundary adjustments to enhance its saleability; the separate parts were then duly put back together, and it was put on the market as a single unit of development land. Although I had some advice from our estate agents, in the end it fell to me to approach a number of property companies who had expressed an interest in the land; one of these whom I saw in London even offered to buy it sight unseen, signing a valid contract there and then for half our asking price and paying cash the next day. But it was with another property company that I did the final negotiating, and because of anticipated changes in the law, this involved a late night dash down into Hampshire to meet their board of directors and get the contract signed before midnight. The purchasers failed to complete on time and I had the uncomfortable duty of phoning them every day to ask them if they were ready to do so, until they did finally fulfil their obligation. In the event the scheme of breaking up Windmill Park had reduced its value by about 80 per cent and the charge for Estate Duty accordingly. The sale of Duke's Meadow to another developer involved few complications and went through smoothly; Michael insisted that the proceeds of the sale should be shared equally between us. We three brothers, Michael, myself and J, were now the joint equal owners of what we called Alford Joint Assets, which included the Great West Road properties, together with the proceeds of our land sales, much of which was held initially as local authority deposits with Guildford Borough Council. Most of these funds were then invested in two further shop properties, one in Isleworth in Middlesex, the other in West Wickham in Kent. Meanwhile the original tenant of our 4,000 sq ft office block – York House – had left and we let it as offices to a company which proceeded to spend a lot of money on upgrading it. Later we bought another property next door to York House and converted this into a small office building, Star House. It is important to remember that in property market terms all these properties were small and of secondary quality, although substantial assets to us.

The management of these assets fell upon myself and my older brother Michael; as an architect he naturally took responsibility for planning matters and for all structural aspects (and there was a steady trickle of things that went wrong and which we as the owners had to put right). I dealt with purchases and sales, leases and rent revisions, supported most efficiently by Peter Cooper of Staffurth & Bray, our solicitors in Bognor Regis. I had to use estate agents and valuers for local market information, but I was not impressed by their speed or their commitment and nearly all our operations were negotiated by myself directly with the other principals. J, who was an engineer, was content to leave the property management to Michael and myself. It was fortunate that we all had equal shares in Alford Joint Assets, were agreed on our general strategy and got on well together.

It was concern over Estate Duty on our father's estate that first led me to consult Ash Wheatcroft but, as mentioned earlier, this led to many pleasant lunches together and broader discussions of Estate Duty and its avoidance. Several years later, sitting next to him at one of the Director's Dinners at the School, he confided to me that the main form of Estate Duty avoidance was in fact break-up schemes such as the one that he had advised us on for Windmill Park. But his help to us had gone well beyond this and had included a most detailed analysis of the whole legal position of our father's estate, covering many pages and going into the most refined details of tax law. When our father's affairs were finally settled I had to decide how best to show my thanks to Ash as a colleague. In the event I went to Fortnum & Mason and from their list of Scotch whiskies I had them make up a case of one each of the most expensive brands for delivery to his home. His response showed that I had made a sound decision.

Income Revealed

I am by nature a hoarder and I have a long run of financial records with only a few gaps; it seemed a pity not to use these figures to provide some of what Leonard Woolf believed to be so important to truthful biography. This requires tables and graphs and these are in Appendix 4. There **Table A** summarises the income side of my personal financial history – denoted by **RA** – from the time I came on to the staff of the London School of Economics in October 1952, bringing in the income of Toni – **ABA** – from March 1960 when we were married. This data runs from the tax year 1952–53, past my retirement in October 1992, up to 2007–08; this table is followed by explanatory notes. One series, my salary/pensions in **Column 2**, is shown as a graph in **Table C**. There it reveals a fairly stable rate of growth in my salary throughout my career at the School; then erratic movement for six years after my retirement (explained in the Notes to Table A) when, in addition to my USS and state pensions, I was paid for running a number of courses for the School; then falling to the level of my pensions which over the years have risen slowly due to indexation. **Column 10** in Table A shows the financial impact of our pre-tax investment income, mainly from Alford Joint Assets and from our portfolio of securities which was its successor. Depending on the method of calculation, this amounted to between 58 and 60 per cent of our annual joint pre-tax earned income over the years 1960–61 to 2007–08.

This whole picture looks rather different when my salary (**Column 2**) and our total income (**Column 9**) in Table A are adjusted for changes in the general level of prices. This is done in **Table B** where first we link calendar years to tax years by maximum overlap (**Column 11**) and then use the National Statistics long term Consumer Price Indicator Series CDKO (**Column 12**) converted into a price inflator (**Column 13**) to restate these as 'real' series at 2007 prices. For ease of comparison **Table B** again shows my salary at current prices (here in **Column 14**) and then my real salary (**Column 15**) and our total real income (**Column 16**). These are all shown as graphs in **Table C**. But while my salary – on this scale – shows a nearly stable rate of growth up to my retirement (marked by the vertical line at 1992), my real salary shows not far from linear growth (ignoring the temporary rise in 1960–62 when I was being paid by the Bank of England) up to 1970, then a gentle decline for 7 years followed by a slight recovery and then rough stability for the next 13 years to retirement. A rather dispiriting performance in an economy which had real income growth of around 50% over these 21 years. Our total real income series is well above my real salary but latterly rather erratic, for reasons which will be explained.

Table B, Column 17 shows my LSE 'career years' with 1952–53 as year 1 (in fact this is a tax year and I started at its mid point – October 1952). I have continued the series after my retirement until 1997–98 because during this time I was still active in running a number of courses for the School. It seemed a pity to stop there, as in these following years I still did a few very minor tasks for the School as well as regularly attending Charles Goodhart's Financial Regulation Seminar. But to indicate that the character of this series changes, there is an underline after 1997–98 and it is continued in *italics*.

A Turn for the Worse

Even at the beginning of Alford Joint Assets I was well aware that our portfolio was concentrated on real property; we did a small degree of diversification into equities but good advice was hard to find and we retreated to the field which we were more comfortable with and knew best. In the early 1980s I did raise with Mike the possibility of a wider spread of assets, but he was by temperament and training focussed upon real property and our experience up to that time seemed to bear out his preference. With my career at the School and a family to think about, I did not feel sufficiently strongly to press for any change in our policy which in retrospect proved to be a mistake.

The property income of Alford Joint Assets progressed reasonably well up to 1989, but we then received an unexpected blow. We had let York House to a public company, Finlay PLC, as its head office. It was a newsagent chain with 185 shops and over 1,000 staff, run by an accountant. On 17 October 1989 Michael was astonished to read in the *Evening Standard* that Finlay had called in the receivers. These were Arthur Andersen & Co who later made a statement blaming cash flow problems for the collapse of the company. Efforts by the receivers to sell Finlay's lease on York House came to nothing; the receivers remained in occupation and paying the rent until their work there was finished in March 1990. When we then came to assess the situation it became clear that Finlay, and indeed their predecessors, had fulfilled few of their obligations to maintain York House in good and lettable condition.

The property market along the Great West Road was becoming very difficult; many developers had seen it as a promising corridor leading from central London out to Heathrow and this had resulted in an excessive supply of office space and growing problems in letting at any reasonable rent. As so often, the problem we faced was not just one adverse factor, the bankruptcy of a tenant, but simultaneously a second and unrelated one, the dire state of the local market for office space. One consequence was that when the receivers left York House it was unoccupied for about a year and then until 1994–5 only some single floors could be let on short informal leases; for business rates this required negotiation for re-rating. The smallest of these tenancies was unusual; Carnival Films leased the ground floor of York House for three days in June 1993 to use it for a television series they called *Anna Lee*; this young lady, played by an actress named Imogen Stubbs: appeared to be fighting the burgeoning crime of West London all by herself, with York House as her headquarters. For this three day lease we received £500. In due course Toni and I watched the film on television, but the ground floor of York House did not have quite the starring role we had hoped for. Our other Great West Road properties also had a rather erratic record in these years including not only vacancies but also defaults – by one tenant for £20,000 and by another for £7,000. The first of these we did not pursue because he had been a good tenant but suddenly his business was on the verge of bankruptcy, his business partner resigned, his wife left him and his whole life seemed to have collapsed. Pressing him for payment might well have precipitated him into bankruptcy and we could not bring ourselves to worsen his woeful situation. The second default, by a tenant in the pop music business, we judged to be not worth pursuing.

These problems are reflected in the sharp fall after 1989–90 in our income from Alford Joint Assets in **Column 6** of Table A. But loss of a major tenant and therefore of rental income was only part of the story; normal expenses for properties include (1) repairs and refurbishment, and (2) occasional unoccupied rates. Revalued at 2007 prices, the expense of these two items over the 25 years 1965–66 to 1989–90 (excluding the conversion of Star House), were an annual average of £2,800 and £500 respectively. Following the bankruptcy of Finlay, over the 7 years 1990–91 to 1997–98 the comparable figures £16,200 and £9,100, a very large rise in expenses against a fall in rental income. Fortunately, in my own case this fall in income from Alford Joint Assets after the Finlay bankruptcy was cushioned to some extent by other changes.

It finally became clear that even with York House fully restored to a lettable state, its prospects for letting were not good, as the property market along the Great West Road continued to be in a dire state with much unlet office space. We came to the conclusion that the time had come to sell all of these properties. We placed them on the market but found little interest, and at auction they attracted no enthusiasm. Finally we sold them privately to one of the few who had made himself known to us at the auction and who wanted them for his own company's occupation; by then it was a relief to see them go. We sold the only remaining shop property to the sitting tenant in July 2001. These events produced a disappointing phase in capital value of Alford Joint Assets. Meanwhile the situations of Mike, J and myself were diverging. J and I each had three children, Mike was unmarried, and I was becoming concerned about prospective Inheritance Tax. It seemed better that we should each manage our own financial assets, so these sales proceeds were distributed between us; Alford Joint Assets had served its purpose and now ceased to exist.

Behind the figures set out in Appendix 4 there were other changes. We were advised quite early on that for tax purposes I should transfer some of my share of Alford Joint Assets to Toni, and I did so. This for a time split our affairs into Alford Joint Assets 1 and 2; in the latter, to keep our family shares equal, Mike, Toni and J's wife Audrey (referred to jocularly by our solicitor as Michael and his wives) had equal shares. In my own case we started looking to the future by taking out Second Survivor life policies to help our children pay future Inheritance Tax; this was becoming more significant as the value of 7 Aldersey Road rose in value from its 1963 price of £7,625. If its price rise had been purely inflationary, in line with our old friend CDKO, by 2007 it would have risen 14 times to £106,750; in fact it was valued at £1.1 million that year. One side of me saw this rise as rather satisfactory; my other side saw it as evidence of disgraceful mismanagement of Britain's property market by government, allowing mortgage lending to grow and drive up house prices while deliberately restricting the availability of development land, thus constraining the construction of new houses; the effect was an artificial boom in house prices watched idly by government, greatly raising their price relative to consumer prices and incomes. This was clear enough at the time. Indeed, in July 2004 I had a letter published in the *Financial Times* pointing out that the Bank of England had only one tool (interest rates) and one target (the overall rate of inflation); action to cool the housing boom therefore remained the responsibility of the Treasury and there were tools to achieve this directly: for banks, higher capital requirements against housing loans, and for borrowers, higher minimum down payments and/or lower maximum loan to income ratios. Nothing was done and later many house owners were to experience the painful consequences of this inaction.

We bought 7 Aldersey Road with a 25 year interest-only mortgage of £4,250 and since I expected inflation to continue and probably worsen, and interest rates therefore to rise, I opted for a fixed interest rate of 6 per cent, with repayment by a life policy with minor profits. Unusually, this mortgage ran to its full 25 year term and the policy fully repaid the mortgage with a margin over. After some years of inflation our fixed mortgage interest and life policy premiums had become hardly noticeable, and we were a correspondingly bad investment for those who had lent us the money.

Summing Up

But where did our income from Alford Joint Assets go to? A significant part was taken by tax; we were soon well into the higher tax bands but we have no regular records of tax payments. This we left to our accountant, John Smith, who agreed our tax with the Inland Revenue and we paid it as he instructed. At one stage a significant part went on fees for private schools; our daughter Annabel was at Guildford High School, a day school, and our sons after prep school both went to Charterhouse and overlapped there by a year. All of them then went on to higher education requiring further expenditure. In their early years Toni largely dressed all three in clothes from the excellent local jumble sales and from second-hand shops run by their schools.

So, was our income from Alford Joint Assets worth the burden on me of managing its properties? This income and our own lifestyle with its instinctive care over expenditure meant that Toni and I never had any worrying sense of financial stringency. Of course, this income would have been much less than the income that a number of my colleagues would have gained from having a working spouse. For us it meant that there was no pressure on Toni to earn, and I am sure the family gained greatly from having her contentedly at home as the children grew up. And our assets provided us with a comforting cushion of capital, although this and the rise in house prices then began to raise concerns about Inheritance Tax. I have always been willing to speak out on some issues, something fostered by my life at the School, and our degree of financial independence further encouraged this. Managing a very small but sometimes demanding property portfolio gave me practical acquaintance with one corner of commercial life as well as experience and confidence in negotiation and in the handling of larger sums of money. All of these were gains which made the burden of managing Alford Joint Assets well worthwhile. Did its claims on my time divert my energy from academic work and promotion? Perhaps to some degree (although its most demanding period was after I had retired). In any case I had already begun to find a life dominated by 'publish or perish' rather arid and unappealing, and had started to concentrate upon things which I found more rewarding – deepening my understanding of the constantly changing British monetary and financial system, teaching this subject, and participating in the affairs of the School. On balance, therefore, I consider that Alford Joint Assets and its successor portfolio presented myself and Toni, and in due course our children, with a clear positive gain.

Appendix 1

Academic Work at University

The central feature of being an undergraduate at a university is your academic work. Here I will propose a number of guidelines and make some other suggestions which should help you to develop intelligent self-management in organising both your time and your work effectively. Your lecturers in the Department of Economics support the advice given here, and your Tutor and other teachers may well have further suggestions.

It is an unfortunate fact that every year a certain number of students admit that they have done badly in their exams because they have not worked hard enough. This is the least acceptable of excuses and shows a lack of appreciation of the invaluable opportunity of studying at a university. The guidelines set out here will help you to take a suitably responsible attitude towards your academic opportunities at the School.

Hours of Work

The first question is how much work should you do in terms of hours per week. I would suggest that you should aim to do 35 hours per week in term time; this covers lectures, classes, seminars and tutorials (ALL of which you should attend regularly) which normally amount to perhaps 10–11 hours per week, leaving around 25 hours per week mainly for reading but also for doing exercises, assignments, essays and other academic activities.

How do you know if you are achieving this amount of work? One way is to keep a work diary, setting down truthfully day by day the amount of effective work you have done in each subject, to the nearest quarter of an hour. Such a work diary can give an alarming picture at first, showing just how little work you are really doing. However, when you do achieve the suggested 35 hours per week, your total hours of work begin to mount up in a most encouraging way, so that a work diary provides both a discipline and a reward. It also has another advantage: it helps you to keep a balance between different subjects. In principle, you should aim to divide your time equally between your subjects and only for some good reason (one that convinces your Tutor) should you deviate significantly from this.

Weekends

For all students an important part of their working week is the weekend, when work can be done with fewer interruptions and distractions than on week days. One way of structuring the weekend is to divide Saturday and Sunday each into three sessions – two hours in the morning, two hours in the afternoon and two in the evening (note how much free time there is between these sessions). Depending on how your work is going, you then decide how many of these sessions you need to devote to work (for most students three would be a minimum) and how many you will use for relaxation. Structuring the weekend in this way makes it much easier to manage your time effectively over these two days.

Academic Work in Vacations

What about vacations? In the Christmas vacation I would suggest a total of 40 hours over the average four week vacation, and some people may prefer to concentrate most of these hours in the period after Christmas and before term begins. The Easter vacation is another matter; by the end of the Lent Term most lecture courses and classes have been substantially completed and, with the work done in term time, you should have an overall view of the main features and topics in each course. It is the eight to ten weeks over the Easter vacation and the first half of the Summer Term, leading up to the examinations, when most undergraduates fill in the final gaps in their course work and really consolidate their grasp of their subjects. This is a time for maximum effort, and I would suggest that the 35 hours per week should apply throughout this period, except perhaps for a few days off immediately after the end of the Lent Term and a few more days over Easter itself. Short but complete breaks of this kind in the Christmas and Easter vacations can be really refreshing and help you to get back to work with renewed vigour.

Not only is the Easter vacation and the first half of the Summer Term a time for maximum effort (helped by the threat of examinations ahead) but for most undergraduates it is also a period of a growing sense that they are at last beginning to gain a real understanding of their subjects. Experience certainly seems to show that if an undergraduate works steadily, hours worked accumulate more or less linearly over the academic year, but understanding grows rather slowly at first and then begins to accelerate sometime in the Lent Term, continuing through the crucial 8 to 10 week period leading up to exams. This means that early in the academic year a lot of work has to be done with only a limited immediate reward in terms of understanding, and in the early part of the Lent Term this disparity between work done and understanding achieved probably reaches a maximum and may cause your morale to sag. However, as the amount of work done continues to accumulate, understanding begins to accelerate and your morale will recover. Recognising this pattern will help you to avoid relapsing into unnecessary feelings of gloom and doom.

These then are my proposed guidelines on how much time should be devoted to work; it is worth pointing out that there are 168 hours in a week, and even allowing one third of that time for sleep, this still leaves 112 waking hours, of which work would take just under one third, leaving two-thirds for all the varied pleasures of being an undergraduate – pleasures made all the more enjoyable by the knowledge that you really are keeping up with your work.

Organisation of Work

A course (consisting of one or more lecture series and their associated classes) leading to an examination is the unit of academic work, and your annual load is four such courses/exams.

In all subjects, one method of organisation is to have something like a box-file for each course; in each box-file there should be 8–10 folders, each folder relating to a significant topic. Taking a typical folder, at the bottom it might have some lecture notes on the topic (or reference to these notes if you prefer to keep your lecture notes on a course all together as a set); on top of that there would be your notes on relevant articles/chapters from your reading list, then perhaps a class paper or exercise on that topic, some of your own worked examples, outlines on key aspects and miscellaneous notes and course handouts; and finally, at the very top, a single side of A4 with the key points/equations/diagrams summarising that topic. This means that by opening your box-file on a particular course and opening the folder on a particular topic, you have in front of you your own summary outline of that topic, which in turn helps to take your mind down into all the underlying notes, exercises, examples etc. In this way you not only do the work, but you also keep it in a structured form which helps you to recall it to mind when you need it, whether in a class discussion or in an exam. The message is straightforward: good organisation is essential for learning, understanding, revising and recalling; it assists (and reflects) clear thinking.

Keeping your written work in the structured form suggested above makes it clear that work done on a class assignment is a valuable contribution to one of your topic folders. Always do some class preparation so that you can take an active part in class discussion; insufficient active and interested discussion by undergraduates is the main weakness in most classes.

In your essays and class assignments, a clear and logical structure is essential; poor structure is the commonest fault in undergraduate written work, and I believe that (in Economics at any rate) making this organisation explicit – in the form of headings, sections and sub-sections – is always acceptable, and indeed is to be encouraged.

The state of your topic folders can be some guide to the balance of the work you should be doing; a very slim folder late in the year may be a warning that more work needs to be done on that topic. However, while in principle all your courses can claim to be equally important, within a course the topics may well vary considerably in their significance for the subject. Distribution of time and effort between topics will, therefore, require judgement on your part; the amount of attention paid to different topics in the lectures, classes and recommended reading, perhaps explicit guidance from teachers, and your own understanding of the subject, all are sources on which you can draw in making this judgement.

Much of your time will be devoted to reading and many people find that a very useful technique is always to look quickly through any item before settling down to read it. In the case of a book, look through the chapter headings, look at the index for entries of particular interest to you and note entries with many page references. Then, in the case of a chapter or an article, thumb through it page by page; note any section headings, run your eye down the text picking out key words and see what maths, diagrams and tables are used. With practice this technique can yield a lot of information which will help you to absorb the content of an item more quickly and efficiently if you do read it or can warn you that an item is not what you really want, helping you to avoid using scarce time on less useful reading.

When taking notes in lectures or from books and articles, selectivity and relevance are essential; you should always be trying to identify and note down clearly the structure of the argument and its key points, with the dual aim of fixing these in your mind at the time and producing clear and informative notes that will be easy to use later on. Virtually copying out large parts of a book or an article is a poor use of your limited time.

It can be very useful to have your own xerox copies of the more important articles or chapters which you can work on and annotate freely. However, most students still find that writing out their own version of the key points is the most effective way of fixing them in the mind.

Finally, I would emphasise the importance of undergraduates helping each other. Explaining something that you have grasped to another student will help them, but it will also help you, because it will strengthen your own grasp on the topic.

Difficulties and work patterns

However well you organise your work, you will still run into occasional difficulties. When you approach your class teacher or tutor, one common response is for them to ask you to put down on one side of A4 EXACTLY what it is that you do not understand. In a surprisingly large number of cases, specifying your problem clearly and systematically will solve that problem; this is because a large proportion of problems arise not from difficulties in the subject, but because often when you come to a particularly demanding area, energy leaks away, interest declines and morale falters. The 'difficulties', therefore, are usually (though not always) in you rather than in the subject; a determined attempt (perhaps using the 'one side of

A4' approach), when you are feeling fresh and work is going well, will often overcome them.

Recognising this is just one aspect of the intelligent self-management which everyone has to develop. Another is that habitual work patterns vary – some people work best early in the morning, others work best late at night – and we have to get to know our own pattern. Fortunately, most patterns are compatible with successful academic work; however, they should not be allowed to become too bizarre or an excuse for idleness, and experience shows that they can be modified in a sensible way with reasonable self-discipline. It is also important to recognise that, like everyone else, you will go through times when somehow your mind simply will not get into gear, and others when you will awake at the bottom of a page without being able to remember a single thing that you have just read. We all have to find our own solutions to these common problems (switching to work on another subject, a quick walk round the block, etc.); perhaps the most important thing is to maintain a sense of balance and to bear in mind that you will recover from even your most unproductive phases.

Examinations

Passing exams with good marks is not the real objective of a university education; its real objective is to develop your grasp of the subjects you are studying and your insight into them, to increase your capacity for sustained intellectual effort, to raise your intellectual standards and to enhance the effectiveness of your thinking in all its aspects. Your exam results are important because they indicate how far you have achieved these objectives.

Nobody likes exams; they are straining, both for candidates (faced with an unseen paper and a time limit of three hours), and for examiners (faced with a large pile of scripts, some very badly written, and a deadline for the examiners' meeting). Nevertheless, they produce scripts which are the candidates' own unaided work done under controlled conditions, and the careful marking of these produces grades which are the fairest available assessment of candidates' performance.

Students are virtually professional examinees and have been given advice on exam technique (and have applied it successfully) many times; here I mention only certain points which are important in exams (and your tutor and other teachers may well have further points to make):

1. Before each year's exams you will receive 'Notes for Candidates' which tells you about the administrative arrangements, but there are some particular points you should look out for:

   a. The importance of attending an exam even if you produce a poor – or even blank – script; then at least your examinations have been completed, but if you miss an exam then your examinations have not been completed and this can cause even greater problems.

   b. What to do if you are ill and cannot attend an exam.

   c. What to do if you are late for an exam. This can cause much panic and distress; avoid all this by making careful arrangements (such as mutual wake-up calls with friends) to ensure that you are not late for any exam.

2. Everyone knows that empty-minded feeling just before an exam; this is when the knowledge that you have worked hard and systematically over the year can give you an underlying feeling of confidence. Begin the exam by reading the whole question paper through twice at least, including the instructions on the number of questions you have to answer and any restrictions on choice ('at least one question from each section'). Doing this has a calming effect, helps you to make the right choice of questions and seems to start very important subconscious processes working which bring relevant material up into your conscious mind. Setting out notes for your first two answers before beginning any of the answers themselves gives these processes even more time to work.

3. Make sure that you answer the required number of questions. You cannot be given marks for answers you have not written, so that you penalise yourself if you do fewer than the required number (or, indeed, if you do more). Similarly, with each chosen question, read the question carefully several times and ANSWER THAT QUESTION; again, if your answer is off the question as it stands, you will lose marks.

4. How do you gain experience in interpreting exactly what the question is getting at? The best way is by practice in answering unseen questions, and one good source of these is recent exam papers; however, remember that although these can be very helpful, the aim is to prepare yourself for the forthcoming question paper, not just to produce model answers for past ones. Beware of naive forecasts that particular questions are 'certain' to come up this year; this can mislead you into narrowing the scope of your work without realising the risk you are running until it is too late. Beware of becoming the prisoner of your own model answers, so that you trot them out even when they are not quite what the question is asking for.

5. Allocate your time roughly equally between equal questions. Giving more than its fair share of time to one question seldom adds as many marks as you lose on the questions to which you give less time. If you miscalculate and are short of time for the last question, note form is permissible and if well done can produce almost as many marks as a full answer.

Remember the examiners who have to read your script. They will be looking longingly for any signs of merit. Relevant, well-organised, well-expressed (and, in quantitative papers, correct) answers which show evidence of hard work, careful thought, intelligent insight and real understanding, all in very clear handwriting – this is the way to their hearts. Even the sternest examiner capitulates before such an assault and pours out marks.

September 1996

Roger Alford
Department of Economics
London School of Economics

Appendix 2

Letters by Roger Alford Published in *The Times/Financial Times*

07 October 1961	*Times*	Public schools
03 August 1962	*Times*	Reflation
27 December 1975	*Times*	Secondary banks and bureaucracy
05 January 1976	*Times*	Economic policy and bankruptcy
12 April 1976	*Times*	Against AUT attack on 'freeloaders'
17 June 1976	*Times*	The immigration problem
12 February 1977	*Times*	Fees and subsidies to overseas students
22 February 1978	*Times*	The immigration problem
08 July 1992	*Times*	Against contingency fees for lawyers
09 March 1995	*FT*	Role of Lender of Last Resort
26 October 1998	*Times*	Against 'closed list' voting
14 August 1999	*Times*	Obscenity replacing wit
12 October 2000	*FT*	Romantic view of UK land resources
21 February 2002	*Times*	Search for a fair pensions scheme
10 July 2002	*FT*	Wrong policy tool for house price problem
03 September 2002	*Times*	Poverty is low productivity per head
03 December 2002	*Times*	Land for development
05 July 2003	*Times*	Analysis of EU constitution is crucial
23 August 2003	*FT*	Different interests in genome information
15 December 2003	*Times*	Collapse of chaotic EU constitution talks
24 June 2004	*Times*	Role of MEPs should be taken by MPs
05 January 2004	*Times*	Poverty, youthful sympathy and bad government
14 July 2004	*FT*	Tools/targets, inflation and house prices
10 September 2004	*Times*	'Social' Europe or democratic Europe
02 June 2005	*FT*	FT not recommended as fuel for boiling water

07 June 2005	*FT*	Defective procedure for EU constitution
23 August 2005	*Times*	Army underwear sizes: too large or too small
27 Feb 2007	*Times*	Costs of planning
19 Sep 2007	*FT*	Moral hazard
18 Oct 2007	*FT Online*	Health of the banking system

Appendix 3

Scott's Field – Some History

In February 1947 my father Frank Alford bought Scott's Field in Hook
Lane, Nyetimber, West Sussex, in the name of my older brother Michael.
This brought us a bundle of documents (Conveyances, Abstracts of
Title, Indentures, Mortgages, Wills) giving some of its history. Since
the sixteenth century the title to such properties had been increasingly held
in a form called copyhold; in this, title was attested by a copy of the
entry of the owner's name on the Roll of the Manorial Court, made by
the Steward of the Manor with the consent of the Lord of the Manor.
Sale of a piece of land was done by the seller surrendering his entry on
the Court Roll to the Lord of the Manor who would then give his consent
for the admission on to the Court Roll of the name of the purchaser.
Giving this consent provided the Lord of the Manor with an occasion
for levying customary 'fines', custom limiting his power in doing this.
One ancient fine which appears on some of these documents is heriot,
the customary right of the Lord of the Manor to have the best beast
belonging to the new entrant on the Roll. This would be commuted to a
sum of money if the person concerned had no animals. During the
nineteenth century many copyholds were already being converted into
freeholds and all those remaining were finally converted by the Law of
Property Act 1922.

The earliest document we have is from 1747 recording the sale of
Scotsfield (and two other fields not relevant here) by Thomas Faulkner to
George Scardefield who was a maltster or brewer. With the legal repetitions
removed, as below, and accepting its deliberate lack of punctuation (which

makes careful reading and re-reading necessary), this document has a sonorous dignity in its wording:

> **Nyetimber Manor** A special Court Baron of John Ballett there holden for the Manor the five and twentieth day of September in the one and twentieth year of the reign of our Sovereign Lord George the second by the Grace of God King of Great Britain etc [*sic*] and in the year of our Lord one thousand seven hundred and forty seven before John Farhill Esq Steward of the Court of the Manor.
>
> The Homage aforesaid upon their oaths do present that this present day Thomas Faulkner did surrender into the hands of the Lord of the Manor by the acceptance of the Steward one Close of land called Scotsfield within the Manor To the use and behoof of George Scardefield of Nyetimber in the parish of Pagham in the County of Sussex Maltster and of his heirs for ever according to the Custom of the Manor (Whereupon happened to the Lord two heriots 10 shillings, because he had no animal) and thereupon came here into Court the said George Scardefield and prayed to be admitted to the premises with the appurtenances To whom the Lord of the Manor by his Steward hath granted to have and to hold by Copy of Court Roll at the Will of the Lord according to the Custom of the Manor by the several rents heriots when they shall happen the best of beasts and other Services and Customs therefore first due and of right accustomed and thus he is admitted Tenant thereof hath Seizin by the Rod and did to the Lord Fealty and for a fine upon his admission gave to the Lord £25 10s 0p.

A Court Baron was held by the Lord of the Manor, here John Ballett. Its role was to ensure that the customs of the Manor were observed and the Homage mentioned means the quorum of Copyholders present at the meeting of the Court to witness its proceedings. 'Seizin by the rod' was a symbolic part of the process of title transfer; here the Steward of the Manor would hold out a wooden rod which was briefly grasped by the purchaser/entrant. By the late nineteenth century the Steward was often a lawyer and the whole process would be conducted in his office; then it was enough for the Steward to use anything wooden – a pencil, for example –

as the rod. The fine upon this particular admission would cover the two other fields as well, but still seems quite a large sum.

Thus in 1747 Scotsfield passed from Thomas Faulkner into the ownership of Josiah Scardefield; then with minor variants in its spelling (although Scots Mead in 1817) it passed into the hands of Philip Lawrance in 1762 but in 1796 it was back in the hands of the Scardefield family, now in the name of Joseph; by 1813 it was in the name of Josephus followed by another Josiah in 1817. By 1853 it was owned by the Collins family who were still holding it in 1891 when it was identified also as field no. 173 in the Tithe Commutation Award.

The rod, pole and perch were names formerly used for what became the standardised 5.5 yard unit of length, but they were often used to mean that length squared – 30.25 square yards – as a measure of area. Less commonly known is the rood which was one quarter of an acre. In Scott's Field we see most of these in use, its area in 1891 being given as '4 acres, 1 rood and 16 perches Statutory Measure'. This last qualification is important because it would mean 160 (square) perches, rods or poles to the acre, while in one of the documents of 1825 it refers to a different customary measure of six score – 120 – (square) rods to the acre. In 1928 the field passed into the hands of the Ockenden family; its measurement then was given as '4 acres, 2 roods and 21 poles'. It was from one of the Ockendens that in February 1947 my father bought Scott's Field in the name of my brother Michael. It was then also designated as part of Ordnance Survey Field 248. Its title was at that point registered with the Land Registry, making all the earlier documents of title redundant.

However the accumulation of documents did not end there, because shortly after it was bought, the Town and Country Planning Act 1947 led to a vast amount of bureaucratic activity all over Britain. For Scott's Field – one small meadow deep in Sussex this included a large four page buff form from the Central Land Board, filled with detailed questions, on which to claim for the depreciation of the value of land, buildings and minerals due to the Act. This led to further correspondence and forms from the Inland Revenue Mineral Valuer, Southern Minerals Section, about the valuation of mineral rights on Scott's Field (these were for brick earth and were in connexion with my father's Lion Brick Company nearby). These came under the heading 'Near-ripe Minerals: Development Charge' which proceeded from a proposed 'No development value' to an objection and a final proposed figure of £490 for the mineral development value and a further £60 for general development value; in April 1954 these figures were noted as 'unagreed' and after that silence descends. At about the same time my father, who was renting Scott's Field from my brother Michael, changed its name to Dukes Meadow and started developing it into the upmarket caravan park it had become by the time he died in 1962. Michael sold Dukes Meadow in 1965 and our connexion with its history ended.

One curiosity is that in documents of 1796 and 1797 there appears:

> ... our Sovereign Lord George the third by the Grace of God of Great Britain France and Ireland King Defender of the Faith...

This claim to France was perhaps concealed behind the 'etc' in the document of 1747 quoted above; it was dropped from the documents of 1813 and later.

Appendix 4

Nominal and Real Income – Tables

Table A
RA and ABA Income Data
Notes on Table A

Table B
RA and ABA Real Income

Table C
RA and ABA Nominal and
Real Income – Graph

Note: the data that follows has to reconcile calendar years, tax years and academic years (October to September). This has been done pragmatically and is unlikely to have distorted the data to any significant degree.

Table A

1 Tax year	2 RA Salary	3 RA Net Fees	4 RA Pre-tax Earned Income	5 ABA Pre-tax Earned Income	6 RA+ABA Joint Assets Inv Inc	7 RA+ABA ISA Inv Inc	8 RA+ABA Other Inv Inc	9 RA+ABA Total Income	10 RA+ABA Inv Inc as % of Earned Income
52–53	250		250					250	
53–54	525	163	688					688	
54–55	623	209	832					832	
55–56	700	353	1053					1053	
56–57	724	172	896					896	
57–58	915	207	1122					1122	
58–59	1035	174	1209					1209	
59–60	1085	87	1172					1172	
60–61	1959	65	2024				46	2070	2
61–62	2237	–17	2220				36	2256	2
62–63	1649	65	1714				226	1940	13
63–64	1785	79	1864				254	2118	14
64–65	2417	45	2462				131	2593	5
65–66	2755	99	2854		1386		273	4513	58
66–67	3092	316	3408		1845		273	5526	62
67–68	3172	–41	3131		2887		410	6428	105
68–69	3325	20	3345		2181		468	5994	79
69–70	3692	22	3714		1965		108	5787	56
70–71	4694	–53	4641		2022		171	6834	47
71–72	4903	150	5053		2142		182	7377	46
72–73	5316	–80	5236		2056		128	7420	42
73–74	5694	–120	5574		1314		22	6910	24
74–75	6455	295	6750		1664		9	8423	25
75–76	7568	116	7684		3620		143	11447	49
76–77	8454	–91	8363		6269		306	14938	79
77–78	8561	344	8905		3042		447	12394	39
78–79	10045	–1	10044		8797		323	19164	91

1 Tax year	2 RA Salary	3 RA Net Fees	4 RA Pre-tax Earned Income	5 ABA Pre-tax Earned Income	6 RA+ABA Joint Assets Inv Inc	7 RA+ABA ISA Inv Inc	8 RA+ABA Other Inv Inc	9 RA+ABA Total Income	10 RA+ABA Inv Inc as % of Earned Income
79–80	12231	286	12517		8918		316	21751	74
80–81	14161	-380	13781		10612		506	24899	81
81–82	17057	-393	16664	312	10701		590	28267	67
82–83	17900	-530	17370	765	9463		359	27958	54
83–84	17093	-381	16712	756	13428		225	31121	78
84–85	17842	-337	17505	900	15119		37	33561	82
85–86	18852	-547	18305	1214	16034		99	35653	83
86–87	19911	-406	19505	964	18115		2189	40773	99
87–88	23264	-693	22571	973	18138		2257	43939	87
88–89	23042	84	23126	1488	23668		3435	51717	110
89–90	24868	1512	26380	1382	22195		9950	59907	116
90–91	26781	546	27327	1837	5902	700	7101	42867	47
91–92	30130	-1319	28811	3607	-1699	700	3248	34667	7
92–93	29782	969	30751	2946	9217	2000	2339	47253	40
93–94	24745	504	25249	1995	4937	2200	1692	36073	32
94–95	34941	3790	38731	1977	5950	3500	1960	52118	28
95–96	40941	-582	40359	2020	758	3000	2037	48174	14
96–97	39157	-1505	37652	2097	1155	5000	2109	48013	21
97–98	53798	12876	66674	2140	3215	7000	4858	83887	22
98–99	22866	7536	30402	2218	3400	7500	7170	50690	55
99–00	23596	524	24120	2289	3508	7933	9503	47353	79
00–01	24015		24015	2315	958	10387	4963	42638	62
01–02	25145		25145	2478		10607	3954	42184	53
02–03	25522	383	25905	2580		13571	3257	45313	59
03–04	25991	145	26136	2655		18544	4622	51957	80
04–05	26972		26972	2815		17361	4080	51228	72
05–06	27546	22	27568	2815		28842	3287	62512	106
06–07	28619	30	28649	2996		45207	3743	80595	155
07–08	29678	30	29708	3114		30079	2820	65721	100

Notes on Table A

The columns in Table A make clear to whom they relate: to myself, Roger Alford (**RA**), to Toni Alford (**ABA**, since Toni is really Antoinette Beatrix) or the two of us together (**RA+ABA**).

Column 1 shows the Tax Year, which runs from 6 April in one calendar year to 5 April in the next calendar year.

Column 2 shows my annual salary from the School which appears on my annual P60 form which has to be provided by every employer or private pension provider; these figures appear in my annual tax return. But note:

  a. for tax year 1952–53 it covers only half a year, October to 5 April, since I only came onto the staff in October 1952.

  b. for 1960–62 most of it is my salary from the Bank of England.

  c. for the years before my retirement, it shows just my School salary at the then current salary scale, certain additional fees paid by the School (for acting as Evening Dean and for examining) which they treated as salary, have here been moved into **Column 3** which covers my net pre-tax freelance earnings.

  d. for 1992–93 to 1997–98, my first six years of retirement, the distinction between salary and fees is arbitrary. This is because after I retired in September 1992 (shown by the vertical line in Table C) I ran a number of courses for the School, particularly courses on banking and finance for young Russians and later courses for young Indian businessmen. Some payments for this work arrived as salary, others as fees, and delays caused them to bunch together creating an artificial peak in 97–98 and spilling over into fees for 98–99. As a warning, for these six years my salary (**Column 2**) and fees (**Column 3**) are in *italics*. Starting with 98–99 my 'salary' consists entirely of my University Superannuation Scheme pension and state pension.

Column 3 shows my pre-tax freelance earnings *less* expenses: books, periodicals, travel, IT equipment and use of part of home as an office. This figure can be erratic due to 'lumpiness' in some components and it can be negative because some general expenses can be allowed to exceed freelance earnings.

Column 4 shows my pre-tax earned income, the sum of my salary and net fees.

Column 5 shows Toni's income as a part-time medical receptionist, which only started in 81–82 (after our two older children had left school and the youngest was away at boarding school) and later consists of just her state pension.

From our share of Alford Joint Assets pre-tax income, **Column 6,** and from capital, we later started to build up a portfolio of securities. Part of this was held in the tax-efficient form of Personal Equity Plans (PEPs) which started in 1990 and were later joined by, and then converted into, Investment Savings Accounts (ISAs) which is the name used here. The gross income (interest and dividends) received from these ISAs is shown in **Column 7,** where the figure for 2006–07 is unduly high due to the unusual incidence of some special dividends. This income did not have to be reported in our annual tax returns so that the early figures were not so carefully preserved. Consequently the figures before tax year 1999–2000 have been estimated from portfolio holdings and yield data, and are shown in *italics* as a warning. Some of our portfolio was held outside ISAs and the gross income from this is shown in **Column 8** as other investment income.

Column 9 gives the total of all our sources of income, before tax.

Column 10 shows our total investment income (**Columns 6, 7 and 8**) as a percentage of our earned income (**Columns 4 and 5**) both of them before tax. This is a rough indicator of the contribution of our investment income to our potential standard of living. The figure varies widely but over the years 1960–61 to 2007–08, depending upon the method of calculation, it amounted to 58 or 60 per cent of our earned income. If it were to be calculated net of tax it would be considerably lower, although after 1990–91 the tax status of our ISA income would have the opposite effect.

Table B

1 Tax year	11 Calendar year with max overlap	12 CDKO annual index no	13 CDKO* inflator: 2007 index no/ yr index no	14 RA Salary	15 RA Real Salary	16 RA+ABA Total Real Income	17 RA: LSE 'career years' 1952–53 =1
52–53	1952	39.3	20.7	250	5184	5184	1
53–54	1953	40.5	20.1	525	10565	13845	2
54–55	1954	41.3	19.7	623	12294	16418	3
55–56	1955	43.1	18.9	700	13237	19912	4
56–57	1956	45.3	18.0	724	13026	16120	5
57–58	1957	46.9	17.4	915	15900	19497	6
58–59	1958	48.4	16.8	1035	17428	20358	7
59–60	1959	48.6	16.8	1085	18195	19654	8
60–61	1960	49.1	16.6	1959	32517	34359	9
61–62	1961	50.8	16.0	2237	35889	36189	10
62–63	1962	53.0	15.4	1649	25357	29832	11
63–64	1963	54.0	15.1	1785	26940	31964	12
64–65	1964	55.8	14.6	2417	35302	37868	13
65–66	1965	58.4	14.0	2755	38447	62983	14
66–67	1966	60.7	13.4	3092	41515	74198	15
67–68	1967	62.3	13.1	3172	41496	84090	16
68–69	1968	65.2	12.5	3325	41563	74924	17
69–70	1969	68.7	11.9	3692	43799	68654	18
70–71	1970	73.1	11.1	4694	52334	76194	19
71–72	1971	80.0	10.2	4903	49949	75155	20
72–73	1972	85.7	9.5	5316	50555	70564	21
73–74	1973	93.5	8.7	5694	49632	60229	22
74–75	1974	108.5	7.5	6455	48487	63272	23
75–76	1975	134.8	6.0	7568	45756	69209	24
76–77	1976	157.1	5.2	8454	43857	77494	25
77–78	1977	182.0	4.5	8561	38336	55501	26
78–79	1978	197.1	4.1	10045	41536	79241	27

1	11	12	13	14	15	16	17
Tax year	Calendar year with max overlap	CDKO annual index no	CDKO* inflator: 2007 index no/ yr index no	RA Salary	RA Real Salary	RA+ABA Total Real Income	RA: LSE 'career years' 1952–53 =1
79–80	1979	223.5	3.6	12231	44601	79317	28
80–81	1980	263.7	3.1	14161	43766	76952	29
81–82	1981	295.0	2.76	17057	47124	78093	30
82–83	1982	320.4	2.54	17900	45532	71116	31
83–84	1983	335.1	2.43	17093	41572	75689	32
84–85	1984	351.8	2.32	17842	41334	77750	33
85–86	1985	373.2	2.18	18852	41169	77859	34
86–87	1986	385.9	2.11	19911	42051	86110	35
87–88	1987	402.0	2.03	23264	47165	89080	36
88–89	1988	421.7	1,93	23042	44532	99950	37
89–90	1989	454.5	1.79	24868	44593	107425	38
90–91	1990	497.5	1.64	26781	43872	70224	39
91–92	1991	526.7	1.55	30130	46622	53643	40
92–93	1992	546.4	1.49	29782	44422	70481	41
93–94	1993	555.1	1.47	24745	36331	52963	42
94–95	1994	568.5	1.43	34941	50091	74717	43
95–96	1995	588.2	1.39	40941	56727	66750	44
96–97	1996	602.4	1.35	39157	52976	64958	45
97–98	1997	621.3	1.31	53798	70570	110040	46
98–99	1998	642.6	1.27	22866	29001	64289	47
99–00	1999	652.5	1.25	23596	29472	59146	48
00–01	2000	671.8	1.21	24015	29134	51727	49
01–02	2001	683.7	1.19	25145	29974	50285	50
02–03	2002	695.1	1.17	25522	29924	53129	51
03–04	2003	715.2	1.14	25991	29618	59207	52
04–05	2004	736.5	1.11	26972	29847	56688	53
05–06	2005	757.3	1.08	27546	29645	67275	54
06–07	2006	781.5	1.04	28619	29846	84050	55
07–08	2007	815.0	1.00	29678	29678	65721	56

Table C

Nominal and Real Income

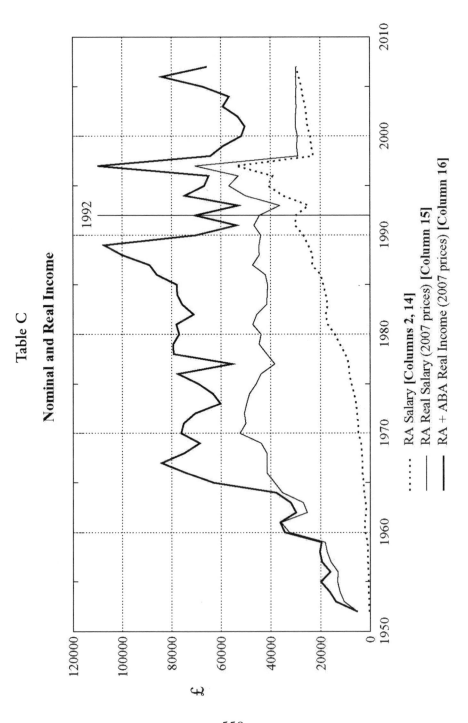

.... RA Salary [Columns 2, 14]

—— RA Real Salary (2007 prices) [Column 15]

—— RA + ABA Real Income (2007 prices) [Column 16]

Appendix 5

7 ALDERSEY ROAD
GUILDFORD

SKETCH PLAN OF THE GARDEN

ALDERSEY ROAD

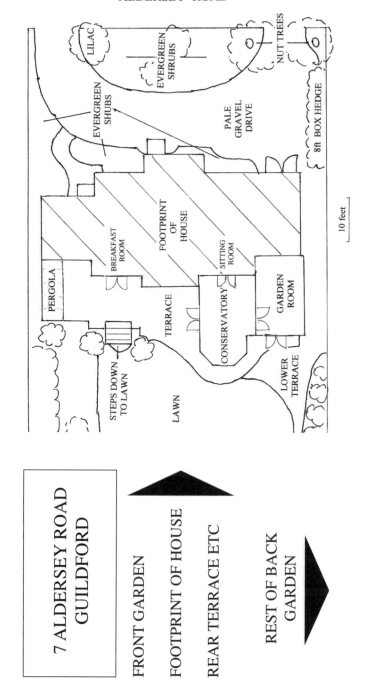

7 ALDERSEY ROAD
GUILDFORD

FRONT GARDEN

FOOTPRINT OF HOUSE

REAR TERRACE ETC

REST OF BACK
GARDEN

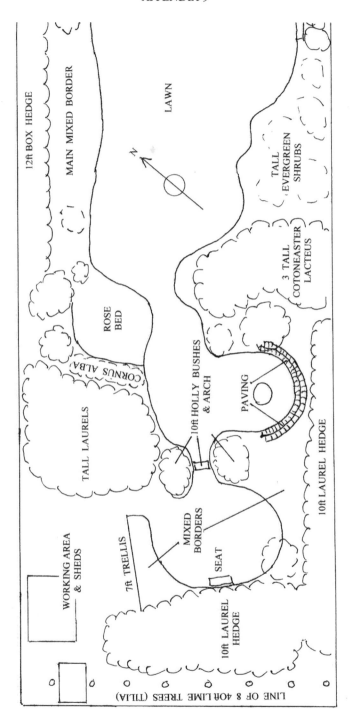

Index